ASCENT®
CENTER FOR TECHNICAL KNOWLEDGE

CATIA V5-6R2022
Generative Structural Analysis

Learning Guide
1st Edition

ASCENT - Center for Technical Knowledge®

CATIA V5-6R2022

Generative Structural Analysis

1st Edition

Prepared and produced by:

ASCENT Center for Technical Knowledge
630 Peter Jefferson Parkway, Suite 175
Charlottesville, VA 22911

866-527-2368
www.ASCENTed.com

Lead Contributor: Iouri Apanovitch

ASCENT - Center for Technical Knowledge is a division of Rand Worldwide, Inc., providing custom developed knowledge products and services for leading engineering software applications. ASCENT is focused on specializing in the creation of education programs that incorporate the best of classroom learning and technology-based training offerings.

We welcome any comments you may have regarding this guide, or any of our products. To contact us please email: feedback@ASCENTed.com.

AS-56CAT22-GSA1-SG // RS-56CAT22-GSA1-SG

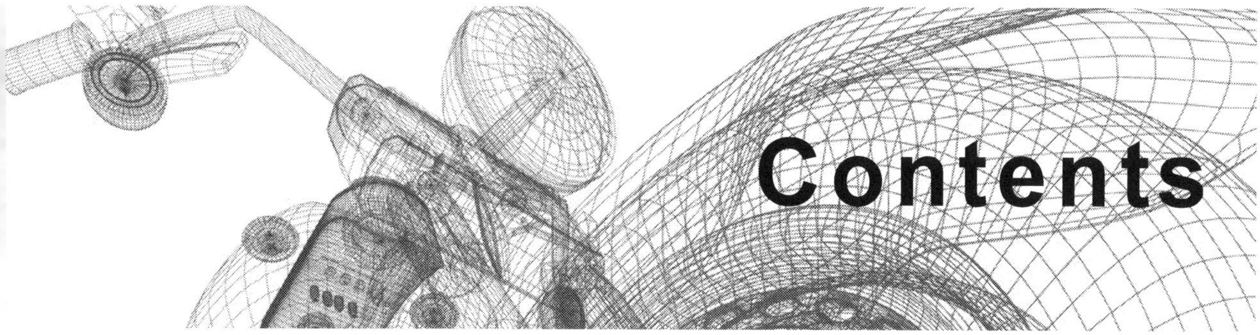

Contents

Preface

This guide covers the fundamentals of the Generative Structural Analysis (GSA) workbench in CATIA. It provides you with the knowledge to effectively use CATIA for structural finite element analysis and simulation, thereby reducing design time. This is an extensive hands-on learning guide, in which you have the opportunity to apply your knowledge through real-world scenarios and examples.

Topics Covered

- FEA fundamentals
- Basic modeling and analysis
- Types of loads and restraints
- Mesh refinement and adaptivity
- Virtual parts
- Assembly modeling and analysis
- Contact analysis
- Simulation of fastened assemblies
- Shell idealizations
- Frequency analysis

Prerequisites

- Access to the CATIA V5-6R2022 software. The practices and files included with this guide might not be compatible with prior versions.
- *CATIA V5-6: Introduction to Modeling* or equivalent CATIA experience. Some FEA knowledge is beneficial, but not a strict requirement.

Note on Software Setup

This learning guide assumes a standard installation of the software using the default options and preferences during installation. Lectures and practices require the use of the following CATIA licenses:

- Any Platform 2 configuration for the basic mechanical design, such as MD2 or HD2
- GPS - Generative Part Structural Analysis
- GAS - Generative Assembly Structural Analysis

Lead Contributor: Iouri Apanovitch

Iouri has been specializing in finite element analysis and simulation for over 30 years, with experience on multiple CAD and FEA systems, including CATIA, Creo, and Abaqus. Iouri uses his extensive knowledge and skills to develop instructor-led and web-based training products.

Iouri holds a Ph.D. degree in mechanical engineering from the National Academy of Sciences, Minsk, Belarus, as well as a Professional Engineer certification in Ontario, Canada.

Iouri Apanovitch has been the lead contributor for *CATIA: Generative Structural Analysis* since 2015.

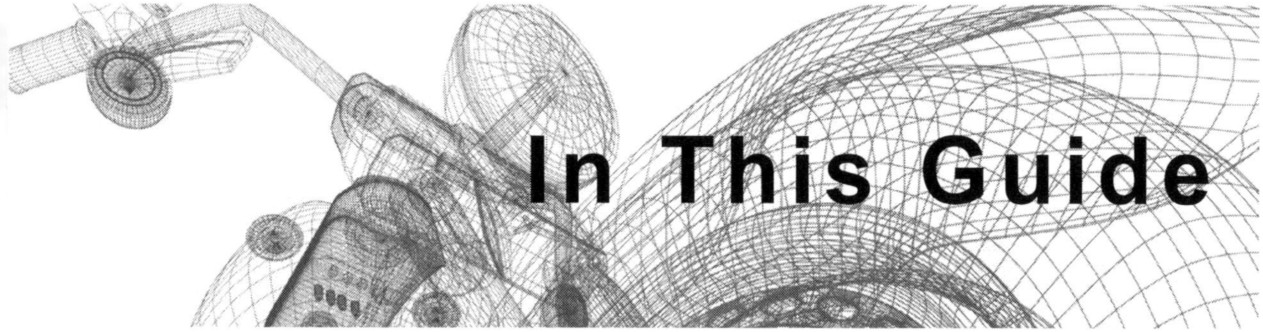

In This Guide

The following highlights the key features of this guide.

Feature	Description
Practice Files	The Practice Files page includes a link to the practice files and instructions on how to download and install them. The practice files are required to complete the practices in this guide.
Chapters	A chapter consists of the following - Learning Objectives, Instructional Content, and Practices. • **Learning Objectives** define the skills you can acquire by learning the content provided in the chapter. • **Instructional Content**, which begins right after Learning Objectives, refers to the descriptive and procedural information related to various topics. Each main topic introduces a product feature, discusses various aspects of that feature, and provides step-by-step procedures on how to use that feature. Where relevant, examples, figures, helpful hints, and notes are provided. • **Practice** for a topic follows the instructional content. Practices enable you to use the software to perform a hands-on review of a topic. It is required that you download the practice files (using the link found on the Practice Files page) prior to starting the first practice.

Practice Files

To download the practice files for this guide, use the following steps:

1. Type the URL ***exactly as shown below*** into the address bar of your Internet browser, to access the Course File Download page.

   Note: If you are using the ebook, you do not have to type the URL. Instead, you can access the page simply by clicking the URL below.

   https://www.ascented.com/getfile/id/scatophagusPF

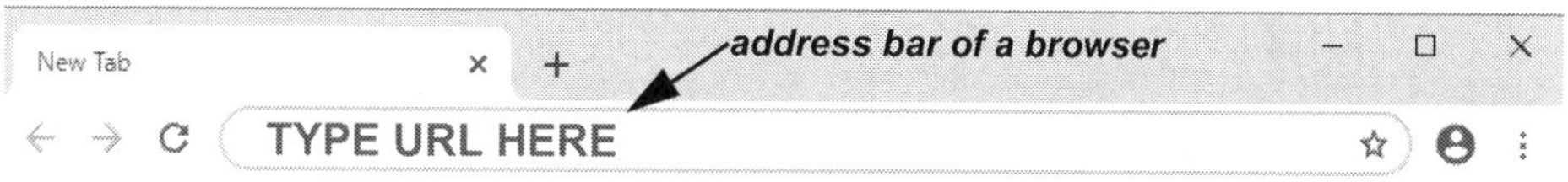

2. On the Course File Download page, click the **DOWNLOAD NOW** button, as shown below, to download the .ZIP file that contains the practice files.

3. Once the download is complete, unzip the file and extract its contents.

   The recommended practice files folder location is:
   C:\CATIA Generative Structural Analysis Practice Files

   Note: It is recommended that you do not change the location of the practice files folder. Doing so may cause errors when completing the practices.

Stay Informed!

To receive information about upcoming events, promotional offers, and complimentary webcasts, visit:

www.ASCENTed.com/updates

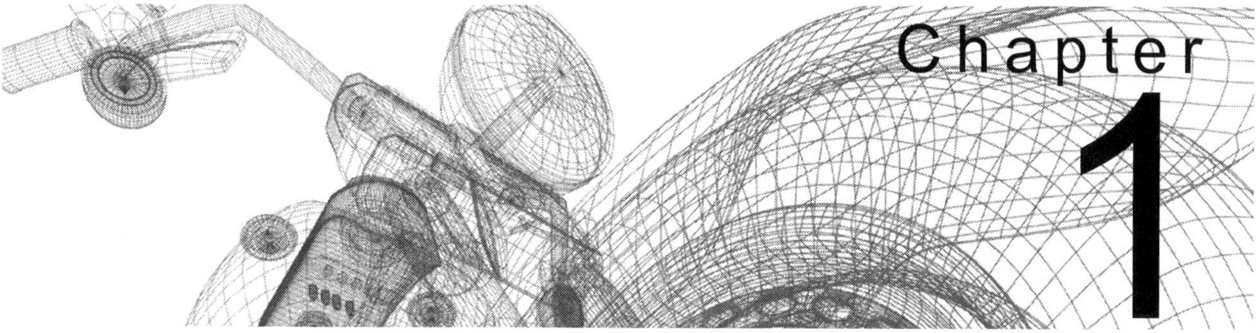

Chapter 1

Introduction to Generative Structural Analysis (GSA) Workbench

The Generative Structural Analysis (GSA) workbench in CATIA is a powerful software tool that enables you to simulate structural behavior of your design to understand and improve the design's performance.

Learning Objectives in This Chapter

- Review the CATIA FEA portfolio.
- Understand the concept of FEA.
- Understand the FEA solution refinement.
- Learn about the GSA analysis assumptions and limitations.
- Review the FEA process.

1.1 CATIA Finite Element Analysis Portfolio

CATIA portfolio offers several workbenches and multiple products related to the finite element analysis (FEA) and simulation. The summary is presented in the following table.

Workbench	Product	Description
Generative Structural Analysis 	**GPS** (Generative Part Structural Analysis)	Basic structural analysis for parts
	GAS (Generative Assembly Structural Analysis)	Basic structural analysis for assemblies
	EST (Elfini Structural Analysis)	Advanced options for GPS and GAS
	GDY (Generative Dynamic Response Analysis)	Dynamic Time Response and Frequency Response analyses
Advanced Meshing Tools 	**FMS** (FEM Surface)	Advanced surface meshing tools
	FMD (FEM Solid)	Advanced solid meshing tools
Nonlinear Structural Analysis 	**ANL** (SIMULIA Nonlinear Structural Analysis)	ABAQUS nonlinear structural analysis integrated with CATIA
Thermal Analysis 	**ATH** (SIMULIA Thermal Analysis)	ABAQUS thermal analysis integrated with CATIA

Each product listed above requires a license. Depending on your company's CATIA licensing setup, either the license may be included into a configuration or it exists as a shareable product (i.e., on-demand). For example, the SA2 configuration automatically includes GPS, GAS, and EST licenses, while the HD2 configuration does not. If the product you intend to use in your FEA simulation is not automatically included in your CATIA configuration, it may be available as a shareable license, activated via **Tools>Options>General>Shareable Products**.

This training course covers the GPS and GAS products; therefore, ensure that you have appropriate licenses in order to be able to perform the hands-on practices in this guide.

1.2 Finite Element Analysis (FEA)

Finite element analysis (FEA) is a numerical mathematical method based on the following process:

- Discretize (i.e., divide) the model into smaller and more simplified volumes (tetrahedra, bricks, wedges, etc.) called *finite elements*. The collection of finite elements approximates the shape of the model and is called *finite element mesh*, or just *mesh*. An example of a meshed model is shown in Figure 1–1.

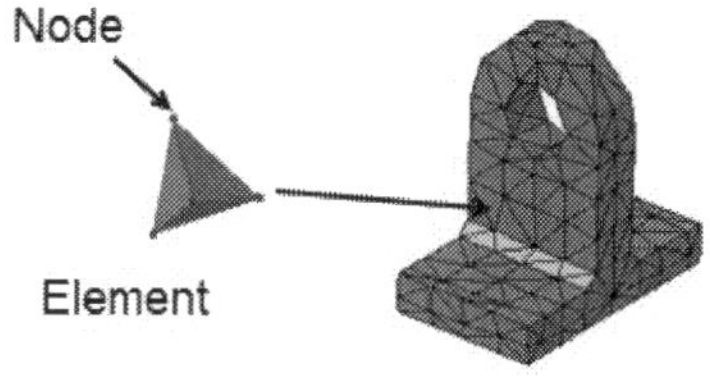

Figure 1–1

- Approximate the variation of the principal quantity of interest (such as displacement, stress, etc.) within each finite element with polynomials. These polynomials are typically called *local approximation functions* or *shape functions*.

- Connect the finite elements across the inter-element boundaries, thus effectively *sewing* elemental polynomials together. The *sewn* local polynomials now approximate a variation of the quantity of interest over the entire model and, therefore, comprise the global approximation function in the form of a piece-wise polynomial.

- Solve the governing equations and boundary conditions (i.e., a boundary value problem) for the global approximation function and find the best-fitting solution. In structural mechanics, the principle of minimum total potential energy is typically used to find the best-fitting solution, which results in solving a large number (sometimes hundreds of thousands) of simultaneous linear equations.

- Present the results for this approximate solution.

Therefore, the key FEA concept is the use of piece-wise polynomials to approximate the sought field quantity in the model, which effectively replaces a continuum problem with an infinite number of degrees of freedom (DOF) with a discrete problem with a finite number of DOF (hence the terms *finite elements* and *discretization*).

For example, consider how the FEA method works when applied to calculate deflections in a simple beam, as shown in Figure 1–2. The beam is clamped at the left end, has a couple of supports in the middle, and is loaded by a couple of transversal forces and a moment. The bottom graph shown in Figure 1–2 represents the unknown true deflection of the beam, which you are trying to determine using the FEA method.

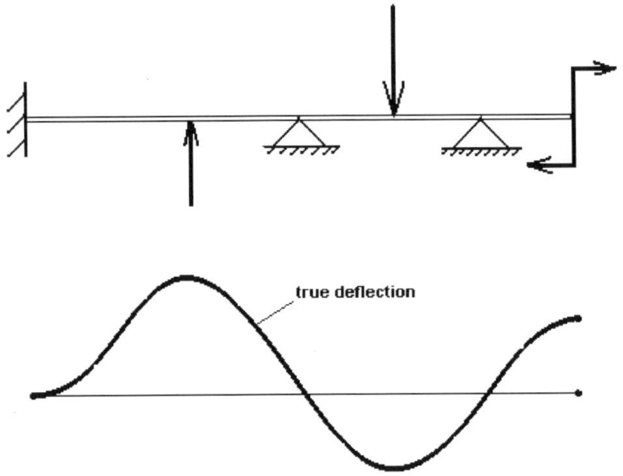

Figure 1–2

The first step in the process (shown in the example in Figure 1–3) is to mesh the beam by breaking it into a collection of shorter pieces (i.e., finite elements) connected at their ends (i.e., the nodes).

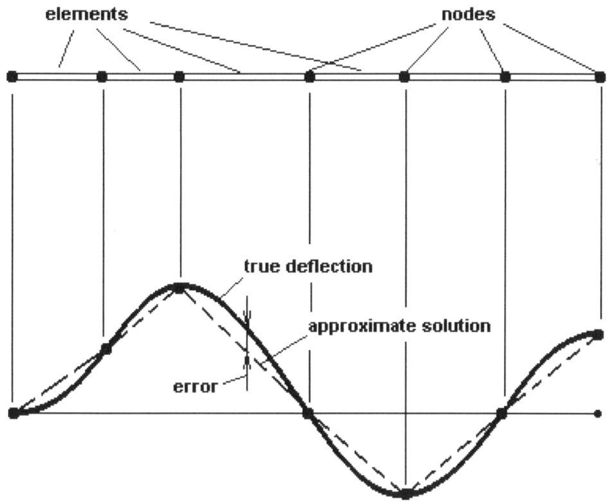

Figure 1–3

Next, the deflection ***Y*** within each finite element is approximated by a polynomial. In this example, you use linear polynomial $Y = a_0 + a_1X$, which means that deflection within each element is approximated by essentially a straight line.

Sewing local polynomials at the nodes ensures continuity of the global approximation function and, therefore, of the FEA solution for the deflection over the entire beam.

Next, the local linear polynomials are sewn together at the nodes, creating a global approximation function in the form of a piece-wise linear polynomial, which is a polyline.

Finally, the global approximation function is best-fit to satisfy both the bending differential equations and beam boundary conditions (loads and constraints). The resulting function (the dashed line shown in Figure 1–3) now represents the FEA solution for the true deflection (the solid line shown in Figure 1–3) in the beam.

It is important to note that your FEA result contains a certain amount of error, which is the deviation between the true deflection (the solid line shown in Figure 1–3) and the FEA solution (the dashed line shown in Figure 1–3), and which is called the *discretization error.*

Any FEA solution is just an approximation, which means it always contains a discretization error. Therefore, in the FEA process, it is critical to know how to estimate, how to control, and how to reduce this unavoidable approximation error to acceptable levels.

1.3 FEA Solution Refinement

The process of bringing the FEA approximation error to acceptable levels is typically called *solution refinement*. There are two alternative ways in which an FEA solution can be refined.

The first option involves increasing the order of polynomials within the finite elements, without changing the elements' sizes.

Consider the beam shown previously in Figure 1–3. If you use second-degree polynomials $Y = a_0 + a_1X + a_2X^2$ to approximate the deflection within each element, it results in a more accurate solution without needing to make the finite elements smaller, as shown in Figure 1–4.

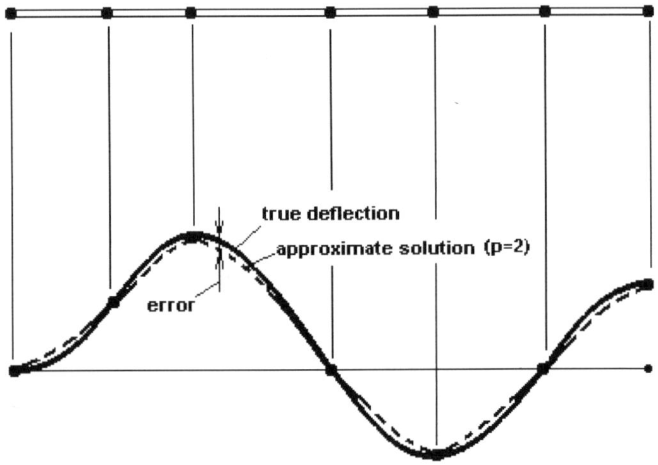

Figure 1–4

CATIA GSA software has limited ability to work with the order of polynomials within the finite elements; the only available options are linear elements that use 1st degree polynomials and parabolic elements that use 2nd degree polynomials.

The second option involves making the finite elements in the mesh progressively smaller while maintaining the order of polynomials within each element.

Again, consider the example of the beam shown previously in Figure 1–3. If you make the finite elements smaller without changing anything else, the approximation error becomes smaller as well, as shown in Figure 1–5.

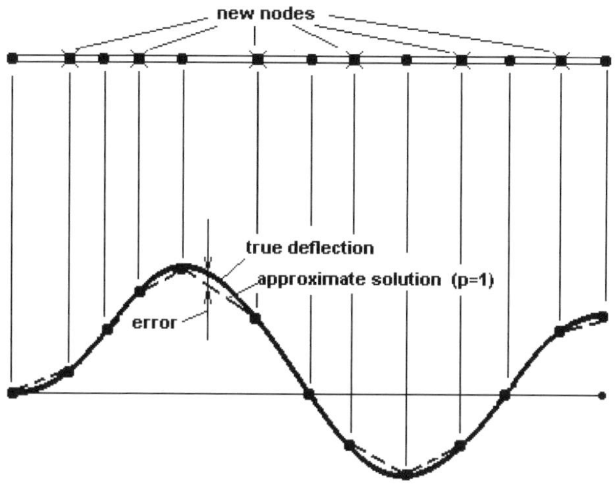

Figure 1–5

This approach is the one that is predominantly used in the GSA workbench for improving the FEA solution.

1.4 GSA Assumptions and Limitations

The GSA's intended users are design engineers rather than FEA experts. The software is intended to be used mostly for linear analyses rather than for complex nonlinear simulations requiring a high level of specialized expertise. As such, its use is subject to the following assumptions and limitations.

Linear Material Model

The materials in the analysis are assumed to be linear elastic (i.e., the relationship between the stress and the strain follows Hooke's law). The elastic materials are characterized by two properties: Young's modulus (also called Modulus of Elasticity) and Poisson's ratio.

The nonlinear material behaviors such as plasticity, hyper-elasticity, or visco-elasticity (or creep) are not supported.

Small Displacements and Strains

All translations and rotations in the model are assumed small, which means that the equilibrium equations in the analysis are solved on the original (i.e., undeformed) geometry. Also, the strains are assumed small (i.e., under 2,000 microstrain).

The geometrically nonlinear simulations involving large displacements and rotations are not supported.

Geometrically Linear Contact

The word "contact" in FEA refers to varying with the load (i.e., nonlinear) boundary conditions and interactions between the parts. A simple example of such a condition would be an assembly in which initially there is a clearance between the parts, but this clearance gets eliminated and the parts start pressing against each other once the load exceeds a certain magnitude.

Although GSA software has some contact analysis capabilities, it is limited to only geometrically linear contact, in which the sliding between the parts in contact is negligible.

Geometrically nonlinear contact, such as with finite sliding, is not supported.

1.5 FEA Process

A typical FEA analysis process in GSA consists of three main steps, as shown in Figure 1–6:

- **Pre-processing:** All input data for the analysis is prepared, such as material properties, loads, and restraints.
- **Solution:** The model is checked for errors, and the analysis computation is performed.
- **Post-processing:** The analysis results are reviewed and verified. A report is prepared.

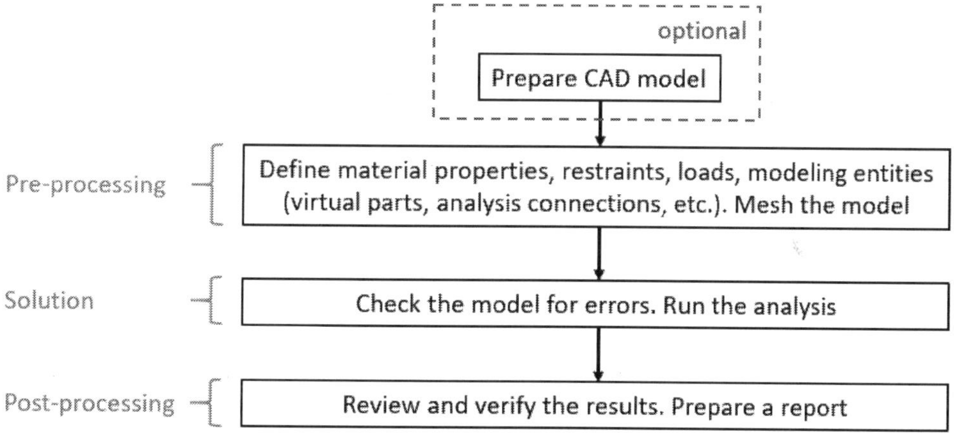

Figure 1–6

The CAD model preparation step is optional. It might not be required, depending on the complexity of the model and whether you intend to use idealizations such as shell or beam elements.

1.6 CAD Model Preparation

A CAD model is developed to provide detailed information for manufacturing. All of the required information related to fillets, rounds, holes, and threads must be included. Processing steps and surface finishes are indicated, and dimensions are fully specified.

An FEA model is developed to determine model behavior under a specific set of loading and boundary conditions. To analyze a model effectively, an FEA model is often different from a model developed for manufacturing. The symmetry of a model can often be exploited. Minor features, such as rounds, fillets, chamfers, and holes, can often be ignored unless they are expected to have a large effect on the result. Therefore, the general recommendation is to use the simplest model possible that is going to yield reliable results at the lowest computational time and cost.

In the example shown in Figure 1–7, the area of interest is the stress in the weld between two pipes due to high pressure. The FEA model for the component is shown on the right. In this case, the symmetry of the component (1/2 of the component) is used for the FEA model. The minor rounds, fillets, chamfers, and holes are also ignored.

Note that the FEA model would be different if the area of interest was the stress at the intersection of lips and pipes.

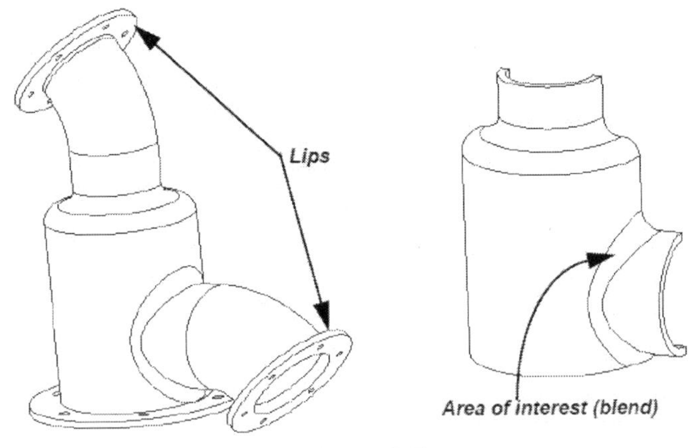

Figure 1–7

It must be emphasized that CAD model simplification is **optional**. If your model is not overly complex, and could be computed within a reasonable time, it is best to solve it “as is”, without any simplification or defeaturing.

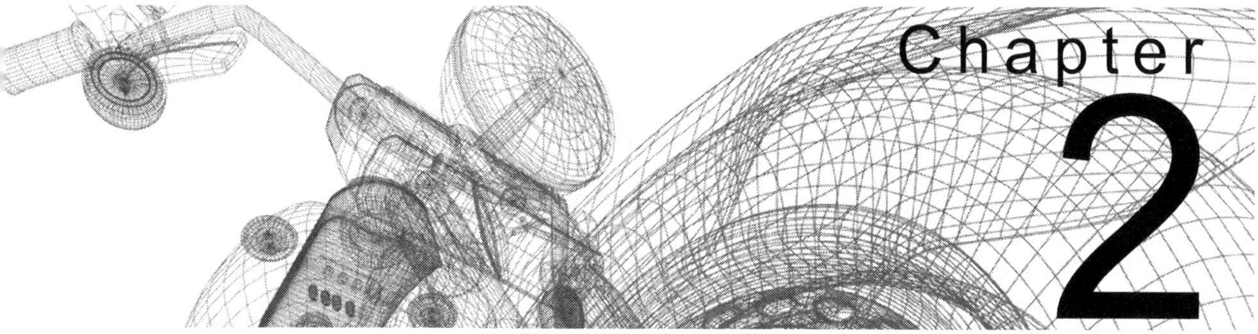

Chapter 2

Basic GSA Modeling

In this chapter, you learn about the tools and processes required to set up your model for a basic static stress analysis. You also learn how to run the computation and then view the results.

Learning Objectives in This Chapter

- Understand the Finite Element Analysis (FEA) process.
- Launch the Generative Structural Analysis (GSA) workbench.
- Apply materials.
- Mesh the model.
- Apply restraints and loads.
- Run the analysis.
- Visualize analysis results.
- Create analysis sensors.
- Create analysis report.

2.1 FEA Process

The FEA process contains three different components: pre-processing, computation, and post-processing. Each component contains several steps, as shown in Figure 2–1.

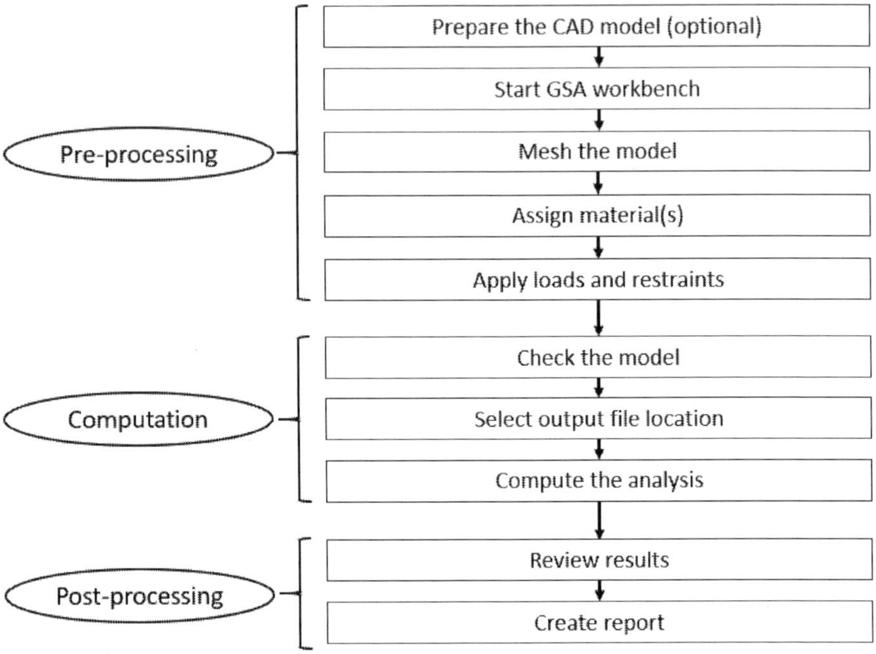

Figure 2–1

The pre-processing involves preparing all the data necessary for the analysis, such as mesh, material properties, loads, and restraints. This stage may optionally involve CAD model preparation, such as simplification and defeaturing, and creating auxiliary geometry, such as mid-surfaces, points, and lines used for specifying load directions, etc.

The computation stage is a batch-like process. Once the model is prepared and checked for errors and the location for the result and computation files is specified, the computation is done by the GSA solver automatically, without any user involvement. Computation time may vary from seconds to hours to days. The major contributing factor is the number of finite elements in the model, so care should be taken to avoid creating a mesh with too many elements.

The post-processing stage involves visualization and validation of the analysis results. Should the accuracy of the results be inadequate, the user might have to go back to the pre-processing stage and modify the model (e.g., refine the mesh, modify the simulation features, etc.), then re-compute the analysis and check the results again. This process may take several iterations, until the desired accuracy is attained.

Lastly, once the analysis is validated, the analysis report is issued.

2.2 Starting the GSA Workbench

To access the GSA workbench, open your **CATPart** or **CATProduct** and select **Start>Analysis & Simulation> Generative Structural Analysis**, as shown in Figure 2–2.

*If this option is not available in the **Start** menu, it means you do not have a license for this CATIA product.*

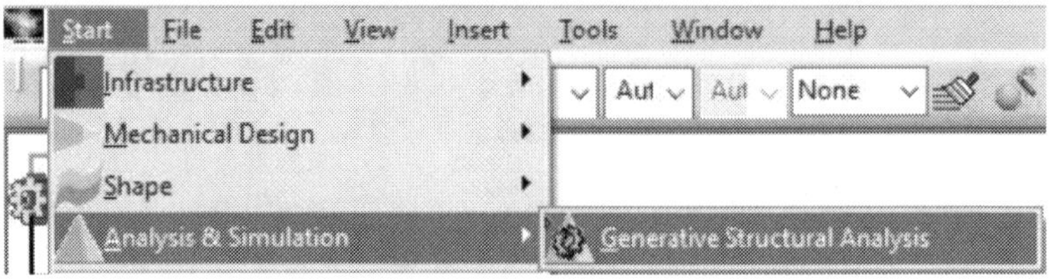

Figure 2–2

The New Analysis Case dialog box opens, as shown in Figure 2–3. Select the analysis case type from the list and click **OK** to start the GSA workbench.

Figure 2–3

CATIA opens a new **CATAnalysis** document and the workbench icon changes to  (Generative Structural Analysis for designers). The **CATAnalysis** document is linked to your part or product, similarly to how a CATDrawing document is linked to its parent part or product (i.e., when you make a design change in your part or product, the analysis will be aware of that change and will require an update).

The user interface is shown in Figure 2–4.

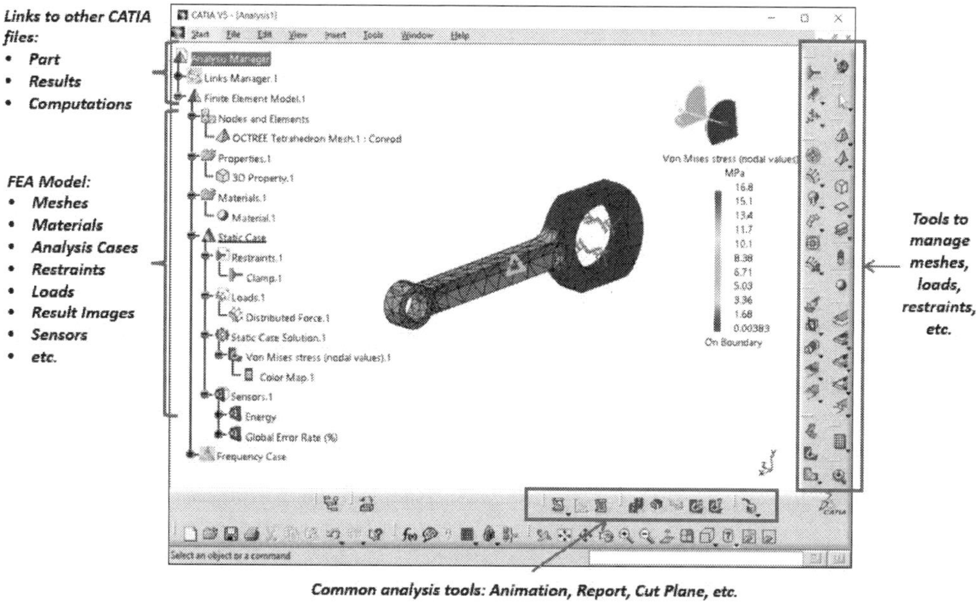

Figure 2–4

CATIA provides for a quick way to switch between the Part Design and GSA workbenches. To switch to the Part Design workbench in order to modify your part, expand **Links Manager.1** and double-click on the part in the tree. To return to the GSA workbench, double-click on **Finite Element Model.1** in the tree, as shown in Figure 2–5.

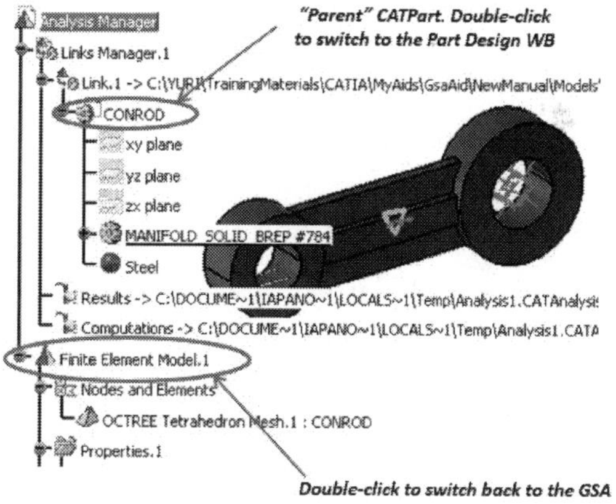

Figure 2–5

Note that once the part is modified, the analysis does not get updated automatically. The analysis must be re-computed upon the user's explicit request.

2.3 Applying Materials

There are two options for applying the material for the analysis:

- Apply the material to your CAD model while in the Part Design workbench.
- Apply the material in your analysis document while in the GSA workbench. Note that this overrides the material applied in the Part Design workbench, if any.

How To: Apply Materials in the Part Design Workbench

1. In the Apply Material toolbar, click  (Apply Material). The **Default Material Catalog** opens, as shown in Figure 2–6.

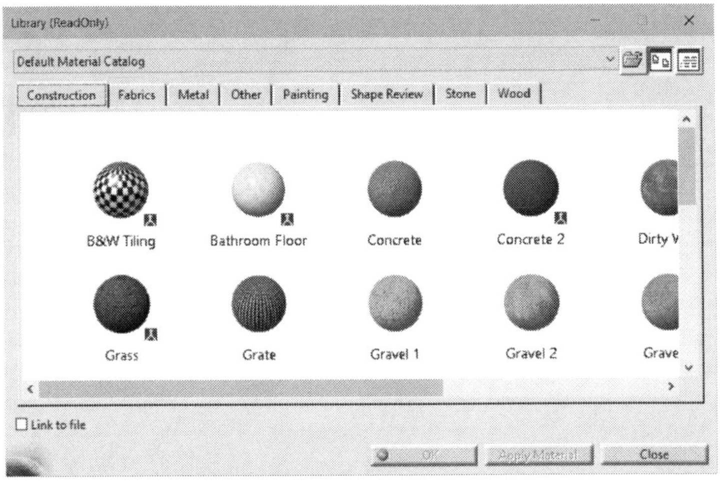

Figure 2–6

2. If you want to use a different material catalog, rather than the default one, select  (Open a material library) and browse to another material catalog.
3. Select a material in the library, select the part in the tree (as shown in Figure 2–7), and click **OK** to apply the material to the part and close the material library.

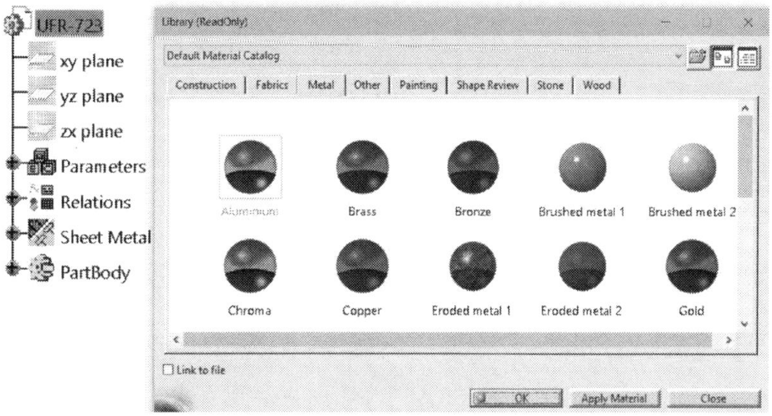

Figure 2–7

4. The applied material is displayed in the tree, as shown in Figure 2–8.

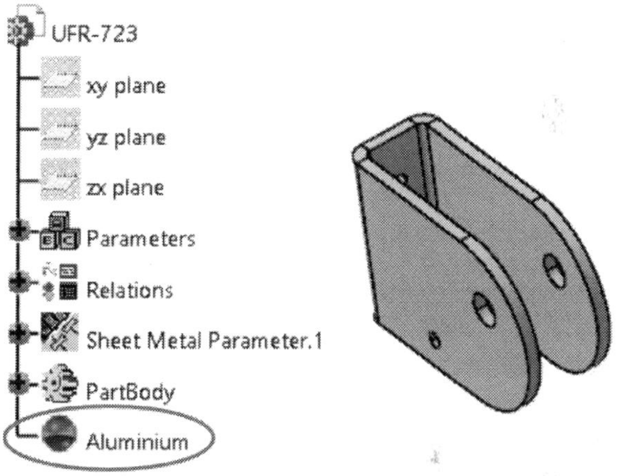

Figure 2–8

The material applied to your CAD model is automatically carried over into the analysis. You can double-click on **Material.1** in the analysis tree to verify, as shown in Figure 2–9.

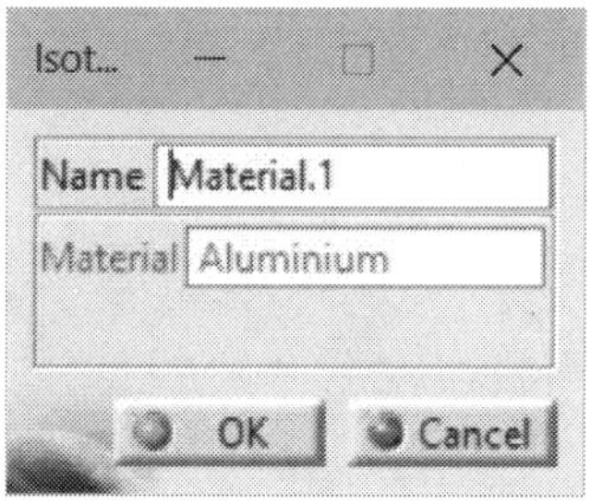

Figure 2–9

Also, the material is automatically assigned to the mesh, as shown in Figure 2–10. You can verify this by double-clicking on **3D Property.1** in the analysis tree.

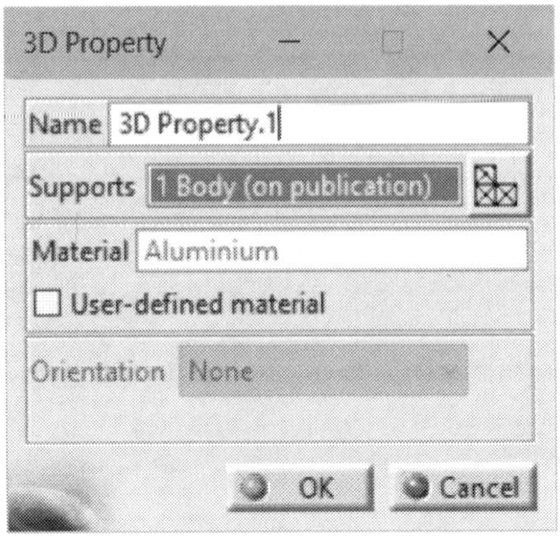

Figure 2–10

How To: Apply Materials in the GSA Workbench

1. In the Model Manager toolbar, click (User Material). The same **Default Material Catalog** opens as shown previously in Figure 2–7. Similarly, if you want to use a different material catalog, rather than the default one, select (Open a material library) and browse to another material catalog.
2. Select a material in the library and click **OK** to import the material into the analysis and close the material library.
3. The imported material appears as **User Material.1** in the tree, as shown in Figure 2–11.

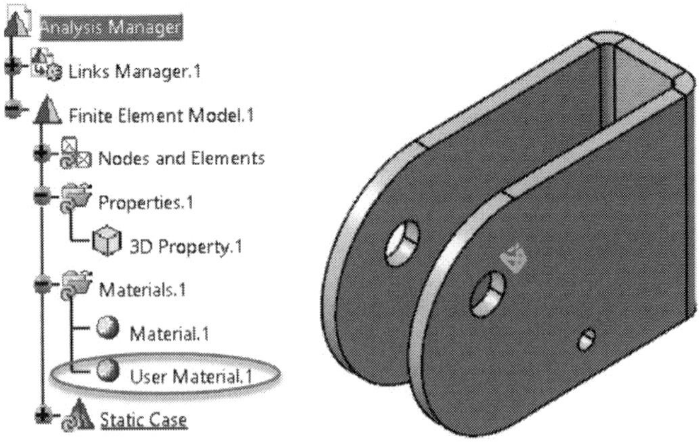

Figure 2–11

The user-defined material overrides the material definition applied to the CAD model, if any.

4. To assign the user material to the mesh, double-click on **3D Property.1**, activate the **User-defined material** option (as shown in Figure 2–12), and select the user material in the tree.

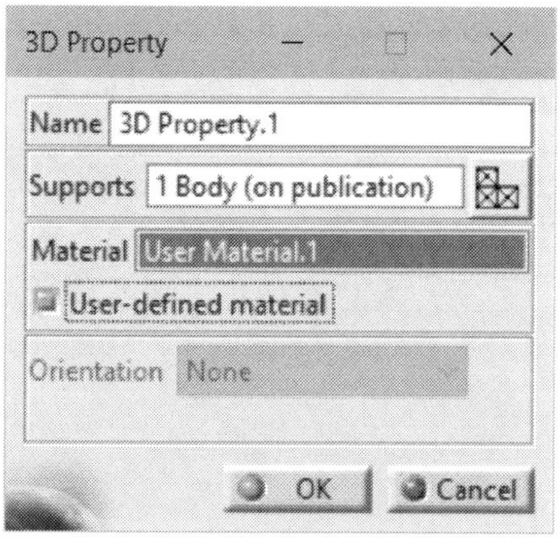

Figure 2–12

To verify the material properties, double-click on the material object in the tree to open the Properties dialog box and select the *Analysis* tab, as shown in Figure 2–13.

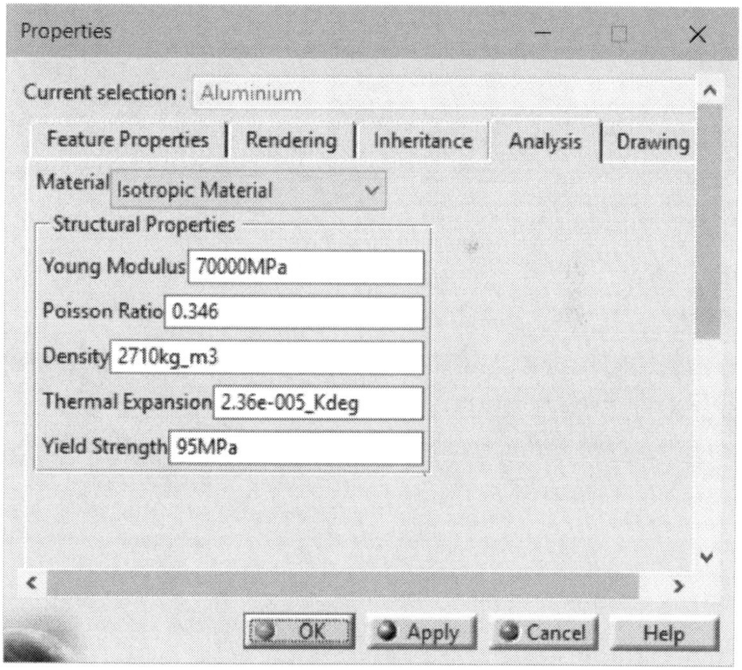

Figure 2–13

The Material drop-down list at the top of the dialog box contains several different material types, such as Orthotropic, Fiber, etc., as shown in Figure 2–14. However, in the GSA workbench, you can only use **Isotropic Material**; the other material types are reserved for CATIA's Composite Part Design workbench.

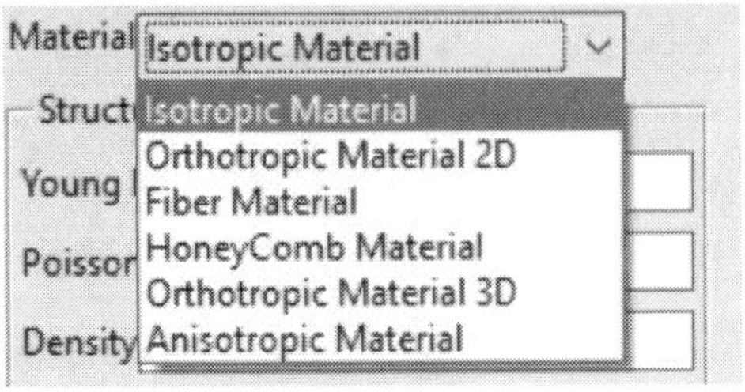

Figure 2–14

Also note that the **Yield Strength** property is for reference only. The GSA solver assumes all materials in the model are linear elastic; therefore, the **Yield Strength** is unused in the analysis computation.

2.4 Meshing the Model

CATIA automatically creates a mesh specification object for the part upon starting the GSA workbench, as shown in Figure 2–15.

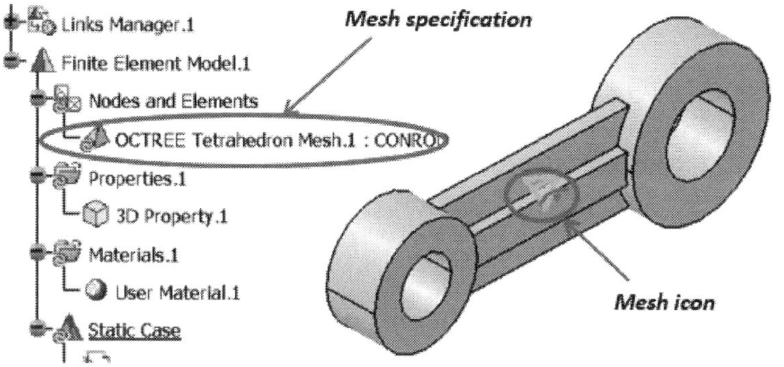

Figure 2–15

Important: A body other than the part body cannot be meshed in the GSA workbench. If your model is multi-body, you must assemble all the bodies into the part body to be able to mesh them.

Initially, the mesh parameters (finite element size, etc.) are determined by CATIA based only on the physical dimensions of the part and are seldom optimal in terms of analysis accuracy. Therefore, mesh parameters should always be checked and adjusted by the user prior to running the analysis.

To modify mesh parameters, either double-click on the mesh object in the tree or double-click on the mesh icon in the model. The OCTREE Tetrahedron Mesh dialog box opens, as shown in Figure 2–16.

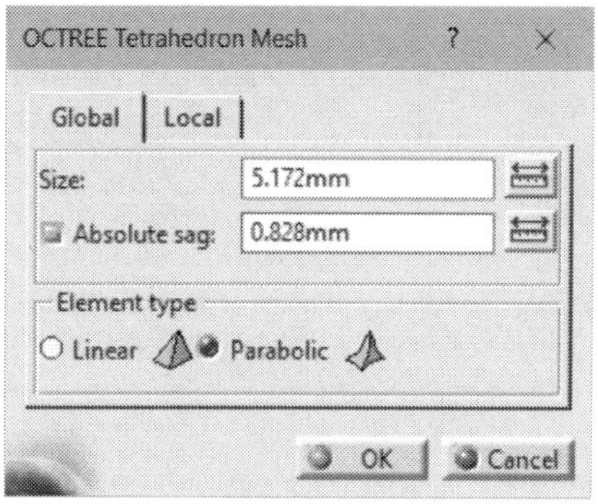

Figure 2–16

The OCTREE Tetrahedron Mesh dialog box contains the following parameters:

- **Element type:** Linear or Parabolic
    - **Linear** elements have four mesh nodes per element and their edges are straight lines, as shown in Figure 2–17. The linear elements use 1st order polynomials to approximate the displacement field within each element, which makes them poorly suitable for capturing bending effects in thin-walled parts. However, linear elements could be used for massive solid parts, provided you use sufficiently refined mesh. The linear elements solve faster than parabolic elements.
    - **Parabolic** elements have ten mesh nodes per element and their edges are curves, which makes them more suitable for accurate modeling of curved geometry, as shown in Figure 2–17. More importantly, parabolic elements use 2nd order polynomials for displacement approximation, which makes them more accurate than linear elements and well suited for all kinds of parts, including thin-walled parts. Parabolic elements are the generally recommended choice for structural stress analysis.

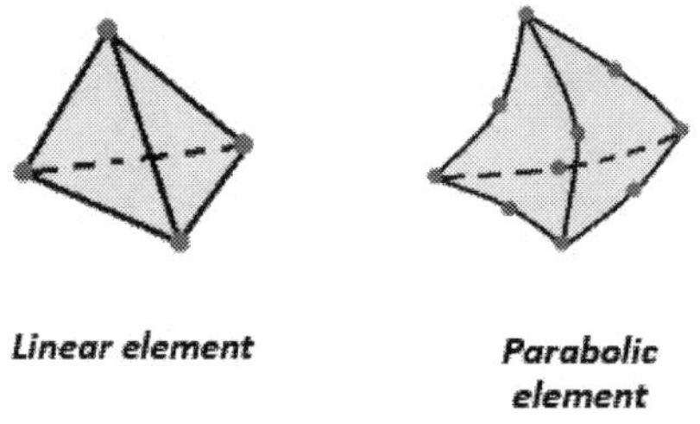

Figure 2–17

- **Size:** This is the characteristic size of the elements in the mesh, which is defined as the length of the longest edge in an element, as shown in Figure 2–18. Using a smaller element size results in a greater number of elements in the model and thus in a more accurate analysis, but at the cost of longer computation time. The recommendation is to try to strike a balance between the two – use the fewest number of elements in the model that would yield acceptable analysis accuracy.

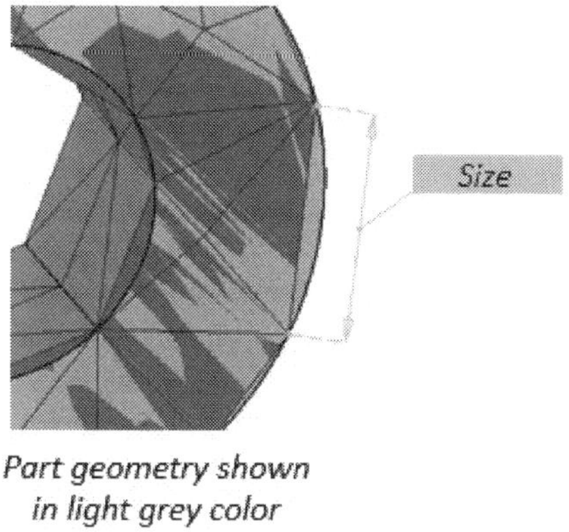

Figure 2–18

- **Absolute sag:** The sag is the allowed deviation between the mesh and the part geometry, as shown in Figure 2–19. This parameter affects the accuracy of the curved geometry representation in the mesh – the smaller the sag value, the more elements are used along the curved edges and surfaces of the part, hence the more accurately the mesh represents the surface geometry. However, care should be taken to not create too many elements in the model, as this may lead to unacceptably long computation time.

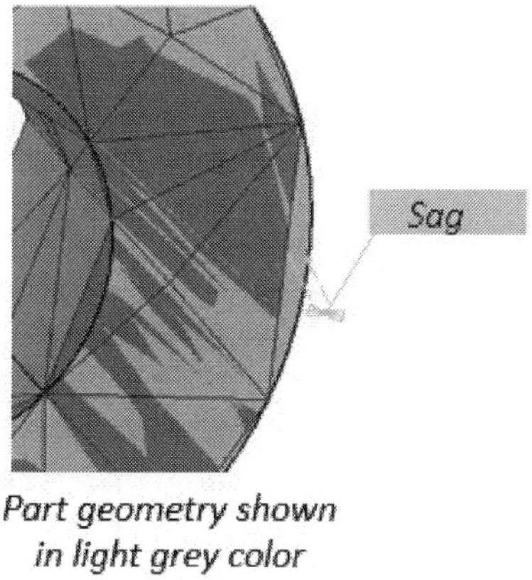

Figure 2–19

Once the mesh specification is finalized, the actual mesh is created automatically when the analysis is run.

Alternatively, if you want to review the mesh prior to running the analysis, right-click on **Nodes and Elements** in the tree and select **Mesh Visualization** in the contextual menu, as shown in Figure 2–20.

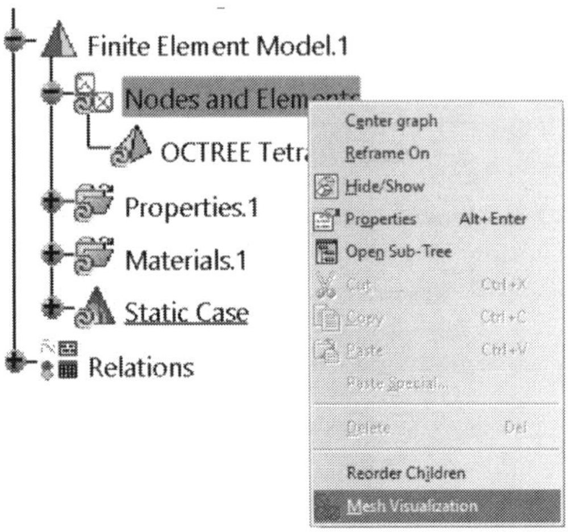

Figure 2–20

The model is now meshed, and the mesh is displayed in CATIA similar to that shown in Figure 2–21.

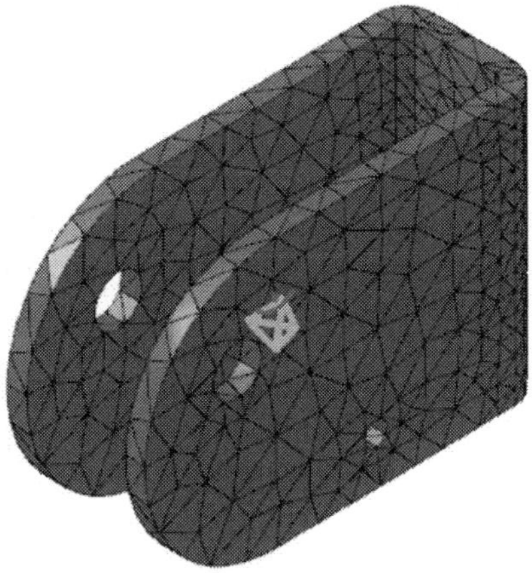

Figure 2–21

To remove the mesh image from the screen and return to the model view, right-click on **Mesh.1** in the tree and select **Delete** in the contextual menu, as shown in Figure 2–22. Note that this only deletes the mesh image but keeps the actual mesh in the model.

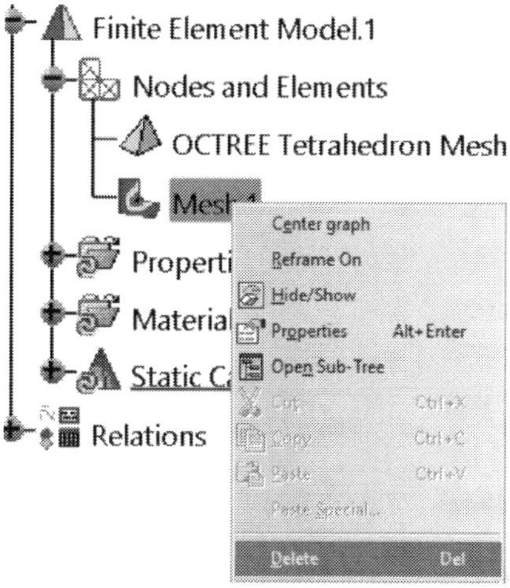

Figure 2–22

2.5 Applying Loads and Restraints

Loads and restraints in the GSA workbench cannot be applied directly to the mesh. Instead, loads and restraints must be applied to the model geometry, such as surfaces, edges, or points.

If you try to apply loads or restraints to the mesh, the mouse cursor displays the “no entry” symbol, as shown in Figure 2–23. Delete or deactivate the mesh image to return to the model view, then apply the load or restraint to the part geometry.

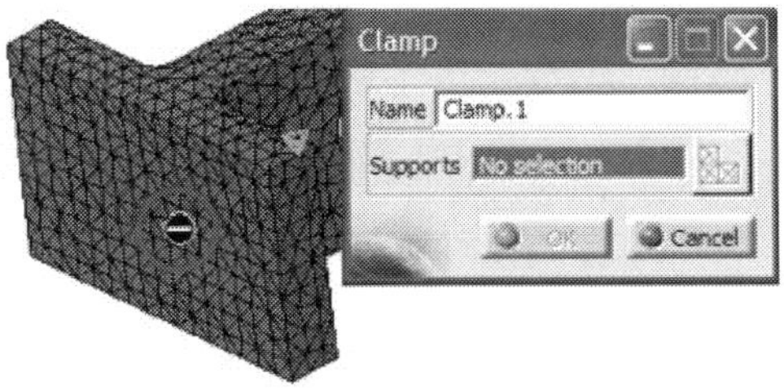

Figure 2–23

Restraints simulate supports and other boundary conditions, such as symmetry, in your model. Restraints can be applied to the part’s surfaces, edges, or points. The following table presents a summary of the restraints that can be created in GSA.

Restraint	Description
Clamp	Models an “immovable” boundary condition, with all degrees of freedom restrained
Surface Slider	Models the ability of a part to slide along a surface
Slider	Models a sliding motion along a direction; only applicable to Virtual Parts
Sliding Pivot	Models a sliding motion and rotation along a direction; only applicable to Virtual Parts
Ball Joint	Models a ball joint; only applicable to Virtual Parts
Pivot	Models a rotation about a direction; only applicable to Virtual Parts

User-defined Restraint	Enables the user to control restrained translations and rotations independently
Isostatic Restraint	Creates so-called minimal support for systems with balanced loads

Loads in your analysis are intended to simulate the actual loading conditions in your model. Loads can be applied to the part's surfaces, edges, or points. The following table presents a summary of the loads that can be applied in GSA.

Load	**Description**
Pressure	Applies pressure load on surfaces
Distributed Force	Distributes the specified total force over the geometrical entity
Moment	Applies a moment load, such as torque
Acceleration	Applies gravity load
Rotation Force	Applies centrifugal load
Line Force Density	Applies distributed force to edges and curves
Surface Force Density	Applies distributed force to surfaces
Volume Force Density	Applies distributed force to volumes
Force Density	Applies distributed force as computed from the total force
Enforced Displacement	Enforces specific displacement on a geometrical entity

2.6 Checking the Model

The GSA's **Model Checker** ( ) tool verifies whether all the pre-processing steps are done and whether the model is ready for computation.

If any data is missing, the **Model Checker** dialog box displays a icon and shows a **KO** status against that row in the dialog box, as shown in Figure 2–24. It also displays a detailed explanation at the bottom of the dialog box.

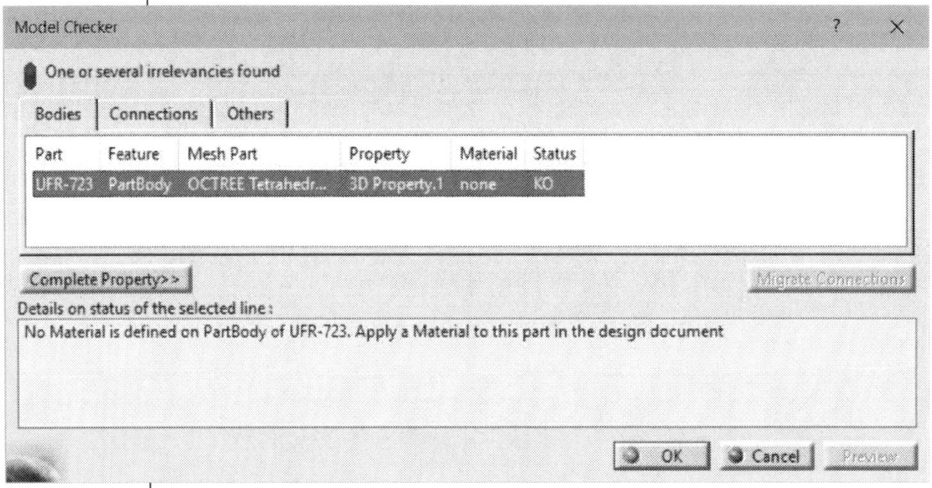

Figure 2–24

2.7 Selecting Output Files' Location

During the computation, the GSA solver creates additional files. The relationship between various files involved in the analysis is shown in Figure 2–25.

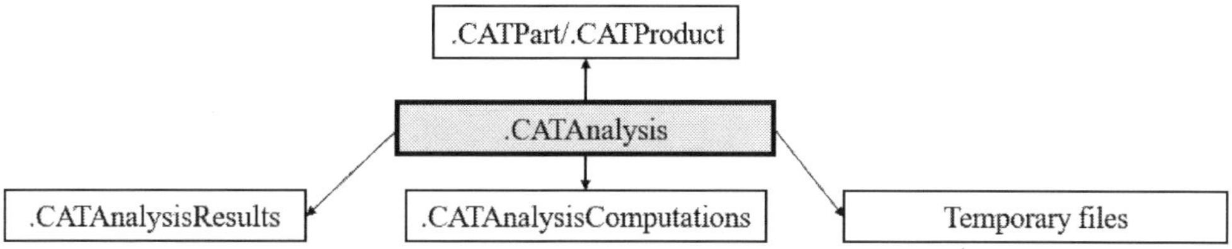

Figure 2–25

The **.CATAnalysis** file contains all the analysis specifications, such as mesh, materials, loads, restraints, etc. It is linked to, but does not contain, your CAD model.

The **.CATAnalysisResults** file stores all the data necessary for the post-processing tasks, such as result visualization, animation, cut plane analysis, etc. If this file is misplaced or deleted, the analysis must be re-computed in order to view the results.

The **.CATAnalysisComputations** file stores some intermediate solver data with the intent of shortening the computation time on subsequent analysis runs. It is not required for viewing the results, so it can be deleted once the analysis is completed and validated.

To specify the location for the **.CATAnalysisResults** and **.CATAnalysisComputations** files, in the Solver Tools toolbar select  (External Storage) to open the External Storage dialog box, as shown in Figure 2–26. Click **Modify** and browse to the directory of your choice.

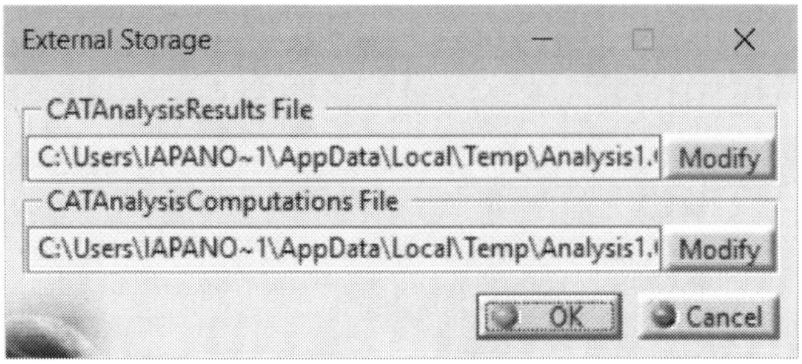

Figure 2–26

To delete the files, select  (External Storage Clean-up) in the Solver Tools toolbar to open the External Storage Clean-up dialog box, as shown in Figure 2–27. Use the options in the dialog box to delete either the computation file only, or both computation and result files.

Figure 2–27

The temporary files are created and deleted "on the fly" while the GSA solver is running, and those files can take up a lot of hard disk space. You can control the location for the files by clicking  (Temporary External Storage) in the Solver Tools toolbar to open the **Temporary External Storage** dialog box, then clicking **Modify** to select a directory of your choice, as shown in Figure 2–28.

Figure 2–28

The locations for the files can also be selected automatically by implementing a specific policy through the **Tools>Options> Analysis & Simulation>External Storage** options, as shown in Figure 2–29.

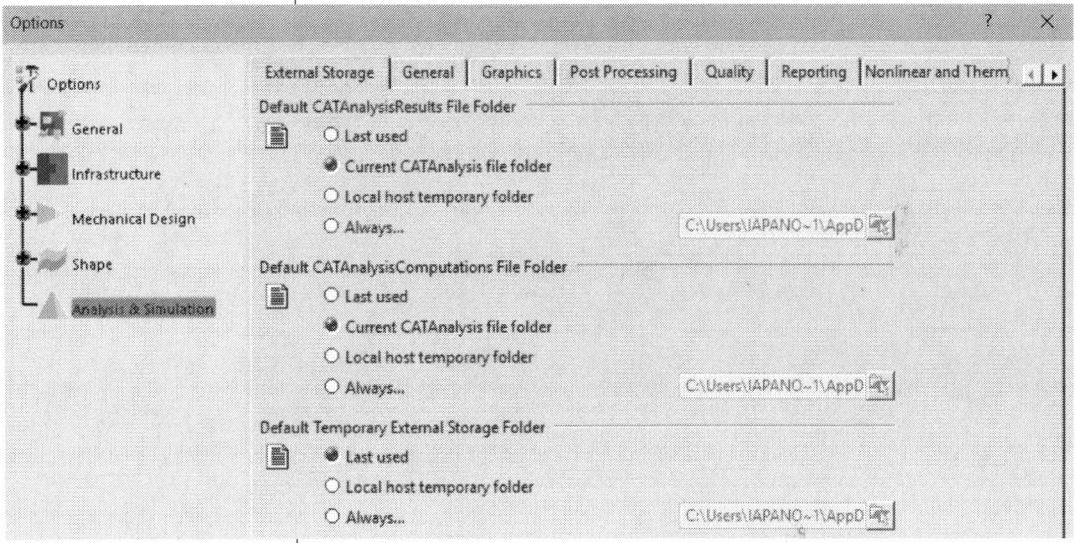

Figure 2–29

2.8 Computation

To start the analysis computation, select  (Compute) in the Compute toolbar. The Compute dialog box opens, as shown in Figure 2–30.

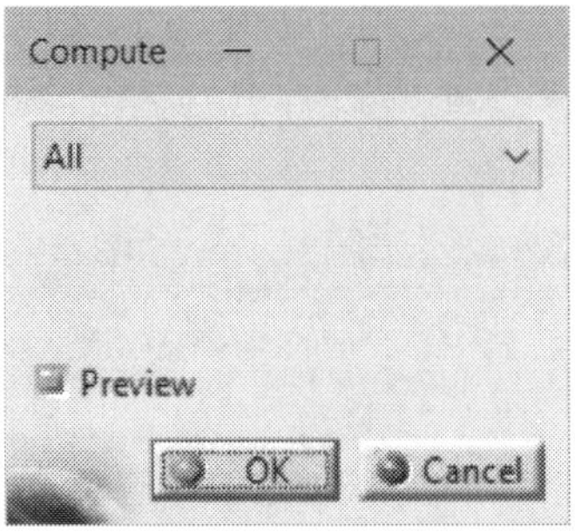

Figure 2–30

The drop-down list at the top of dialog box contains the following options, as shown in Figure 2–31:

- **All:** Solves the entire analysis model for all of the analysis cases
- **Mesh Only:** Only meshes the model, without solving
- **Analysis Case Solution Selection:** Solves only the selected analysis case

Figure 2–31

To start the computation, click **OK** and wait until the Computation Resources Estimation dialog box displays (it may take some time), as shown in Figure 2–32.

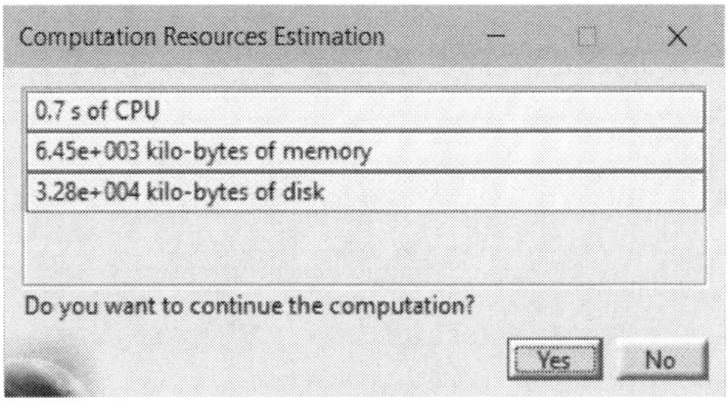

Figure 2–32

The following information is displayed in the dialog box:

- Amount of CPU time, in seconds, necessary to carry out the computation
- Amount of RAM for the computation
- Amount of hard disk space for the computation

Click **Yes** to continue the computation. CATIA displays a series of messages (meshing, factorization, etc.), informing you about the status of the computation. Wait until the computation is complete.

2.9 Results Visualization

The GSA workbench enables you to visualize many different types of results, such as deformations, displacements, and stresses. The following table summarizes the tools used to display the results, which are found in the Image toolbar.

Tool		Description
	Deformation	Displays the deformed mesh
	Von Mises Stress	Displays Von Mises Stress
	Displacement	Displays displacements
	Principal Stress	Displays principal stress
	Precision	Displays discretization error plot, used as the aid in mesh refinement

Once a result plot is displayed, you can double-click on it to open the Image Edition dialog box, which reveals additional visualization options. For example, double-clicking on the **Principal Stress** plot opens options to display the result as a color plot or as a vector plot, to select between various stress criteria (Principal shearing, Principal value, etc.), to select specific stress components (using the Component drop-down list), etc., as shown in Figure 2–33.

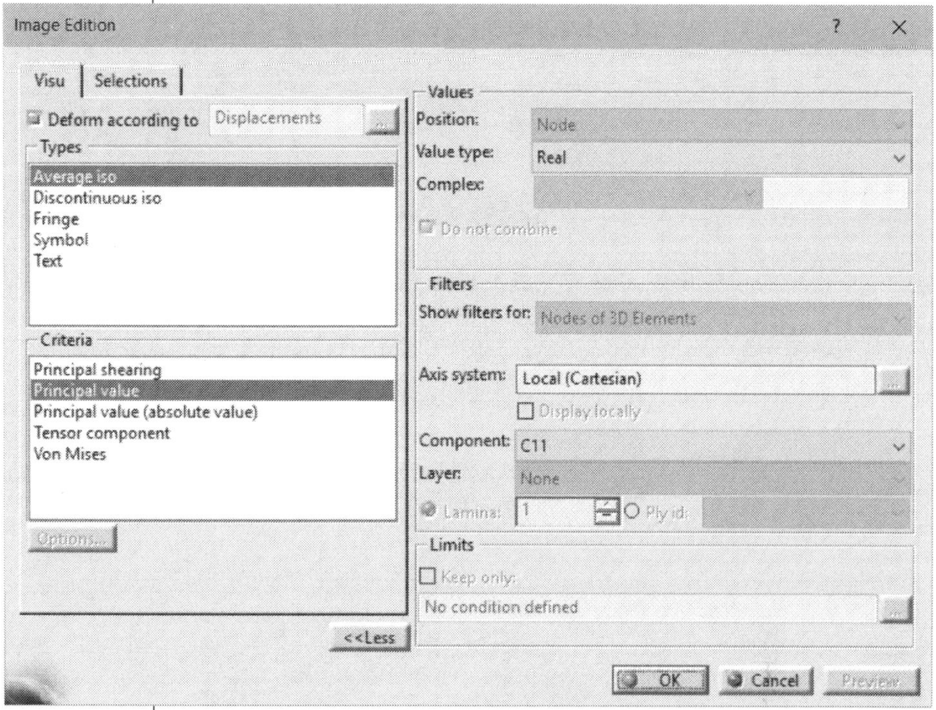

Figure 2–33

In addition, the result plots can be animated for better understanding of model deformation, cross-sectioned with a cut plane, annotated with the minimum and maximum stress labels, etc. The following table lists these tools, which are found in the Analysis Tools toolbar.

Tool		Description
	Animate	Animates the result image
	Cut Plane Analysis	Cuts the result image with a cross-section plane
	Amplification Magnitude	Scales the displayed deformation up or down, for better visualization
	Image Extrema	Finds locations of minimum and maximum values in the image
	Information	Displays the summary information about a result plot

2.10 Result Sensors

The result sensors in CATIA GSA are, essentially, "virtual gauges" that you can place on your analysis model to monitor quantities of interest at specific locations.

There are two types of result sensors that you can create:

- **Global Sensors:** These are the quantities computed for the entire model.
- **Local Sensors:** These are the quantities computed for a specific location in your model.

To create a global sensor, right-click on the **Sensors.1** object in the tree and select **Create Global Sensor**, as shown in Figure 2–34.

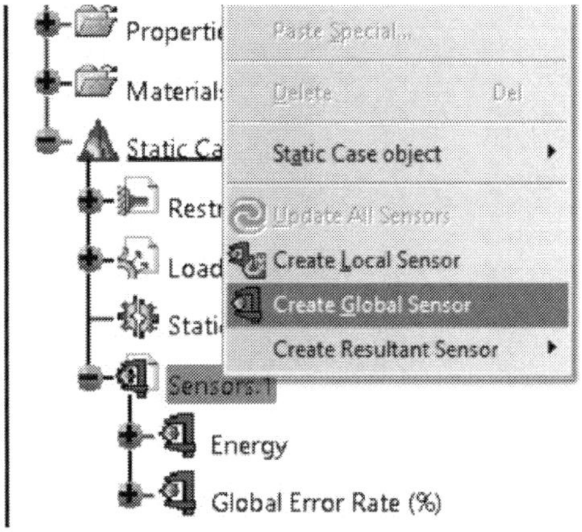

Figure 2–34

In the Create Sensor dialog box, select the quantity in the list and click **OK**, as shown in Figure 2–35.

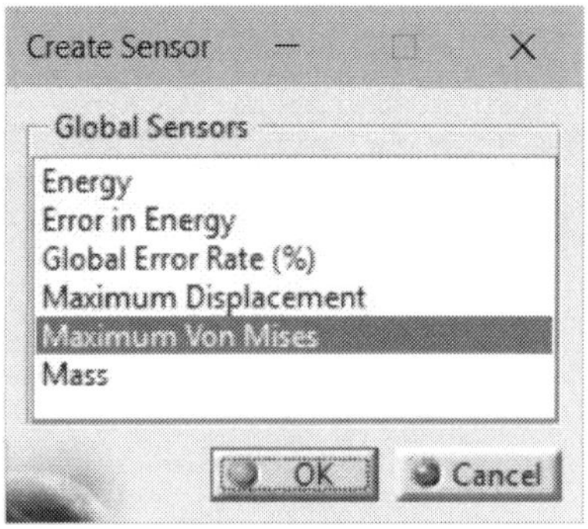

Figure 2–35

If the sensor does not display the value, activate the Tools> Options>Parameters and Measures> Knowledge> Parameter Tree View> With value option.

The sensor is displayed in the tree, as shown in Figure 2–36.

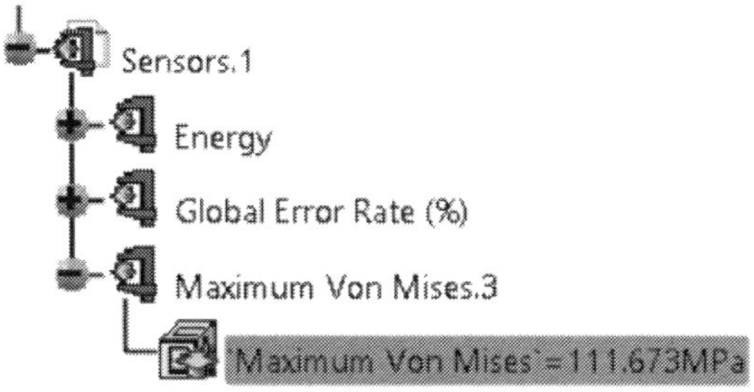

Figure 2–36

To create a local sensor, right-click on the **Sensors.1** object in the tree and select **Create Local Sensor** in the contextual menu. Select the quantity in the Create Sensor dialog box and click **OK**, as shown in Figure 2–37.

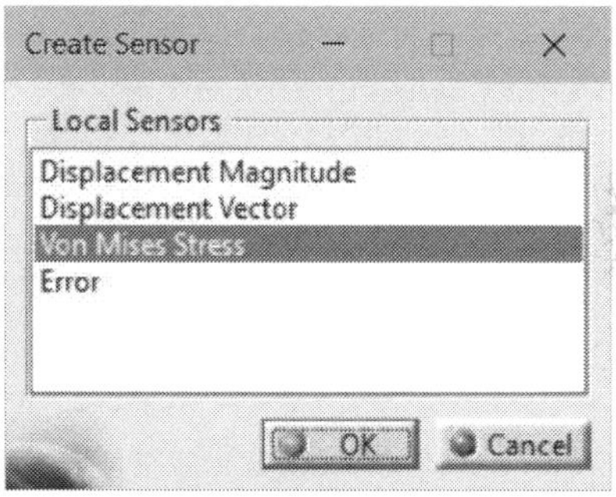

Figure 2–37

The new sensor displays in the tree with the exclamation symbol (as shown in Figure 2–38), meaning that it is still incomplete.

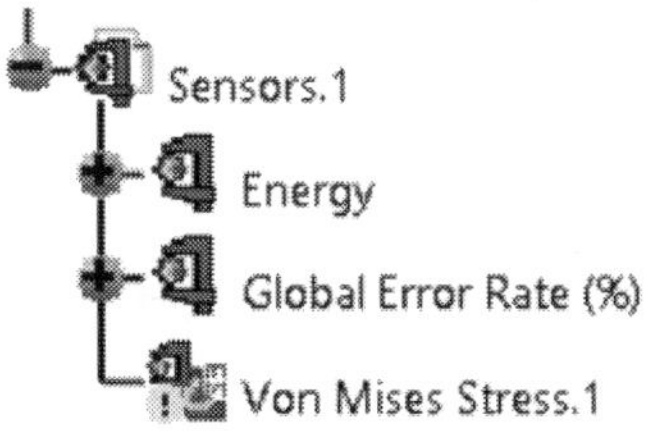

Figure 2–38

To complete the local sensor, double-click on the sensor object in the tree. In the Local Sensor dialog box that opens, make the following selections, as shown in Figure 2–39:

- **Supports:** Select a location in the model on which to compute the sensor. This could be a surface, an edge, or a point.
- **Post-Treatment:** If a point is the sensor support, the Post-Treatment must be set to **None**. If a surface or an edge has been selected as the sensor support, select whether to obtain the **Maximum**, **Minimum**, or **Average** value on that surface or edge.
- **Create Parameters:** Select this option in order to have the sensor's value displayed in the tree.

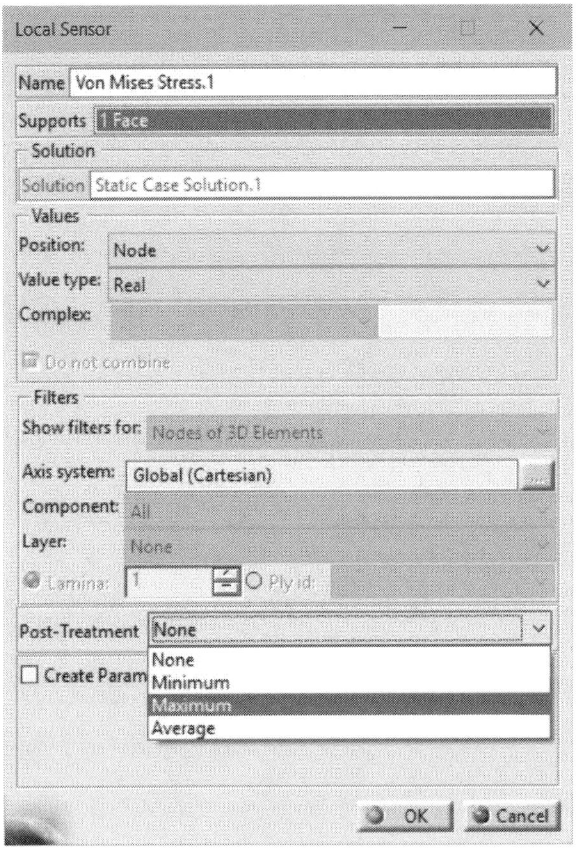

Figure 2–39

Click **OK** to close the Local Sensor dialog box. The sensor now displays the value in the tree and in the model, as shown in Figure 2–40.

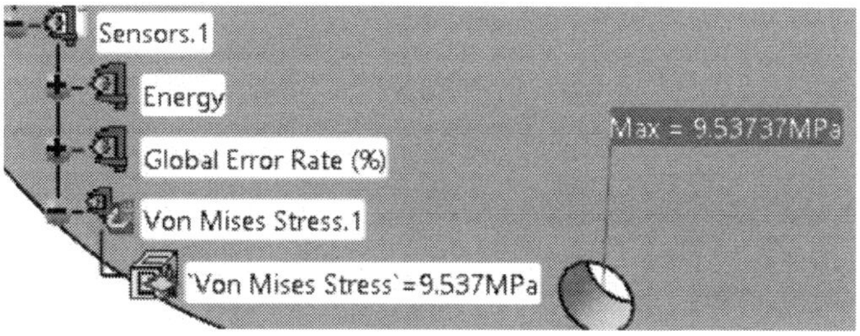

Figure 2–40

2.11 Creating a Report

To create an analysis report in HTML format, click (Generate Report) in the Analysis Results toolbar. The Report Generation dialog box opens, as shown in Figure 2–41.

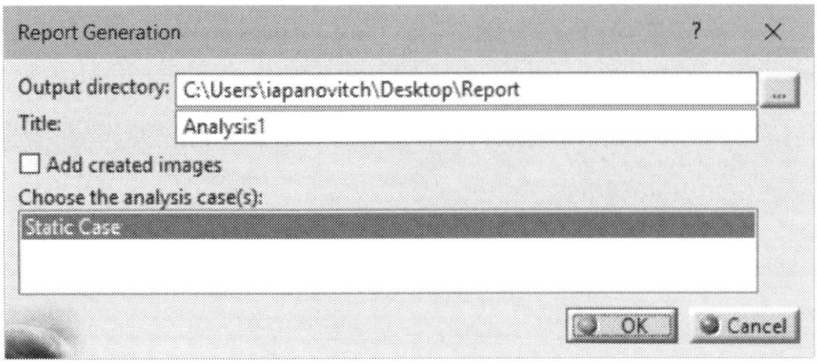

Figure 2–41

To select the output directory for the report, click the ellipsis button (...) and browse to the folder of your choice.

Enter the report title and select the analysis case for the report. Once you click **OK**, the report files are saved in the output directory, and the report opens in your default web browser, as shown in Figure 2–42.

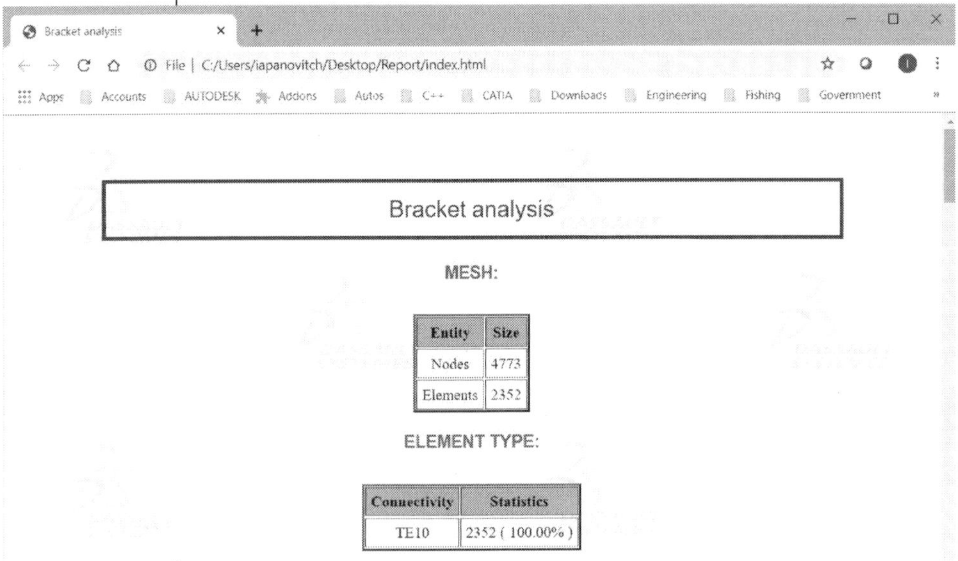

Figure 2–42

By default, the report contains the following sections:

- Information about the mesh
- Material properties
- Boundary conditions (loads and restraints)
- Computation data (loads summary, factorization, equilibrium, etc.)
- Deformed mesh image
- Von Mises Stress image

To add more result images to the report, you must first create those images so they display in the tree, then activate the **Add created images** option in the Report Generation dialog box.

Practice 2a Static Stress Analysis of a Bracket

Practice Objectives

- Apply the material.
- Mesh the model.
- Set up loads and restraints.
- Compute the analysis.
- Display the results.
- Modify the part dimensions and re-compute the analysis.
- Create an analysis report.

In this practice, you will set up and run a static stress analysis on a simple bracket model, shown in Figure 2–43. You will also examine the analysis results, make a design change, and re-run the analysis to validate the design change.

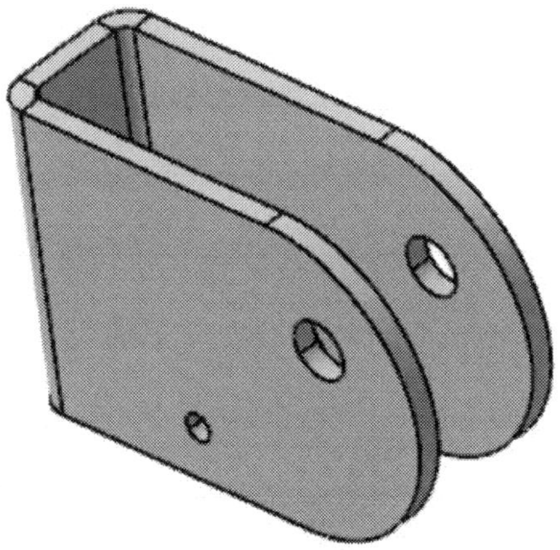

Figure 2–43

Task 1 - Open the part in CATIA.

1. Open **UFR-723_02.CATPart** from the *CATIA Generative Structural Analysis Practice Files\Ch02* folder.

2. Set the model display as (Shading with Edges). The part displays as shown in Figure 2–44.

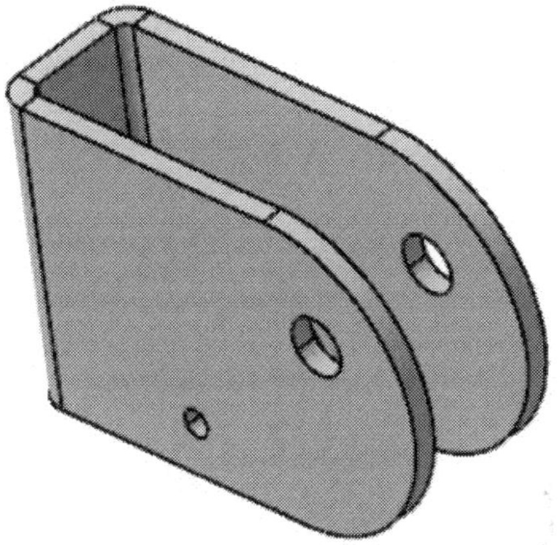

Figure 2–44

3. Select **Tools>Options>Parameters and Measures>Units** and set the units as follows:

   - Length: **Millimeter (mm)**
   - Force: **Newton (N)**
   - Moment: **Newton x Meter (Nxm)**
   - Pressure: **Megapascal (MPa)**

Task 2 - Apply the material.

In this task, you will select the material for the bracket.

1. In the Apply Material toolbar, click  (Apply Material). The **Default Material Catalog** opens, as shown in Figure 2–45.

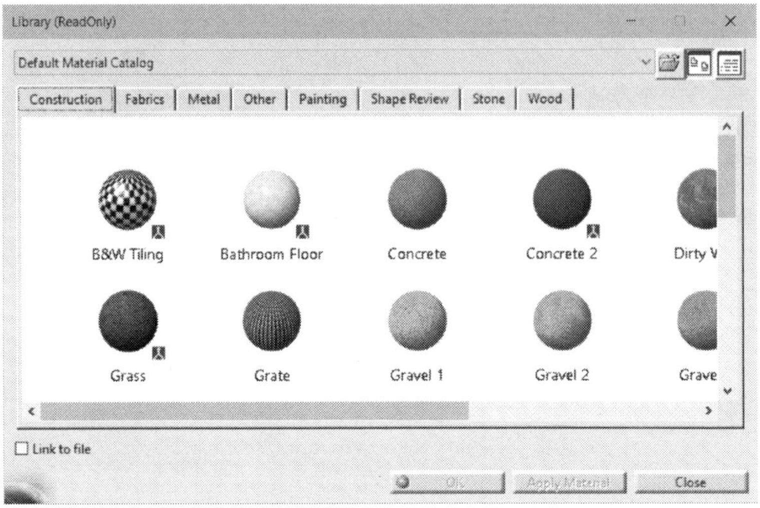

Figure 2–45

2. Select the *Metal* tab and click **Aluminium**. Select the **UFR-723** part in the tree, as shown in Figure 2–46, and click **OK** to apply the material to the part and close the Library dialog box.

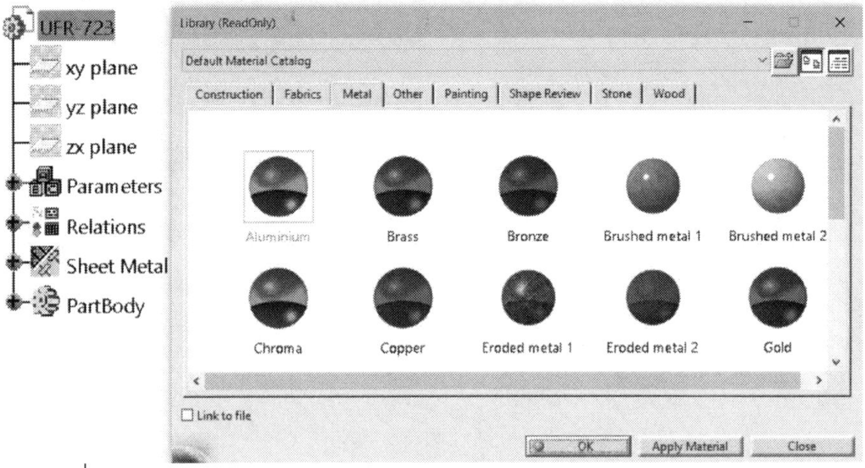

Figure 2–46

3. Double-click on **Aluminium** in the tree to open the Properties dialog box. Select the *Analysis* tab. Note that the **Aluminium** material has the following mechanical properties, as shown in Figure 2–47:

    - Material: **Isotropic Material**
    - Young Modulus: **70000MPa**
    - Poisson Ratio: **0.346**
    - Density: **2710kg/m^3**
    - Thermal Expansion: **2.36e-005/Kdeg**
    - Yield Strength: **95MPa**

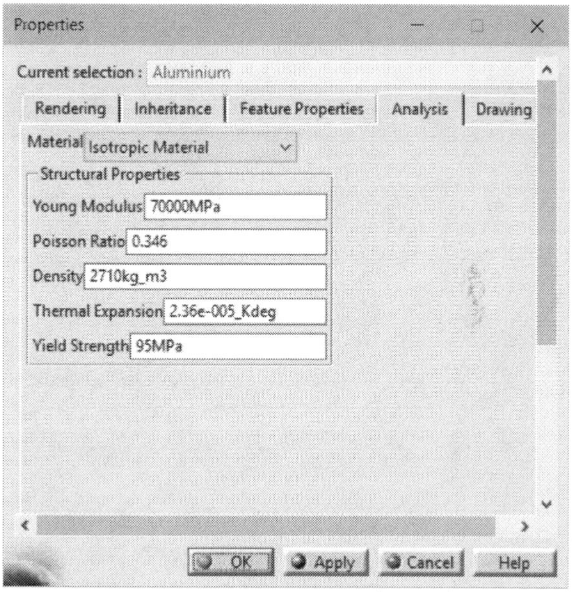

Figure 2–47

4. Click **OK** to close the Properties dialog box.

Task 3 - Launch the GSA workbench.

1. Select **Start>Analysis & Simulation>Generative Structural Analysis**, as shown in Figure 2–48.

Note: *If this option is not available, you do not have a license for this CATIA product.*

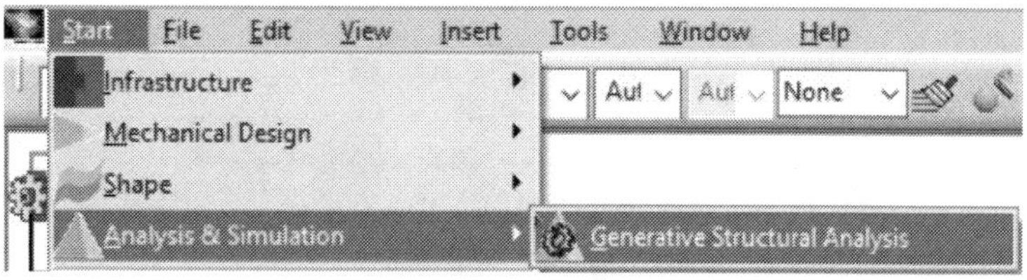

Figure 2–48

2. In the New Analysis Case dialog box, select **Static Analysis** and click **OK**, as shown in Figure 2–49.

Figure 2–49

3. CATIA opens a new analysis document, named **Analysis1.CATAnalysis**, and the workbench icon changes to .

4. Examine the specification tree of the **Analysis1** document and note that CATIA created the following entities, as shown in Figure 2–50:

   - **OCTREE Tetrahedron Mesh.1: UFR-723:** This is the default mesh specification. It is created automatically whenever there is a non-empty **PartBody** in the model.
   - **3D Property.1:** This assigns the material properties to the mesh.
   - **Material.1:** This is the material specification imported from the part model. You applied the material to the part in Task 2. Double-clicking on **Material.1** reveals that the imported material is indeed Aluminium.
   - **Static Case:** This is the default analysis case. Note that the Restraints.1 and Loads.1 nodes in the Static Case are still empty, since you have not applied any loads or restraints yet.

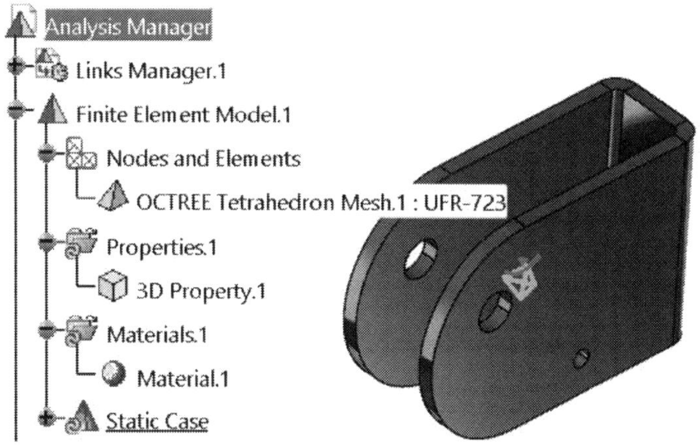

Figure 2–50

Task 4 - Mesh the bracket part.

In this task, you will mesh the bracket, which enables you to check prior to the analysis whether CATIA is able to mesh your model. You will also link the mesh parameters to the bracket thickness using CATIA formulas.

1. Select **Tools>Options>Infrastructure>Part Infrastructure> Display** and activate the **Parameters** display, as shown in Figure 2–51.

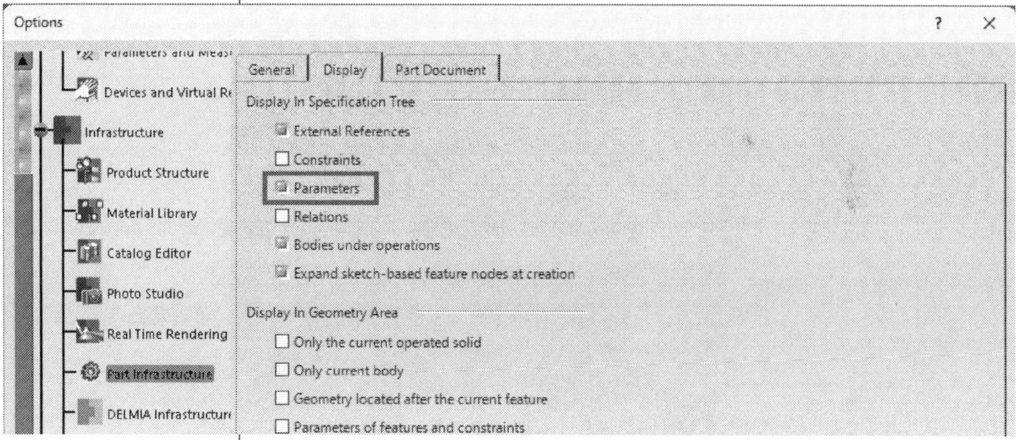

Figure 2–51

Activating these options ensures that the parameters and formulas that will be created in the next steps are shown in the specification tree.

2. Select **Tools>Options>Analysis & Simulation>General** and activate the **Show parameters** and **Show relations** options, as shown in Figure 2–52. Click **OK** to close the Options dialog box.

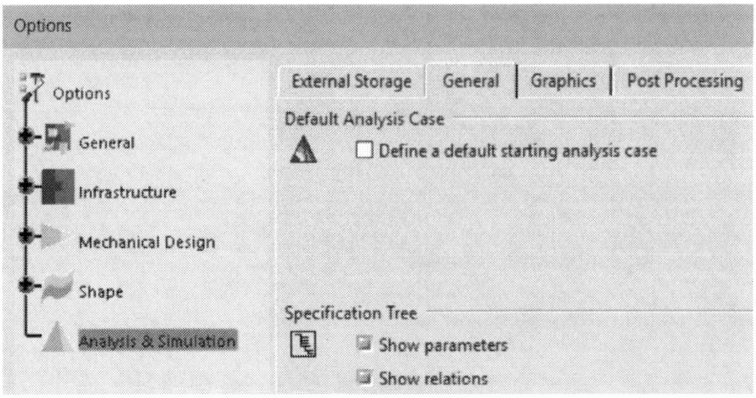

Figure 2–52

3. Double-click on **OCTREE Tetrahedron Mesh.1: UFR-723** in the tree. The OCTREE Tetrahedron Mesh dialog box opens, as shown in Figure 2–53, which displays the default mesh size and sag.

CATIA selects the default mesh parameters as a percentage of the size of the part.

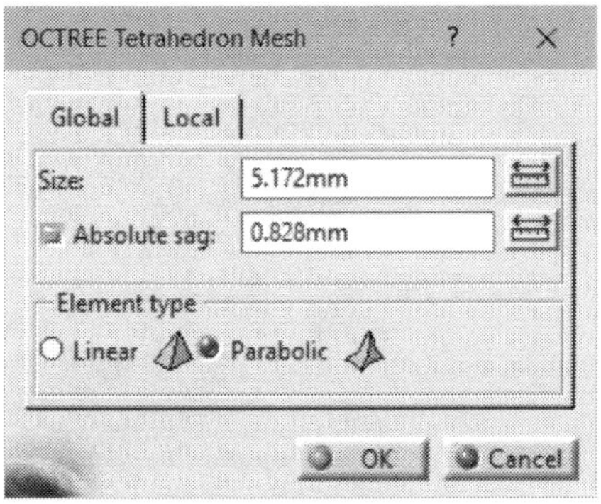

Figure 2–53

4. Ensure that the *Element type* is set to **Parabolic**.

In the following steps, you will link the mesh parameters to the part thickness, which will ensure that the correct mesh is created whenever the part thickness is modified.

5. Right-click in the *Size* field and select **Edit formula** in the contextual menu, as shown in Figure 2–54.

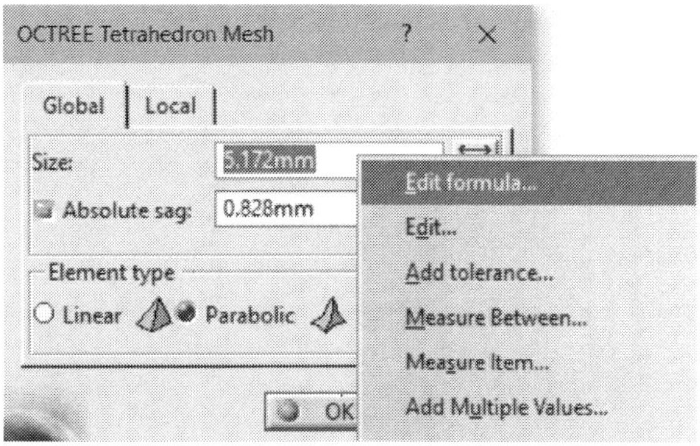

Figure 2–54

6. The Formula Editor dialog box opens, as shown in Figure 2–55.

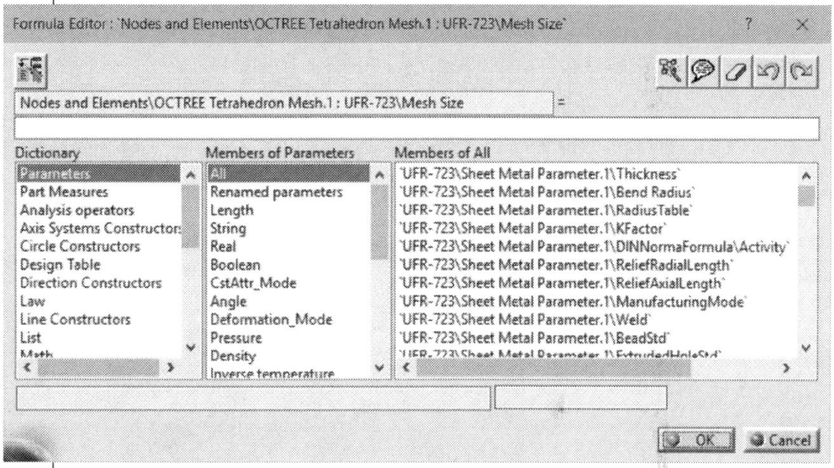

Figure 2–55

For thin-walled parts, the rule of thumb is to use a mesh size that is between 1.5 and 1.8 times the part thickness. This ensures good analysis accuracy without creating an excessive number of finite elements.

7. Expand the tree and click the parameter named **Thickness** in the part model, which will put this parameter into the formula. Multiply the parameter by **1.8**, as shown in Figure 2–56, which will ensure that the mesh size is 1.8 times the part thickness.

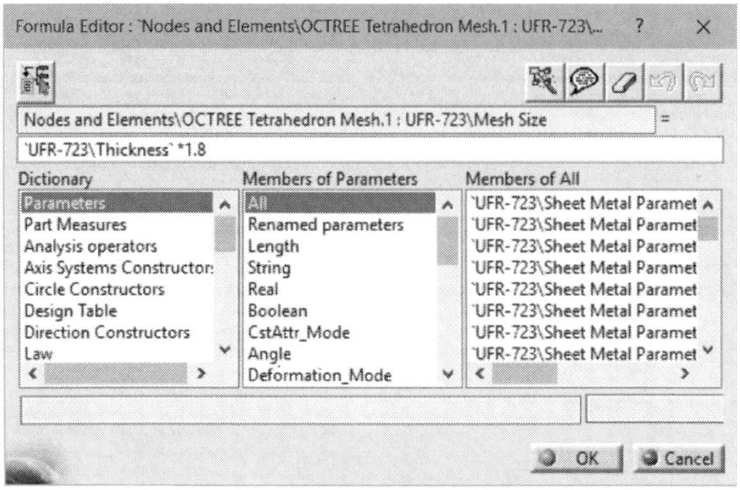

Figure 2–56

8. Click **OK** to close the Formula Editor dialog box and return to the OCTREE Tetrahedron Mesh dialog box.

In the following steps, you will link the mesh sag and size parameters with a formula.

9. Right-click in the *Absolute sag* field and select **Edit formula** in the contextual menu, as shown in Figure 2–57.

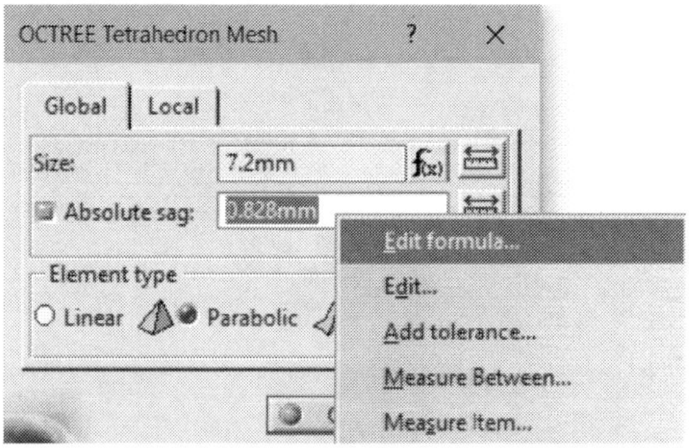

Figure 2–57

10. The Formula Editor dialog box opens, as shown in Figure 2–58.

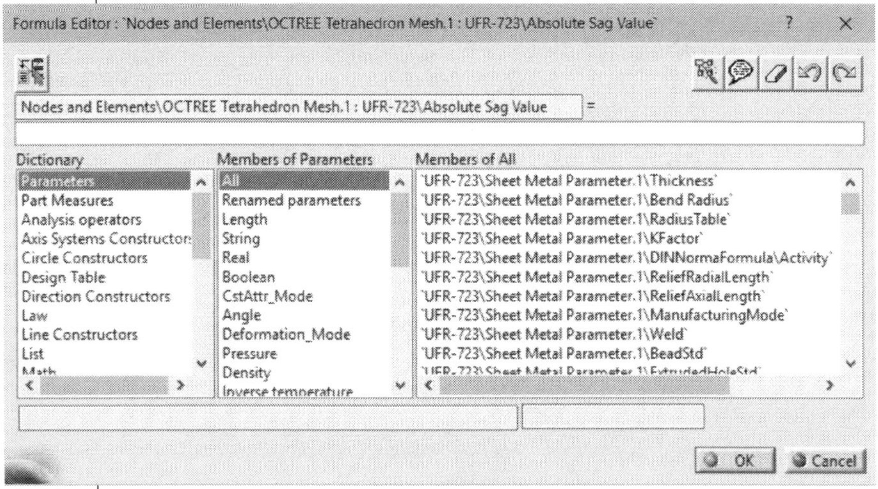

Figure 2–58

11. Select **OCTREE Tetrahedron Mesh.1: UFR-723** in the tree. This filters the parameters displayed in the Formula Editor dialog box, so now the **Members of All** column only lists parameters in the selected entity, which is the mesh specification.

The rule of thumb for the mesh sag is between 0.15 and 0.2 of the mesh size. This ensures good mesh on curved surfaces without creating an excessive number of finite elements.

12. Double-click on the **Nodes and Elements\OCTREE Tetrahedron Mesh.1: UFR-723\Mesh Size** parameter in the **Members of All** column, which puts this parameter into the formula. Multiply the parameter by **0.15**, as shown in Figure 2–59, which will ensure that the mesh sag is 0.15 times the mesh size.

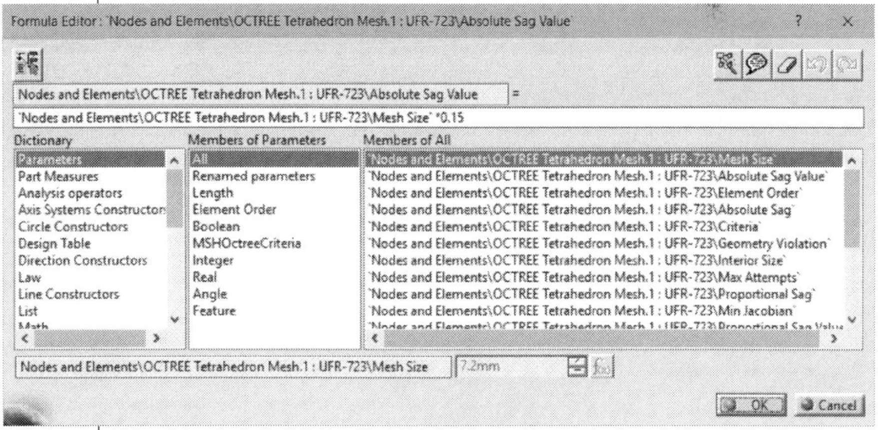

Figure 2–59

13. Click **OK** to close the Formula Editor box. The OCTREE Tetrahedron Mesh dialog box displays, as shown in Figure 2–60.

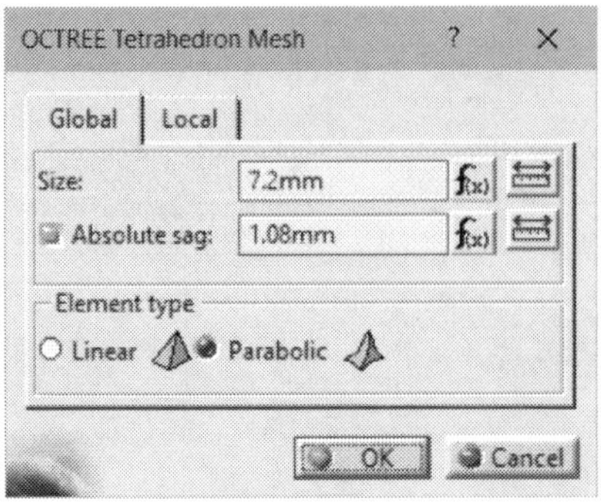

Figure 2–60

14. Click **OK** to close the OCTREE Tetrahedron Mesh dialog box. Note that there are two new formulas created in the **Relations** node in the tree, as shown in Figure 2–61.

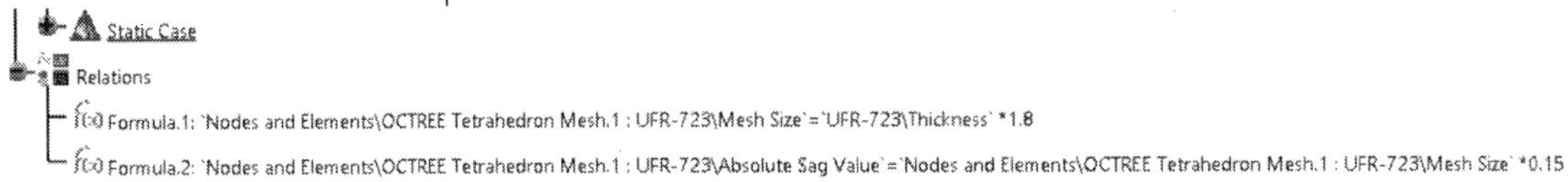

Figure 2–61

15. Right-click on **Nodes and Elements** in the tree and select **Mesh Visualization** in the contextual menu, as shown in Figure 2–62.

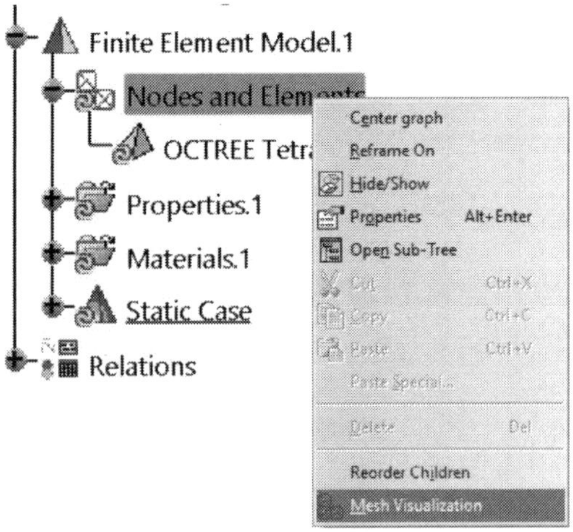

Figure 2–62

16. Click **OK** in the Warnings dialog box that displays in order to proceed with the meshing of the model.

17. The mesh is displayed, as shown in Figure 2–63. Rotate the model and examine the mesh in various areas of the part.

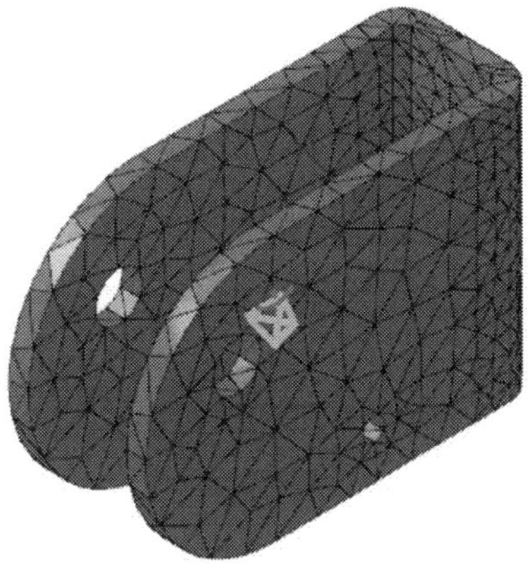

Figure 2–63

This only deletes the mesh image but keeps the actual mesh in the model.

18. Right-click on **Mesh.1** in the tree and select **Delete** in the contextual menu, as shown in Figure 2–64.

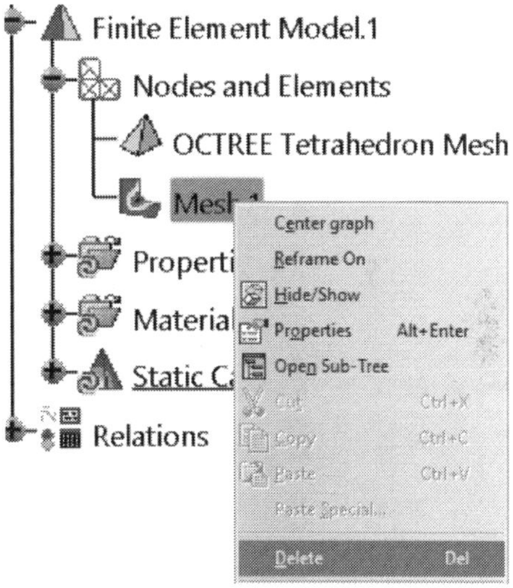

Figure 2–64

Task 5 - Apply restraints.

In this task, you will apply the Clamp restraint to the two holes in the middle of the bracket. This models the bracket being rigidly bolted to the adjoining structure.

1. Select  (Clamp) in the Restraints toolbar. The Clamp dialog box opens, as shown in Figure 2–65.

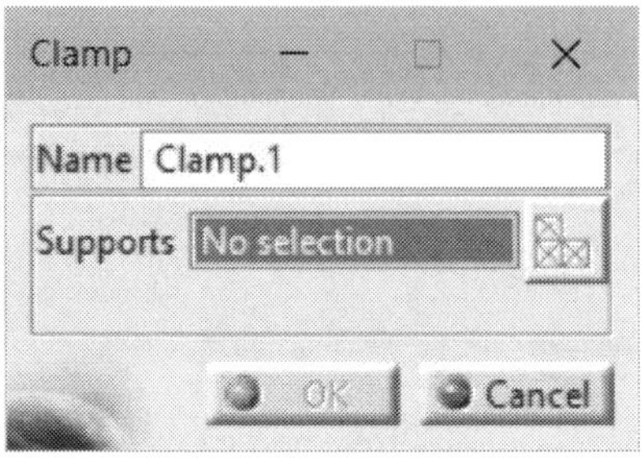

Figure 2–65

2. Select the inside surfaces of the two holes, as shown in Figure 2–66.

Figure 2–66

3. Click **OK** to close the Clamp dialog box.

Task 6 - Apply loads.

In this task, you will apply a 500N vertical force to the bracket.

1. Select  (Distributed Force) in the Forces toolbar. The Distributed Force dialog box opens, as shown in Figure 2–67.

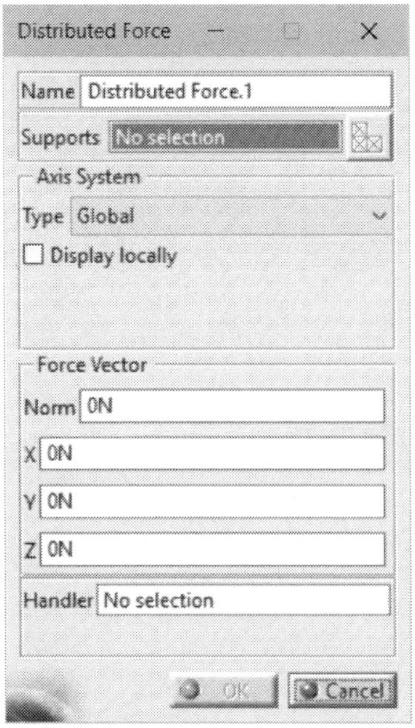

Figure 2–67

2. Select the inside surfaces of both large holes in the flanges of the part and enter **-500N** in the **Z** field of the *Force Vector* area, as shown in Figure 2–68.

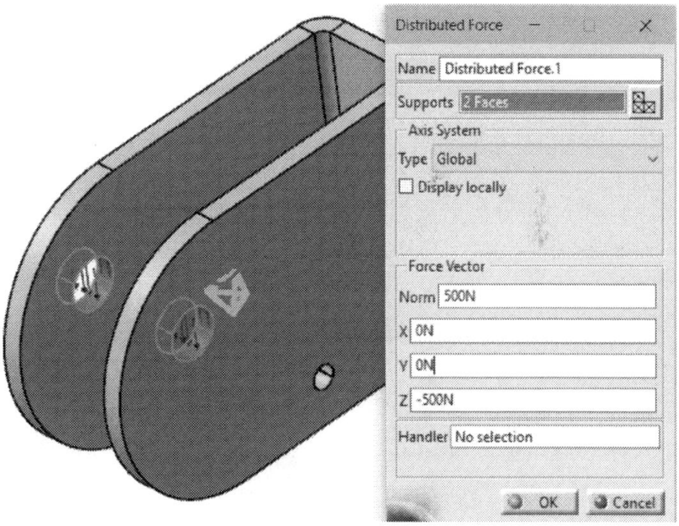

Figure 2–68

3. Click **OK** to close the Distributed Force dialog box. The model displays as shown in Figure 2–69.

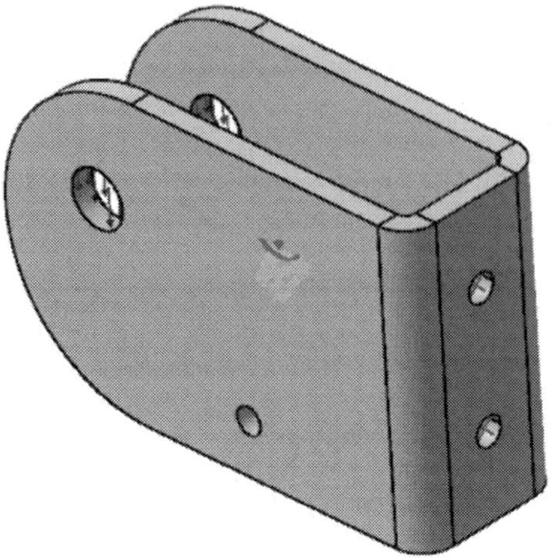

Figure 2–69

Task 7 - Run the analysis.

In this task, you will check the model for errors and run the analysis.

1. In the Model Manager toolbar, select (Model Checker). CATIA checks the model for errors and inconsistencies and displays the summary in the Model Checker dialog box, as shown in Figure 2–70.

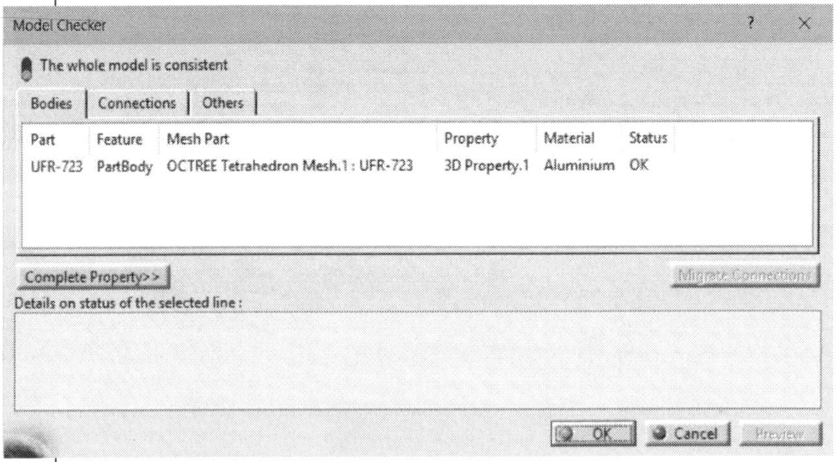

Figure 2–70

2. Note that the message at the top is "**The whole model is consistent**" and the *Status* is **OK**. Click **OK** to close the Model Checker dialog box.
3. In the Compute toolbar, select  (Compute). The Compute dialog box opens, as shown in Figure 2–71.

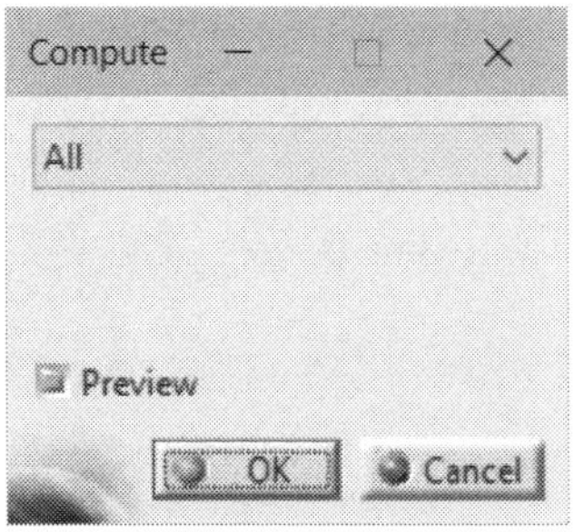

Figure 2–71

4. Ensure that **All** is selected in the drop-down list at the top of the dialog box and the **Preview** option is activated. Click **OK** to start the computation.
5. CATIA performs the CPU time and memory requirements calculation and displays the estimation in the Computation Resources Estimation dialog box, as shown in Figure 2–72.

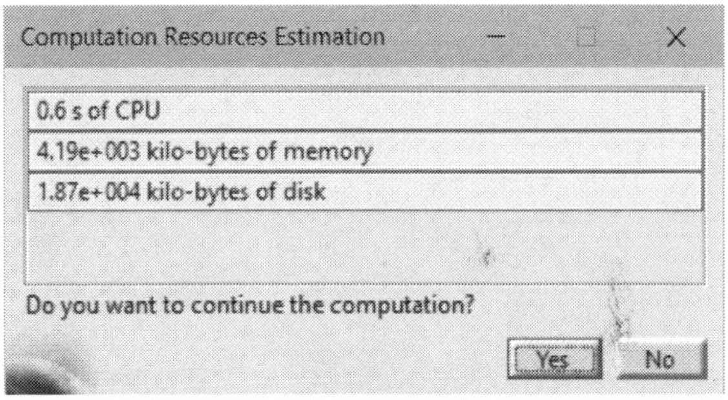

Figure 2–72

6. Click **Yes** to continue the computation. CATIA runs the analysis, which, depending on the number of finite elements, may take some time. For this model, the computation time should be under 1 second.
7. Note that after the computation is completed, the **Static Case Solution.1** object in the tree no longer displays the  (Update) symbol.

Task 8 - Change the view mode.

In this task, you will change the view mode to Shading with Material. This is necessary in CATIA for proper display of color plots.

1. In the View toolbar>View mode sub-toolbar, select  (Customize View Parameters).

2. In the View Mode Customization dialog box that opens, select the options **Edges and points**, **Shading**, and **Material**, as shown in Figure 2–73.

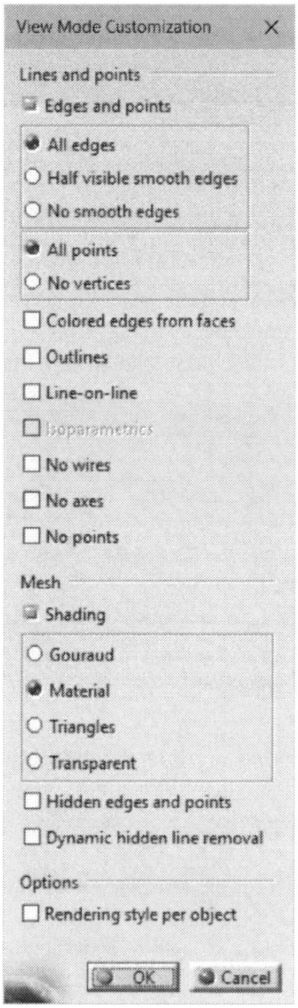

Figure 2–73

3. Click **OK** to close the View Mode Customization dialog box.

Task 9 - Display the deformed mesh.

In this task, you will display the model deformation as computed in the analysis.

1. In the Image toolbar, select  (Deformation). The deformed mesh image displays, as shown in Figure 2–74.

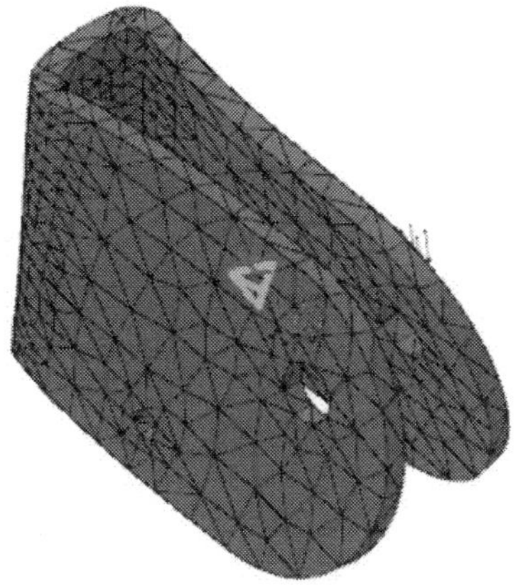

Figure 2–74

2. In the tree, right-click on **Links Manager.1** and select **Hide/Show** in the contextual menu. The deformed mesh is now overlaid over the undeformed model, as shown in Figure 2–75.

Overlaying the deformed mesh over the undeformed model helps to visualize the overall shape and direction of the model deformation under the applied loads.

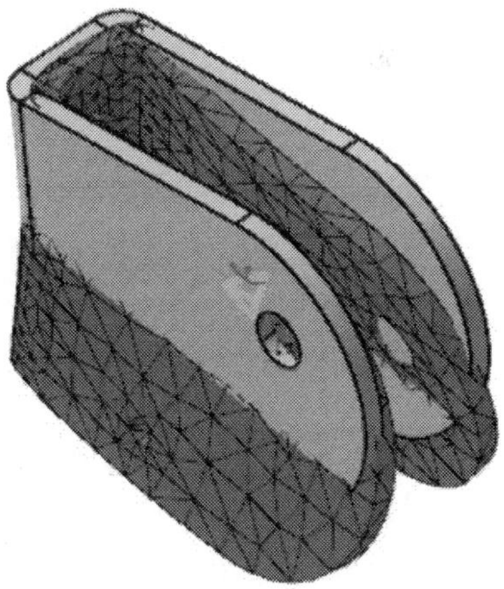

Figure 2–75

CATIA scales up (i.e., exaggerates) the displayed deformation of the model. The Amplification Magnitude tool lets you control the scaling factor.

3. In the Analysis Tools toolbar, select (Amplification Magnitude). The Amplification Magnitude dialog box opens, as shown in Figure 2–76.

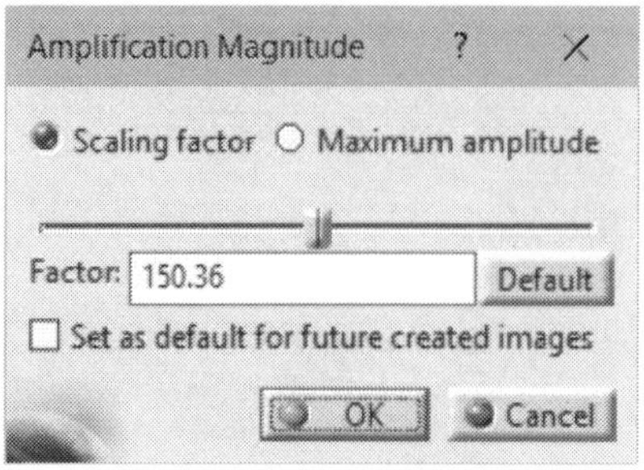

Figure 2–76

4. Drag the slider in the Amplification Magnitude dialog box to see how it affects the displayed deformation. Set the **Factor** value to **50**, which means the displayed deformation will be 50 times the actual deformation under the given loads, and click **OK** to close the dialog box. The model displays as shown in Figure 2–77.

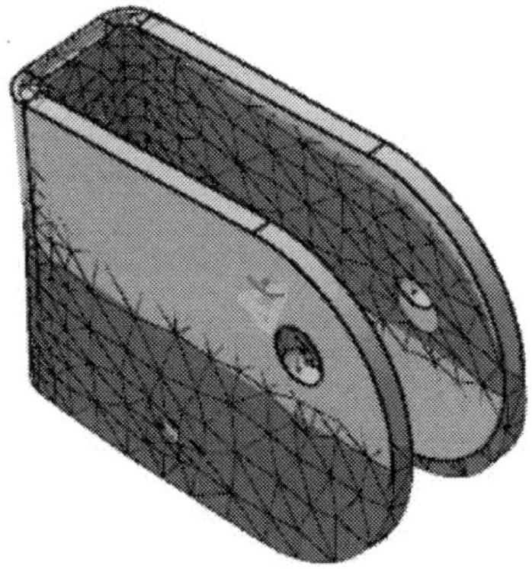

Figure 2–77

Task 10 - Display the displacements.

In this task, you will display the model displacements as computed in the analysis.

1. In the Image toolbar, select (Displacement). The displacement vector image displays, as shown in Figure 2–78.

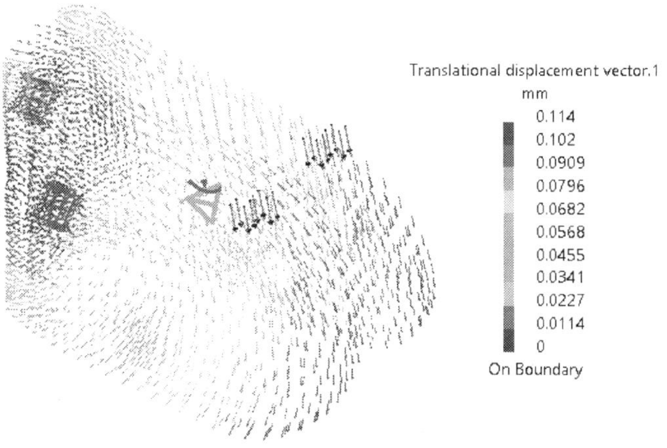

Figure 2–78

2. The model displacements are displayed as a collection of vectors, with each vector originating at a mesh node. Zoom in on the image and point the mouse to any of the vectors. The mouse tooltip displays the displacement components in **X-**, **Y-**, and **Z-directions**, as shown in Figure 2–79.

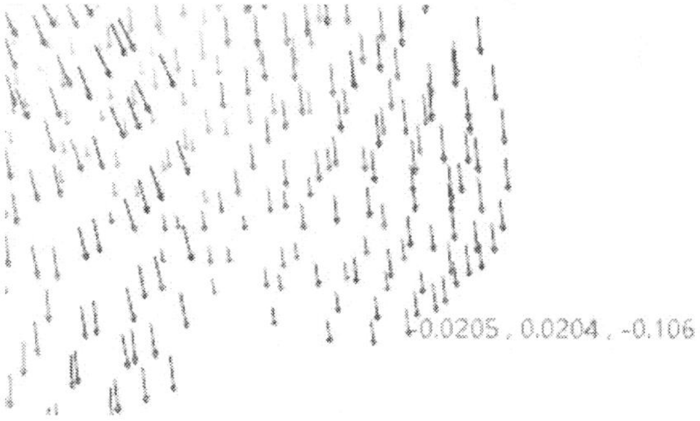

Figure 2–79

3. Double-click on the **Translational displacement vector.1** object in the tree. The Image Edition dialog box opens, as shown in Figure 2–80.

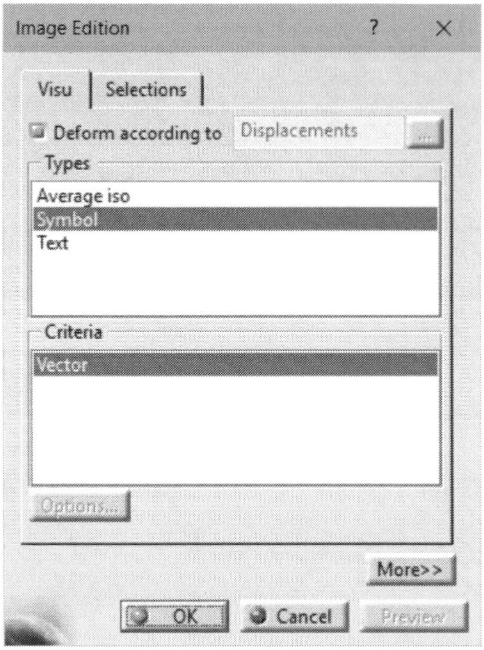

Figure 2–80

4. Select **Average iso** in the *Types* list and click **OK** to close the Image Edition dialog box. The image is now displayed as a color plot of the translational displacement magnitude, as shown in Figure 2–81.

   • **Note:** The displacement magnitude ***D*** is computed from the nodal displacement components D_x, D_y, and D_z with the following equation:

$$D = \sqrt{D_x^2 + D_y^2 + D_z^2}$$

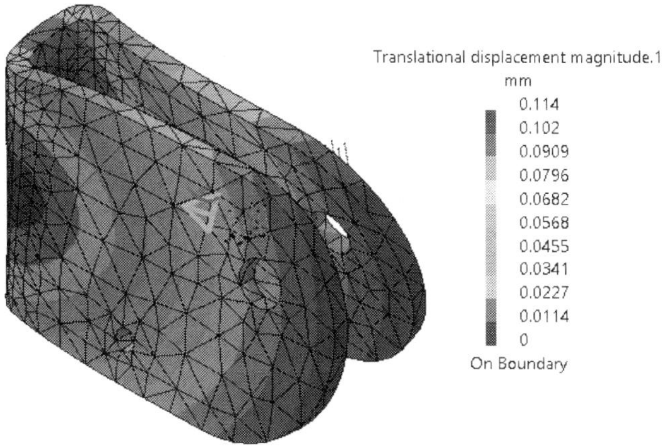

Figure 2–81

5. Note that the maximum displacement magnitude under the 500N load is **0.114mm**. In the next step, you will display the vertical displacement D_z alone.

6. Double-click on the **Translational displacement magnitude.1** object in the tree. The Image Edition dialog box opens, as shown in Figure 2–82.

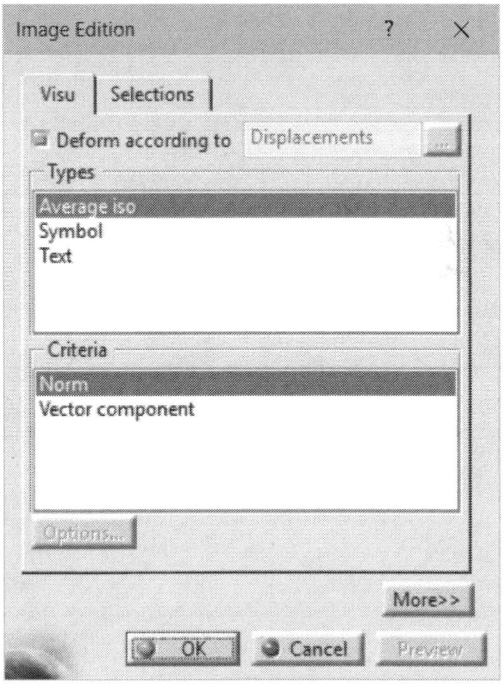

Figure 2–82

*The **C3** component in the Global Cartesian Axis System is the **Z** component.*

7. Click **More** to expand the dialog box. Select **Vector component** in the *Criteria* field and **C3** in the Component drop-down list, as shown in Figure 2–83.

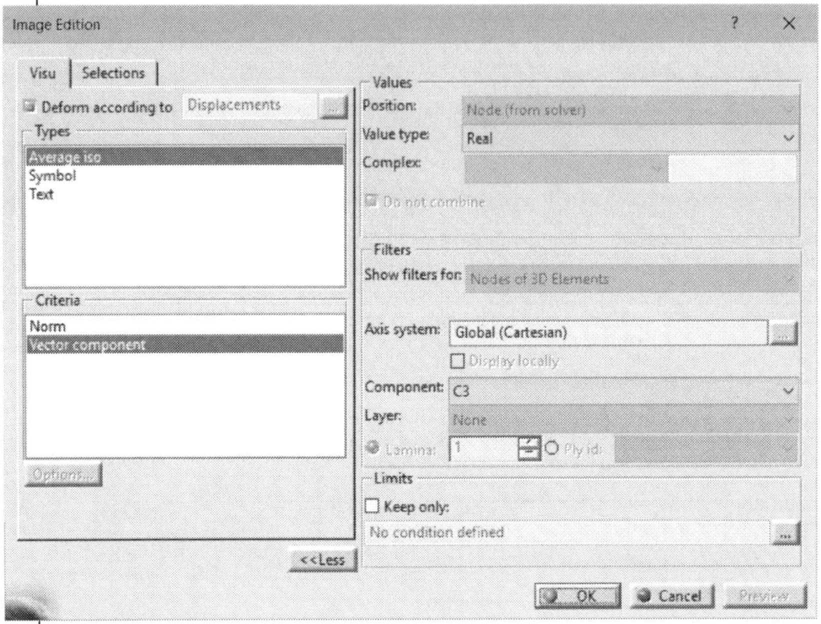

Figure 2–83

8. Click **OK** to close the Image Edition dialog box. The image is displayed as shown in Figure 2–84.

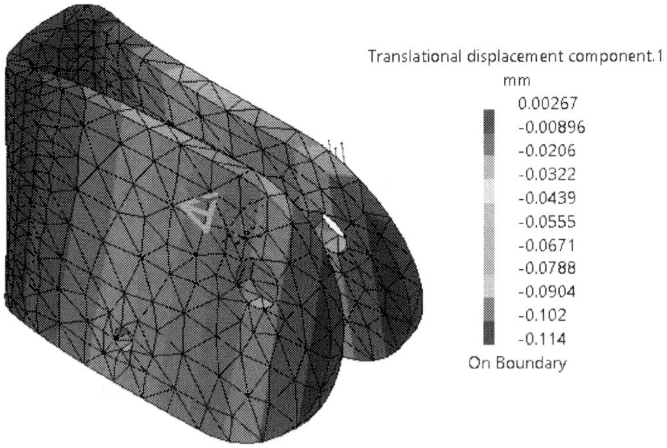

Figure 2–84

9. Note that the maximum displacement in the vertical Z-direction is **-0.114mm**. This is the same as the maximum displacement magnitude, which indicates that vertical displacement is the dominant mode of deformation in the bracket under the given load.

Task 11 - Display the stresses.

In this task, you will display the Von Mises stress in the model. Von Mises stress is a value used to determine if the material will yield and is mostly used for ductile materials such as metals. The bracket is made of Aluminium, which is a ductile metal; therefore, Von Mises stress would be an appropriate criterion to predict the bracket's failure.

1. In the Image toolbar, select  (Von Mises Stress). The stress image displays, as shown in Figure 2–85.

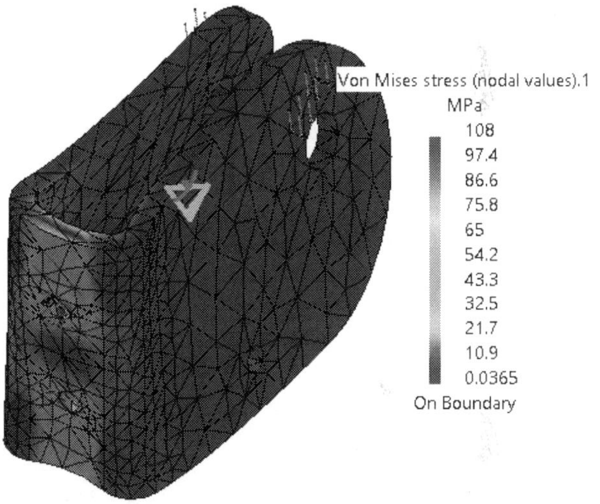

Figure 2–85

2. Rotate the model to examine the location of the maximum stress, which is around the clamped holes in the bracket. Note that CATIA displays the stress values at the mesh nodes when you move the mouse cursor over the image, as shown in Figure 2–86.

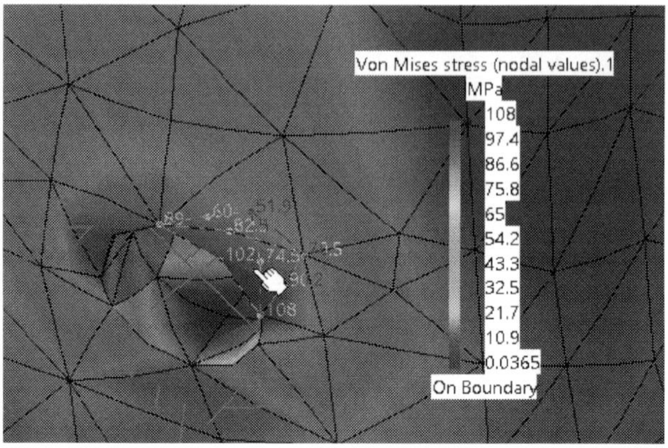

Figure 2–86

3. In the Analysis Tools toolbar, select (Information) and click the **Von Mises stress (nodal values).1** object in the tree. The Information dialog box displays, as shown in Figure 2–87.

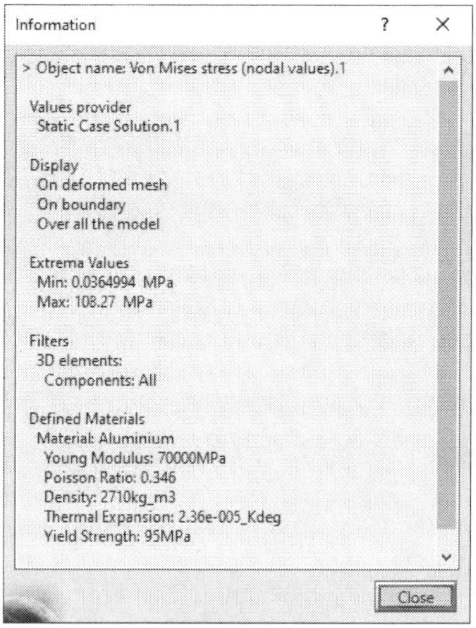

Figure 2–87

4. Note that the **Yield Strength** of the material is **95MPa**, while the maximum stress in the model is **108.27MPa**, which is greater than the material's yield strength. Therefore, the bracket is predicted to fail under the given loading. Click **Close** to close the Information dialog box.

In the next step, you will locate the areas in the model that should fail.

5. Expand the tree and double-click on the **Color Map** object located under the **Von Mises stress (nodal values).1** node. The Color Map Edition dialog box displays, as shown in Figure 2–88.

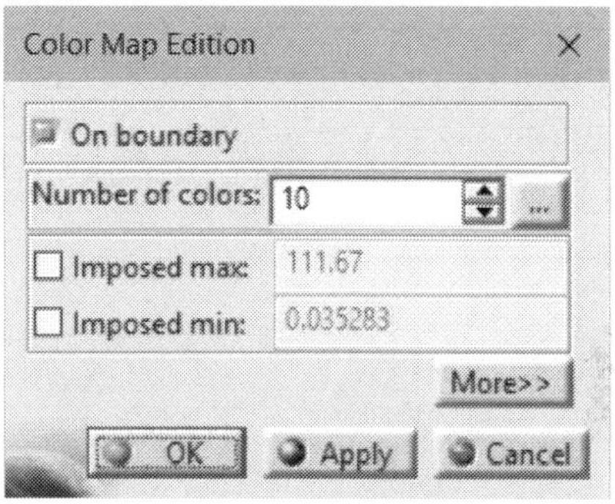

Figure 2–88

*Deselecting the **Smooth** option will help to visually discern the areas of different stress levels in the model.*

6. Click the ellipsis button (**...**). In the Color Edition dialog box that opens, deselect the **Smooth** option, as shown in Figure 2–89, and click **OK** to close the dialog box.

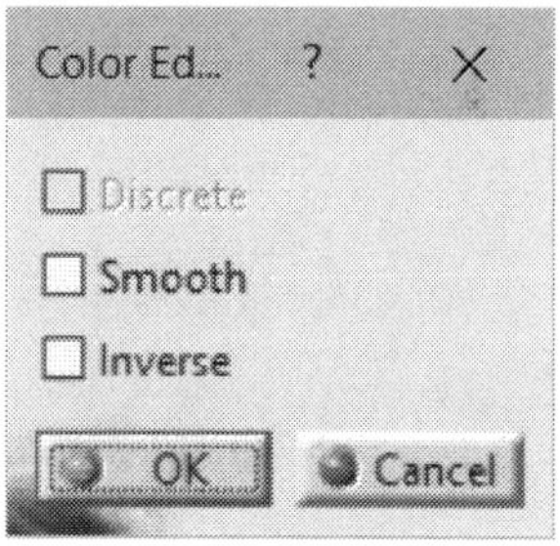

Figure 2–89

Note: In the Color Map Edition dialog box, select the **Imposed max** option and enter the value **95** in the corresponding field, as shown in Figure 2–90.

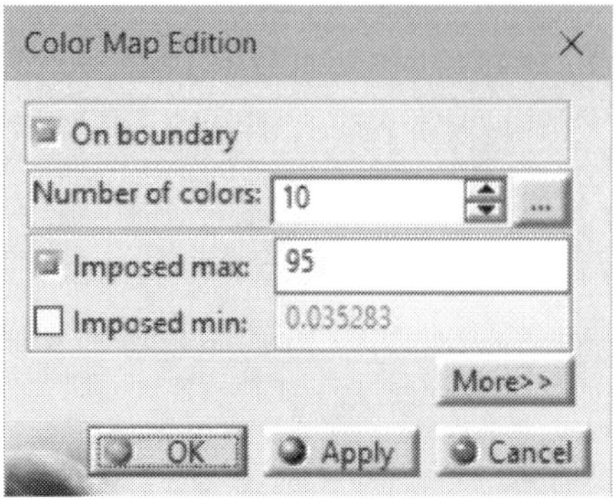

Figure 2–90

7. Click **OK** to close the Color Map Edition dialog box. The stress image displays as shown in Figure 2–91.

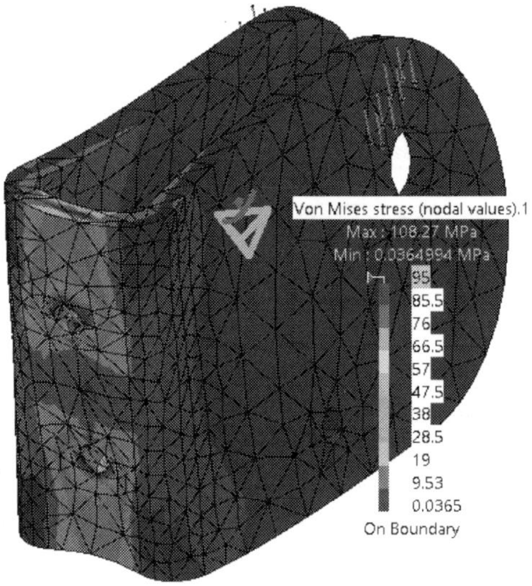

Figure 2–91

8. Zoom in on one of the clamped holes. The dark red color now indicates the areas where the stress exceeds 95MPa, which is the yield strength of the material, as shown in Figure 2–92.

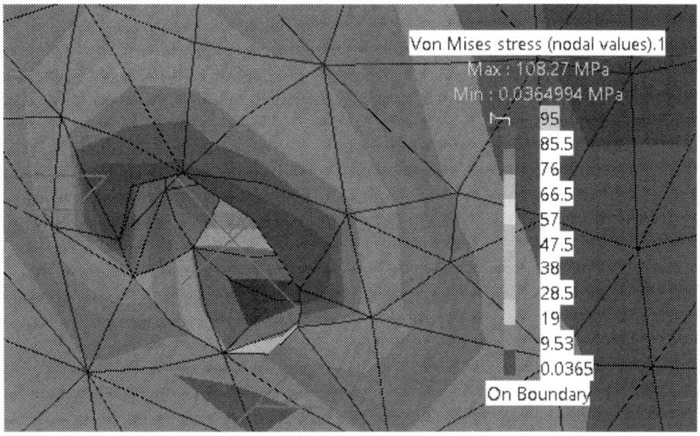

Figure 2–92

9. Right-click on **Von Mises stress (nodal values).1** in the tree and select **Activate/Deactivate** to deactivate the stress image and return to the model view.

Task 12 - Create a factor of safety parameter.

In this task, you will create a factor of safety (FoS) parameter that will indicate whether the maximum stress in the analysis exceeds the material strength, using the following formula:

FoS = <material_yield_strength> / <maximum_stress_in_analysis>

Therefore, **FoS > 1** indicates that the maximum stress does not exceed the material strength, and the part is safe under the given loads. Alternatively, **FoS < 1** indicates that the part is predicted to fail.

You will use this parameter to check whether the part is safe once you modify the bracket's thickness.

1. In the tree, right-click on **Sensors.1** and select **Create Global Sensor**, as shown in Figure 2–93.

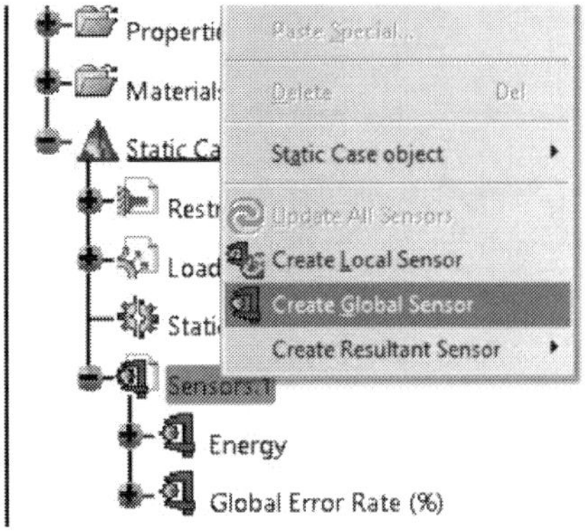

Figure 2–93

2. The Create Sensor dialog box opens, as shown in Figure 2–94. Select **Maximum Von Mises** in the list and click **OK**.

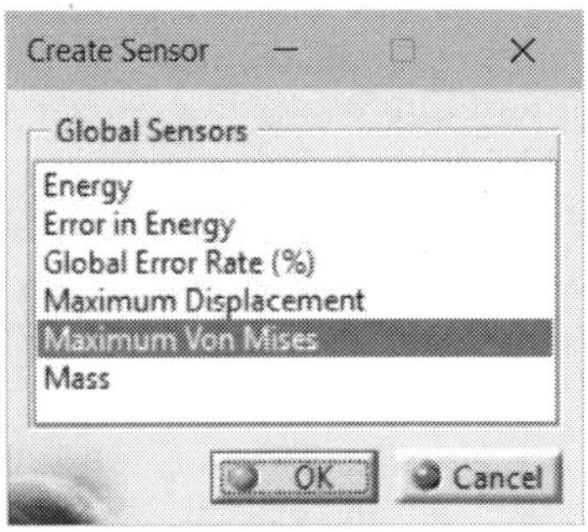

Figure 2–94

3. The **Maximum Von Mises** sensor displays in the tree, as shown in Figure 2–95.

If the sensor does not display the value, activate the Tools> Options>Parameters and Measures> Knowledge>Parameter Tree View>With value option.

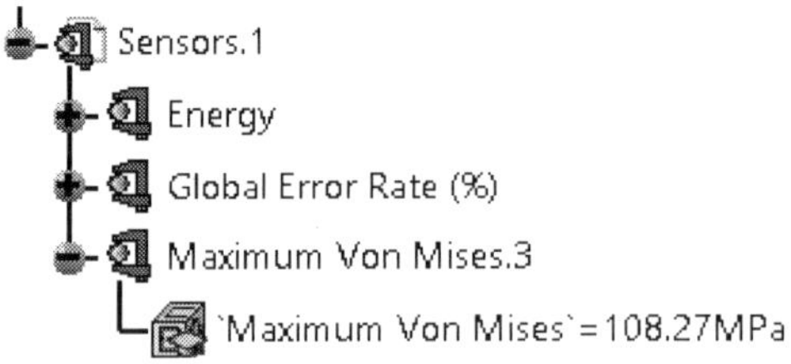

Figure 2–95

4. In the Knowledge toolbar, select (Formula). The Formulas dialog box opens, as shown in Figure 2–96.

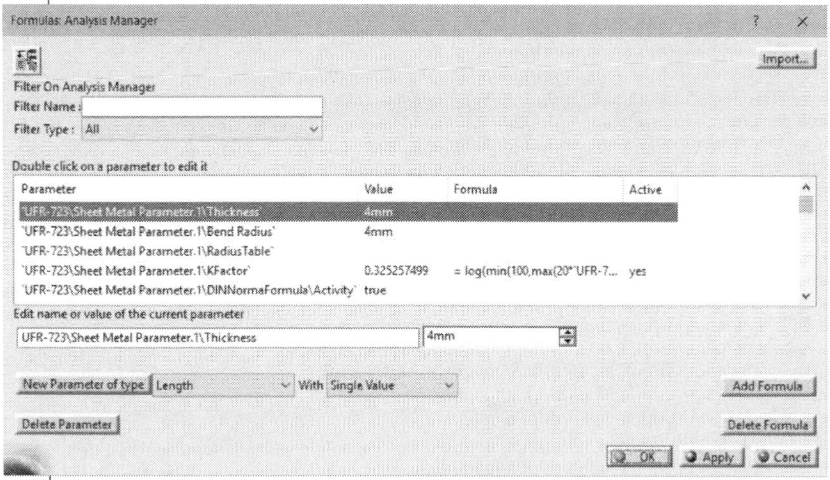

Figure 2–96

*The **Real** type means the parameter has no units associated with it.*

5. In the drop-down list near the **New Parameter of type** button, select **Real**, then click **New Parameter of type**, as shown in Figure 2–97.

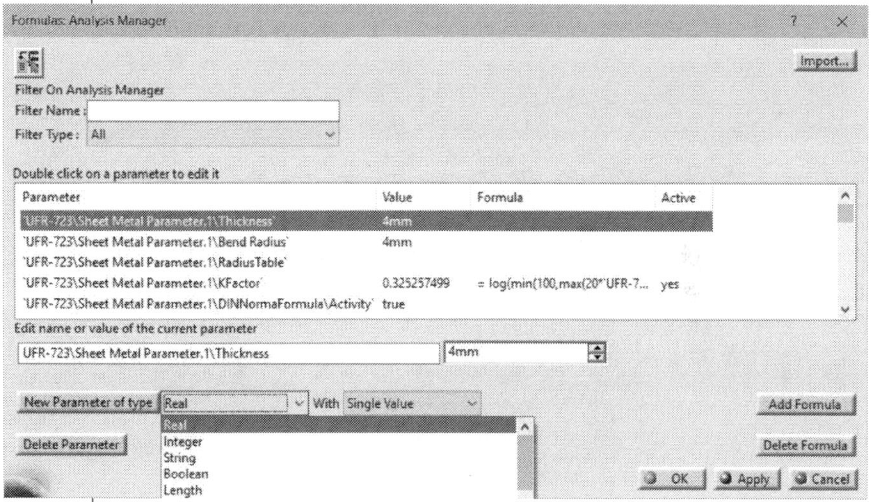

Figure 2–97

6. Rename the created parameter from **Real.1** to **FoS**, as shown in Figure 2–98, then click **Add Formula**.

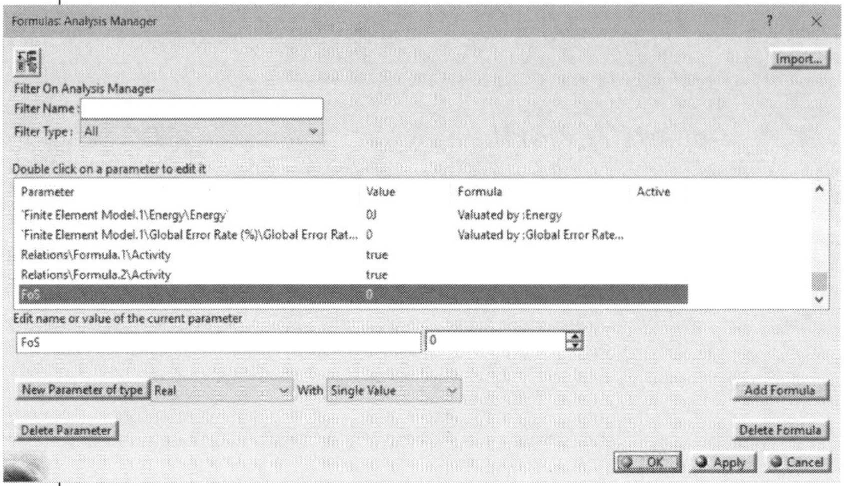

Figure 2–98

7. Once the Formula Editor dialog box opens, expand the tree and select the **Aluminium** material in the part. This filters the parameters displayed in the **Members of All** column, so now it only lists parameters in the selected entity, which are the **Aluminium** properties.

8. Double-click on the **UFR-723\Aluminium\Aluminium.1\ Yield Strength** parameter in the **Members of All** column, which puts this parameter in the formula. Add the division operator "/" at the end, as shown in Figure 2–99.

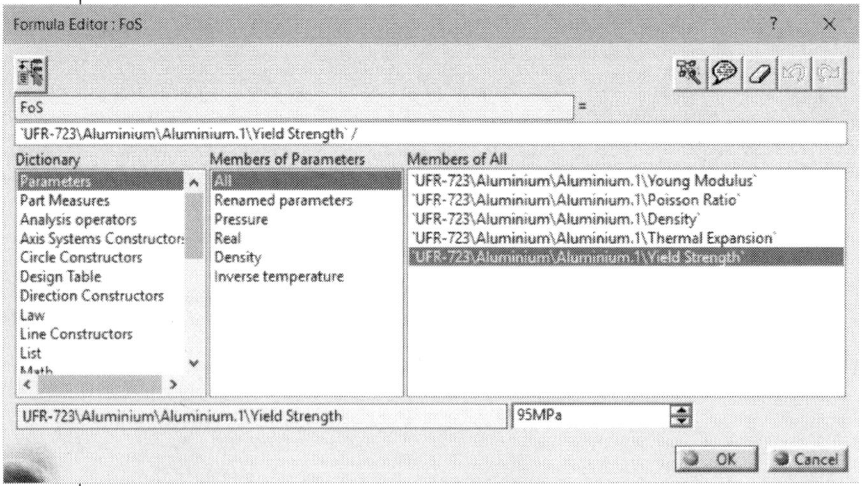

Figure 2–99

9. Select the **Maximum Von Mises** parameter in the tree. This will put the parameter into the formula after the division operator "/", as shown in Figure 2–100.

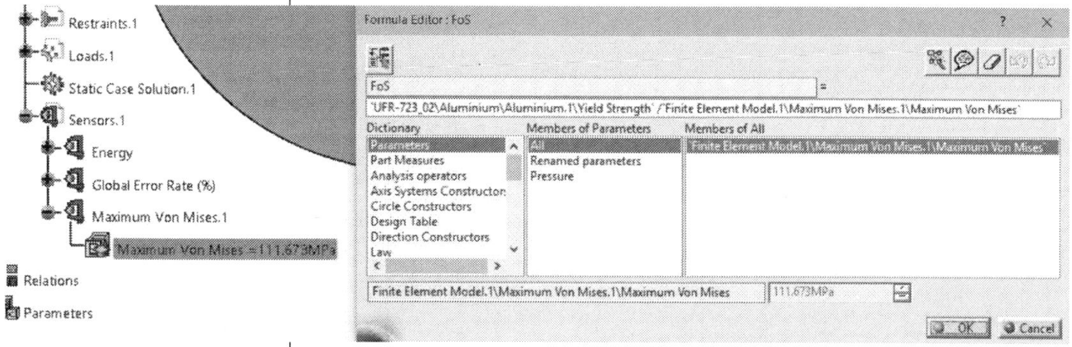

Figure 2–100

10. Click **OK** twice to close the Formula Editor and Formulas dialog boxes. The **FoS** parameter displays in the tree, as shown in Figure 2–101. Note that the current **FoS** value is approximately **0.877**, which is less than **1.0** and means that the part is predicted to fail.

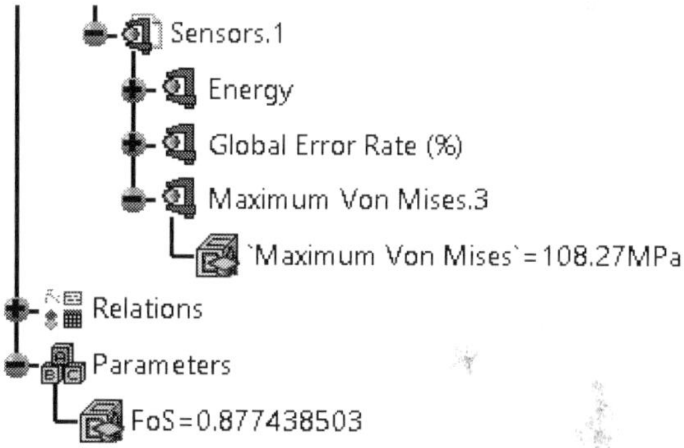

Figure 2–101

Task 13 - Modify the bracket thickness.

In this task, you will modify the bracket dimensions in order to bring the stress levels to below the yield strength of the material.

1. In the tree, expand **Links Manager.1>Link.1** and double-click on the **UFR-723** part, as shown in Figure 2–102. This automatically hides the analysis model and switches CATIA to the **Part Design** workbench.

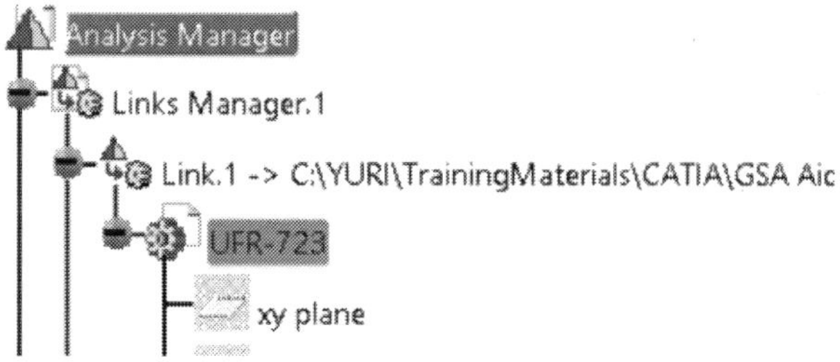

Figure 2–102

2. Double-click on the **Thickness** parameter in the **Parameters** node in the tree to open the Edit Parameter dialog box. Change the value from 4mm to **4.5mm**, as shown in Figure 2–103.

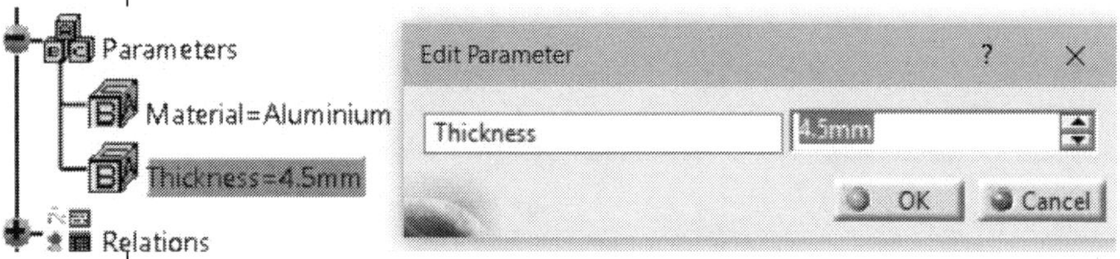

Figure 2–103

It is not possible to predict how thick the bracket should be to bring the stress down to within the material's strength. Therefore, several design-analysis iterations might be required here.

3. Click **OK** to close the Edit Parameter dialog box. CATIA regenerates the model, so the bracket part is now 4.5mm thick.

Task 14 - Re-run the analysis.

1. Double-click on the **Finite Element Model.1** in the tree in order to switch back to the GSA workbench.

2. In the Compute toolbar, select  (Compute) and re-run the analysis.

3. Note that after the analysis completes, the **Maximum Von Mises** sensor displays a value of **68MPa**, and the **FoS** parameter is approximately **1.39**, as shown in Figure 2–104. This is greater than 1.0, so the redesigned bracket is now predicted to withstand the 500N load.

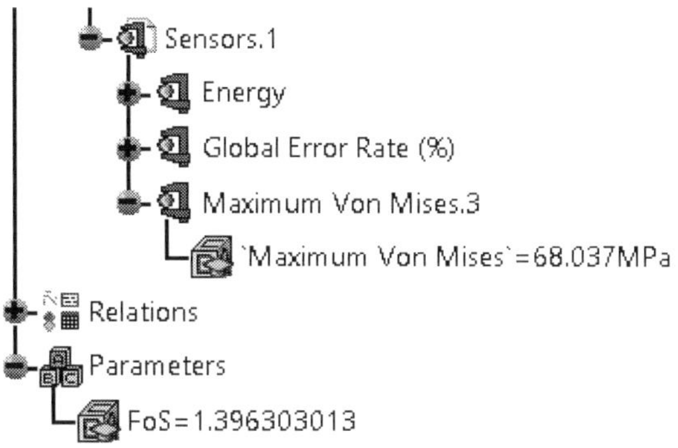

Figure 2–104

Task 15 - Display the Von Mises stress.

In this task, you will visualize the Von Mises stress in the modified model.

1. In the tree, right-click on the **Von Mises stress (nodal values).1** object and select **Activate/Deactivate** in the contextual menu to activate the stress image. The Von Mises stress result plot displays as shown in Figure 2–105. Note that now there are no areas in the image colored deep red, which means there are no areas where the stress exceeds 95MPa.

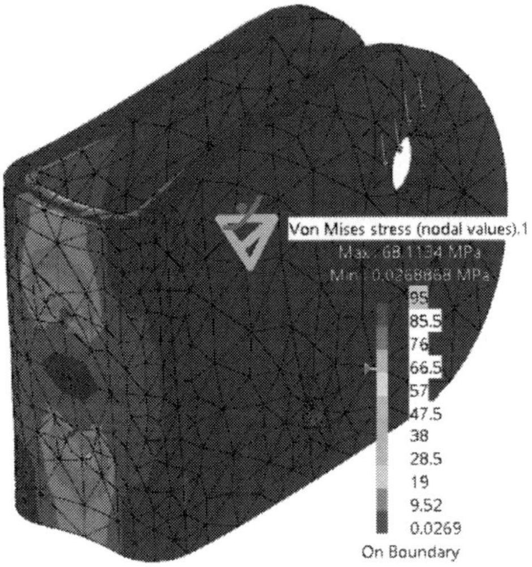

Figure 2–105

2. In the Analysis Tools toolbar, select  (Information), then click the **Von Mises stress (nodal values).1** object in the tree. The Information dialog box displays, as shown in Figure 2–106.

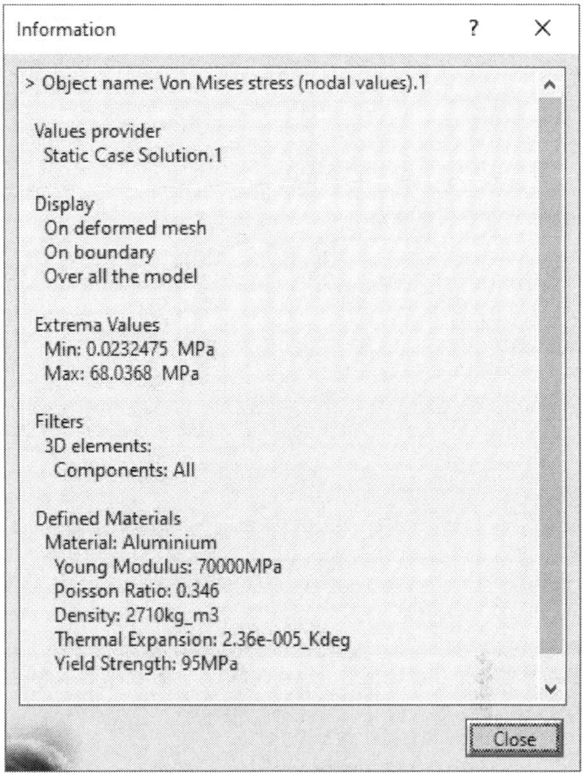

Figure 2–106

3. Note that now the maximum stress in the model is **68MPa**, which is below the material's yield strength of **95MPa**. Therefore, the bracket can now be deemed safe for the 500N vertical load.

4. Click **Close** to close the Information dialog box.

5. Right-click on the **Von Mises stress (nodal values).1** and select **Activate/Deactivate** to deactivate the stress image and return to the model view.

Task 16 - Create the analysis report.

1. In the Analysis Results toolbar, select  (Generate Report). The Report Generation dialog box opens as shown in Figure 2–107.

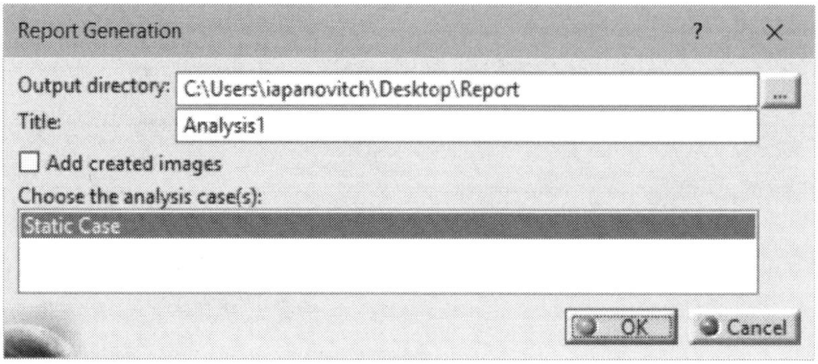

Figure 2–107

2. Click the ellipsis button (**...**) and select an output folder of your choice for the report. Enter **Bracket analysis** as the *Title*, as shown in Figure 2–108.

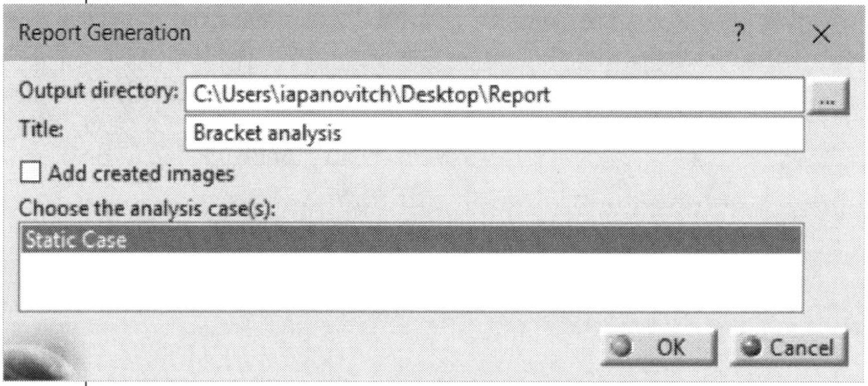

Figure 2–108

3. Click **OK**. The report opens in your default web browser, as shown in Figure 2–109.

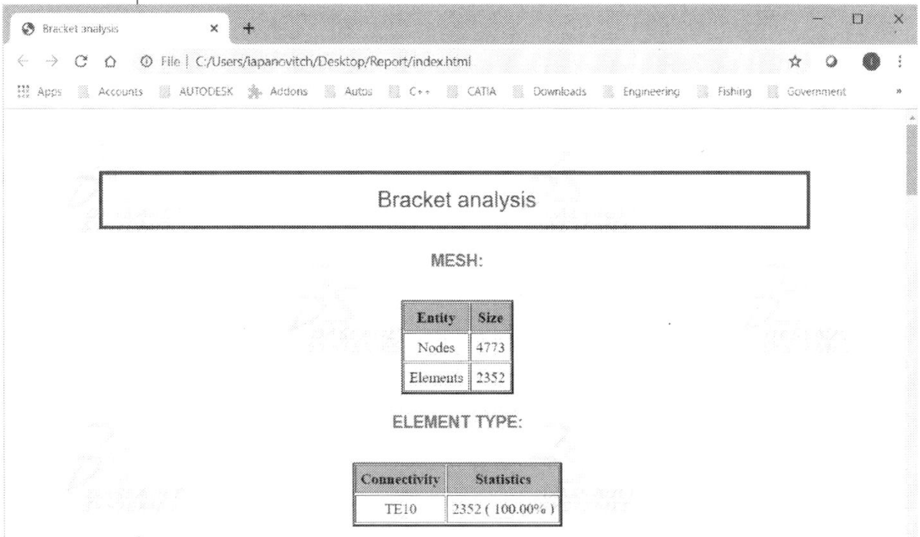

Figure 2–109

4. Scroll down and examine the contents of the analysis report.

Task 17 - Save and close the files.

1. Optionally, save the analysis document and the redesigned part for future reference.
2. Close both the analysis and the part documents.

Practice 2b Static Stress Analysis of a Hanger

Practice Objectives

- Apply the material.
- Mesh the model.
- Apply loads and restraints.
- Compute the analysis.
- Display and animate deformation and displacements.
- Display Von Mises stress and principal stress.
- Locate maximum stresses.
- Create a local stress sensor.
- Perform a cut plane analysis.
- Create the analysis report.

In this practice, you will set up and run a static stress analysis on the hanger part shown in Figure 2–110.

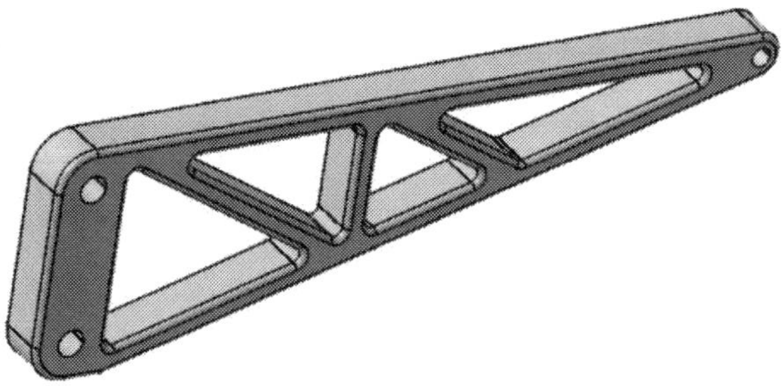

Figure 2–110

Task 1 - Open the part in CATIA.

1. Open **Hanger_02.CATPart** from the *CATIA Generative Structural Analysis Practice Files\Ch02* folder.

2. Set the model display as  (Shading with Edges). The part displays as shown in Figure 2–111.

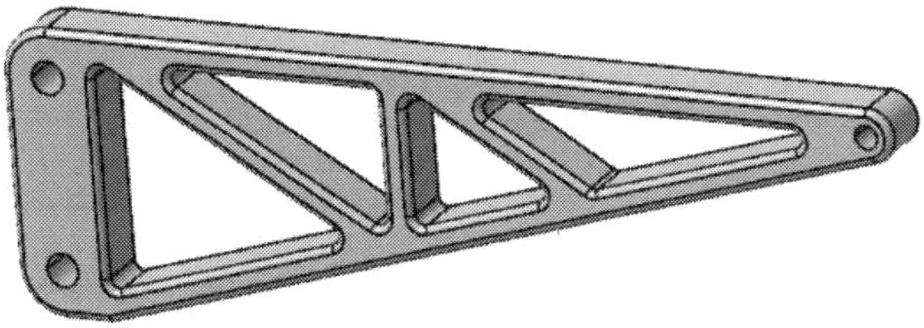

Figure 2–111

3. Select **Tools>Options>Parameters and Measures>Units** and set the units as follows:
   - Length: **Millimeter (mm)**
   - Force: **Newton (N)**
   - Moment: **Newton x Meter (Nxm)**
   - Pressure: **Megapascal (MPa)**

Task 2 - Apply the material.

In this task, you will select the material for the hanger.

1. In the Apply Material toolbar, click  (Apply Material). The **Default Material Catalog** opens, as shown in Figure 2–112.

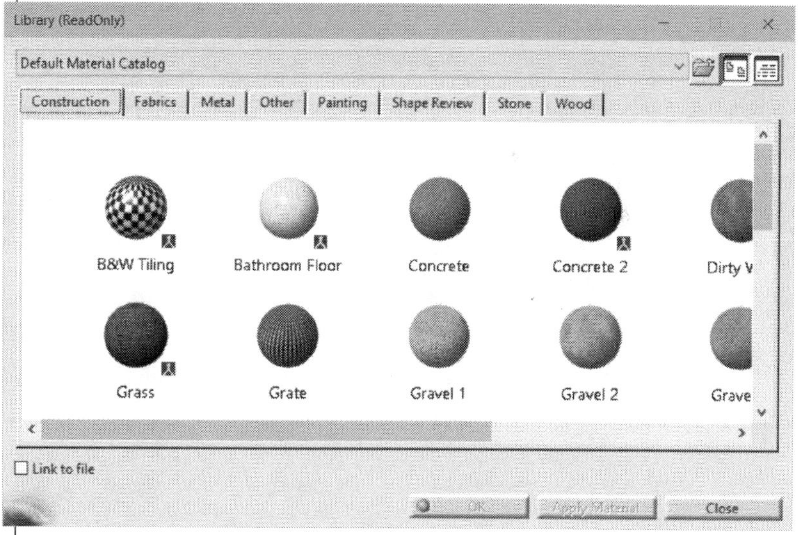

Figure 2–112

2. Select the *Metal* tab and click **Steel**. Select the **Hanger** part in the tree, as shown in Figure 2–113, and click **OK** to apply the material to the part and close the Library dialog box.

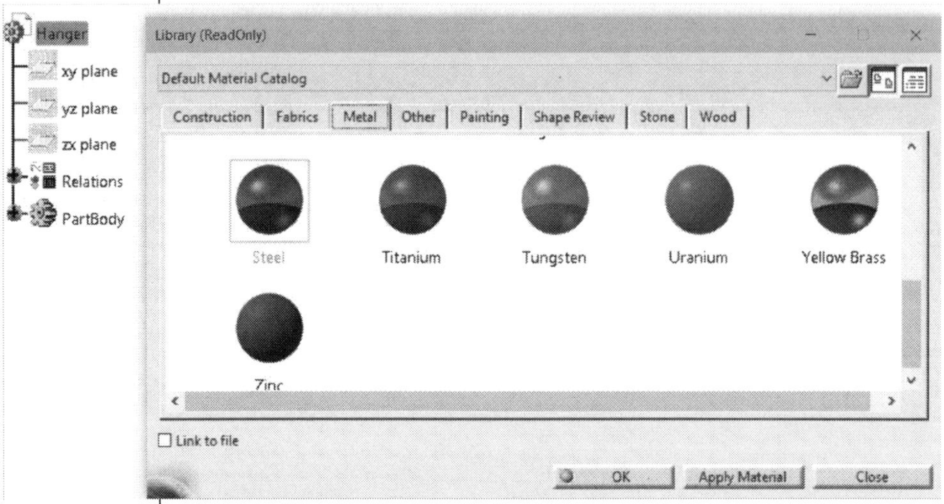

Figure 2–113

3. Double-click on **Steel** in the tree to open the Properties dialog box. Select the *Analysis* tab. Note that the Steel material has the following mechanical properties, as shown in Figure 2–114:

- Material: **Isotropic Material**
- Young Modulus: **200000MPa**
- Poisson Ratio: **0.266**
- Density: **7860kg/m^3**
- Thermal Expansion: **1.17e-005/Kdeg**
- Yield Strength: **250MPa**

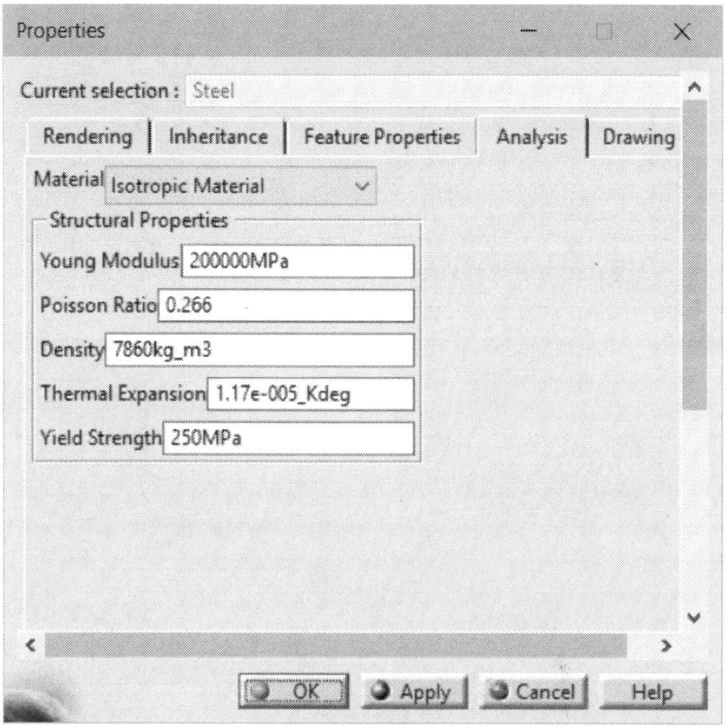

Figure 2–114

4. Click **OK** to close the Properties dialog box.

Task 3 - Launch the GSA workbench.

1. Select **Start>Analysis & Simulation>Generative Structural Analysis**, as shown in Figure 2–115.

If this option is not available, you do not have a license for this CATIA product.

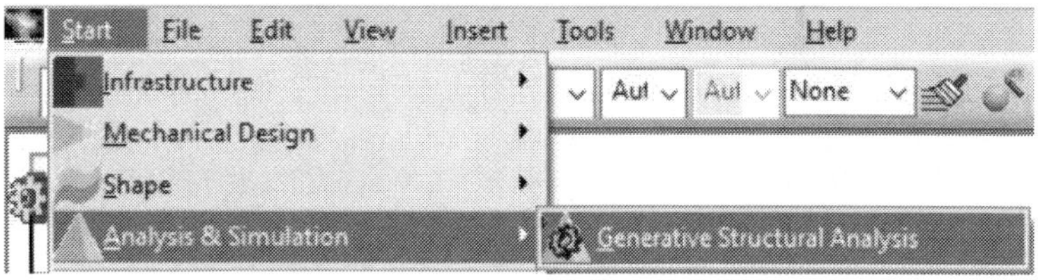

Figure 2–115

2. In the New Analysis Case dialog box, select **Static Analysis** and click **OK**, as shown in Figure 2–116.

Figure 2–116

3. CATIA opens a new analysis document named **Analysis1.CATAnalysis** and the workbench icon changes to .

Task 4 - Mesh the hanger part.

In this task, you will mesh the hanger part, which enables you to check prior to the analysis whether CATIA is able to mesh your model.

1. Double-click on **OCTREE Tetrahedron Mesh.1: Hanger** in the tree. The OCTREE Tetrahedron Mesh dialog box opens, as shown in Figure 2–117, which displays the default mesh size and sag.

CATIA selects the default mesh parameters as a percentage of the size of the part.

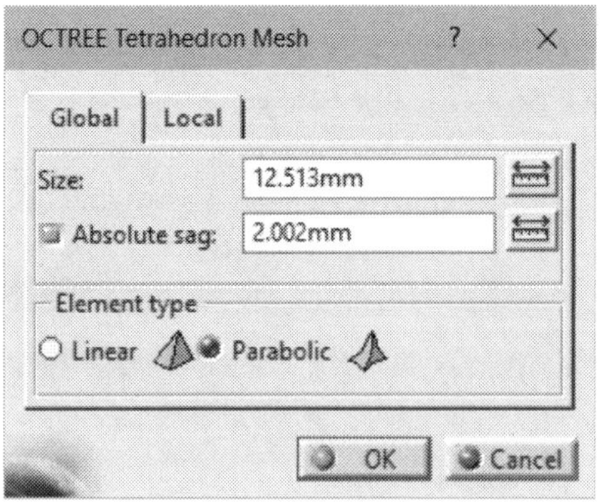

Figure 2–117

2. Ensure that the *Element type* is set to **Parabolic**.

3. Enter **3mm** as the *Size*, as shown in Figure 2–118.

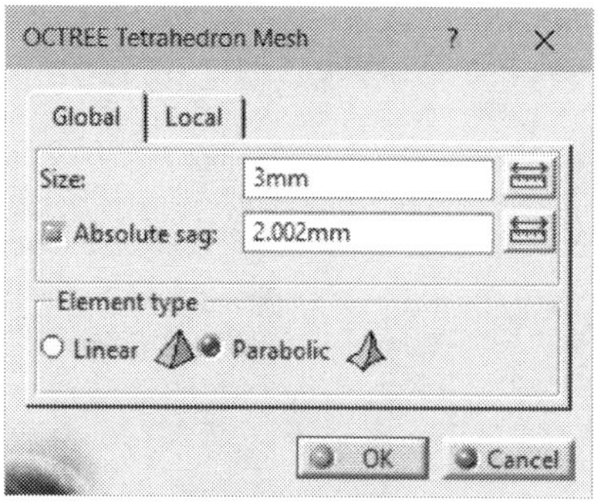

Figure 2–118

4. Right-click in the *Absolute sag* field and select **Edit formula** in the contextual menu, as shown in Figure 2–119.

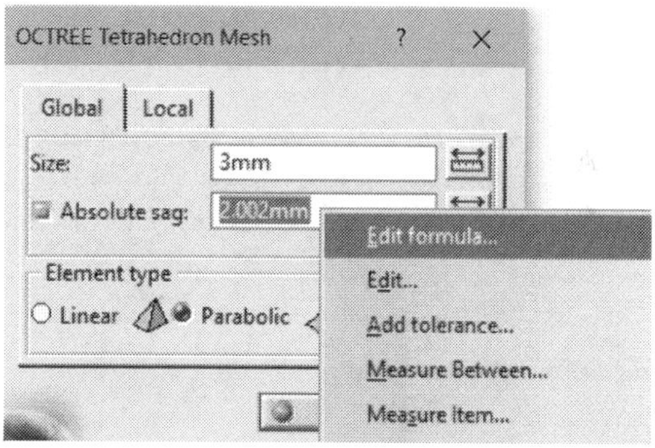

Figure 2–119

In the following steps, you will link the mesh sag and size parameters with a formula.

5. The Formula Editor dialog box opens, as shown in Figure 2–120.

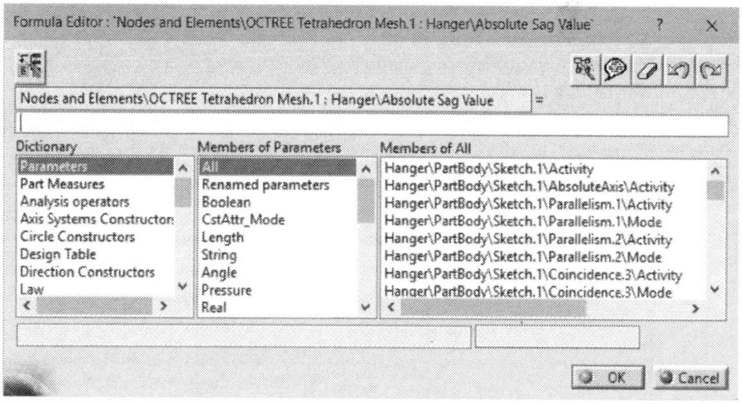

Figure 2–120

6. Select **OCTREE Tetrahedron Mesh.1: Hanger** in the tree. This filters the parameters displayed in the Formula Editor dialog box, so now the **Members of All** column only lists parameters in the selected entity, which is the mesh specification.

The rule of thumb for the mesh sag is between 0.15 and 0.2 of the mesh size. This ensures good mesh on curved surfaces without creating an excessive number of finite elements.

7. Double-click on the **Nodes and Elements\OCTREE Tetrahedron Mesh.1: Hanger\Mesh Size** parameter in the **Members of All** column, which puts this parameter into the formula. Multiply the parameter by **0.15**, as shown in Figure 2–121, which will ensure that the mesh sag is 0.15 times the mesh size.

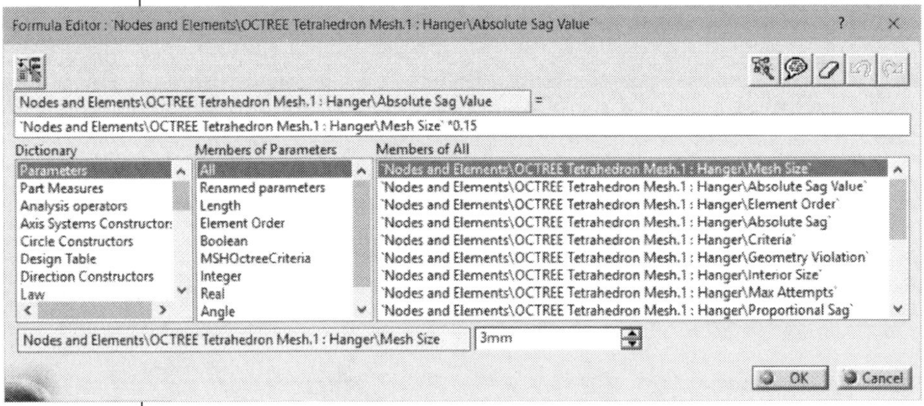

Figure 2–121

8. Click **OK** to close the Formula Editor dialog box. The OCTREE Tetrahedron Mesh dialog box displays as shown in Figure 2–122.

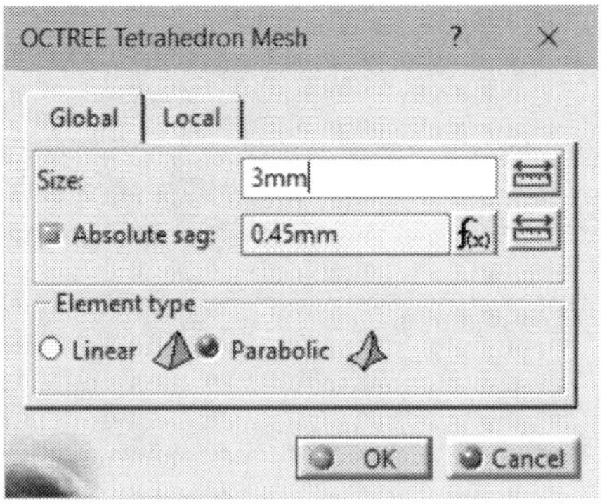

Figure 2–122

9. Click **OK** to close the OCTREE Tetrahedron Mesh dialog box.
10. Right-click on **Nodes and Elements** in the tree and select **Mesh Visualization** in the contextual menu.
11. Click **OK** in the Warnings dialog box that appears to proceed with the meshing of the model.
12. The mesh is displayed, as shown in Figure 2–123.

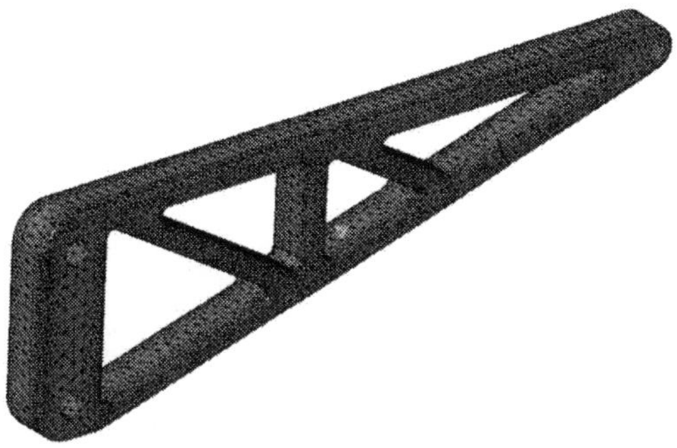

Figure 2–123

The Shrink Coefficient is only a visualization tool that enables you to better see the shape of the finite elements in the mesh. It does not affect the analysis results.

13. Double-click on **Mesh.1** in the tree. In the Image Edition dialog box that opens, activate the **Display nodes of elements** option and set the **Shrink Coefficient** to **0.9**, as shown in Figure 2–124.

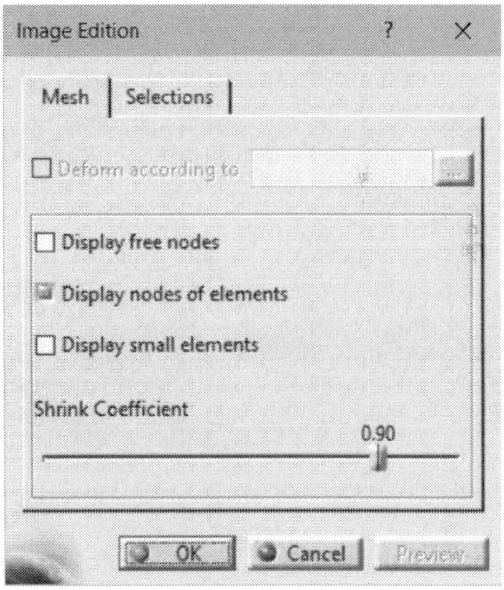

Figure 2–124

14. Click **OK** to close the Image Edition dialog box. Rotate and zoom in on the model to examine the mesh in various areas of the part, as shown in Figure 2–125. The red dots indicate the mesh nodes. Note there are three nodes per element edge since the elements are **Parabolic**.

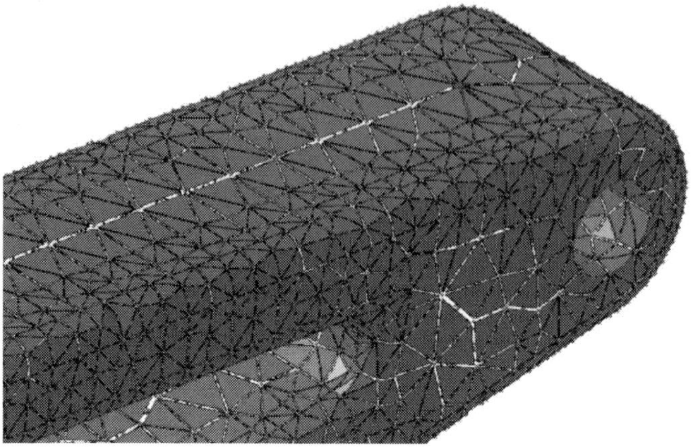

Figure 2–125

15. Right-click on **Mesh.1** in the tree and select **Delete** in the contextual menu to remove the mesh image and return to the model view.

Task 5 - Apply restraints.

In this task, you will apply the Clamp restraint to the two holes on one end of the hanger. This models the hanger being rigidly bolted to the adjoining structure.

1. Select  (Clamp) in the Restraints toolbar. The Clamp dialog box opens, as shown in Figure 2–126.

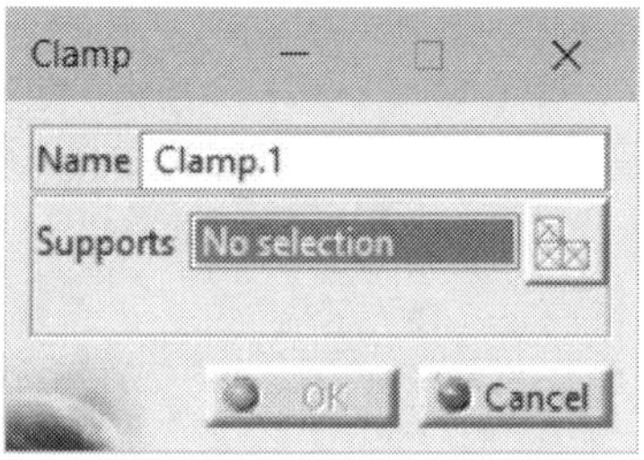

Figure 2–126

2. Select the inside surfaces of the two holes, as shown in Figure 2–127.

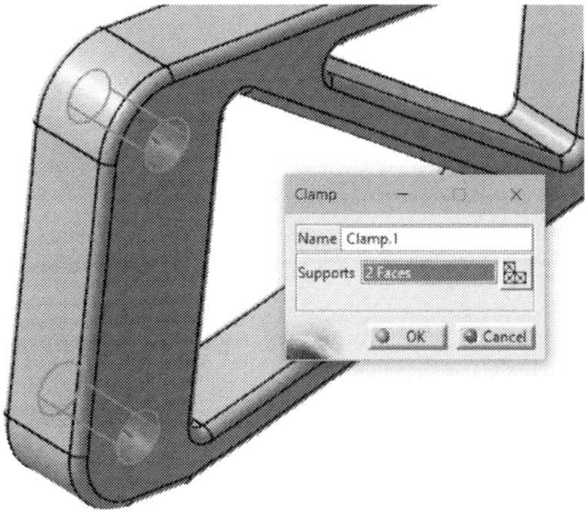

Figure 2–127

3. Click **OK** to close the Clamp dialog box.

Task 6 - Apply loads.

In this task, you will apply a 1000N vertical force to the hole on the other end of the hanger.

1. Select 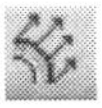 (Distributed Force) in the Forces toolbar. The Distributed Force dialog box opens, as shown in Figure 2–128.

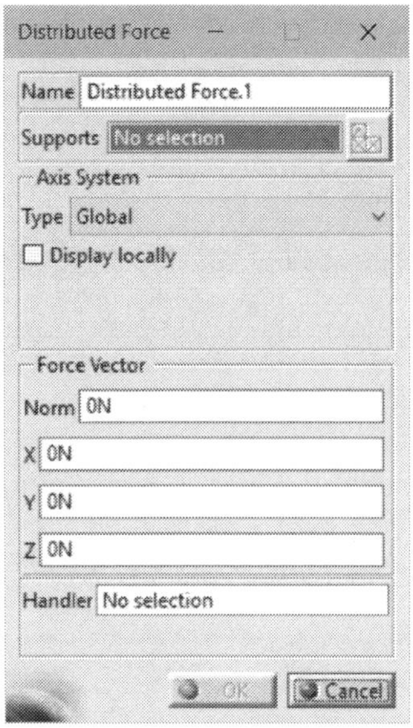

Figure 2–128

2. Select the inside surface of the hole and enter **-1000N** in the **Z** field in the *Force Vector* area, as shown in Figure 2–129.

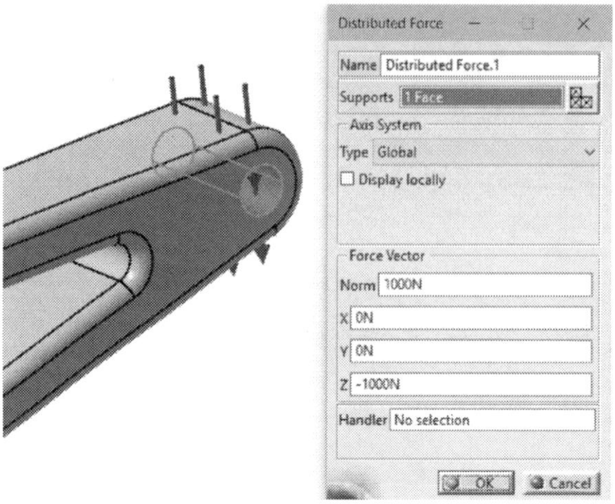

Figure 2–129

3. Click **OK** to close the Distributed Force dialog box. The model displays as shown in Figure 2–130.

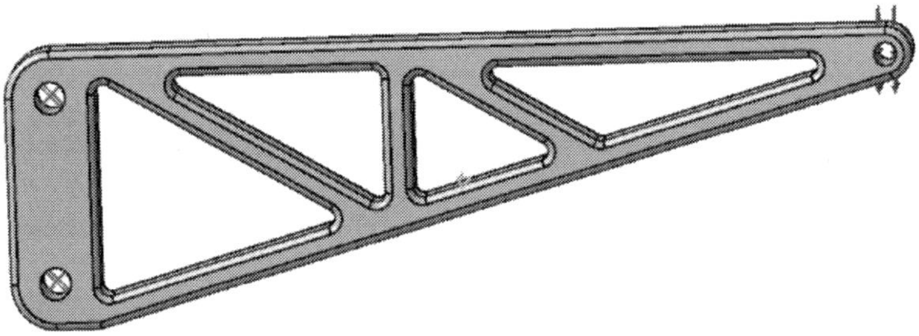

Figure 2–130

Task 7 - Run the analysis.

In this task, you will check the model for errors and run the analysis.

1. In the Model Manager toolbar, select  (Model Checker). CATIA checks the model for errors and inconsistencies and displays the summary in the Model Checker dialog box, as shown in Figure 2–131.

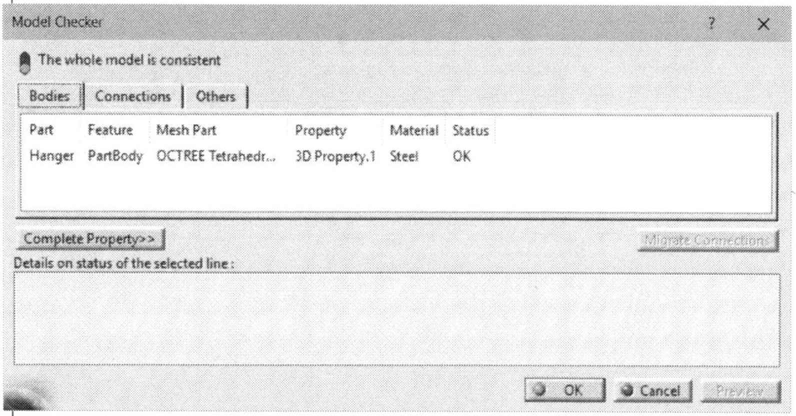

Figure 2–131

2. Note that the message at the top is "**The whole model is consistent**" and the *Status* is **OK**. Click **OK** to close the Model Checker dialog box.

3. In the Compute toolbar, select  (Compute). The Compute dialog box opens, as shown in Figure 2–132.

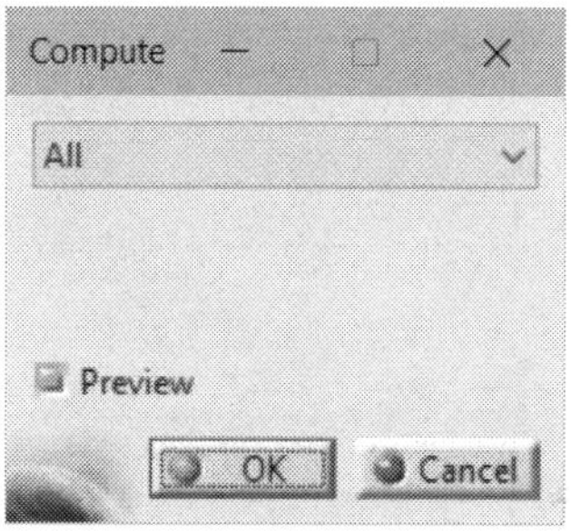

Figure 2–132

4. Ensure that **All** is selected in the drop-down list at the top of the dialog box and the **Preview** option is activated. Click **OK** to start the computation.

5. CATIA performs the CPU time and memory requirements calculation and displays the estimation in the Computation Resources Estimation dialog box, as shown in Figure 2–133.

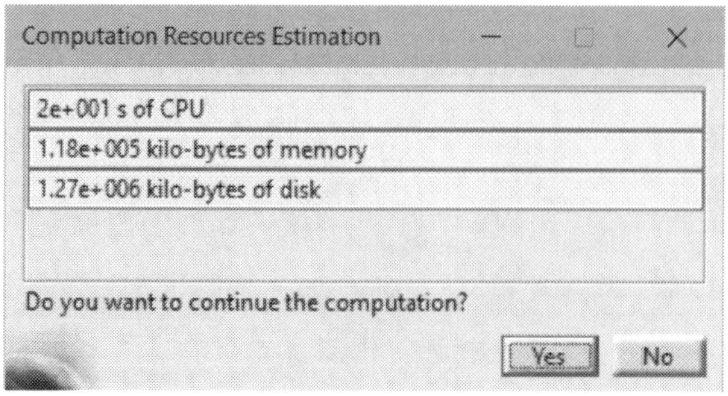

Figure 2–133

6. Click **Yes** to continue the computation. For this model, the computation time should be under 30 seconds.

7. Note that after the computation is completed, the **Static Case Solution.1** object in the tree no longer displays the  (Update) symbol.

Task 8 - Change the view mode.

The Shading with Material mode is necessary for the correct display of color result plots.

1. In the View toolbar, select  (Shading with Material).

Task 9 - Display and animate the displacements.

1. In the Image toolbar, select  (Displacement). The displacement vector image displays, as shown in Figure 2–134.

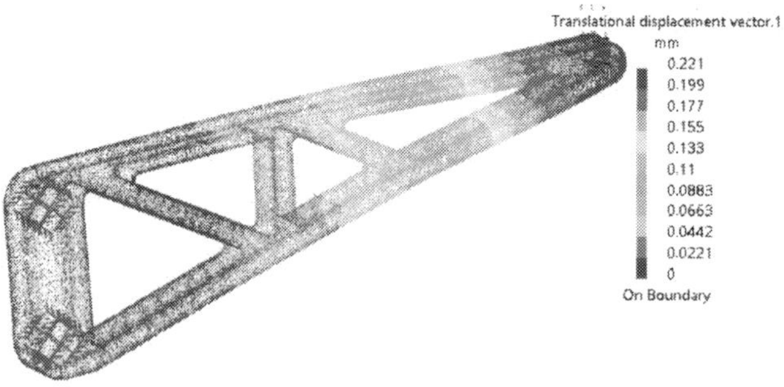

Figure 2–134

2. Double-click on the **Translational displacement vector.1** object in the tree. The Image Edition dialog box opens, as shown in Figure 2–135.

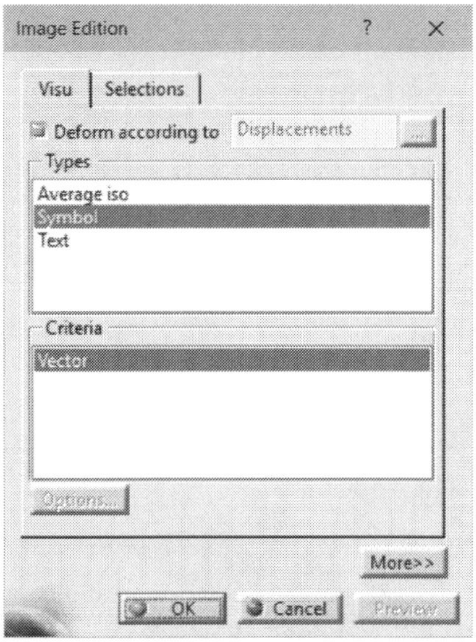

Figure 2–135

3. Select **Average iso** in the *Types* list and click **OK** to close the Image Edition dialog box. The image is now displayed as a color plot of the translational displacement magnitude, as shown in Figure 2–136.

   Note that the maximum displacement magnitude under the 1000N load is **0.221mm**.

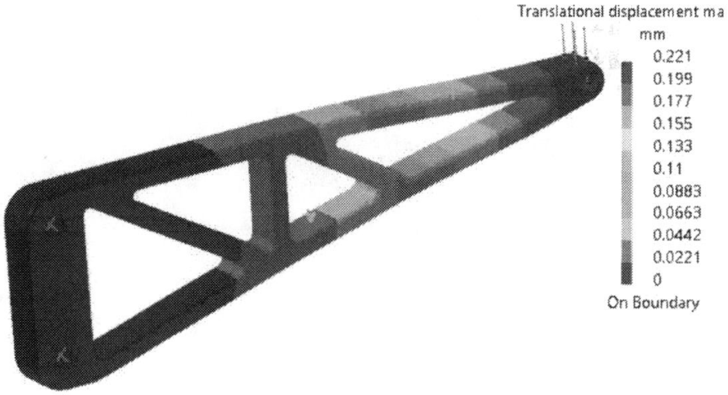

Figure 2–136

4. In the Analysis Tools toolbar, select  (Animate). The Animation dialog box opens, as shown in Figure 2–137, and the displacement magnitude result is now animated.

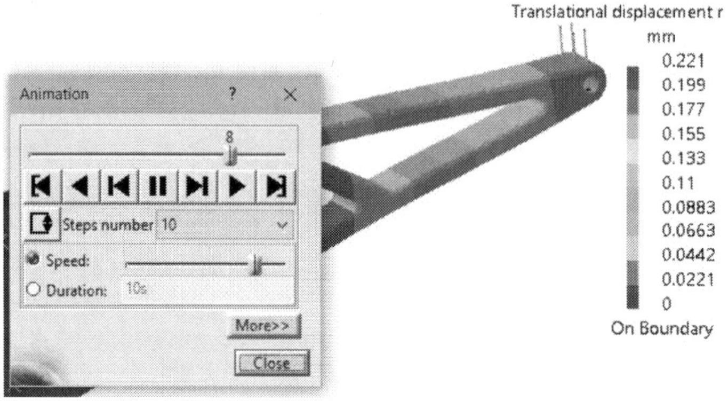

Figure 2–137

You can use Tools> Image>Video to record and save the animation to an .AVI file.

5. Using the controls in the Animation dialog box, pause and restart the animation, then step through the animation frame-by-frame.

6. Click **More** to expand the Animation dialog box, as shown in Figure 2–138. Experiment with the **Animate colors** and **Animate deformation** options to see their effect on the animation.

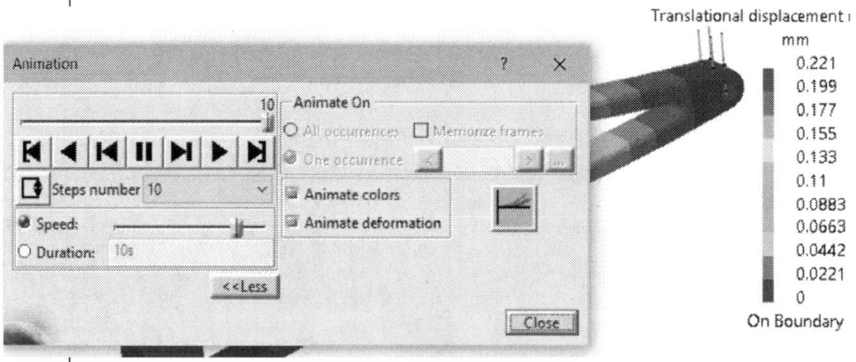

Figure 2–138

7. Click **Close** to close the Animation dialog box and stop the animation.

Task 10 - Display Von Mises stress.

Von Mises stress is a value used to determine if the material will yield and is mostly used for ductile materials such as metals. The hanger is made of Steel, which is a ductile metal; therefore, Von Mises stress would be an appropriate criterion to predict the hanger's failure.

1. In the Image toolbar, select  (Von Mises Stress). The stress image displays as shown in Figure 2–139.

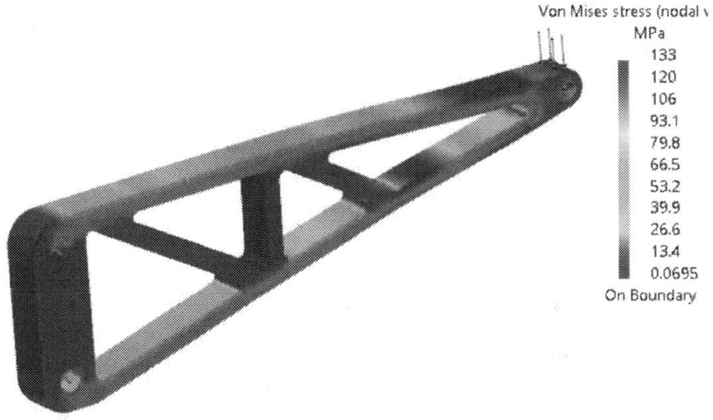

Figure 2–139

2. Rotate and visually examine the stress plot. Note that the maximum Von Mises stress is occurring in the triangular pocket near the loaded hole. You will later use the **Extrema** tool to precisely locate the area of maximum stress.

3. In the Analysis Tools toolbar, select (Information) and click the **Von Mises stress (nodal values).1** object in the tree. The Information dialog box displays, as shown in Figure 2–140.

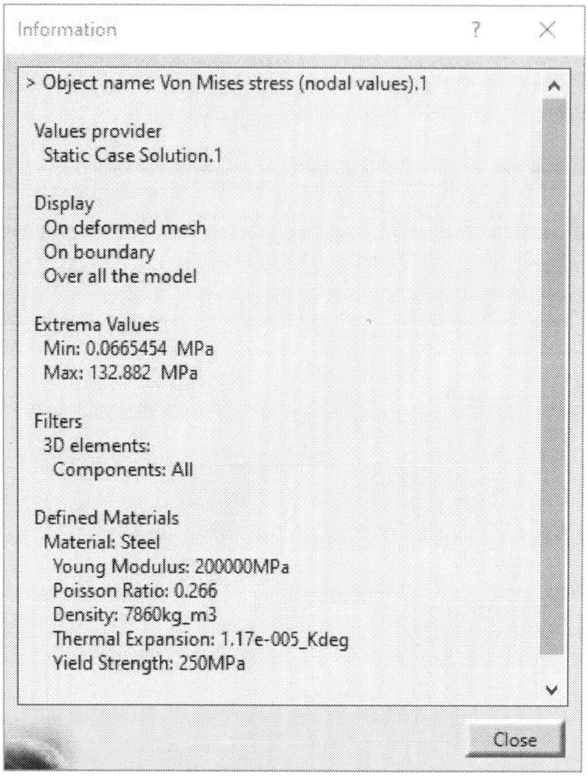

Figure 2–140

4. Note that the maximum Von Mises stress in the model is approximately **132.9MPa**, which is well below the material's **Yield Strength** of **250MPa**. Therefore, the part is predicted to withstand the load without failure. Click **Close** to close the Information dialog box.

Task 11 - Perform cut plane analysis.

1. In the Analysis Tools toolbar, select (Cut Plane Analysis). The Cut Plane Analysis dialog box opens, as shown in Figure 2–141.

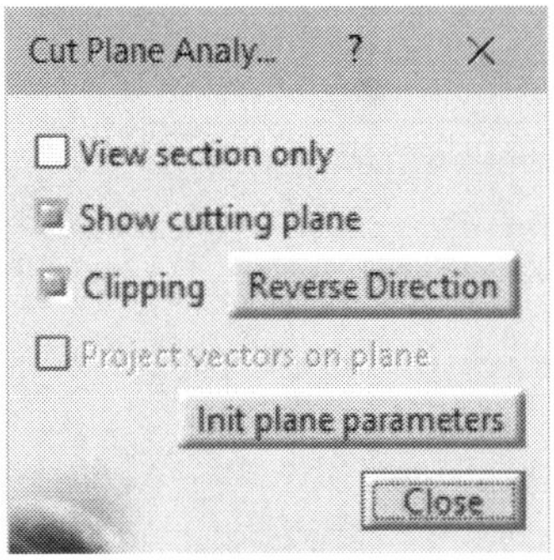

Figure 2–141

2. Deselect **Show cutting plane** and click **Init plane parameters**. The result plot displays as shown in Figure 2–142.

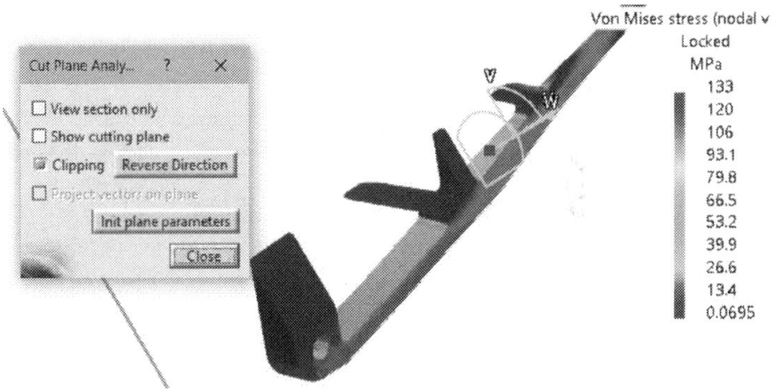

Figure 2–142

3. Right-click on the red square in the compass and select **Edit** in the contextual menu, as shown in Figure 2–143.

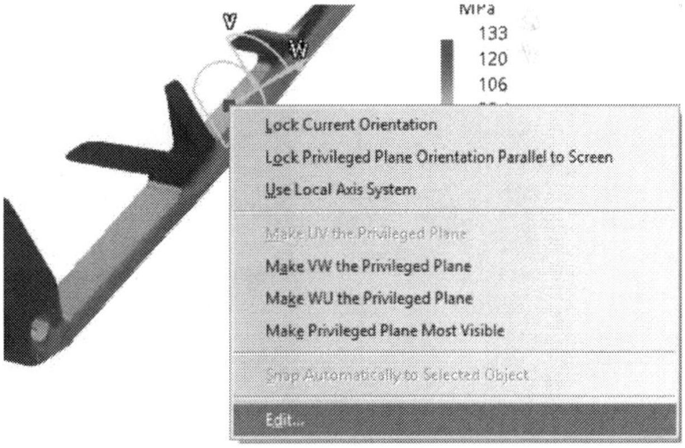

Figure 2–143

4. The Parameters for Compass Manipulation dialog box opens, as shown in Figure 2–144.

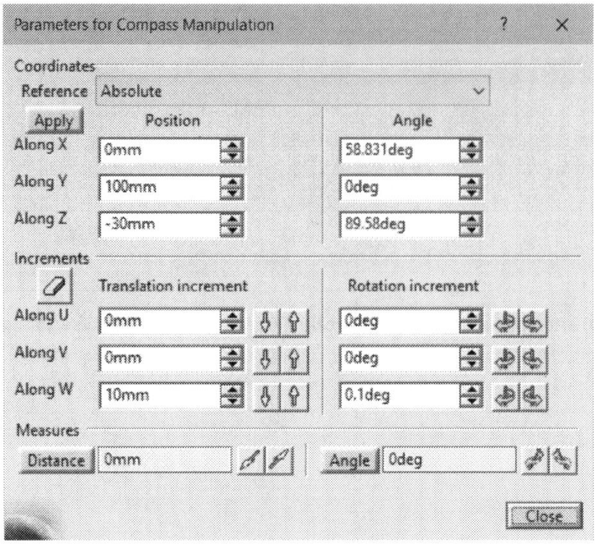

Figure 2–144

5. In the *Coordinates* section of the dialog box, enter the coordinates and angles as shown in Figure 2–145.

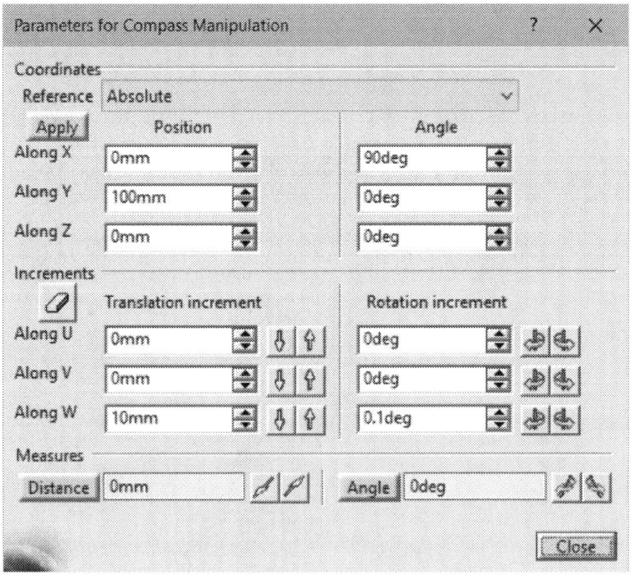

Figure 2–145

6. Click **Apply**, then click **Close**. The model displays as shown in Figure 2–146.

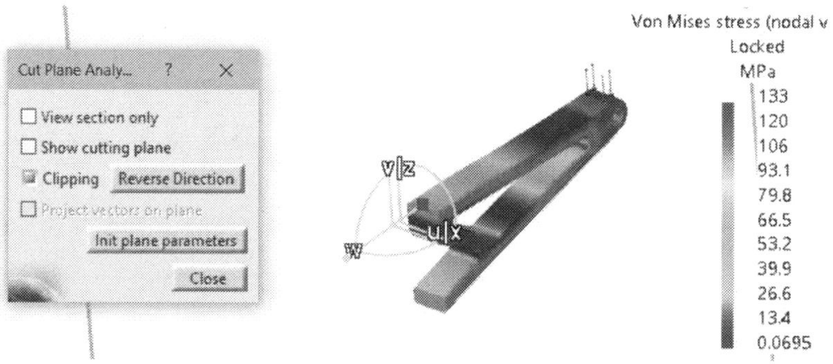

Figure 2–146

7. Drag the **W** axis in the compass to move the cut plane through the model. Examine stress in the cross-sections as you proceed.

8. Click **Close** in the Cut Plane Analysis dialog box to finish.

Task 12 - Create local stress sensor.

Rotate the model and note that there is an area of higher stress on the bottom surface of the bracket, as shown in Figure 2–147.

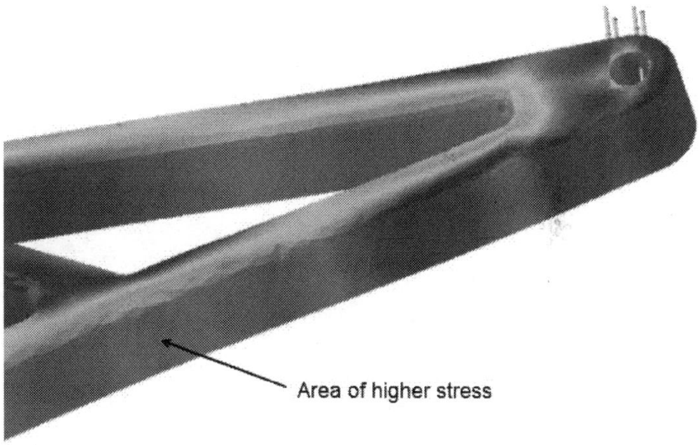

Figure 2–147

In this task, you will measure the maximum stress on the bottom surface using the local stress sensor tool.

1. Right-click on **Von Mises stress (nodal values).1** in the tree and select **Activate/Deactivate** to deactivate the stress image and return to the model view.

2. Right-click on **Sensors.1** in the tree and select **Create Local Sensor**, as shown in Figure 2–148.

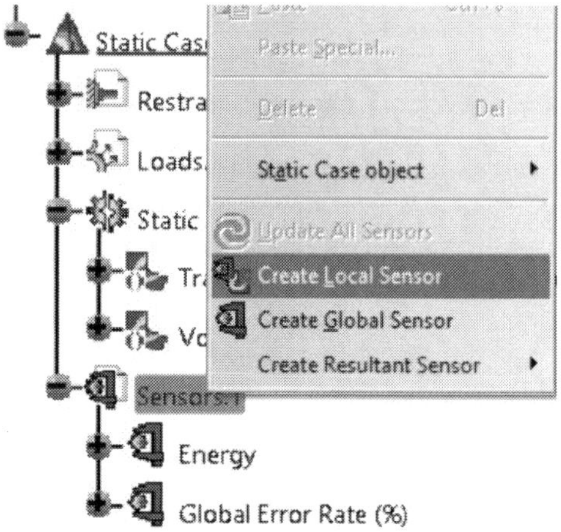

Figure 2–148

3. In the Create Sensor dialog box, select **Von Mises Stress** and click **OK**, as shown in Figure 2–149.

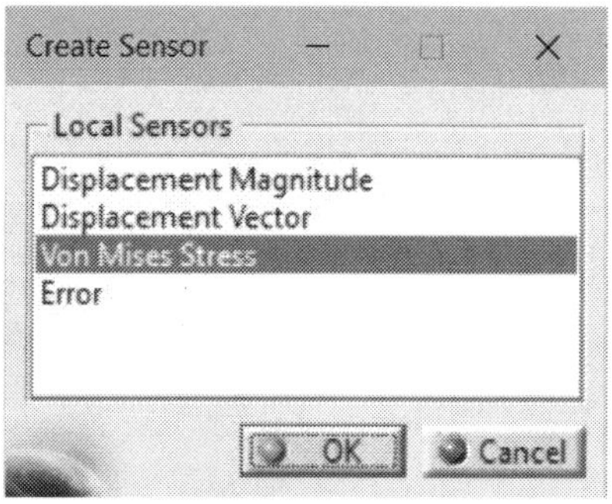

Figure 2–149

4. Double-click on the **Von Mises Stress.1** sensor in the tree. The Local Sensor dialog box opens, as shown in Figure 2–150.

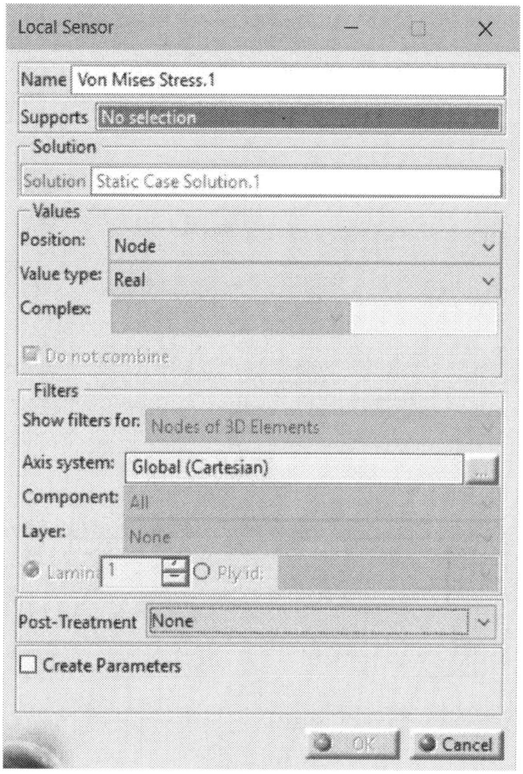

Figure 2–150

5. Select the bottom surface of the bracket as the *Supports*, as shown in Figure 2–151.

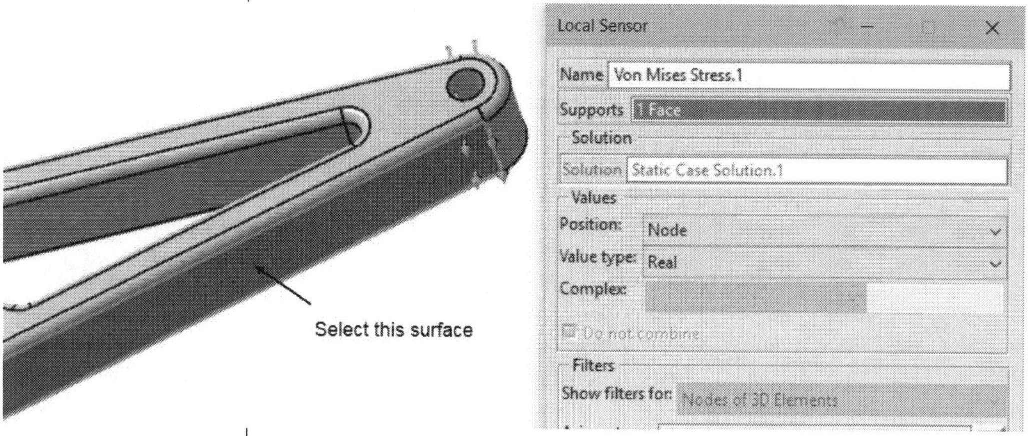

Figure 2–151

6. In the Post-Treatment drop-down list, select **Maximum**. Select the **Create Parameters** option, as shown in Figure 2–152.

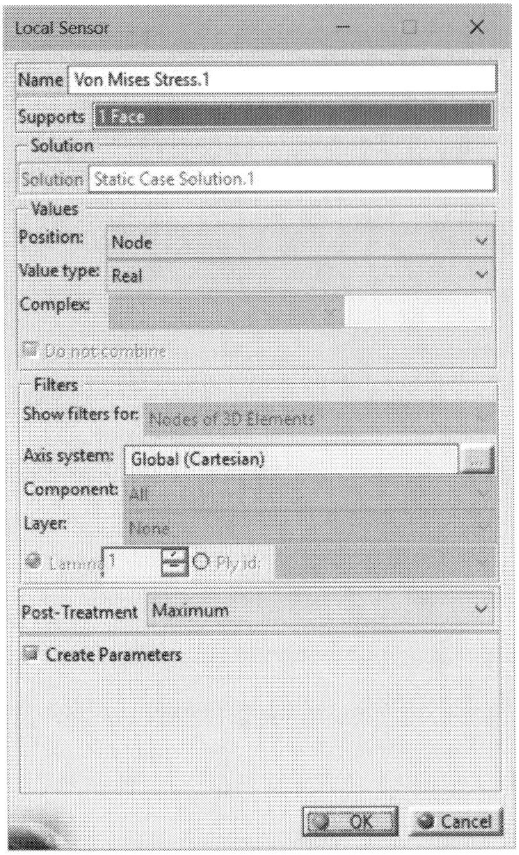

Figure 2–152

7. Click **OK** to close the Local Sensor dialog box. CATIA creates a new stress sensor in the tree but does not update it yet.

8. Right-click on the **Von Mises Stress.1** sensor and select **Update Sensor**, as shown in Figure 2–153.

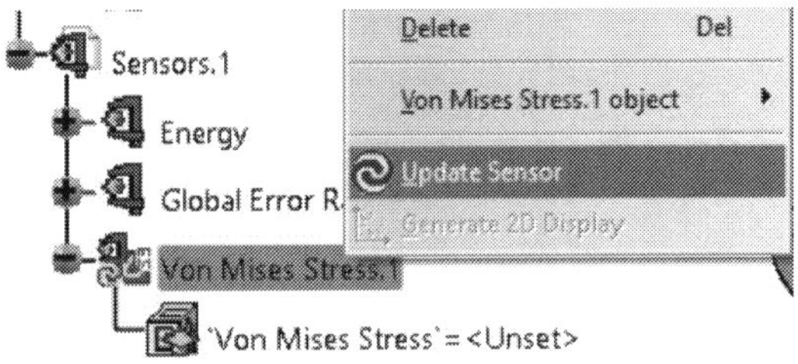

Figure 2–153

9. CATIA updates the sensor and shows the value in the tree and in the model, as shown in Figure 2–154.

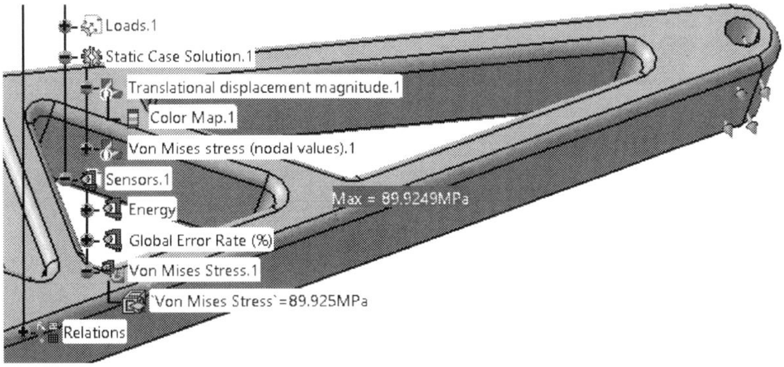

Figure 2–154

10. Right-click on the **Von Mises Stress.1** sensor and select **Hide/Show** to remove the label from the model view.

Task 13 - Display principal stress.

The Von Mises stress is a scalar value and, as such, it does not differentiate between tension and compression. It is always positive.

In some cases, it is the tensile stress that causes material failure, not the compressive stress. Therefore, it may be important to know where the material is in tension, and where it is in compression. Such cases include working with brittle materials that are less strong in tension than in compression, as well as dealing with metal fatigue, where it is the tensile normal stress that causes the crack initiation.

To differentiate between tensile and compressive stresses, we need to look at the principal stresses, not just the Von Mises stress.

The principal stresses are the so-called stress invariants and there are three at each infinitesimal point in the model: S_1, S_2, and S_3. S_1 is the maximum normal stress at the point and it typically is the tensile stress. S_3 is the minimum normal stress at a point and it typically is the compressive stress. S_2 is the stress in between and is seldom used in material strength estimations.

1. In the Image toolbar, select 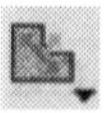 (Principal Stress). The result image displays as shown in Figure 2–155.

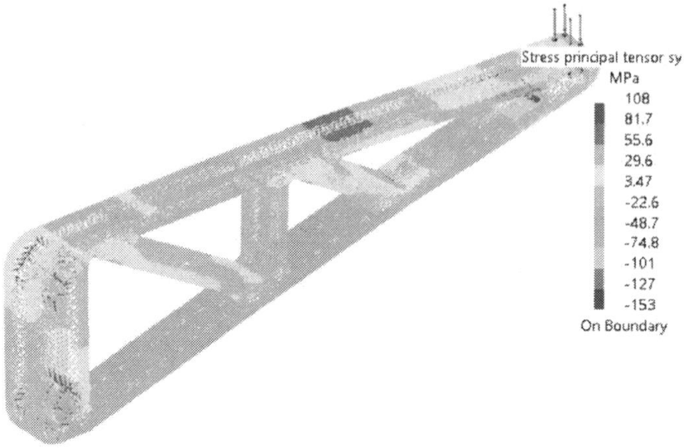

Figure 2–155

2. Zoom in on any area in the model. Note that the results are represented as three vectors at each mesh node, as shown in Figure 2–156. These are the three principal stresses, with the outward arrows indicating tension and inward arrows indicating compression.

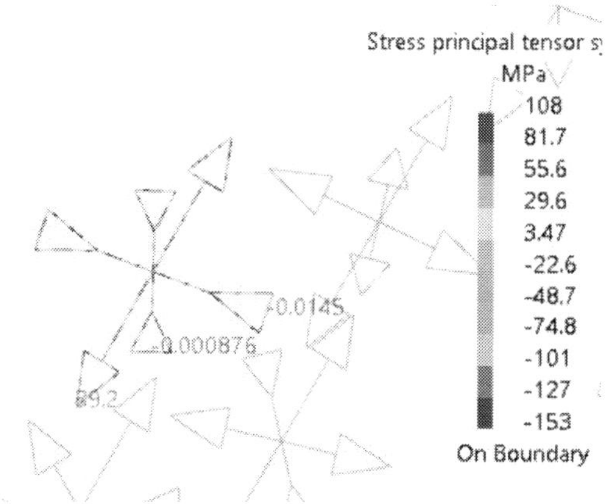

Figure 2–156

3. Double-click on the **Stress principal tensor symbol.1** object in the tree. The Image Edition dialog box opens, as shown in Figure 2–157.

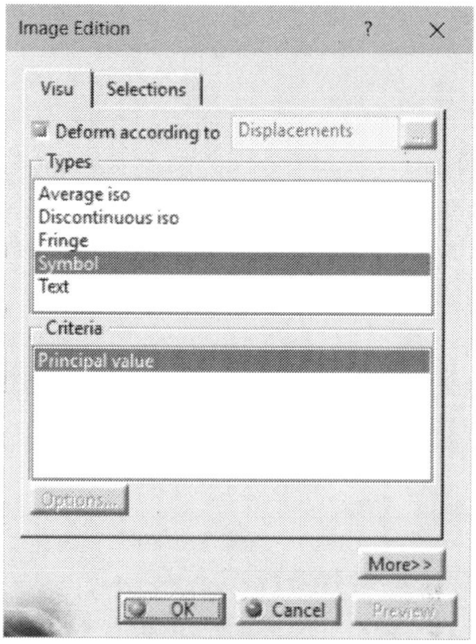

Figure 2–157

4. Click **More** to expand the dialog box. Select **C11** in the Component drop-down list, as shown in Figure 2–158.

*In CATIA's notation, **C11** corresponds to maximum principal stress S_1, **C22** corresponds to medium principal stress S_2, and **C33** corresponds to the minimum principal stress S_3.*

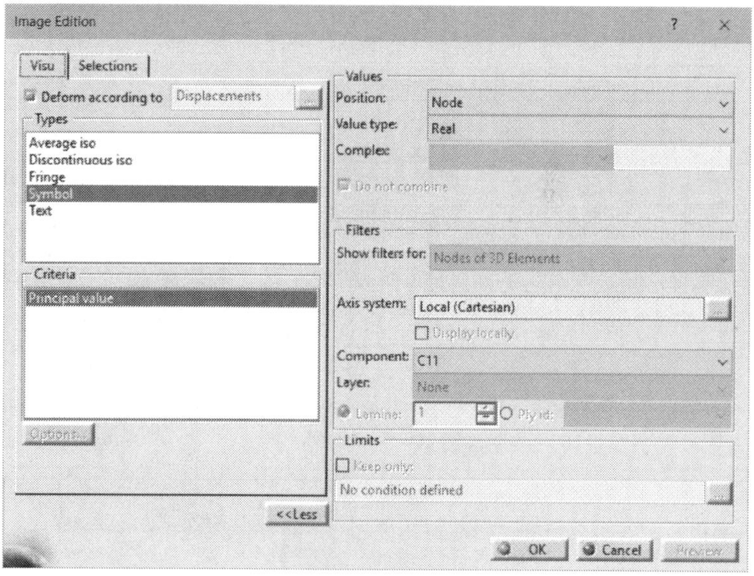

Figure 2–158

5. Click **OK**. The result image displays as shown in Figure 2–159.

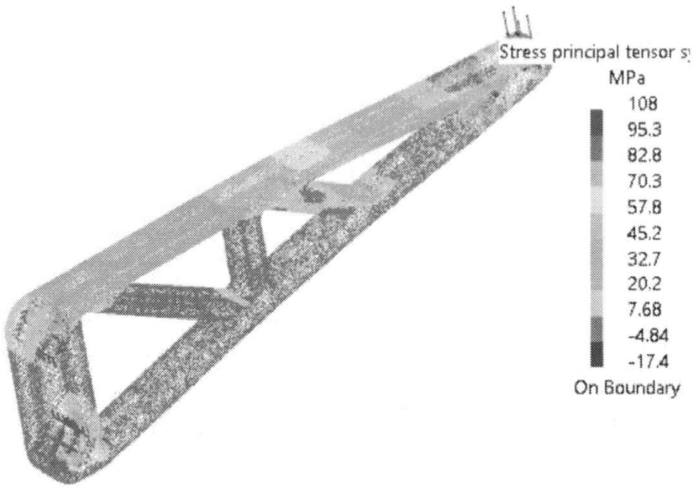

Figure 2–159

6. Select the **Front View** and zoom in on the area near the loaded hole, as shown in Figure 2–160. Note that now there is only one vector shown at each mesh node, which is the maximum normal stress, and the vector's direction indicates the stress's direction.

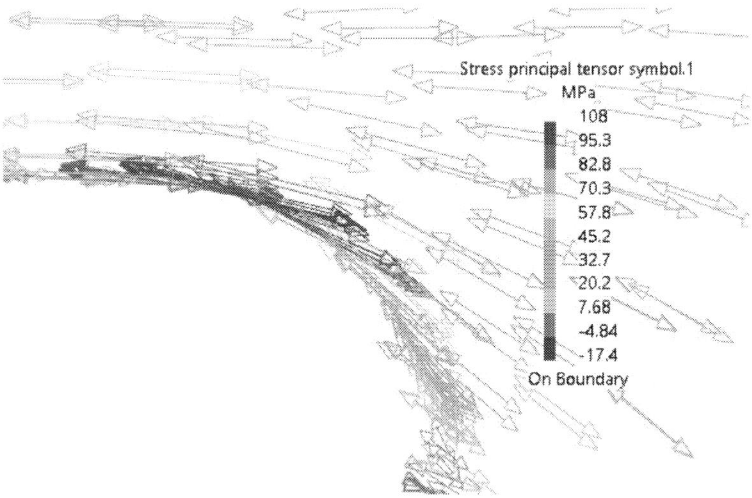

Figure 2–160

7. Double-click on the **Stress principal tensor symbol.1** object in the tree. Change the image type to **Average iso**, as shown in Figure 2–161.

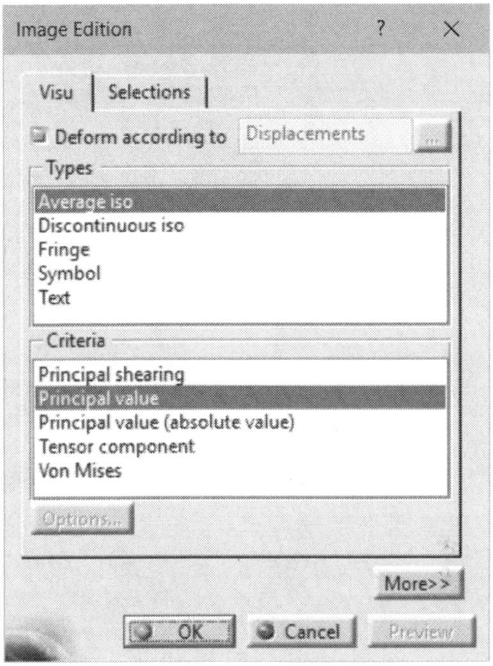

Figure 2–161

8. Click **OK**. The maximum principal stress image is now displayed as a color plot, as shown in Figure 2–162.

Figure 2–162

Task 14 - Locate areas of maximum tensile stress.

In this task, you will locate the areas of maximum tensile stress using the **Image Extrema** tool. The tool can be used to find global maximums and minimums (i.e., throughout the model), as well as local maximums and minimums. The local extrema are the local "peaks" in stress compared to the surrounding area.

1. In the Analysis Tools toolbar, select (Image Extrema). In the Extrema Creation dialog box that opens, request **1** global maximum and **10** local maximums, as shown in Figure 2–163.

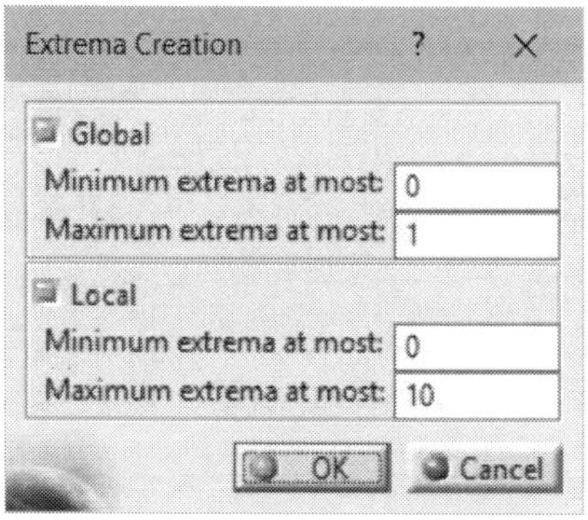

Figure 2–163

2. Click **OK**. The result plot displays as shown in Figure 2–164. Note that the extrema objects are also created in the tree, under the **Stress principal tensor component (nodal values).1** object.

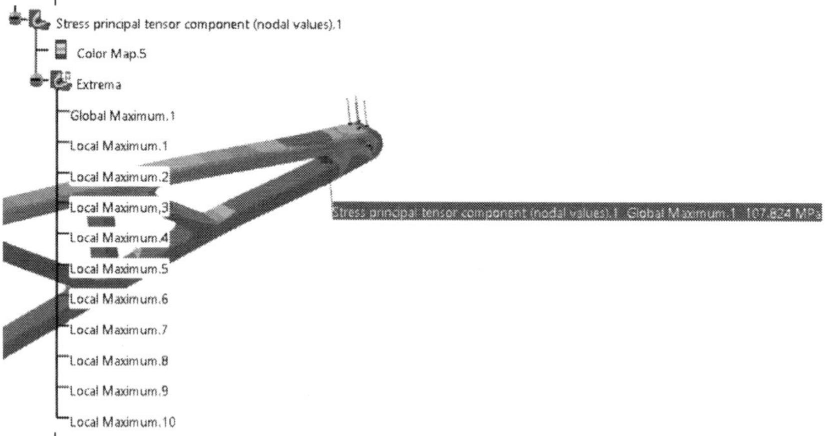

Figure 2–164

3. Rotate the model to locate the area that is indicated with a label, which is the fillet in the pocket nearest to the loaded hole, as shown in Figure 2–165.

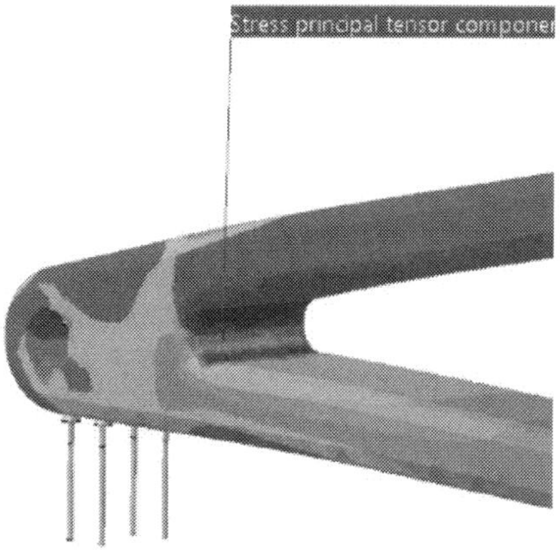

Figure 2–165

4. Double-click on **Global Maximum.1** in the tree. In the Extremum Edition dialog box that opens, shorten the label text so it only reads the stress value **107.768MPa**, as shown in Figure 2–166.

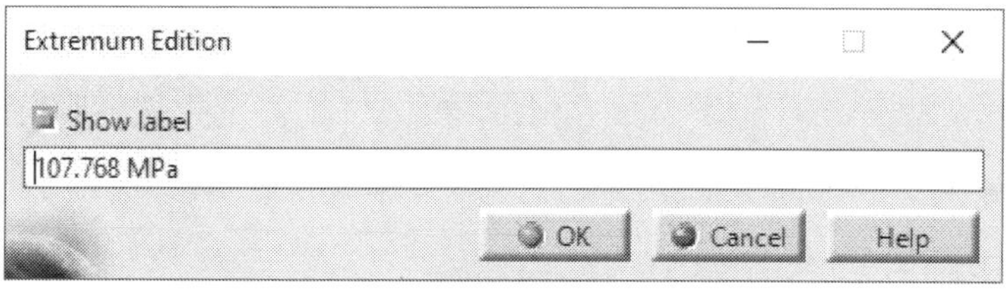

Figure 2–166

5. Click **OK**. The result image displays as shown in Figure 2–167.

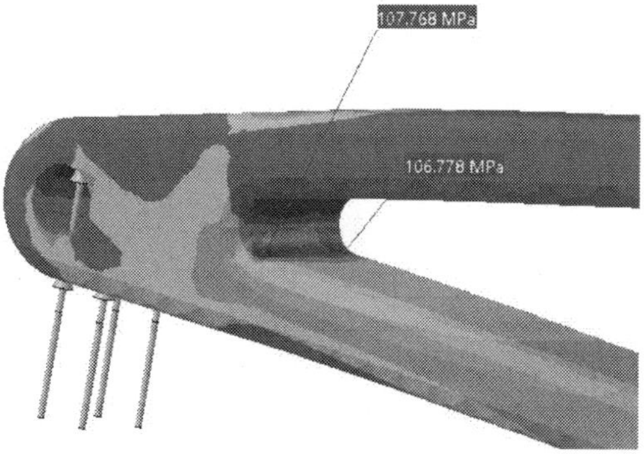

Figure 2–167

6. Double-click on **Local Maximum.1** in the tree. In the Extremum Edition dialog box that opens, activate the **Show label** option and shorten the label text so it only reads the stress value **106.778MPa**, as shown in Figure 2–168.

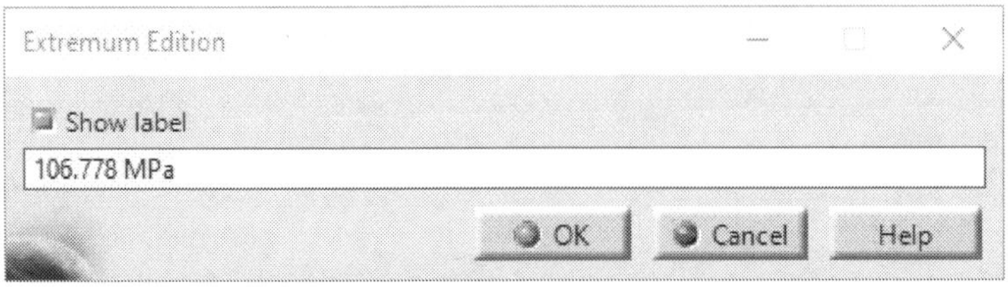

Figure 2–168

7. Click **OK**. The **Local Maximum.1** is now also labeled in the result image, as shown in Figure 2–169.

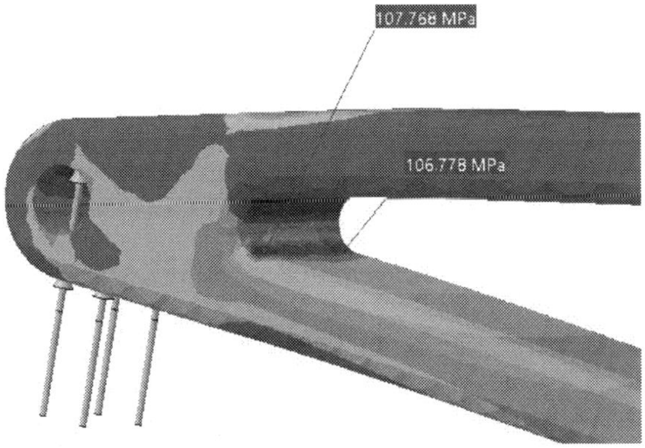

Figure 2–169

8. To adjust the position of the new label on the screen, double-click on it. While the Extremum Edition dialog box is open, point to the label with your mouse and, once you see the two crossing arrows, left-click and drag the label to a new position, as shown in Figure 2–170.

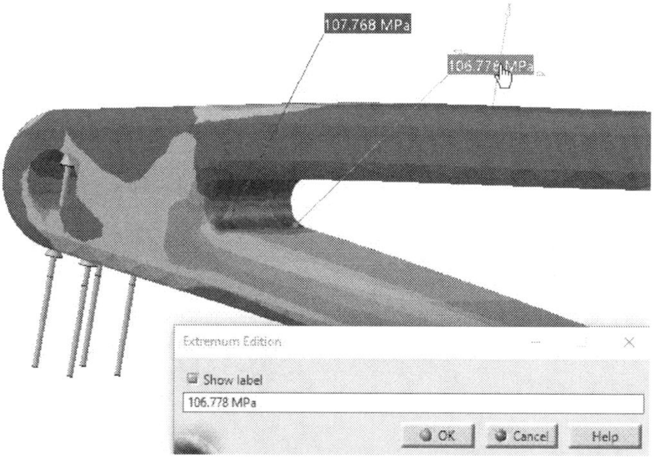

Figure 2–170

9. To label another local maximum (e.g., **Local Maximum.9**), right-click on it in the tree and select **Focus On** in the contextual menu, as shown in Figure 2–171.

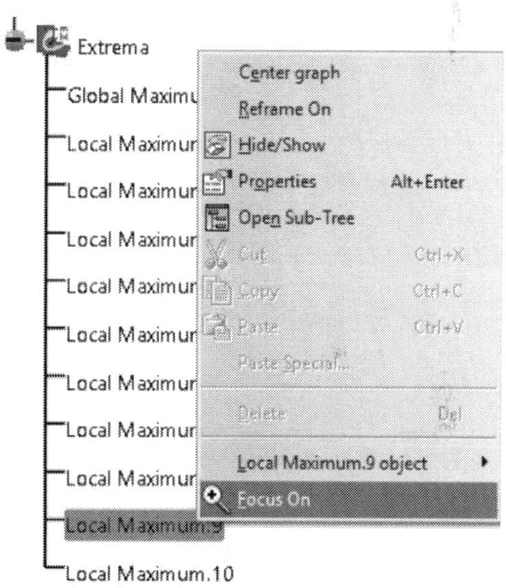

Figure 2–171

10. CATIA rotates and zooms in on the location, as shown in Figure 2–172. The local maximum is shown as a small colored sphere.

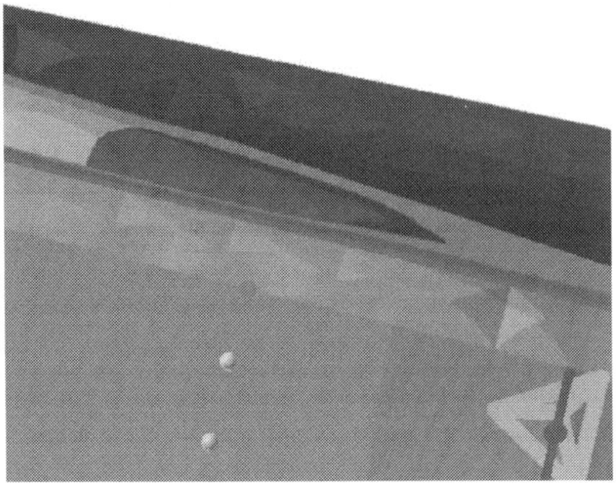

Figure 2–172

11. Double-click on **Local Maximum.9** in the tree. In the Extremum Edition dialog box that opens, activate the **Show label** option and, optionally, shorten the label text, as shown in Figure 2–173.

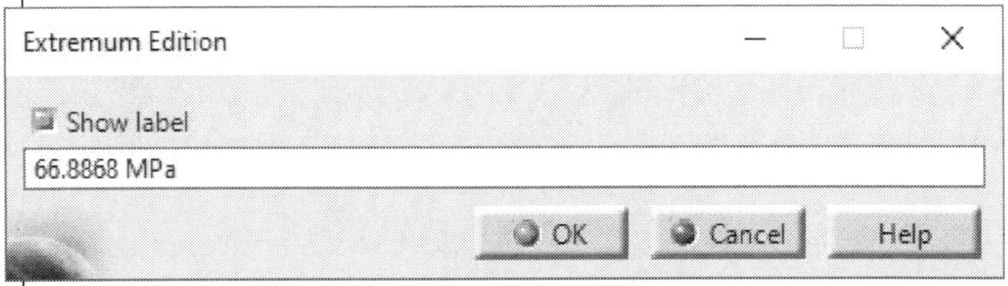

Figure 2–173

12. Click **OK**. The **Local Maximum.9** is now also labeled in the result image, as shown in Figure 2–174.

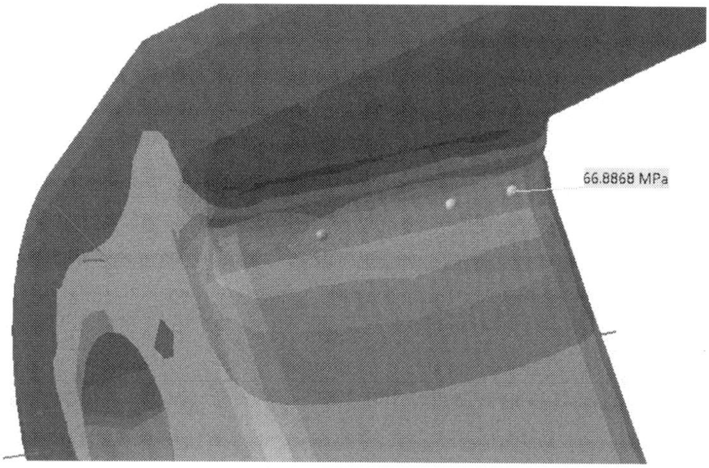

Figure 2–174

13. To adjust the position of the new label on the screen, double-click on it. While the Extremum Edition dialog box is open, point to the label with your mouse and, once you see the two crossing arrows, left-click and drag the label to a new position, as shown in Figure 2–175.

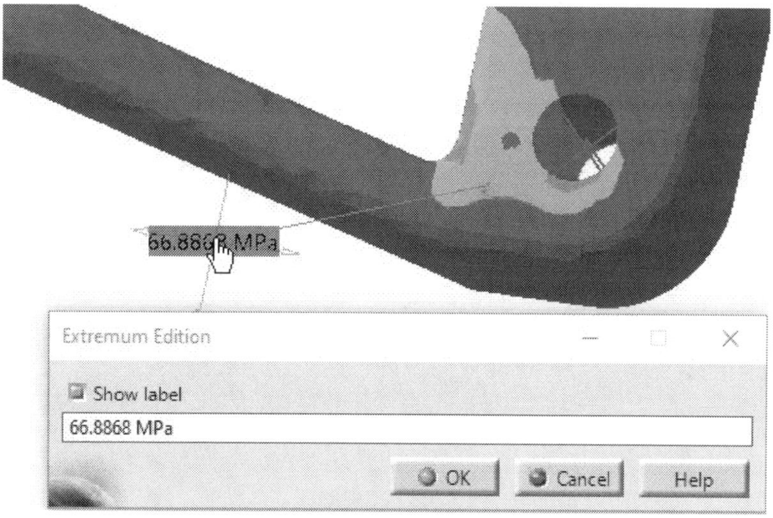

Figure 2–175

14. Right-click on the **Stress principal tensor component (nodal values).1** and select **Activate/Deactivate** to deactivate the principal stress image and return to the model view.

Task 15 - Create the analysis report.

1. In the Analysis Results toolbar, select (Generate Report). In the Report Generation dialog box that opens, click the ellipsis button (**...**) and select an output folder of your choice for the report. Enter **Hanger analysis** as the *Title*, as shown in Figure 2–176.

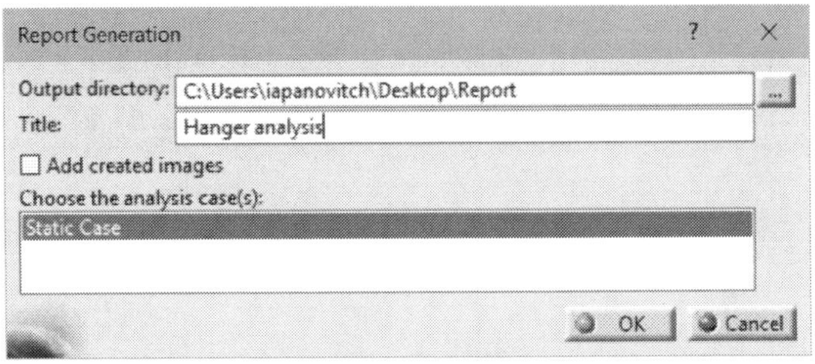

Figure 2–176

2. Click **OK**. The report opens in your default web browser, as shown in Figure 2–177.

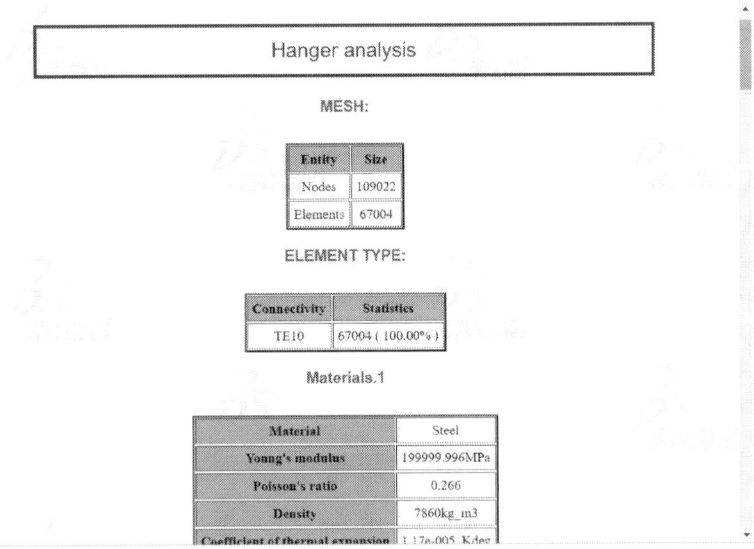

Hanger analysis

MESH:

Entity	Size
Nodes	109022
Elements	67004

ELEMENT TYPE:

Connectivity	Statistics
TE10	67004 (100.00%)

Materials.1

Material	Steel
Young's modulus	199999.996MPa
Poisson's ratio	0.266
Density	7860kg_m3
Coefficient of thermal expansion	1.17e-005_Kdeg

Figure 2–177

3. Scroll down and examine the contents of the analysis report.

Task 16 - Save and close the files.

1. Optionally, save the analysis document and the part for future reference.
2. Close both the analysis and the part documents.

Practice 2c

Static Stress Analysis of a Pin

Practice Objectives

- Prepare the model for the analysis.
- Run the analysis.
- Visualize the analysis results.
- Create the analysis report.

In this practice, you will set up and run a static stress analysis on the pin model shown in Figure 2–178 with minimum instruction.

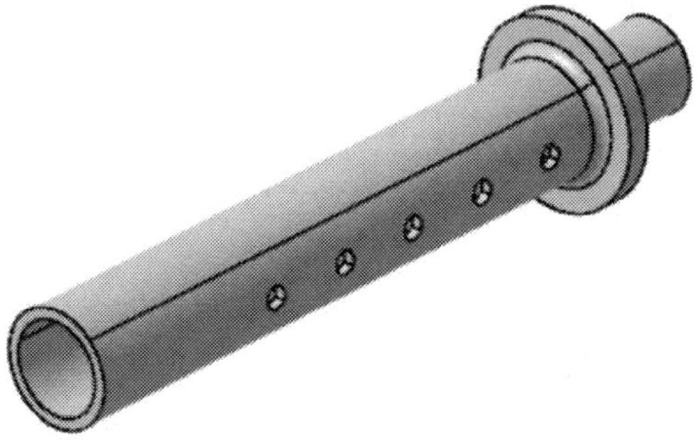

Figure 2–178

Task 1 - Prepare the model for the analysis.

1. Open **Pin_02.CATPart** from the *CATIA Generative Structural Analysis Practice Files\Ch02* folder.
2. Apply the **Steel** material to the part.
3. Start the GSA workbench.
4. Mesh the model with the following parameters:
   - Element type: **Parabolic**
   - Size: **5mm**
   - Sag: 20% of the mesh size
5. Visually examine the mesh.

6. Clamp the surface shown in Figure 2–179.

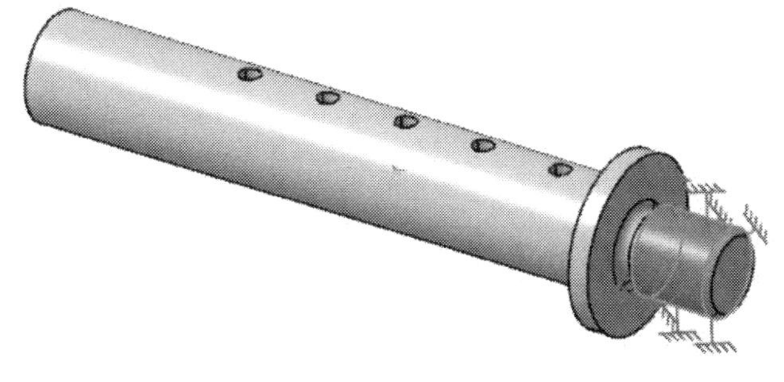

Figure 2–179

7. Apply **1500N** distributed force in **+Y** direction to the end surface of the pin, as shown in Figure 2–180.

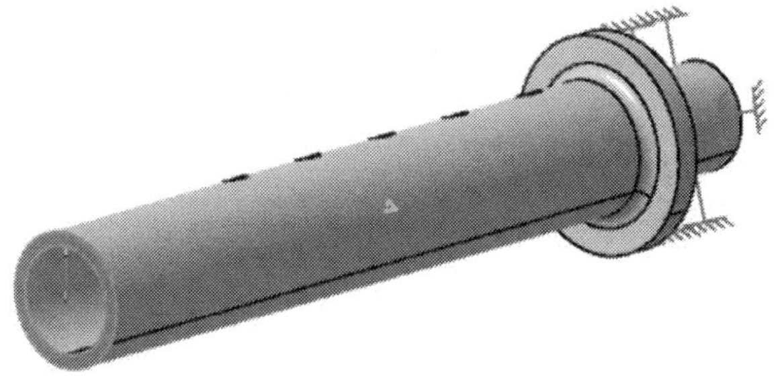

Figure 2–180

Task 2 - Run the analysis.

1. Check the model for inconsistencies.
2. Run the analysis.

Task 3 - Visualize and examine the analysis results.

1. Visualize and animate the deformed mesh. Does the part deform according to the applied loads?
2. Display the displacement magnitude color plot. What is the value of the maximum displacement in the model?

Factor of Safety value is obtained by dividing the material's yield strength by the maximum stress in the model.

3. Display the Von Mises color plot. Does the maximum stress exceed the yield strength of the material? What is the value of the factor of safety of the part?

4. Find the location of the maximum stress. Can you think of design changes that would lead to a decrease in the stress level in that area?

5. Do the transverse holes cause stress concentration? Should it be a design concern?

6. Close the model without saving.

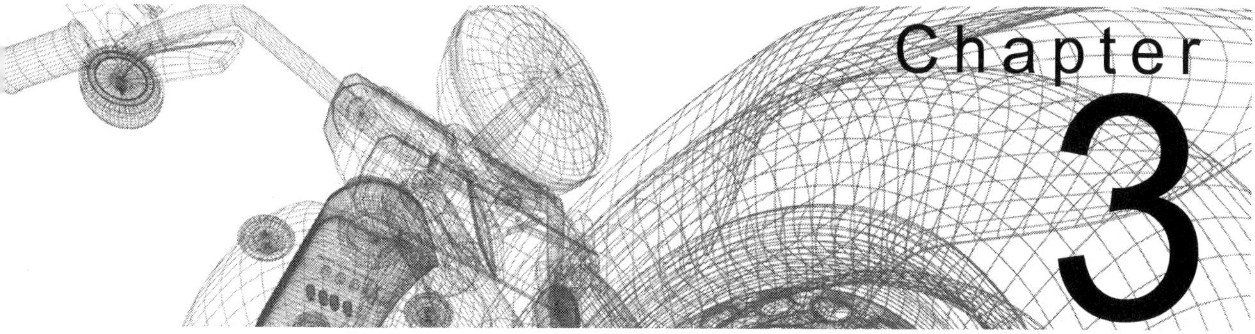

Loads and Restraints

Loads and restraints are the boundary conditions that the product experiences in its working environment. Selecting the correct boundary conditions for your FEA model is a critical aspect of developing an accurate simulation. Therefore, when you are analyzing a model, the loads and restraints placed on it must realistically represent the operating conditions of your product.

In this chapter, you learn about the tools available for applying restraints and loads in an analysis.

Learning Objectives in This Chapter

- Understand the rigid body motions.
- Create clamp and surface slider restraints.
- Create user-defined and isostatic restraints.
- Use the symmetry restraints.
- Create distributed force and moment loads.
- Create pressure and force density loads.
- Create acceleration and rotation loads.
- Apply enforced displacement.
- Create surface patches to apply loads and restraints.
- Obtain reaction forces in restraints.

3.1 Restraints

In CATIA GSA, a restraint is a form of boundary condition in which a *prescribed displacement* is assigned to one or more geometrical entities in the model. Prescribed displacement means that the displacement of the geometrical entity to which it is applied is enforced throughout the simulation. A prescribed displacement (i.e., restraint) can be of a zero value, which is typically used to simulate all kinds of supports in the analysis model, or of a non-zero value, which is typically used to enforce a specific motion in the model.

Restraints are commonly used to model a true support, such as where a structure is fixed to a rigid foundation or adjoining structure. Another common use is to simulate symmetry conditions.

Although restraints are essential for structural analyses, it is usually preferable to avoid the use of unnecessary restraints. Since the essence of structural FEA is to calculate displacements (along with the corresponding strains and stresses), the prescribed displacements effectively force an assumed solution onto some of the geometrical entities in the model. Therefore, unnecessary restraints might unnaturally stiffen the model and, consequently, the stresses might typically err on the low side.

Rigid Body Motions

In static structural analysis, it is necessary to provide sufficient supports to prevent rigid body motions (RBMs), which are the movements of parts of the structure that do not produce strain. An example of a simply supported beam is shown in Figure 3–1.

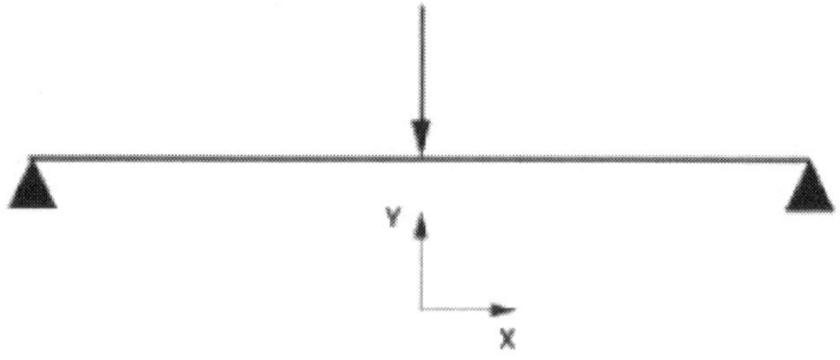

Figure 3–1

When using handbook formulas to calculate deflections and stresses in the beam, the only supports required are those in the Y-direction. Since no loads are applied in the X-direction, a support in that direction is not necessary. However, in FEA the lack of support in the X-direction results in a fatal error, since the beam is unconstrained against moving in the X-direction as a rigid body.

When CATIA detects an RBM in the model, an error message is issued as shown in Figure 3–2.

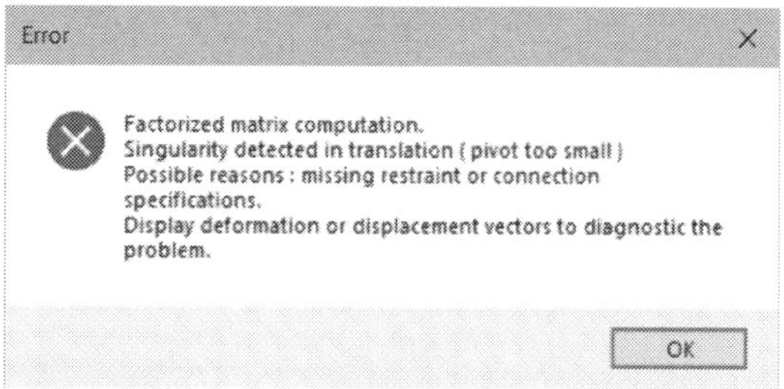

Figure 3–2

The number of possible RBMs varies from one model to another. For a single part in 3D, there are six possible RBMs: three translations and three rotations. For an assembly, the number could be much greater, since each part now has six possible RBMs that have to be eliminated by applying restraints and connections between the parts.

Clamp Restraint

The clamp restraint applied to a geometrical entity renders that entity completely immovable – all translations and rotations are blocked.

To apply a clamp, select  (Clamp) in the Restraints toolbar and select the entities you want to restrain as the *Supports*, as shown in Figure 3–3.

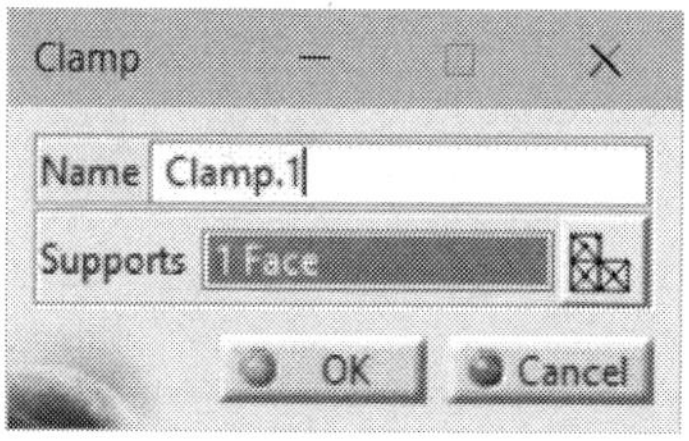

Figure 3–3

The clamp restraint can be applied to surfaces, edges, points, or Virtual Parts in your model.

Surface Slider Restraint

The surface slider restraint applied to a surface restrains displacements normal to the surface direction at every mesh node on that surface. The tangent to the surface directions, however, are not restrained.

An example of the surface slider restraint applied to a planar surface is shown in Figure 3–4. Since only normal to the plane displacements are blocked, the model with this restraint can still experience the in-plane motions, which are two translations and one rotation within the plane.

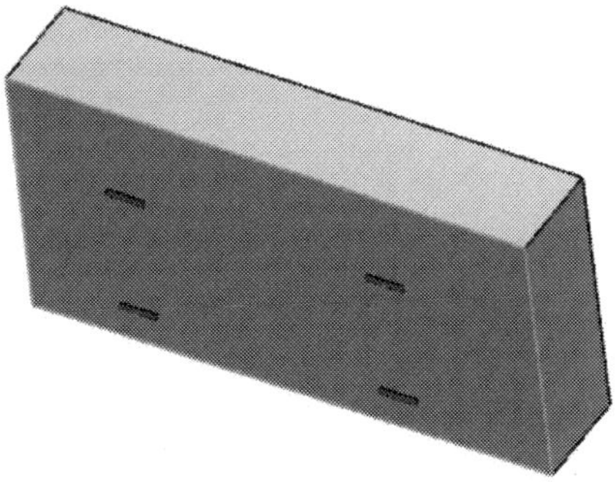

Figure 3–4

An example of the surface slider restraint applied to a cylindrical surface is shown in Figure 3–5. Since normal to the cylinder displacements are blocked, which are displacements in the radial direction, the model with this restraint can experience the following free motions:

- Sliding along the axis of the hole
- Rotation around the axis of the hole

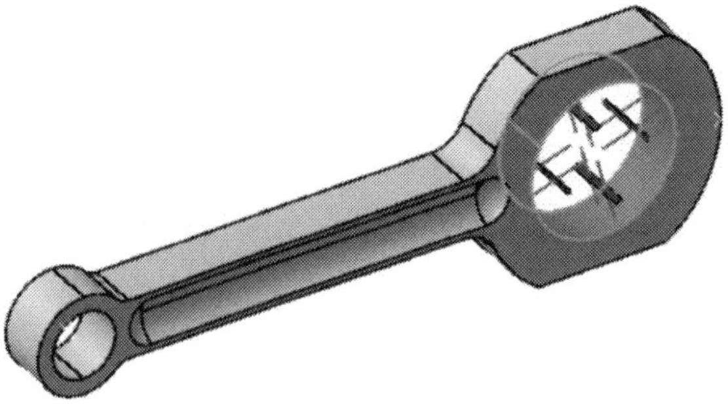

Figure 3–5

To apply a surface slider restraint, select (Surface Slider) in the Restraints toolbar and select the *Supports*, as shown in Figure 3–6.

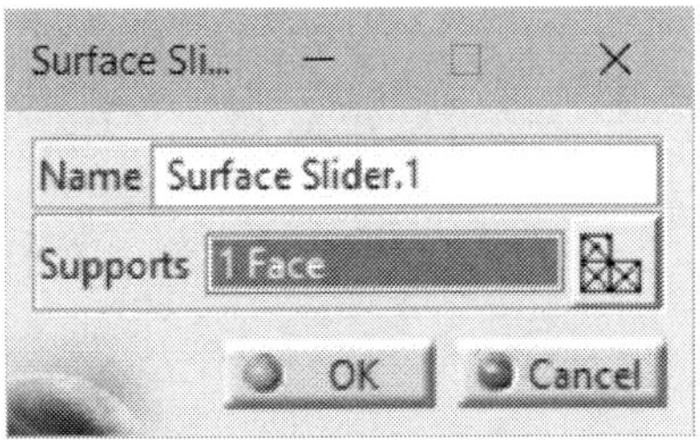

Figure 3–6

User-defined Restraint

The user-defined restraint enables the user to individually select in which directions to restrain the displacements. Any combination of the restrained directions can be modeled.

To apply a user-defined restraint, select (User-defined Restraint) in the Restraints toolbar to open the User-defined Restraint dialog box, as shown in Figure 3–7.

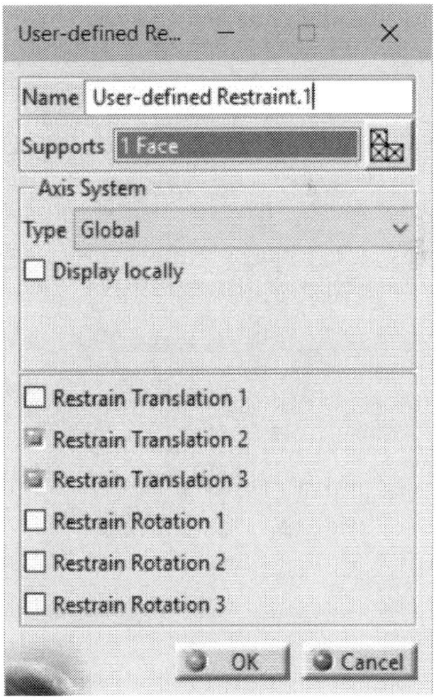

Figure 3–7

The bottom section of the dialog box contains six checkboxes: **Restrain Translation 1** through **Restrain Rotation 3**. Selecting a corresponding checkbox constrains the mesh nodes on the selected geometry against movement in that direction. Clearing a checkbox permits the mesh nodes to move in that direction when the model deforms.

Note that mesh nodes of 3D solid elements, such as tetrahedral or hexahedral, do not carry rotational degrees of freedom, therefore cannot be restrained against rotations. Only nodes of structural finite elements, such as shells, plates, or beams, can be restrained against rotations. If you select the rotational checkboxes when applying a user-defined restraint to a 3D solid mesh, the selections are ignored by the GSA and a notification message is issued, as shown in Figure 3–8.

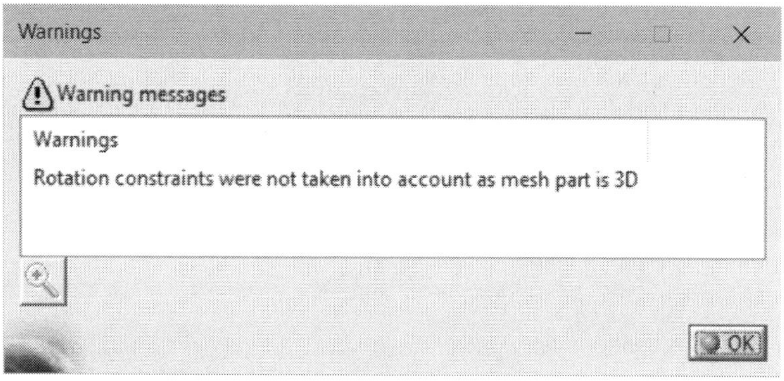

Figure 3–8

The directions 1, 2, and 3 are determined based on the coordinate system selected in the Axis System drop-down list as follows:

- **Global**: Directions 1, 2, and 3 are the global **X**, **Y**, and **Z** directions.
- **User**: The user selects another axis system, and directions 1, 2, and 3 are interpreted according to the axis system type.
    - **Cartesian**: Directions 1, 2, and 3 are the axis system's **X**, **Y**, and **Z**.
    - **Cylindrical**: Directions 1, 2, and 3 are interpreted as directions **r**, **Θ**, and **Z** of the cylindrical coordinate system.
    - **Spherical**: Directions 1, 2, and 3 are interpreted as directions **r**, **Θ**, and φ of the spherical coordinate system

- **Implicit**: Directions 1, 2, and 3 are interpreted according to the so-called parametric directions **U**, **V**, and **n** on the part surface.
    - Parametric directions **U** and **V** are in-plane of the surface and depend on the surface type (whether it is a plane or a cylinder, etc.). The directions are determined internally by CATIA. The user has no control over the parametric directions **U** and **V**.
    - Direction **n** is always normal to the surface.

You can preview the directions on the surface by activating the **Display locally** checkbox.

Isostatic Restraint

The isostatic restraint is specifically designed for analysis models with *balanced* systems of loads.

In a balanced system of loads, all the applied forces cancel each other, so the model is said to be in the state of equilibrium without involvement of the reactions in restraints.

As an example, consider loading of a bar under tension, as shown in Figure 3–9. The same amount of force is applied on either end of the bar, but in opposite directions. As a result, the two forces cancel each other and the model is in equilibrium.

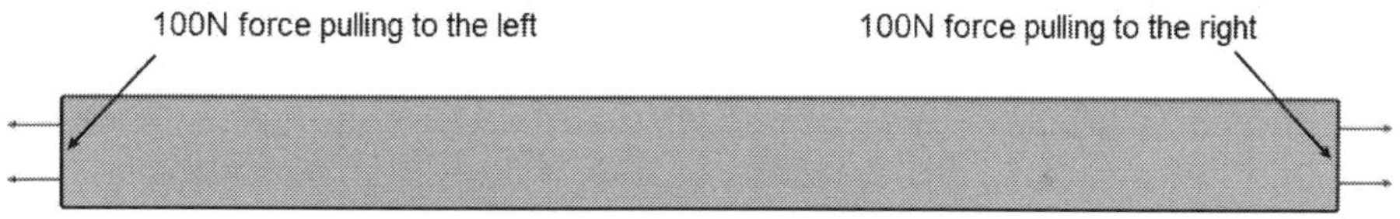

Figure 3–9

In such a case, the model should be minimally supported, just enough to eliminate possible rigid motions, to ensure a successful computation.

The isostatic restraint automatically, behind the scenes, creates such a "minimal" support scheme by applying three user-defined restraints to three nodes on the mesh. No user involvement to select the nodes or directions is required.

To apply an isostatic restraint, select  (Isostatic Restraint) in the Restraints toolbar and click **OK**, as shown in Figure 3–10.

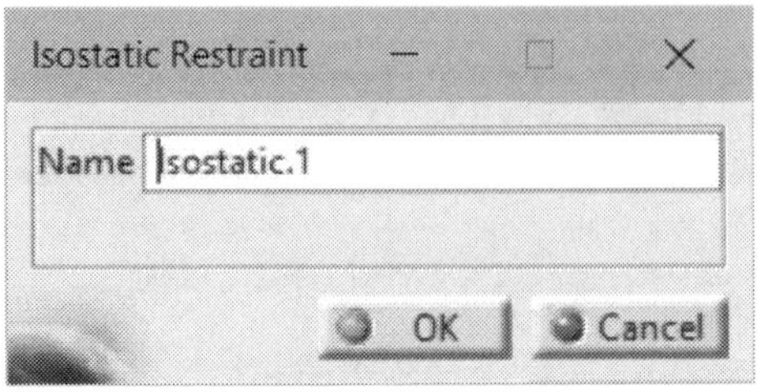

Figure 3–10

Note: Exercise caution as to not use isostatic restraints with unbalanced systems of loads.

Mechanical Restraints

The Mechanical Restraints sub-toolbar of the Restraints toolbar contains the following restraints:

-  (Slider): Allows sliding motion along a specific direction.
-  (Sliding Pivot): Allows sliding motion and rotation along a specific direction.
-  (Pivot): Allows rotation about a specific direction, without sliding along that direction.
-  (Ball Joint): Allows rotations about a point, without translations.

The mechanical restraints are only applicable to Virtual Parts, which will be discussed in detail in Chapter 5.

Symmetry Restraint

Using symmetry restraints, you can take advantage of the model's symmetry to reduce the number of finite elements and therefore the analysis time. In essence, symmetry restraints enable you to analyze a segment of the model and project the result onto the entire model.

The symmetry restraint requires that the model exhibit a *reflective* symmetry about a plane (i.e., the geometry, loads, and restraints on one side of the plane must mirror the geometry, loads, and restraints on the other side of the plane). The model may have one, two, or even three planes of symmetry.

For example, the model shown in Figure 3–11 exhibits reflective symmetry about the horizontal plane through the center of the part.

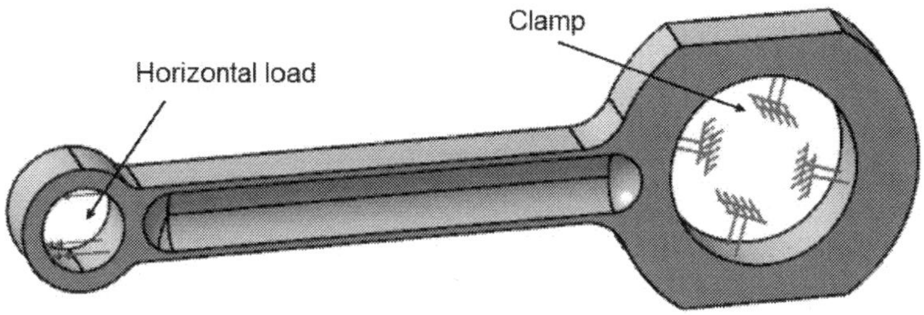

Figure 3–11

Therefore, you could take advantage of the symmetry and solve half of the model, as shown in Figure 3–12.

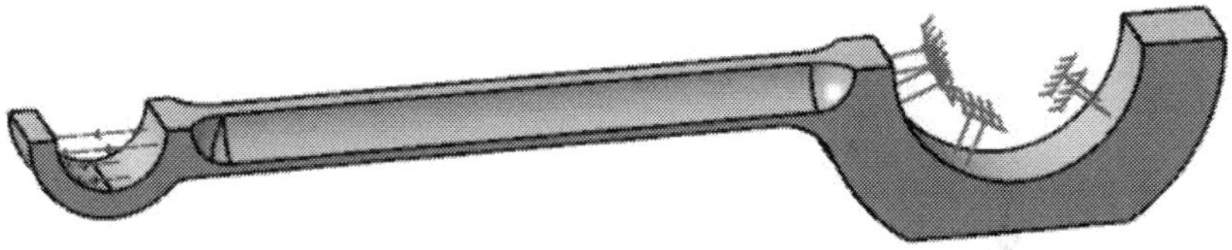

Figure 3–12

However, the same part with a different loading, as shown in Figure 3–13, does not exhibit reflective symmetry because the loading is not symmetrical. Therefore, this model cannot be solved as half of the part.

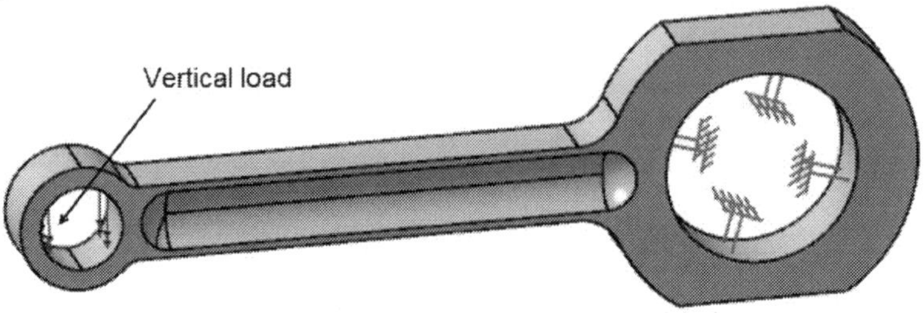

Figure 3–13

The symmetry restraint is applied on the surfaces that lie in the plane of symmetry, and it simulates the effect of the other half of the part, as if it were still in the analysis model.

To figure out which directions to restrain, visualize which motions would be possible and which motions would not be possible for infinitesimal material particles on the plane of symmetry. The restricted motions on the plane of symmetry are shown in Figure 3–14.

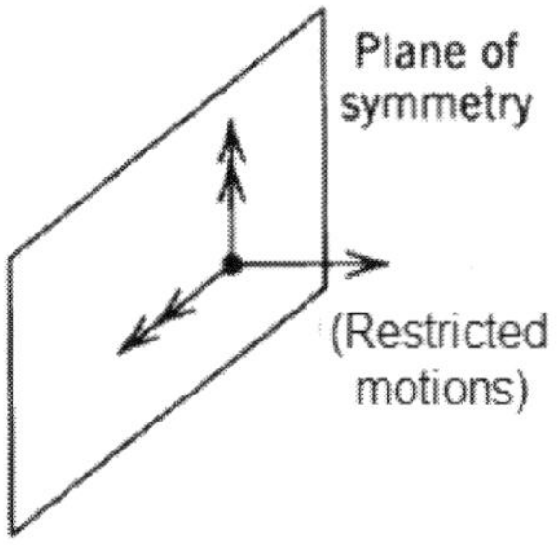

Figure 3–14

For solid meshes, this means that only the normal to the symmetry plane direction must be restrained. This can be accomplished by applying the surface slider restraint on the surfaces that lie in the plane of symmetry, as shown in Figure 3–15.

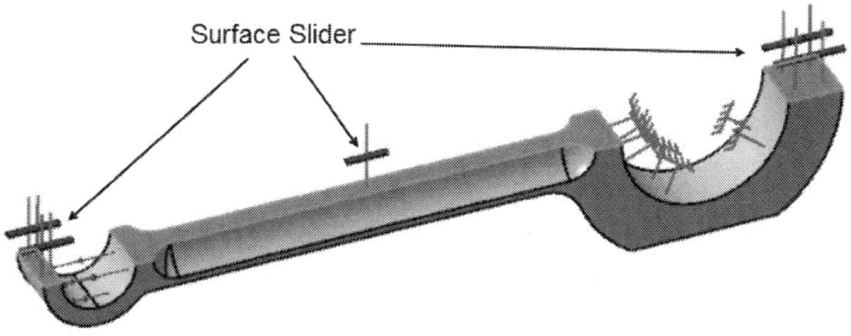

Figure 3–15

3.2 Loads

Unsatisfactory representation of the loading is a common cause of inaccurate analysis results. Therefore, gathering adequate information about the magnitude of the loads is a critical aspect of developing an accurate simulation. It should be noted that in a linear analysis, the stresses and deformations are directly proportional to the magnitude of the loading. For example, a possible error in loading of 20% leads to a minimum 20% error in stresses and deflections.

Pressure Load

A pressure load is a distributed surface force that acts in the normal to the part surface direction, even if the surface is curved. The positive load direction is toward the part body.

To apply a pressure load, select  (Pressure) in the Loads toolbar to open the Pressure dialog box, as shown in Figure 3–16. Select the surfaces to which you want to apply the load, enter the pressure value, and click **OK**.

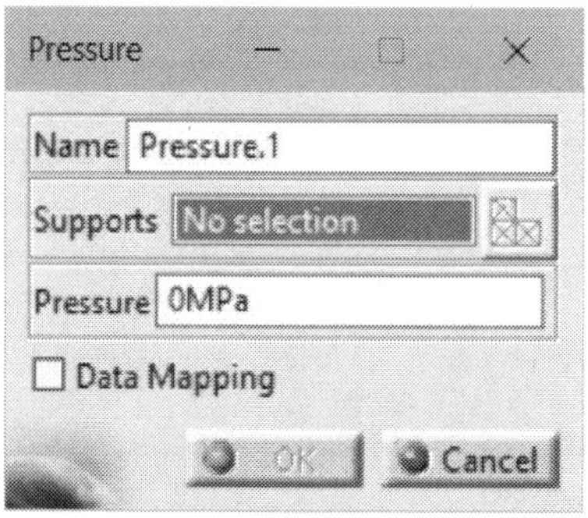

Figure 3–16

The pressure load is assumed to be distributed evenly over the selected surfaces. The **Data Mapping** option enables an uneven pressure distribution, which requires creating an external file (such as an Excel spreadsheet) containing coordinates for a cloud of points on the surface, along with the pressure scaling coefficients for each point. That data is then mapped onto the part surface to obtain the required uneven pressure distribution. The Data Mapping option requires the EST license.

Distributed Force Load

A distributed force load applies a system of forces on the mesh nodes of the selected geometrical supports. This system of nodal forces is made *statically equivalent* to the given concentrated force located at the selected handler point. “Statically equivalent” means that the resultant force of all the nodal forces is equal to the given concentrated force at the handler point (i.e., it will exert the same effect).

If no handler point is selected by the user, an implicit handler point is created at the centroid of the geometrical supports. This, in most cases, results in a uniform force distribution.

If a handler point is selected by the user and it is located away from the centroid of the geometrical supports, the nodal force distribution will depend on the exact location of the handler point.

Consider the example of a beam under tensile distributed force without a handler point, as shown in Figure 3–17.

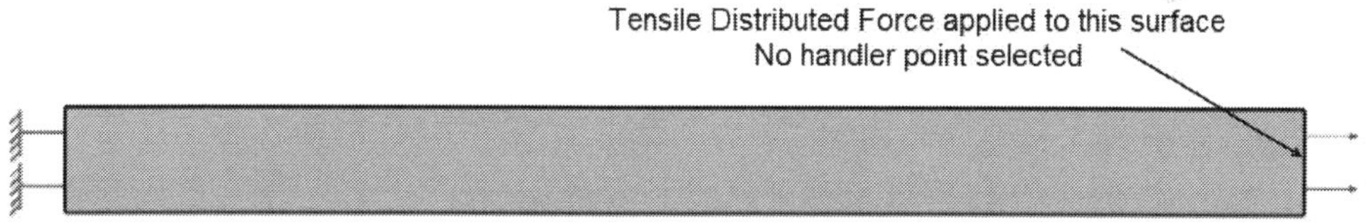

Figure 3–17

The nodal force distribution over the surface is uniform, as shown in Figure 3–18.

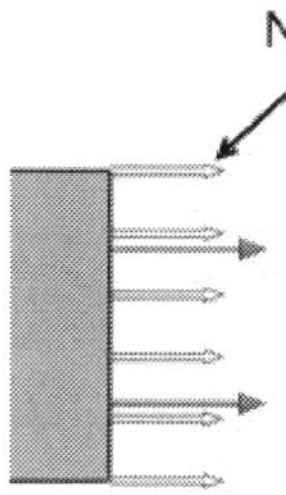

Figure 3–18

This results in a pure tension of the beam, as shown in Figure 3–19.

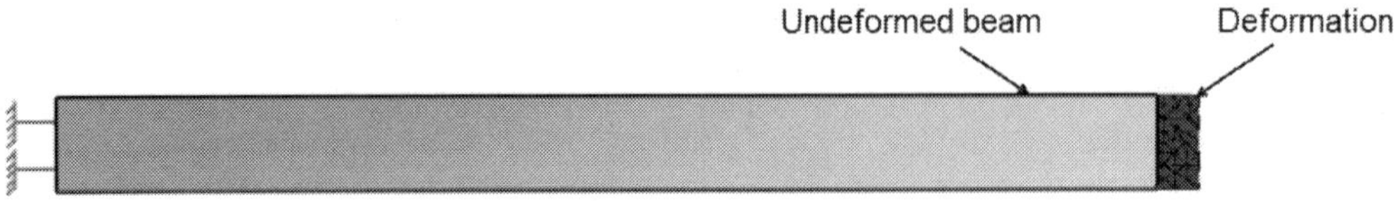

Figure 3–19

Consider the same beam with the same distributed force, but now with a handler point located on the bottom edge of the loaded surface, as shown in Figure 3–20. Since the handler point is off the centroid of the loaded surface, this should cause bending of the beam in the vertical direction, along with the tension.

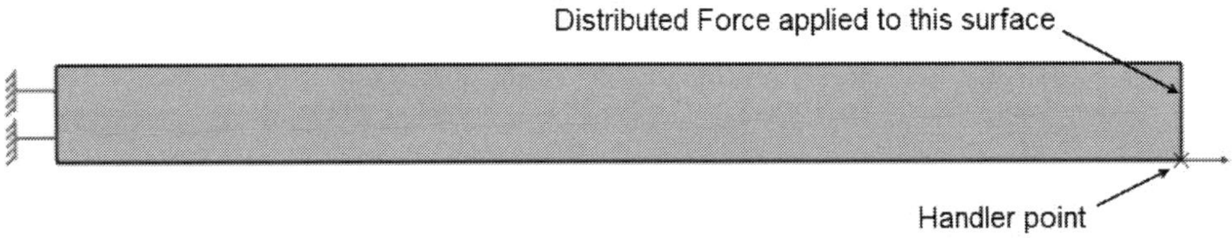

Figure 3–20

The nodal force distribution over the surface is non-uniform, as shown in Figure 3–21. Note that now the nodal forces are applied in such a way as to create a bending moment as well.

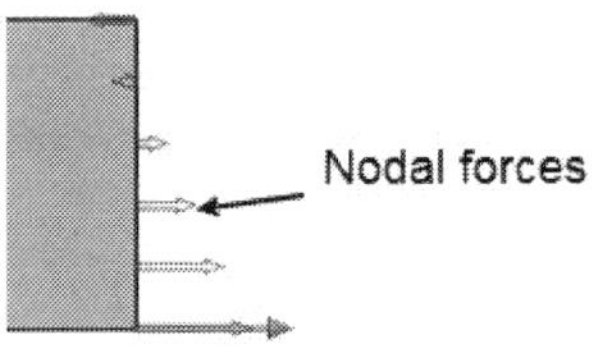

Figure 3–21

This results in both tension and bending of the beam, as shown in Figure 3–22.

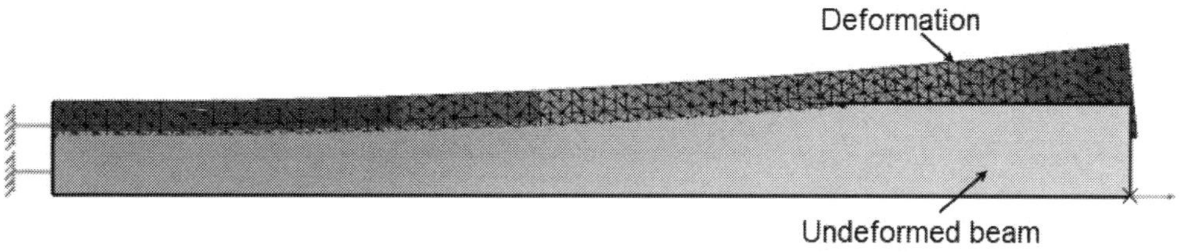

Figure 3–22

To apply a distributed force, select  (Distributed Force) in the Loads toolbar. In the Distributed Force dialog box that opens, select the entities to which you want to apply the load, select the *Axis System*, and enter the **X**, **Y**, and **Z** components of the *Force Vector*, as shown in Figure 3–23. Optionally, select the *Handler* point, and click **OK**.

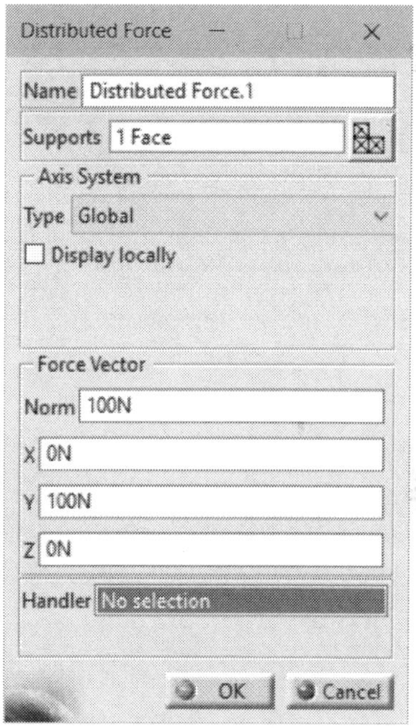

Figure 3–23

The Axis System drop-down list provides the following options:

- **Global**: Uses the global **X**, **Y**, and **Z** directions.
- **User**: Uses the **X**, **Y**, and **Z** directions of the user-selected axis system.

Moment Load

A moment load applies a system of forces on the mesh nodes of the selected geometrical supports. This system of nodal forces is made *statically equivalent* to the given concentrated moment (force couple) located at the selected handler point. "Statically equivalent" means that the resultant force of all the nodal forces is equal to the given moment at the handler point (i.e., it will exert the same effect).

If no handler point is selected by the user, an implicit handler point is created at the centroid of the geometrical supports. The resultant force of all the nodal forces in this case is nil.

If a handler point is selected by the user and it is located away from the centroid of the geometrical supports, the resultant force of all the nodal forces is not nil. The exact behavior depends on the location of the handler point.

To apply a moment load, select  (Moment) in the Loads toolbar. In the Moment dialog box that opens, select the entities to which you want to apply the load, select the *Axis System*, and enter the **X**, **Y**, and **Z** components of the *Moment Vector*, as shown in Figure 3–24.

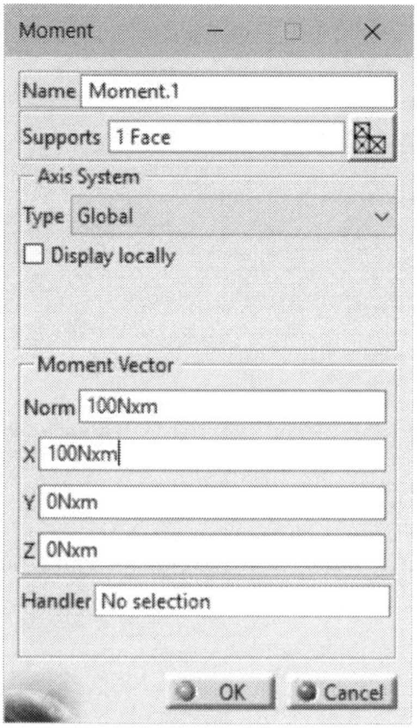

Figure 3–24

The Axis System drop-down list provides the following options:

- **Global**: Uses the global **X**, **Y**, and **Z** directions.
- **User**: Uses the **X**, **Y**, and **Z** directions of the user-selected axis system.

Line Force Density Load

A line force density load applies a force intensity of uniform magnitude to the selected edges of the solid body.

To apply a line force density load, select  (Line Force Density) in the Loads toolbar. In the Line Force Density dialog box that opens, select the entities to which you want to apply the load, select the *Axis System*, and enter the **X**, **Y**, and **Z** components of the *Force Vector*, as shown in Figure 3–25.

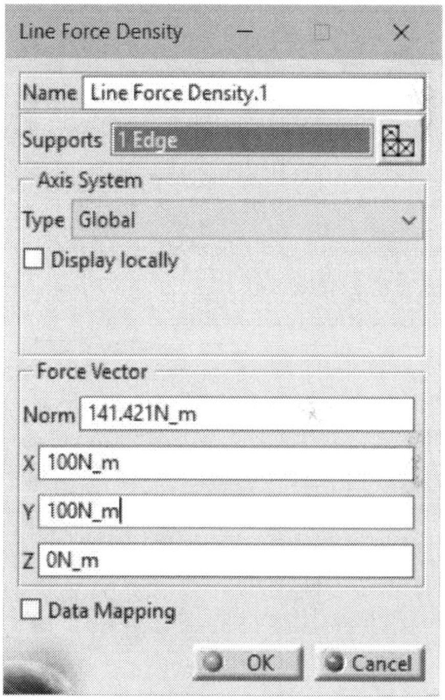

Figure 3–25

The force directions **X**, **Y**, and **Z** are interpreted according to the coordinate system selected in the Axis System drop-down list as follows:

- **Global**: These are the global **X**, **Y**, and **Z** directions.
- **User**: The user selects another axis system, and directions are interpreted according to the axis system type.
  - **Cartesian**: Directions **X**, **Y**, and **Z** are the axis system's **X**, **Y**, and **Z**.
  - **Cylindrical**: Directions **X**, **Y**, and **Z** are interpreted as directions **r**, **Θ**, and **Z** of the cylindrical coordinate system.
  - **Spherical**: Directions **X**, **Y**, and **Z** are interpreted as directions **r**, **Θ**, and φ of the spherical coordinate system
- **Implicit**: Directions **X**, **Y**, and **Z** are interpreted according to the parametric directions on the edge.
  - The 1st parametric direction is along the edge.
  - The 3rd parametric direction bisects the angle between the surfaces joined at this edge.
  - The 2nd parametric direction is determined by the cross-product of the 3rd and the 1st parametric directions.

You can preview the directions by activating the **Display locally** checkbox.

The force density load is assumed to be distributed evenly over the selected edge. The **Data Mapping** option enables an uneven load distribution, which requires creating an external file (such as an Excel spreadsheet) containing coordinates for a cloud of points on the edge, along with the force density vector for each point. That data is then mapped onto the edge to obtain the required non-uniform load distribution. The Data Mapping option requires the EST license.

Surface Force Density Load

A surface force density load applies a force intensity of uniform magnitude to the selected surfaces.

To apply a surface force density load, select  (Surface Force Density) in the Loads toolbar. In the Surface Force Density dialog box that opens, select the entities to which you want to apply the load, select the *Axis System*, and enter the **X**, **Y**, and **Z** components of the *Force Vector*, as shown in Figure 3–26.

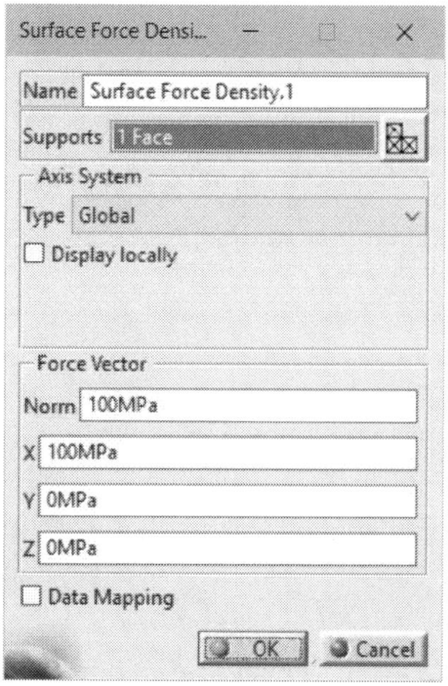

Figure 3–26

The force directions **X**, **Y**, and **Z** are interpreted according to the coordinate system selected in the Axis System drop-down list as follows:

- **Global**: These are the global **X**, **Y**, and **Z** directions.
- **User**: The user selects another axis system and directions are interpreted according to the axis system type.
    - **Cartesian**: Directions **X**, **Y**, and **Z** are the axis system's **X**, **Y**, and **Z**.
    - **Cylindrical**: Directions **X**, **Y**, and **Z** are interpreted as directions **r**, **Θ**, and **Z** of the cylindrical coordinate system.
    - **Spherical**: Directions **X**, **Y**, and **Z** are interpreted as directions **r**, **Θ**, and φ of the spherical coordinate system
- **Implicit**: Directions **X**, **Y**, and **Z** are interpreted according to the parametric directions **U**, **V**, and **n** on the part surface.
    - Parametric directions **U** and **V** are in-plane of the surface and depend on the surface type (whether it's a plane or a cylinder, etc.). The directions are determined internally by CATIA. The user has no control over the parametric directions **U** and **V**.
    - Direction **n** is always normal to the surface.

You can preview the directions by activating the **Display locally** checkbox.

The force density load is assumed to be distributed evenly over the selected surface. The **Data Mapping** option enables an uneven load distribution, which requires creating an external file (such as an Excel spreadsheet) containing coordinates for a cloud of points on the surface, along with the force density vector for each point. That data is then mapped onto the surface to obtain the required non-uniform load distribution. The Data Mapping option requires the EST license.

Force Density Load

A force density load is equivalent to either a line force density or a surface force density; the only difference being that the input value is a total force instead of a force intensity.

To apply a force density load, select  (Force Density) in the Loads toolbar. In the Force Density Defined by Force Vector dialog box that opens, select the entities to which you want to apply the load, select the *Axis System*, and enter the **X**, **Y**, and **Z** components of the *Force Vector*, as shown in Figure 3–27.

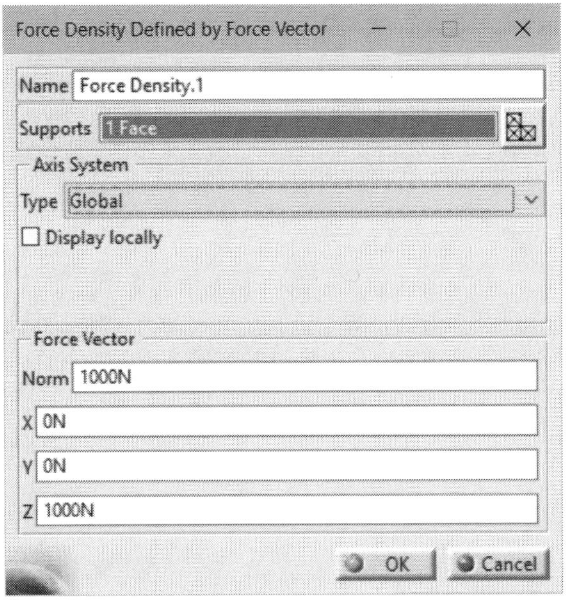

Figure 3–27

The Axis System drop-down list provides the following options:

- **Global**: Uses the global **X**, **Y**, and **Z** directions.
- **User**: Uses the **X**, **Y**, and **Z** directions of the user-selected axis system.

Acceleration Load

An acceleration load simulates the body force created by the acceleration or deceleration of your model. One of the typical applications is the gravity force.

To apply an acceleration load, select  (Acceleration) in the Loads toolbar. In the Acceleration dialog box that opens, select the bodies to which you want to apply the load, select the *Axis System*, and enter the **X**, **Y**, and **Z** components of the *Acceleration Vector*, as shown in Figure 3–28.

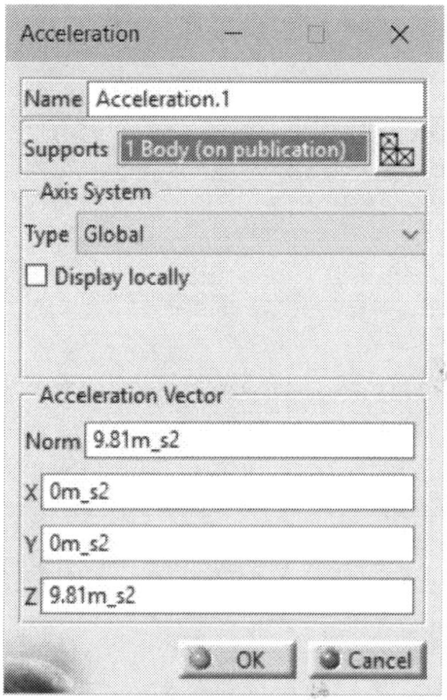

Figure 3–28

The acceleration directions **X**, **Y**, and **Z** are interpreted according to the coordinate system selected in the Axis System drop-down list as follows:

- **Global**: These are the global **X**, **Y**, and **Z** directions.
- **User**: The user selects another axis system and directions are interpreted according to the axis system type.
  - **Cartesian**: Directions **X**, **Y**, and **Z** are the axis system's **X**, **Y**, and **Z**.
  - **Cylindrical**: Directions **X**, **Y**, and **Z** are interpreted as directions **r**, **Θ**, and **Z** of the cylindrical coordinate system.
  - **Spherical**: Directions **X**, **Y**, and **Z** are interpreted as directions **r**, **Θ**, and φ of the spherical coordinate system

Rotation Force Load

A rotation force load simulates the body force created by the rotation of your model, such as centrifugal force. Both angular velocity and acceleration can be applied.

To apply a rotation force load, select  (Rotation Force) in the Loads toolbar. In the Rotation Force dialog box that opens, select the bodies to which you want to apply the load, select the *Rotation Axis*, and enter the *Angular Velocity* and *Angular Acceleration* values, as shown in Figure 3–29.

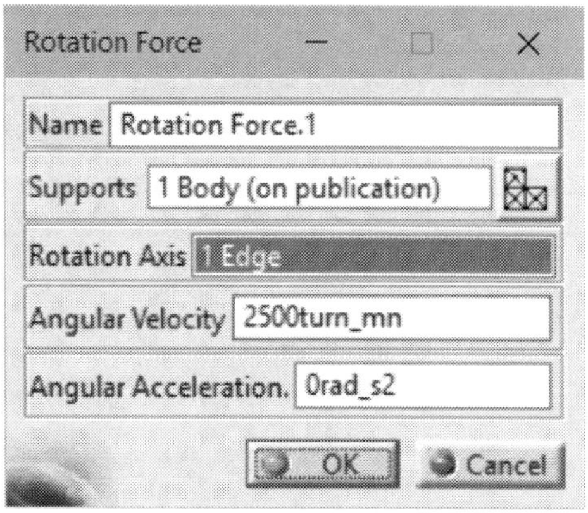

Figure 3–29

Enforced Displacement Load

An enforced displacement load enforces a specific motion on one or more geometrical entities in your model. The enforced displacement stays constant (i.e., it does not change) through the simulation.

In GSA, the enforced displacement load is always associated with a restraint object, and it assigns non-zero values to displacements in previously restrained directions.

Therefore, the first step when creating an enforced displacement load is to create a user-defined restraint. In the user-defined restraint, only restrain the directions in which you want to enforce the displacement, as shown in Figure 3–30.

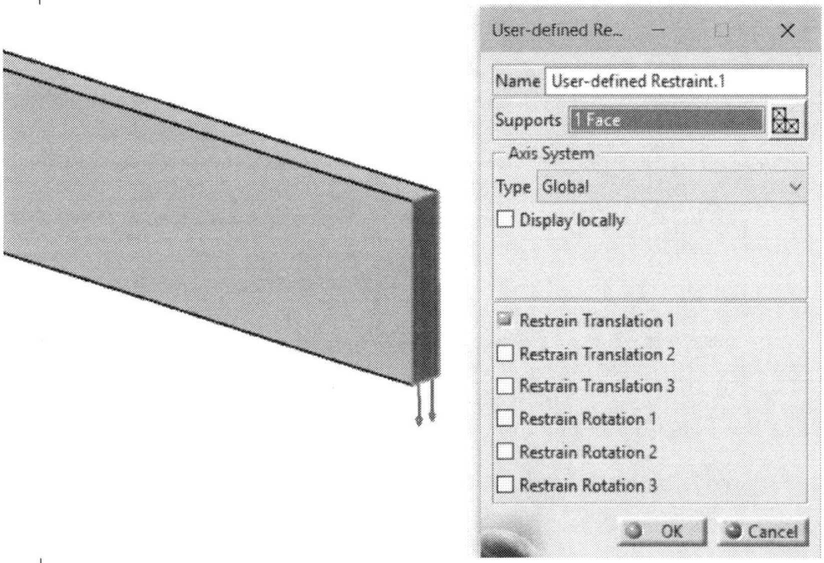

Figure 3–30

In the second step, you apply an enforced displacement to that user-defined restraint. Select 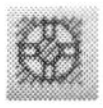 (Enforced Displacement) in the Loads toolbar. In the Enforced Displacement dialog box that opens, select the user-defined restraint and enter the value of the displacement, as shown in Figure 3–31.

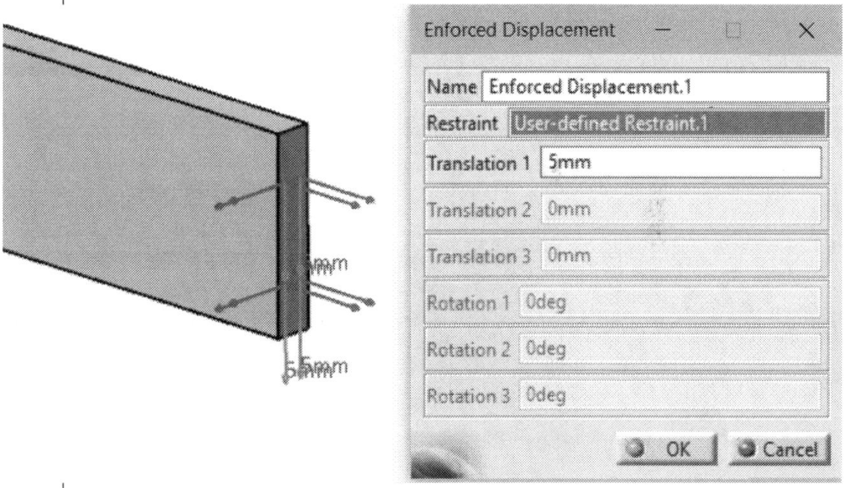

Figure 3–31

3.3 Applying Loads and Restraints on Surface Patches

In some analysis models, you might need to apply loads and restraints on the portions of the part surfaces rather than on whole surfaces. For example, for the model shown in Figure 3–32, the restraints must be applied over the weldment area only, which is a thin strip of the part surface going around the entire part. The load also must be applied over a patch on the part surface, as shown in Figure 3–32.

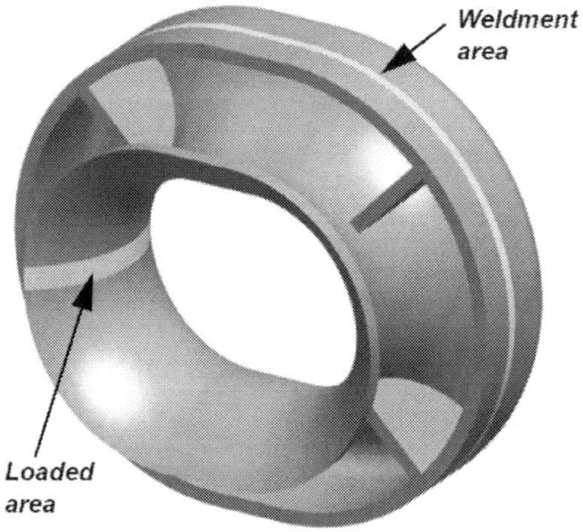

Figure 3–32

Creating geometrical supports for such loads and restraints is a multi-step process, as follows:

1. Create a boundary for the surface patch. On planar surfaces, use a sketch. On curved surfaces, you can use projections, intersections, or other tools as suitable. The boundary of the patch must be a closed contour and must lie on the surface of the part. For example, to simulate the clamping action of the bolt head around a hole, the boundary of the area under the bolt head can be sketched, as shown in Figure 3–33.

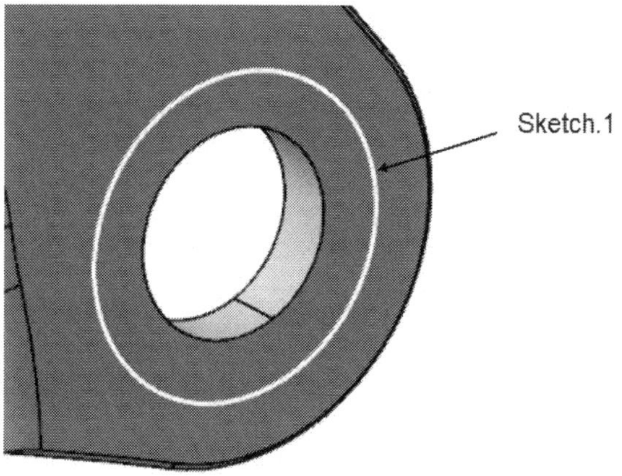

Figure 3–33

2. In the Generative Shape Design (GSD) 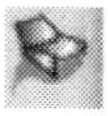 workbench, using the  (Extract) tool, extract the solid surface on which you want to create the surface patch. The result, with the **PartBody** hidden, is shown in Figure 3–34.

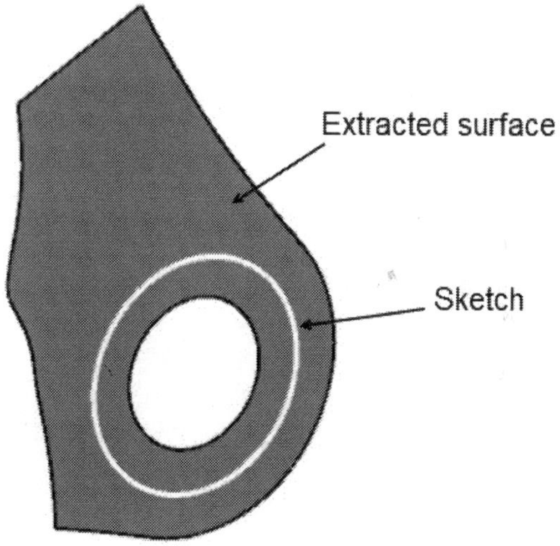

Figure 3–34

3. Using the  (Split) tool in the GSD workbench, split the extracted surface with the patch's boundary, keeping the side that is inside the patch boundary, as shown in Figure 3–35.

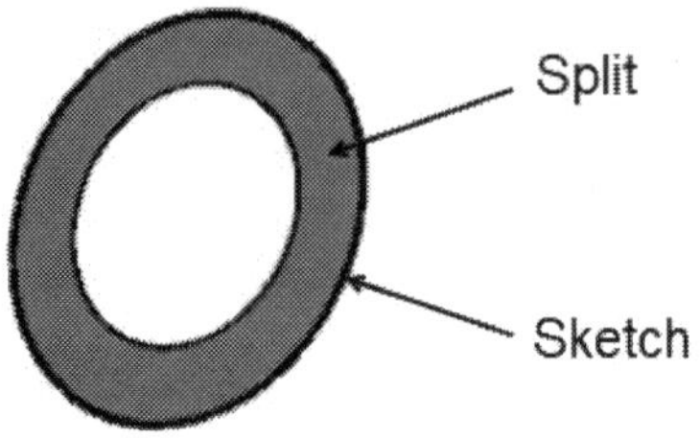

Figure 3–35

4. Switch to the Part Design  workbench. Unhide and activate the **PartBody**.

*If the **Simplify geometry** option is activated, CATIA will not separate the surface patch from the rest of the solid's surface.*

5. In the Surface-Based Features toolbar, select  (Sew Surface). In the Sew Surface Definition dialog box that opens, select the split surface as the *Object to sew* and deactivate the **Simplify geometry** checkbox. Make sure the orange arrow in the preview points toward the solid body. The model displays as shown in Figure 3–36.

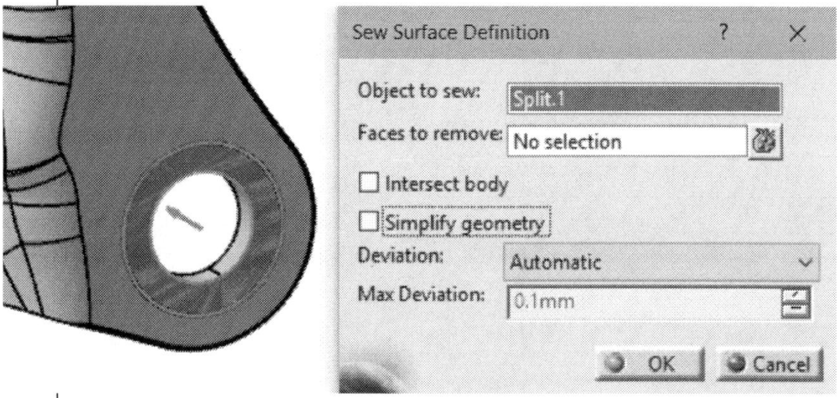

Figure 3–36

6. Click **OK** to complete the operation. Hide the split surface and the sketch. The model displays as shown in Figure 3–37. Note that the surface patch area is now separate from the rest of the part surface.

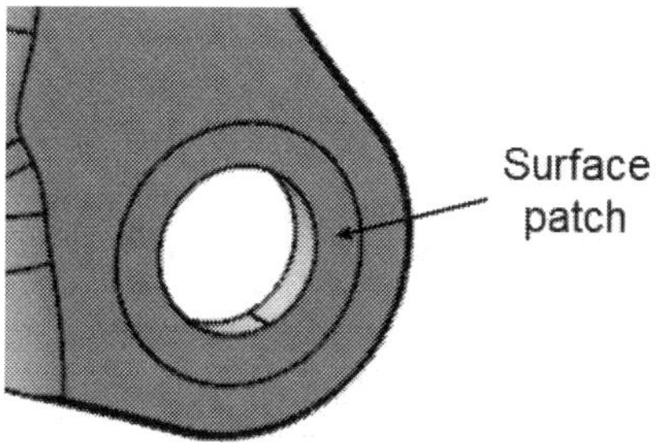

Figure 3–37

Now you can apply a load or a restraint to the created surface patch, as shown in Figure 3–38.

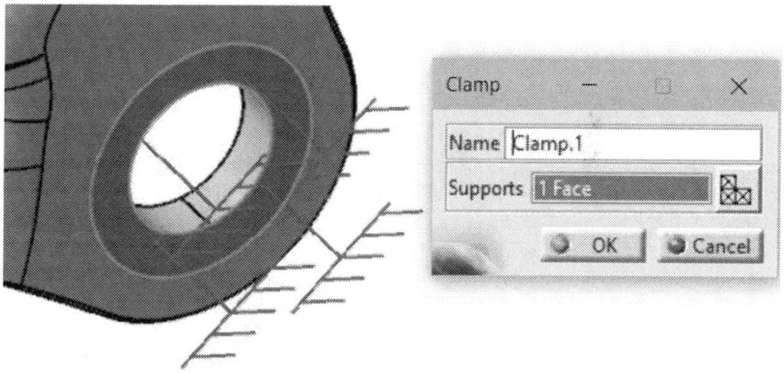

Figure 3–38

3.4 Obtaining Reaction Forces in Restraints

Once the analysis is solved, you can use a reaction sensor to obtain the force and moment reactions in a restraint.

To create a reaction sensor, right-click on **Sensors.1** in the tree and select **Create Resultant Sensor>Reaction Sensor** in the contextual menu, as shown in Figure 3–39.

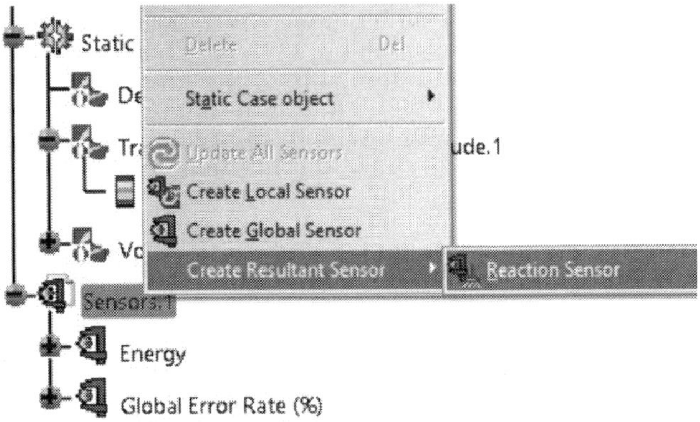

Figure 3–39

In the Reaction Sensor dialog box that opens, select a restraint and click **Update Results**. CATIA calculates the reaction forces and moments in the restraint and displays the results, as shown in Figure 3–40.

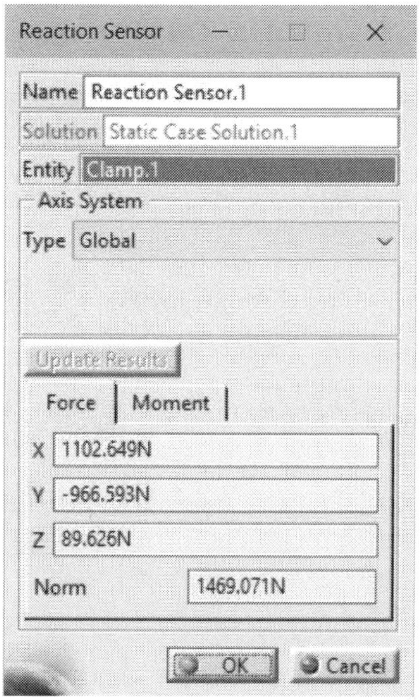

Figure 3–40

The **Reaction Sensor** also displays in the tree, as shown in Figure 3–41.

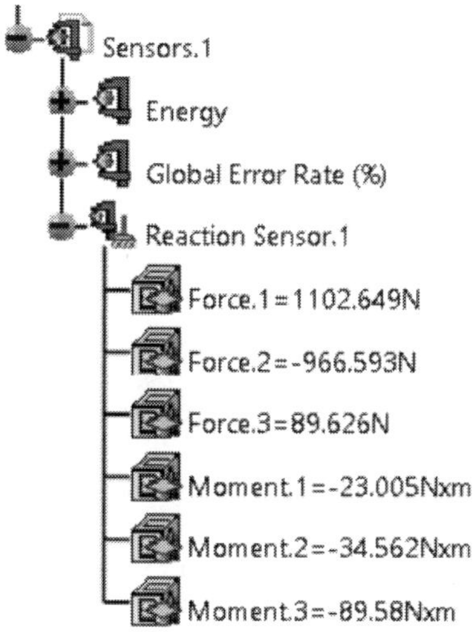

Figure 3–41

Practice 3a Stress Analysis of a Crank

Practice Objectives

- Apply the material and mesh the model.
- Apply force load in a specific direction.
- Simulate pin and bushing supports with a surface slider restraint.
- Apply a user-defined restraint in a cylindrical axis system.
- Deal with the detected rigid body motions.
- Display and animate the analysis results.

In this practice, you will set up and run a static stress analysis on the crank part shown in Figure 3–42. The part is restrained by a pin support in the lower boss and by two bushing supports at the ends of the lower rod. This way, the lower beam of the part is not constrained against rotation at its ends, similar to a simply supported beam.

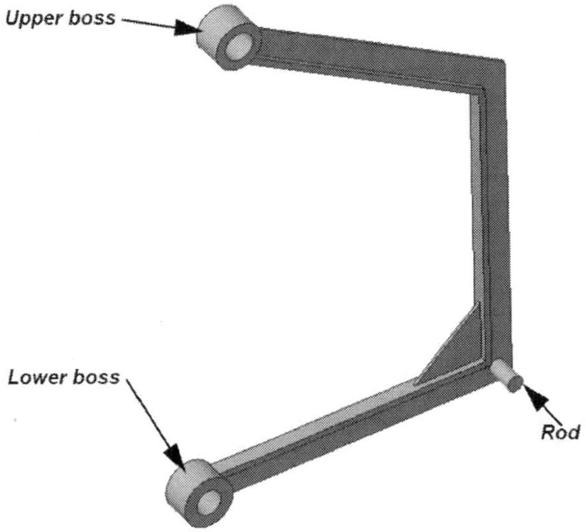

Figure 3–42

Task 1 - Open the part in CATIA.

1. Open **Crank_03.CATPart** from the *CATIA Generative Structural Analysis Practice Files\Ch03* folder.

2. Set the model display as  (Shading with Edges). The part displays as shown in Figure 3–43.

Figure 3–43

3. Select **Tools>Options>Parameters and Measures>Units** and set the units as follows:

   - Length: **Millimeter (mm)**
   - Force: **Newton (N)**
   - Moment: **Newton x Meter (Nxm)**
   - Pressure: **Megapascal (MPa)**

Task 2 - Apply the material.

1. Apply the **Steel** material from the **Default Material Catalog** to the part. Verify that the applied material has the following properties:

   - Young Modulus: **200000MPa**
   - Poisson Ratio: **0.266**
   - Density: **7860 kg/m^3**
   - Thermal Expansion: **1.17e-005/Kdeg**
   - Yield Strength: **250MPa**

Task 3 - Start the GSA workbench.

1. Select **Start>Analysis & Simulation>Generative Structural Analysis**.
2. Select **Static Analysis** as the new analysis case.

Task 4 - Mesh the part.

1. Measure the thickness of the part's profile, as shown in Figure 3–44.

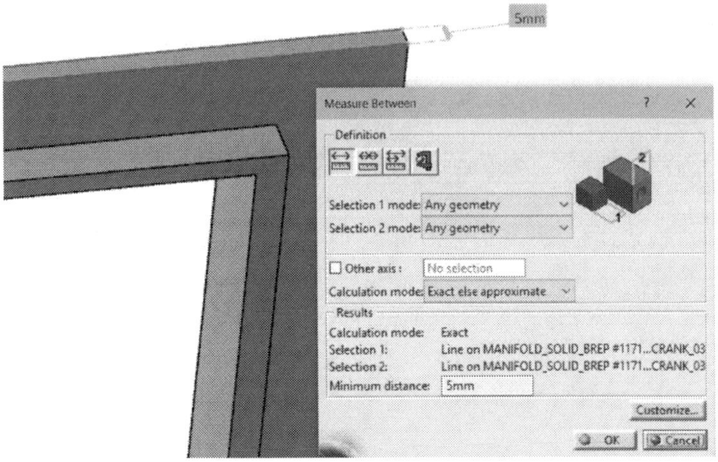

Figure 3–44

A size of 9mm is 1.8 times the thickness of the part, which is the recommended ratio for thin-walled parts. A sag of 1.8mm is 20% of the size, which is the rule of thumb for most of the parts.

2. Double-click on **OCTREE Tetrahedron Mesh.1: CRANK_03** in the tree. The OCTREE Tetrahedron Mesh dialog box displays, as shown in Figure 3–45. Select **Parabolic** as the *Element type*, enter the *Size* as **9mm** and the *Absolute sag* as **1.8mm**.

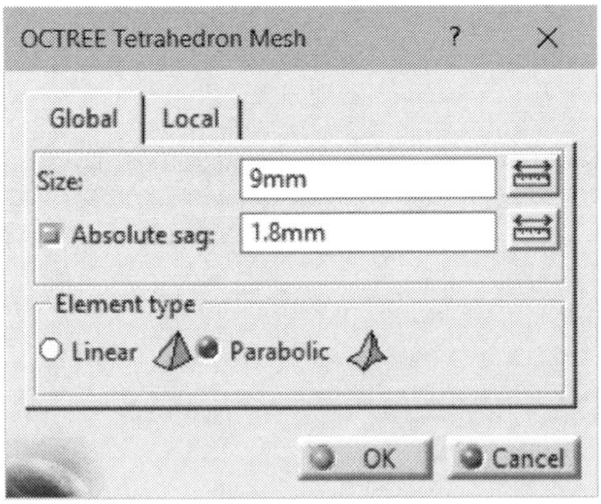

Figure 3–45

3. Click **OK** to close the OCTREE Tetrahedron Mesh dialog box.

4. Right-click on **Nodes and Elements** in the tree and select **Mesh Visualization**. The part mesh is displayed, as shown in Figure 3–46. Rotate the model and examine the mesh in various areas of the part.

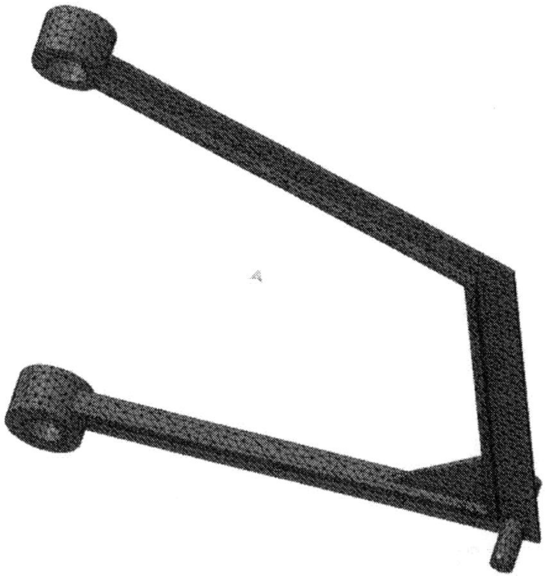

Figure 3–46

5. Right-click on **Mesh.1** in the tree and select **Delete** to delete the mesh visualization and return to the model view.

Task 5 - Apply the load.

In this task, you will apply a 500N force to the hole in the upper boss, acting in-plane of the crank and in a specified direction. The force direction is specified by a line that you will need to create prior to applying the load.

1. In the tree, expand **Links Manager.1>Link.1** and double-click on the **CRANK_03** part. This automatically hides the analysis model and switches CATIA to the Part Design workbench.

2. Create a new geometrical set (**Geometrical Set.1**).

3. Using the **Circle/Sphere/Ellipse center** option, create two points (**Point.1** and **Point.2**) at the centers of the circles on both sides of the upper boss, as shown in Figure 3–47.

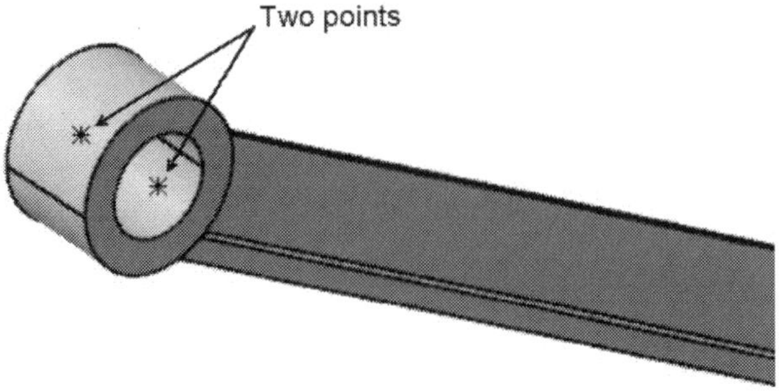

Figure 3–47

4. Using the **Between** option, create the middle point (**Point.3**) between **Point.1** and **Point.2**, as shown in Figure 3–48.

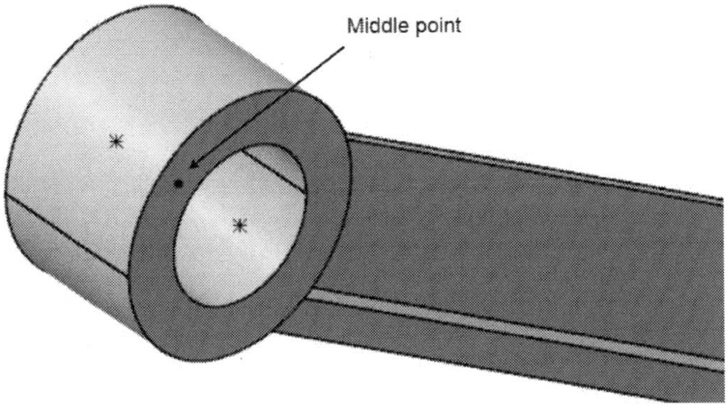

Figure 3–48

5. Using the **Coordinates** option, create the fourth point (**Point.4**) with coordinates **-100mm**, **-150mm**, **0mm** and **Point.3** as the **Reference** point, as shown in Figure 3–49.

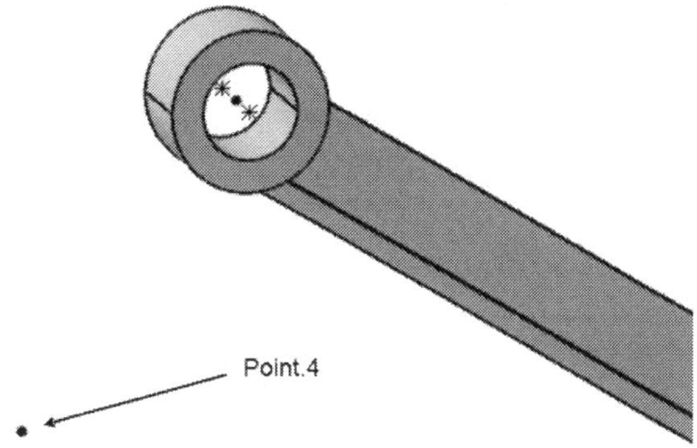

Figure 3–49

6. Create a line (**Line.1**) from **Point.3** to **Point.4**, as shown in Figure 3–50.

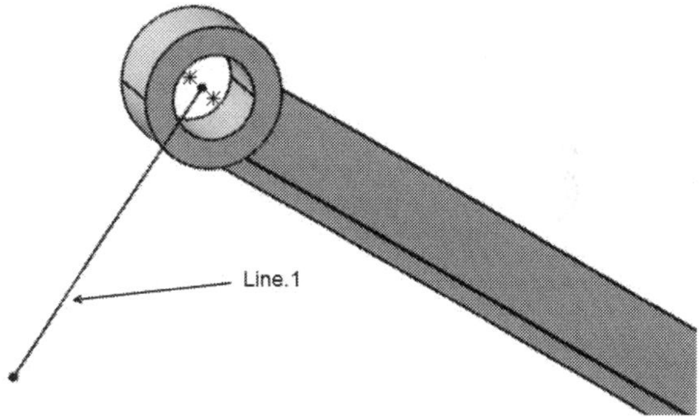

Figure 3–50

7. Create a new axis system, with **Origin** at **Point.3**, **X axis** direction along **Line.1**, and **Z axis** direction normal to **XY plane**. Rename the axis system as **Axis System Load**. Hide **Geometrical Set.1** and the model displays as shown in Figure 3–51.

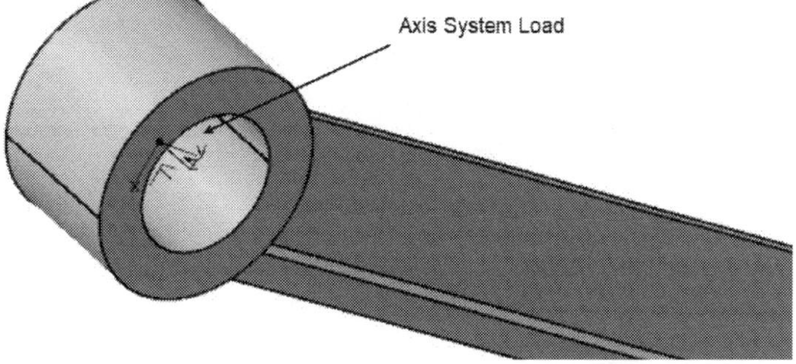

Figure 3–51

8. Double-click on **Finite Element Model.1** in the tree to go back to the GSA workbench.

9. Select 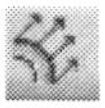 (Distributed Force) in the Forces toolbar. Once the Distributed Force dialog box opens, select the inside surface of the boss as the *Supports*, as shown in Figure 3–52.

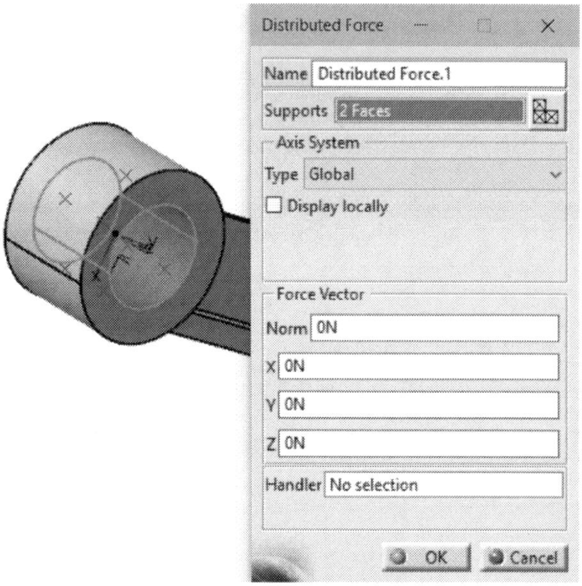

Figure 3–52

*Since the X-axis of the **Axis System Load** system has been aligned with **Line.1** (created in Step 6), the **500N** load gets applied along the direction of **Line.1**.*

10. In the Axis System drop-down list, select **User**, then select **Axis System Load**. Enter **500N** in the **X** field of the *Force Vector* section, as shown in Figure 3–53.

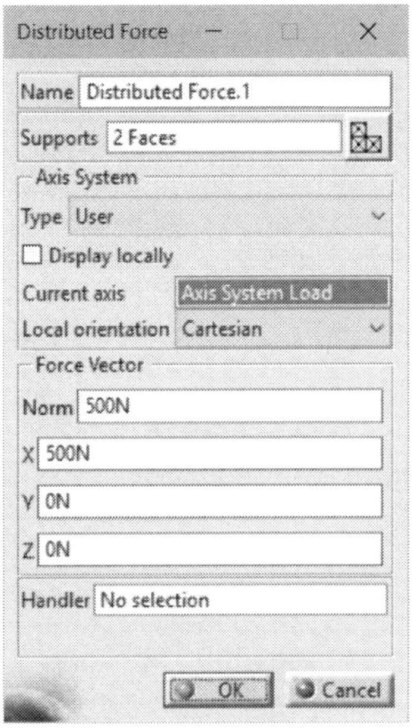

Figure 3–53

11. Click **OK** to close the Distributed Force dialog box. The load displays as shown in Figure 3–54.

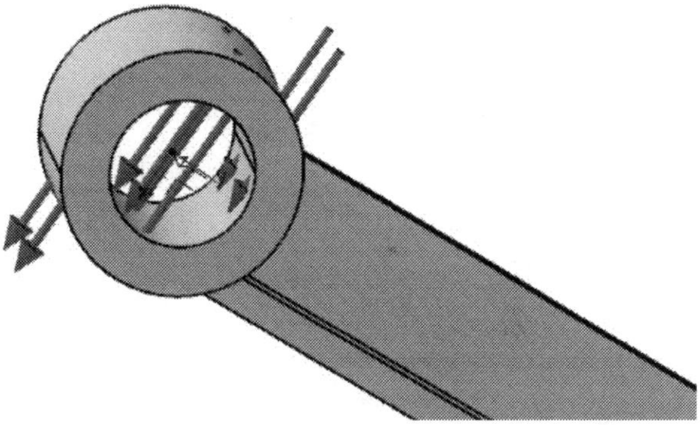

Figure 3–54

Task 6 - Apply the restraints.

In this task, you will apply surface slider restraints to the lower boss and to the lower rod. The surface slider restrains displacement in the normal to the surface direction, which is the radial direction on the boss and the rod, while allowing the tangential to the surface motions. This models pin support on the boss and bushing supports on the rod, so the lower beam of the part is not constrained against rotation at its ends, similar to a simply supported beam.

1. Select  (Surface Slider) in the Restraints toolbar. The Surface Slider dialog box opens, as shown in Figure 3–55.

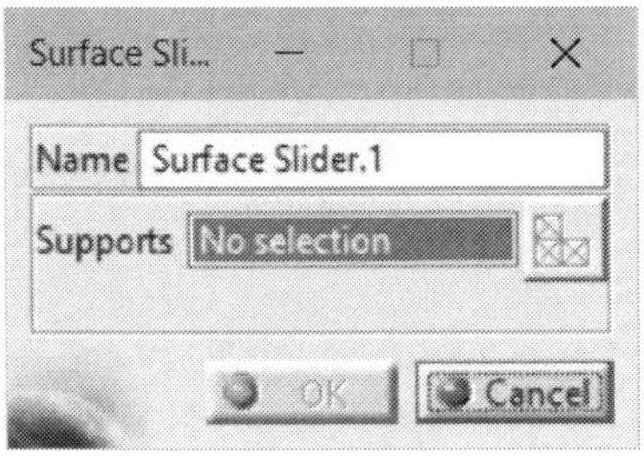

Figure 3–55

2. Select the outer diameter (OD) surfaces of the rod, as shown in Figure 3–56.

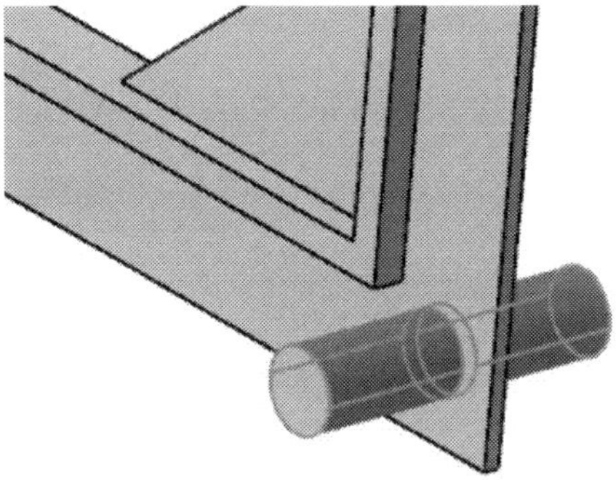

Figure 3–56

3. Click **OK** to close the Surface Slider dialog box. The model displays as shown in Figure 3–57.

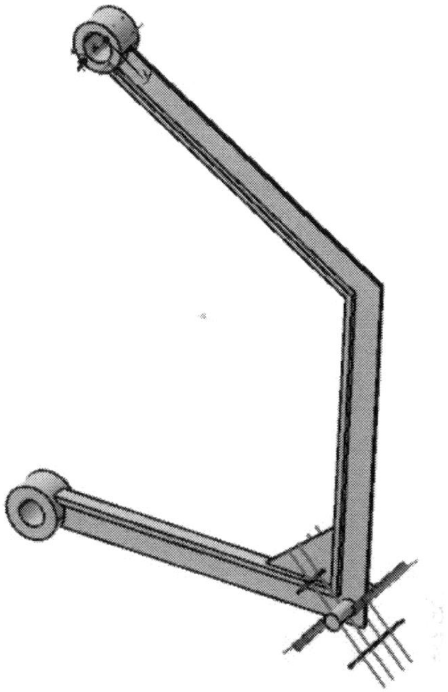

Figure 3–57

4. Repeat Steps 1 to 3 to apply another surface slider restraint to the inner diameter (ID) surfaces of the lower boss, as shown in Figure 3–58.

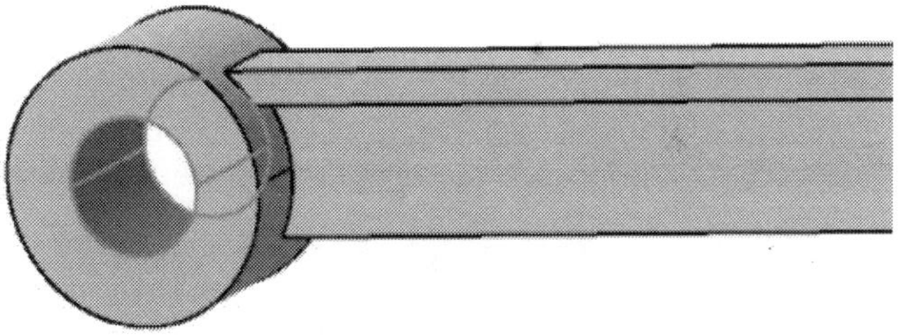

Figure 3–58

Task 7 - Run the analysis.

1. Select  (Model Checker) to check your model for errors and inconsistencies. The Model Checker reports that "**The whole model is consistent**" and ready for the computation, as shown in Figure 3–59.

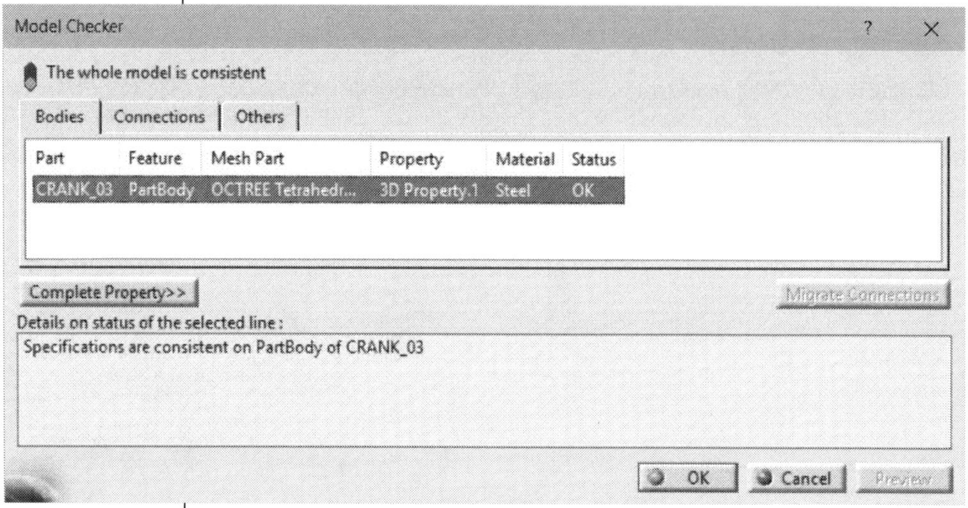

Figure 3–59

2. Select  (Compute) to run the analysis. Ensure that **All** is selected in the drop-down list at the top of the dialog box and that the **Preview** option is activated. Click **OK** to start the computation.

The warning message is issued because ***Surface Slider****, behind the scenes, also applies restraints to the rotational motions of the mesh nodes, which would only be applicable to shell or beam meshes. Since this model only has solid elements (and therefore mesh nodes only have translational degrees of freedom), those rotational restraints are ignored, which is correct.*

3. CATIA displays the Computation Resources Estimation dialog box as well as the Warnings dialog box (shown in Figure 3–60).

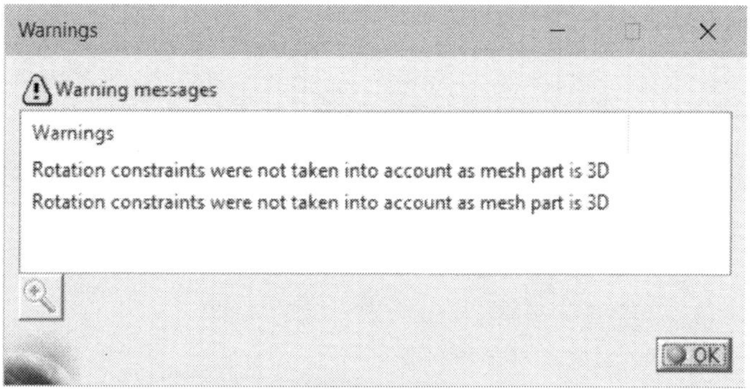

Figure 3–60

4. Click **OK** and **Yes** to close both dialog boxes and continue the computation. CATIA displays a series of messages informing you on the progress of the computation, and then displays the error message shown in Figure 3–61.

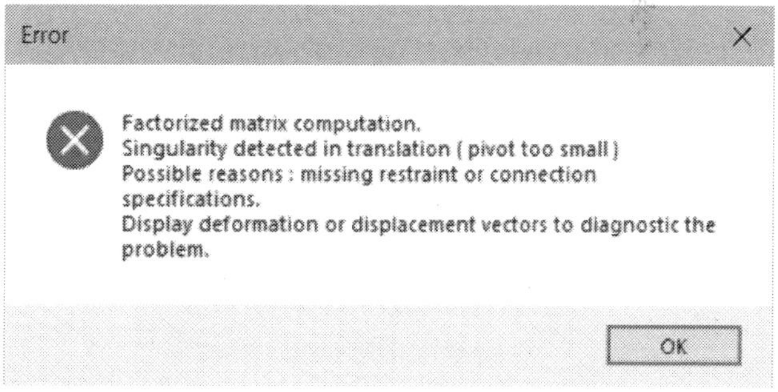

Figure 3–61

This error message is displayed whenever CATIA detects a rigid body motion in the model (i.e., that the model is insufficiently restrained).

Note that the **Model Checker** tool you used in Step 1 was unable to detect this error. This is because rigid body motions can only be detected when the analysis is solved, not before.

5. Click **OK** to close the error message.

Task 8 - Display the detected rigid body motion.

1. Note that in the Image toolbar, the **Von Mises Stress** icon is grayed-out, which means that stresses could not be displayed. But both the **Deformation** and **Displacement** icons are active, as shown in Figure 3–62.

Figure 3–62

2. Select  (Deformation) to display the deformed mesh image. Unhide the **Links Manager.1** to visualize the part. Animate the deformed mesh. CATIA displays the detected rigid body motion, which is the sliding motion along the **Z**-direction, as shown in Figure 3–63.

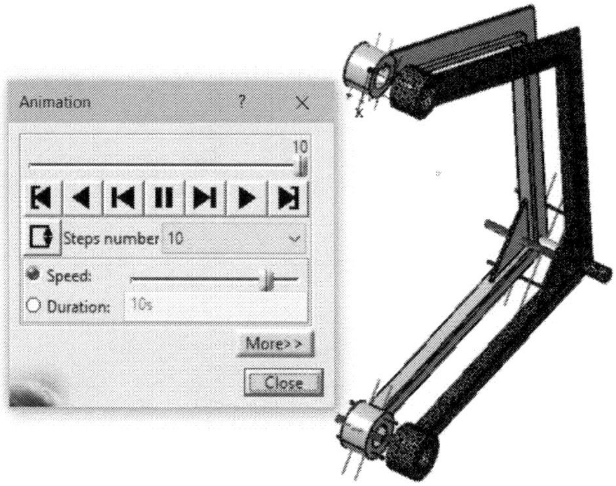

Figure 3–63

This rigid body motion exists because the surface slider restraint was applied to both the boss and the rod. Consider this:

- The surface slider restrains displacements of the mesh nodes in normal to the surface direction, which is the radial direction on the cylindrical surfaces of the rod and the boss. This prevents the rod and the boss from free translations in the X- and Y-directions, which is the intended effect of this restraint.

- However, the surface slider does not restrain displacements in the tangential to the surface directions.
- The first unrestrained tangential direction is around the circumferences of the boss and rod surfaces, which enables both the rod and the boss to freely rotate around their respective axes – this also is the desired effect in this simulation.
- The second unrestrained tangential direction is along the axes of the rod and the boss, which allows the part to freely slide along that direction without creating any strain – this is the detected rigid body motion. This is an undesired effect, and this motion must be restrained for a successful computation.

There are several possible ways to eliminate the detected rigid body motion while enabling the rotations of the rod and the boss, as intended in the analysis. In this practice, you will use one possible method, which is using a user-defined restraint with a cylindrical coordinate system on one end of the lower beam.

3. Delete the **Deformed Mesh.1** image and **Surface Slider.2** restraint, which is the restraint on the lower boss.

Task 9 - Create axis system.

A cylindrical coordinate system ***r,Θ,z*** specifies the position of a point in 3D space by the radial distance ***r*** from a reference axis ***z***, the angle ***Θ*** from a reference axis ***x***, and the coordinate along the reference axis ***z***, as shown in Figure 3–64.

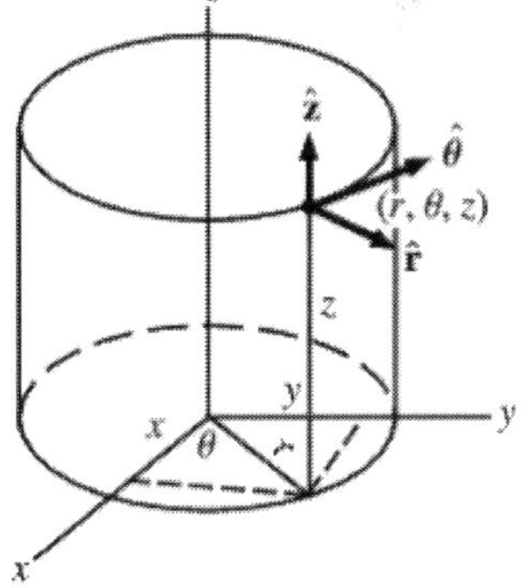

Figure 3–64

Therefore, if we create an axis system in CATIA with the origin on the axis of the lower boss and Z-direction along the axis of the boss, and interpret this axis system as cylindrical, then we could enable rotation about the axis while preventing translational motions, including sliding along the axis of the boss, by the following:

- Restraining the ***r*** and ***z*** directions – this would block all the translational motions of the lower boss.
- Leaving the ***Θ*** direction free – this would enable the rotation about the axis of the cylinder.

1. In the tree, expand **Links Manager.1>Link.1** and double-click on the **CRANK_03** part. This automatically hides the analysis model and switches CATIA to the Part Design workbench.
2. Create a new geometrical set (**Geometrical Set.2**).
3. Using the **Circle/Sphere/Ellipse center** option, create a point (**Point.5**) at the center of the hole of the lower boss, as shown in Figure 3–65.

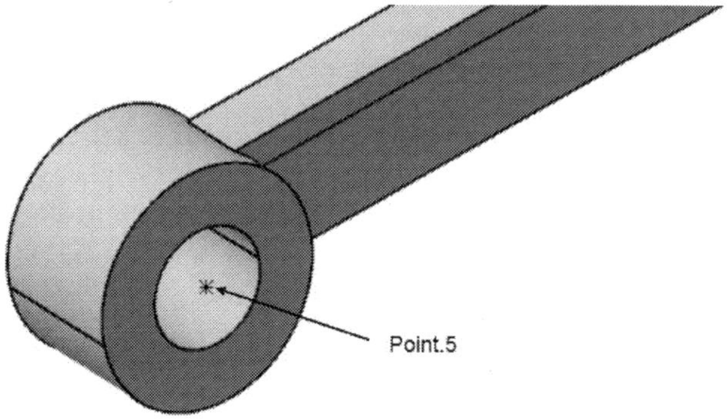

Figure 3–65

4. Create a new axis system, with **Origin** at **Point.5**, **X axis** normal to **YZ plane**, and **Z axis** normal to **XY plane**. Rename the axis system to **Axis System Cyl**. Hide **Geometrical Set.2** and the model displays as shown in Figure 3–66.

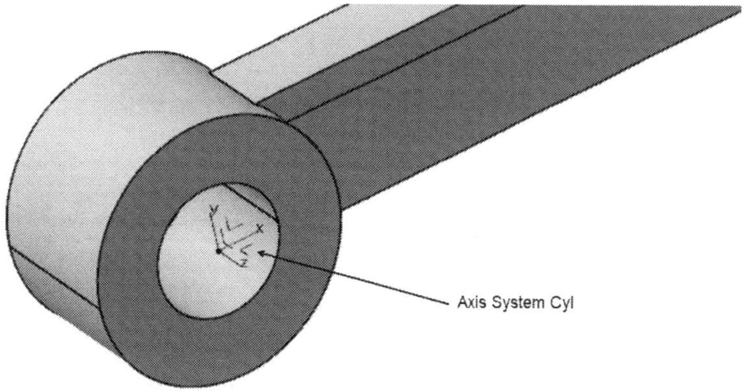

Figure 3–66

5. Double-click on **Finite Element Model.1** in the tree to switch back to the GSA workbench.

Task 10 - Apply the user-defined restraint.

1. Select  (User-defined Restraint) in the Restraints toolbar. In the User-defined Restraint dialog box, select the inside surface of the lower boss as shown in Figure 3–67.

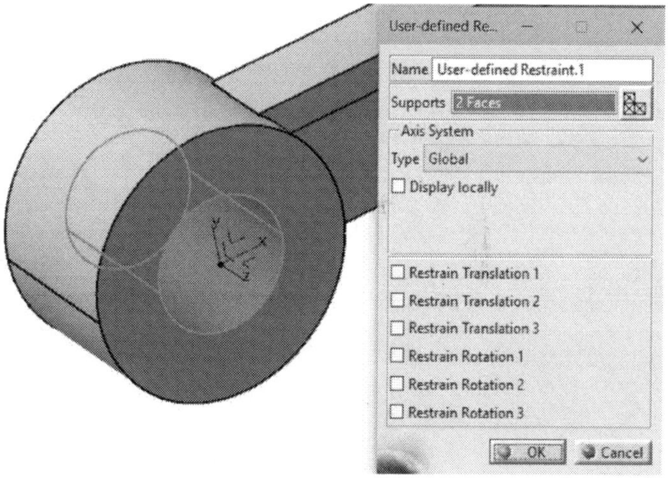

Figure 3–67

Translation 1 *corresponds to the* ***r*** *direction and* ***Translation 3*** *corresponds to the* ***z*** *direction of the cylindrical coordinate system.* ***Translation 2*** *corresponds to the* ***Θ*** *direction and it remains free.*

2. In the Axis System drop-down list, select **User**, then select **Axis System Cyl**. Select **Cylindrical** in the Local orientation drop-down list. Select the **Restrain Translation 1** and **Restrain Translation 3** checkboxes, as shown in Figure 3–68.

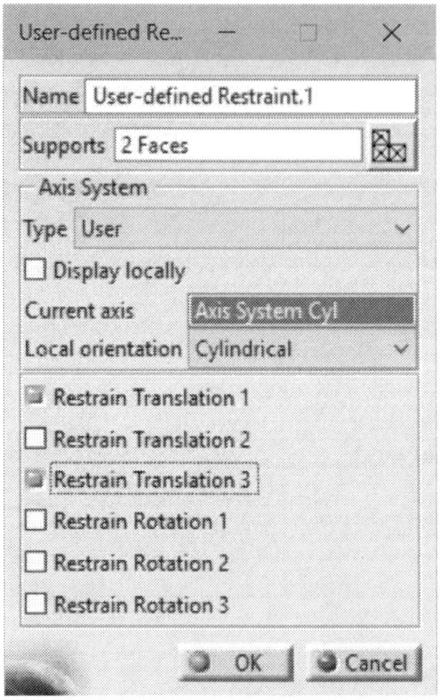

Figure 3–68

3. Click **OK**. The model displays as shown in Figure 3–69.

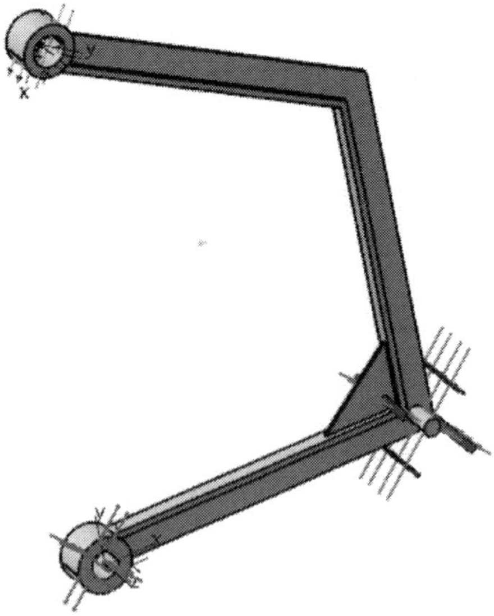

Figure 3–69

Task 11 - Run the analysis.

1. Select  (Compute) and run the analysis. Note that now CATIA completes the computation successfully, without issuing any error messages.

Task 12 - Display and animate the deformation.

1. In the Image toolbar, select  (Deformation). The deformed mesh image displays, as shown in Figure 3–70.

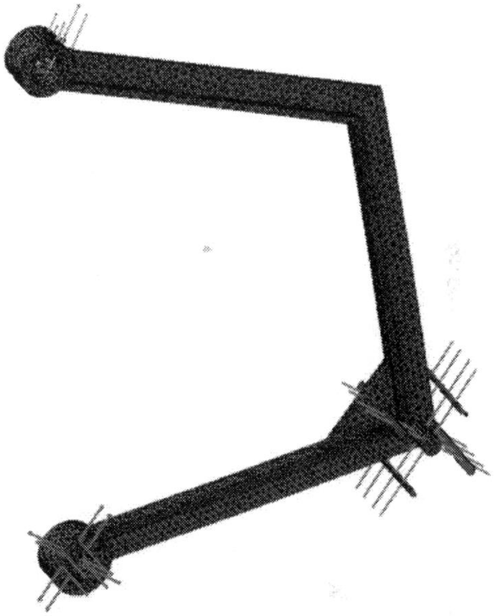

Figure 3–70

2. Unhide **Links Manager.1** to overlay the deformed mesh over the CAD model.

3. Using the (Amplification Magnitude) tool, set the scaling factor to **20**, as shown in Figure 3–71.

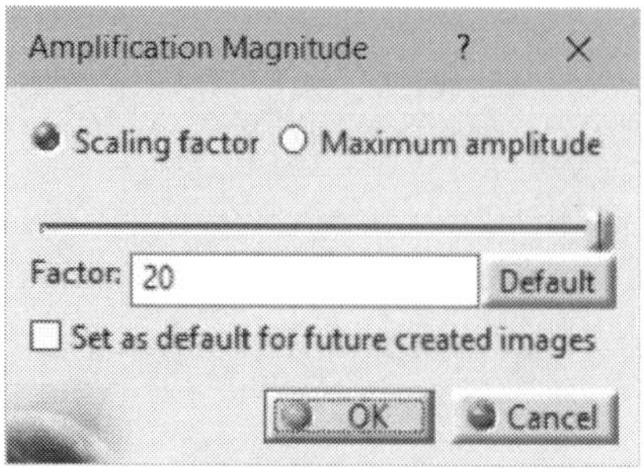

Figure 3–71

4. Run the animation. Zoom in on the rod, as shown in Figure 3–72. Note that the rod's rotation is not restricted, as if it were supported by sleeve bearings or bushings. This results from applying the surface slider restraint to the rod's surface.

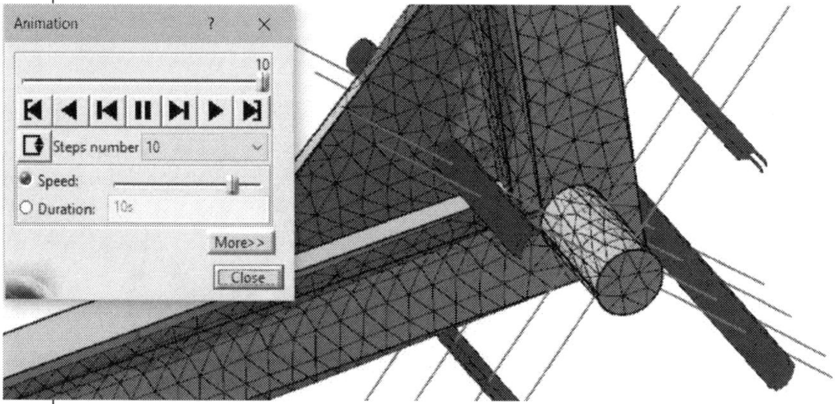

Figure 3–72

5. Zoom in on the lower boss and note that its rotation is not restricted either, as if it were supported by a rigid pin.

6. Close the animation.

Task 13 - Change the view mode.

Shading with Material mode is necessary for the correct display of color result plots.

1. In the View toolbar, select (Shading with Material).

Task 14 - Visualize the displacement magnitude.

1. In the Image toolbar, select (Displacement). Once the displacement vector image is displayed, double-click on the **Translational displacement vector.1** object in the tree and select **Average iso** in the Image Edition dialog box. The image is now displayed as a color plot of the translational displacement magnitude, as shown in Figure 3–73.

   Note that the maximum displacement magnitude under the 500N load is **6.91mm**.

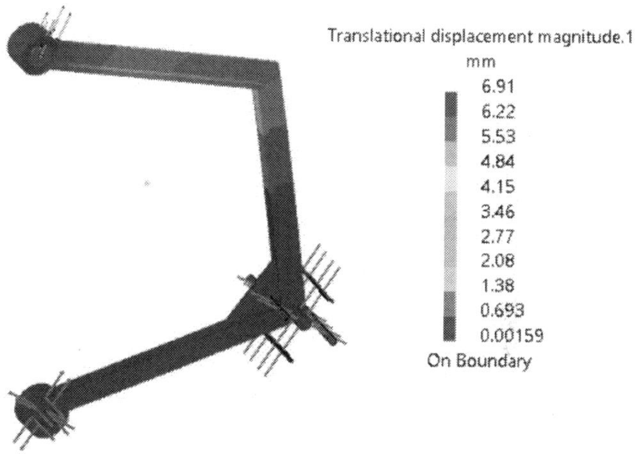

Figure 3–73

Task 15 - Display Von Mises stress.

1. In the Image toolbar, select (Von Mises Stress). The stress image displays as shown in Figure 3–74.

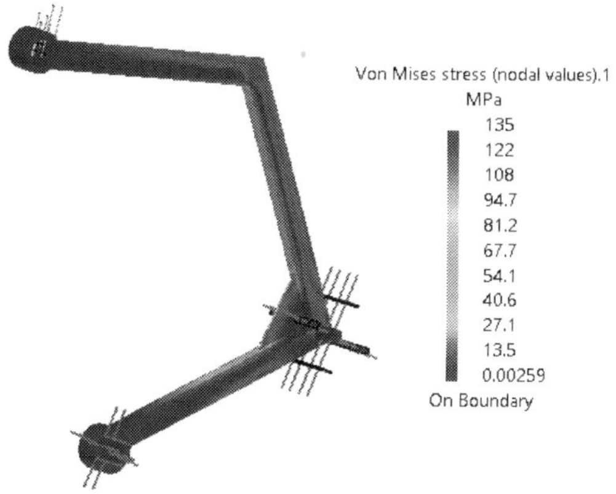

Figure 3–74

2. In the Analysis Tools toolbar, select  (Information) and click the **Von Mises stress (nodal values).1** object in the tree. The Information dialog box displays, as shown in Figure 3–75.

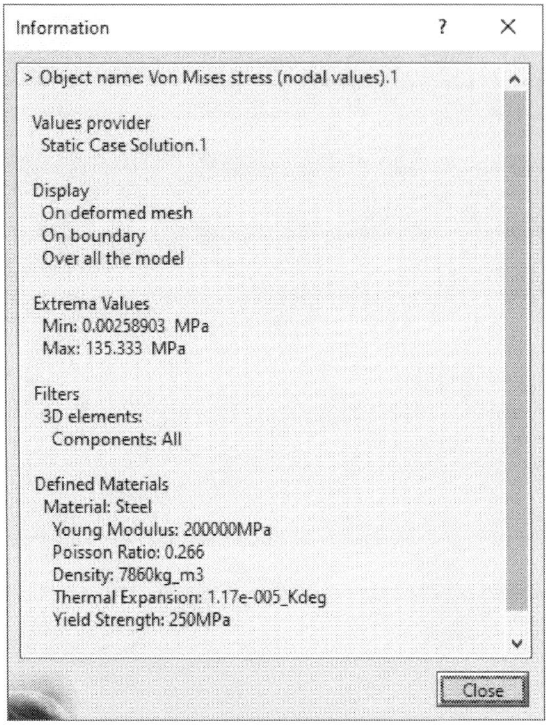

Figure 3–75

3. Note that the maximum Von Mises stress in the model is approximately **135.3MPa**, which is well below the material's **Yield Strength** of **250MPa**. Therefore, the part is predicted to withstand the load without failure. Close the Information dialog box.

Task 16 - Adjust the color map.

1. Expand the tree and double-click on the **Color Map** object located under the **Von Mises stress (nodal values).1** node. In the Color Map Edition dialog box, change the *Number of colors* to **6**, as shown in Figure 3–76.

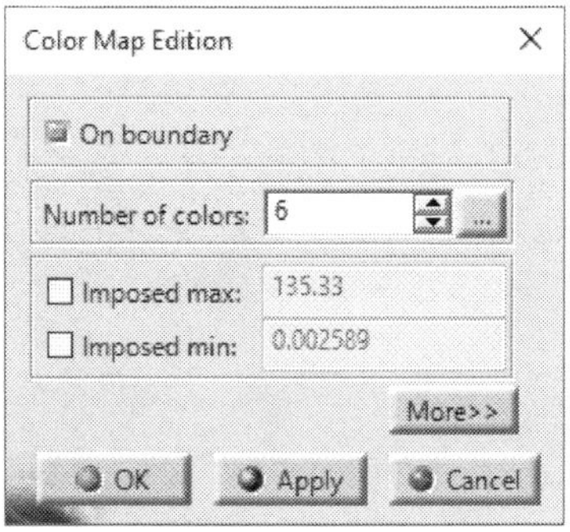

Figure 3–76

2. Click the ellipsis button (**...**). In the Color Edition dialog box that opens, deselect the **Smooth** option, as shown in Figure 3–77, and click **OK** to close.

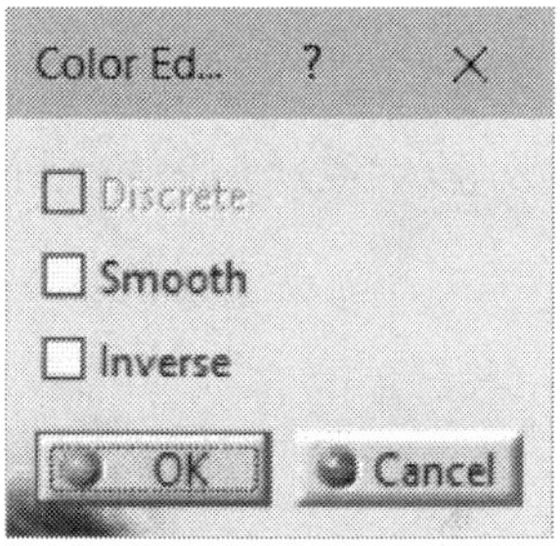

Figure 3–77

3. Click **OK** to close the Color Map Edition dialog box. Hide the restraints.

4. Review the stress in various areas of the model. Note that now the color map has six colors, and the stress ranges associated with each color are easily identifiable in the image, as shown in Figure 3–78.

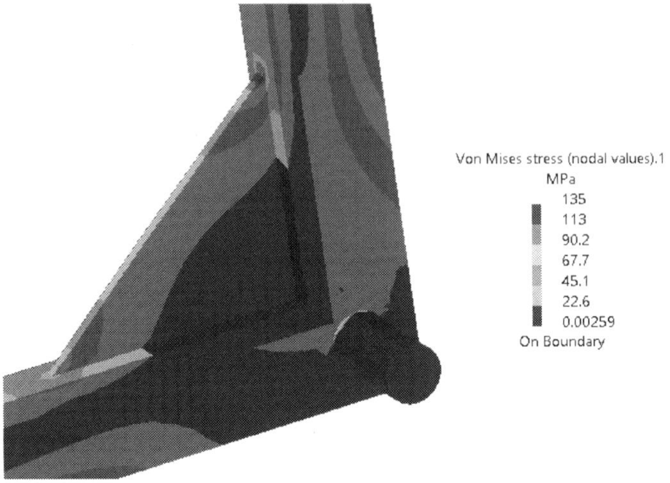

Figure 3–78

Task 17 - Locate areas of maximum stress.

1. In the Analysis Tools toolbar, select (Image Extrema). In the Extrema Creation dialog box that opens, request **1** global maximum and no local maximums, as shown in Figure 3–79.

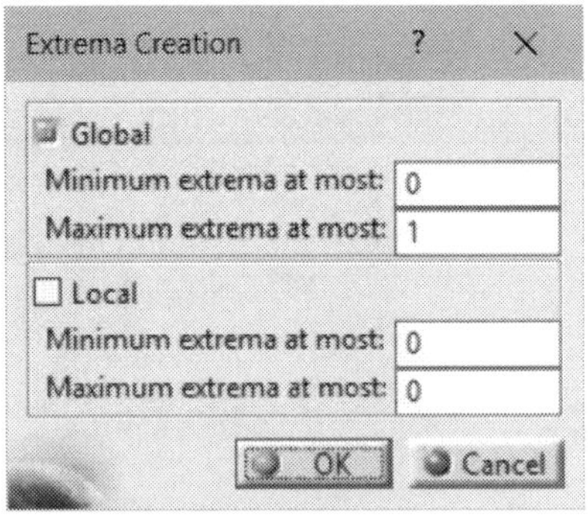

Figure 3–79

2. Click **OK**. Right-click on **Global Maximum.1** in the tree and select **Focus On** in the contextual menu. CATIA rotates and zooms in on the maximum stress location, as shown in Figure 3–80.

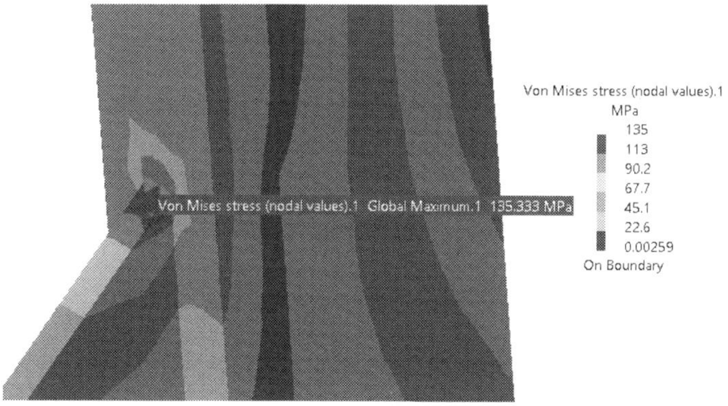

Figure 3–80

3. Double-click on **Global Maximum.1** in the tree to open the Extremum Edition dialog box. Shorten the label so it only shows the stress value, and, using the left mouse button, move the label to another location on the screen, as shown in Figure 3–81.

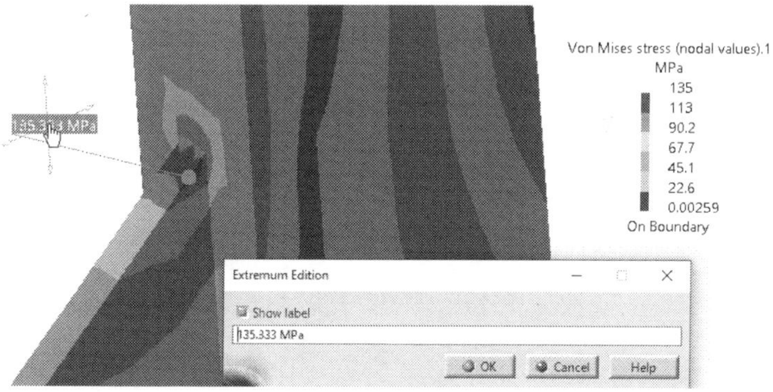

Figure 3–81

4. Click **OK** to close the Extremum Edition dialog box.

Task 18 - Capture the image of the maximum stress location.

1. Select **Tools>Image>Capture**. The Capture toolbar displays, as shown in Figure 3–82.

Figure 3–82

2. Ensure that  (Pixel Mode) is enabled.

3. Click  (Select Mode) and drag a "rubber" rectangle around the area of maximum stress, as shown in Figure 3–83.

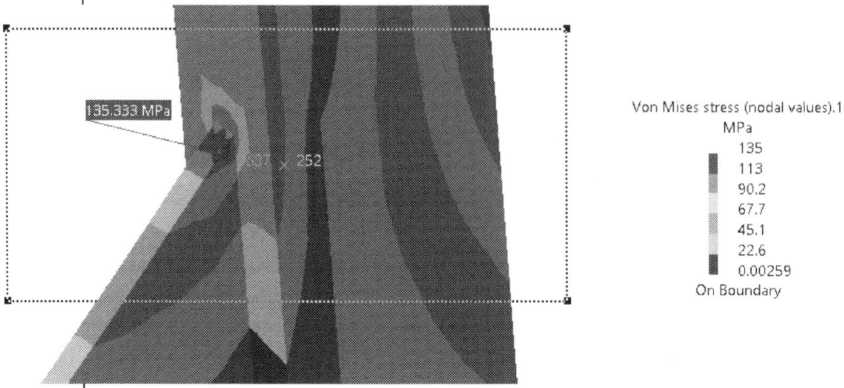

Figure 3–83

4. Click 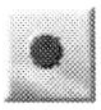 (Capture) to capture the image of the selected area. The Capture Preview window opens, as shown in Figure 3–84.

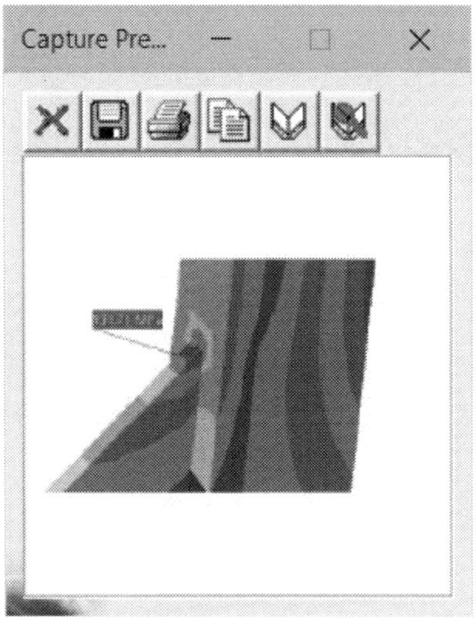

Figure 3–84

5. While the capture preview is open, you can use (Save As) to save the capture to a file, (Print) to print the capture, or (Copy) to copy the capture onto the Windows clipboard then paste into another document, such as PowerPoint or Excel.

6. Click (Cancel) to cancel the capture, then close the Capture toolbar.

7. Right-click on the **Extrema** object in the tree and select **Hide/Show** to hide the maximum stress label.

Task 19 - Return to the model view.

1. Right-click on **Von Mises stress (nodal values).1** in the tree and select **Activate/Deactivate** to delete the stress image from the screen and return to the model view.

Task 20 - Save and close the files.

1. Optionally, save the analysis document and the part for future reference.

2. Close both the analysis and the part documents.

Practice 3b

Bracket Loaded with a Remote Force

Practice Objectives

- Apply the material and mesh the model.
- Apply the remote force load using a handler point.
- Compute the analysis.
- Visualize the analysis results.
- Obtain reaction forces in the restraints.

In this practice, you will set up and run a static stress analysis on a bracket, which is a part in the assembly shown in Figure 3–85. The bracket is restrained at the four holes in the top and bottom flanges, and the end of the shaft is loaded with a 400N force acting in the horizontal direction.

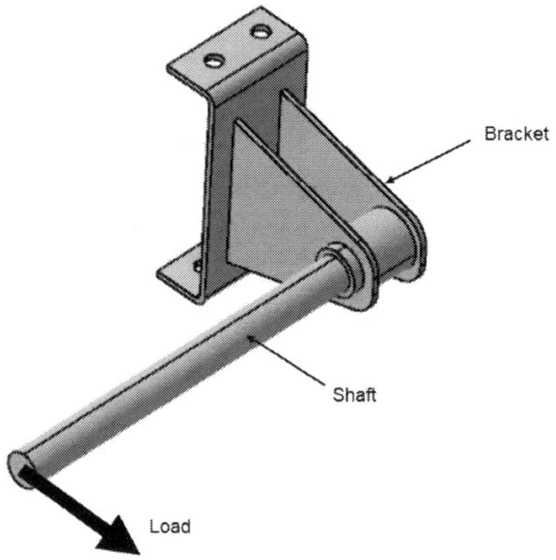

Figure 3–85

Task 1 - Open the part in CATIA.

1. Open **BRACKET_03.CATPart** from the *CATIA Generative Structural Analysis Practice Files\Ch03* folder.

2. Set the model display as  (Shading with Edges). The part displays as shown in Figure 3–86.

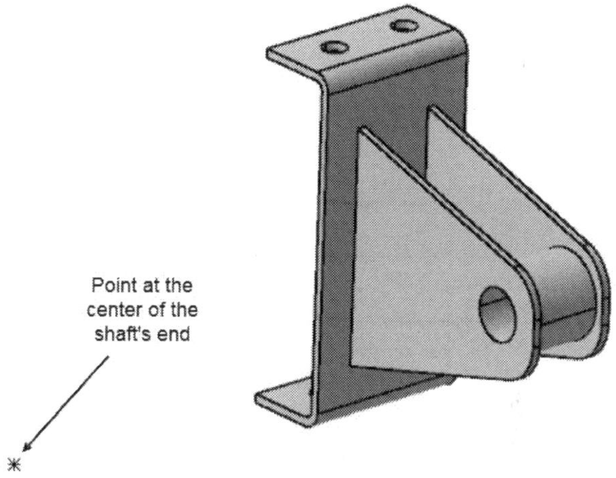

Figure 3–86

Note that the shaft part will not be included in the analysis model. Instead, the load on the shaft will be applied at the remote point **Point.1**, which is located at the center of the shaft's end.

3. Select **Tools>Options>Parameters and Measures>Units** and set the units as follows:

   - Length: **Millimeter (mm)**
   - Force: **Newton (N)**
   - Moment: **Newton x Meter (Nxm)**
   - Pressure: **Megapascal (MPa)**

Task 2 - Apply the material.

1. Apply the **Steel** material from the **Default Material Catalog** to the part. Verify that the applied material has the following properties:
   - Young Modulus: **200000MPa**
   - Poisson Ratio: **0.266**
   - Density: **7860kg/m^3**
   - Thermal Expansion: **1.17e-005/Kdeg**
   - Yield Strength: **250MPa**

Task 3 - Start the GSA workbench.

1. Select **Start>Analysis & Simulation>Generative Structural Analysis**.
2. Select **Static Analysis** as the new analysis case.

Task 4 - Mesh the part.

1. Measure the thickness of the part's profile, as shown in Figure 3–87.

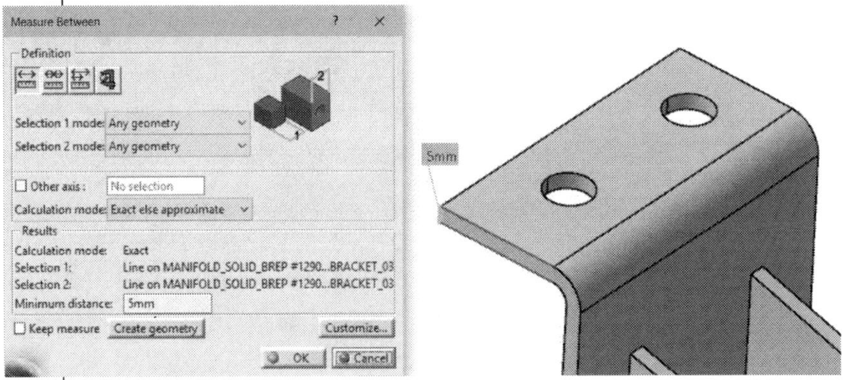

Figure 3–87

A size of 9mm is 1.8 times the thickness of the part, which is the recommended ratio for thin-walled parts. A sag of 1.8mm is 20% of the size, which is the rule of thumb for most of the parts.

2. Double-click on **OCTREE Tetrahedron Mesh.1: BRACKET_03** in the tree to open the OCTREE Tetrahedron Mesh dialog box. Select **Parabolic** as the *Element type*, enter the *Size* as **9mm** and the *Absolute sag* as **1.8mm**, as shown in Figure 3–88.

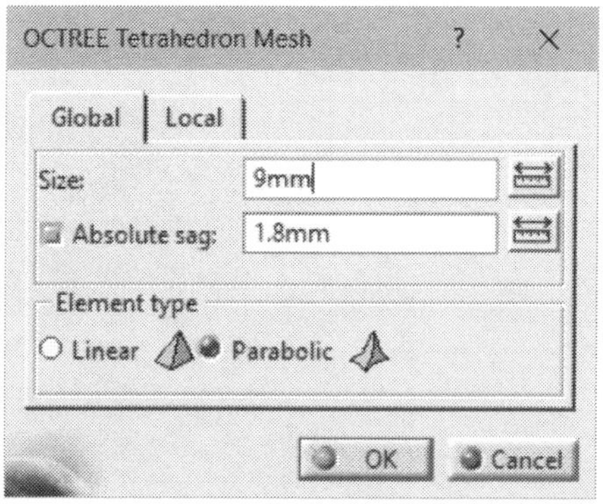

Figure 3–88

3. Click **OK** to close the OCTREE Tetrahedron Mesh dialog box.

4. Right-click on **Nodes and Elements** in the tree and select **Mesh Visualization**. The part mesh is displayed, as shown in Figure 3–89.

Figure 3–89

5. Double-click on **Mesh.1** in the tree. In the Image Edition dialog box that opens, activate the **Display nodes of elements** option, as shown in Figure 3–90.

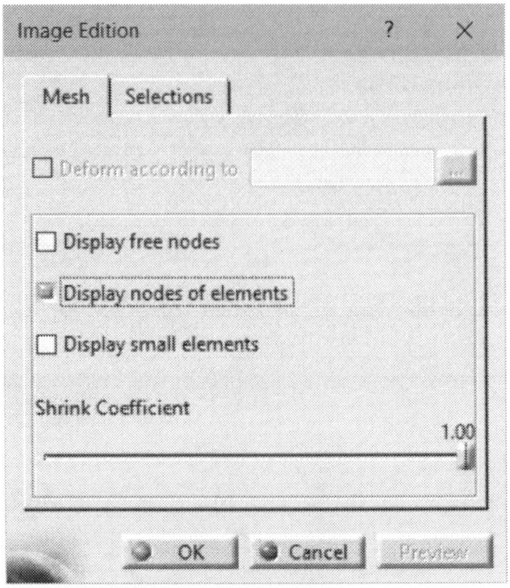

Figure 3–90

6. Click **OK** to close the Image Edition dialog box. Rotate and zoom in on the model to examine the mesh in various areas of the part, as shown in Figure 3–91. The red dots indicate the mesh nodes, three nodes per element edge since the elements are **Parabolic.**

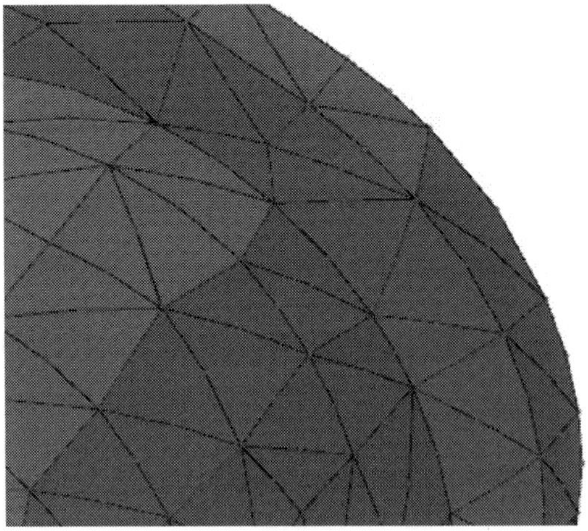

Figure 3–91

7. Right-click on **Mesh.1** in the tree and select **Delete** to delete the mesh visualization and return to the model view.

Task 5 - Apply restraints.

In this task, you will apply clamp restraints to the four holes in the bracket. You will create a separate restraint for each hole in order to facilitate separate reaction force extraction for each hole.

1. Select  (Clamp) in the Restraints toolbar and restrain the inside surface of the first hole in the top flange of the bracket, as shown in Figure 3–92.

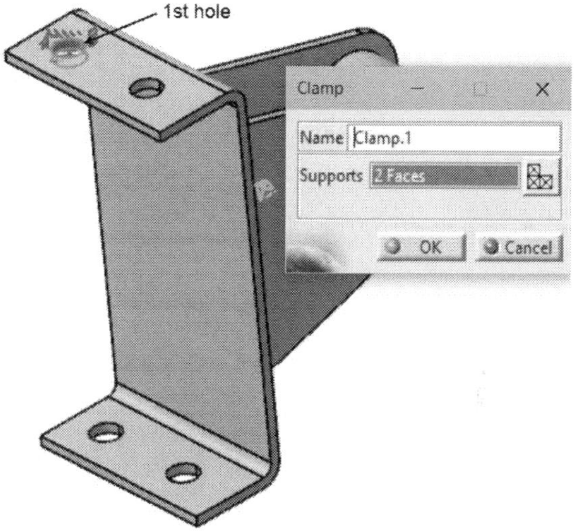

Figure 3–92

2. Repeat Step 1 three more times for the remaining three holes, as shown in Figure 3–93.

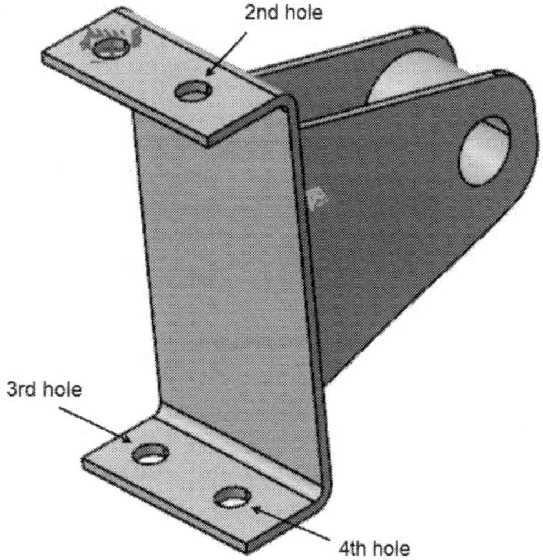

Figure 3–93

3. The model displays as shown in Figure 3–94.

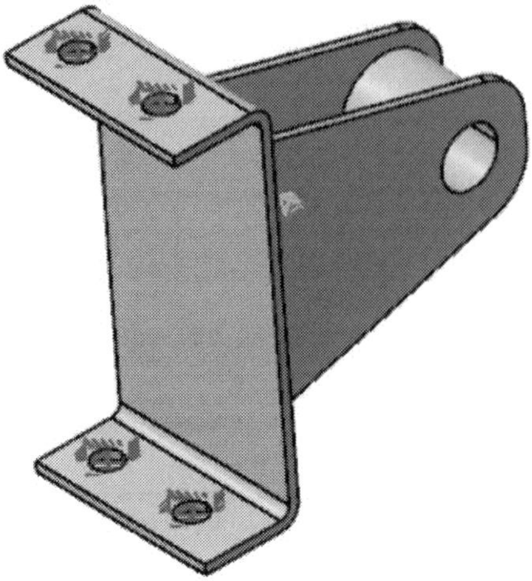

Figure 3–94

Task 6 - Apply the load.

1. Select (Distributed Force) in the Forces toolbar. Select the inside surface of the boss as the *Supports*, as shown in Figure 3–95.

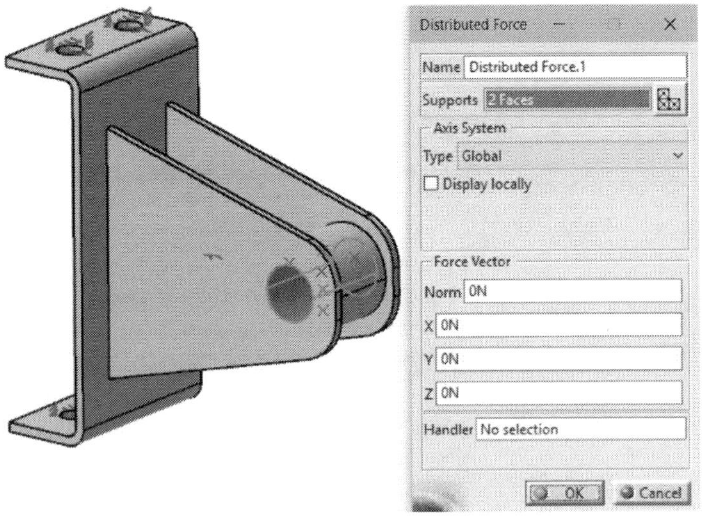

Figure 3–95

*With this setup, CATIA will transfer the **400N** force from the remote point (**Point.1**) to the inside surface of the boss (the load's **Supports**), by creating a system of forces on the mesh nodes in the boss that is **statically equivalent** to the force applied on the remote point.*

2. Click in the **Handler** field and select **Point.1**. Enter **400N** in the **X** field of the *Force Vector* section of the dialog box, as shown in Figure 3–96. Click **OK** to finish.

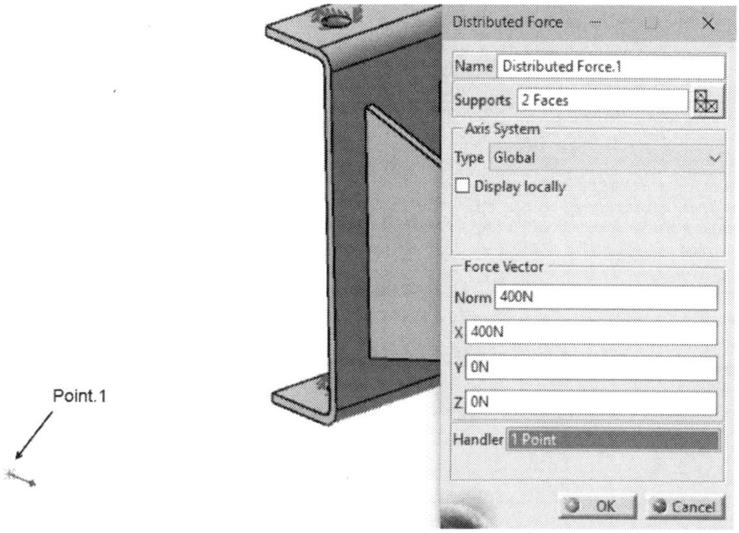

Figure 3–96

Task 7 - Run the analysis.

1. Check your model for errors and inconsistencies.
2. Run the analysis and wait until it completes. The computation time should be within a few seconds.

Task 8 - Display and animate the deformed mesh.

1. Select  (Deformation) to display the deformed mesh image. Unhide the **Links Manager.1** to overlay the mesh over the undeformed part, as shown in Figure 3–97.

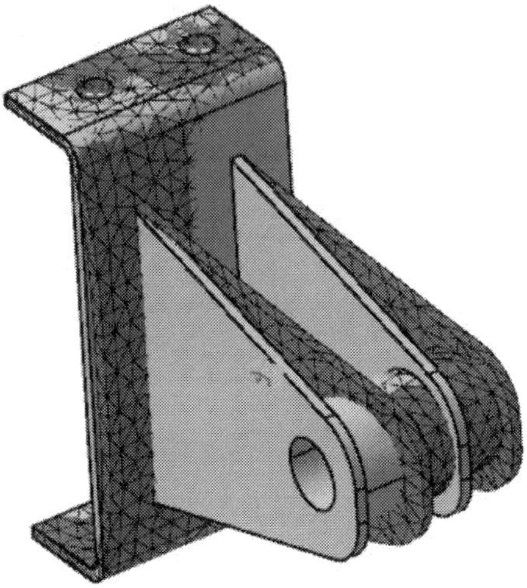

Figure 3–97

2. Using the  (Amplification Magnitude) tool, set the scaling factor to **150.**

3. Animate the deformed mesh. Note that the model deforms according to the applied load, as if the 400N force was indeed applied at the tip of the shaft shown previously in Figure 3–85. The deformed mesh at step 10 of the animation is shown in Figure 3–98.

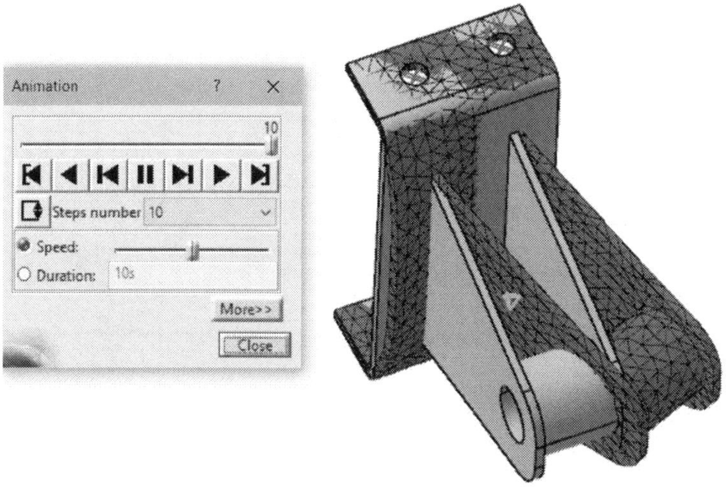

Figure 3–98

4. Close the animation.

Task 9 - Change the view mode.

1. In the View toolbar, select  (Shading with Material).

Task 10 - Visualize the displacement magnitude.

1. Select  (Displacement) to display the displacements, then change the image type to **Average iso**. The translational displacement magnitude image is displayed, as shown in Figure 3–99.

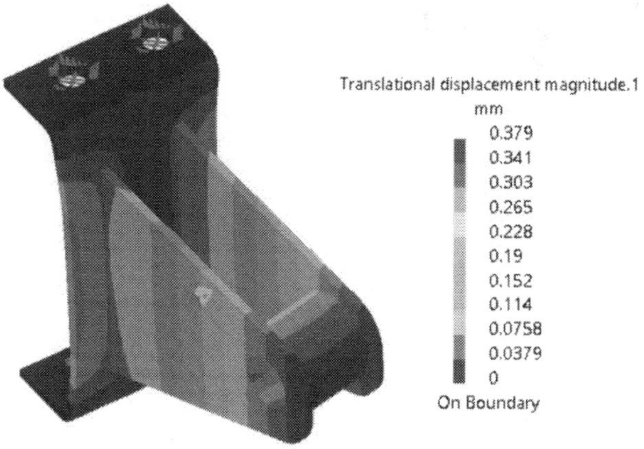

Figure 3–99

Note that the maximum displacement magnitude under the given load is approximately **0.38mm**.

Task 11 - Display Von Mises stress.

1. Select (Von Mises Stress) to display the stress image, as shown in Figure 3–100.

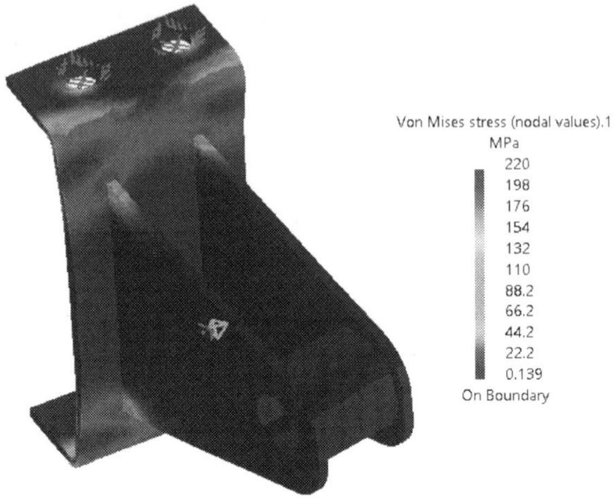

Figure 3–100

2. In the Analysis Tools toolbar, select (Information) and click the **Von Mises stress (nodal values).1** object in the tree. Note that the maximum Von Mises stress (**220.26MPa**) is below the material's Yield Strength (**250MPa**), which means that the bracket is not expected to fail under the 400N load.

3. Close the Information dialog box.

Task 12 - Locate areas of maximum stress.

1. Select (Image Extrema). In the Extrema Creation dialog box that opens, request **1** global maximum and **3** local maximums, as shown in Figure 3–101.

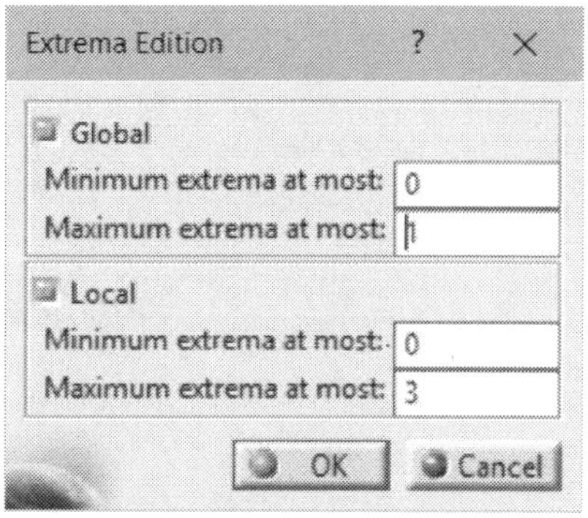

Figure 3–101

2. Display and edit the labels of the found maximums (**Global Maximum.1** through **Local Maximum.3**). Rearrange the labels on the screen approximately as shown in Figure 3–102.

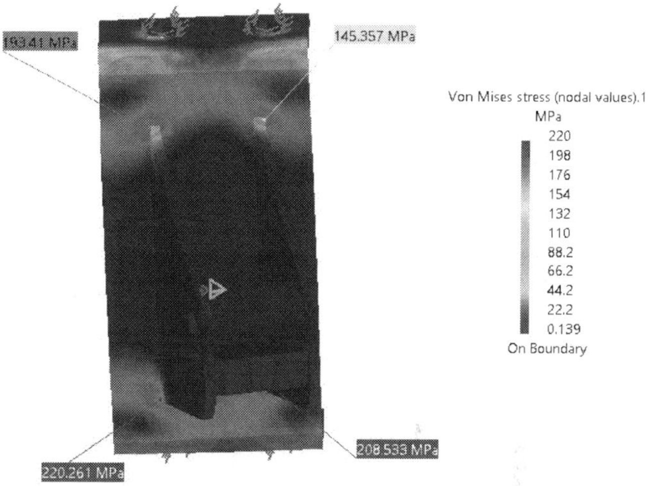

Figure 3–102

Note that the maximum stresses in the model occur at the four corner points as shown above.

3. Optionally, capture the stress image with the labels, and copy and paste it into PowerPoint or Excel.

4. Right-click on **Extrema** in the tree and select **Hide/Show** to hide the labels.

Task 13 - Perform a cut plane analysis.

This ensures that the cutting plane cross-sections the result plot on the undeformed (i.e., as in your CAD model) geometry of the part.

1. Double-click on the **Von Mises stress (nodal values).1** in the tree and deselect the **Deform according to** option, as shown in Figure 3–103.

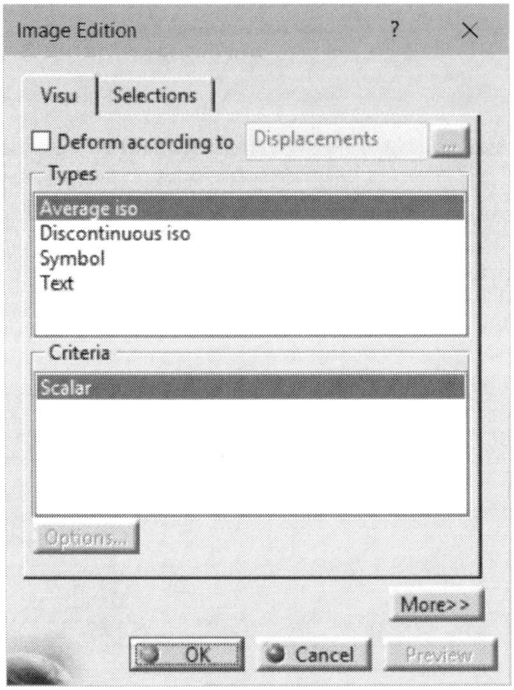

Figure 3–103

2. Select  (Cut Plane Analysis). In the Cut Plane Analysis dialog box that opens, deselect **Show cutting plane** and click **Init plane parameters**. The model displays as shown in Figure 3–104.

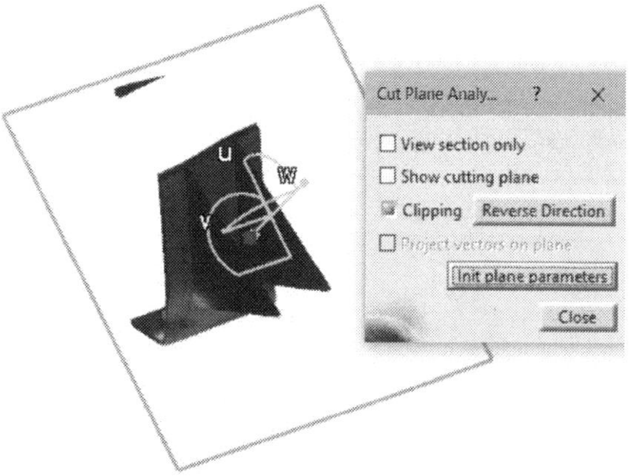

Figure 3–104

3. Right-click on the red square in the compass and select **Edit** in the contextual menu.

4. In the Parameters for Compass Manipulation dialog box that opens, enter the coordinates and angles as shown in Figure 3–105.

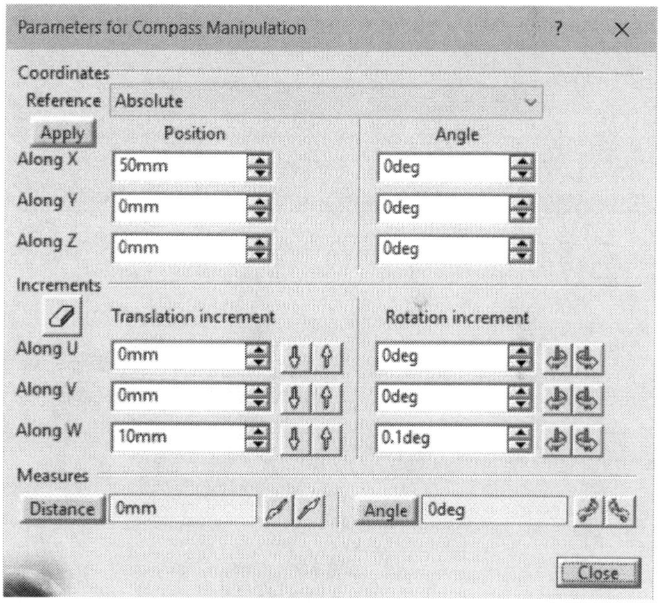

Figure 3–105

5. Click **Apply**, but do not close the Parameters for Compass Manipulation dialog box yet. The model displays as shown in Figure 3–106.

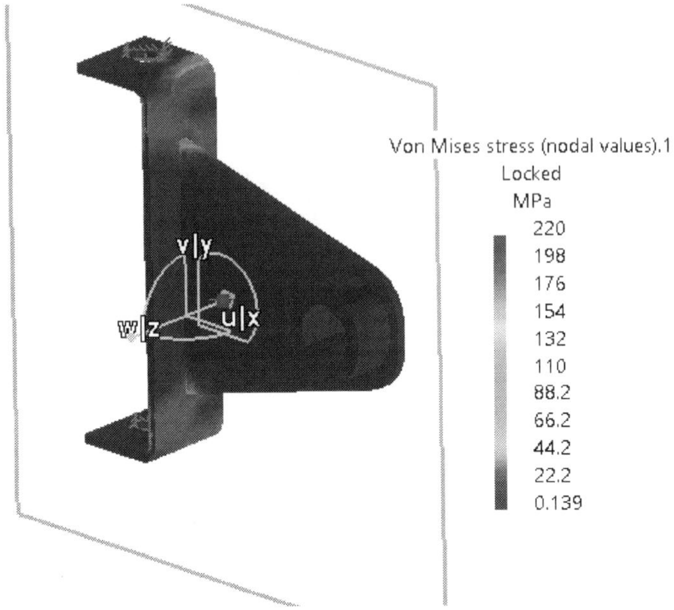

Figure 3–106

6. In the *Along W* field, enter **10mm**. Use the and buttons to move the cutting plane back and forth through the model in 10mm increments.

7. Click **Close** twice to close the Parameters for Compass Manipulation and the Cut Plane Analysis dialog boxes to finish the cut plane analysis.

8. Right-click on **Von Mises stress (nodal values).1** in the tree and select **Activate/Deactivate** to delete the stress image from the screen and return to the model view.

Task 14 - Obtain reactions in restraints.

In this task, you will create reaction sensors in order to obtain the amounts of force carried by each restraint under the given load on the bracket. This information would help you with proper sizing of the fasteners used for mounting the bracket through the holes.

1. Right-click on **Sensors.1** in the tree and select **Create Resultant Sensor>Reaction Sensor** in the contextual menu, as shown in Figure 3–107.

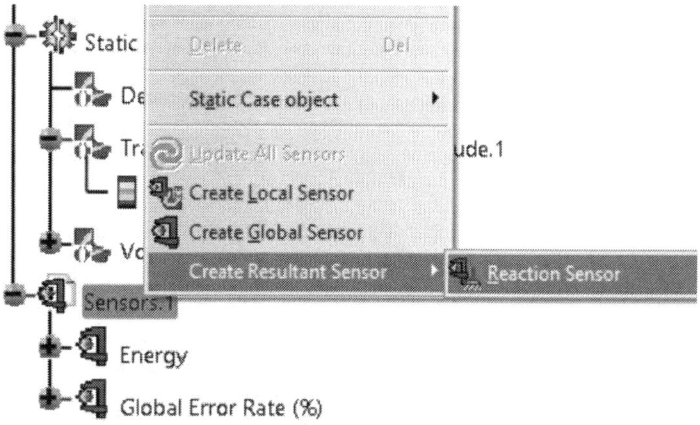

Figure 3–107

2. The Reaction Sensor dialog box opens, as shown in Figure 3–108.

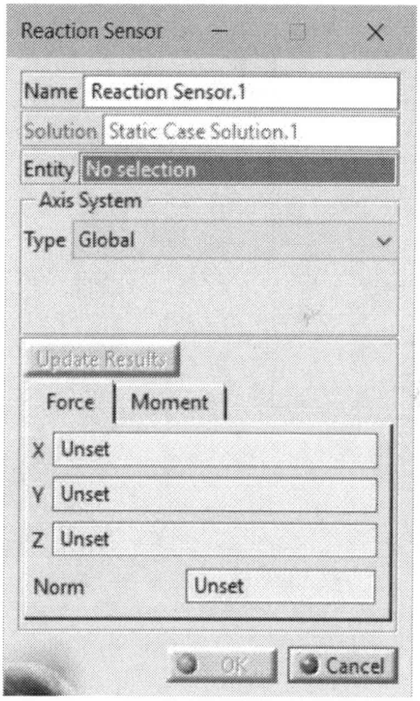

Figure 3–108

3. Select **Clamp.1** in the tree and click **Update Results**. CATIA calculates the reaction forces and moments in the restraint and displays the results, as shown in Figure 3–109.

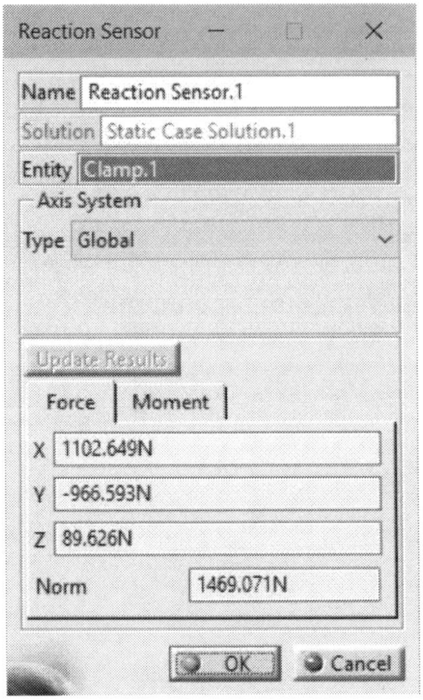

Figure 3–109

Note that the reaction magnitude on the first clamped hole in the bracket is approximately **1470N**, and it is predominantly in the **X** and **Y** directions.

4. Click **OK**. The **Reaction Sensor.1** displays in the tree, as shown in Figure 3–110.

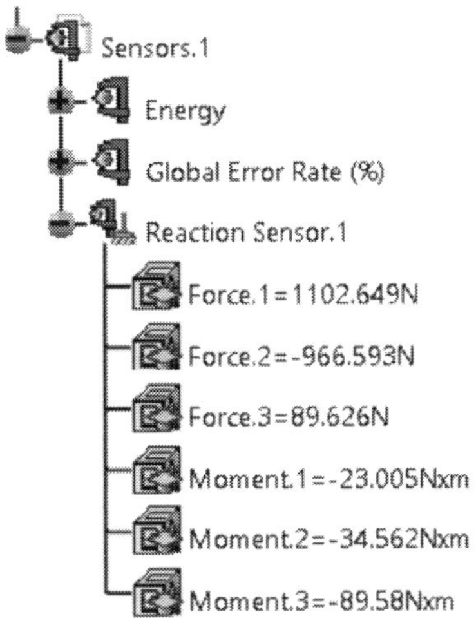

Figure 3–110

5. Repeat Steps 1 to 4 for the remaining three holes (**Clamp.2**, **Clamp.3, Clamp.4**). The sensors are displayed in the tree, as shown in Figure 3–111.

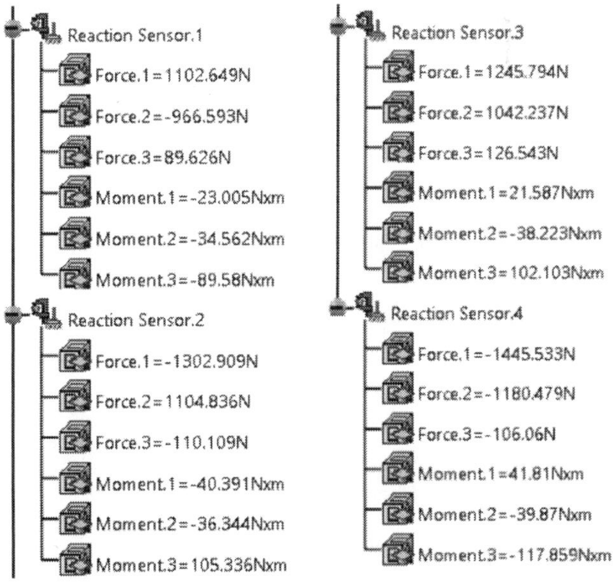

Figure 3–111

Task 15 - Save and close the files.

1. Optionally, save the analysis document and the part for future reference.

2. Close both the analysis and the part documents.

Practice 3c

Loads and Restraints on Surface Patches

Practice Objectives

- Create surface patches using the Sew Surface tool.
- Apply the material and mesh the model.
- Apply a symmetry restraint.
- Apply loads.
- Compute the analysis.
- Display the results.

In this practice, you will set up and run a static stress analysis on a mooring chock that is used for fastening ships to piers. The model is shown in Figure 3–112. The chock is welded into the hull of the ship over an area 1 inch wide going around the outside surface, and loaded by a mooring line over a 2-inch area, as shown in Figure 3–112.

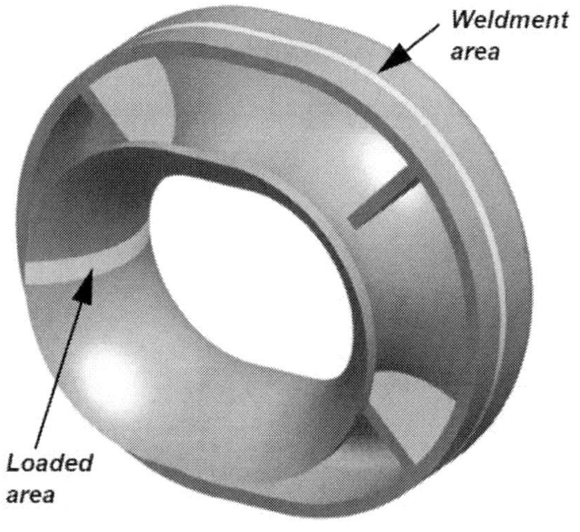

Figure 3–112

You will use the Sew Surface tool in the Part Design workbench to create the surface patches shown in Figure 3–112 for applying loads and restraints.

Task 1 - Open the part in CATIA.

1. Open **Chock_03.CATPart** from the *CATIA Generative Structural Analysis Practice Files\Ch03* folder.

2. Set the model display as  (Shading with Edges). The part displays as shown in Figure 3–113.

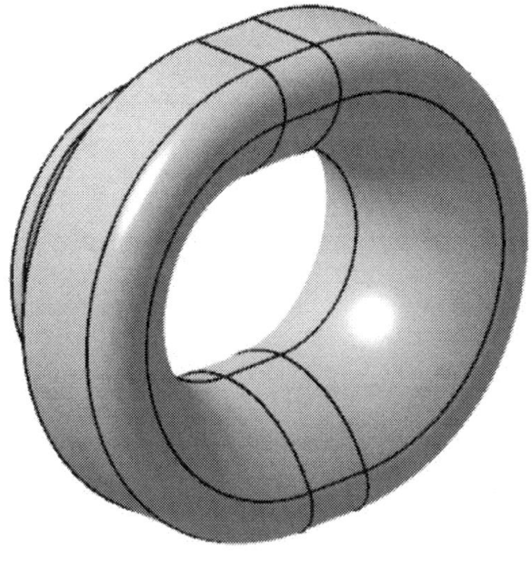

Figure 3–113

3. Select **Tools>Options>Parameters and Measures>Units** and set the units as follows:
   - Length: **Millimeter (mm)**
   - Force: **Newton (N)**
   - Moment: **Newton x Meter (Nxm)**
   - Pressure: **Megapascal (MPa)**

Task 2 - Split the part in half.

The part geometry and the boundary conditions in this analysis exhibit mirror symmetry (i.e., the geometry, loads, and restraints on the upper half of the chock mirror the geometry, loads, and restraints on the lower half). In this task, you will split the part in half along the symmetry plane and keep the bottom half to take advantage of symmetry restraints later in the analysis.

1. Ensure the current workbench is **Part Design** .

2. In the Surface-Based Features toolbar, select (Split). The Split Definition dialog box opens, as shown in Figure 3–114.

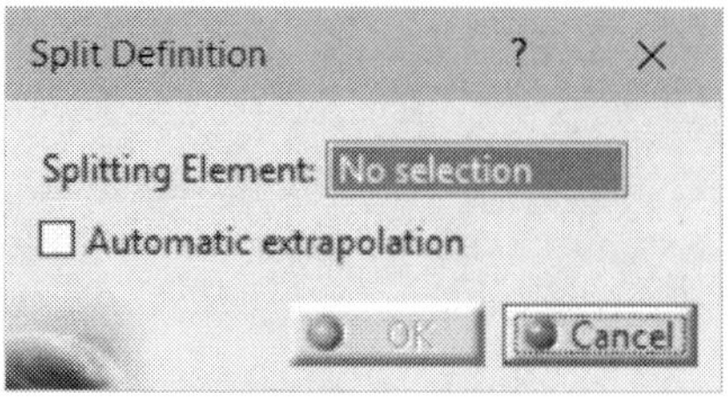

Figure 3–114

3. Select **zx plane** as the *Splitting Element*. Make sure the **orange arrow** points down, opposite to the Y-direction. If not, click on the orange arrow to flip the direction. The model displays as shown in Figure 3–115.

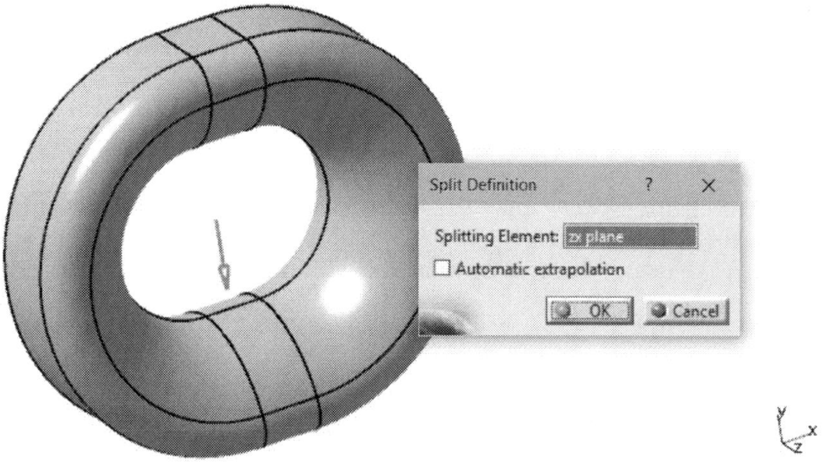

Figure 3–115

4. Click **OK**. The part displays, as shown in Figure 3–116.

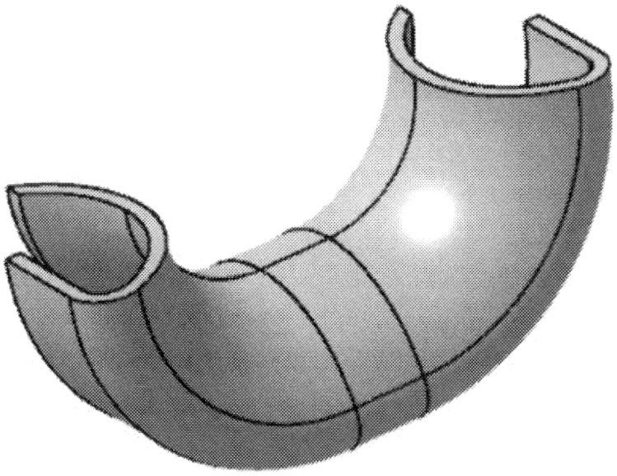

Figure 3–116

Task 3 - Create a surface patch for the weldment area.

In this task, you will split the part surface in order to separate the welded area from the rest of the solid's surface. The process essentially consists of two steps:

- First, you create a patch of the surface by extracting and splitting the PartBody's surface
- Second, you sew that patch back onto the PartBody using the Sew Surface tool.

1. Switch to the **Generative Shape Design**  workbench.
2. Create a new geometrical set named **GS weldment**.
3. Create two new planes:
    - **Plane.1:** Offset by **88.9mm** (3.5") from **xy plane** toward the positive Z-direction.
    - **Plane.2:** Offset by **114.3mm** (4.5") from **xy plane** toward the positive Z-direction.

4. The model displays as shown in Figure 3–117.

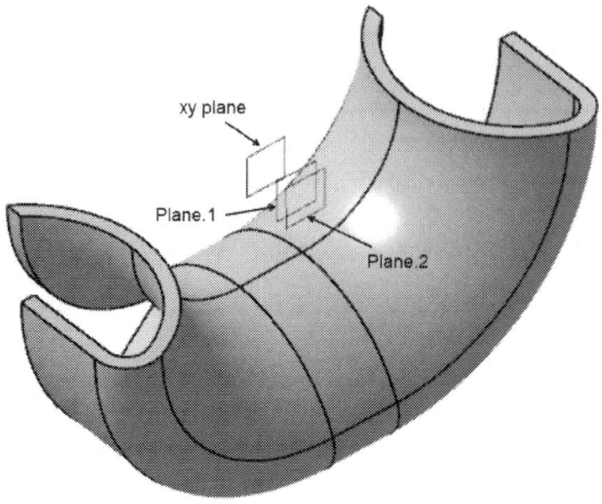

Figure 3–117

5. Extract and join the three outside surfaces. The result, **Join.1**, is shown in Figure 3–118.

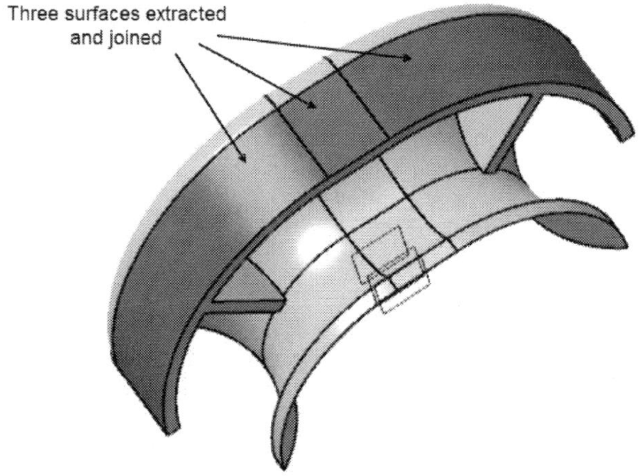

Figure 3–118

6. Split **Join.1** with **Plane.1**, keeping the side toward the positive Z-direction. The result, **Split.1**, is shown in Figure 3–119.

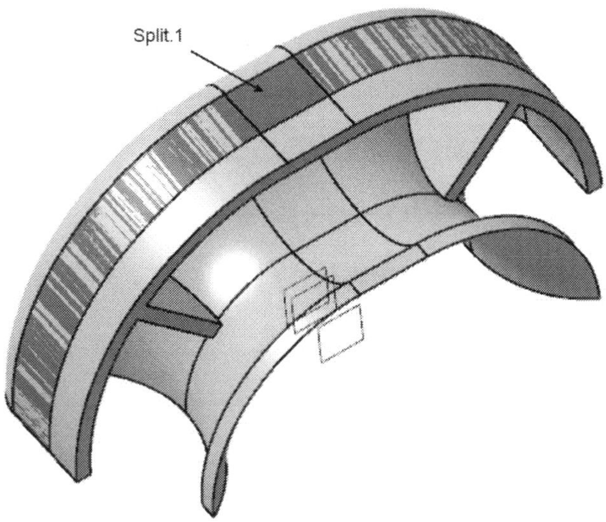

Figure 3–119

7. Split the **Split.1** surface with **Plane.2**, keeping the side toward the negative Z-direction. The result, **Split.2**, is shown in Figure 3–120.

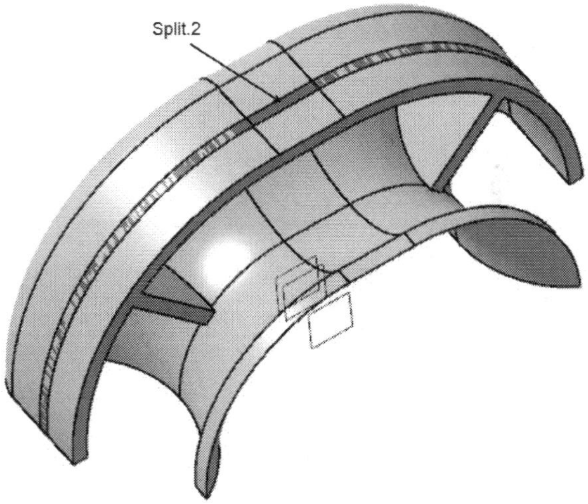

Figure 3–120

8. Switch to the **Part Design**  workbench.

9. Right-click on the **PartBody** and select **Define In Work Object** in the contextual menu.

10. In the Surface-Based Features toolbar, select  (Sew Surface). The Sew Surface Definition dialog box opens, as shown in Figure 3–121.

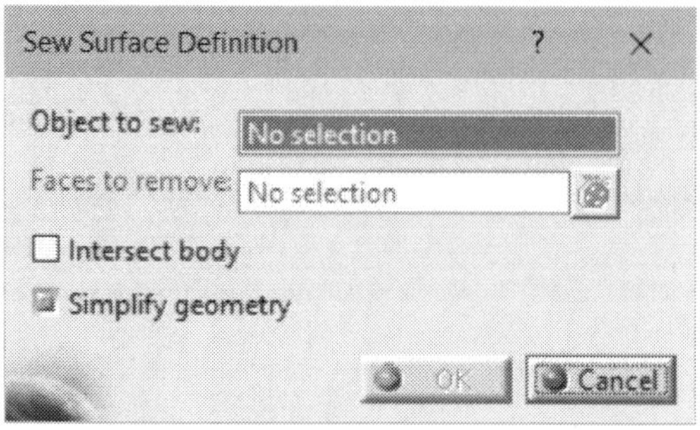

Figure 3–121

*If the **Simplify geometry** option is activated, CATIA will not split the surface patch from the rest of the solid's surface.*

11. Select **Split.2** as the *Object to sew* and deselect the **Simplify geometry** option. Make sure the orange arrows in the preview point toward the solid body. The model displays as shown in Figure 3–122.

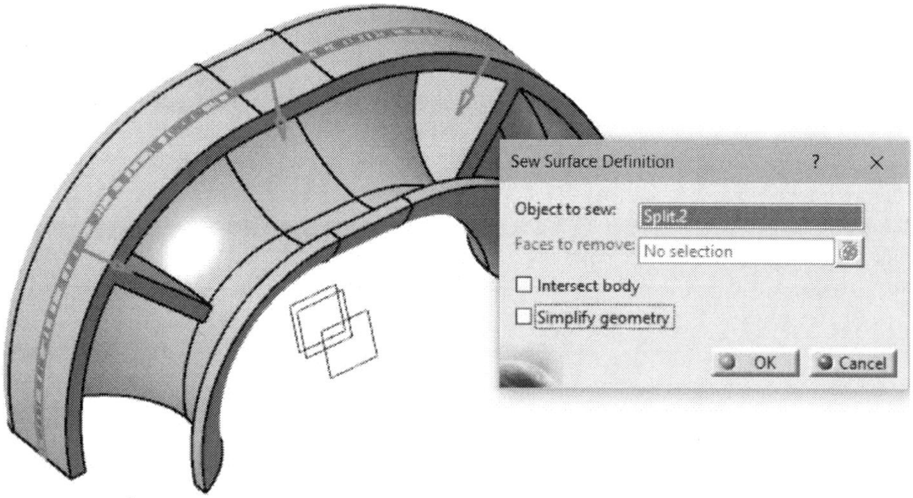

Figure 3–122

12. Click **OK**. Hide the **GS weldment** geometrical set. The model displays as shown in Figure 3–123. Note that the weldment area is now separate from the rest of the part surface.

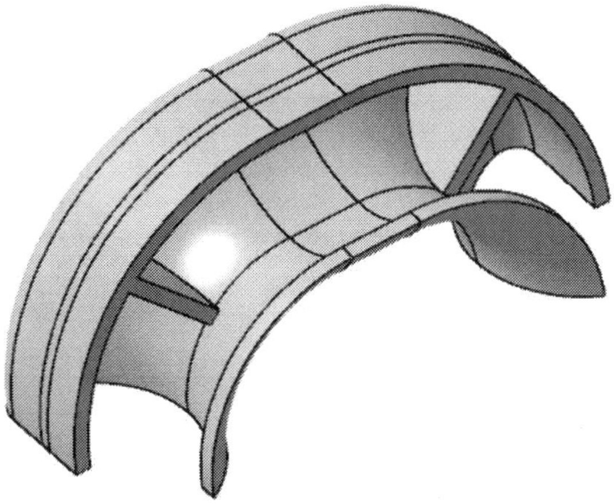

Figure 3–123

Task 4 - Create a surface patch for the loaded area.

In this task, you will split the part surface again, in order to separate the loaded area from the rest of the solid's surface. The process is very similar to Task 3 above; the only difference will be how you create the boundary of the surface patch.

1. Switch to the **Generative Shape Design**  workbench.
2. Create a new geometrical set named **GS load**.

3. Create a sketch (**Sketch.1**) on the **yz plane**, with the dimensions shown in Figure 3–124.

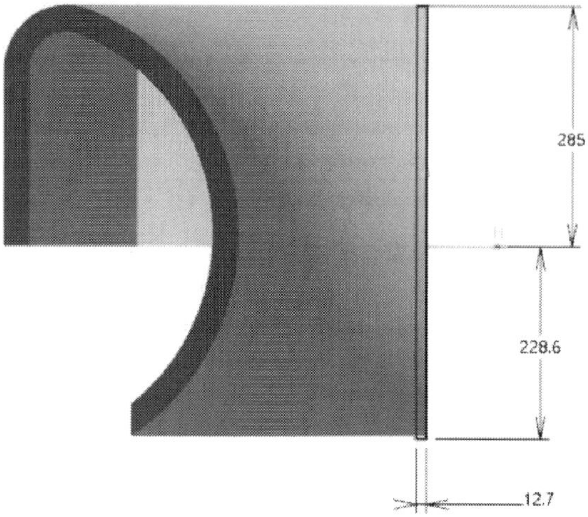

Figure 3–124

4. Exit the **Sketcher** workbench. The model displays as shown in Figure 3–125.

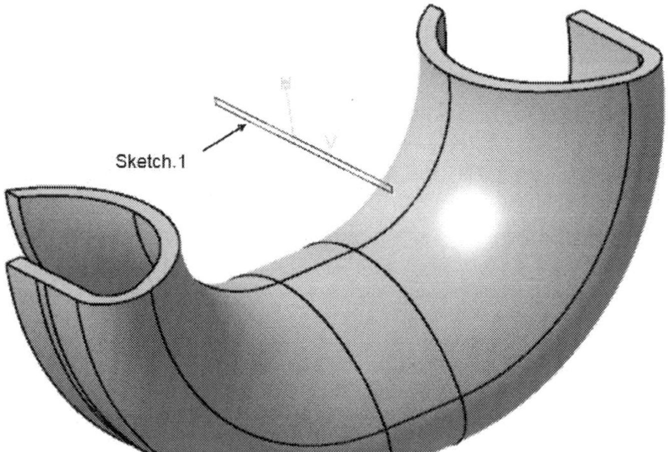

Figure 3–125

5. Extract and join the two inside surfaces that are toward the positive X-direction. The result, **Join.2**, is shown in Figure 3–126.

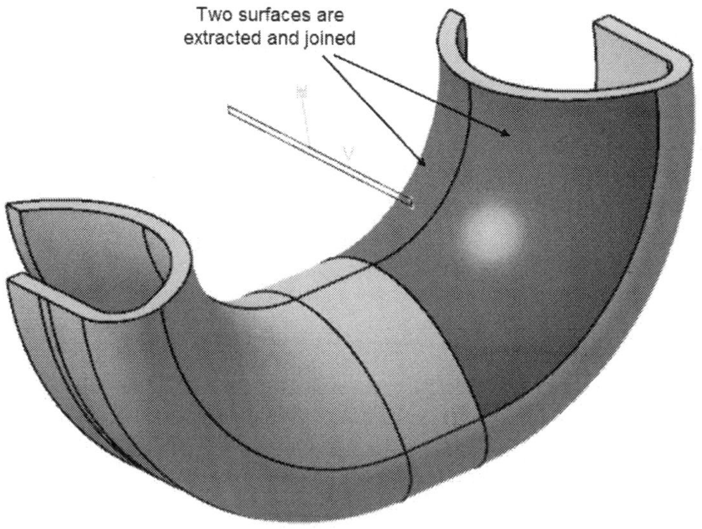

Figure 3–126

6. Project **Sketch.1** onto **Join.2** using the following parameters:

   - Projection type: **Along a direction**
   - Projected: **Sketch.1**
   - Support: **Join.2**
   - Direction: **X Component**

   The result, **Project.1**, is shown in Figure 3–127.

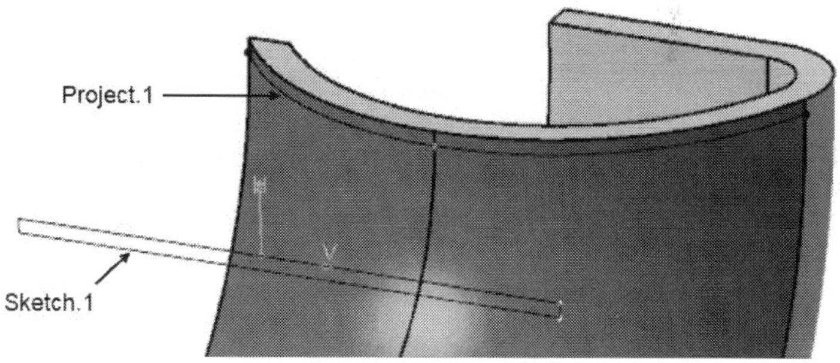

Figure 3–127

7. Split **Join.2** with **Project.1**, keeping the side that is inside **Project.1**. The result, **Split.3**, is shown in Figure 3–128.

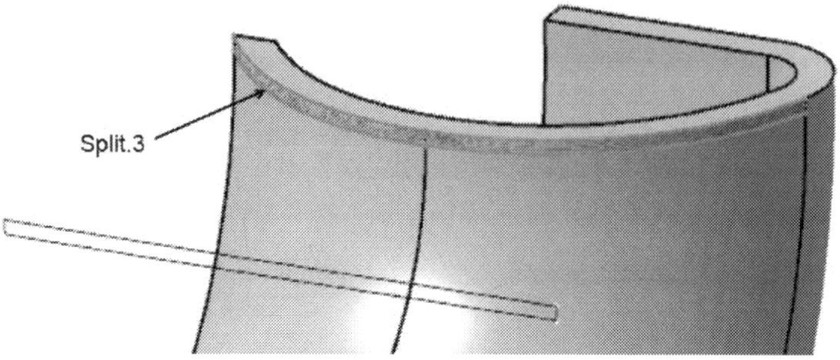

Figure 3–128

8. Switch to the **Part Design**  workbench.

9. Right-click on the **PartBody** and select **Define In Work Object** in the contextual menu.

10. In the Surface-Based Features toolbar, select  (Sew Surface). Select **Split.3** as the *Object to sew* and deselect the **Simplify geometry** option. Make sure the orange arrows in the preview point toward the solid body. The model displays as shown in Figure 3–129.

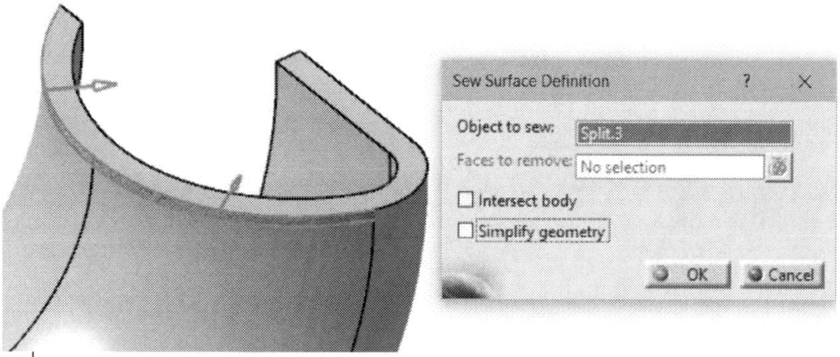

Figure 3–129

11. Click **OK**. Hide the **GS load** geometrical set. The model displays as shown in Figure 3–130. Note that the loaded area is now separate from the rest of the part surface.

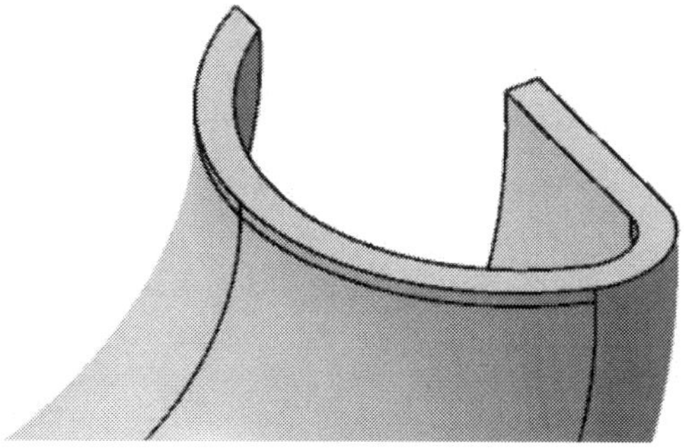

Figure 3–130

Task 5 - Apply the material.

1. Apply the **Steel** material from the **Default Material Catalog** to the part. Verify that the applied material has the following properties:

   - Young Modulus: **200000MPa**
   - Poisson Ratio: **0.266**
   - Density: **7860kg/m^3**
   - Thermal Expansion: **1.17e-005/Kdeg**
   - Yield Strength: **250MPa**

Task 6 - Start the GSA workbench.

1. Select **Start>Analysis & Simulation>Generative Structural Analysis**.
2. Select **Static Analysis** as the new analysis case.

Task 7 - Mesh the part.

1. Double-click on **OCTREE Tetrahedron Mesh.1: CHOCK_03** in the tree and adjust the mesh parameters as following:

   - Element type: **Parabolic**
   - Size: **22mm**
   - Absolute sag: **2mm**

2. Right-click on **Nodes and Elements** in the tree and select **Mesh Visualization**. The part mesh is displayed, as shown in Figure 3–131. Zoom in on the image and examine the mesh near the surface patches. Note that the surface patches' boundaries are clearly visible in the mesh.

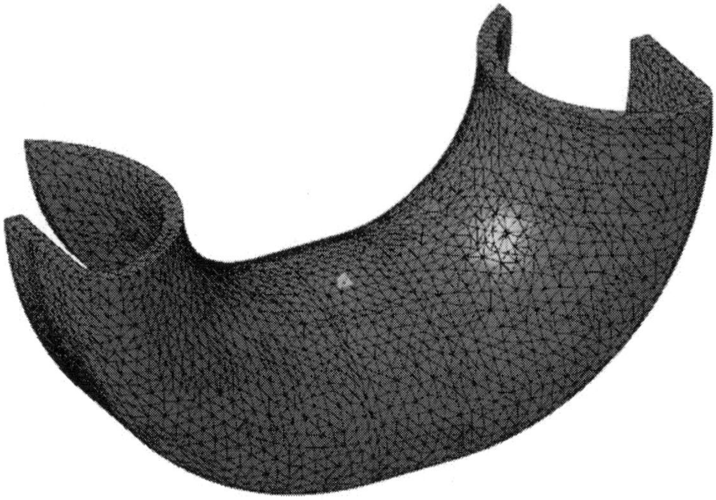

Figure 3–131

3. Right-click on **Mesh.1** in the tree and select **Delete** to delete the mesh visualization and return to the model view.

Task 8 - Apply a symmetry restraint.

Since only one half of the part has been included in the analysis, in this task you will apply a symmetry restraint, which simulates the effect of the other half of the part as if it were still in the model. The symmetry restraint must restrict motion of the material particles out of the plane of symmetry and permit motions in the plane of symmetry. This can be accomplished by applying a surface slider restraint on the cutout surfaces.

1. Select (Surface Slider) in the Restraints toolbar and select the two cutout surfaces, as shown in Figure 3–132.

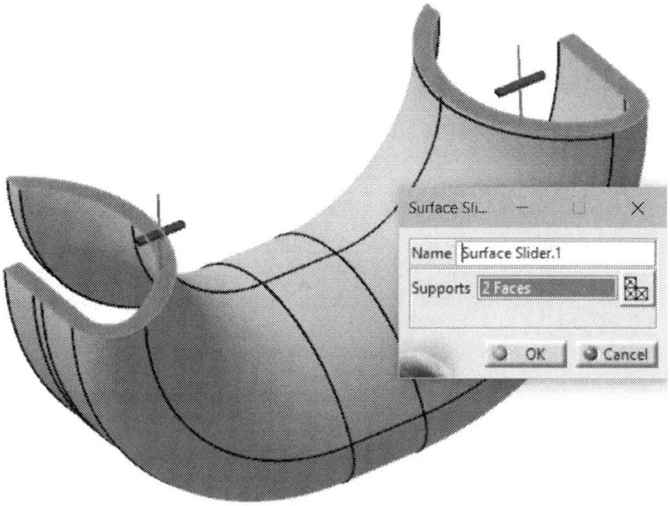

Figure 3–132

2. Click **OK** to finish.

Task 9 - Apply weldment restraint.

1. Select (Clamp) and restrain the three surfaces of the weldment surface patch, as shown in Figure 3–133.

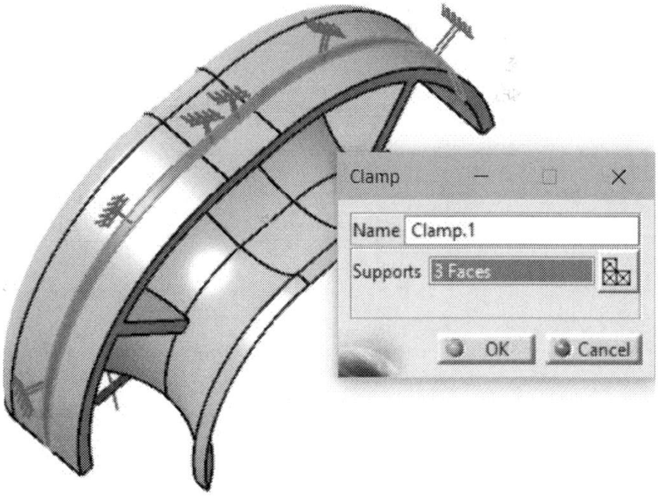

Figure 3–133

Task 10 - Apply the load.

The force exerted by the mooring line onto the chock is 80,000 lbs. Therefore, the amount of force applied to a half of the chock is 80,000/2 = 40,000 lbs., which is approximately 178,000N.

1. Select (Distributed Force) in the Forces toolbar. Select the loaded surface patch as the *Supports*, and apply **178000N** force in the **X** direction, as shown in Figure 3–134.

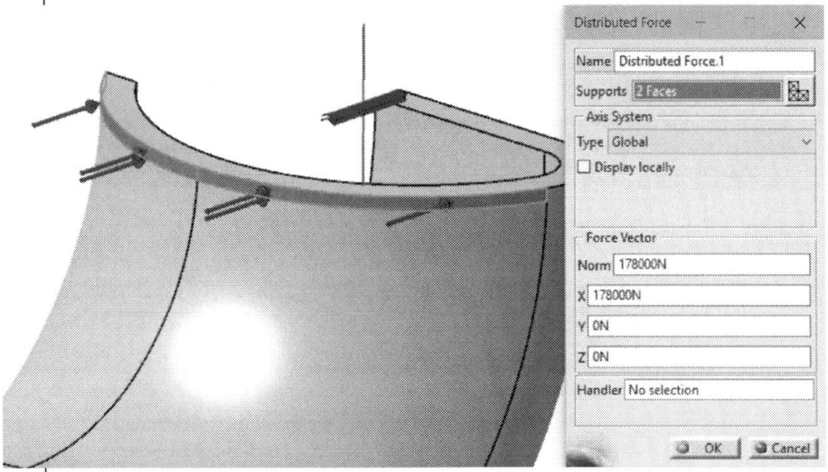

Figure 3–134

Task 11 - Run the analysis.

1. Using (Model Checker), check your model for errors and inconsistencies.
2. Start the computation. CATIA displays the Computation Resources Estimation dialog box as well as the Warnings dialog box, saying that "Rotation constraints were not taken into account ..., etc." The warning message is issued because surface slider, behind the scenes, also applies restraints to the rotational motions of the mesh nodes, which would only be applicable to shell or beam meshes. This model only has solid elements, therefore mesh nodes only have translational degrees of freedom. Those rotational restraints are ignored, which is correct.
3. Close the Warnings dialog box and click **Yes** to continue the computation. Wait until the analysis completes, which should be within 30 seconds.

Task 12 - Display the displacement magnitude.

1. Change the view mode to (Shading with Material).
2. Visualize the displacement magnitude image, overlaid on the CAD model, as shown in Figure 3–135.

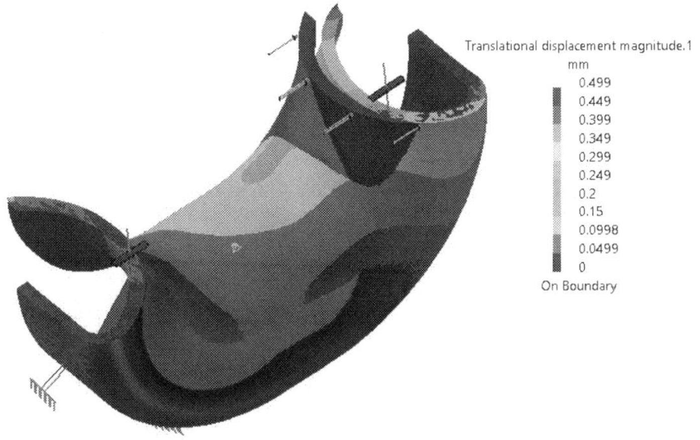

Figure 3–135

3. Start the animation. Check whether the applied boundary conditions behave correctly. Note that the displacements on the plane of symmetry are only in-plane, not out-of-plane.

Task 13 - Display Von Mises stress.

1. Hide **Restraints** and **Loads**.
2. Display the **Von Mises Stress** image. Modify the **Color Map** so that it displays 8 colors and is not smooth, as shown in Figure 3–136.

Figure 3–136

3. Verify whether the maximum Von Mises stress exceeds the material's yield strength.

4. Using the **Image Extrema** tool, locate the maximum stress area, as shown in Figure 3–137.

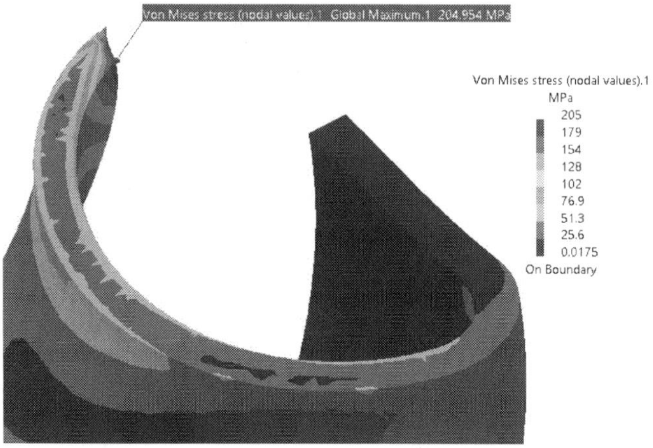

Figure 3–137

5. Right-click on **Von Mises stress (nodal values).1** in the tree and select **Activate/Deactivate** to delete the stress image from the screen and return to the model view.

Task 14 - Save and close the files.

1. Optionally, save the analysis document and the part for future reference.

2. Close both the analysis and the part documents.

Practice 3d Loads and Restraints on Points

Practice Objectives

- Apply the material and mesh the model.
- Apply loads and restraints on points.
- Run the analysis.
- Display the results.
- Create a local analysis sensor to measure displacement under the loaded point.

In this practice, you will set up and run a static stress analysis on the simple L-bracket shown in Figure 3–138. The bracket is clamped at the two holes and loaded at the point on the lower flange, as shown in Figure 3–138.

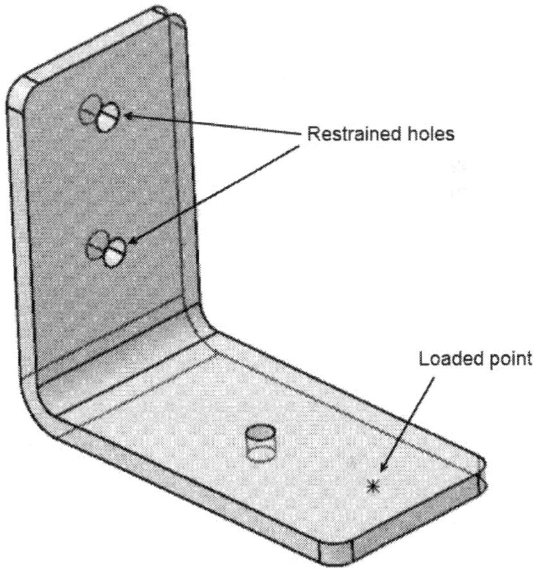

Figure 3–138

Task 1 - Open the part in CATIA.

1. Open **L-Bracket_03.CATPart** from the *CATIA Generative Structural Analysis Practice Files\Ch03* folder.

2. Set the model display as  (Shading with Edges). The part displays as shown in Figure 3–139.

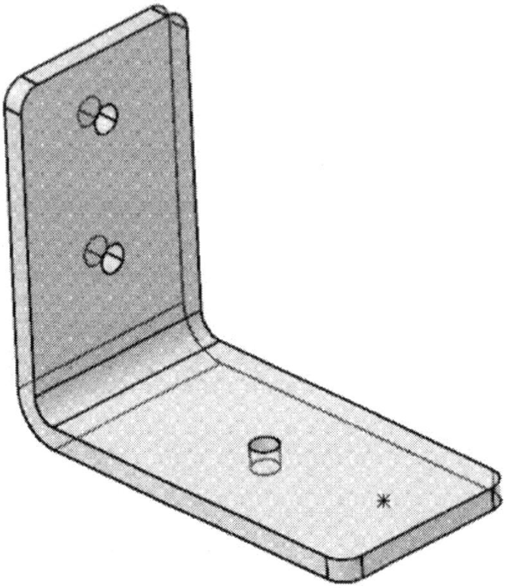

Figure 3–139

3. Select **Tools>Options>Parameters and Measures>Units** and set the units as follows:

   - Length: **Millimeter (mm)**
   - Force: **Newton (N)**
   - Moment: **Newton x Meter (Nxm)**
   - Pressure: **Megapascal (MPa)**

Task 2 - Apply the material.

1. Apply the **Aluminium** material from the **Default Material Catalog** to the part. Verify that the applied material has the following properties:

   - Young Modulus: **70000MPa**
   - Poisson Ratio: **0.346**
   - Density: **2710kg/m^3**
   - Thermal Expansion: **2.36e-005/Kdeg**
   - Yield Strength: **95MPa**

Task 3 - Start the GSA workbench.

1. Select **Start>Analysis & Simulation>Generative Structural Analysis**.

2. Select **Static Analysis** as the new analysis case.

Task 4 - Mesh the part.

1. Double-click on **OCTREE Tetrahedron Mesh.1: L-Bracket_03** in the tree and set the mesh parameters as follows:

   - Element type: **Parabolic**
   - Size: **12mm**
   - Absolute sag: **2mm**

Task 5 - Apply the restraints.

1. Select  (Clamp) and restrain the inside surfaces of the two holes, as shown in Figure 3–140.

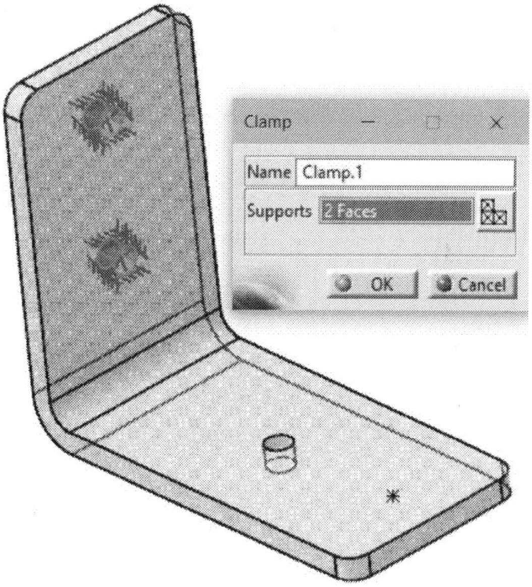

Figure 3–140

Task 6 - Apply the load.

1. Select  (Distributed Force) in the Forces toolbar. Select the point on the bottom flange of the part (**Point.2**) and apply **-200N** force in the **Y** direction, as shown in Figure 3–141.

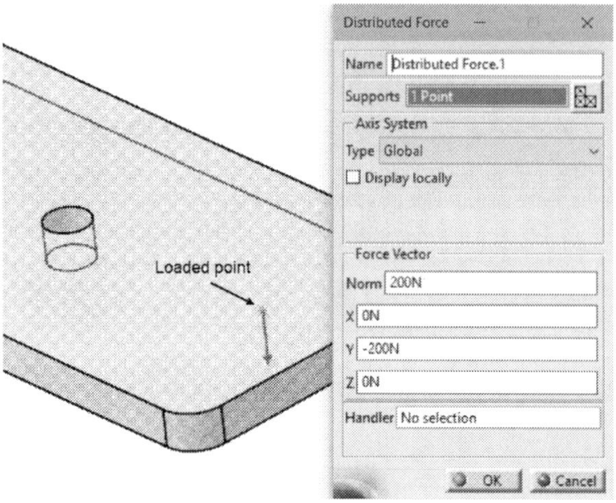

Figure 3–141

Task 7 - Run the analysis.

1. Select  (Compute) and start the computation. CATIA displays the Warnings dialog box, as shown in Figure 3–142.

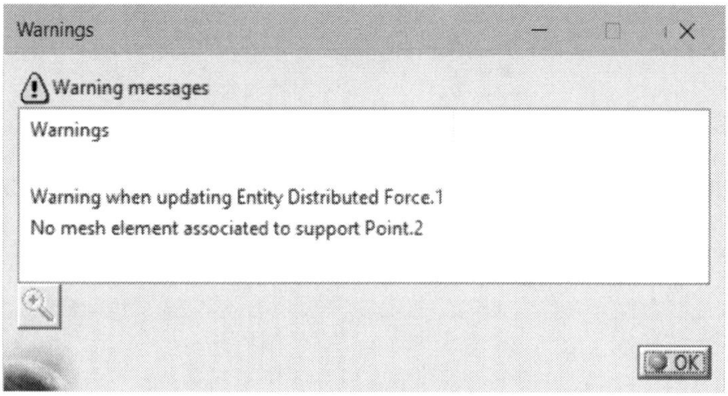

Figure 3–142

During the computation, CATIA transfers all the loads and constraints from the CAD geometry to the mesh. In this case, there was a problem transferring the load that was applied to the point in Task 6 to the mesh.

2. Click **OK** to close the Warnings dialog box and click **No** in the Computation Resource Estimation dialog box to abort the computation.

Task 8 - Visualize the mesh.

1. Right-click on **Nodes and Elements** in the tree and select **Mesh Visualization** to display the part mesh.

2. Double-click on **Mesh.1** in the tree and activate the **Display nodes of elements** option, as shown in Figure 3–143.

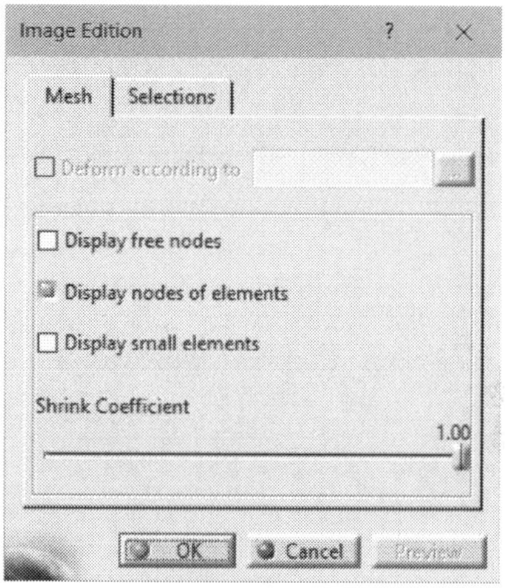

Figure 3–143

3. Click **OK**. The mesh is displayed, as shown in Figure 3–144. The red dots in the image indicate the mesh nodes.

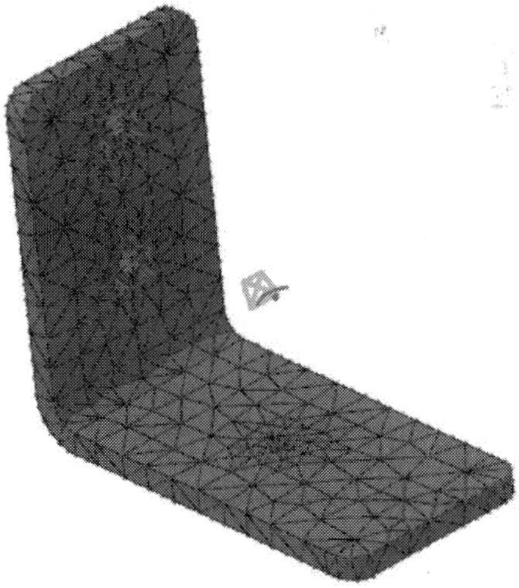

Figure 3–144

4. Unhide the **Links Manager.1** to show the CAD model. Zoom in on the loaded point and note that there is no mesh node matching the point, as shown in Figure 3–145.

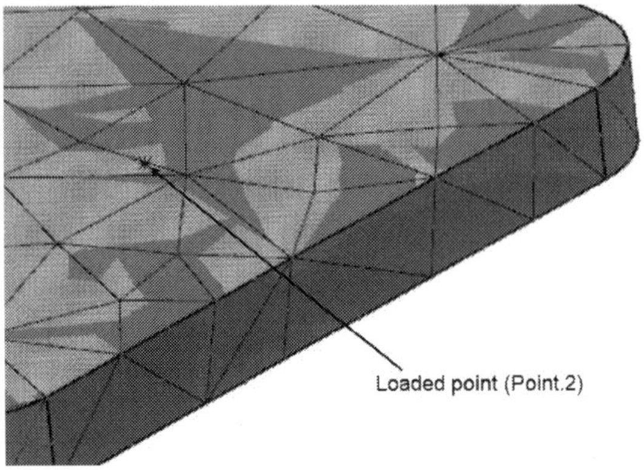

Figure 3–145

This is because, by default, CATIA does not include points on the surface of the part into the mesh. Therefore, the load applied to **Point.2** in Task 6 was unable to transfer to a mesh node, which caused an error.

Task 9 - Create an imposed point.

In this task, you will force CATIA to include the loaded point into the mesh of the part.

1. Right-click on **Mesh.1** in the tree and select **Activate/Deactivate** to deactivate the mesh visualization and return to the model view.

2. Double-click on **OCTREE Tetrahedron Mesh.1: L-Bracket-03** in the tree to display the OCTREE Tetrahedron Mesh dialog box. Click the *Local* tab, as shown in Figure 3–146.

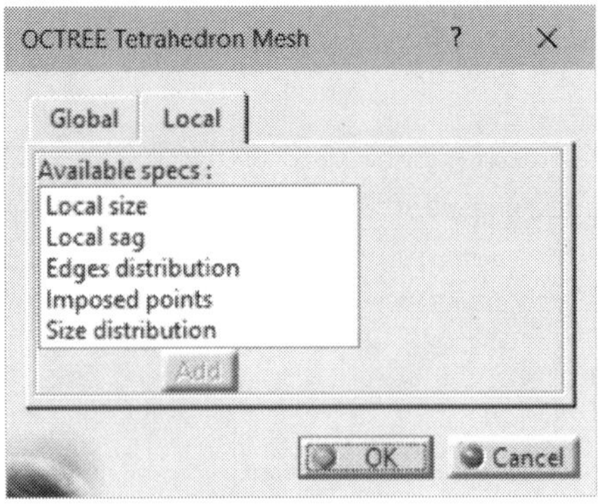

Figure 3–146

3. Select **Imposed points** in the *Available specs* list and click **Add**, as shown in Figure 3–147.

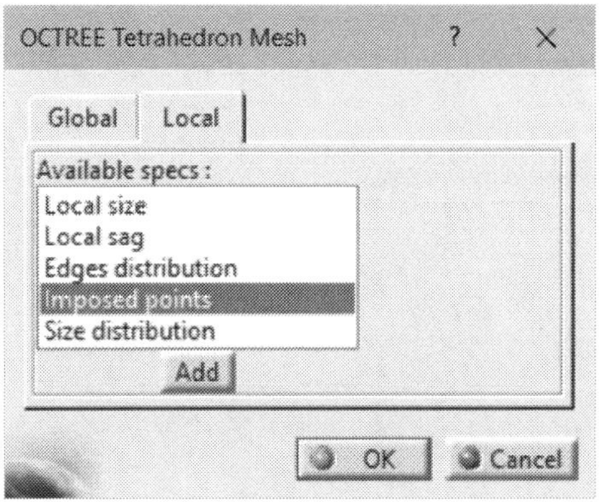

Figure 3–147

4. Once the Imposed Points dialog box opens, select the loaded point, as shown in Figure 3–148.

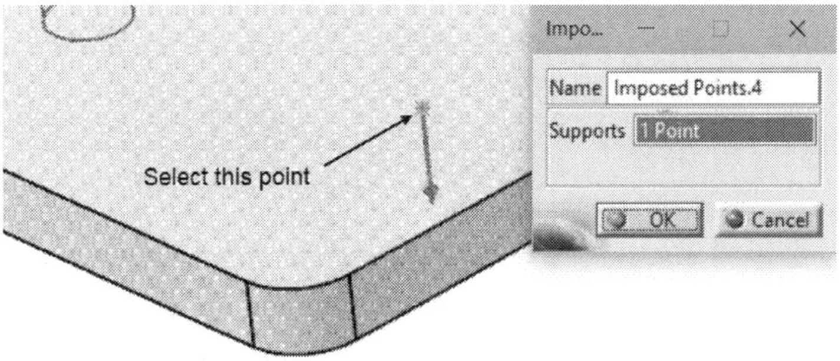

Figure 3–148

5. Click **OK** twice to close both the Imposed Points and OCTREE Tetrahedron Mesh dialog boxes.

6. Right-click on **Mesh.1** in the tree and select **Activate/Deactivate** to update and visualize the mesh.

7. Unhide the **Links Manager.1** to show the CAD model. Zoom in on the loaded point and note that now there is a mesh node matching the point, as shown in Figure 3–149.

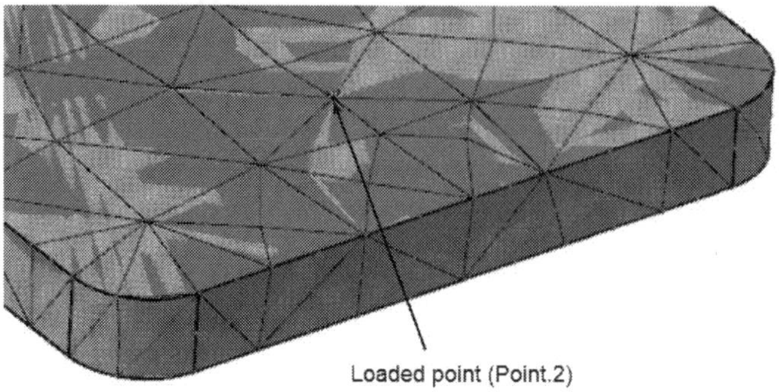

Figure 3–149

8. Right-click on **Mesh.1** in the tree and select **Delete** to delete the mesh visualization and return to the model view.

Task 10 - Run the analysis.

1. Select  (Compute) and run the analysis. Note that now CATIA completes the computation successfully, without issuing any error messages.

Task 11 - Display the displacement magnitude.

1. Change the view mode to  (Shading with Material).
2. Visualize the displacement magnitude **Average iso** image, as shown in Figure 3–150.

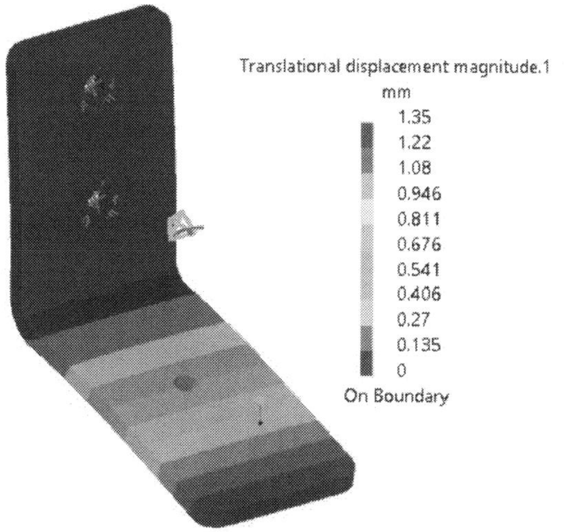

Figure 3–150

Note that the maximum displacement magnitude at the tip of the bottom flange is **1.35mm**. In the next task, you will measure displacement magnitude directly under the load.

Task 12 - Create local displacement sensor.

1. Right-click on **Translational displacement magnitude.1** in the tree and select **Activate/Deactivate** to deactivate the displacement image and return to the model view.

2. Right-click on **Sensors.1** in the tree and select **Create Local Sensor**, as shown in Figure 3–151.

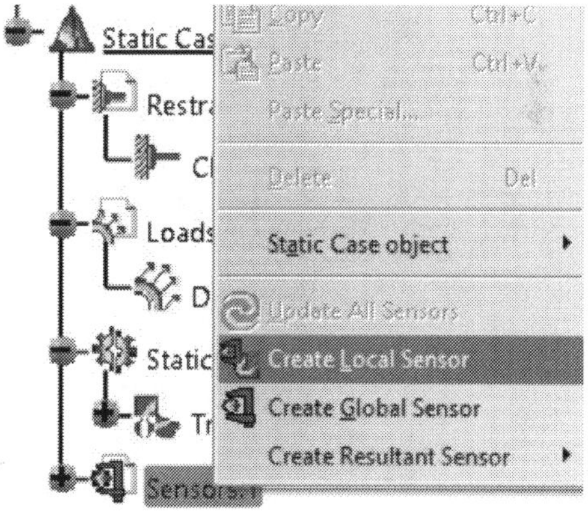

Figure 3–151

3. In the Create Sensor dialog box, select **Displacement Magnitude** and click **OK**, as shown in Figure 3–152.

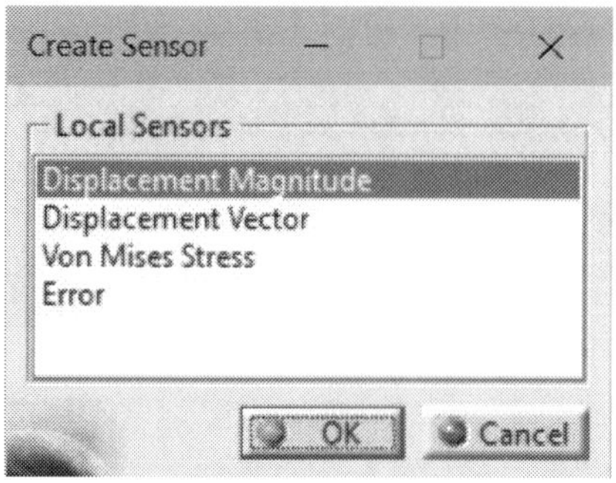

Figure 3–152

4. Double-click on the **Displacement Magnitude.1** sensor in the tree. In the Local Sensor dialog box that opens, select **Point.2** as the *Supports*. Select **None** from the Post-Treatment drop-down list and activate the **Create Parameters** option, as shown in Figure 3–153.

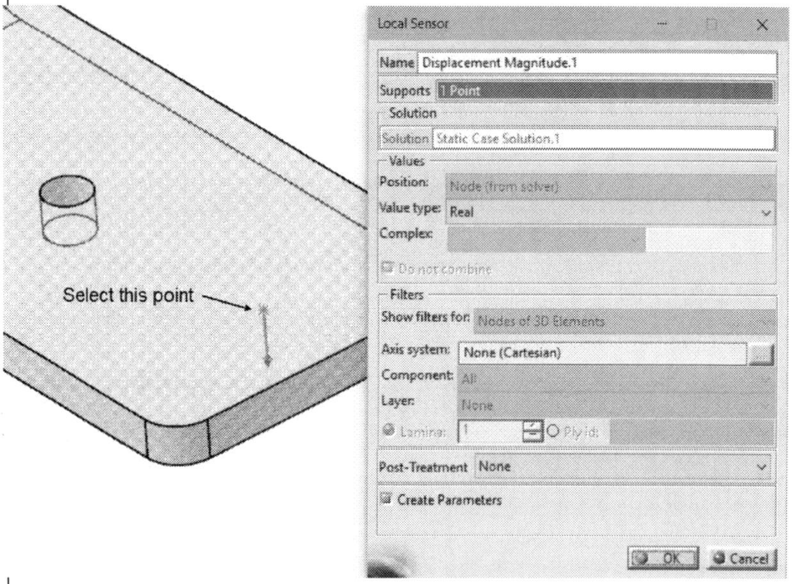

Figure 3–153

5. Click **OK** to close the Local Sensor dialog box. CATIA creates a new **Displacement Magnitude.1** sensor in the tree but does not update it yet.

6. Right-click on the **Displacement Magnitude.1** sensor and select **Update Sensor** in the contextual menu. CATIA updates the sensor and shows the value in the tree, as shown in Figure 3–154.

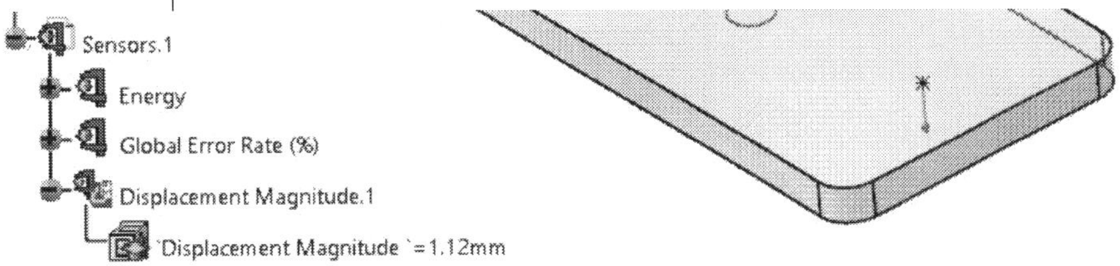

Figure 3–154

Task 13 - Display Von Mises stress.

1. Hide **Restraints** and **Loads**.
2. Display and animate the **Von Mises Stress** plot. On step 10 of the animation, the stress image displays as shown in Figure 3–155.

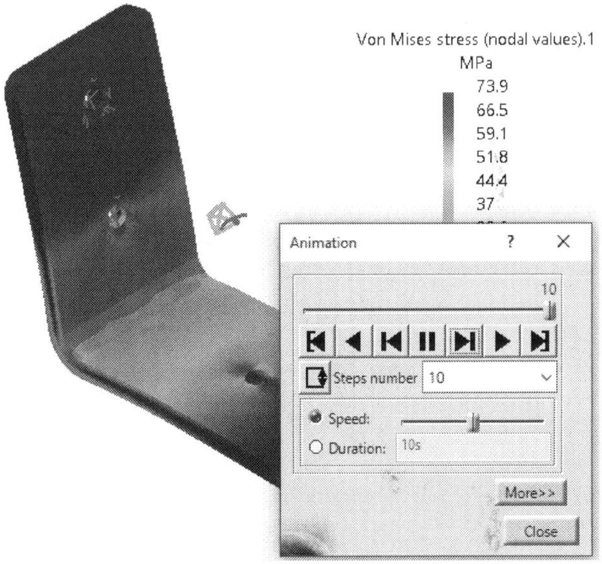

Figure 3–155

3. Close the animation.
4. Right-click on **Von Mises stress (nodal values).1** in the tree and select **Activate/Deactivate** to delete the stress image from the screen and return to the model view.

Task 14 - Save and close the files.

1. Optionally, save the analysis document and the part for future reference.
2. Close both the analysis and the part documents.

Practice 3e Stress Analysis of a Pressure Vessel

Practice Objectives

- Apply the material and mesh the model.
- Apply symmetry restraints.
- Apply pressure load.
- Run the analysis and display the results.

In this practice, you will set up and run a static stress analysis on the pressure vessel shown in Figure 3–156, with minimum instruction.

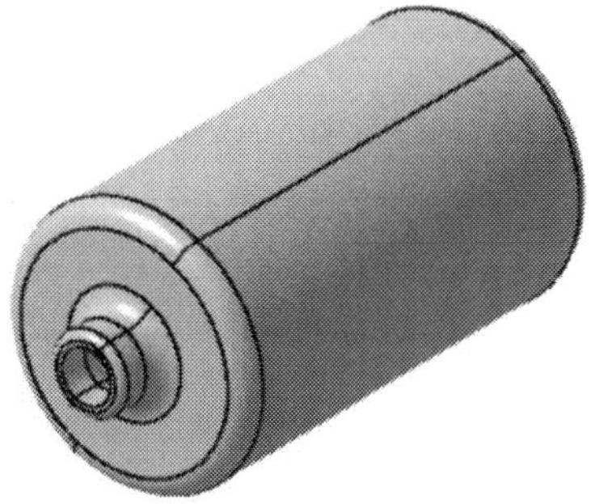

Figure 3–156

Task 1 - Prepare the CAD model.

1. Open **Tank_03.CATPart** from the *CATIA Generative Structural Analysis Practice Files\Ch03* folder.

2. From the full model, create the 45 deg segment (i.e., 1/8) of the model, as shown in Figure 3–157.

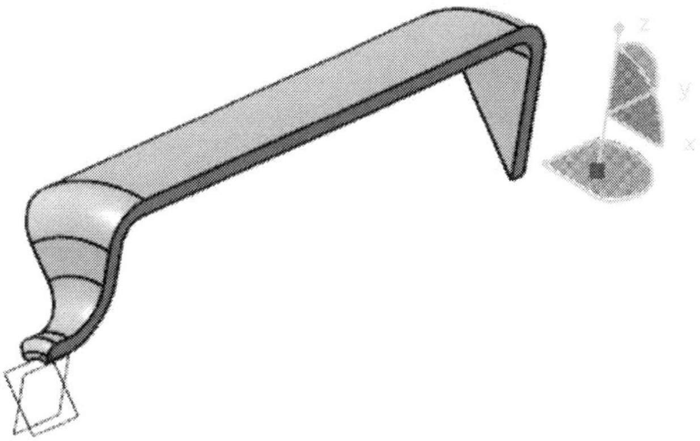

Figure 3–157

3. Apply the **Steel** material to the part.

Task 2 - Prepare the analysis model.

1. Start the GSA workbench.
2. Mesh the model with the following parameters:
   - Element type: **Parabolic**
   - Size: 1.8 times the thickness of the tank
   - Sag: 10% of the mesh size
3. Visually examine the mesh.
4. Using  (Surface Slider), apply symmetry restraints on both cutout surfaces, as shown in Figure 3–158.

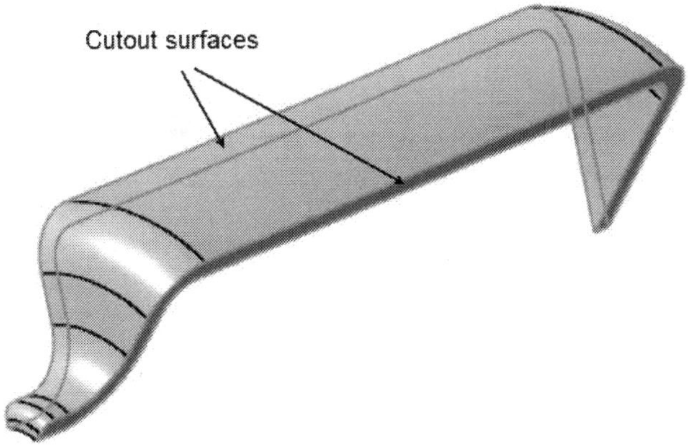

Figure 3–158

5. Using  (User-defined Restraint), restrain the end surface of the tank in the **Y** direction, as shown in Figure 3–159.

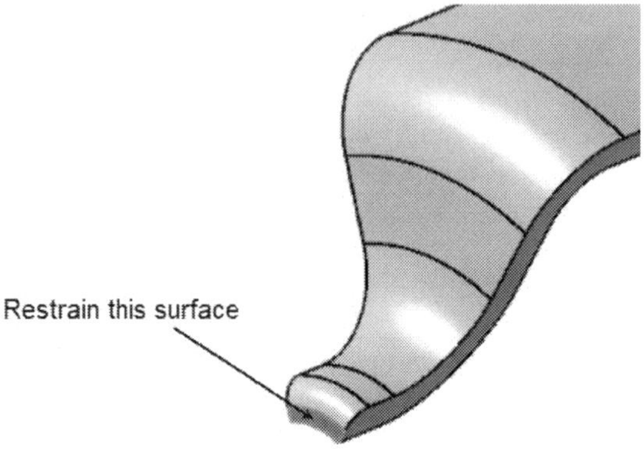

Figure 3–159

6. Apply **800psi** pressure to all of the inside surfaces of the tank, as shown in Figure 3–160.

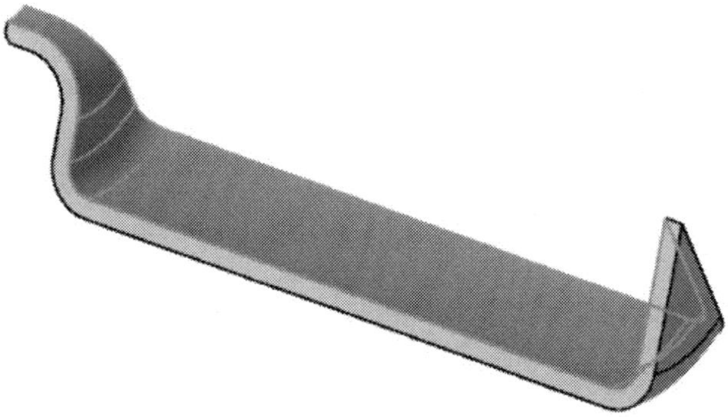

Figure 3–160

Task 3 - Run the analysis.

1. Check the model for inconsistencies.
2. Run the analysis.

Task 4 - Visualize and examine the analysis results.

Factor of Safety value is obtained by dividing the material's yield strength by the maximum stress in the model.

1. Visualize and animate the deformed mesh. Does the part deform according to the applied loads?
2. Display the displacement magnitude color plot. What is the value of the maximum displacement in the model?
3. Display the Von Mises color plot. Does the maximum stress exceed the yield strength of the material? What is the value of the factor of safety for the part?
4. Find the location of the maximum stress. Can you think of design changes that would lead to a decrease in the stress level in that area?
5. Close the model without saving.

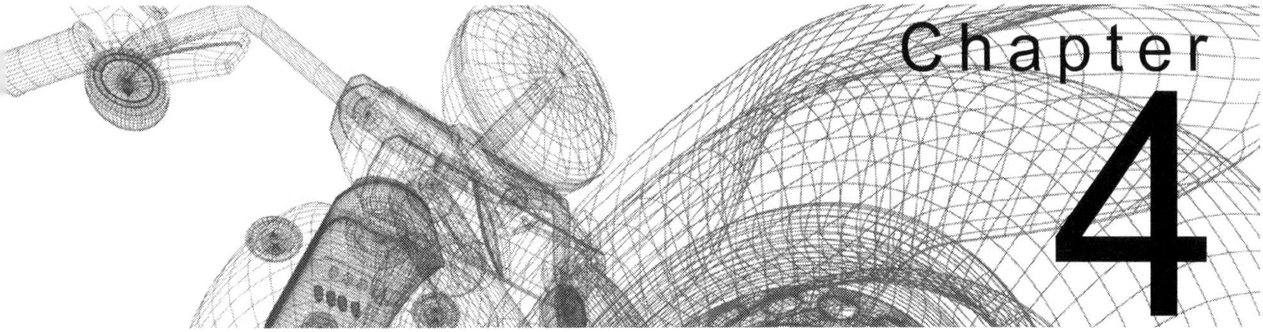

Mesh Refinement and Adaptivity

Any FEA solution is an approximation, which means it always contains some amount of error. Bringing the FEA approximation error to acceptable levels is a critical aspect of developing an accurate simulation.

In this chapter, you learn about the tools available for the FEA solution refinement in CATIA's GSA workbench.

Learning Objectives in This Chapter

- Understand the discretization error.
- Understand the Global Error Rate sensor.
- Understand the difference between linear and parabolic element types.
- Learn how to refine the mesh manually.
- Use the mesh Adaptivity tool to refine the mesh automatically.

4.1 Precision Image

In structural FEA, the approximation functions are built in such a way that displacement continuity across inter-element boundaries is guaranteed.

The stress contours are then computed based on the relative displacements of the nodes of each element and are not necessarily continuous from one finite element to the next. Essentially, this discontinuity of the stress contour from one element to another is the discretization error. As the size of each element is reduced during the mesh refinement process, the discretization error decreases too.

The amount of stress discontinuity at each mesh node can be used as a measure of the stress error at that node. CATIA integrates the stress error over the volume of each element and reports it as a strain energy error.

Select  (Precision) in the Image toolbar to display the strain energy error result plot, as shown in Figure 4–1.

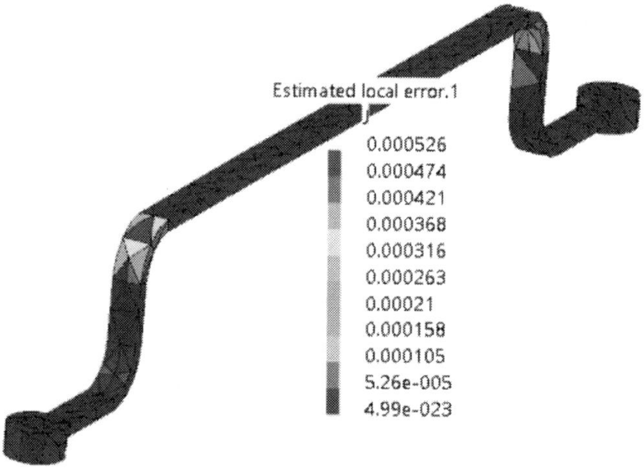

Figure 4–1

The strain energy error image represents a visual map of the discretization error for a given computation. The image provides an insight as to the areas in the model where the results are relatively accurate and where they are not.

- The areas with the greater strain energy error (red- and yellow-colored finite elements) are least accurate. The mesh in those areas should be refined.
- The areas with the lower strain energy error (blue-colored finite elements) are relatively accurate.

The image provides qualitative rather than quantitative information to the user. The value of the strain energy error cannot be directly related to, for instance, error in stress.

4.2 Global Error Rate

Additionally, CATIA sums the energy error for each element and reports a total energy error for the entire model as the percentage of the total strain energy in the model. The measure is called **Global Error Rate** and is located in the **Sensors.1** section of the specification tree, as shown in Figure 4–2.

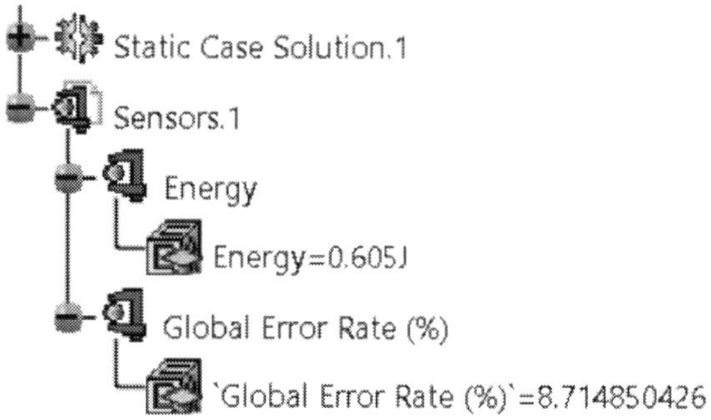

Figure 4–2

Large values of energy error imply that the stress field is very discontinuous, and small values of energy error imply a more continuous stress field.

While there are no absolutes regarding permissible values for energy error, a maximum percentage error of 5% is typically recommended in the literature for the general-purpose structural analysis.

4.3 Changing Element Type

As discussed in Chapter 2, you can use either linear elements or parabolic elements in the GSA analysis.

The use of linear elements results in faster computation time. However, linear elements also result in a much larger discretization error than parabolic elements and should be used with caution.

If you used linear elements in your analysis and the global error rate is unsatisfactory, the first recommended action is that you change the element type to **Parabolic**.

To do so, double-click on the mesh object in the tree to open the OCTREE Tetrahedron Mesh dialog box and activate **Parabolic** as the *Element type*, as shown in Figure 4–3.

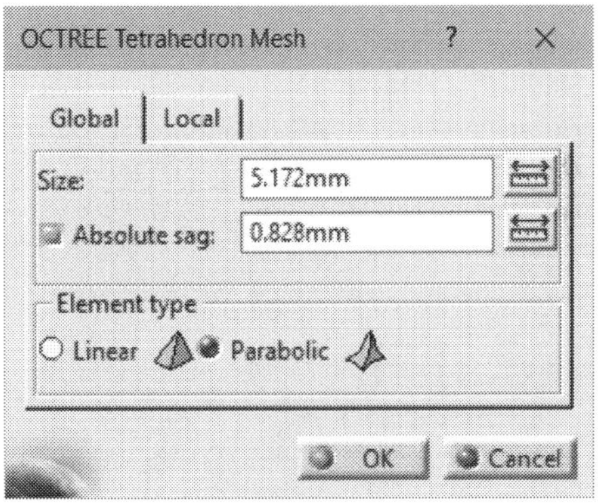

Figure 4–3

Alternatively, you can select  (Element Type) in the Model Manager toolbar and select **Parabolic** in the Element Type dialog box, as shown in Figure 4–4.

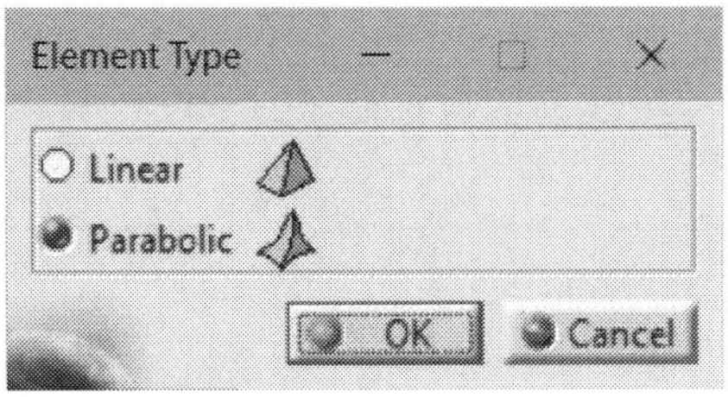

Figure 4–4

If you used parabolic elements in your analysis and the error rate is still unsatisfactory, the only course of action is to use a denser mesh.

4.4 Mesh Refinement Process

Refining the mesh in order to obtain the required analysis accuracy is an iterative process, as shown in Figure 4–5.

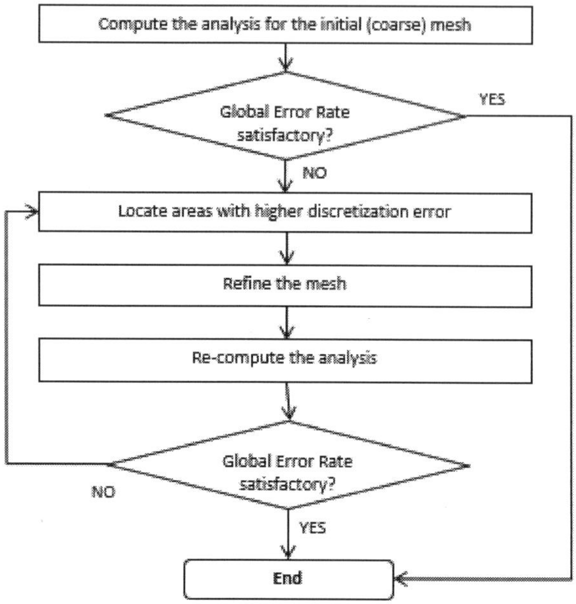

Figure 4–5

The process starts with performing an initial computation with a coarse mesh and checking the global error rate value.

If the error rate is too high, the next steps are:

1. Using the Precision result plot, locate the areas with the higher discretization error.
2. Refine the mesh accordingly.
3. Re-compute the analysis and re-check the global error rate.

Since it is extremely difficult to predict the mesh size that will yield the necessary analysis accuracy, these steps may have to be repeated several times, thus decreasing the error to the acceptable level in iterations.

4.5 Global and Local Mesh Refinement

The mesh in your model could be refined globally or locally.

With global mesh refinement, the mesh size is reduced evenly throughout the entire volume, as shown in Figure 4–6.

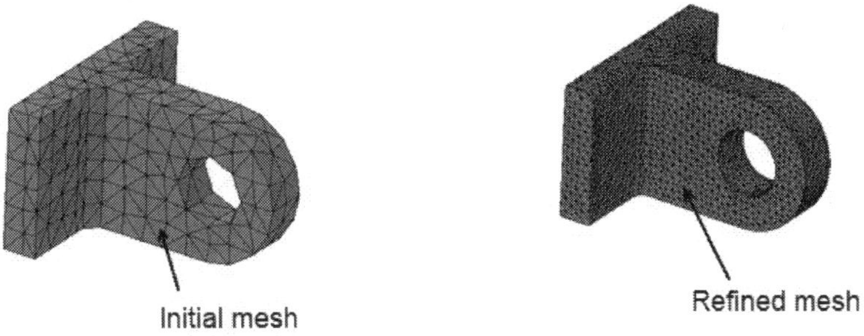

Figure 4–6

Global mesh refinement is a workable but uneconomic strategy, since analysis computation time and memory requirements will increase exponentially.

With local mesh refinement, the mesh is only made denser in local areas with higher discretization error, as shown in Figure 4–7.

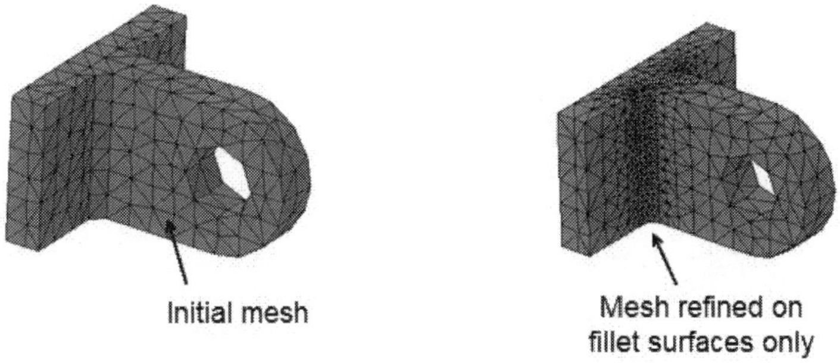

Figure 4–7

Local mesh refinement is the most efficient strategy that achieves an accurate solution with the least expense in terms of computation time and memory.

Global Mesh Specification

The global mesh specification is in the *Global* tab of the OCTREE Tetrahedron Mesh dialog box, as shown in Figure 4–8.

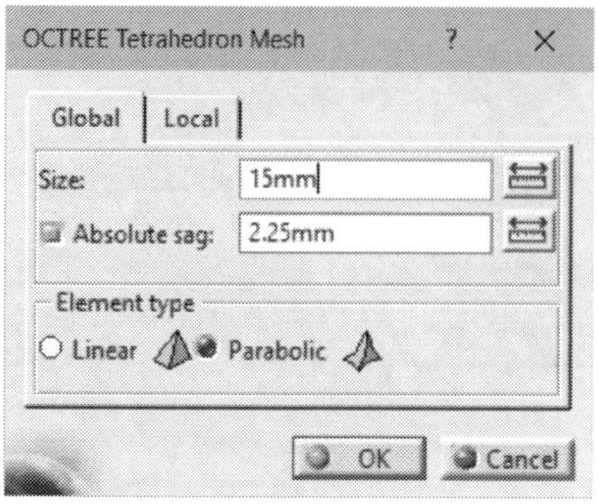

Figure 4–8

To increase the mesh density globally, throughout your entire model, reduce the *Size* and, optionally, the *Absolute sag* values.

Local Mesh Specification

The local mesh specifications are in the *Local* tab of the OCTREE Tetrahedron Mesh dialog box, as shown in Figure 4–9.

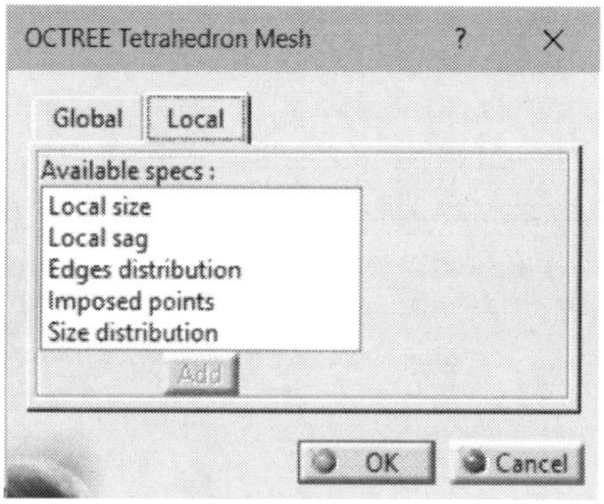

Figure 4–9

The available local mesh specification options are described in the following table.

Mesh Specification	Description
Local size	Applies local mesh size on selected surfaces or edges
Local sag	Applies local mesh sag on selected surfaces or edges
Edges distribution	Specifies number of mesh nodes along selected edges
Imposed points	Creates mesh nodes at the selected surface points
Size distribution	Specifies mesh edges size on selected edges

To apply a local mesh specification, select an option from the list, click **Add**, and select the geometrical support, such as a surface or an edge in the model. For example, the dialog box for the **Local size** specification is shown in Figure 4–10.

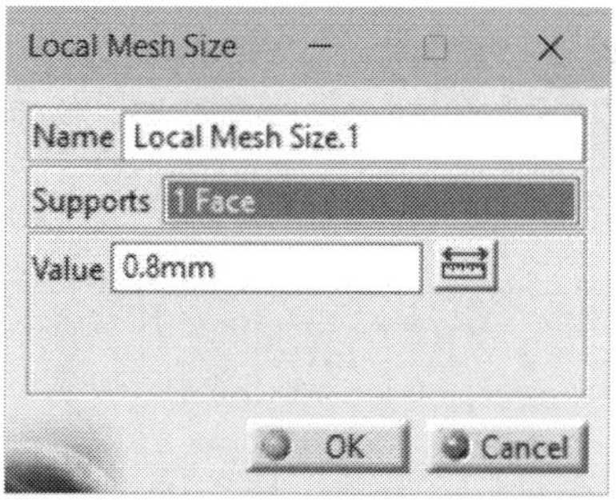

Figure 4–10

4.6 Mesh Adaptivity

The iterative mesh refinement process described previously in Figure 4–5 can be fully automated in GSA, using the **Adaptivity** tool.

The Adaptivity tool automatically, without user involvement, refines the mesh based on the discretization error map. The algorithm implements a computational technique called *predictive error estimation*.

1. Once the analysis is computed, the discretization error map is calculated, similarly to the Precision result plot.
2. Based on the discretization error map, the new mesh size is estimated for the areas with higher error and a new mesh size map is created.
3. The mesh is refined and the analysis is re-computed.
4. The process continues until either the accuracy objective is achieved or the user-set limit on the number of mesh refinement iterations is reached.

Running an analysis with mesh adaptivity is a two-step process.

First, you set up the accuracy objective. In the Adaptivity toolbar, select  (New Adaptivity Entity) and select the mesh, or meshes, in your model. The Global Adaptivity dialog box displays the **Current Error** in the model, and you enter your **Objective Error**, as shown in Figure 4–11.

For assemblies, you must select all meshes in the model as the adaptivity Supports.

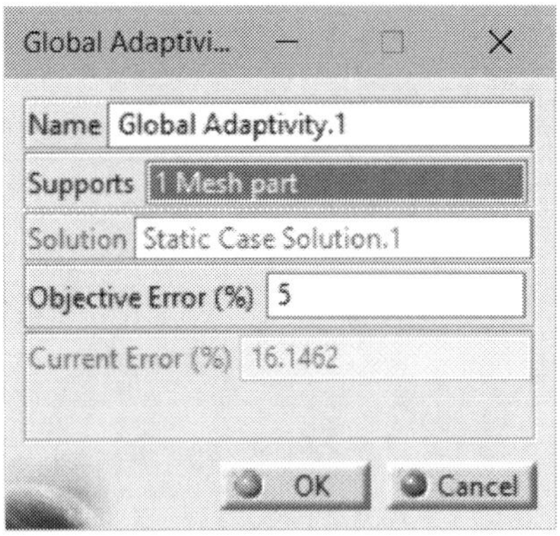

Figure 4–11

The computation does not yet start when you click **OK** to close the Global Adaptivity dialog box.

To start the computation, select  (Compute with Adaptivity) in the Compute toolbar. In the Adaptivity Process Parameters dialog box, enter the computation parameters and click **OK**, as shown in Figure 4–12.

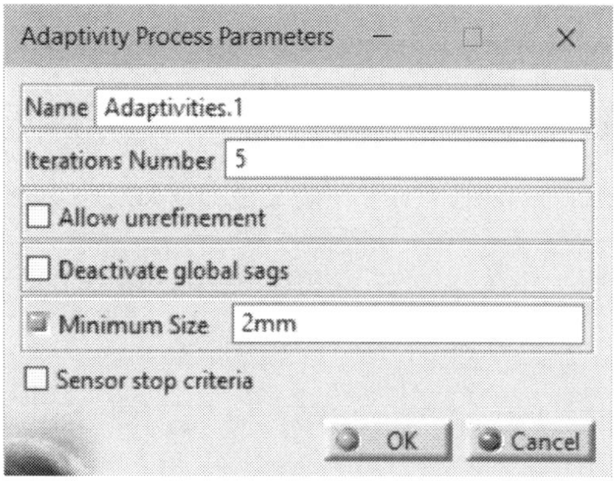

Figure 4–12

The adaptivity process parameters are described in the following table.

Option or Parameter	Description
Iterations Number	Maximum number of mesh refinement iterations. This is a “hard” limit; the process stops even if the user-specified accuracy objective has not yet been achieved.
Allow unrefinement	Enables CATIA to “unrefine” the mesh (i.e., make elements larger where appropriate).
Deactivate global sags	Enables deactivation of the mesh sag parameter while unrefining.
Minimum Size	Imposes a minimum size of elements. This is a “hard” limit; the process stops with a warning message whenever CATIA determines that a smaller element size would be required in order to achieve the accuracy objective.

Note that adaptive computation may take considerable time, depending on the complexity of the model, the accuracy objective, and the number of iterations.

Practice 4a Mesh Refinement

Practice Objectives

- Apply the material and mesh the model.
- Apply loads and restraints.
- Run the analysis and display the results.
- Use local mesh refinement to achieve the required analysis accuracy.

In this practice, you will set up and run a static stress analysis on the link part shown in Figure 4–13. You will also refine the mesh in order to achieve analysis accuracy to within 2% of the Global Error Rate.

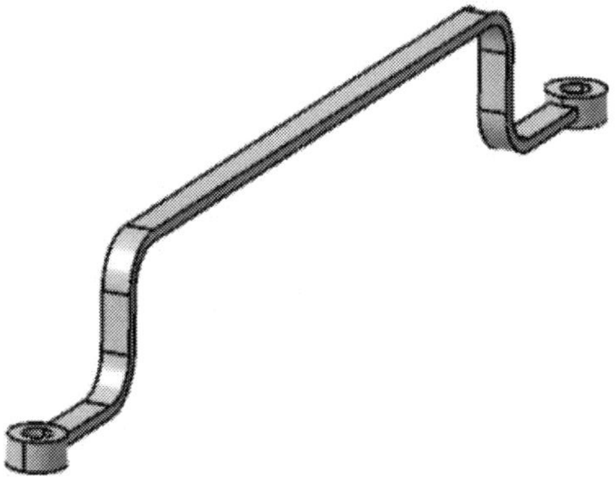

Figure 4–13

Task 1 - Open the part in CATIA.

1. Open **Link_04.CATPart** from the *CATIA Generative Structural Analysis Practice Files\Ch04* folder.

2. Set the model display as  (Shading with Edges). The part displays as shown in Figure 4–14.

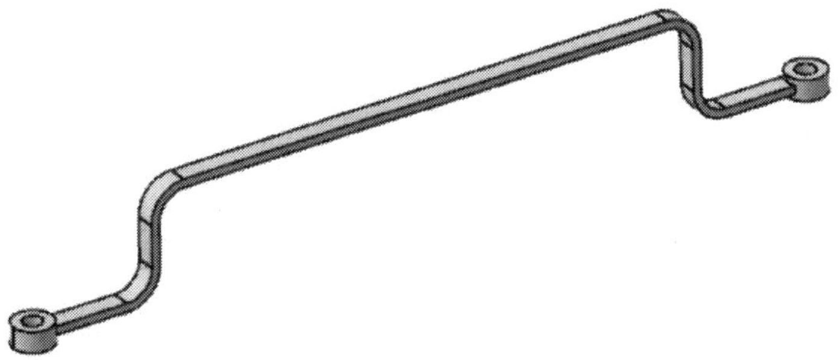

Figure 4–14

3. Select **Tools>Options>Parameters and Measures>Units** and set the units as follows:

   - Length: **Millimeter (mm)**
   - Force: **Newton (N)**
   - Moment: **Newton x Meter (Nxm)**
   - Pressure: **Megapascal (MPa)**

Task 2 - Apply the material.

1. Apply the **Titanium** material from the **Default Material Catalog** to the part. Verify that the applied material has the following properties:

   - Young Modulus: **114000MPa**
   - Poisson Ratio: **0.34**
   - Density: **4460kg/m^3**
   - Thermal Expansion: **9.5e-006/Kdeg**
   - Yield Strength: **825MPa**

Task 3 - Start the GSA workbench.

1. Select **Start>Analysis & Simulation>Generative Structural Analysis**.

2. Select **Static Analysis** as the new analysis case.

Task 4 - Mesh the part.

1. Double-click on **OCTREE Tetrahedron Mesh.1: Link_04** in the tree and set up the mesh parameters as shown in Figure 4–15:

   - Element type: **Linear**
   - Size: **15mm**
   - Absolute sag: 15% of the size

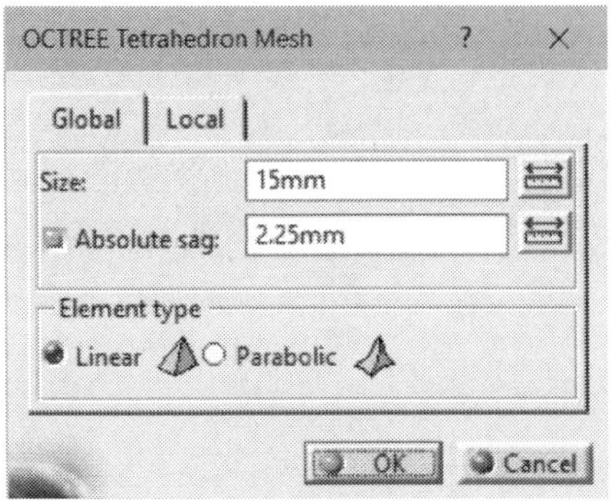

Figure 4–15

2. Right-click on **Nodes and Elements** in the tree and select **Mesh Visualization** to display the mesh.

3. Double-click on **Mesh.1** in the tree and activate the **Display nodes of elements** option. The part mesh is displayed, as shown in Figure 4–16.

Figure 4–16

The red dots indicate the mesh nodes. Note that element edges do not have middle nodes, because the element type is **Linear**.

4. Right-click on **Mesh.1** in the tree and select **Activate/Deactivate** to deactivate the mesh visualization and return to the model view.

Task 5 - Apply restraints.

1. Select  (Clamp) and restrain the inside surface of the hole on one end, as shown in Figure 4–17.

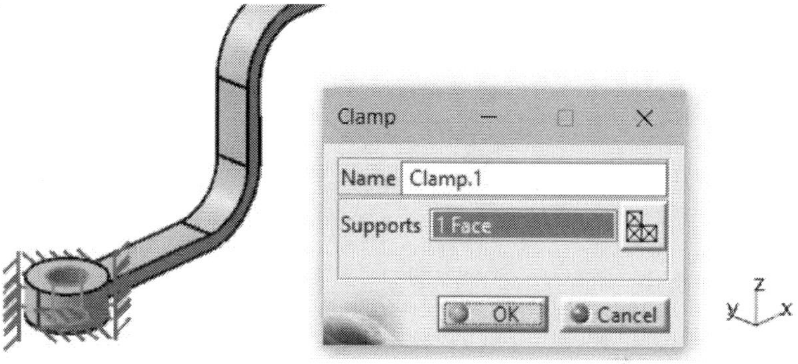

Figure 4–17

Task 6 - Apply loads.

1. Select  (Distributed Force) and apply **100N** force in the **X** direction to the inside surface of the hole on the other end of the part, as shown in Figure 4–18.

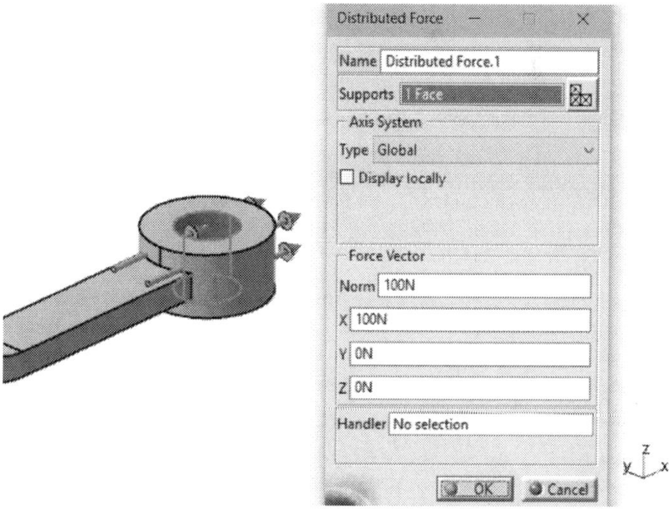

Figure 4–18

Task 7 - Run the analysis.

1. Run the analysis and wait until it completes.
2. Expand the tree and note that the value of the **Global Error Rate** sensor is approximately **66%**, as shown in Figure 4–19. This means that the analysis has a very poor accuracy; the recommended Global Error Rate value for general-purpose stress analysis should be within 5%.

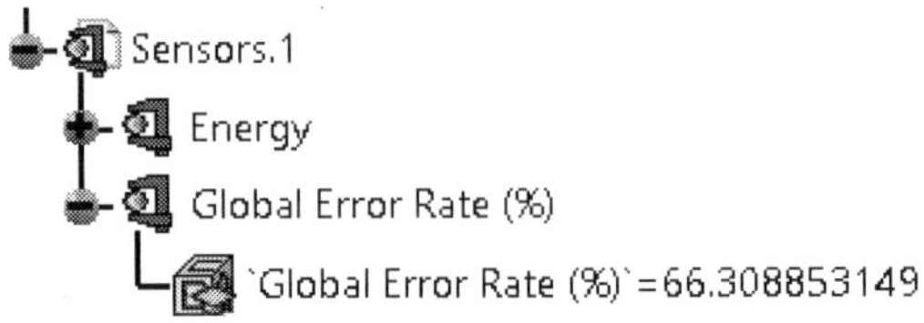

Figure 4–19

Task 8 - Change element type.

1. Double-click on **OCTREE Tetrahedron Mesh.1: Link_04** in the tree and change the *Element type* to **Parabolic**, as shown in Figure 4–20.

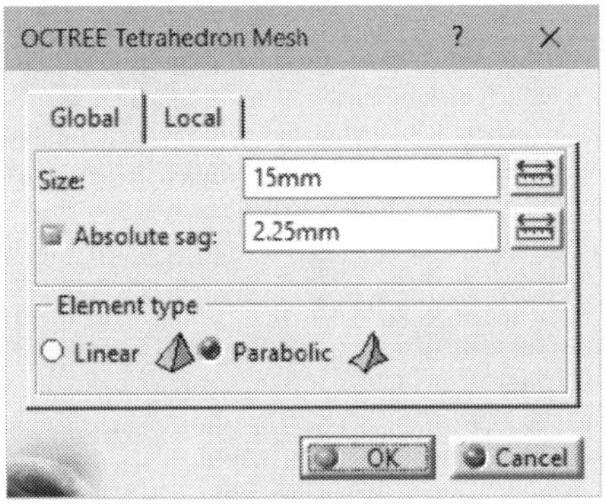

Figure 4–20

2. Re-run the analysis.

Parabolic elements provide much better accuracy than Linear elements, with the same mesh size. Therefore, Parabolic elements are the recommended option for the general-purpose stress analysis.

3. Note that the value of the **Global Error Rate** sensor has decreased from 66% to **10.3%**, as shown in Figure 4–21.

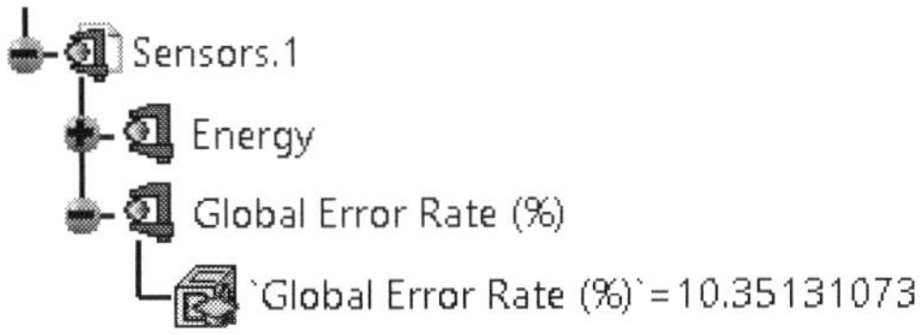

Figure 4–21

Task 9 - Refine the mesh.

The target error rate in this analysis is 2% or less. The current error rate of 10.3% could be brought down to under 2% by:

- Global mesh refinement, in which the element size is made smaller globally (i.e., in the entire model). This is a workable but inefficient strategy, as it typically leads to an unnecessarily large number of finite elements.
- Local mesh refinement, in which the mesh is only refined in the inaccurate areas of the model, leaving the mesh in the already accurate areas unchanged. This is the most efficient strategy, leading to good accuracy with the least computational expense.

In this task, you will perform local mesh refinement.

1. In the Image toolbar, select (Precision). The **Estimated local error** result plot displays, as shown in Figure 4–22.

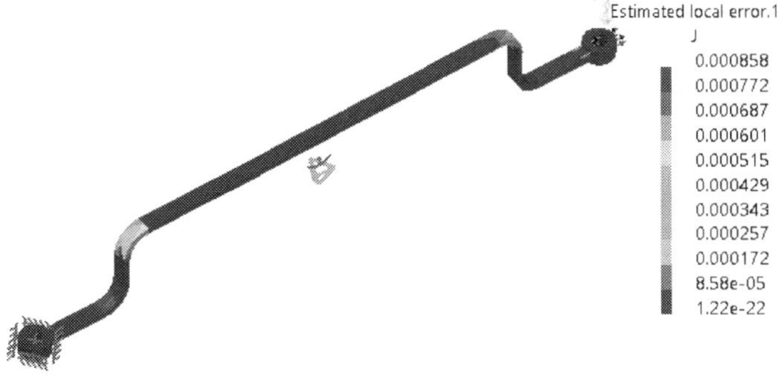

Figure 4–22

The image displays distribution of strain energy error throughout the model, and it provides information as to which areas of the mesh should be refined in order to improve the analysis accuracy. The elements colored in red or yellow should be refined, while the elements colored in blue should be left intact.

2. Note that the red and yellow elements are concentrated around the upper bends in the part, as shown in Figure 4–23. This is where you will refine the mesh.

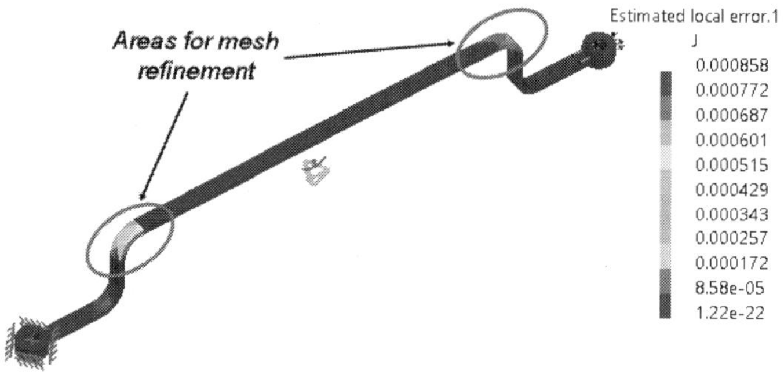

Figure 4–23

3. Right-click on the **Estimated local error.1** in the tree and select **Activate/Deactivate** to return to the model view.

4. Double-click on **OCTREE Tetrahedron Mesh.1: Link_04** in the tree to open the OCTREE Tetrahedron Mesh dialog box. Select the *Local* tab, as shown in Figure 4–24.

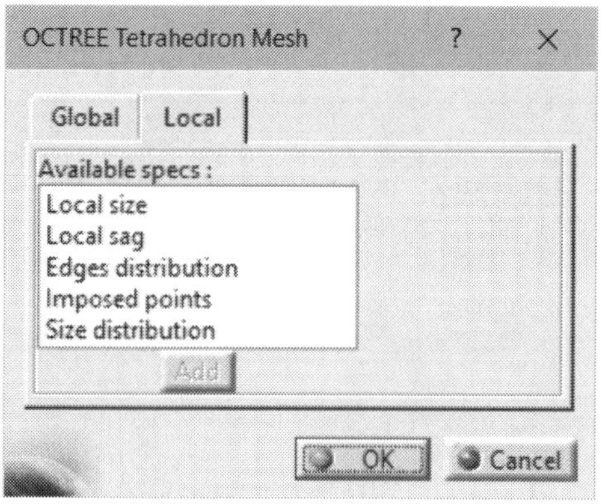

Figure 4–24

5. Select **Local size** and click **Add**, as shown in Figure 4–25.

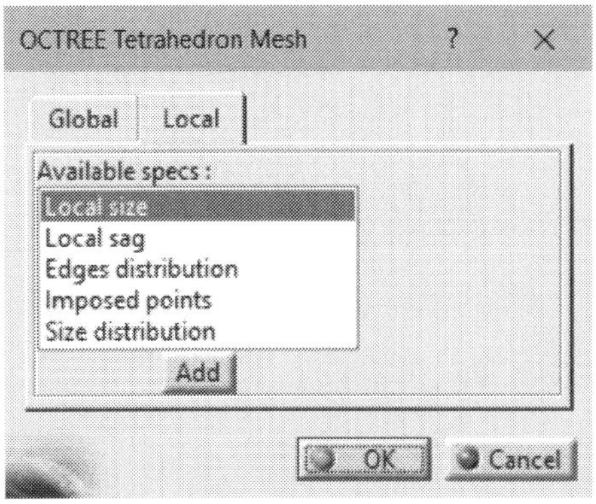

Figure 4–25

It is nearly impossible to predict exactly which mesh size would yield the desired analysis accuracy. Therefore, it may require several mesh refinements, gradually moving from larger to even smaller elements, to achieve the desired accuracy. The 5mm size will be your first attempt.

6. Once the Local Mesh Size dialog box opens, select the four surfaces on both upper bends in the part and enter **5mm** as the *Value*, as shown in Figure 4–26.

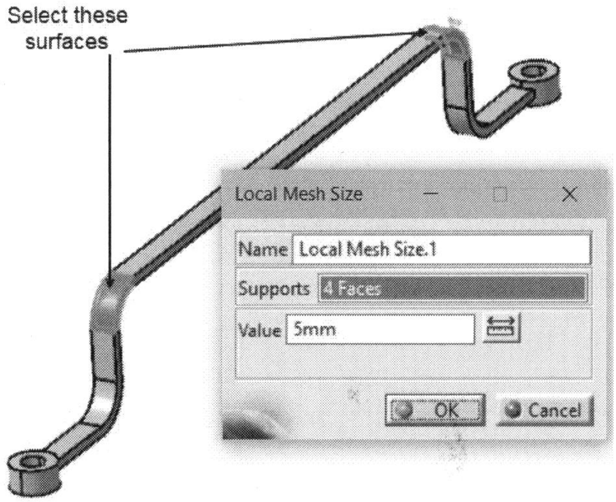

Figure 4–26

7. Click **OK** twice to close both the Local Mesh Size and OCTREE Tetrahedron Mesh dialog boxes.

8. Right-click on **Mesh.1** in the tree and select **Activate/Deactivate**. CATIA updates and displays the mesh. Zoom in on one of the bends and note the finer mesh in the area, as shown in Figure 4–27.

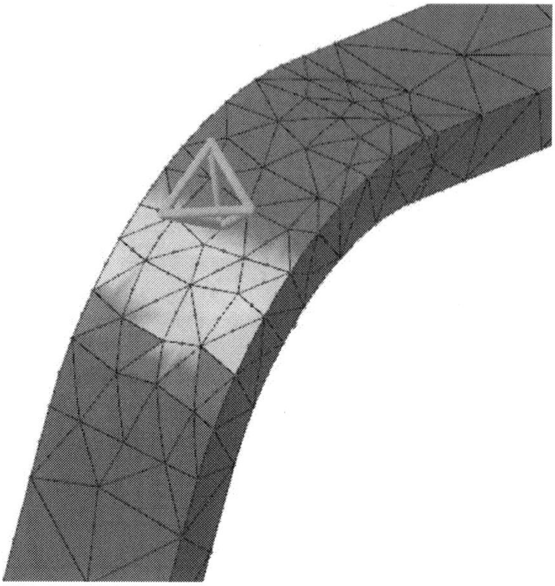

Figure 4–27

9. Right-click on **Mesh.1** in the tree and select **Activate/Deactivate** to return to the model view.

Task 10 - Re-run the analysis.

1. Re-run the analysis.

2. Note that the value of the **Global Error Rate** sensor has decreased from 10.3% to **2.7%**, as shown in Figure 4–28. This is a much better accuracy, but it is still short of the 2% error objective for this specific analysis.

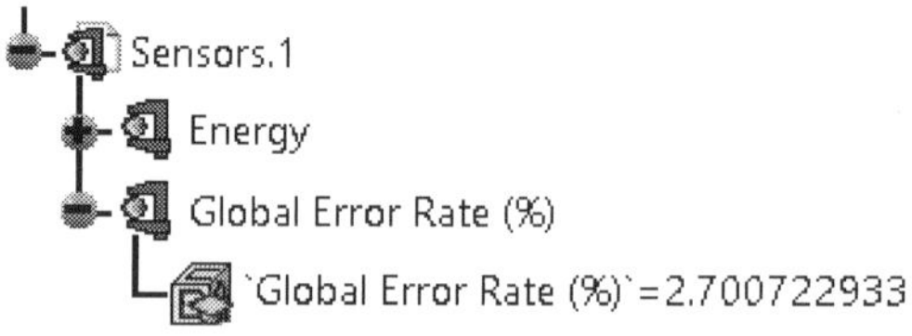

Figure 4–28

Task 11 - Refine the mesh.

In this task, you will further refine the mesh in order to achieve your objective of 2% or less error rate. Note that in general cases, this process may require several mesh refinement iterations, with the mesh progressively refined to a smaller and smaller size, until the desired accuracy is achieved.

1. Right-click on **Estimated local error.1** in the tree and select **Activate/Deactivate** to visualize the **Estimated local error** image. Examine the error image and note that now the elements that display the highest level of error are located just below the upper bends, as shown in Figure 4–29. Also, the elements in the upper bends, which you refined in Task 9, still exhibit a noticeable amount of error.

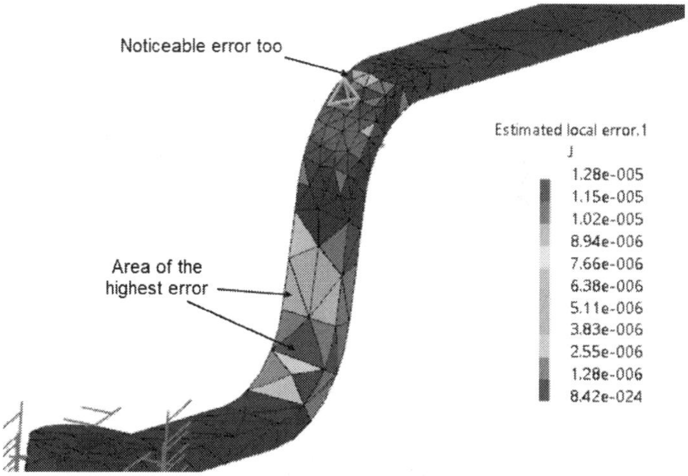

Figure 4–29

2. Right-click on **Estimated local error.1** in the tree and select **Activate/Deactivate** to return to the model view.

3. Double-click on **Local Mesh Size.1** in the tree and change the *Value* from 5mm to **2mm**, as shown in Figure 4–30. This will further refine the mesh in the upper bends.

Figure 4–30

4. Double-click on **OCTREE Tetrahedron Mesh.1: Link_04** in the tree, switch to the *Local* tab, and apply **4mm Local size** to the eight surfaces, as shown in Figure 4–31.

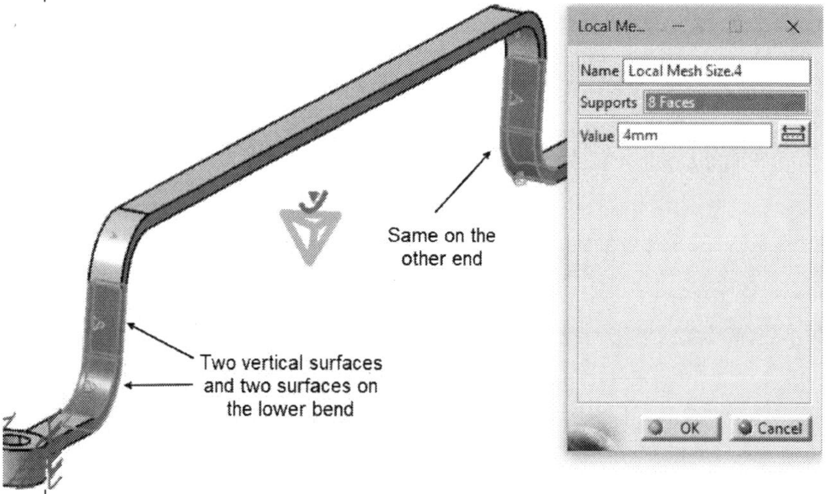

Figure 4–31

5. Visualize and examine the refined mesh, as shown in Figure 4–32.

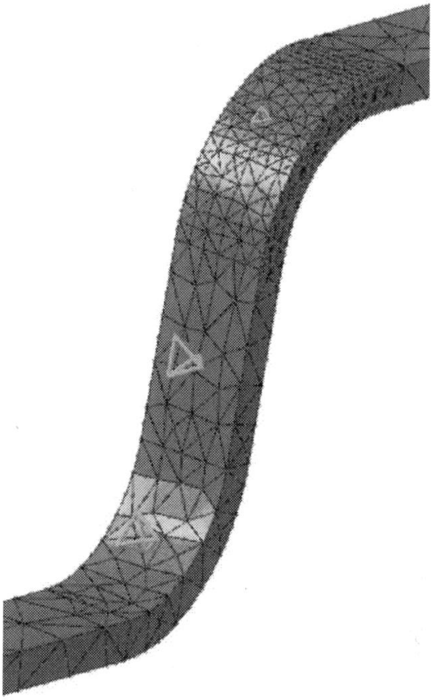

Figure 4–32

6. Right-click on **Mesh.1** in the tree and select **Activate/Deactivate** to return to the model view.

Task 12 - Re-run the analysis.

1. Re-run the analysis.

2. Note that the value of the **Global Error Rate** sensor has decreased from 2.7% to **1%**, as shown in Figure 4–33. This is well within the target value of 2%, so you can now proceed to reviewing the analysis results.

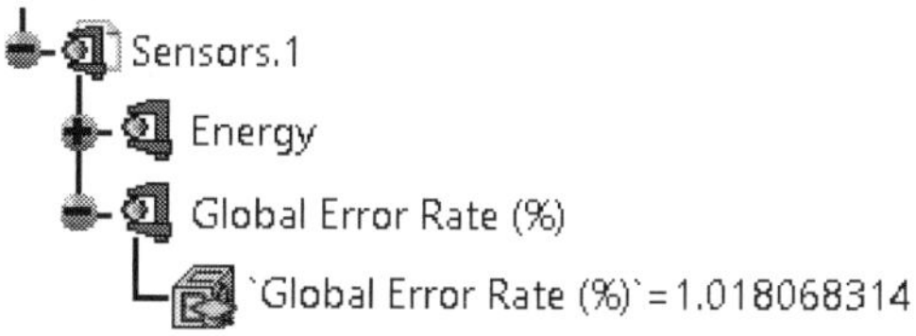

Figure 4–33

Task 13 - Display the displacement magnitude.

1. Change the view mode to (Shading with Material).
2. Right-click on **Nodes and Elements** and select **Hide/Show** to hide the mesh symbols in the model view.
3. Visualize the displacement magnitude image, overlaid over the CAD model, as shown in Figure 4–34.

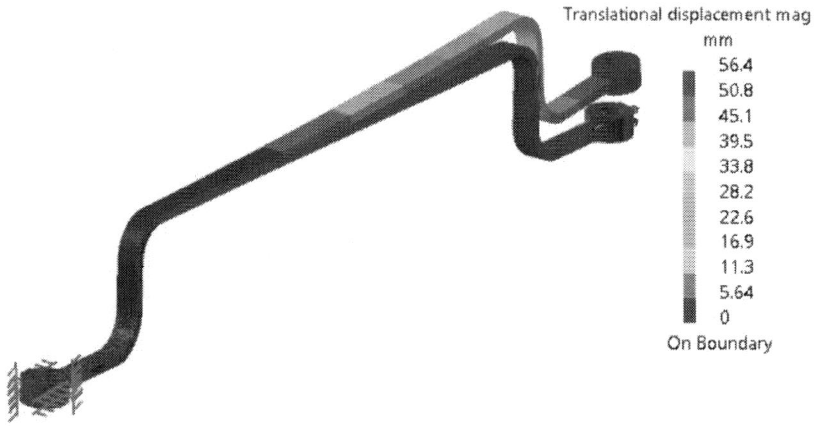

Figure 4–34

4. Animate the displacement magnitude. Check whether the applied loads and restraints behave correctly.

Task 14 - Display Von Mises stress.

1. Display the **Von Mises Stress** image, as shown in Figure 4–35. Does the maximum stress exceed the yield strength of the material?

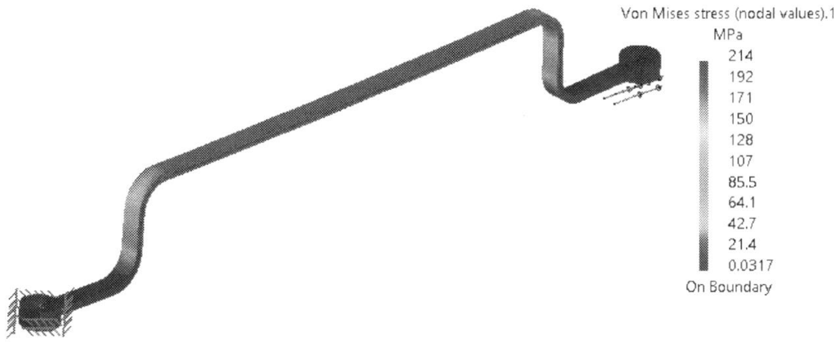

Figure 4–35

2. Using the **Image Extrema** tool, locate the maximum stress area, as shown in Figure 4–36. Note that the maximum stress occurs on the inside surface of the upper bend, and this is where you refined the mesh the most.

Figure 4–36

3. Right-click on **Von Mises stress (nodal values).1** in the tree and select **Activate/Deactivate** to delete the stress image from the screen and return to the model view.

Task 15 - Save and close the files.

1. Optionally, save the analysis document and the part for future reference.
2. Close both the analysis and the part documents.

Practice 4b Mesh Adaptivity

Practice Objectives

- Apply the material and mesh the model.
- Apply loads and restraints.
- Run the analysis and display the results.
- Use mesh adaptivity to achieve the required analysis accuracy.

In this practice, you will set up and run a static stress analysis on the part shown in Figure 4–37. The part is restrained through the two smaller holes on one end and is loaded with a torque moment applied to the bigger hole on the other end. You will also use the mesh Adaptivity tool in order to achieve analysis accuracy within 5% of the Global Error Rate.

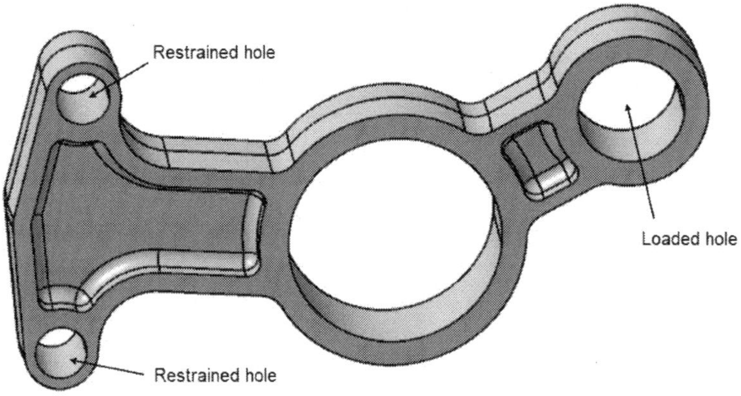

Figure 4–37

Task 1 - Open the part in CATIA.

1. Open **P10205_04.CATPart** from the *CATIA Generative Structural Analysis Practice Files\Ch04* folder.

2. Set the model display as (Shading with Edges). The part displays as shown in Figure 4–38.

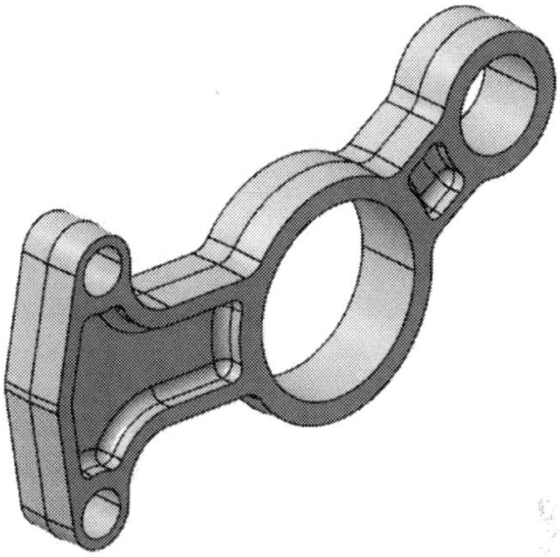

Figure 4–38

3. Select **Tools>Options>Parameters and Measures>Units** and set the units as follows:

   - Length: **Millimeter (mm)**
   - Force: **Newton (N)**
   - Moment: **Newton x Meter (Nxm)**
   - Pressure: **Megapascal (MPa)**

Task 2 - Create axis system.

In this task, you will create an axis system that you will later use to apply the torque load to the part.

1. Create a new geometrical set (**Geometrical Set.1**).

2. Using the **Circle/Sphere/Ellipse center** option, create two points (**Point.1** and **Point.2**) at the centers of the circles on both sides of the loaded hole, as shown in Figure 4–39.

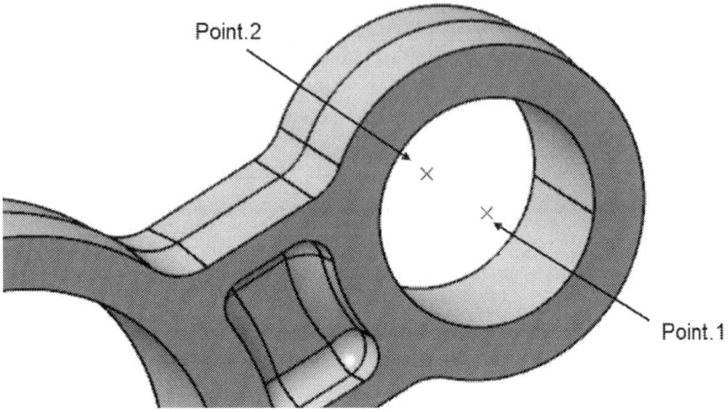

Figure 4–39

3. Using the **Between** option, create the middle point (**Point.3**) between **Point.1** and **Point.2**, as shown in Figure 4–40.

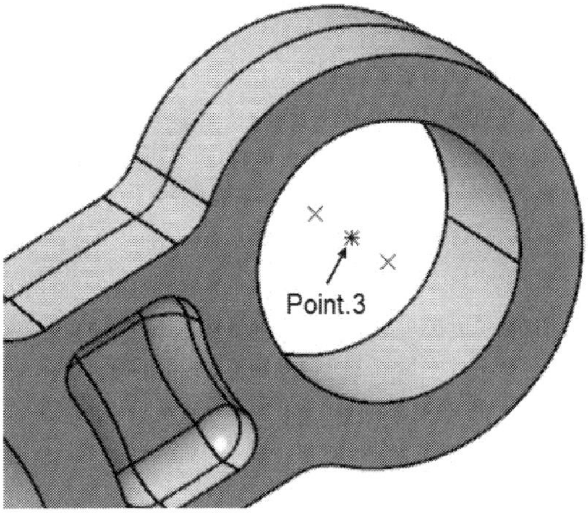

Figure 4–40

4. Repeat Steps 2 and 3 to create three points in the large center hole, as shown in Figure 4–41.

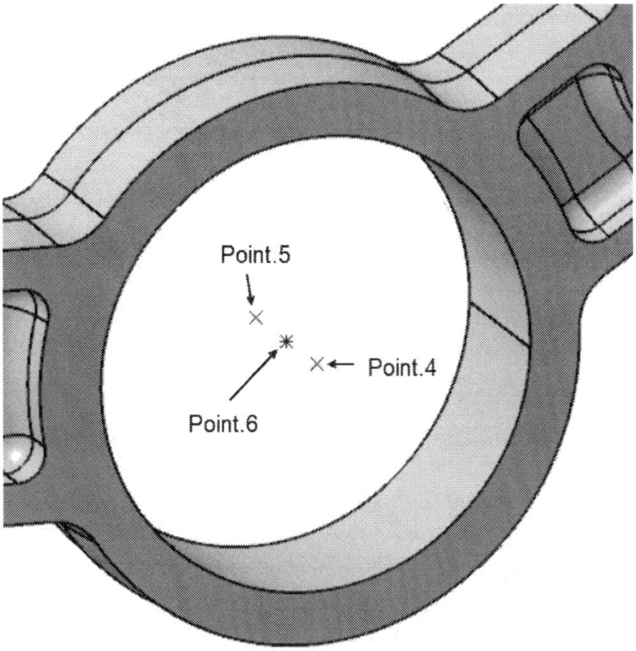

Figure 4–41

5. Create a line (**Line.1**) from **Point.3** to **Point.6**, as shown in Figure 4–42.

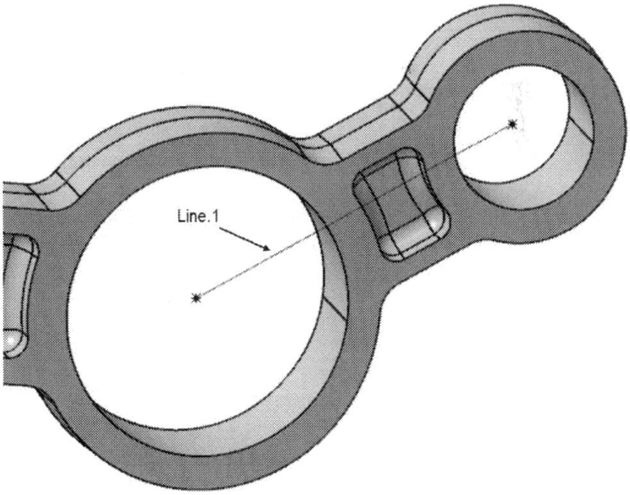

Figure 4–42

6. Create an axis system (**Axis System.1**), with the **Origin** at **Point.3**, **X axis** direction along **Line.1**, and **Z axis** direction normal to **YZ plane**. Hide **Geometrical Set.1** and the model displays as shown in Figure 4–43.

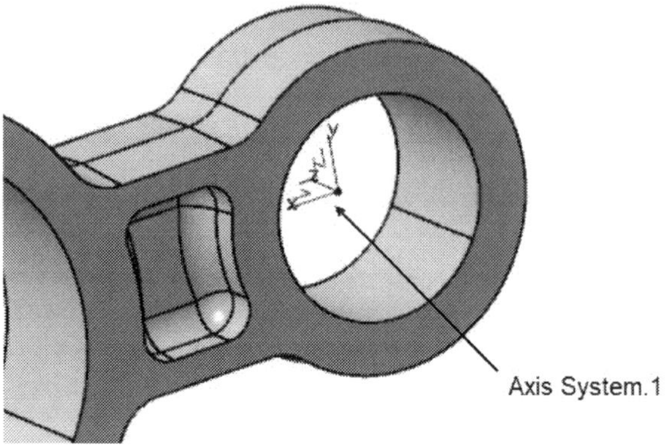

Figure 4–43

Task 3 - Apply the material.

1. Apply the **Aluminium** material from the **Default Material Catalog** to the part. Verify that the applied material has the following properties:

   - Young Modulus: **70000MPa**
   - Poisson Ratio: **0.346**
   - Density: **2710kg/m**^{3}
   - Thermal Expansion: **2.36e-005/Kdeg**
   - Yield Strength: **95MPa**

Task 4 - Start the GSA workbench.

1. Select **Start>Analysis & Simulation>Generative Structural Analysis**.

2. Select **Static Analysis** as the new analysis case.

Task 5 - Mesh the part.

The element size in this analysis will be selected automatically by CATIA's Adaptivity tool. Therefore, in this task you will only select the element type and link the Sag and the Size parameters with a formula.

1. Double-click on **OCTREE Tetrahedron Mesh.1: P10205_04** in the tree and select **Parabolic** as the *Element type*, as shown in Figure 4–44.

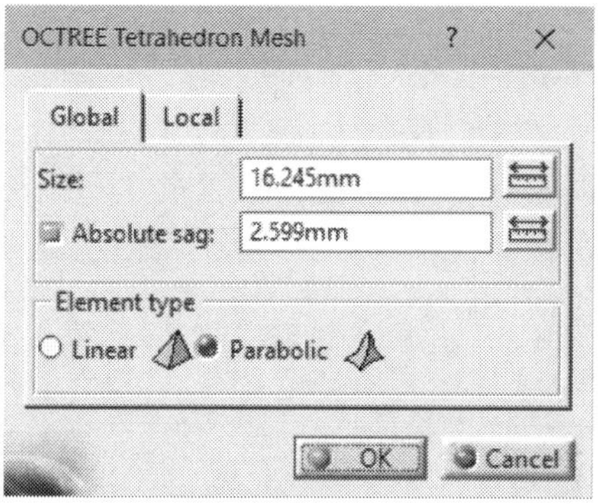

Figure 4–44

2. Right-click in the *Absolute sag* field, select **Edit formula**, and create a formula that sets the **Sag** value as **15%** of the **Size** value, as shown in Figure 4–45.

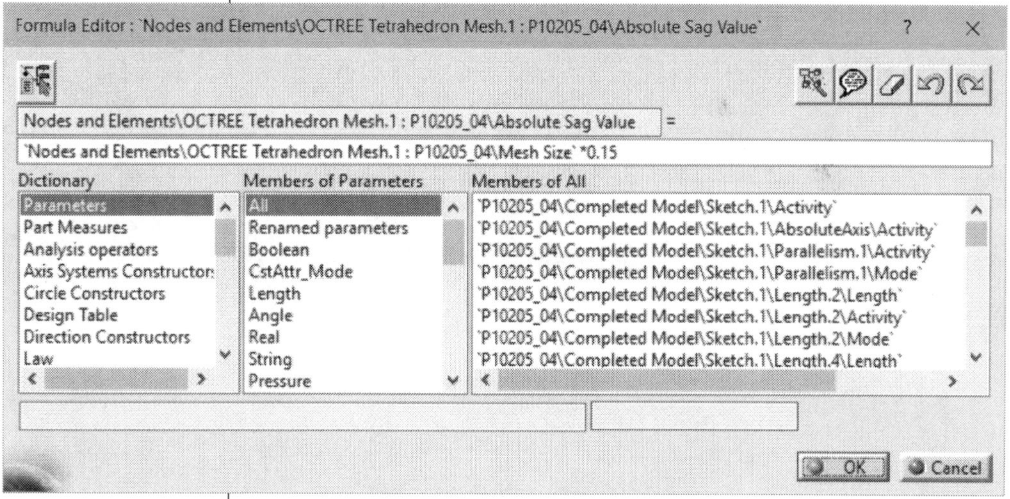

Figure 4–45

3. Click **OK** to close the Formula Editor dialog box. The OCTREE Tetrahedron Mesh dialog box displays as shown in Figure 4–46.

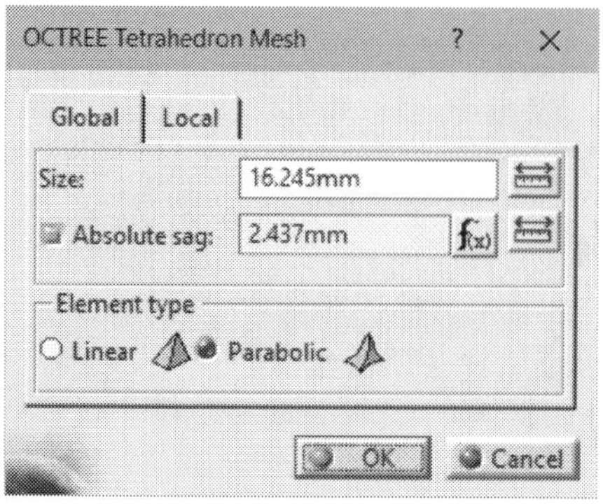

Figure 4–46

4. Click **OK** to close the OCTREE Tetrahedron Mesh dialog box.

5. Right-click on **Nodes and Elements** in the tree and select **Mesh Visualization** to display the mesh, as shown in Figure 4–47. Rotate the model and review the mesh in various areas.

Figure 4–47

6. Right-click on **Mesh.1** in the tree and select **Activate/Deactivate** to deactivate the mesh visualization and return to the model view.

Task 6 - Apply restraints.

1. Select (Clamp) and restrain the inside surfaces of the two smaller holes, as shown in Figure 4–48.

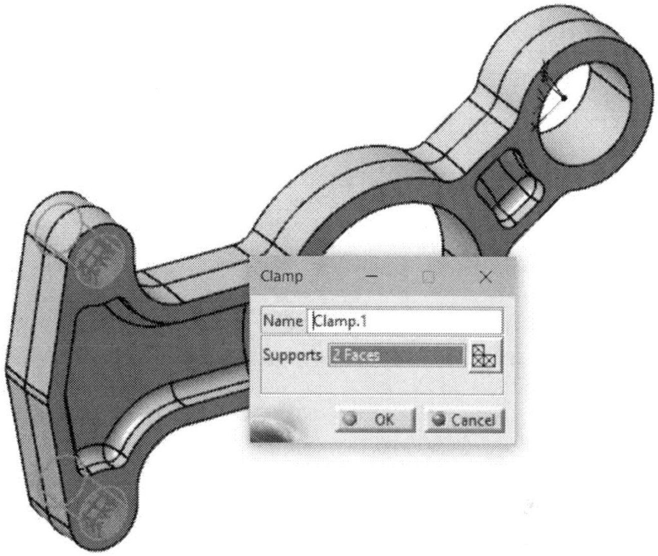

Figure 4–48

Task 7 - Apply loads.

1. In the Forces toolbar, select (Moment). In the Moment dialog box that opens, select the inside surface of the hole on the other end of the part, as shown in Figure 4–49.

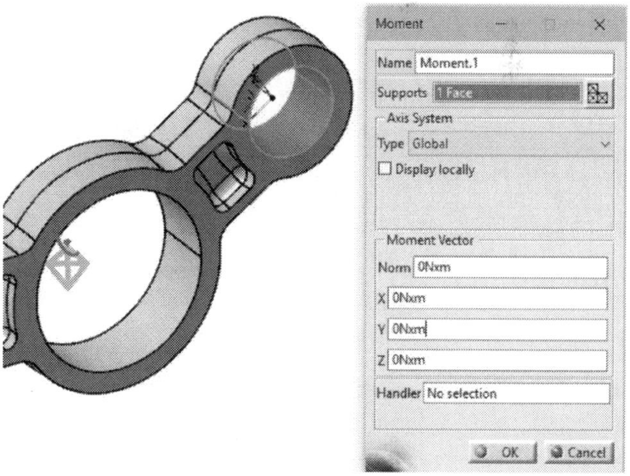

Figure 4–49

*Since the X-axis of **Axis System.1** has been aligned with **Line.1** (created in Task 2), the **120Nxm** moment applies the torque around the direction of **Line.1**.*

2. In the Axis System drop-down list, select **User**, then select **Axis System.1**. Enter **120Nxm** in the **X** field of the *Moment Vector* section, as shown in Figure 4–50.

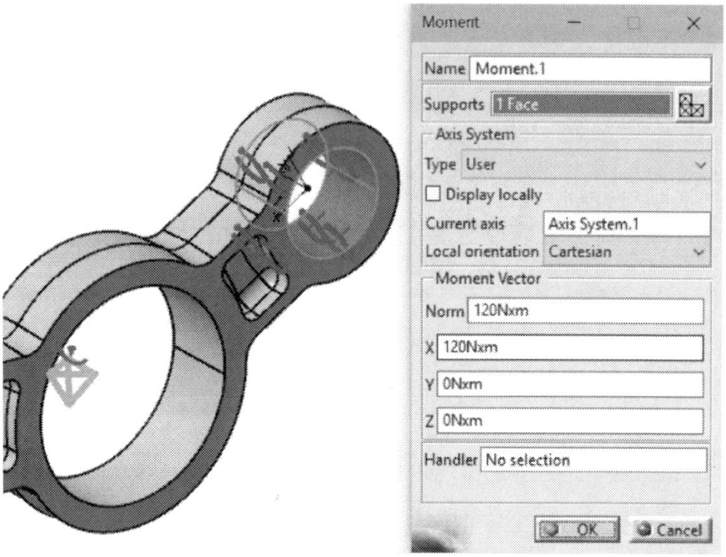

Figure 4–50

3. Click **OK** to close the Moment dialog box.

Task 8 - Run the analysis.

1. Run the analysis.

2. Expand the tree and note that the value of the **Global Error Rate** sensor is approximately **16.1%**, as shown in Figure 4–51.

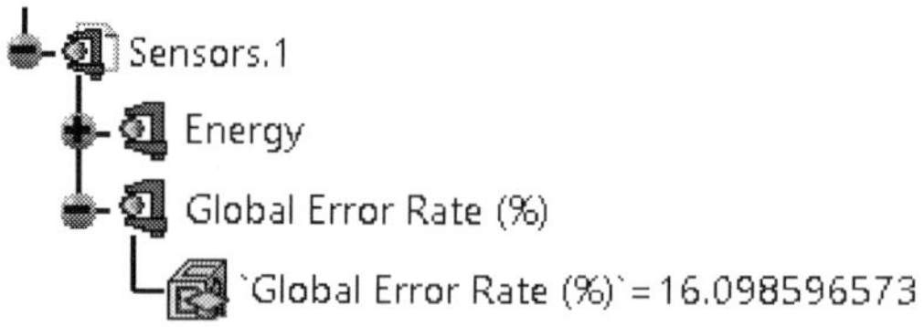

Figure 4–51

Task 9 - Set up Global Adaptivity.

The target error rate in this analysis is 5% or less. In this task, you will create a Global Adaptivity object and request the 5% error as the objective.

1. In the Adaptivity toolbar, select  (New Adaptivity Entity). The Global Adaptivity dialog box opens, as shown in Figure 4–52.

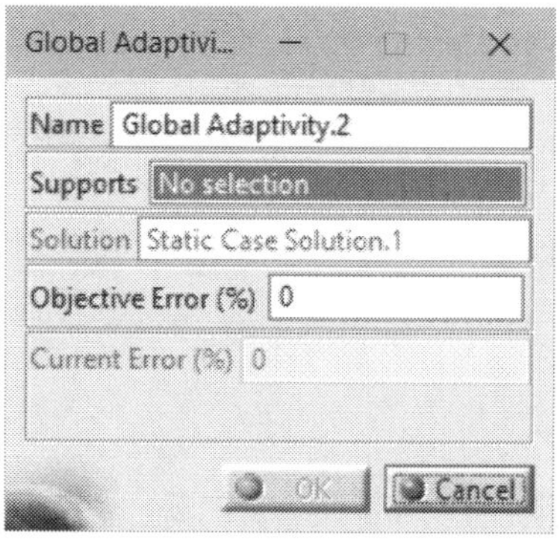

Figure 4–52

2. Select **OCTREE Tetrahedron Mesh.1: P10205_04** as the *Supports* and enter **5** in the *Objective Error* field, as shown in Figure 4–53.

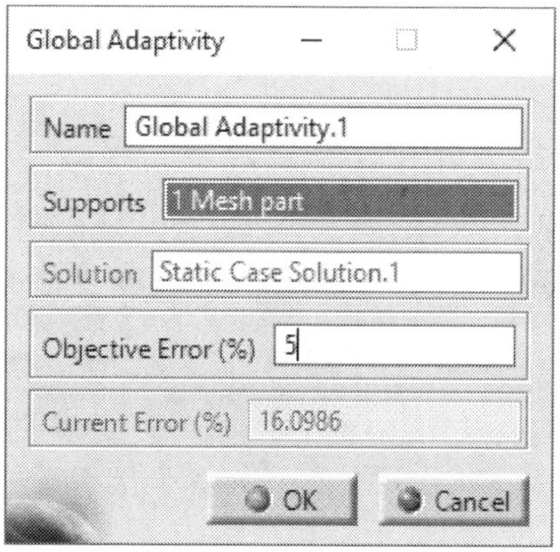

Figure 4–53

3. Click **OK** to close the Global Adaptivity dialog box.

Task 10 - Run the analysis with adaptivity.

The Global Adaptivity entity sets up the accuracy objective, but it does not run the adaptivity process. In this task, you will run the adaptivity computation.

1. In the Compute toolbar, select  (Compute with Adaptivity). The Adaptivity Process Parameters dialog box opens, as shown in Figure 4–54.

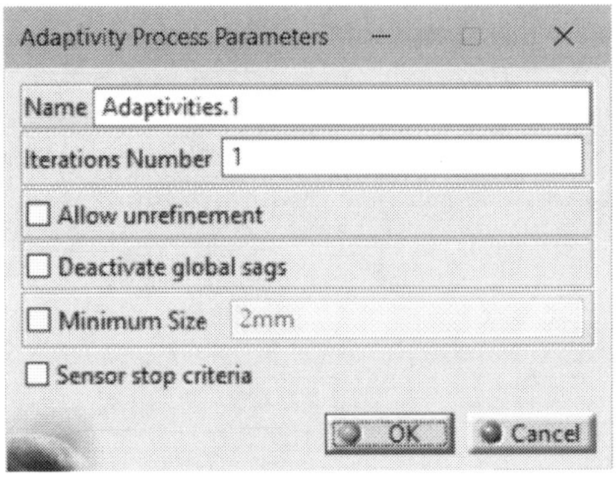

Figure 4–54

2. Enter **5** in the *Iterations Number* field, activate the **Minimum Size** option, and enter **2mm** as the minimum element size, as shown in Figure 4–55.

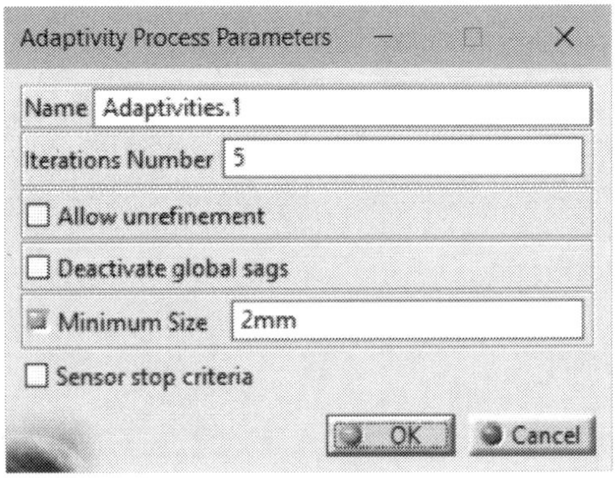

Figure 4–55

- The mesh adaptivity process runs in iterations, and it is not known in advance how many iterations CATIA will need to perform in order to achieve your objective. The **Iterations Number** parameter sets the hard limit on the number of iterations (i.e., the process will stop even if the accuracy objective has not been reached). In that case, you might continue the iterations by running the computation with adaptivity again.
- The **Minimum Size** parameter sets the hard limit on the minimum element size during the adaptivity process (i.e., the process would stop with a warning message if the error objective could not be reached with a mesh size equal or larger than the minimum size). In that case, you might reduce the **Minimum Size** value and re-start the computation.

3. Click **OK** to close the dialog box and start the computation. CATIA displays a series of messages informing you on the status of the computation process. Wait until computation completes, which may take some time depending on the complexity of your model and the accuracy objective.

Task 11 - Review the adaptivity results.

1. Expand the tree under **Nodes and Elements** and note the **Local Mesh Size Map.1** entity, as shown in Figure 4–56. This is the mesh refinement map created during the adaptivity process. Deleting **Local Mesh Size Map.1** would undo the adaptivity process.

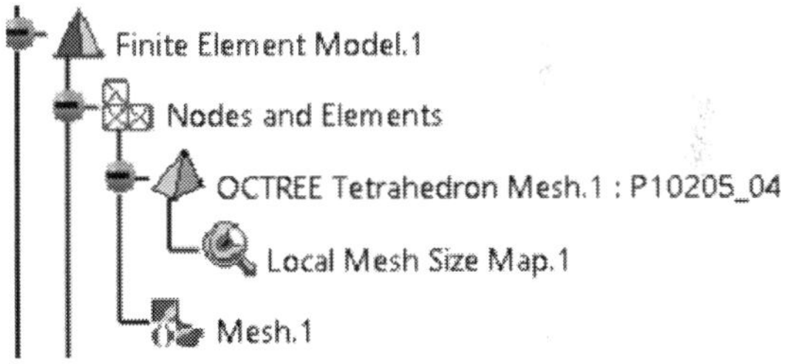

Figure 4–56

2. CATIA may or may not automatically update the analysis sensors once the computation finishes. To update all the sensors, right-click on **Sensors.1** in the tree and select **Update All Sensors**, as shown in Figure 4–57.

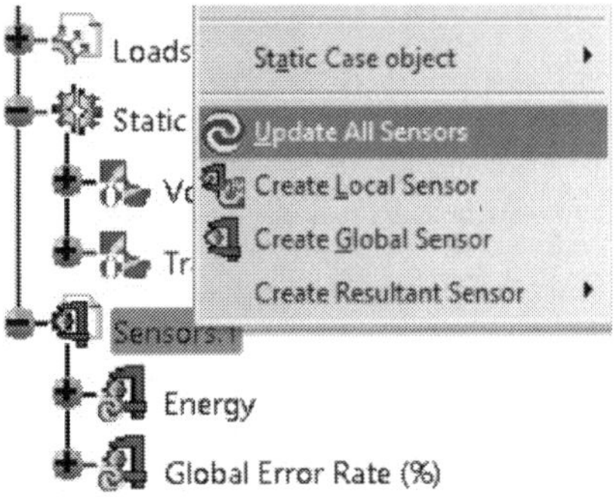

Figure 4–57

3. Expand **Sensors.1** in the tree and note that the value of the **Global Error Rate** sensor now reads **4.2%**, as shown in Figure 4–58. This is below the objective error in this analysis, which was 5%, so the adaptivity process has succeeded.

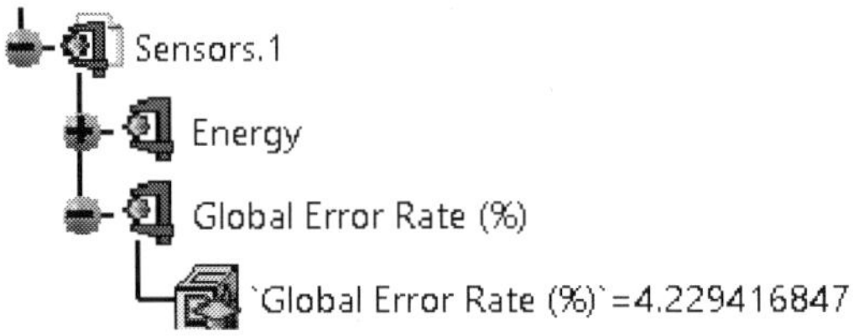

Figure 4–58

4. In the Analysis Results toolbar, select  (Historic of Computations). The Convergence of computation visualization window opens, as shown in Figure 4–59.

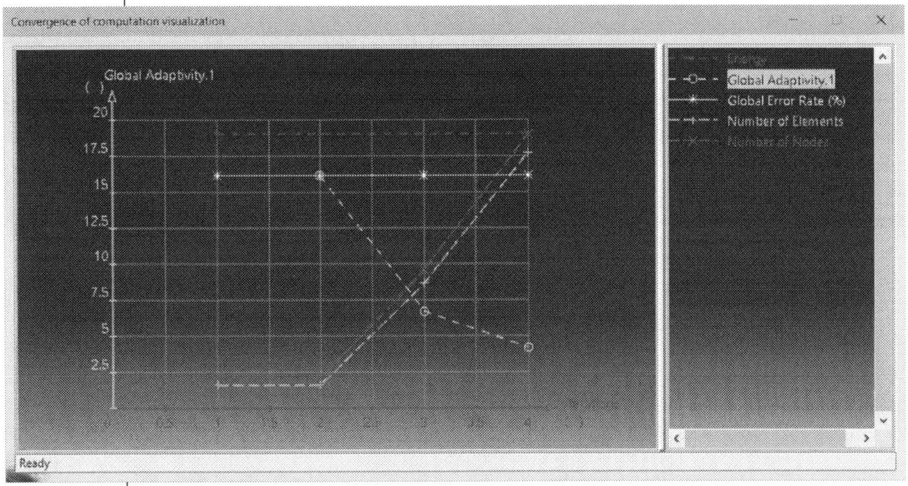

Figure 4–59

5. Note that CATIA performed two adaptivity iterations, during which the error rate (**Global Adaptivity.1** graph) was reduced from **16.1%** to approximately **7%** in the first iteration, and then down to **4.2%** in the second iteration. At the same time, the count of finite elements (**Number of Element**s graph) increased from under **5,000** to over **35,000**.

6. Close the Convergence of computation visualization window.

Task 12 - Display the analysis results.

1. Change the view mode to  (Shading with Material).

2. Hide **Loads** and **Restraints**.

3. Visualize and animate the displacement magnitude image, overlaid on the CAD model, as shown in Figure 4–60. Does the model deform according to the applied loads and restraints?

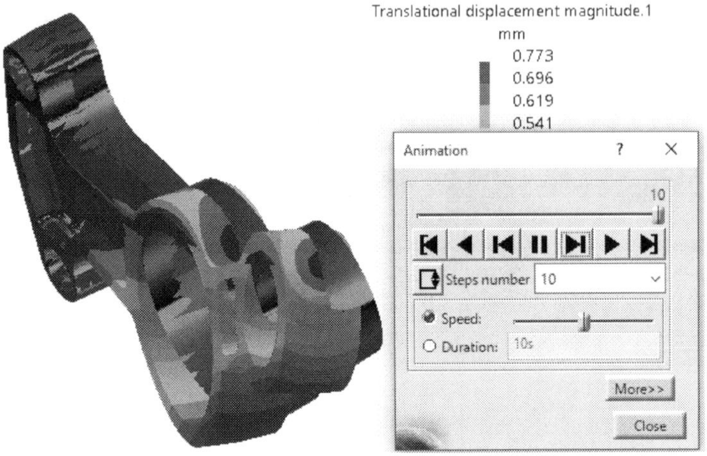

Figure 4–60

4. Display the **Von Mises Stress** image, as shown in Figure 4–61. Does the maximum stress exceed the yield strength of the material?

Figure 4–61

5. Using the **Image Extrema** tool, locate the maximum stress area, as shown in Figure 4–62.

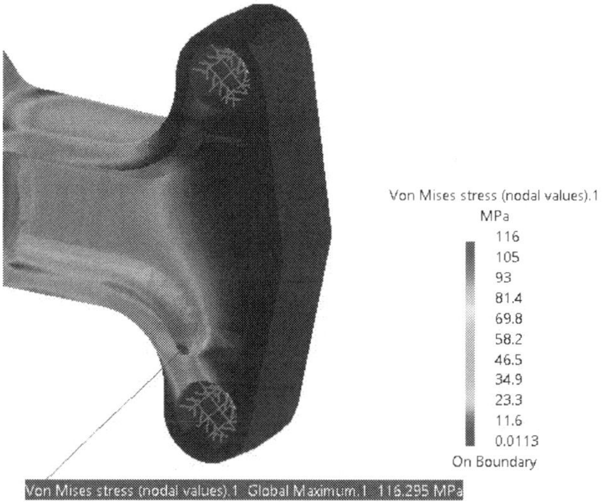

Figure 4–62

6. Right-click on **Von Mises stress (nodal values).1** in the tree and select **Activate/Deactivate** to delete the stress image from the screen and return to the model view.

Task 13 - Save and close the files.

1. Optionally, save the analysis document and the part for future reference.

2. Close both the analysis and the part documents.

Practice 4c Solid Bracket with Adaptivity

Practice Objectives

- Prepare the model for the analysis.
- Compute the analysis with mesh adaptivity.
- Display the results.

In this practice, you will set up and run a static stress analysis with adaptivity on the solid bracket shown in Figure 4–63, with minimum instruction.

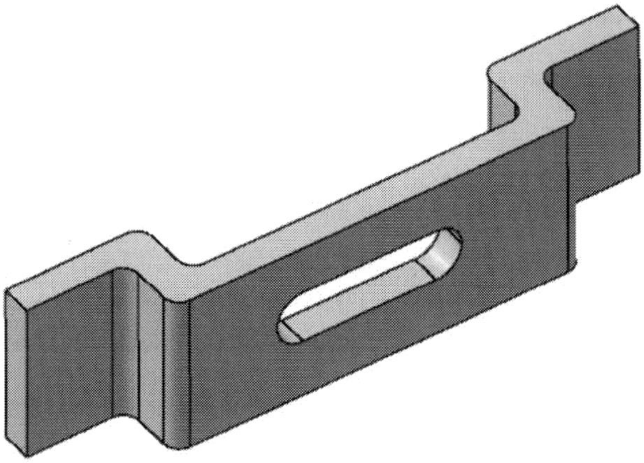

Figure 4–63

Task 1 - Open the part.

1. Open **Solid_Bracket_04.CATPart** from the *CATIA Generative Structural Analysis Practice Files\Ch04* folder.
2. Apply the **Steel** material to the part.

Task 2 - Prepare the analysis model.

1. Start the GSA workbench.
2. Mesh the model with the following parameters:
    - Element type: **Parabolic**
    - Size: Keep the default value
    - Sag: 15% of the mesh size
3. Visually examine the mesh.

4. Clamp the two surfaces shown in Figure 4–64.

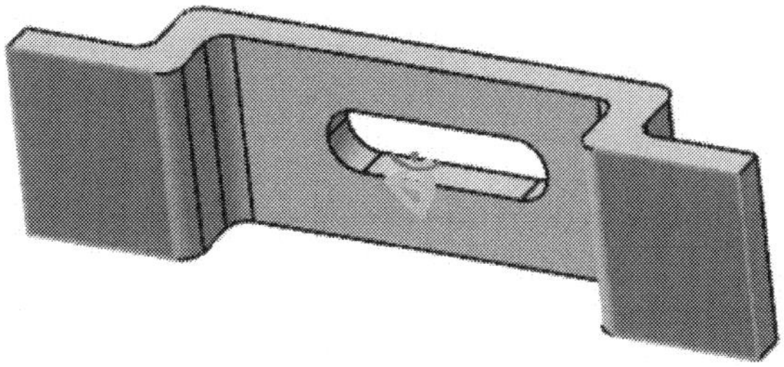

Figure 4–64

5. Apply **-100000N** distributed force in the **Z** direction to the surface shown in Figure 4–65.

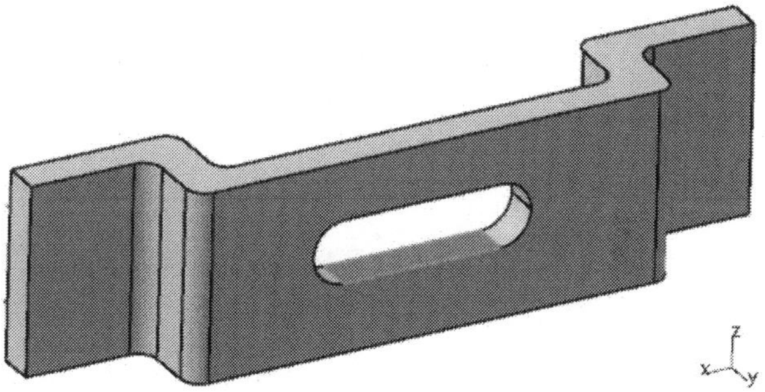

Figure 4–65

Task 3 - Run the analysis.

1. Check the model for inconsistencies.
2. Run the analysis. What is the value of the Global Error Rate with the default mesh size?

Task 4 - Run mesh adaptivity.

1. Set up a **Global Adaptivity** with **5%** objective error.
2. Compute with adaptivity, using the following parameters:
    - Iterations Number: **3**
    - Minimum Size: **3mm**

3. What is the value of the Global Error Rate after computation with adaptivity?
4. Approximately how many finite elements does the refined model contain?

Task 5 - Visualize and examine the analysis results.

1. Visualize and animate the deformed mesh. Does the part deform according to the applied loads?
2. Display the displacement magnitude color plot. What is the value of the maximum displacement in the model?
3. Display the Von Mises color plot. Does the maximum stress exceed the yield strength of the material?
4. Close the model without saving.

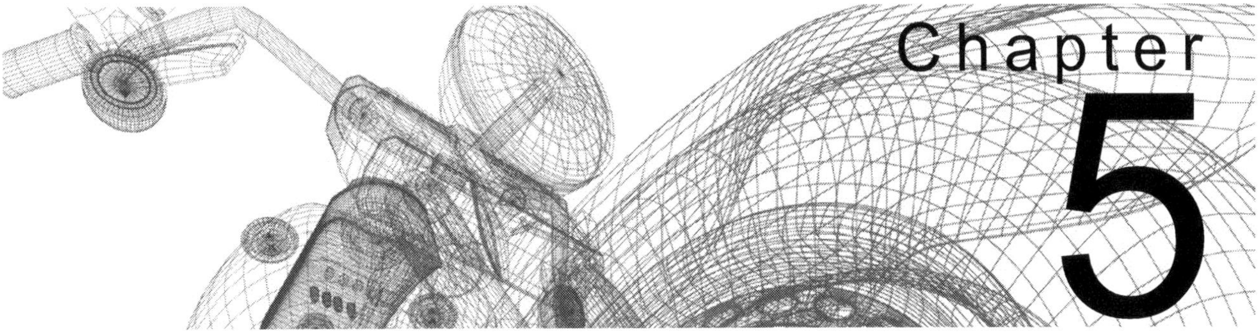

Virtual Parts

Virtual parts in CATIA GSA are the tools designed to simulate parts in the analysis of assemblies without modeling the part's detailed geometrical shape, which results in faster analysis computation time. In this chapter, you learn how to use the virtual parts in GSA.

Learning Objectives in This Chapter

- Understand the concept of a virtual part in GSA.
- Understand the rigid virtual part.
- Understand the rigid spring virtual part.
- Understand the smooth virtual part.
- Understand the smooth spring virtual part.
- Understand the contact virtual part.
- Apply loads and restraints to virtual parts.

5.1 Virtual Part Concepts

A major issue in FEA simulations is computer hardware and analysis runtime limitations. As the count of finite elements increases, due to the necessity to simulate assemblies consisting of many parts and/or to use very dense mesh to achieve accurate results, the computation runtime and computer memory requirements increase exponentially. Meshing and solving models with hundreds of thousands of finite elements may become impractical.

Thus, it may be essential to use special purpose elements and tools in order to decrease the computation's cost when possible.

Consider the example of simulating the dynamic behavior of a pickup truck. The frame of the truck is the main load-bearing structure that bends and twists as the vehicle travels on a rough road. The shape and the size of the frame is essential since it affects the frame's stiffness, and hence the truck's dynamic properties. Therefore, great care must be taken to accurately model the frame with a detailed finite element mesh.

At the same time, the exact shape of the truck engine is not essential; it is the mass of the engine that is important for the simulation. Therefore, the engine could be modeled in the analysis as just a lumped mass placed at the center of gravity of the engine and attached to the engine's multiple mounting locations using, for instance, rigid links.

The Virtual Part features in CATIA's GSA are intended to simulate parts in the analysis of assemblies without modeling the part's detailed geometrical shape. The virtual parts do not have a geometrical representation, such as a solid or a surface, which is why they are called "virtual". And yet virtual parts can approximately model the behavior of the real parts, such as transferring forces, modeling analysis supports, etc.

Consider an example of using a virtual part in CATIA. The assembly to be analyzed is shown in Figure 5–1.

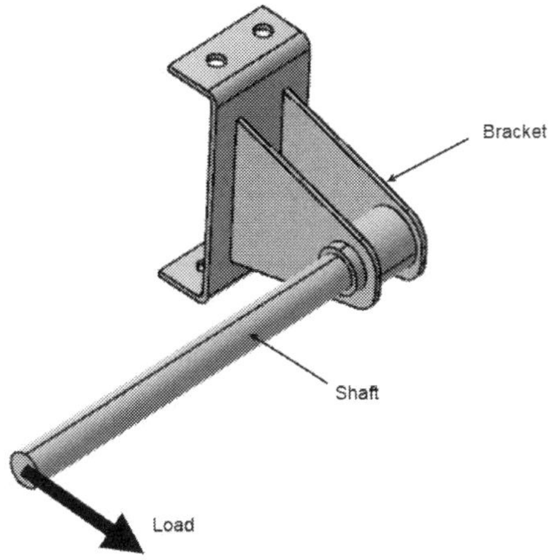

Figure 5–1

The part of interest is the bracket. The load is applied to the end of the shaft and is transferred to the bracket through the shaft. Therefore, the exact location of the point where the load is applied is important, but the other geometrical details of the shaft are irrelevant.

In this case, you could model the shaft with a virtual part, as shown in Figure 5–2.

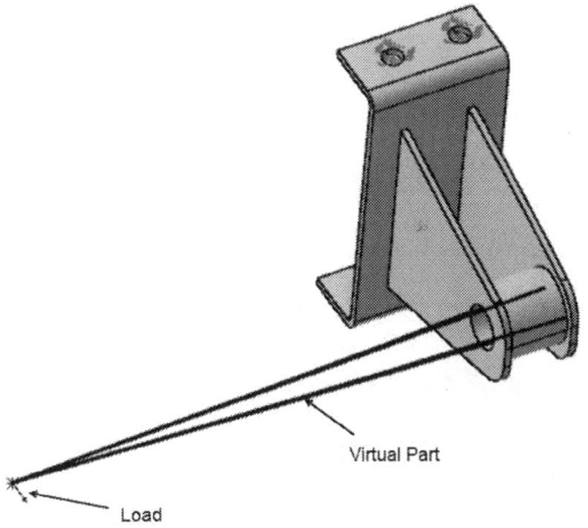

Figure 5–2

Virtual parts are not unique to CATIA. Similar tools and features, although named differently, can be found in other FEA software, such as ABAQUS, ANSYS, or NASTRAN. In fact, the origins of virtual parts can be traced back to the Rigid Body Elements (RBEs) implemented in NASTRAN in the 1960s.

5.2 Rigid Virtual Part

A rigid virtual part uses rigid links to connect one point (called the handler) with all mesh nodes on the virtual part's support, as shown in Figure 5–3.

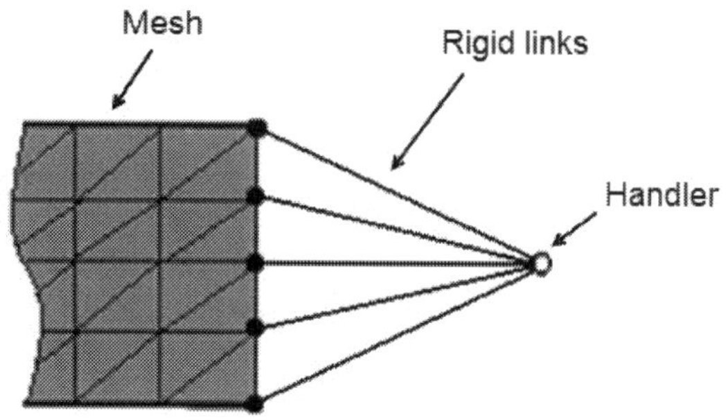

Figure 5–3

A rigid link is a constraint equation (called Multi-Point Constraint, or MPC in short) rather than some kind of rigid beam or other type of finite element connecting the two points. The rigid link cannot stretch or deform in any way, which creates a kinematic (rather than elastic) relationship between motions of the connected nodes. Together, the collection of rigid links in the rigid virtual part effectively makes up a rigid body that is attached to the mesh in your model.

The mesh nodes on the virtual part's support form the dependent side, while the handler point forms the independent side in the virtual part (i.e., controlling the motion of the handler point effectively controls the motions of the dependent nodes, which is due to the kinematic relations between the motions of the nodes).

The handler point has six full degrees of freedom (three translations and three rotations); therefore, it supports rotational restraints and loads.

The rigid virtual part is analogous to the RBE2 element in NASTRAN.

Selecting a handler is optional. If you do not select a handler point, an implicit handler is created at the centroid of the support.

To create a rigid virtual part in CATIA, click  (Rigid Virtual Part) in the Virtual Parts toolbar and select the *Supports* and the *Handler*, as shown in Figure 5–4. The rigid virtual part is indicated by solid thick lines connecting the handler and the support.

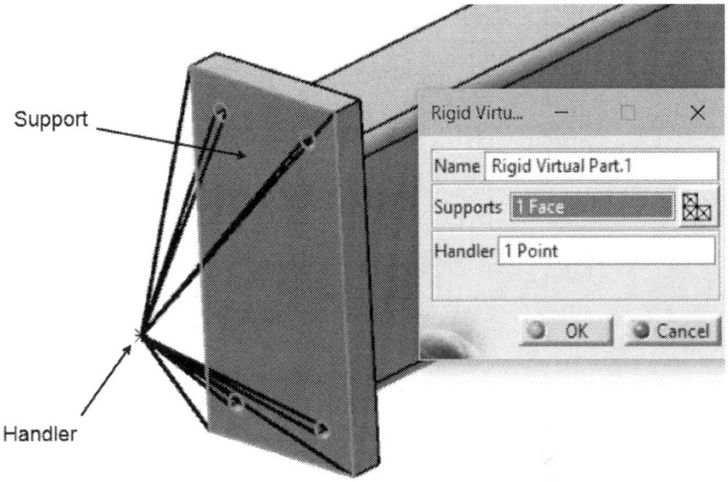

Figure 5–4

The rigid virtual part cannot deform in any way, hence it will locally stiffen the mesh on and near the support. Therefore, exercise caution when applying rigid virtual parts to large areas in your model since this may lead to an over-stiffened model.

One of the typical applications for the rigid virtual part is modeling relatively stiff components, such as the engine mounted on a truck frame.

5.3 Rigid Spring Virtual Part

A rigid spring virtual part, in addition to the rigid links, also includes a spring, as shown in Figure 5–5. In other words, the rigid spring virtual part could be thought of as a rigid virtual part with a spring.

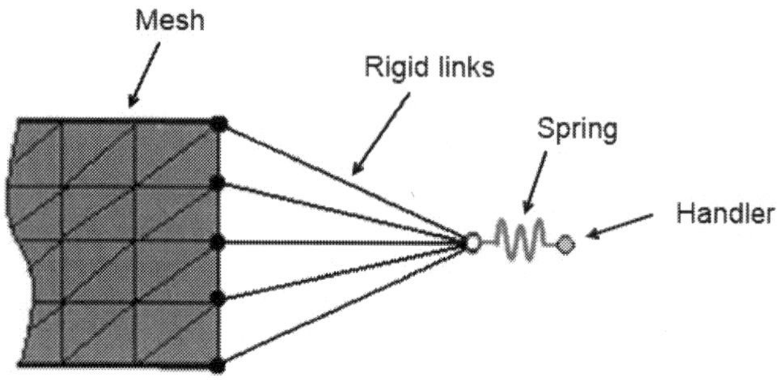

Figure 5–5

Since the spring can stretch and deform, the rigid spring virtual part forms an elastic body rather than an infinitely rigid one. However, the rigid links cannot stretch or deform, hence will locally stiffen the mesh on and near the support.

Selecting a handler is optional. If you do not select a handler point, an implicit handler is created at the centroid of the support.

To create a rigid spring virtual part in CATIA, click  (Rigid Spring Virtual Part) in the Virtual Parts toolbar. Select the *Supports*, the *Handler*, and enter the values for the translation and rotational stiffnesses, as shown in Figure 5–6. The rigid spring virtual part is indicated by solid thick lines connecting the handler and the support and the spring symbol at the handler.

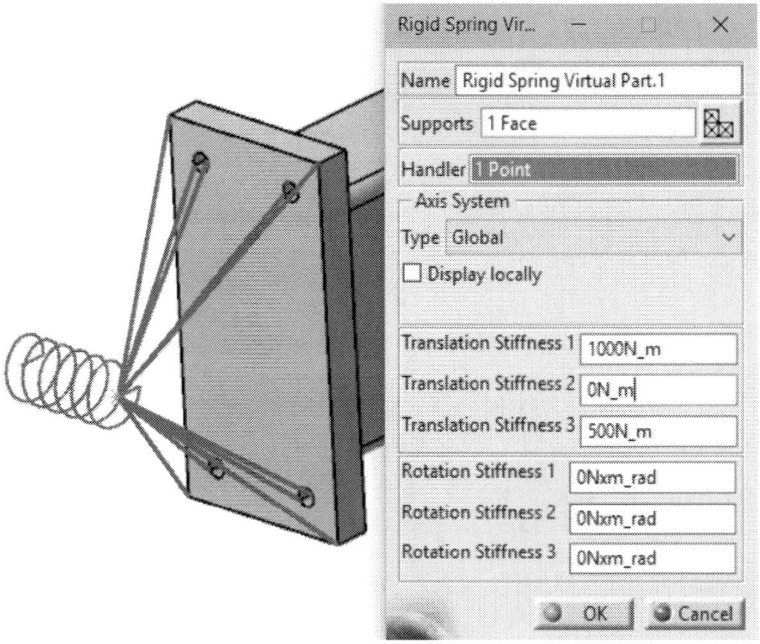

Figure 5–6

One of the typical applications for the rigid spring virtual part is modeling compliant supports, such as rubber mounts and bushings.

5.4 Smooth Virtual Part

A smooth virtual part uses smooth links to connect one point (called the handler) with all mesh nodes on the virtual part's support, as shown in Figure 5–7.

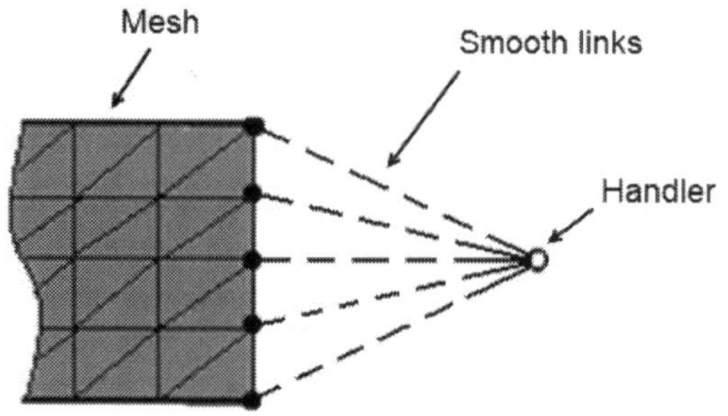

Figure 5–7

The collection of smooth links forms a constraint equation (i.e., an MPC) that interpolates displacements at the handler point as the average of displacements of the nodes on the mesh, using the least-squares method.

The mesh nodes on the virtual part's support form the independent side, while the handler point forms the dependent side in the smooth virtual part (i.e., motions of the mesh nodes on the support (independent side) collectively control the motion of the handler point (dependent side), which is opposite to the behavior of the rigid virtual part).

Since displacements of the mesh nodes are independent of the displacement of the handler, the smooth virtual part does not locally stiffen the mesh on and near the support, making it a complete opposite to the rigid virtual part.

The handler point has a full six degrees of freedom (three translations and three rotations); therefore, it supports rotational restraints and loads.

The smooth virtual part is analogous to the RBE3 element in NASTRAN.

Selecting a handler is optional. If you do not select a handler point, an implicit handler is created at the centroid of the support.

To create a smooth virtual part in CATIA, click  (Smooth Virtual Part) in the Virtual Parts toolbar and select the *Supports* and the *Handler*, as shown in Figure 5–8. The smooth virtual part is indicated by thick dashed lines connecting the handler and the support.

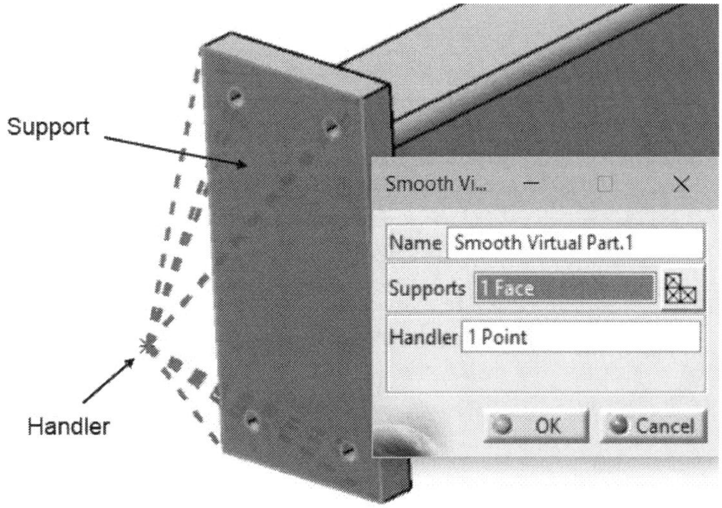

Figure 5–8

One of the typical applications for the smooth virtual part is distributing the effect of a force acting at the handler point over a number of mesh nodes on the support surface without adding stiffness to the structure, as shown in Figure 5–9. Note that using a rigid virtual part in this case would locally stiffen the model by rendering the support surface undeformable.

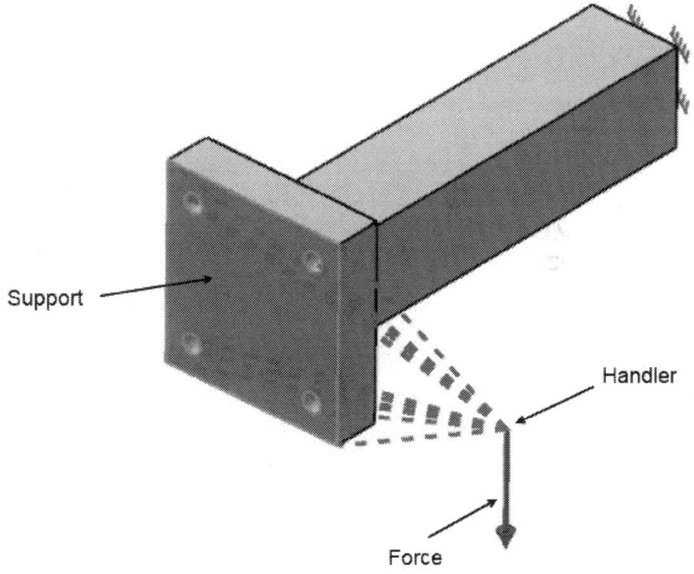

Figure 5–9

5.5 Smooth Spring Virtual Part

A smooth spring virtual part, includes a spring in addition to the smooth links, as shown in Figure 5–10. In other words, the smooth spring virtual part could be thought of as a smooth virtual part with a spring.

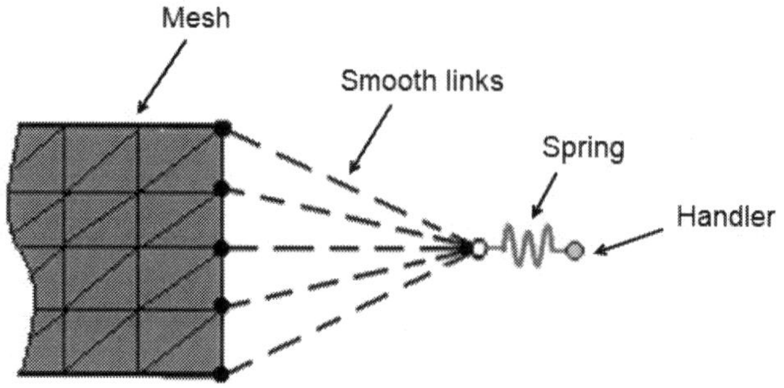

Figure 5–10

Selecting a handler is optional. If you do not select a handler point, an implicit handler is created at the centroid of the support.

To create a smooth spring virtual part in CATIA, click (Smooth Spring Virtual Part) in the Virtual Parts toolbar. Select the *Supports*, the *Handler*, and enter the values for the translation and rotational stiffnesses, as shown in Figure 5–11. The smooth spring virtual part is indicated by solid thick lines connecting the handler and the support and the spring symbol at the handler.

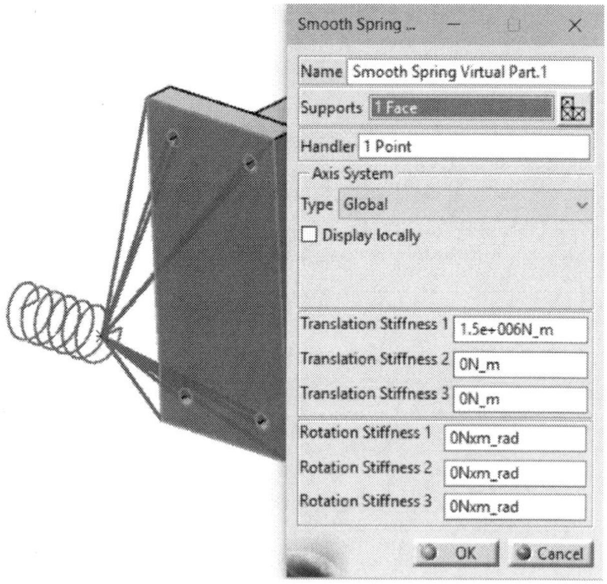

Figure 5–11

One of the typical applications for the smooth spring virtual part is modeling soft supports, such as rubber mounts and bushings.

5.6 Contact Virtual Part

A contact virtual part, like the rigid virtual part, uses rigid links. The difference is that in the contact virtual part, the ends of the rigid links are connected to the mesh nodes via very short 1-dimensional elements called contact rods (or gap elements), as shown in Figure 5–12. In other words, the contact virtual part could be thought of as a rigid virtual part with contact rods.

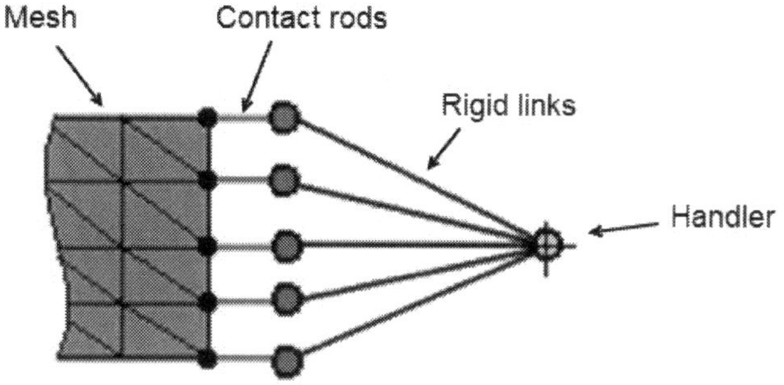

Figure 5–12

The condition that a contact rod element enforces is that the rigid link cannot penetrate into the part mesh. The movements of the rigid links away from or along the parts mesh are not constrained.

Therefore, if a compressive force is applied to the handler, the contact virtual part will not penetrate into the part mesh, as shown in Figure 5–13.

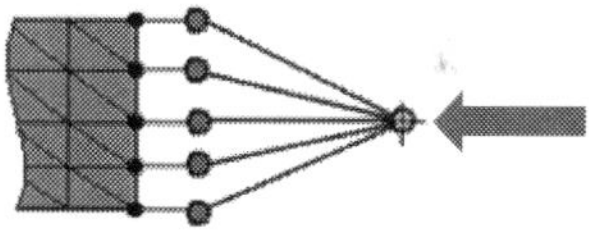

Figure 5–13

If a tensile force is applied, the contact virtual part will separate from the part mesh, as shown in Figure 5–14.

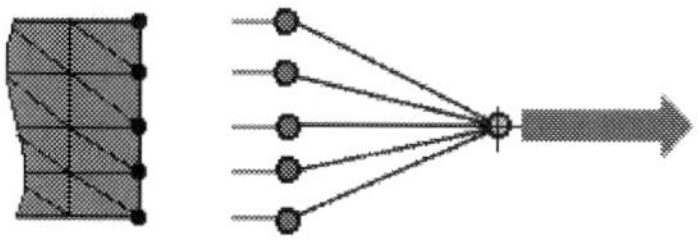

Figure 5–14

If a tangential force is applied, the contact virtual part will slide along the part mesh without friction, as shown in Figure 5–15.

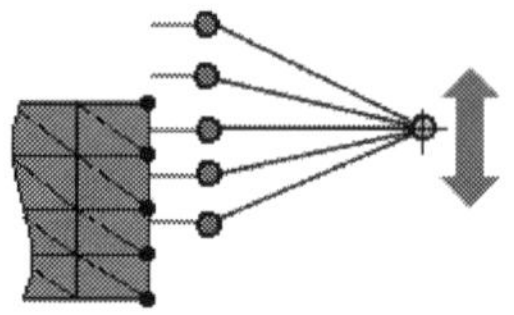

Figure 5–15

Under a more complex loading condition, the contact virtual part may press against the part mesh in some areas, while separating from the part mesh in other areas, as shown in Figure 5–16.

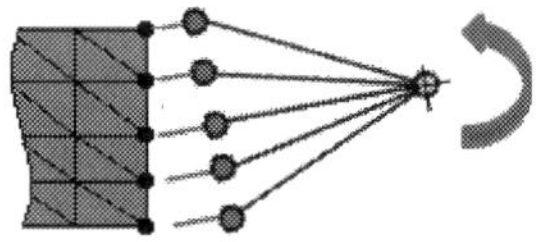

Figure 5–16

A contact virtual part is a non-linear feature. If contact virtual parts are present in the model, the analysis becomes non-linear and generally takes longer computation time. For the same reason, contact virtual parts cannot be used in frequency analysis or any other dynamic analysis, which are strictly linear types of analysis.

Beware of making your model insufficiently restrained (by inadvertently enabling rigid body motions in the model) when using contact virtual parts, due to the ability of contact virtual parts to slide along the mesh without friction, as well as to freely separate from the mesh under tensile load.

Selecting a handler is optional. If you do not select a handler point, an implicit handler is created at the centroid of the support.

To create a contact virtual part in CATIA, click (Contact Virtual Part) in the Virtual Parts toolbar and select the *Supports* and the *Handler*, as shown in Figure 5–17. Optionally, enter the *Clearance* value, which is the amount by which the contact virtual part can freely move toward the mesh, or vice versa, until the gap is closed.

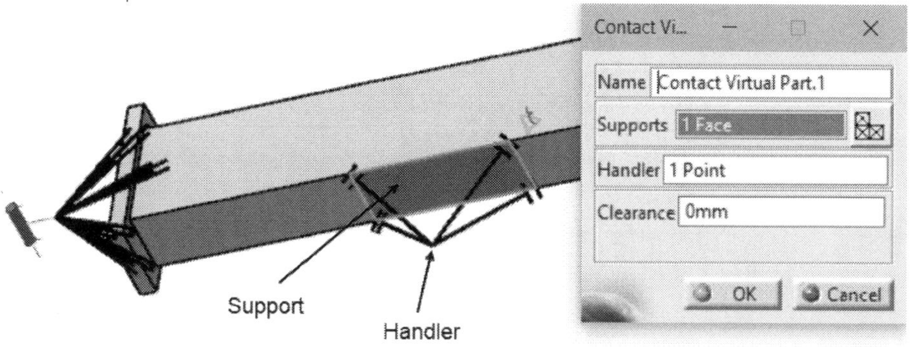

Figure 5–17

A typical application for the contact virtual part is modeling supports that are not bonded or welded to the analyzed structure, so the structure can separate from the support under the applied loads to create a gap.

5.7 Loads and Restraints on Virtual Parts

Loads and restraints can be applied to virtual parts in the same way as to the part geometry. Note that whenever a load or restraint is applied to a virtual part, it is, in fact, applied to its handler point.

There are, however, four types of restraints that can only be applied to virtual parts and never directly to the model geometry: slider, sliding pivot, pivot, and ball joint.

Slider Restraint

The slider restraint leaves only one degree of freedom unblocked, which is translational motion along a user-specified direction. This direction is called the *Released Direction*.

The other five degrees of freedom (two translations and three rotations) are restrained.

To apply a slider restraint, select  (Slider) in the Restraints toolbar, select a virtual part as the *Supports*, and specify the *Released Direction* as an **XYZ** vector, as shown in Figure 5–18.

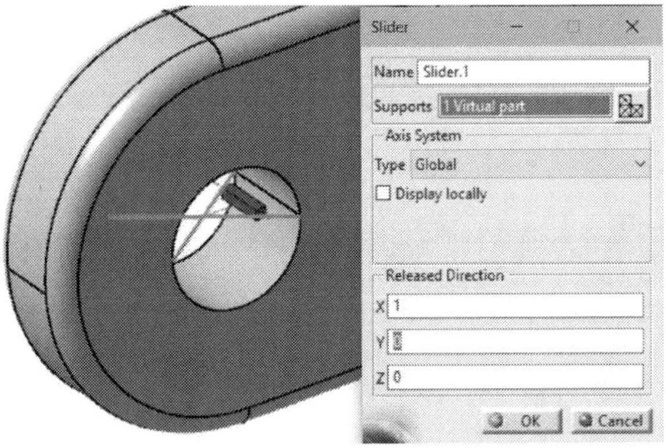

Figure 5–18

Sliding Pivot Restraint

The sliding pivot restraint leaves two degrees of freedom unblocked, which are the translational motion along the released direction and the rotational motion around the released direction.

The other four degrees of freedom (two translations and two rotations) are restrained.

To apply a sliding pivot restraint, select  (Sliding Pivot) in the Restraints toolbar, select a virtual part as the *Supports*, and specify the *Released Direction* as an **XYZ** vector, as shown in Figure 5–19.

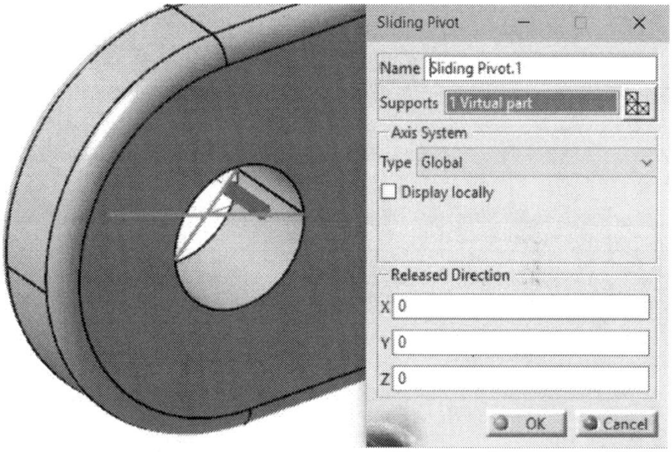

Figure 5–19

Pivot Restraint

The pivot restraint leaves only one degree of freedom unblocked, which is the rotational motion around the released direction.

The other five degrees of freedom (three translations and two rotations) are restrained.

To apply a pivot restraint, select  (Pivot) in the Restraints toolbar, select a virtual part as the *Supports*, and specify the *Released Direction* as an **XYZ** vector, as shown in Figure 5–20.

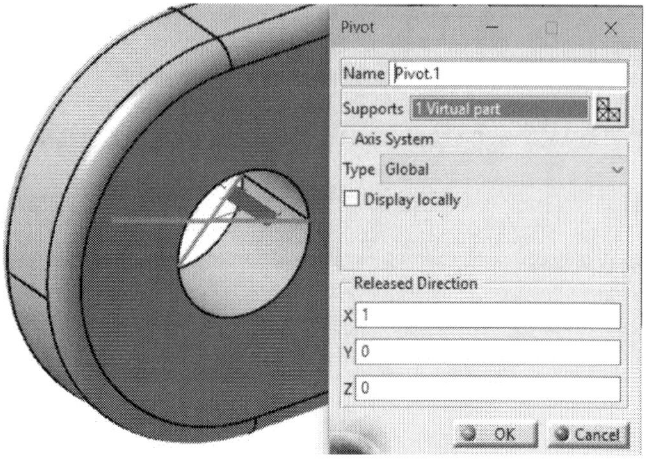

Figure 5–20

Ball Joint Restraint

The ball joint restraint enables free rotation of the virtual part around its handler point, while blocking all translational motions.

To apply a ball joint restraint, select  (Ball Joint) in the Restraints toolbar and select a virtual part as the *Supports*, as shown in Figure 5–21.

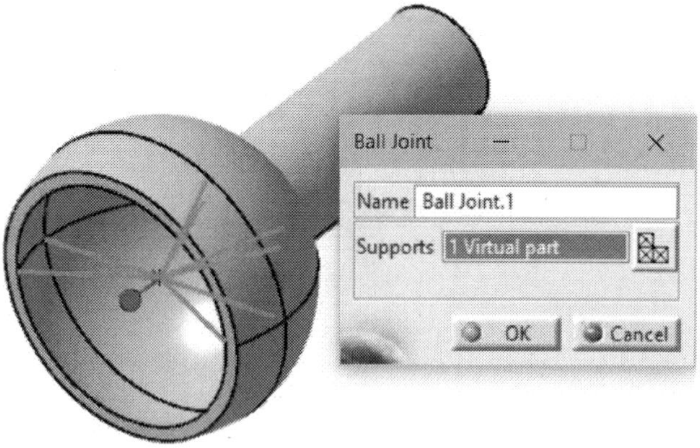

Figure 5–21

Practice 5a

Analysis of a Beam on a Flat Support

Practice Objectives

- Prepare the CAD geometry.
- Create a rigid virtual part.
- Create a contact virtual part.
- Apply a pivot restraint.
- Apply loads.
- Run the analysis and display the results.
- Obtain reactions in restraints.

In this practice, you will set up and run a static analysis of a beam, which is a part in the assembly shown in Figure 5–22. The rocker and the beam are bolted together. The beam is not welded to the support part, but instead is freely resting on the flat top surface of the support. The rocker part is restrained by the rigid pin inserted through the hole, while the support part is rigidly attached to the ground. The beam is loaded with a vertical force on the right end of the beam.

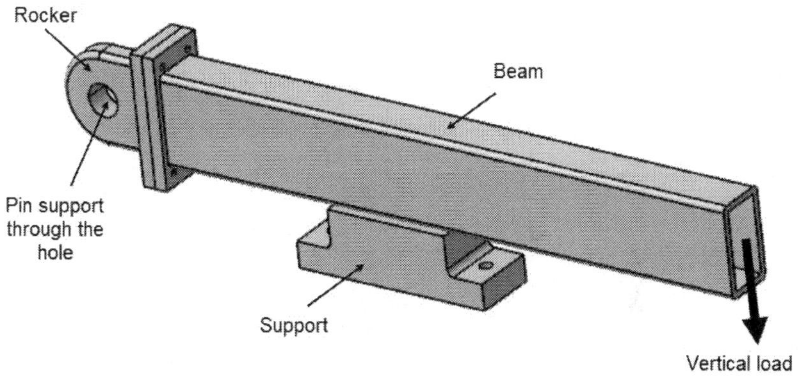

Figure 5–22

The area of interest in this analysis is the beam. The rocker and the support parts are of little concern. Given these considerations, the most efficient way to set up the analysis would be to use a good-quality solid mesh for the beam part in order to get accurate stress results, while using the GSA's virtual parts to model the effects of the rocker and the support parts on the beam.

Task 1 - Open the assembly in CATIA.

1. Open **RockingBeam_05.CATProduct** from the *CATIA Generative Structural Analysis Practice Files\Ch05* folder.

2. Set the model display as  (Shading with Edges). The assembly displays as shown in Figure 5–23.

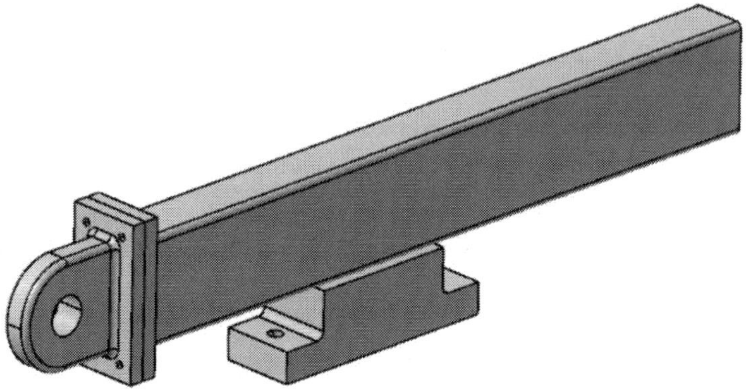

Figure 5–23

3. Select **Tools>Options>Parameters and Measures>Units** and set the units as follows:

   - Length: **Millimeter (mm)**
   - Force: **Newton (N)**
   - Moment: **Newton x Meter (Nxm)**
   - Pressure: **Megapascal (MPa)**

Task 2 - Create reference geometry.

In this task, you will create the geometrical elements in the beam part that reference surrounding parts - the rocker and the support. Namely, you will create the hole center in the rocker part and the contact area between the beam and the support.

1. Double-click on the **Beam_05** part in the tree to activate it, as shown in Figure 5–24. CATIA automatically switches to the Part Design  workbench.

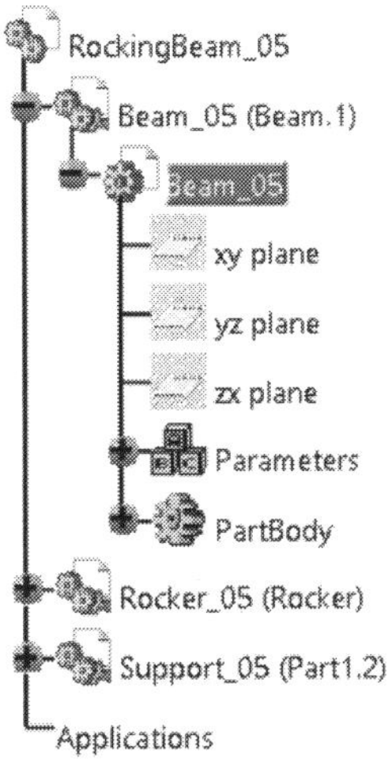

Figure 5–24

2. Create a new geometrical set (**Geometrical Set.1**).

3. Using the **Circle/Sphere/Ellipse center** option, create two points (**Point.1** and **Point.2**) at the centers of the circles on both sides of the hole, as shown in Figure 5–25.

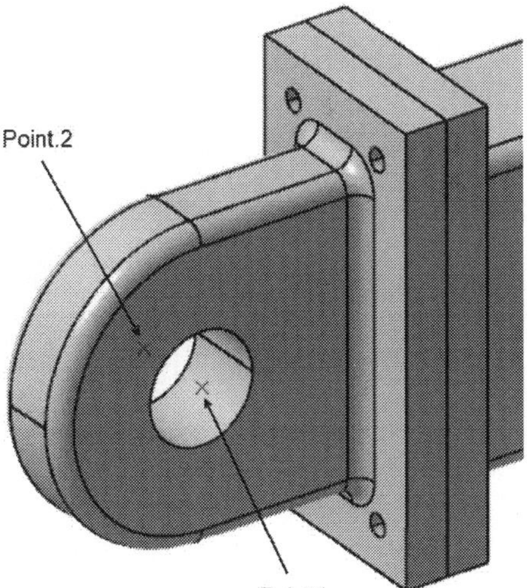

Figure 5–25

4. Using the **Between** option, create the middle point (**Point.3**) between **Point.1** and **Point.2**, as shown in Figure 5–26.

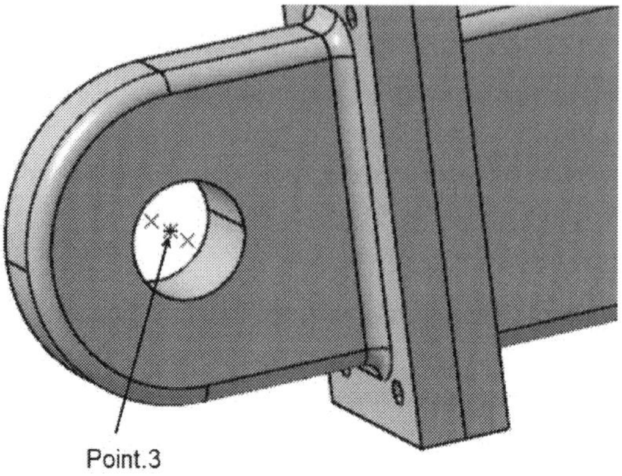

Figure 5–26

5. Hide **Point.1** and **Point.2**.

6. Switch to the **Generative Shape Design**  workbench.

7. Create another geometrical set (**Geometrical Set.2**).

8. Using the **Between** option, create the middle point (**Point.4**) between the two corners of the bottom surface of the support part, as shown in Figure 5–27.

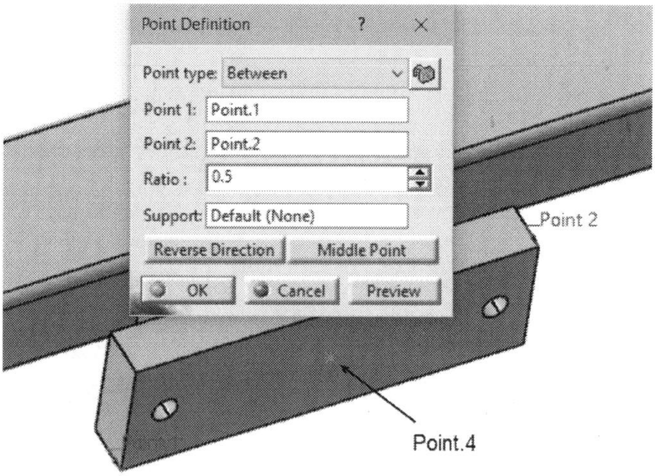

Figure 5–27

9. Extract the bottom surface of the beam (**Extract.1**), as shown in Figure 5–28.

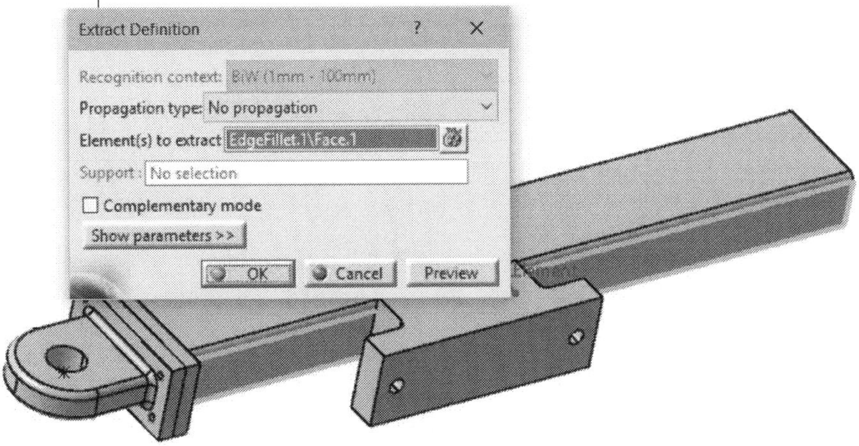

Figure 5–28

10. Project the two contacting edges of the support part onto the extracted surface of the beam, as shown in Figure 5–29.

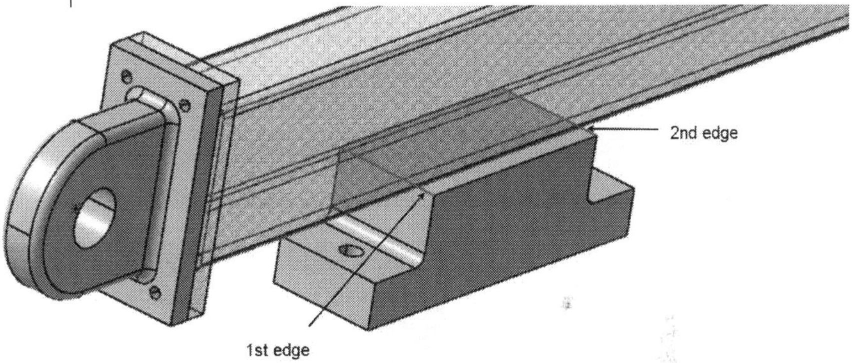

Figure 5–29

11. Hide the **Support_05** part. The model displays as shown in Figure 5–30.

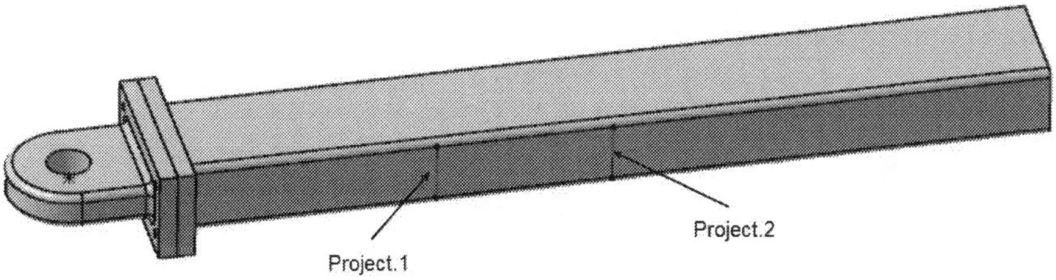

Figure 5–30

12. Split **Extract.1** with **Project.1**, keeping the side that is toward **Project.2**. The result (**Split.1**) is shown in Figure 5–31.

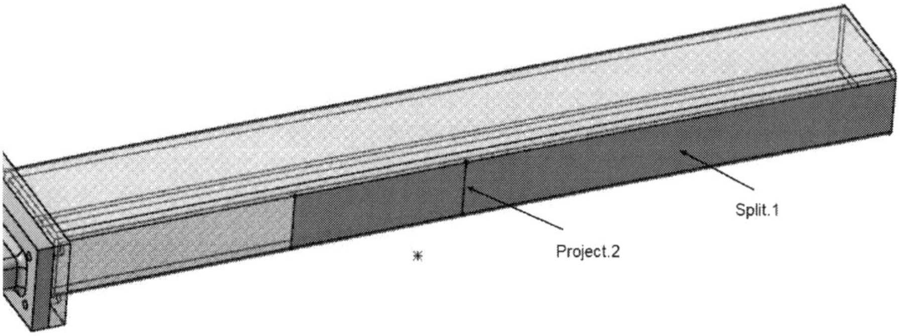

Figure 5–31

13. Split the **Split.1** with **Project.2**, keeping the side that is between **Project.1** and **Project.2**. The result (**Split.2**) is shown in Figure 5–32.

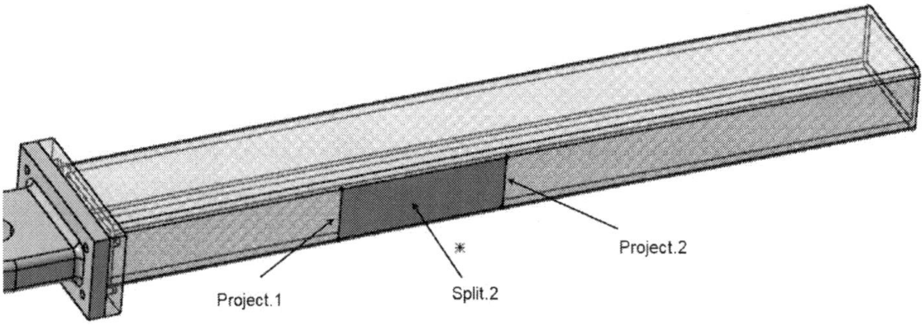

Figure 5–32

14. Switch to the **Part Design** workbench.

15. Right-click on the **PartBody** and select **Define In Work Object** in the contextual menu.

16. In the Surface-Based Features toolbar, select  (Sew Surface). In the Sew Surface Definition dialog box that opens, select **Split.2** as the *Object to sew* and deselect the **Simplify geometry** option, as shown in Figure 5–33.

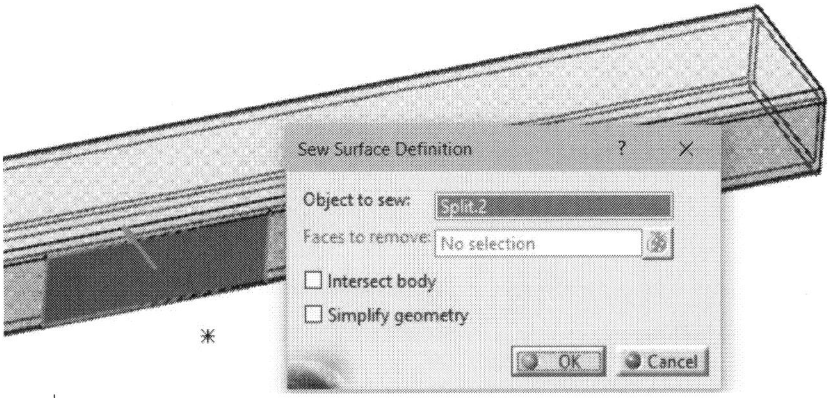

Figure 5–33

17. Click **OK** to complete the Sew Surface operation. Hide **Project.1**, **Project.2**, and **Split.2**.

18. Hide the **Rocker_05** part. The beam part is prepared for the analysis and displays as shown in Figure 5–34.

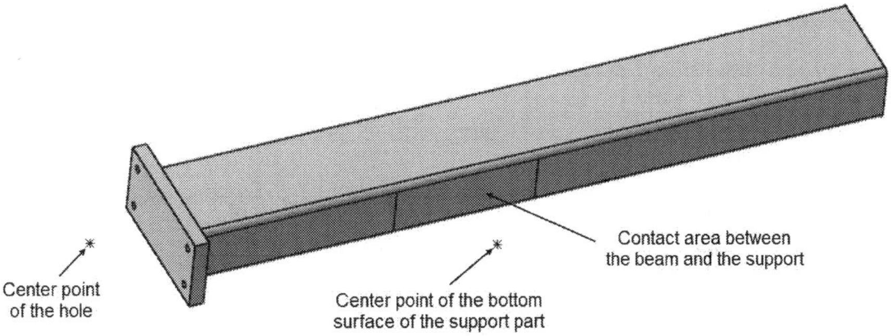

Figure 5–34

19. Open the **Beam_05** part in a new window. From here on, you will be working with the part's model alone.

Task 3 - Apply the material.

1. Apply the **Steel** material from the **Default Material Catalog** to the beam.

Task 4 - Start the GSA workbench.

1. Select **Start>Analysis & Simulation>Generative Structural Analysis**.
2. Select **Static Analysis** as the new analysis case.

Task 5 - Mesh the part.

1. Measure the thickness of the beam profile, as shown in Figure 5–35.

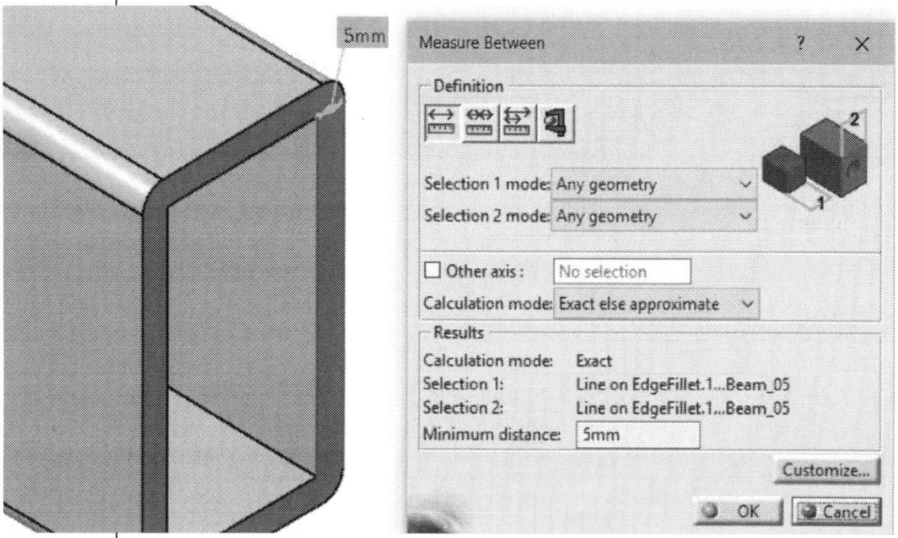

Figure 5–35

2. Double-click on **OCTREE Tetrahedron Mesh.1: Beam_05** in the tree and set the mesh parameters as follows:
   - Element type: **Parabolic**
   - Size: **9mm** (which is 1.8 times the thickness of the part)
   - Absolute sag: **1.8mm** (which is 20% of the size)

3. Display and visually examine the quality of the mesh, as shown in Figure 5–36.

Figure 5–36

4. Right-click on **Mesh.1** in the tree and select **Delete** to delete the mesh visualization and return to the model view.

Task 6 - Create a rigid virtual part.

In this task, you will use a rigid virtual part to model the rocker part in the analysis.

1. In the Virtual Parts toolbar, select  (Rigid Virtual Part). The Rigid Virtual Part dialog box opens, as shown in Figure 5–37.

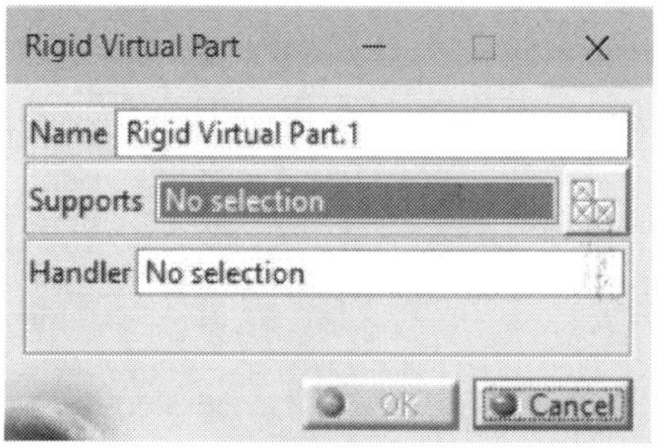

Figure 5–37

2. Select the flange surface of the beam as the *Supports*, and **Point.3** at the center of the hole in the rocker part as the *Handler*, as shown in Figure 5–38.

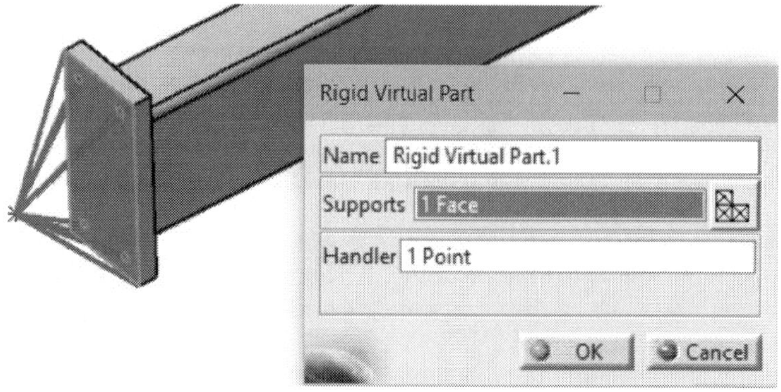

Figure 5–38

3. Click **OK**. The model displays as shown in Figure 5–39.

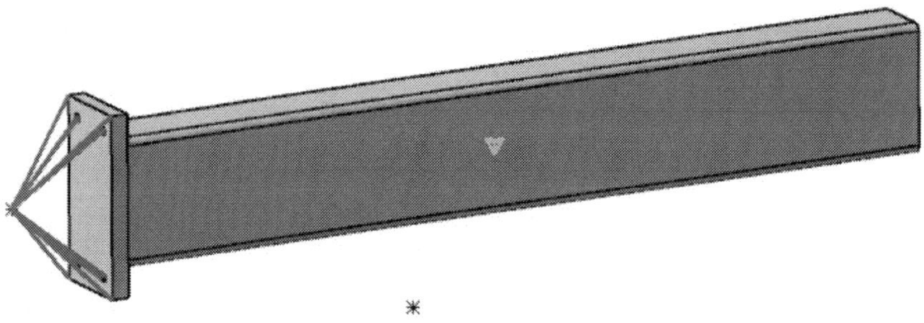

Figure 5–39

Task 7 - Restrain the rigid virtual part.

The rocker part in the assembly is supported by a rigid pin inserted through the hole in the part. Therefore, when a vertical load is applied to the beam, the rocker part should be able to pivot about the center of the hole, which can be accomplished by applying the pivot restraint to the rigid virtual part that models the rocker part. In this task, you will apply a pivot restraint to the rigid virtual part.

1. In the Mechanical Restraints toolbar, select  (Pivot). The Pivot dialog box opens, as shown in Figure 5–40.

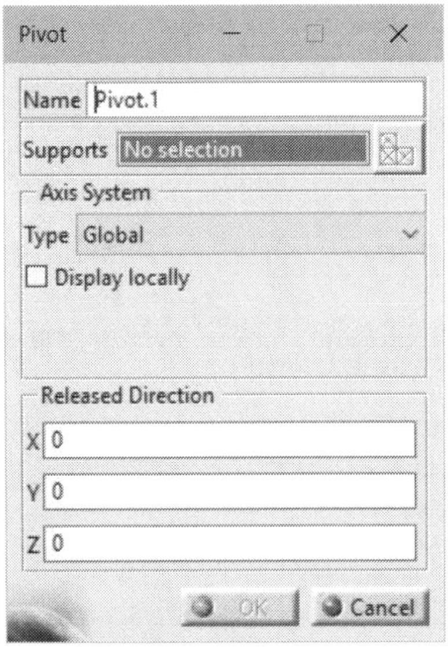

Figure 5–40

*Whenever a restraint or a load is applied to a virtual part, it effectively applies to its handler point, which in this case is the rocker part's pivot point **Point.3**.*

The pivot restraint enables rotation while disabling translation in the Released Direction. Therefore, this setup will enable the Rigid Virtual Part.1 to rotate about the rocker part's pivot point Point.3.

2. Select the **Rigid Virtual Part.1** as the *Supports* and enter **1** in the **X** field of the *Released Direction* section, as shown in Figure 5–41.

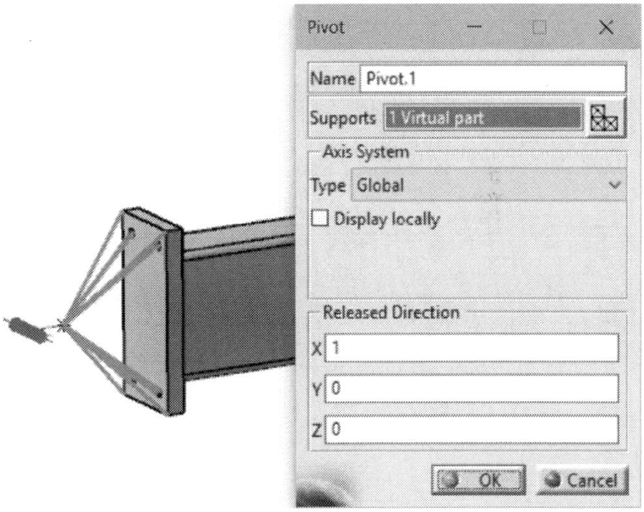

Figure 5–41

3. Click **OK** to close the Pivot dialog box.

Task 8 - Create a contact virtual part.

When the vertical load is applied to the end of the beam, the beam bends and separates from the support part over the initial contact area while remaining in contact along only one of the edges of the support part. This behavior can be simulated with a contact virtual part. In this task, you will use a contact virtual part to model the support part in the analysis.

1. In the Virtual Parts toolbar, select  (Contact Virtual Part). The Contact Virtual Part dialog box opens, as shown in Figure 5–42.

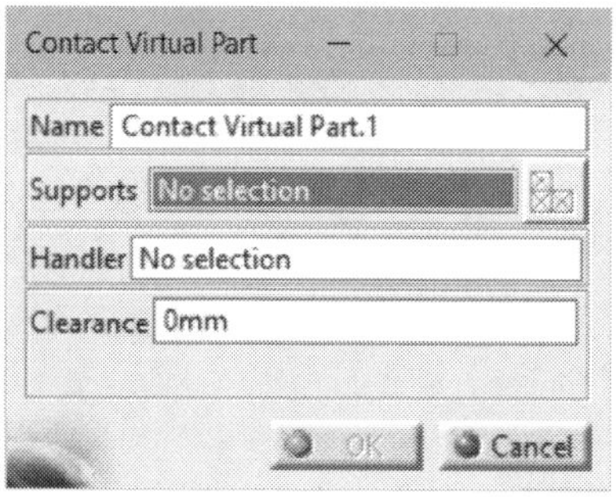

Figure 5–42

2. Select the contact patch on the beam as the *Supports* and select **Point.4** as the *Handler*, as shown in Figure 5–43. Leave the *Clearance* value at **0mm**, which means there is no gap between the virtual part and the beam.

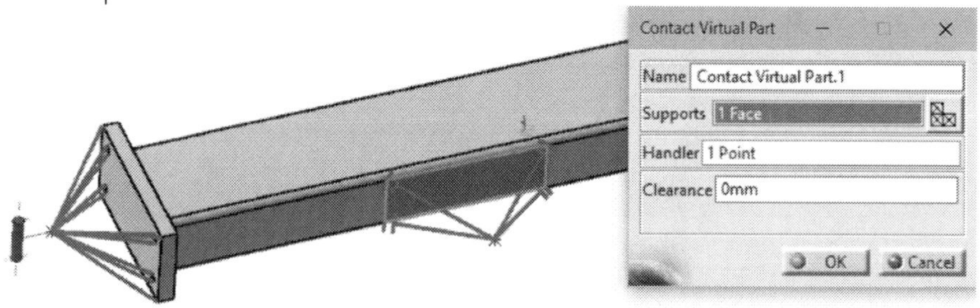

Figure 5–43

3. Click **OK**. The model displays as shown in Figure 5–44.

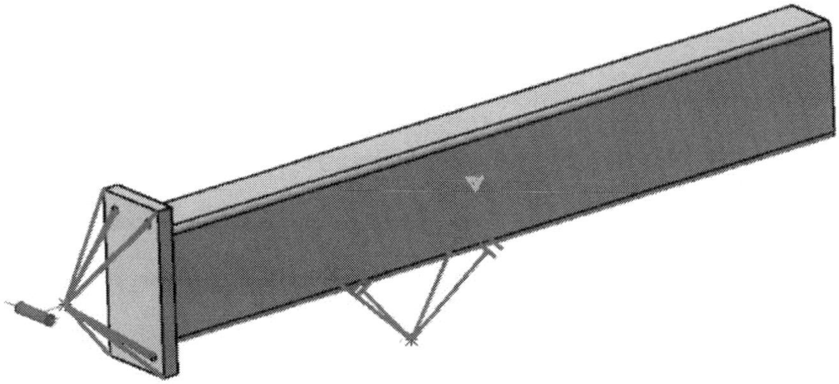

Figure 5–44

Task 9 - Restrain the contact virtual part.

1. Apply (Clamp) to the **Contact Virtual Part.1**, as shown in Figure 5–45. This models the support part being rigidly mounted on the foundation.

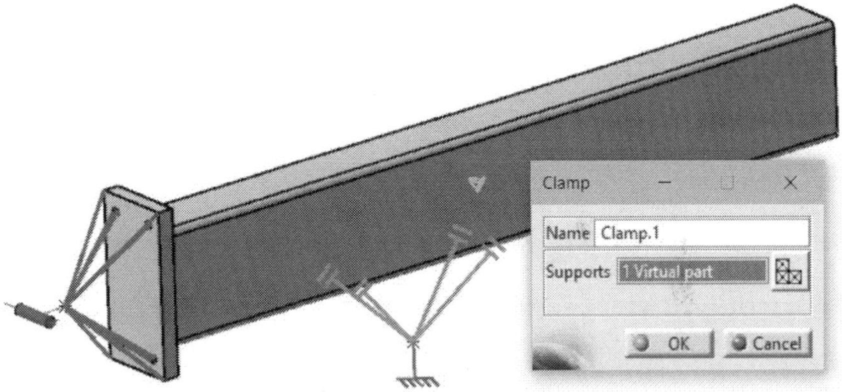

Figure 5–45

Task 10 - Apply loads.

1. Select  (Distributed Force) and apply -**1000N** force in the **Z** direction to the end surface of the beam, as shown in Figure 5–46.

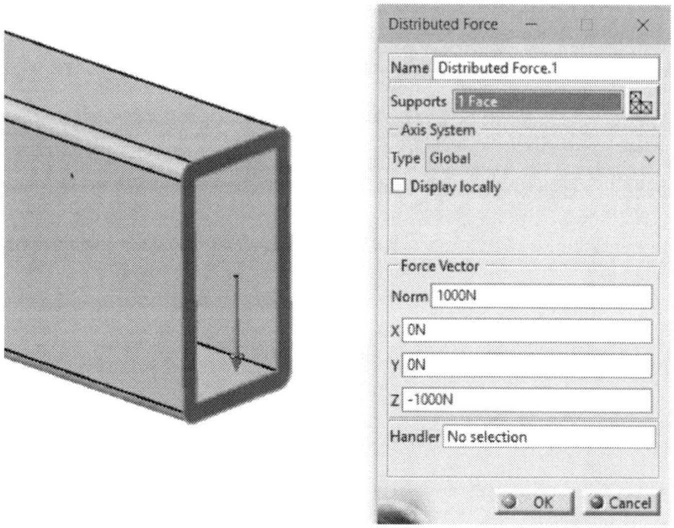

Figure 5–46

Task 11 - Run the analysis.

1. Run the analysis and wait until it completes, which should take less than 30 seconds.

Task 12 - Visualize and animate the deformation.

1. Set the viewpoint to **Front View**.

2. Visualize the model deformation. Set the **Amplification Magnitude** to **500**. The result displays as shown in Figure 5–47.

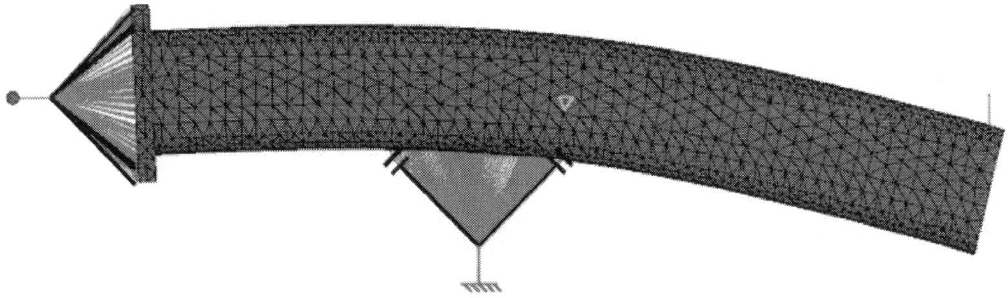

Figure 5–47

3. Animate the deformation and zoom in on the flange area, as shown in Figure 5–48. Note how the flange surface rotates about the pivot point, as was intended in this analysis.

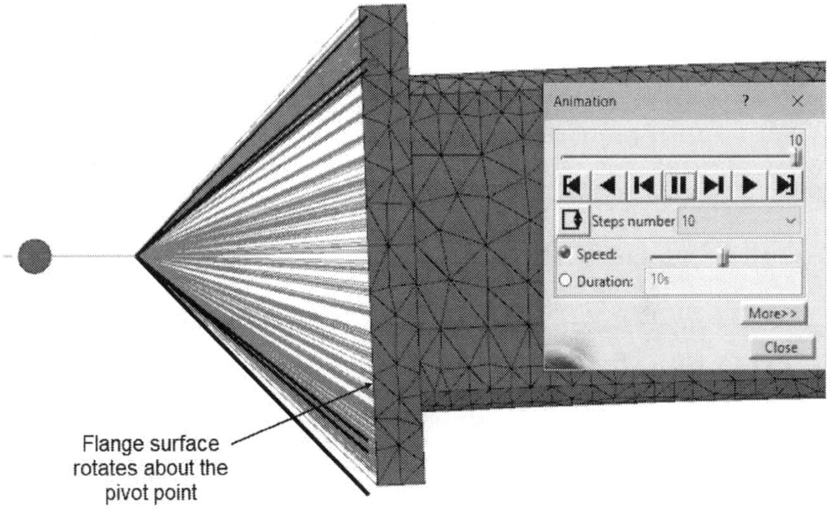

Figure 5–48

4. Zoom in on the contact virtual part area, as shown in Figure 5–49. Note how the beam mesh separates from the Contact Virtual Part on the left end of the contact area while remaining in contact on the right edge of the contact area, which is correct.

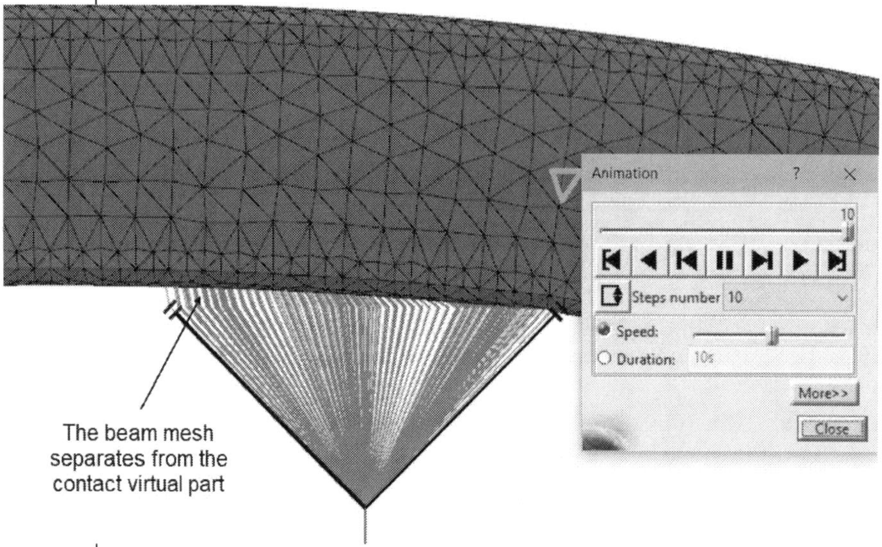

Figure 5–49

5. Close the animation.

Task 13 - Visualize the displacements.

1. Select  (Customize View Parameters) and activate options **Edges and points**, **Shading**, and **Material**.

2. Visualize the displacement magnitude image as **Average Iso**, as shown in Figure 5–50.

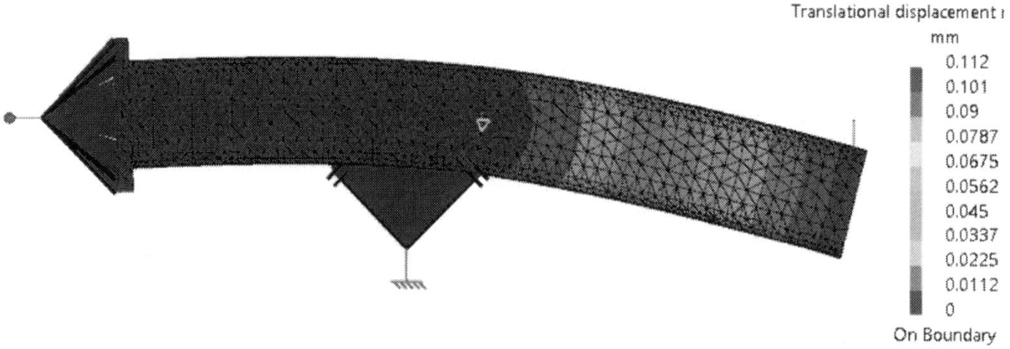

Figure 5–50

Task 14 - Display Von Mises stress.

1. Display the **Von Mises Stress** image, as shown in Figure 5–51.

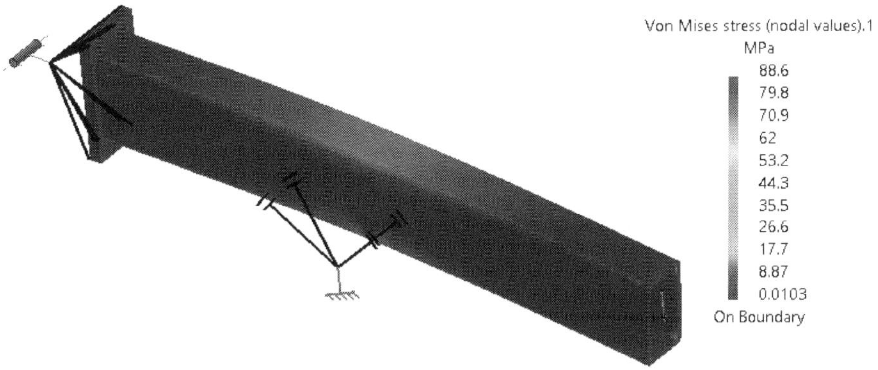

Figure 5–51

2. Using the **Image Extrema** tool, locate the maximum stress area, as shown in Figure 5–52. Note that the maximum stress occurs on the right edge of the contact area, where the beam under the load presses against the sharp edge of the support part.

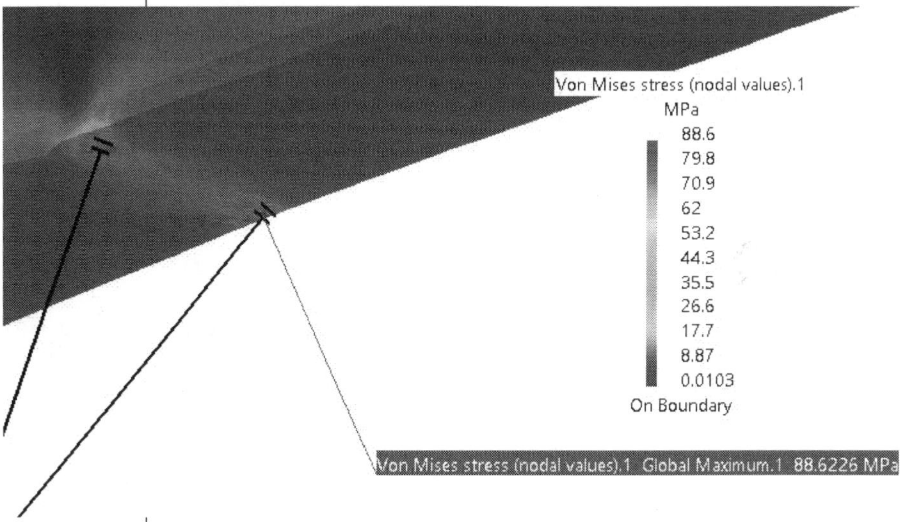

Figure 5–52

3. Right-click on **Von Mises stress (nodal values).1** in the tree and select **Activate/Deactivate** to delete the stress image from the screen and return to the model view.

Task 15 - Obtain reactions in restraints.

In this task, you will create reaction sensors in order to obtain the amounts of force carried by each restraint.

1. Right-click on **Sensors.1** in the tree and select **Create Resultant Sensor>Reaction Sensor** in the contextual menu, as shown in Figure 5–53.

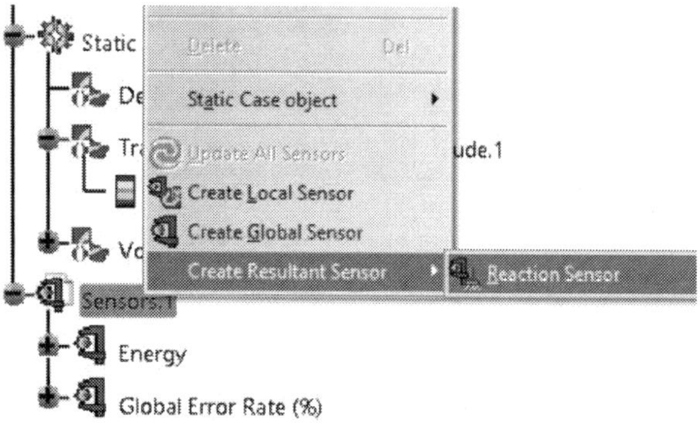

Figure 5–53

2. Once the Reaction Sensor dialog box opens, select **Pivot.1** and click **Update Results**. The reaction forces are displayed, as shown in Figure 5–54.

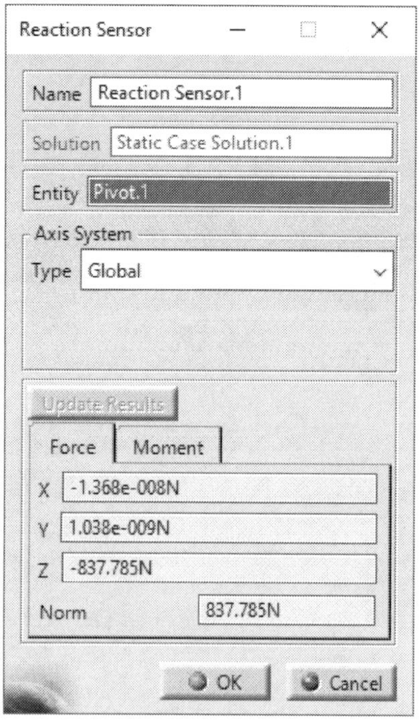

Figure 5–54

Note that the vertical reaction in the pivot is approximately **838N**.

3. Repeat Steps 1 and 2 for the **Clamp.1** restraint. The result is shown in Figure 5–55.

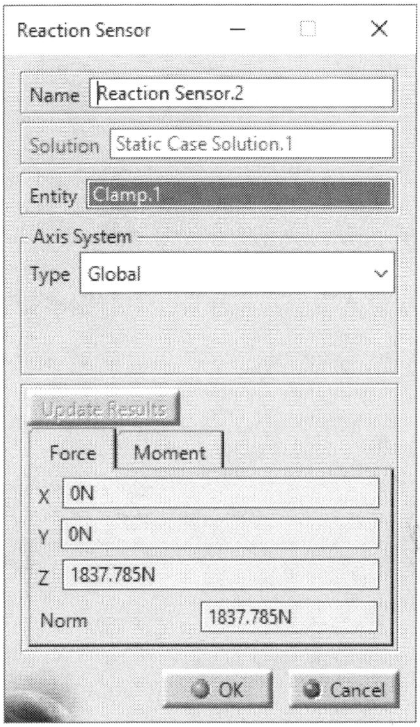

Figure 5–55

Note that the vertical reaction in the clamp is approximately **1838N**, which is more than twice the reaction force in the pivot restraint and which explains why the maximum stress occurs in the contact area between the beam and the support part.

Task 16 - Save and close the files.

1. Optionally, save the analysis document and the part for future reference.

2. Close both the analysis and the part documents.

Practice 5b Stress Analysis of a Steering Knuckle

Practice Objectives

- Create rigid virtual parts.
- Apply loads and restraints to virtual parts.
- Run the analysis and display the results.

In this practice, you will set up and run a static stress analysis on the steering knuckle shown in Figure 5–56. The knuckle is supported by the shock absorber, the lower ball joint, and the steering arm. The load comes from the tire when it hits a pothole: 1200N in the aft direction and 800N in the lateral direction.

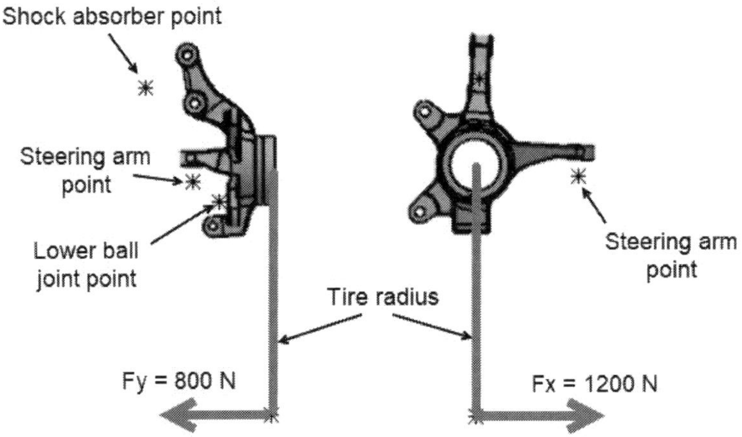

Figure 5–56

Task 1 - Open the part in CATIA.

1. Open **SteeringKnuckle_05.CATPart** from the *CATIA Generative Structural Analysis Practice Files\Ch05* folder. Note that the part has the **Aluminium** material already applied.

2. Set the model display as (Shading with Edges). The part displays as shown in Figure 5–57.

Figure 5–57

3. Select **Tools>Options>Parameters and Measures>Units** and set the units as follows:

   - Length: **Millimeter (mm)**
   - Force: **Newton (N)**
   - Moment: **Newton x Meter (Nxm)**
   - Pressure: **Megapascal (MPa)**

Task 2 - Start the GSA workbench.

1. Select **Start>Analysis & Simulation>Generative Structural Analysis**.

2. Select **Static Analysis** as the new analysis case.

Task 3 - Mesh the part.

1. Double-click on **OCTREE Tetrahedron Mesh.1: SteeringKnuckle_05** in the tree and set up the mesh parameters as following:

   - Element type: **Parabolic**
   - Size: **5mm**
   - Absolute sag: **1mm**

2. Right-click on **Nodes and Elements** in the tree and select **Mesh Visualization** to display the mesh, as shown in Figure 5–58. Rotate the model and visually examine the mesh.

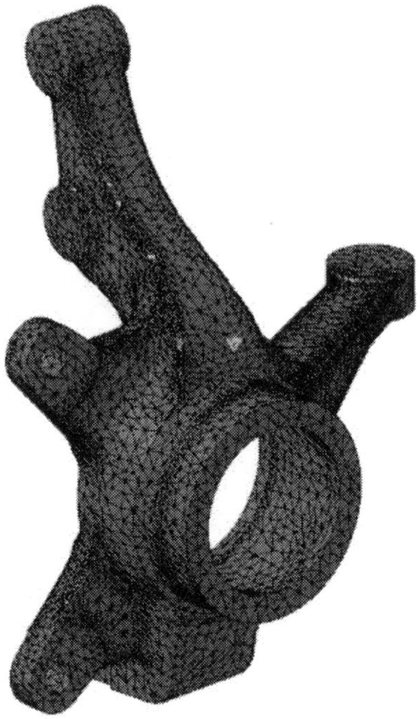

Figure 5–58

3. Right-click on **Mesh.1** in the tree and select **Delete** to delete the mesh visualization and return to the model view.

Task 4 - Create a virtual part.

In this analysis, the adjoining parts to the steering knuckle are simulated with rigid virtual parts. In this task, you create a virtual part that models the wheel rim and the tire diameter, and enables transfer of the pothole impact force from the point at the bottom of the tire to the knuckle part.

1. Select  (Rigid Virtual Part). The Rigid Virtual Part dialog box opens, as shown in Figure 5–59.

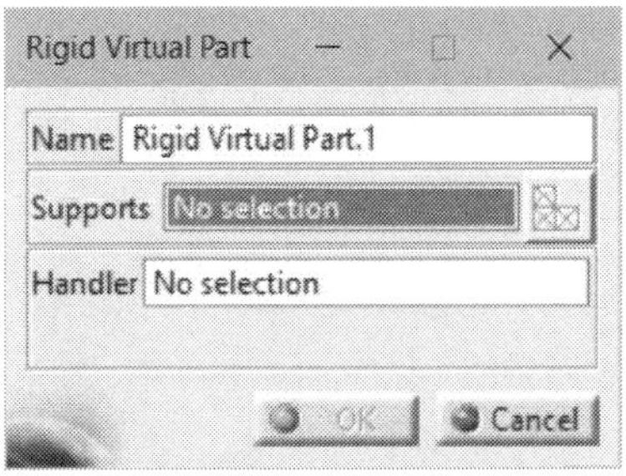

Figure 5–59

2. Select the inside surface of the hub as the *Supports* and the **TirePnt** point as the *Handler*, as shown in Figure 5–60.

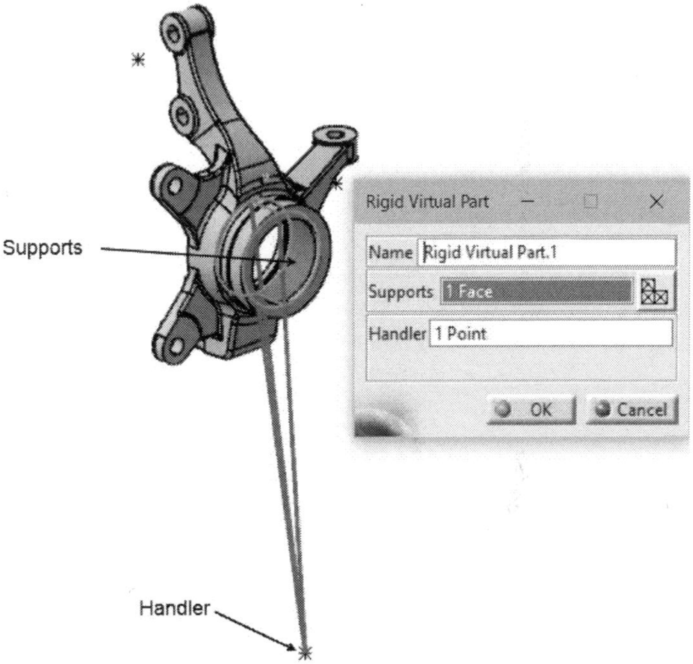

Figure 5–60

3. Click **OK** to close the Rigid Virtual Part dialog box.

Task 5 - Apply load.

When a load is applied to a virtual part, it effectively is applied to the virtual part's handler point.

1. Select  (Distributed Force) and apply **1200N** force in the **X** direction and **800N** force in the **Y** direction to **Rigid Virtual Part.1**, as shown in Figure 5–61.

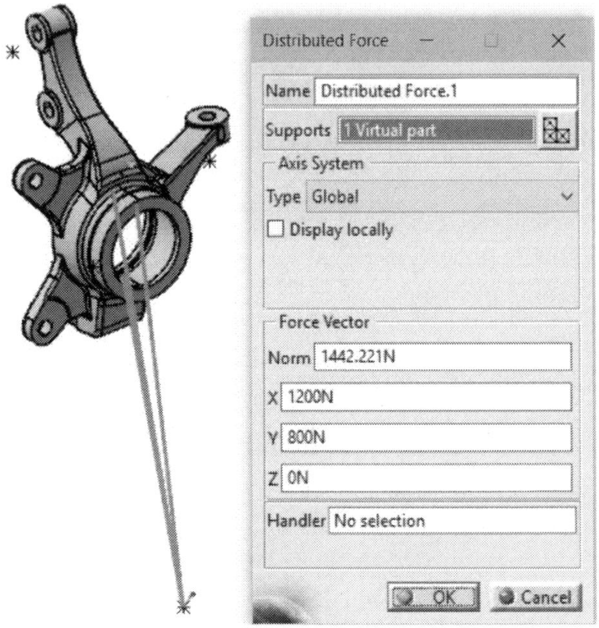

Figure 5–61

Task 6 - Create a virtual part simulating the shock absorber.

In this task, you create a virtual part that models the shock absorber attached to the knuckle through the two upper holes.

1. Select  (Rigid Virtual Part).

2. Select the inside surfaces of the two upper holes as the *Supports* and the **UpperShockPnt** point as the *Handler*, as shown in Figure 5–62. Click **OK** when done.

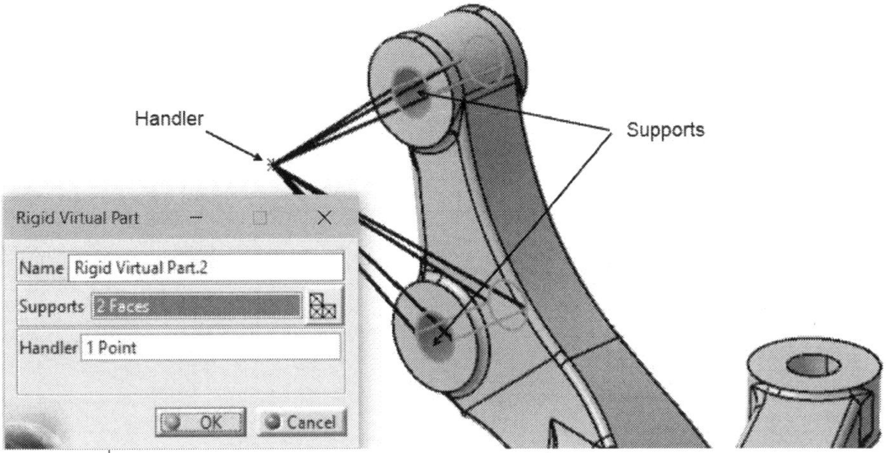

Figure 5–62

Task 7 - Create a virtual part simulating the lower ball joint.

In this task, you create a virtual part that models the lower ball joint attached to the knuckle through the vertical hole at the bottom of the knuckle.

1. Select  (Rigid Virtual Part) and select the inside surface of the bottom hole as the *Supports* and the **LowerBallJointPnt** point as the *Handler*, as shown in Figure 5–63.

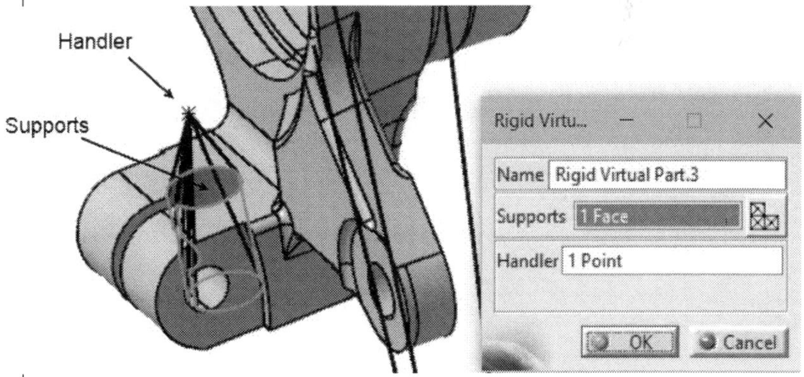

Figure 5–63

Task 8 - Create a virtual part simulating the steering arm.

In this task, you create a virtual part that models the steering arm attached to the knuckle through the vertical hole at the end of the lever.

1. Select (Rigid Virtual Part) and select the inside surface of the hole at the end of the lever as the *Supports* and the **SteeringArmPnt** point as the *Handler*, as shown in Figure 5–64.

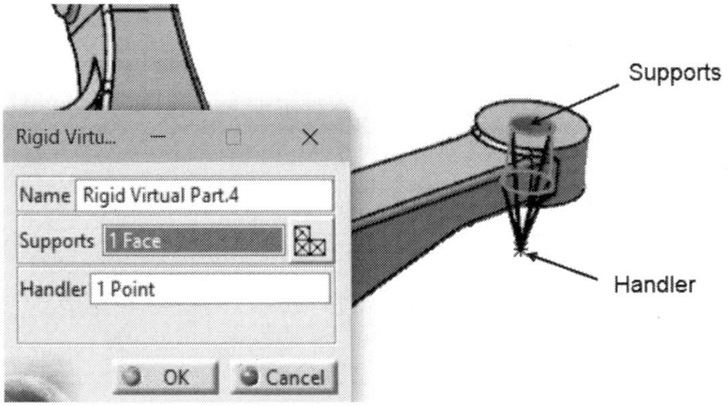

Figure 5–64

Task 9 - Apply restraints.

When a restraint is applied to a virtual part, it effectively is applied to the virtual part's handler point.

1. Select (Clamp) and clamp the virtual part that models the shock absorber (**Rigid Virtual Part.2**).

2. Select (User-defined Restraint) and restrain the **X** and **Y** translations of the virtual part that models the lower ball joint (**Rigid Virtual Part.3**).

3. Select  (User-defined Restraint) and restrain the **Y** translation of the virtual part that models the steering arm (**Rigid Virtual Part.4**).

4. The model displays as shown in Figure 5–65.

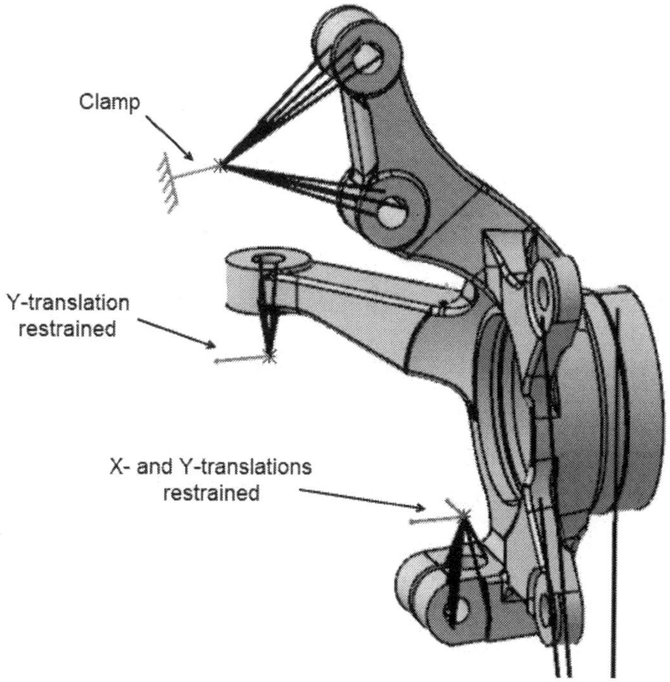

Figure 5–65

Task 10 - Visualize the virtual part meshes.

1. Right-click on **Nodes and Elements** in the tree and select **Mesh Visualization** to display the mesh, as shown in Figure 5–66. Note that each virtual part created its own mesh, which is a collection of rigid links connecting the handler point with the mesh nodes on the virtual part's supports.

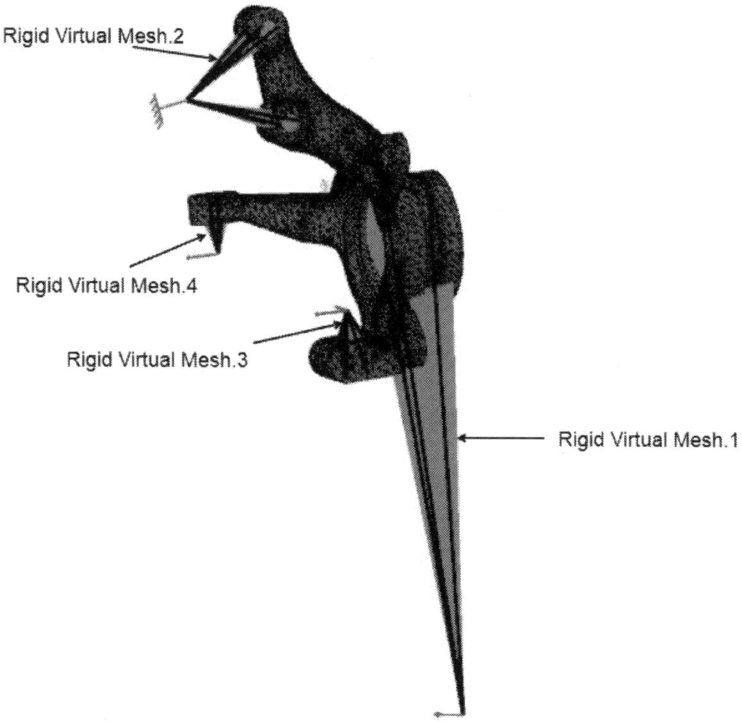

Figure 5–66

2. Right-click **Mesh.1** in the tree and select **Delete** to delete the mesh visualization and return to the model view.

Task 11 - Run the analysis.

1. Run the analysis and wait until it completes.

Task 12 - Display and animate the displacement magnitude.

1. Change the view mode to (Shading with Material).

2. In the Image toolbar, select (Displacement). The displacement vector image displays, as shown in Figure 5–67.

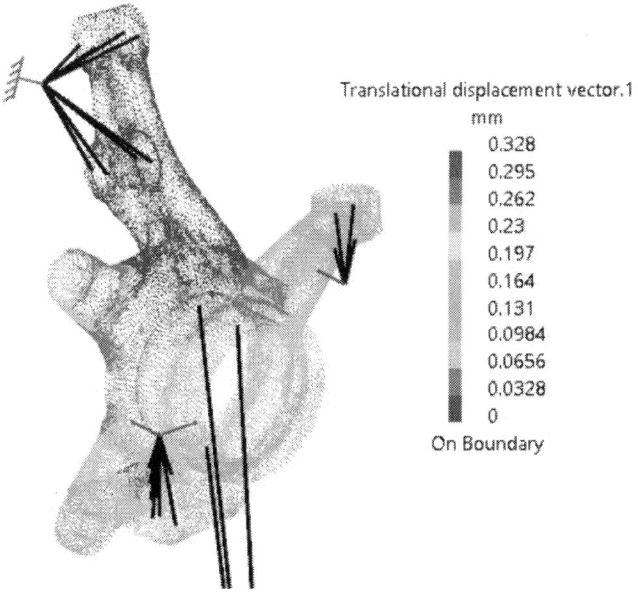

Figure 5–67

3. Double-click on the **Translational displacement vector.1** object in the tree. In the Image Edition dialog box that opens, select **Average iso**. The result image displays as shown in Figure 5–68. Note that now displacements are also shown for the virtual part meshes. Do not close the Image Edition dialog box yet.

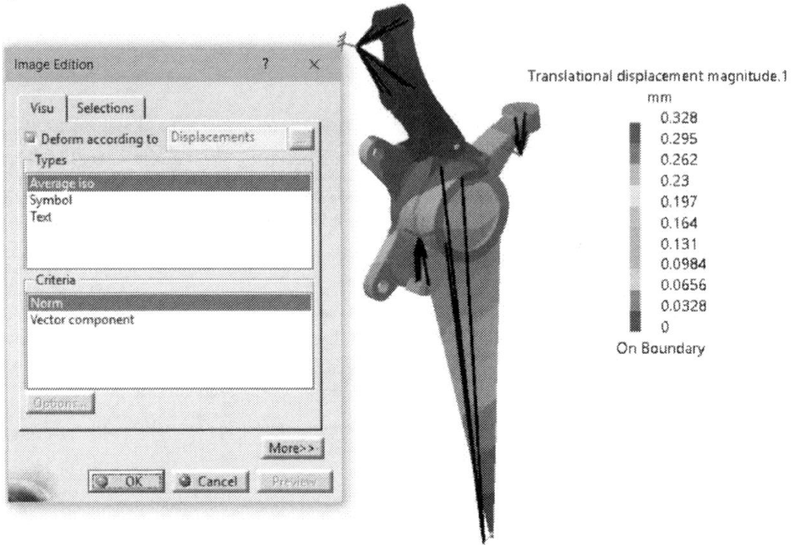

Figure 5–68

4. In the Image Edition dialog box, activate the *Selections* tab. In the *Available Groups* section, select **OCTREE Tetrahedron Mesh.1: SteeringKnuckle_05** and click the  button to move the part mesh into the *Activated Groups* section, as shown in Figure 5–69.

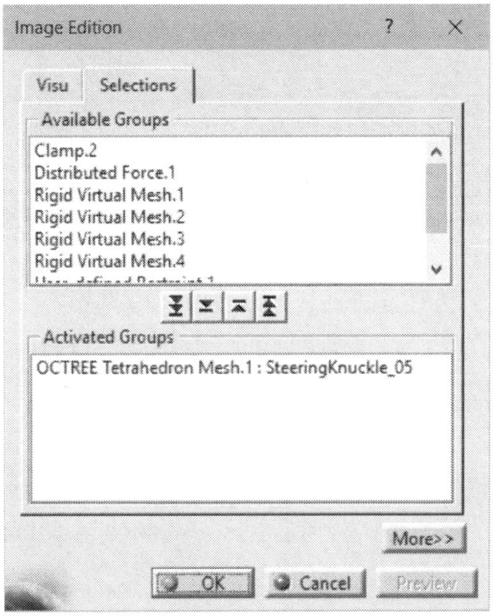

Figure 5–69

5. Click **OK** to close the Image Edition dialog box. The displacement magnitude image displays as shown in Figure 5–70. Note that now the result is only shown for the knuckle part mesh and the virtual part meshes are hidden.

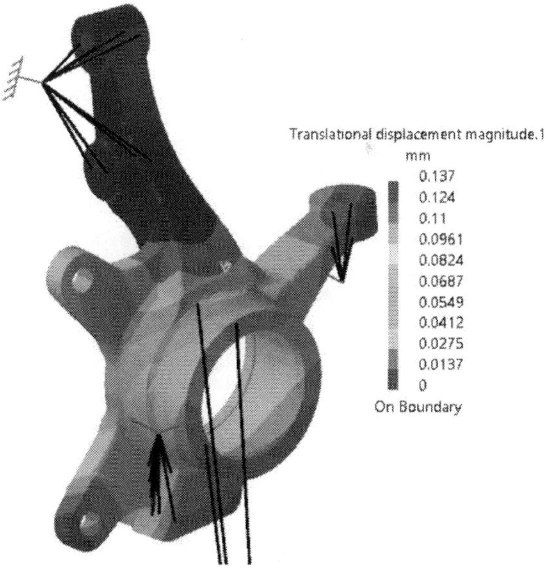

Figure 5–70

6. Using the (Amplification Magnitude) tool, set the **Scaling factor** value to **100**.

7. In the tree, right-click on **Links Manager.1** and select **Hide/Show** in the contextual menu. The displacement magnitude image is now overlaid on the undeformed model, as shown in Figure 5–71.

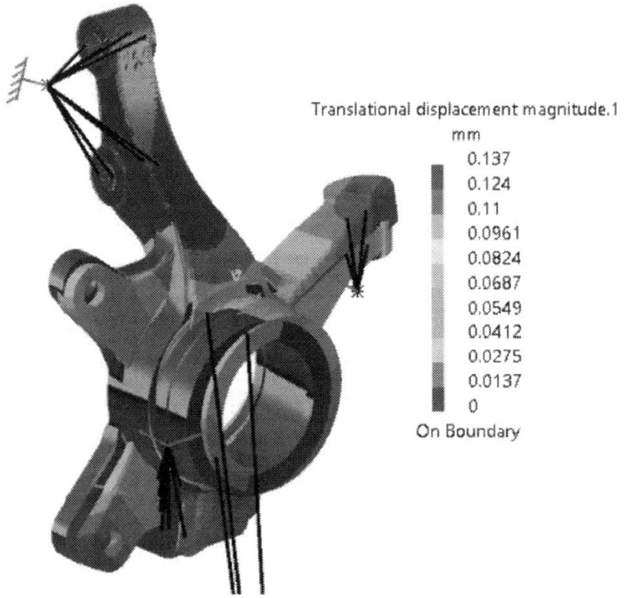

Figure 5–71

8. Animate the displacement magnitude. Check whether the applied loads and restraints behave correctly.

Task 13 - Display Von Mises stress.

1. Display the **Von Mises Stress** image, as shown in Figure 5–72. Does the maximum stress exceed the yield strength of the material?

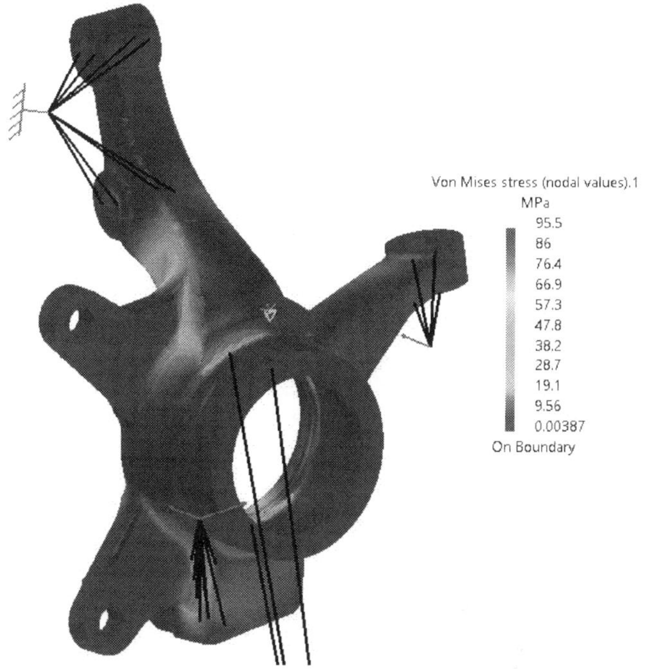

Figure 5–72

2. Using the **Image Extrema** tool, locate the maximum stress area, as shown in Figure 5–73. Note that the maximum stress occurs in the fillet near the lower ball joint attachment.

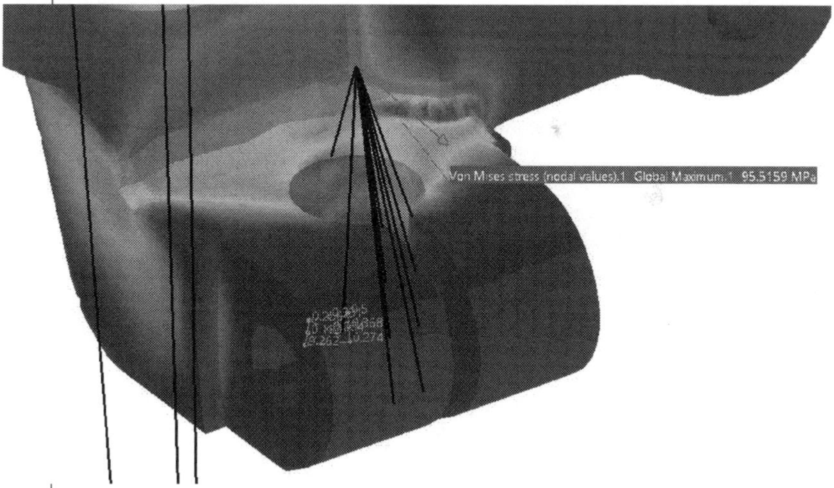

Figure 5–73

3. Right-click on **Von Mises stress (nodal values).1** in the tree and select **Activate/Deactivate** to delete the stress image from the screen and return to the model view.

Task 14 - Save and close the files.

1. Optionally, save the analysis document and the part for future reference.
2. Close both the analysis and the part documents.

Practice 5c Bracket Supported by Rubber Bushings

Practice Objectives

- Create smooth spring virtual parts.
- Apply loads and restraints.
- Run the analysis and display the results.

In this practice, you will set up and run a static stress analysis of the bracket shown in Figure 5–74, with minimum instruction.

The end holes of the bracket are fixed to a rigid foundation, while the middle two holes are supported by rubber bushings in the vertical direction. The bracket is loaded in the horizontal direction at the two holes in the vertical flange.

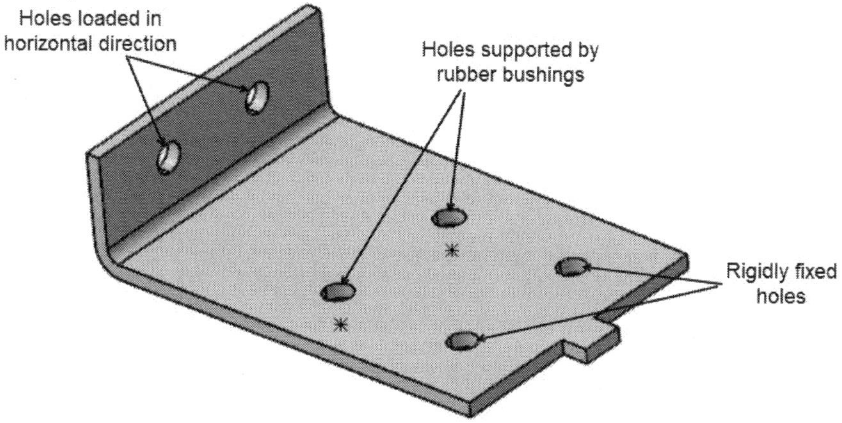

Figure 5–74

Task 1 - Open the part.

1. Open **xbracket_05.CATPart** from the *CATIA Generative Structural Analysis Practice Files\Ch05* folder.
2. Apply the **Aluminium** material to the part.

Task 2 - Prepare the analysis model.

1. Start the GSA workbench.

2. Mesh the model with the following parameters:

   - Element type: **Parabolic**
   - Size: **23mm**
   - Sag: **4mm**

3. Visually examine the mesh.

4. Clamp the inside surfaces of the two end holes, as shown in Figure 5–75.

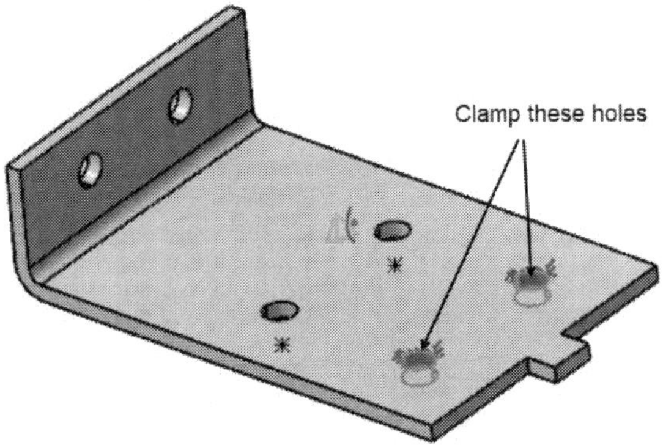

Figure 5–75

Rubber bushings provide compliant supports to the middle holes, which is simulated with springs. Also, the use of smooth virtual parts allows the holes to deform during the loading. In contrast, the holes would not be able to deform if rigid virtual parts were used instead.

5. For the two middle holes, create two smooth spring virtual parts, as shown in Figure 5–76. Use the inside surfaces of each hole as the *Supports*. Use **Point.3** as the *Handler* for the first virtual part and **Point.4** as the *Handler* for the second virtual part. For both virtual parts, use the **1.5e+6 N_m** translation stiffness in the global **X-**direction.

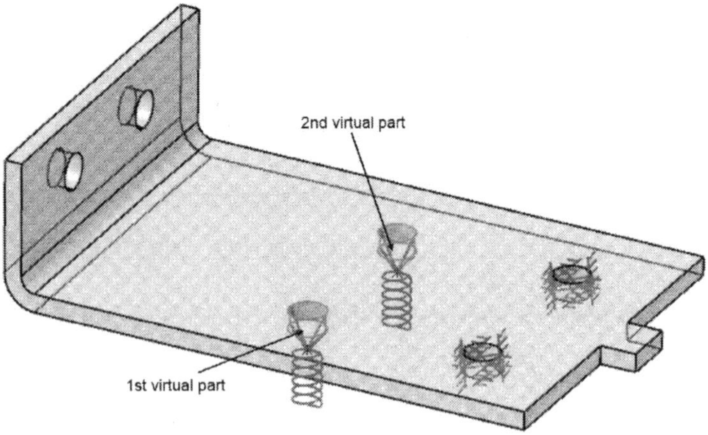

Figure 5–76

6. Apply a clamp to both virtual parts.
7. Apply **5000N** combined force in the **-Y** direction to the holes in the vertical flange, as shown in Figure 5–77.

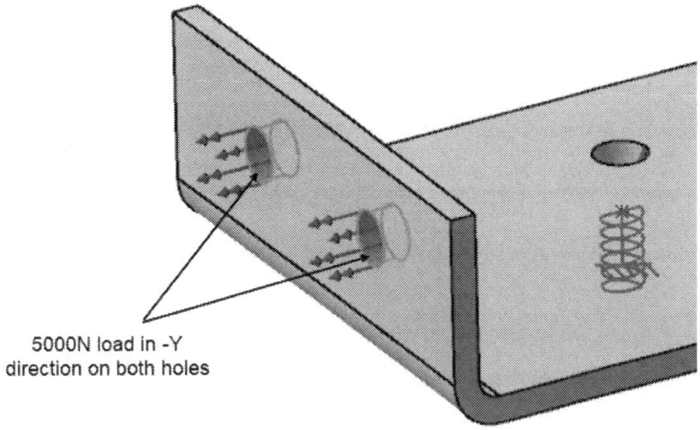

Figure 5–77

Task 3 - Run the analysis.

1. Check the model for inconsistencies.
2. Run the analysis.

Task 4 - Visualize and examine the analysis results.

1. Visualize and animate the Displacement Magnitude. Do the springs correctly simulate compliant supports on the middle holes?
2. Display the Von Mises color plot. In which area in the model are the stresses at maximum? Would you expect the area of maximum stress to move to a different location if rubber bushings with lower stiffness were used?
3. Close the model without saving.

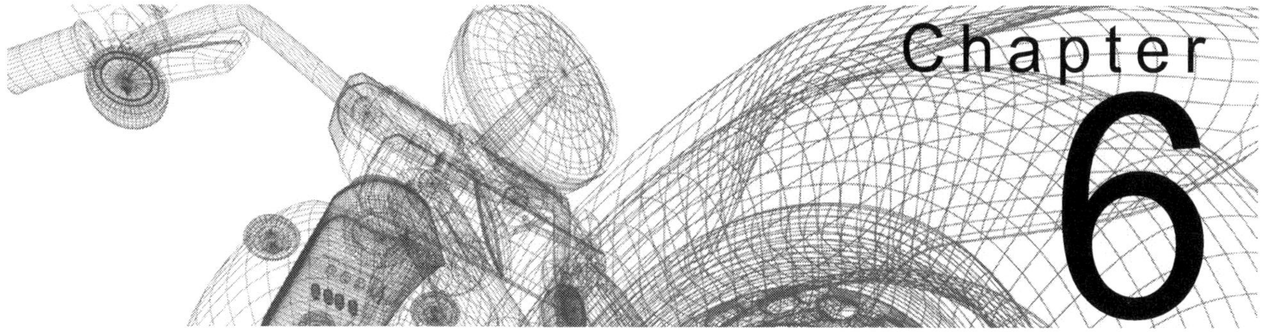

Chapter 6

Assembly Analysis

In this chapter, you learn how to model the analysis connections between assembly components.

Learning Objectives in This Chapter

- Understand the assembly analysis process.
- Review the types of connection properties.
- Use assembly constraints and general analysis connection as supports.
- Understand the fastened and slider connection properties.
- Understand the rigid and smooth connection properties.
- Understand the user-defined connection property.
- Visualize the assembly analysis results.

6.1 Assembly Analysis Process

The assembly analysis process in GSA is shown in Figure 6–1. In general, the process is quite similar to the part analysis, with only two steps being unique to the assembly analysis:

- Switching the assembly to Design mode
- Creating the analysis connections

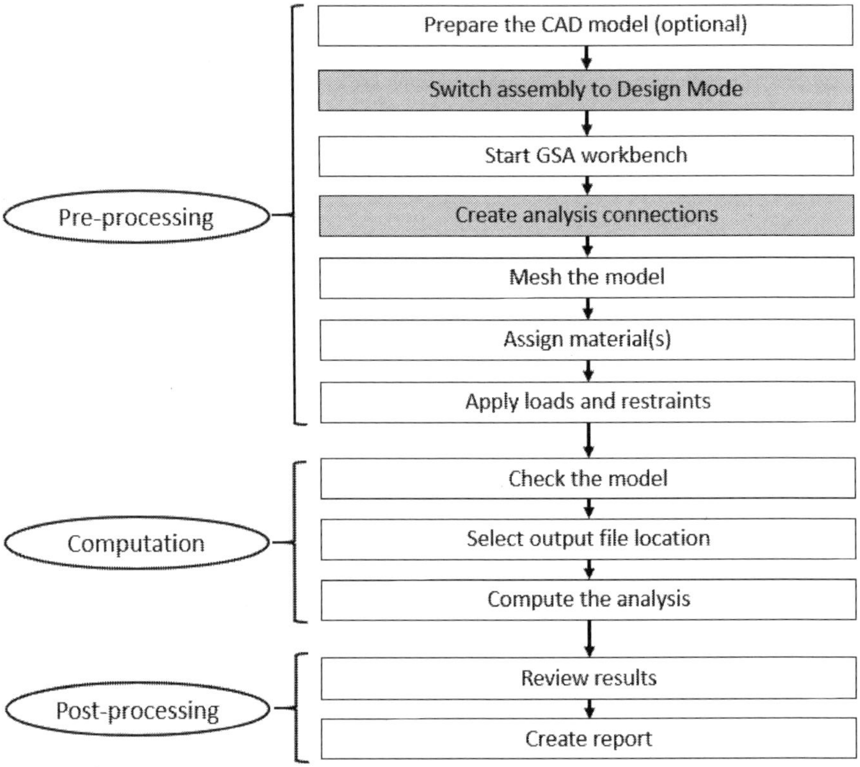

Figure 6–1

Switching to Design Mode

This step is only necessary if you open the assembly in Visualization mode (the option **Tools>Options>Infrastructure> Product Structure>Cache Management>Work with the cache system** is toggled on), since the GSA workbench requires the parts to be in Design mode.

To switch to Design mode, right-click on the root assembly and select **Representations>Design Mode**, as shown in Figure 6–2.

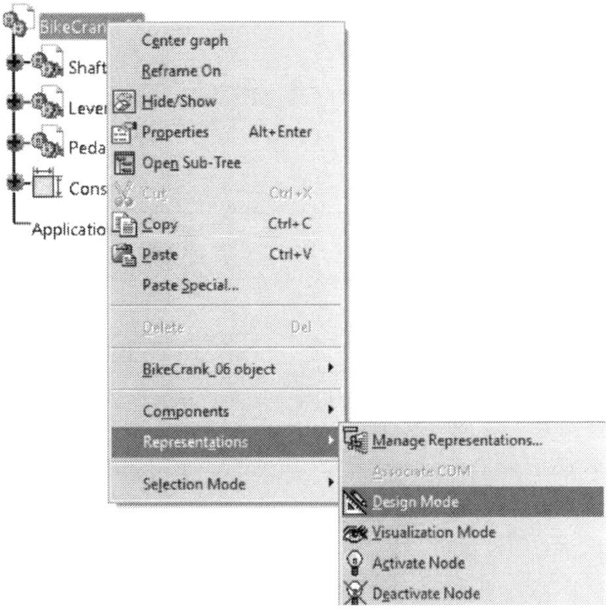

Figure 6–2

Alternatively, activate the **Tools>Options>Analysis & Simulation>General>Disable Product Structure cache system** option, as shown in Figure 6–3. This will automatically switch the assembly to Design mode upon starting the GSA workbench.

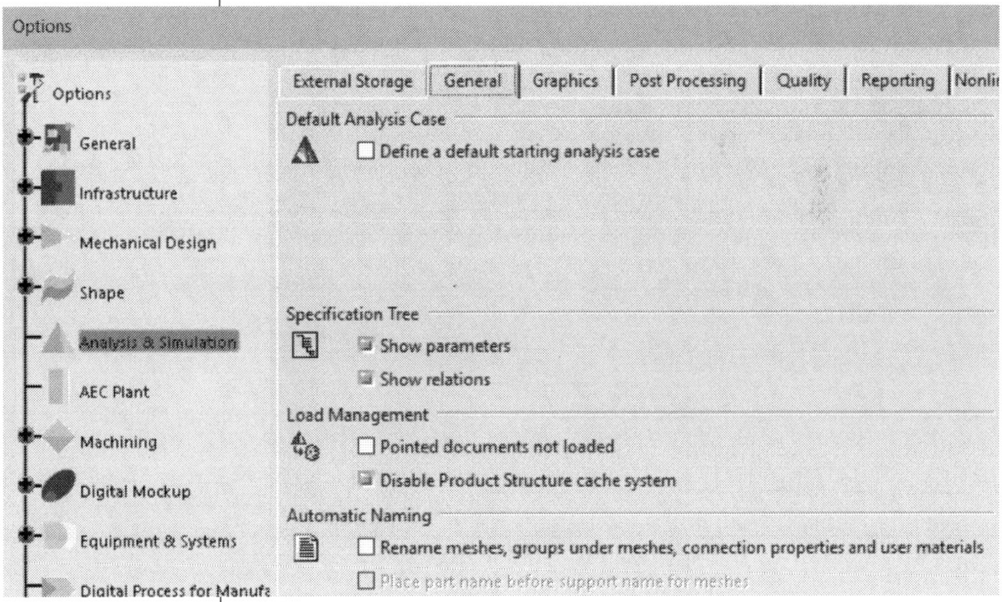

Figure 6–3

Creating Analysis Connections

Initially, CATIA assumes that all parts in the assembly are *disjoint* (i.e., do not interact with each other when a load is applied). Thus, the parts may interpenetrate or separate, etc., when they are not supposed to, and the computation is likely to fail due to parts being able to move as rigid bodies.

The user must explicitly define all part interactions by creating analysis connections.

An analysis connection in GSA is defined by two bits of information:

- A connection support, which describes which geometrical entities are connected.
- A connection property, which describes how those geometrical entities are connected (e.g., are the parts welded to one another or bolted?).

Therefore, creating an analysis connection in GSA is always a two-step process, as shown in Figure 6–4.

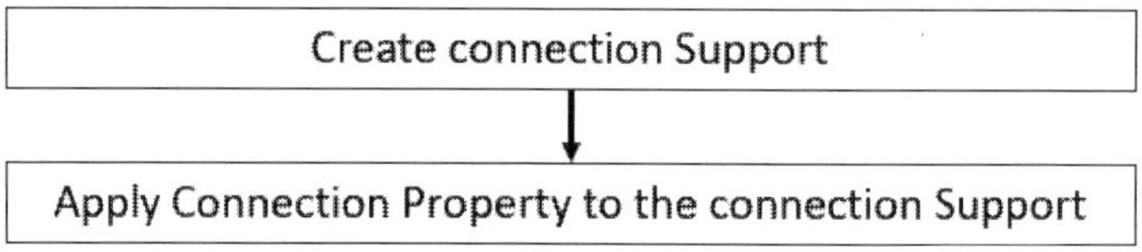

Figure 6–4

6.2 Analysis Connection Supports

There are two options for how you can specify an analysis connection support.

The first option involves reusing assembly constraints (e.g., coincidence, surface contact, etc.) as the connection supports. If you have suitable assembly constraints in your model, you can create a new analysis connection by selecting a connection property and selecting an appropriate assembly constraint.

The second option does not require you to have constraints in your assembly. Instead, you create connection supports using the Analysis Supports toolbar shown in Figure 6–5.

Figure 6–5

The  (Point Analysis Connection),  (Line Analysis Connection), and  (Surface Analysis Connection) tools are designed specifically for the welding connection properties in shell models and are discussed in Chapter 9.

For all other types of connection properties, you use the  (General Analysis Connection) tool.

To create a new connection support, select  (General Analysis Connection). The General Analysis Connection dialog box opens, as shown in Figure 6–6.

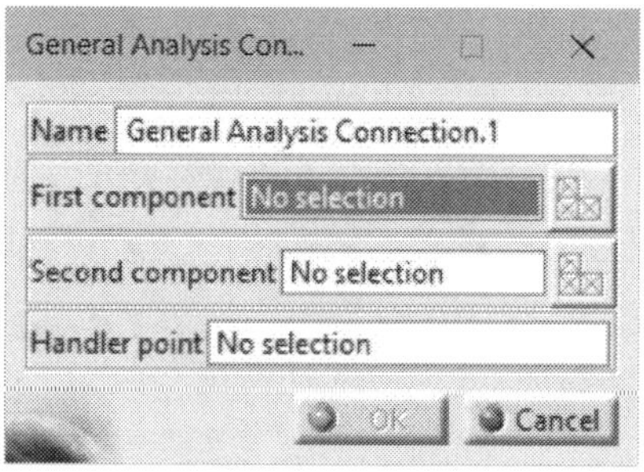

Figure 6–6

Select one or more surfaces or other geometrical entities on the first part as the *First component*, as shown in Figure 6–7.

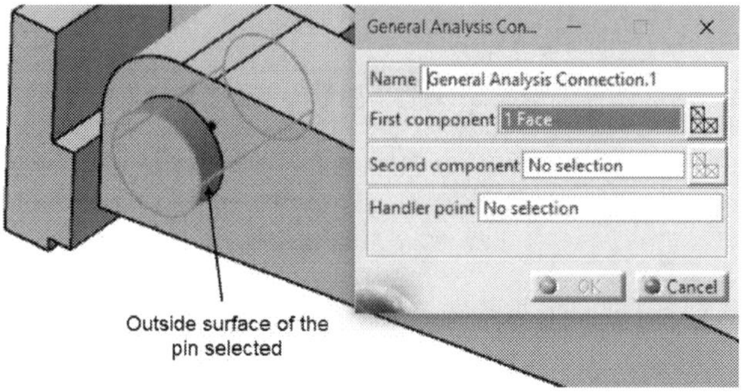

Figure 6–7

Click the *Second component* field to activate it and select one or more geometrical entities on the second part, as shown in Figure 6–8.

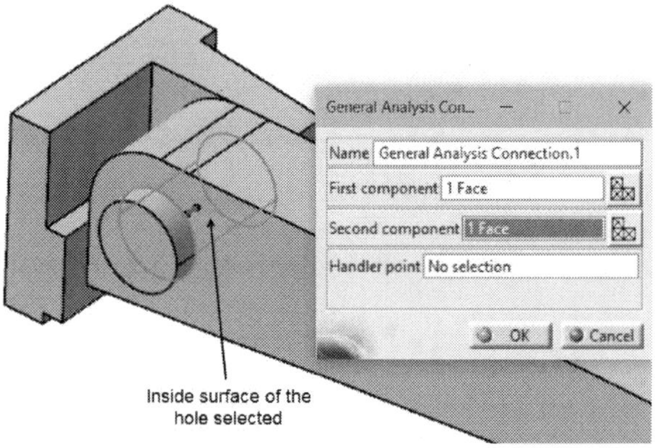

Figure 6–8

The *Handler point* is optional and is only applicable to a few types of connections, such as the rigid connection, smooth connection, and user-defined connection.

Once you have selected your components, click **OK**. The new analysis connection support displays in the **Analysis Connections.1** section in the tree, as shown in Figure 6–9.

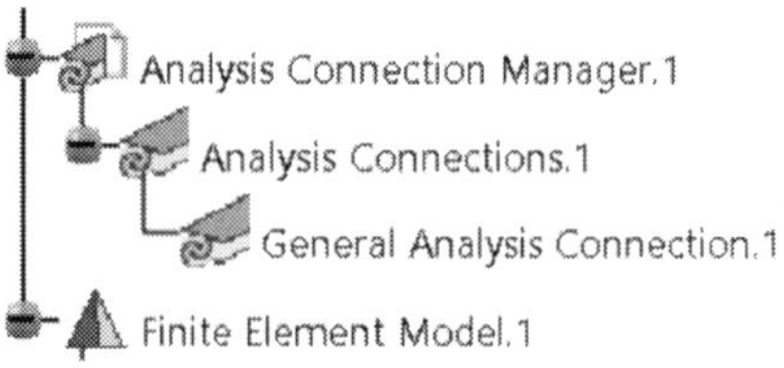

Figure 6–9

6.3 Connection Properties

The connection property types available in GSA are described in the following table.

Name	Description
Slider	Enables the two connected surfaces to slide without friction along each other. Neither the surface inter-penetration nor separation is permitted.
Contact	Prevents inter-penetration of the two connected surfaces, while permitting sliding or separation. Discussed in detail in Chapter 7.
Fastened	Bonds the two surfaces together, so there is neither slippage nor separation occurring between the surfaces.
Fastened Spring	Similar to the fastened connection, but with a linear elastic layer between the connected surfaces.
Pressure Fitting	Similar to the contact connection, but allows initial interference between the connected surfaces. Discussed in detail in Chapter 7.
Bolt Tightening	Enables application of a preload to bolts or screws. Discussed in detail in Chapter 8.
Rigid	Creates an infinitely rigid connection between the parts.
Smooth	Creates a soft connection between the parts.
Virtual Bolt Tightening	Enables application of a preload in fastened assemblies, without having the actual bolts or screws in the model. Discussed in detail in Chapter 8.
Virtual Spring Bolt Tightening	Similar to the virtual bolt tightening connection, but allows simulation of the bolt or screw flexibility with a spring. Discussed in detail in Chapter 8.
User-defined	Allows customization of the connection properties, per the user requirements.
Spot Welding	Simulates spot welds in shell models. Discussed in detail in Chapter 9.
Seam Welding	Simulates continuous welds in shell models. Discussed in detail in Chapter 9.
Surface Welding	Simulates surface welds in shell models. Discussed in detail in Chapter 9.

Fastened Connection Property

The fastened connection property creates a link that makes two parts behave as if they were a single body, so there is neither slippage nor separation occurring on the interface boundary. However, the parts may have different material properties. From the FEA standpoint, this is equivalent to merging two meshes together.

The fastened connection property is suitable for simulating parts that are arc-welded, bonded, fusion-welded, etc.

To create a fastened connection, select  (Fastened Connection Property) in the Connection Properties toolbar and select the *Supports*, as shown in Figure 6–10.

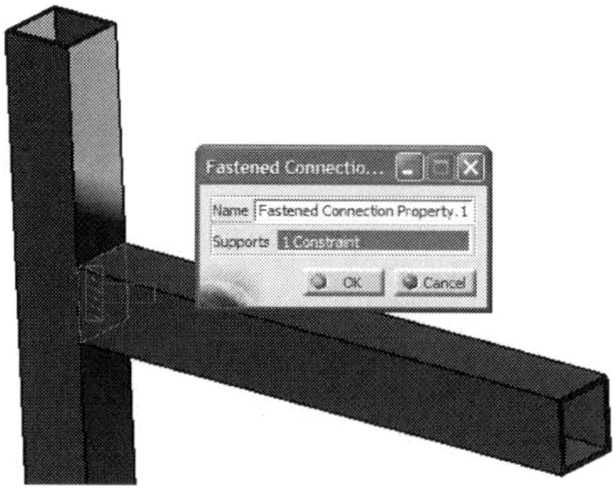

Figure 6–10

Fastened Spring Connection Property

The fastened spring connection property links the two parts similarly to the fastened connection property. However, the difference is that the fastened spring connection property also models a virtual elastic layer between the connected parts, with the user being able to assign the specific stiffness to that elastic layer.

The fastened spring connection property is suitable for simulating thin gaskets, adhesive films, etc., between the parts.

To create a fastened spring connection, select  (Fastened Spring Connection Property) in the Connection Properties toolbar, select the *Supports*, and enter the translation and rotation stiffnesses, as shown in Figure 6–11.

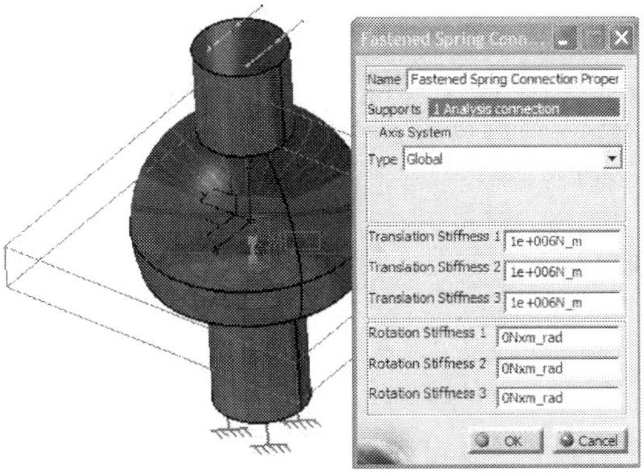

Figure 6–11

Slider Connection Property

The slider connection property enables the two connected parts to slide, without friction, along each other on the common boundary. However, the parts are not permitted either to interpenetrate or to separate while sliding.

The slider connection is suitable for simulating parts that should be permitted to freely slide along each other, with the separation between the interfacing surfaces being negligible.

To create a slider connection, select  (Slider Connection Property) in the Connection Properties toolbar and select the *Supports*, as shown in Figure 6–12.

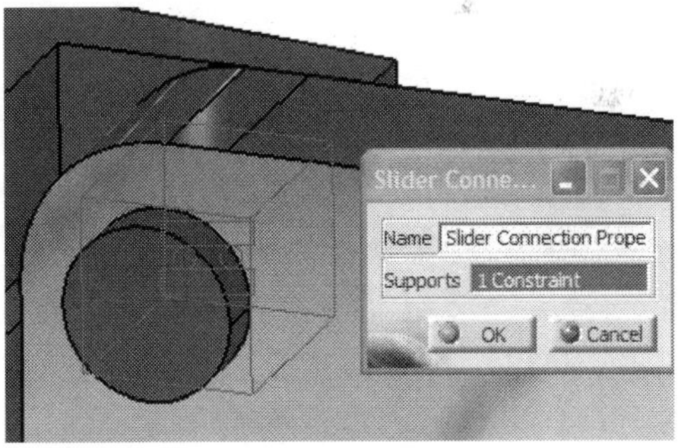

Figure 6–12

Rigid Connection Property

The rigid connection property links the selected geometries with a set of infinitely rigid links, as shown in Figure 6–13.

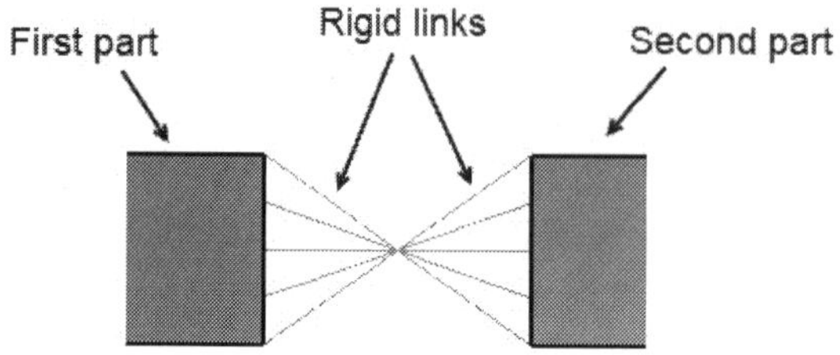

Figure 6–13

Note that the rigid links effectively render the connected geometries completely *undeformable* (i.e., unable to stretch, bend, or somehow else distort). Therefore, this type of connection should be used with caution when applied over extended geometries, such as large surfaces, since the model may be unrealistically over-stiffened.

One of the suitable applications for the rigid connection property is simulating small fasteners (screws, rivets, etc.) in assemblies.

To create a rigid connection, select  (Rigid Connection Property) in the Connection Properties toolbar and select the *Supports*, as shown in Figure 6–14.

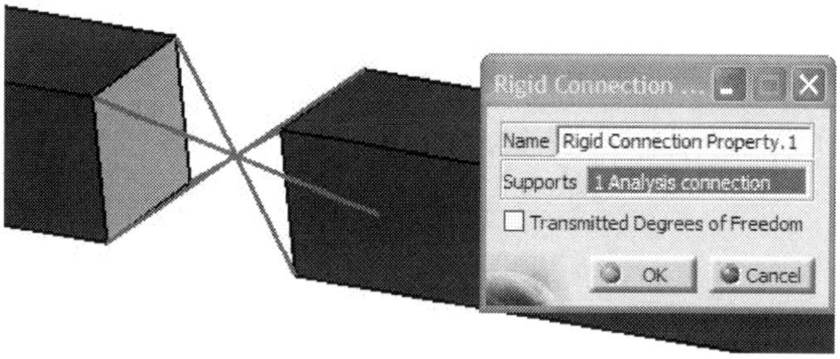

Figure 6–14

Optionally, select the **Transmitted Degrees of Freedom** checkbox to reveal the additional options, as shown in Figure 6–15.

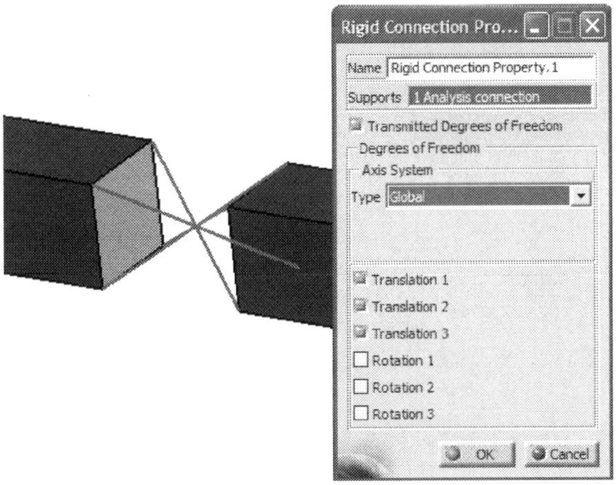

Figure 6–15

The **Transmitted Degrees of Freedom** options enable the user to select in which directions to connect and in which directions to disconnect the parts.

Activating a checkbox connects the parts and deactivating a checkbox disconnects the parts along that specific direction. The directions are determined according to the selected Axis System.

For example, the selections shown in Figure 6–15 effectively model a ball joint connecting the two parts.

Smooth Connection Property

The smooth connection property links the selected geometries with a set of smooth links, as shown in Figure 6–16.

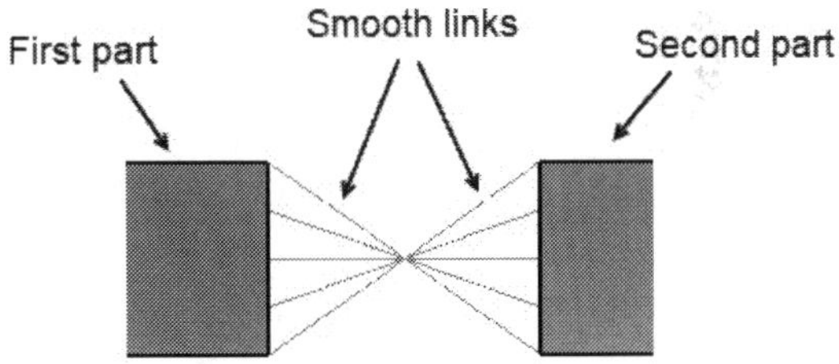

Figure 6–16

Although smooth links are soft (and will let the connected geometries freely deform), their deformations are very approximate. Therefore, this type of connection should be used with caution when applied over large surfaces, since deformation of the model near the connection may be unrealistic.

One of the suitable applications for the smooth connection property is simulating small fasteners (screws, rivets, etc.) in assemblies.

To create a smooth connection, select  (Smooth Connection Property) in the Connection Properties toolbar and select the *Supports*, as shown in Figure 6–17.

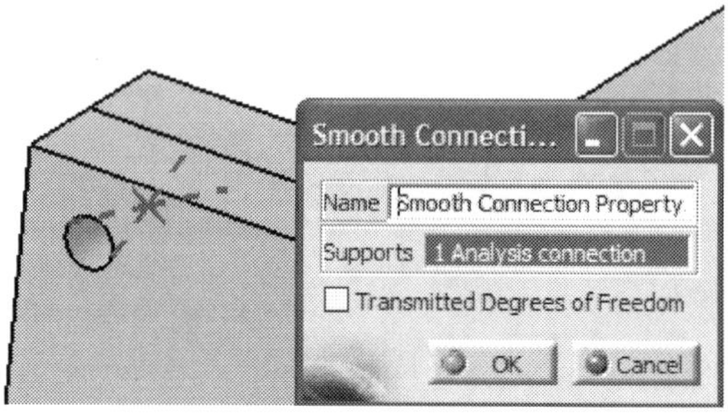

Figure 6–17

Optionally, select the **Transmitted Degrees of Freedom** checkbox to control the connected and disconnected directions, similarly to the rigid connection property.

User-defined Connection Property

The user-defined connection property is essentially a toolbox that enables you to construct the desired type of connection from building blocks.

How it works:

- The connection consists of three parts – the **Start** link, the **End** link, and the **Middle** link, as shown in Figure 6–18.
- Behind the scenes, CATIA creates two points – the first point at the centroid of the first support and the second point at the centroid of the second support.
- The first centroid point is connected to the first support with the Start link, and the second centroid point is connected to the second support with the End link.
- The two centroid points are then connected with the Middle link.

- The user selects which type of link to use for the Start, which type of link to use for the End, and which type of link to use for the Middle. Together, the selected types of links define the connection's properties.

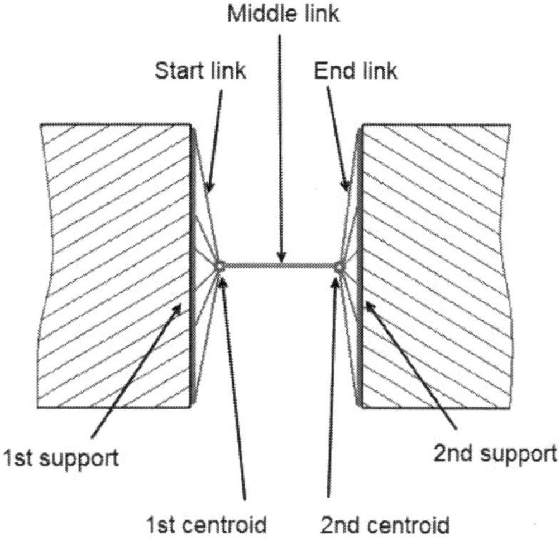

Figure 6–18

To create a user-defined connection, select  (User-defined Distant Connection Property) in the Connection Properties toolbar. Select the **Supports** and, using the drop-down lists in the dialog box, select link types for the *Start*, the *Middle*, and the *End* links, as shown in Figure 6–19.

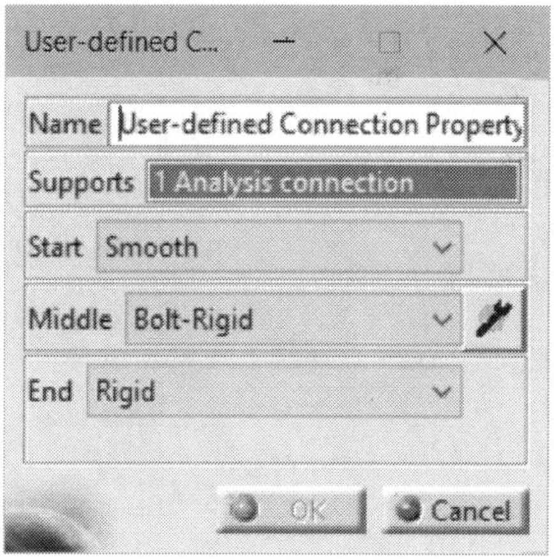

Figure 6–19

The available link types and their properties are described in the following table.

Link	Link Type	Description
Start or **End**	Smooth	Smooth links from the centroid point to the support's mesh.
	Rigid	Rigid links from the centroid point to the support's mesh.
	Spring-Smooth	Spring element, followed by smooth links from the centroid point to the support's mesh.
	Spring-Rigid	Spring element, followed by rigid links from the centroid point to the support's mesh.
	Contact-Rigid	Rigid links, followed by contact rods from the centroid point to the support's mesh.
Middle	Rigid	A rigid link.
	Spring-Rigid-Spring	A chain consisting of a spring, a rigid link, then another spring.
	Rigid-Spring-Rigid	A chain consisting of a rigid link, a spring, then another rigid link.
	Spring-Rigid	A chain consisting of a spring followed by a rigid link.
	Rigid-Spring	A chain consisting of a rigid link followed by a spring.
	Beam	A beam element.
	Spring-Beam-Spring	A chain consisting of a spring, a beam, then another spring.
	Beam-Spring-Beam	A chain consisting of a beam, a spring, then another beam.
	Spring-Beam	A chain consisting of a spring followed by a beam.
	Beam-Spring	A chain consisting of a beam followed by a spring.
	Bolt-Rigid	A chain consisting of a pre-tension element followed by a rigid link. The pre-tension element allows application of a preload, such as in bolted or screwed assemblies.

Middle (cont.)	Rigid-Bolt	A chain consisting of a rigid link followed by a pre-tension element. The pre-tension element allows application of a preload, such as in bolted or screwed assemblies.
	Bolt-Beam	A chain consisting of a pre-tension element followed by a beam. The pre-tension element allows application of a preload, such as in bolted or screwed assemblies.
	Beam-Bolt	A chain consisting of a beam followed by a pre-tension element. The pre-tension element allows application of a preload, such as in bolted or screwed assemblies.
	Bolt-Rigid-Spring	A chain consisting of a pre-tension element, a rigid link, and a spring. The pre-tension element allows application of a preload, such as in bolted or screwed assemblies.
	Spring-Rigid-Bolt	A chain consisting of a spring, a rigid link, and a pre-tension element. The pre-tension element allows application of a preload, such as in bolted or screwed assemblies.

The user-defined connection is a very powerful and flexible tool that enables you to simulate many different types of connection behaviors. However, its use should be reserved for intermediate to advanced users only. It is recommended that you have a good understanding of how each type of link behaves in order to correctly construct the required connection property.

6.4 Result Visualization

The assembly analysis results are visualized in the same way as for the part analysis (i.e., by selecting an appropriate result icon, such as deformation, displacement, or stress). The results are displayed for all of the parts for which there is a mesh in the analysis model.

If you want to display the result for one particular part, double-click on the image object in the tree to open the Image Edition dialog box and switch to the *Selections* tab, as shown in Figure 6–20.

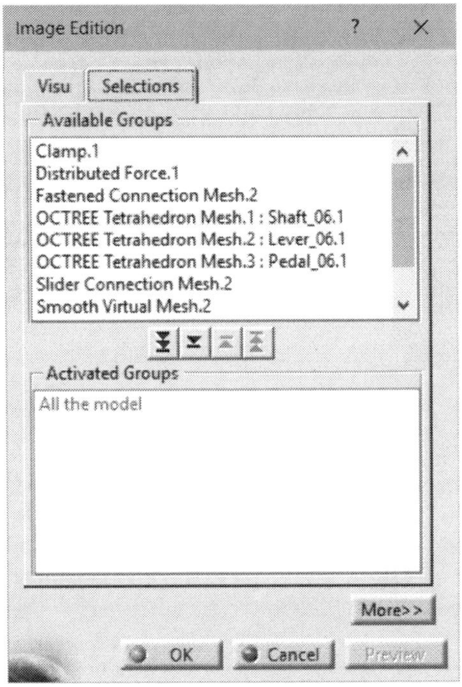

Figure 6–20

In the list of *Available Groups*, select the mesh for the part you want to visualize and move it into the *Activated Groups*, as shown in Figure 6–21.

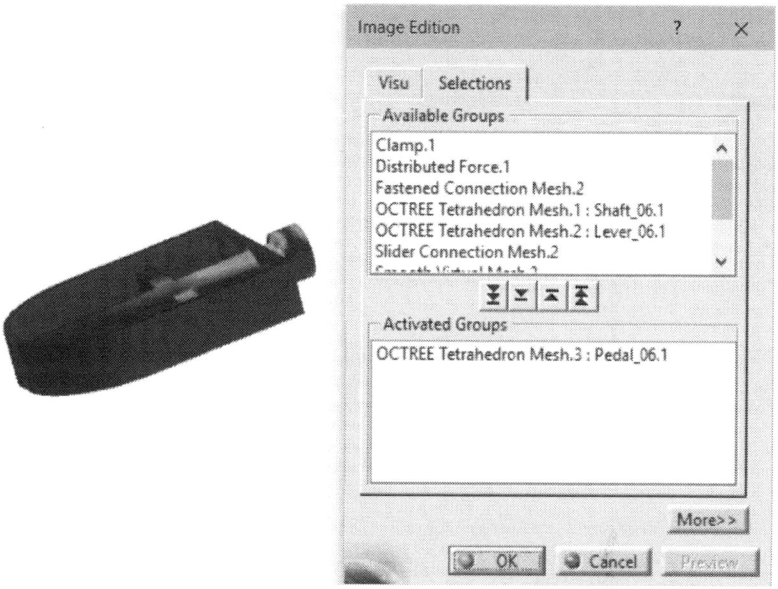

Figure 6–21

Practice 6a Bicycle Crank Assembly

Practice Objectives

- Apply the materials and mesh the model.
- Create assembly analysis connections.
- Apply loads and restraints.
- Compute the analysis with mesh adaptivity.
- Visualize the results.

In this practice, you will set up and run a static stress analysis on a crank assembly for a children's bicycle, shown in Figure 6–22. The shaft part is made of steel, while the crank and the pedal parts are made of aluminum alloy. The assembly is loaded by a vertical force on the pedal.

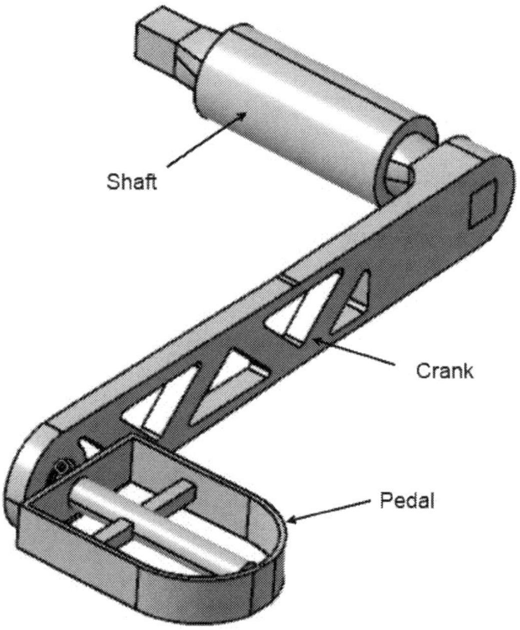

Figure 6–22

Task 1 - Open the assembly in CATIA.

1. Open **BikeCrank_06.CATProduct** from the *CATIA Generative Structural Analysis Practice Files\Ch06* folder.

2. Set the model display as  (Shading with Edges). The assembly displays as shown in Figure 6–23.

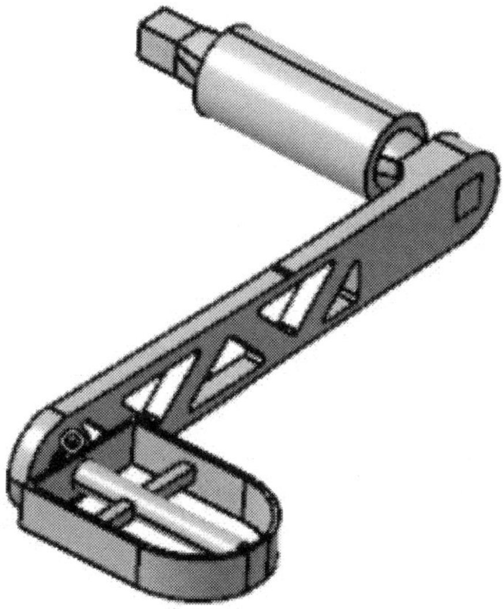

Figure 6–23

3. Select **Tools>Options>Parameters and Measures>Units** and set the units as follows:

    - Length: **Millimeter (mm)**
    - Force: **Newton (N)**
    - Moment: **Newton x Meter (Nxm)**
    - Pressure: **Megapascal (MPa)**

Task 2 - Switch the parts to Design Mode.

You only need to do this task if you opened the assembly in Visualization mode (the toggle **Tools>Options> Infrastructure>Product Structure>Work with the cache system** is on), because the parts must be in Design mode for the analysis.

1. Right-click on the root assembly **BikeCrank_06** and select **Representations>Design Mode** in the contextual menu, as shown in Figure 6–24.

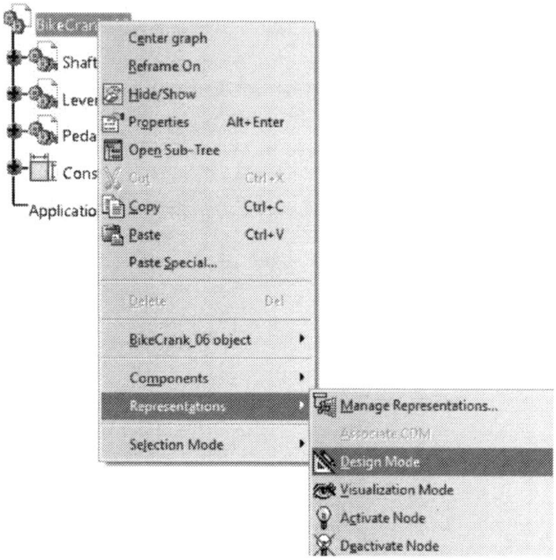

Figure 6–24

Task 3 - Apply the materials.

1. Apply the following materials to the assembly parts (as shown in Figure 6–25):
   - Shaft_06: **Steel**
   - Lever_06: **Aluminium**
   - Pedal_06: **Aluminium**

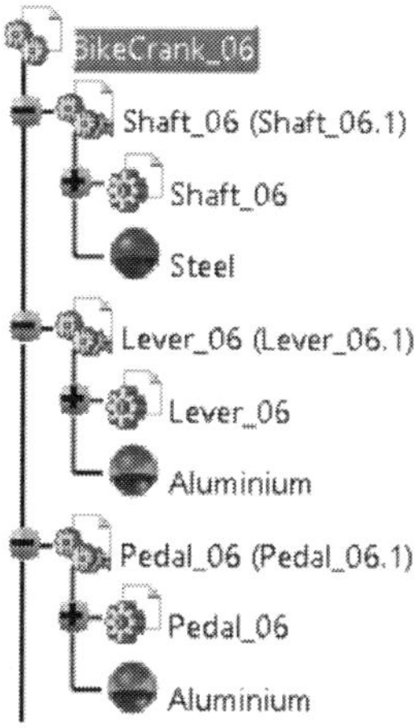

Figure 6–25

Task 4 - Start the GSA workbench.

1. Select **Start>Analysis & Simulation>Generative Structural Analysis**.

2. Select **Static Analysis** as the new analysis case.

Task 5 - Mesh the model.

1. Set the mesh parameters for the assembly parts as follows:

- OCTREE Tetrahedron Mesh.1: Shaft_06.1
    - Element type: **Parabolic**
    - Size: **4mm**
    - Absolute sag: **0.6mm** (i.e., 15% of the size)
- OCTREE Tetrahedron Mesh.1: Lever_06.1
    - Element type: **Parabolic**
    - Size: **4mm**
    - Absolute sag: **0.6mm** (i.e., 15% of the size)
- OCTREE Tetrahedron Mesh.1: Pedal_06.1
    - Element type: **Parabolic**
    - Size: **4mm**
    - Absolute sag: **0.6mm** (i.e., 15% of the size)

2. Right-click on **Nodes and Elements** in the tree and select **Mesh Visualization**. The part mesh is displayed, as shown in Figure 6–26. Rotate the model and examine the mesh in various areas of the assembly.

Figure 6–26

3. Right-click on **Mesh.1** in the tree and select **Delete** to delete the mesh visualization and return to the model view.

Task 6 - Create an analysis connection between the pedal and the crank.

The pedal in a bicycle crank assembly should be able to freely rotate about its axis. This can be accomplished by using a slider connection between the pedal's axis and the crank's hole.

1. Expand the tree and notice the **Coincidence.10** constraint in the assembly. This constraint lines up the axes of the pedal and the crank's hole, as shown in Figure 6–27. Therefore, this constraint can be used as the support for the slider connection.

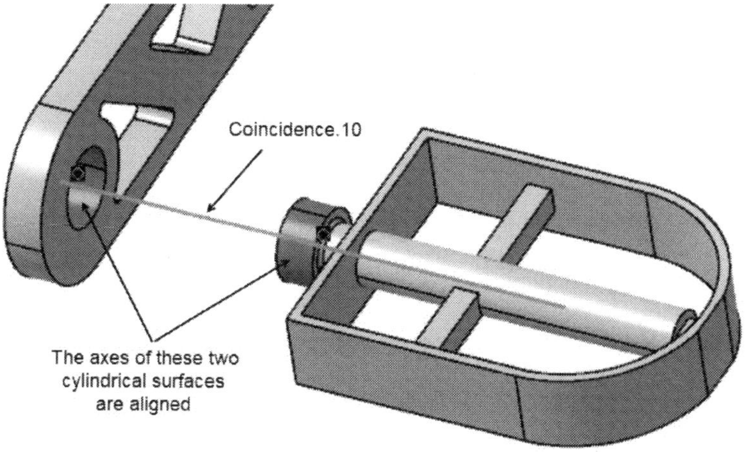

Figure 6–27

2. In the Connection Properties toolbar, select  (Slider Connection Property). The Slider Connection Property dialog box opens, as shown in Figure 6–28.

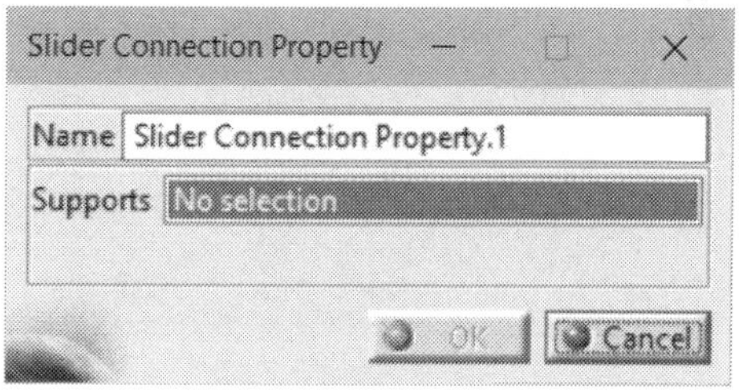

Figure 6–28

3. Select the **Coincidence.10** constraint as the *Supports*, as shown in Figure 6–29, and click **OK**.

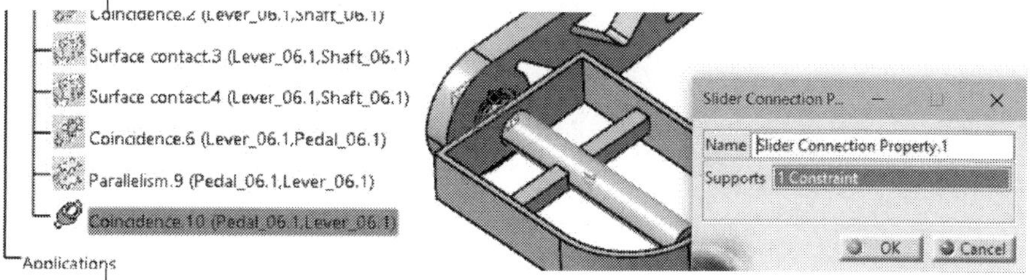

Figure 6–29

4. The created connection property is displayed in the **Properties.1** section of the tree, as shown in Figure 6–30.

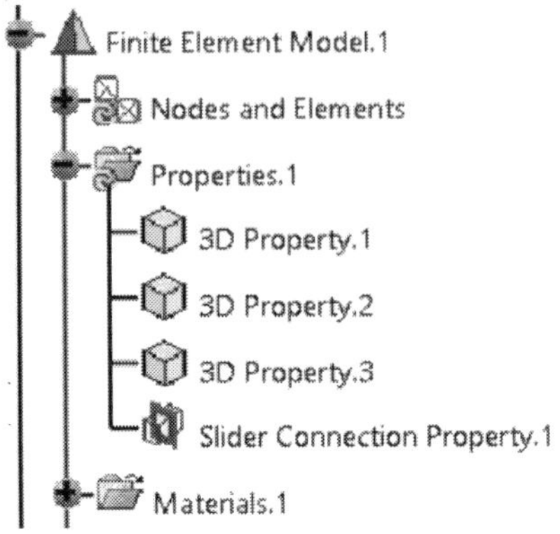

Figure 6–30

Task 7 - Create an analysis connection between the shaft and the crank.

The square end of the shaft is tightly fit into the square hole in the crank, as shown in Figure 6–31 (exploded view shown). The crank is not supposed to detach or slip off the shaft. This type of a connection can be simulated with a fastened connection property between the four surfaces on the shaft and the four surfaces in the square hole.

However, there is no suitable constraint in the assembly to serve as the support for this connection. Therefore, in this task, you will create a general analysis connection as the support for the fastened connection property.

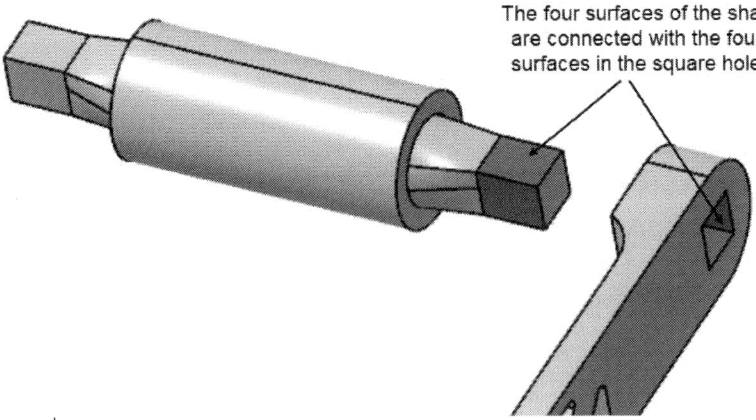

Figure 6–31

1. In the Analysis Supports toolbar, select  (General Analysis Connection). The General Analysis Connection dialog box opens, as shown in Figure 6–32.

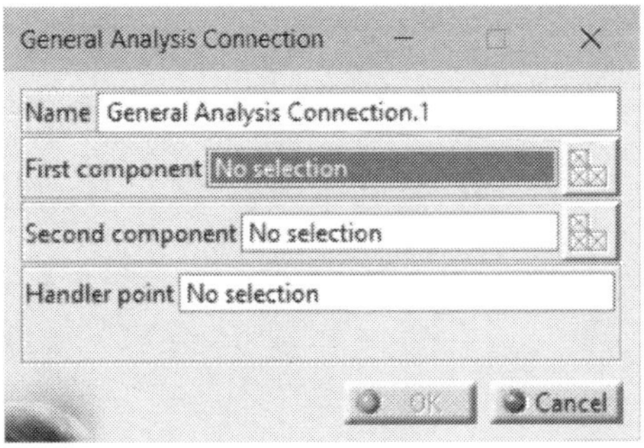

Figure 6–32

Hide and unhide the parts as you go to facilitate the selection.

2. Activate the *First component* field in the dialog box and select the four surfaces, all around, on the square end of the shaft, as shown in Figure 6–33 (exploded view shown).

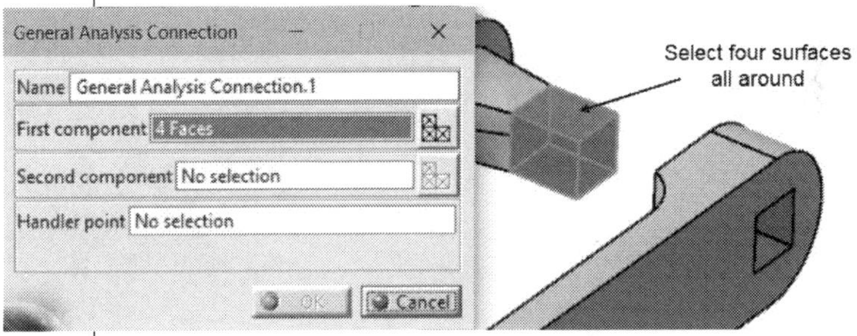

Figure 6–33

3. Activate the *Second component* field in the dialog box and select the four surfaces, all around, in the square hole in the crank, as shown in Figure 6–34 (exploded view shown).

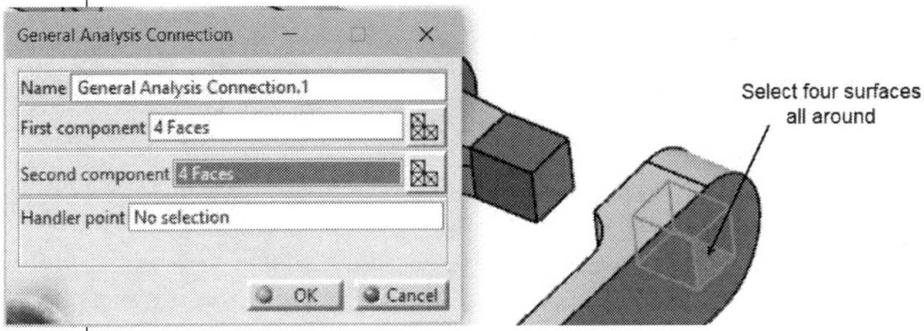

Figure 6–34

4. Click **OK** to finish. **General Analysis Connection.1** is created and displayed in the tree, as shown in Figure 6–35.

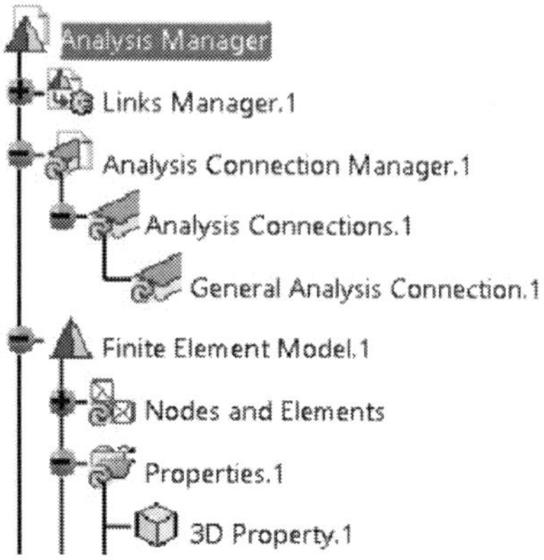

Figure 6–35

5. In the Connection Properties toolbar, select  (Fastened Connection Property). The Fastened Connection Property dialog box opens, as shown in Figure 6–36.

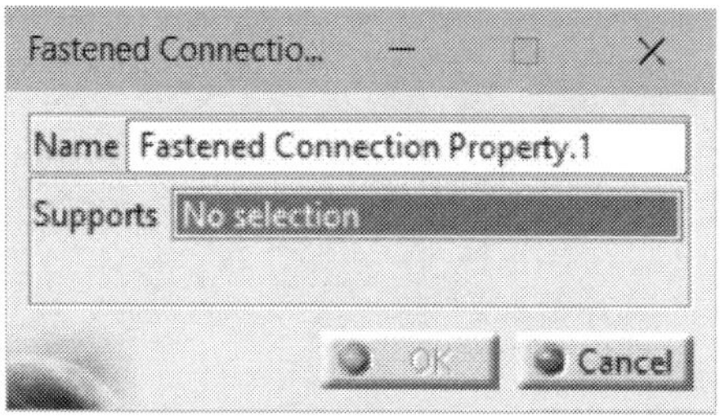

Figure 6–36

6. Select **General Analysis Connection.1** as the *Supports*, as shown in Figure 6–37, and click **OK**.

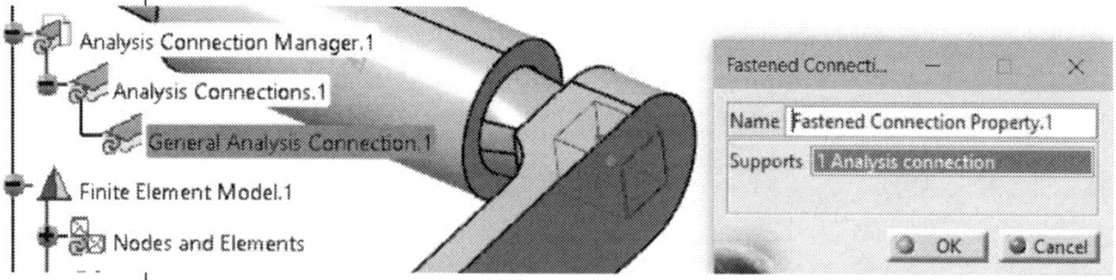

Figure 6–37

7. The created connection property is displayed in the **Properties.1** section of the tree, as shown in Figure 6–38.

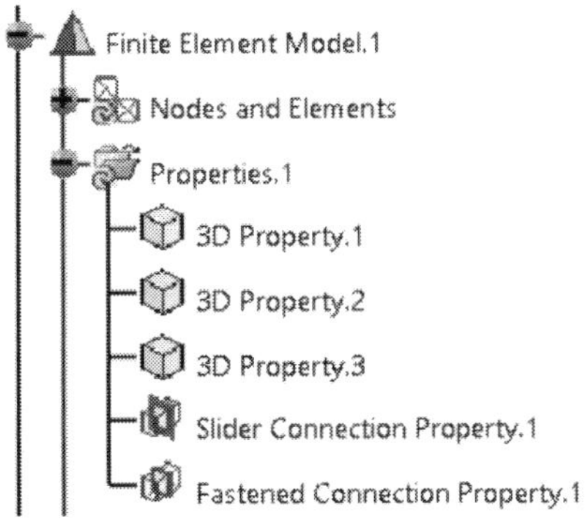

Figure 6–38

Task 8 - Apply the load.

1. Select (Distributed Force) and apply **80N** force in the **-Z** direction to the top surface of the pedal, as shown in Figure 6–39.

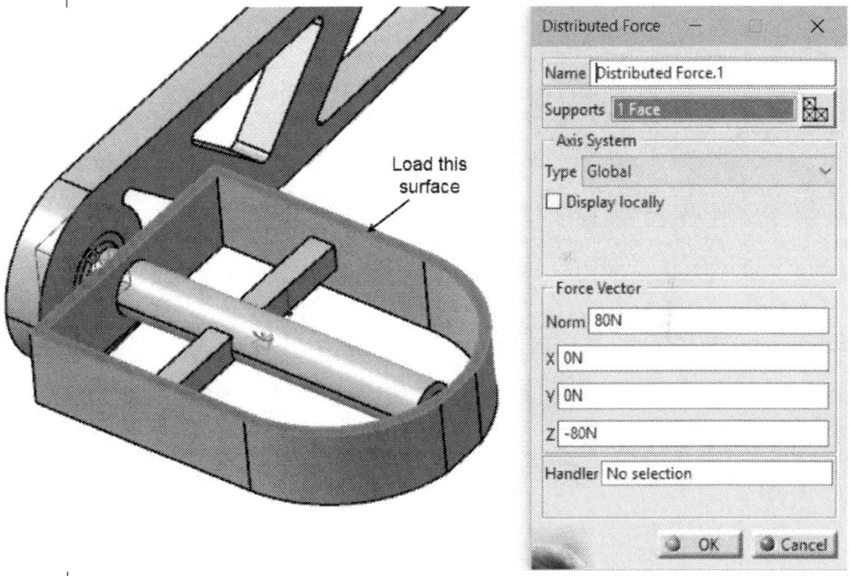

Figure 6–39

Task 9 - Apply the restraints.

This simulates a bushing-type support on this section of the shaft.

1. Apply the  (Surface Slider) restraint to the outside diameter of the shaft, as shown in Figure 6–40.

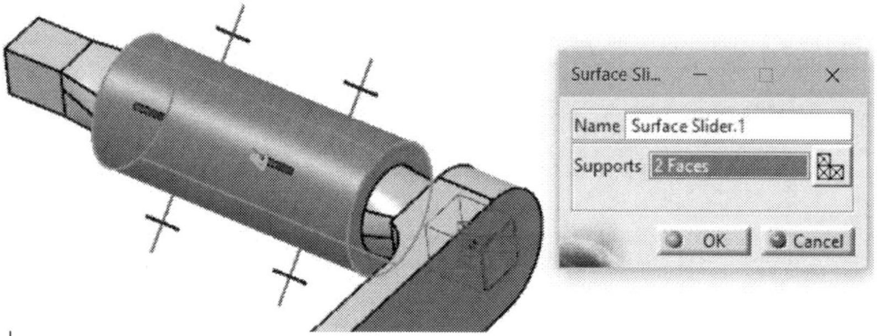

Figure 6–40

2. Apply the  (Clamp) restraint to the four surfaces, all around, on the square end of the shaft, as shown in Figure 6–41.

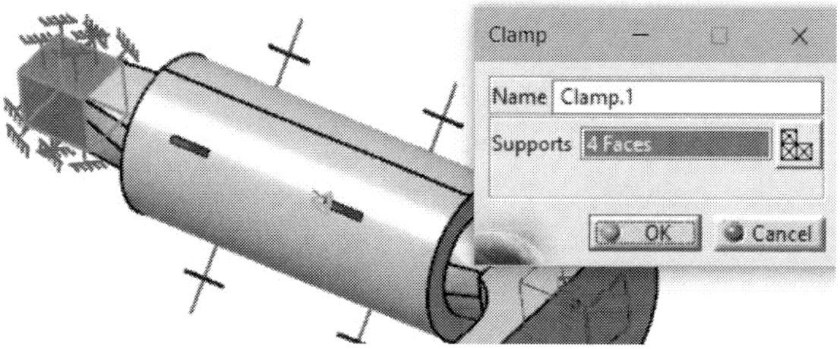

Figure 6–41

3. The model displays as shown in Figure 6–42.

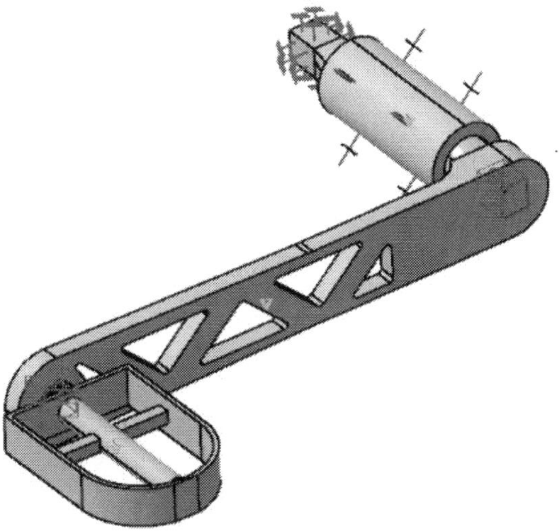

Figure 6–42

Task 10 - Run the analysis.

1. Select  (Compute) and run the analysis. Close the Warnings dialog box that appears in the process.

2. CATIA displays a series of messages informing you on the progress of the computation, then displays the error message shown in Figure 6–43.

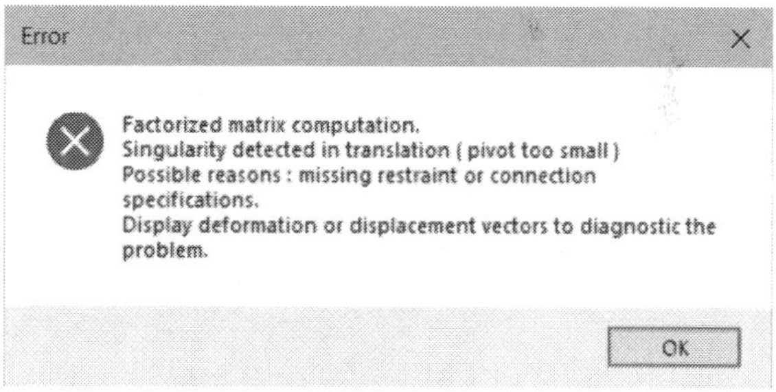

Figure 6–43

This error message is displayed whenever CATIA detects a rigid body motion in the model (i.e., that the model is insufficiently restrained).

3. Click **OK** to close the error message.

Task 11 - Display the detected rigid body motion.

1. Select  (Deformation) to display the deformed mesh image. Unhide the **Links Manager.1** to visualize the undeformed assembly as well. Change the **Amplification Magnitude** to **0.1** and animate the deformed mesh image. CATIA displays the detected rigid body motion, which is the sliding movement of the pedal part along its axis, as shown in Figure 6–44.

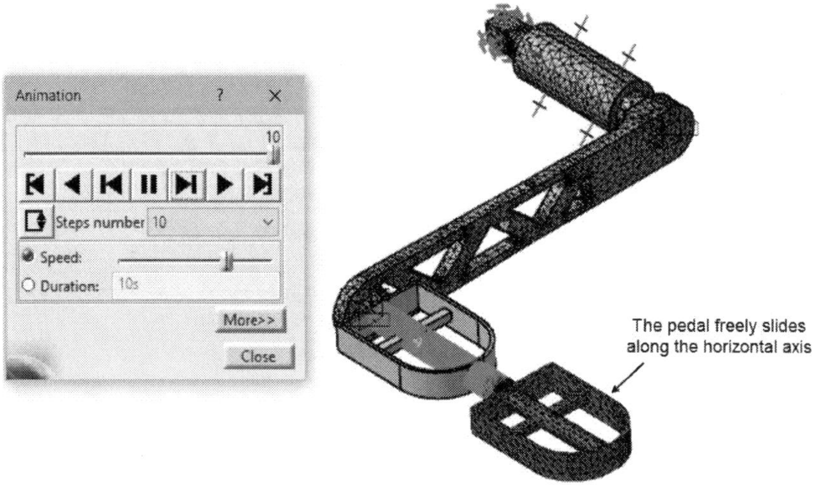

Figure 6–44

   This rigid body motion exists because the slider connection that you created to connect the crank and the pedal in Task 6 only restrains the OD surface of the pedal and ID surface of the crank's hole in normal to the surfaces direction, but allows the two surfaces to freely slide along each other without friction.

   In the following tasks, you will use a smooth virtual part to properly restrain the pedal part.

2. Delete the **Deformed Mesh.1** image to return to the model view.

Task 12 - Create the virtual part handler point.

1. In the tree, expand **Links Manager.1>Link.1** and double-click on the **Pedal_06** part. This automatically hides the analysis model and switches CATIA to the Part Design workbench.

2. Using the **Between** option, create a point (**Point.1**) at the center of the small rectangular surface on the free end of the pedal, as shown in Figure 6–45.

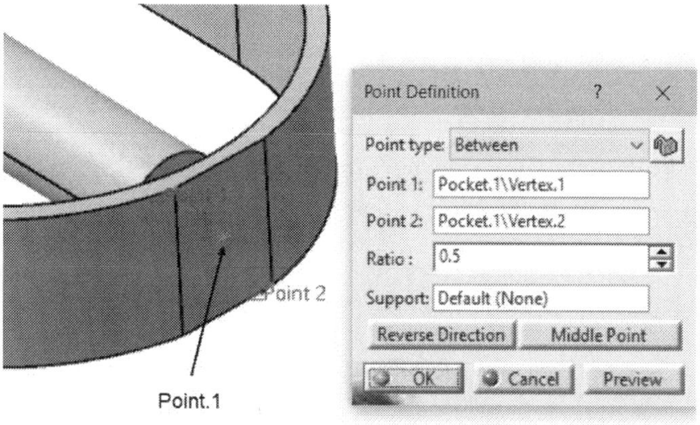

Figure 6–45

Task 13 - Create the virtual part.

1. Double-click on **Finite Element Model.1** in the tree to switch back to the GSA workbench.

2. In the Virtual Parts toolbar, select (Smooth Virtual Part).

3. Select the flat surface at the end of pedal as the *Supports* and select **Point.1** as the *Handler*, as shown in Figure 6–46. Click **OK** to finish.

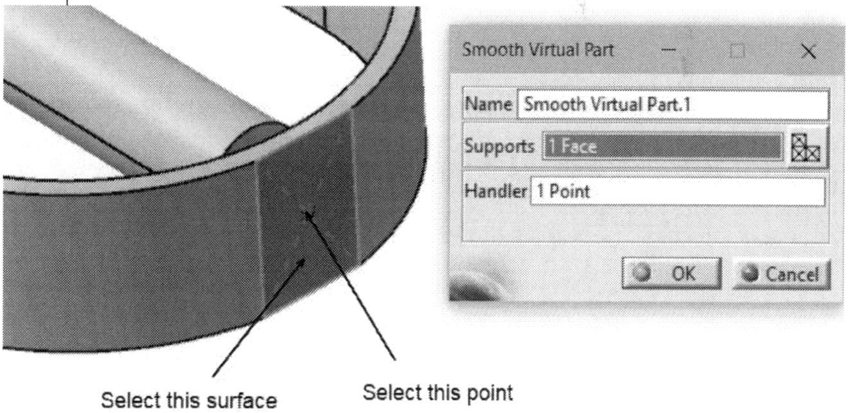

Figure 6–46

Task 14 - Restrain the virtual part.

__Translation 1__ is the translation in the __X__ direction, which is the direction along the pedal's axis. Restraining __Rotation 1__ is necessary in order to block free rotation of the pedal inside the crank's hole.

1. Select (User-defined Restraint) and select the **Smooth Virtual Part.1** as the *Supports*. Restrain only **Translation 1** and **Rotation 1** and leave all other translations and rotations free, as shown in Figure 6–47.

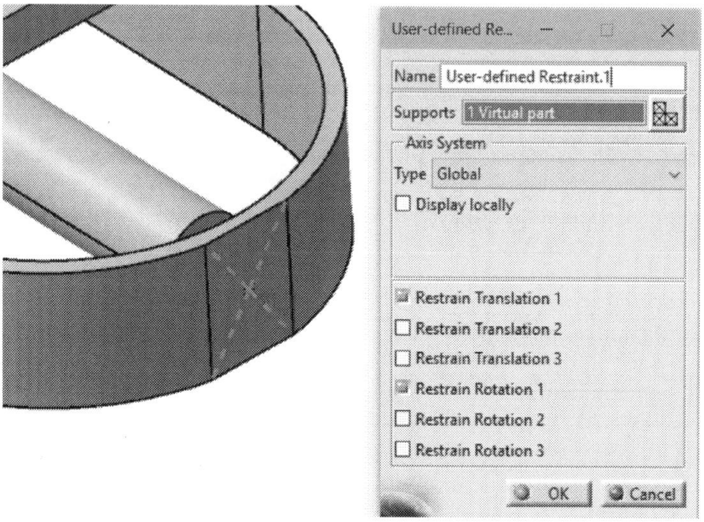

Figure 6–47

Task 15 - Run the analysis.

1. Select (Compute) and run the analysis. Now CATIA completes the computation successfully, without issuing any error messages.

2. Expand **Sensors.1** in the tree. Note that the value of the **Global Error Rate** sensor is about **9.5%**, as shown in Figure 6–48. In the following tasks, you will use the Adaptivity tool to improve the analysis accuracy to under 5% global error rate.

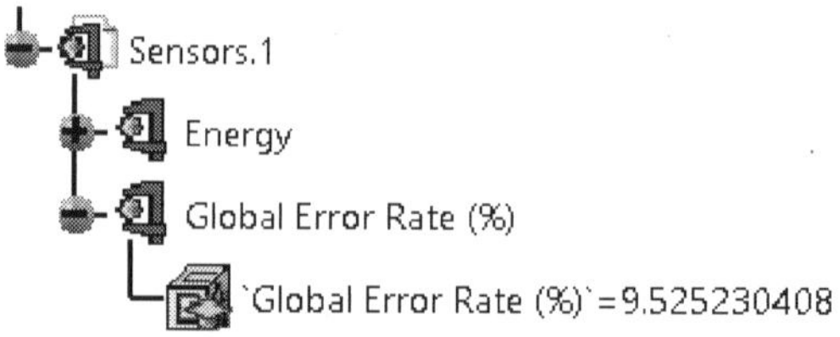

Figure 6–48

Task 16 - Set up Global Adaptivity.

1. Select  (New Adaptivity Entity). In the Global Adaptivity dialog box that opens, select the **OCTREE Tetrahedron Mesh.1: Shaft_06.1**, **OCTREE Tetrahedron Mesh.2: Lever_06.1**, and **OCTREE Tetrahedron Mesh.3: Pedal_06.1** meshes as the *Supports* and enter **5** in the *Objective Error* field, as shown in Figure 6–49. Click **OK** to finish.

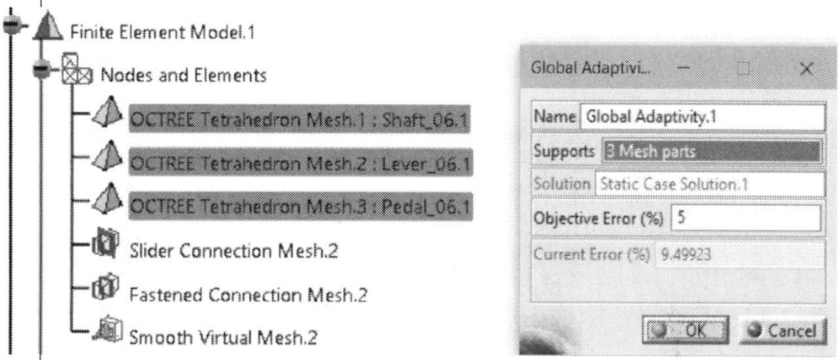

Figure 6–49

Task 17 - Run the analysis with adaptivity.

1. Select  (Compute with Adaptivity). In the Adaptivity Process Parameters dialog box that opens, enter **3** in the *Iterations Number* field, activate the **Minimum Size** option and enter **1mm** as the minimum element size, as shown in Figure 6–50.

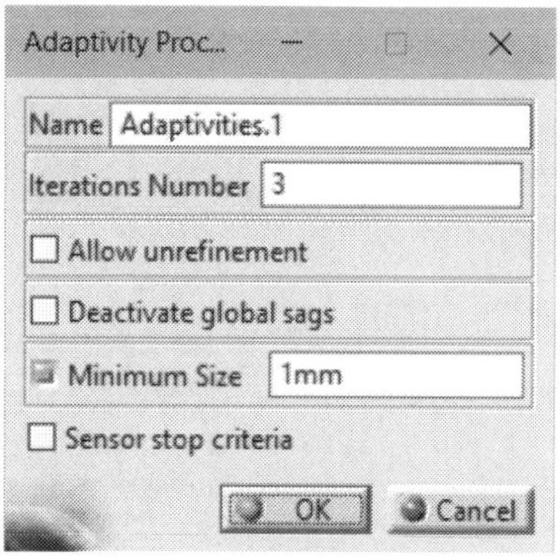

Figure 6–50

2. Click **OK** to start the computation. CATIA displays a series of messages informing you about the status of the computation process. Wait until computation completes, which may take a few minutes.

3. Once the computation is finished, CATIA may or may not automatically update the analysis sensors. To update all the sensors, right-click on **Sensors.1** in the tree and select **Update All Sensors**, as shown in Figure 6–51.

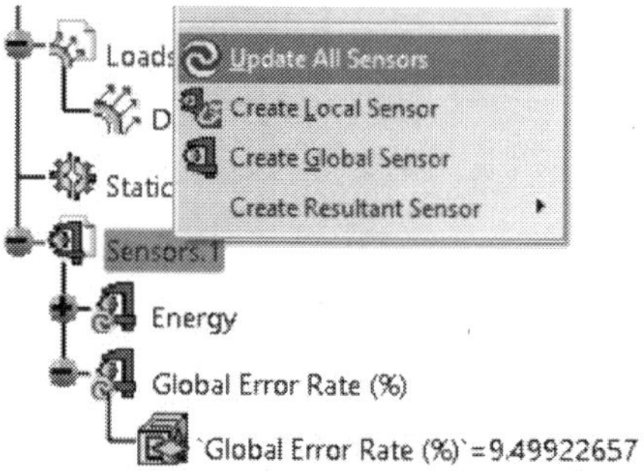

Figure 6–51

4. Expand **Sensors.1** in the tree and note that the value of the **Global Error Rate** sensor now reads **4.38%**, as shown in Figure 6–52. This is below the objective error in this analysis, which was 5%, so the mesh adaptivity process has succeeded.

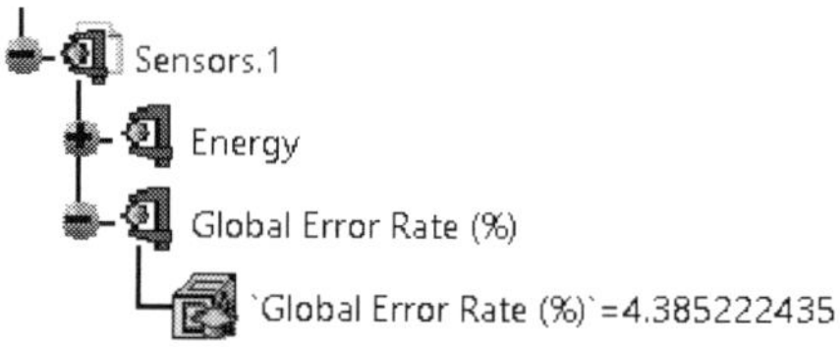

Figure 6–52

Task 18 - Display and animate the displacement magnitude.

1. Change the view mode to (Shading with Material).

2. Hide **Loads** and **Restraints**.

3. Visualize and animate the displacement magnitude image, overlaid on the CAD model, as shown in Figure 6–53. Does the model deform according to the applied loads and restraints?

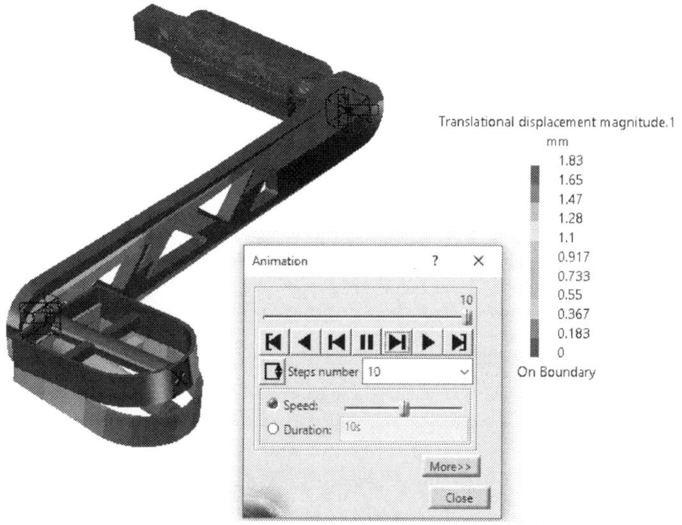

Figure 6–53

Task 19 - Display Von Mises stress in the shaft part.

1. Select  (Von Mises Stress). The stress results for the entire assembly displays as shown in Figure 6–54.

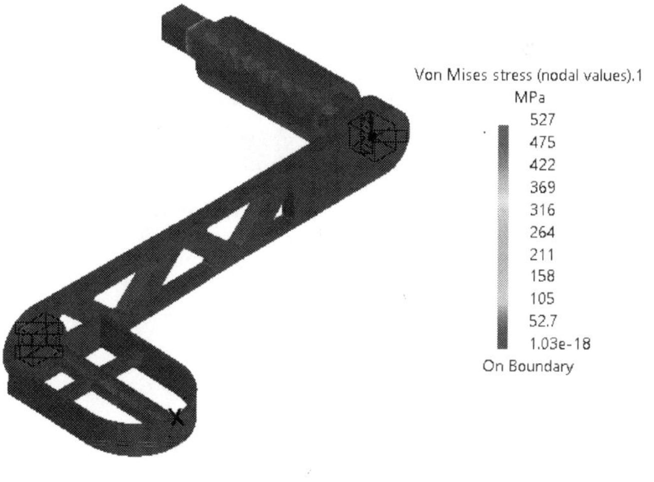

Figure 6–54

2. Double-click on **Von Mises stress (nodal values).1** in the tree. In the Image Edition dialog box that opens, activate the *Selections* tab. In the *Available Groups* section, select **OCTREE Tetrahedron Mesh.1: Shaft_06.1** and click the  button to move the part mesh into the *Activated Groups* section, as shown in Figure 6–55.

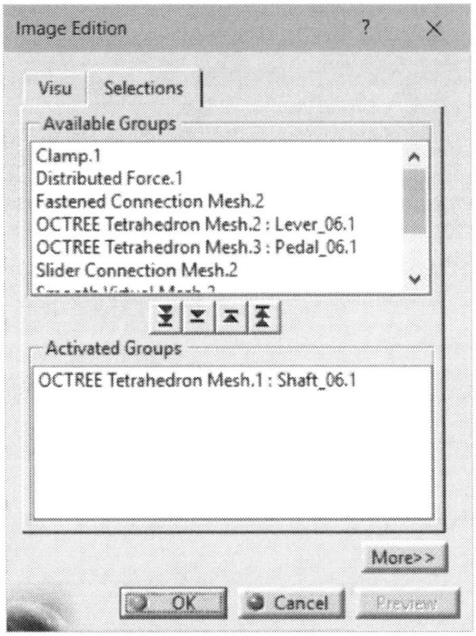

Figure 6–55

3. Click **OK** to close the Image Edition dialog box. Now the stress result is only displayed for the shaft part, as shown in Figure 6–56.

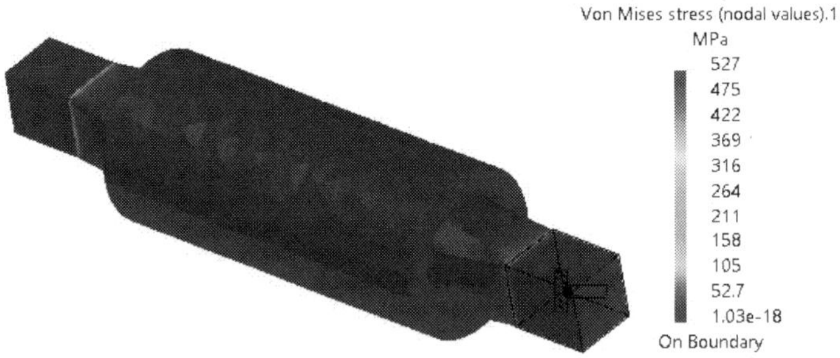

Figure 6–56

4. Using the  (Image Extrema) tool, locate the area of maximum stress in the shaft, as shown in Figure 6–57. Note that the maximum stress occurs where the shaft fits into the crank part.

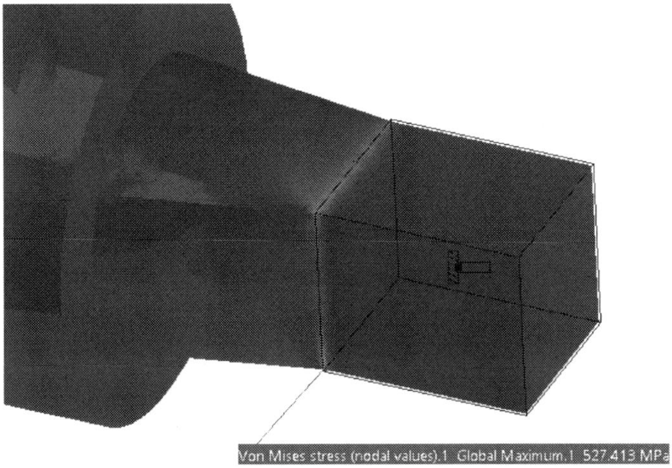

Figure 6–57

Task 20 - Display Von Mises stress in the crank part.

1. Double-click on **Von Mises stress (nodal values).1** in the tree. In the Image Edition dialog box that opens, activate the *Selections* tab. Move the **OCTREE Tetrahedron Mesh.1: Shaft_06.1** mesh from the *Activated Groups* into the *Available Groups s*ection, and move the **OCTREE Tetrahedron Mesh.2: Lever_06.1** mesh from the *Available Groups* into the *Activated Groups*, as shown in Figure 6–58.

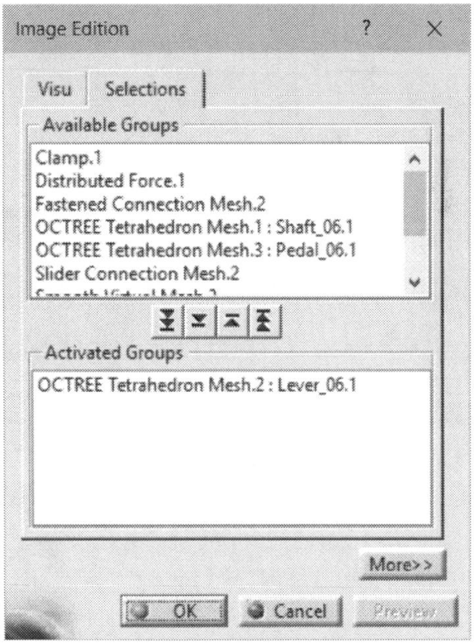

Figure 6–58

2. Click **OK** to close the Image Edition dialog box. Now the stress result is only displayed for the crank part, as shown in Figure 6–59.

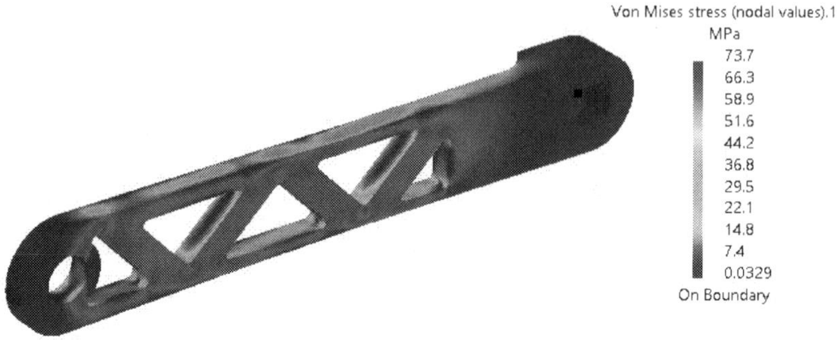

Figure 6–59

3. Select (Information) and click the **Von Mises stress (nodal values).1** object in the tree. The Information dialog box displays, as shown in Figure 6–60.

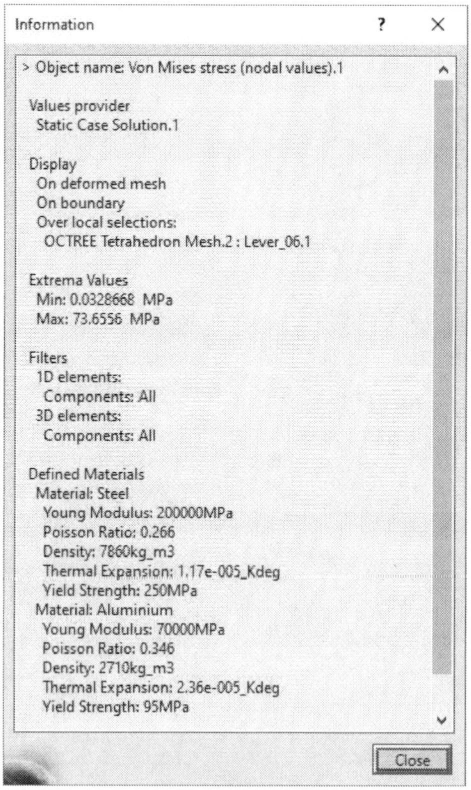

Figure 6–60

4. Note that the maximum Von Mises stress in the crank part is approximately **74MPa**, which is below the Aluminium material's **Yield Strength** of **95MPa**. Therefore, the crank is predicted to withstand the load without failure. Close the Information dialog box.

5. Using the (Image Extrema) tool, locate the area of maximum stress in the crank, as shown in Figure 6–61. Note that the maximum stress occurs where the shaft fits into the crank.

Figure 6–61

Task 21 - Display Von Mises stress in the pedal part.

1. Using the steps in Task 19, display and examine the Von Mises stress in the pedal part.

Task 22 - Return to the model view.

1. Right-click on **Von Mises stress (nodal values).1** in the tree and select **Activate/Deactivate** to delete the stress image from the screen and return to the model view.

Task 23 - Save and close the files.

1. Optionally, save the analysis document and the assembly for future reference.

2. Close both the analysis and the product documents.

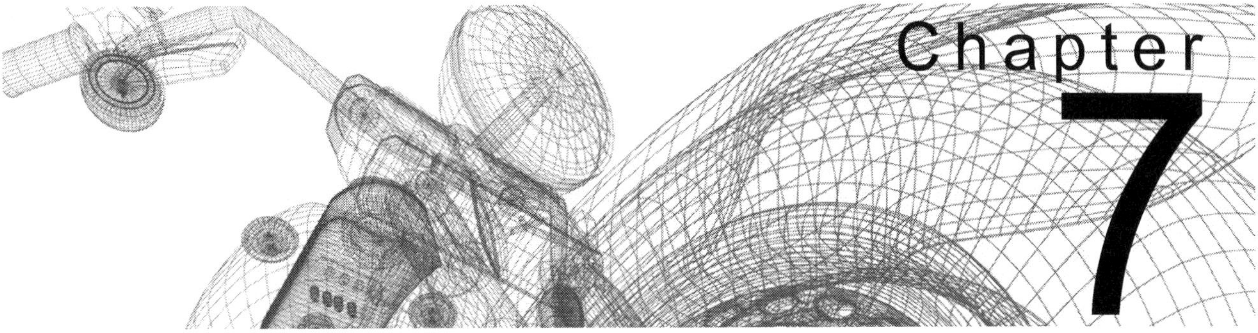

Contact Analysis

In this chapter, you learn how to model contact and press-fit conditions between assembly components.

Learning Objectives in This Chapter

- Understand the contact connection property.
- Understand the pressure fitting connection property.
- Refine the mesh in contact areas.
- Solve contact analysis.
- Visualize contact analysis results.

7.1 Contact Connection Property

In a contact connection, the two parts are free to move apart and/or slide along each other under the applied loading, but they cannot interpenetrate. The parts are initially permitted to be at a clearance, but might come into contact during the analysis. Only compressive normal stresses are transmitted through the contacting surfaces (i.e., the surfaces cannot *pull* each other).

The contact connection is the most realistic model for simulating parts that must remain separate from each other during the analysis, yet do not interpenetrate. From the FEA standpoint, the contact connection represents a boundary condition that changes during the loading. For example, when a chain roller is pressed against a sprocket, the line contact changes to an area contact.

In the example shown in Figure 7–1, there is a gap between the plate and block initially (configuration 1). Once the load has been applied, the plate bends freely until it comes into contact with the block, as shown in configuration 2. If the load is further increased, the area of contact shifts from the edge of the plate to the edge of the block (configuration 3). Therefore, the contact area and location change depending on the amount of load applied.

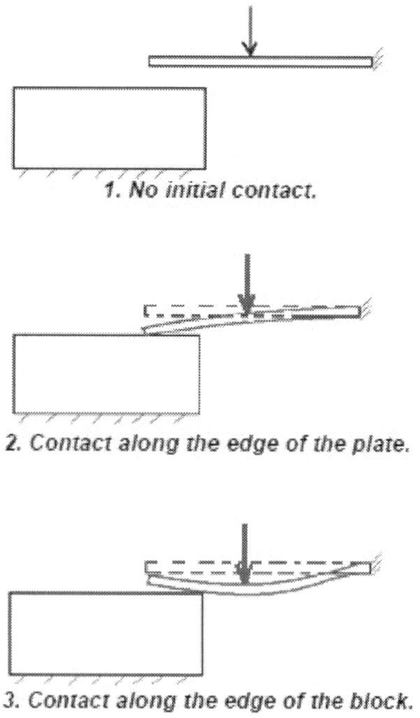

Figure 7–1

Contact in GSA can use or ignore friction. The following friction options are available.

- **None:** Creates a frictionless contact. Only compressive forces are transmitted through a frictionless contact, and the surfaces will slip relative to each other whenever there is a tangential force between them.
- **Friction ratio:** Creates a contact with friction. The surfaces will slip relative to each other only if tangential force exceeds the friction force. The friction force is the coefficient of friction times the compressive force.
- **No sliding:** The interfacing surfaces are able to come apart in the normal direction, but they cannot slip relative to each other.

To create a contact connection, select  (Contact Connection Property) and select the *Supports*, as shown in Figure 7–2.

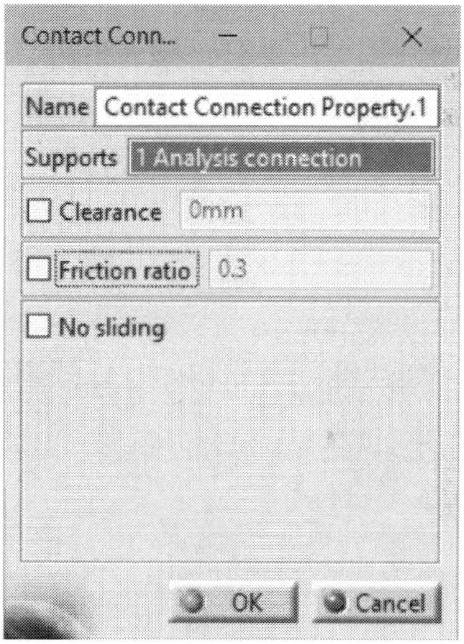

Figure 7–2

To create a contact with friction, toggle on the **Friction ratio** checkbox and enter a friction ratio value, as shown in Figure 7–3.

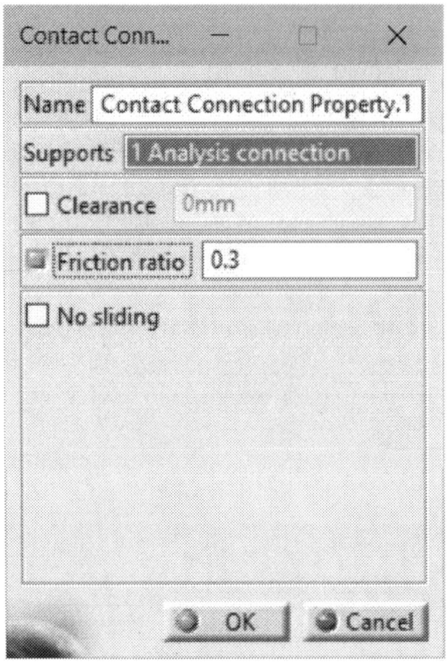

Figure 7–3

To create a contact without sliding, toggle on the **No sliding** checkbox, as shown in Figure 7–4.

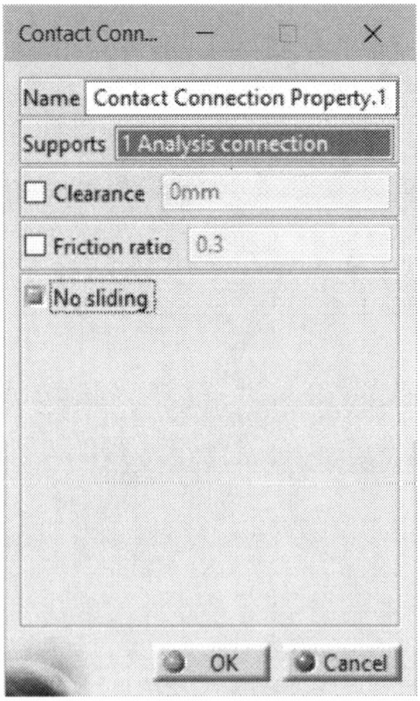

Figure 7–4

Optionally, you can introduce a virtual initial gap between the parts by activating the **Clearance** checkbox, as shown in Figure 7–5. A positive Clearance value means that the surfaces can still come closer until they are considered to be in contact during the analysis.

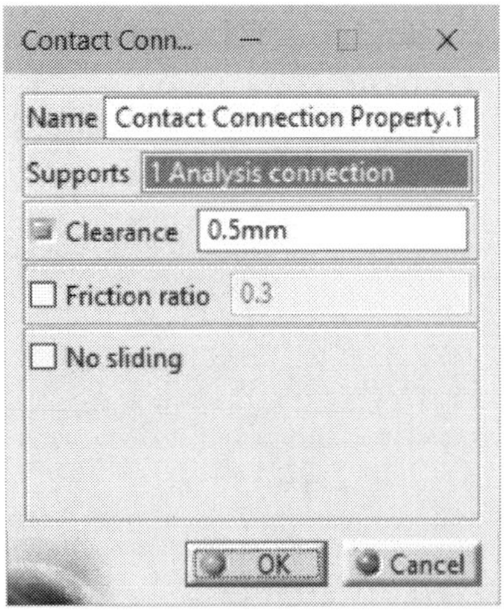

Figure 7–5

7.2 Pressure Fitting Connection Property

The pressure fitting connection allows an initial interference or overlap between the parts. During the analysis, the interference is removed, thus creating strains and stresses in the parts.

The pressure fitting connection behaves as a contact connection along the direction that is normal to the connected surfaces (i.e., the condition of non-penetration is strictly enforced). However, in the tangential direction, the surfaces are linked so there is no sliding or slippage between the parts.

To create a pressure fitting connection, select  (Pressure Fitting Connection Property) and select the *Supports*, as shown in Figure 7–6.

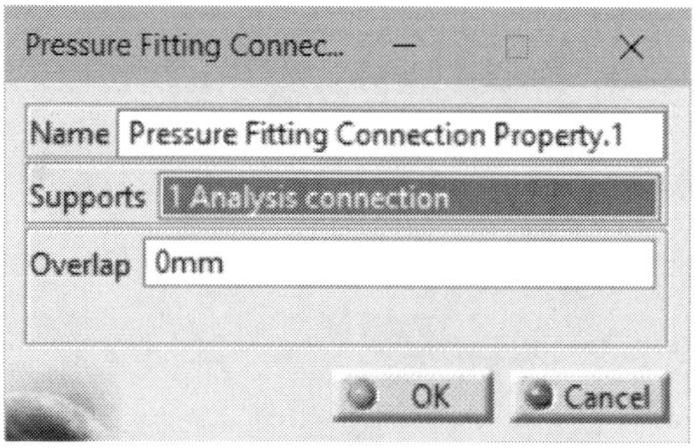

Figure 7–6

Enter the amount of *Overlap* and click **OK** to finish, as shown in Figure 7–7.

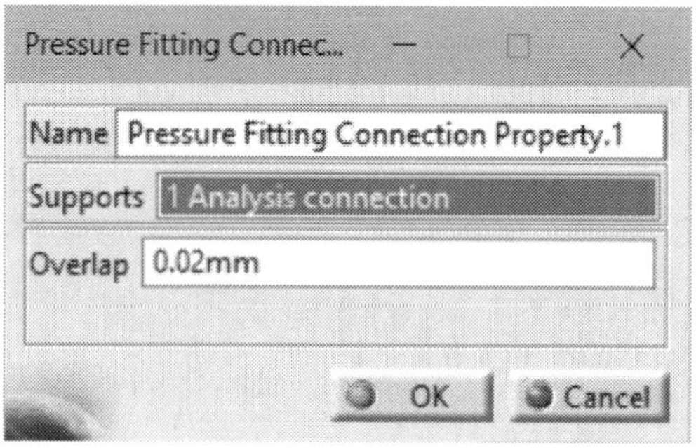

Figure 7–7

7.3 Contact Connections Wizard

The Connections Wizard searches for and automatically creates contact and fastened connections.

To launch the tool, select  (Find interactions) in the Connection Properties toolbar. The Find Connections Wizard: Step 1 dialog box opens, as shown in Figure 7–8.

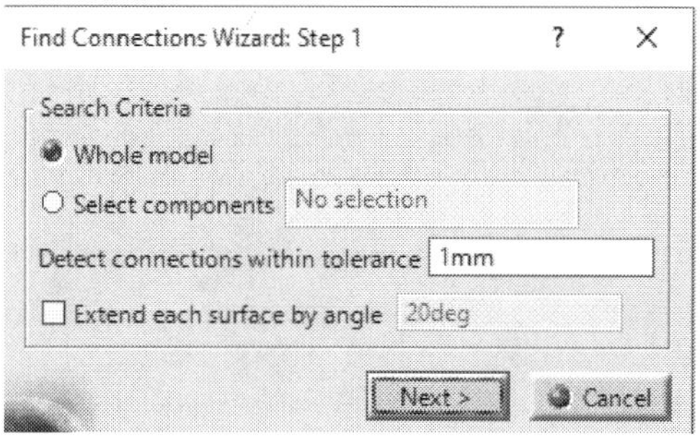

Figure 7–8

Specify the detection tolerance and click **Next**. The Find Connections Wizard dialog updates to Step 2, as shown in Figure 7–9.

Figure 7–9

Select the default type of connection to create and click **Run**. The Find Connections Wizard searches for surfaces within the specified tolerance and displays the result, as shown in Figure 7–10.

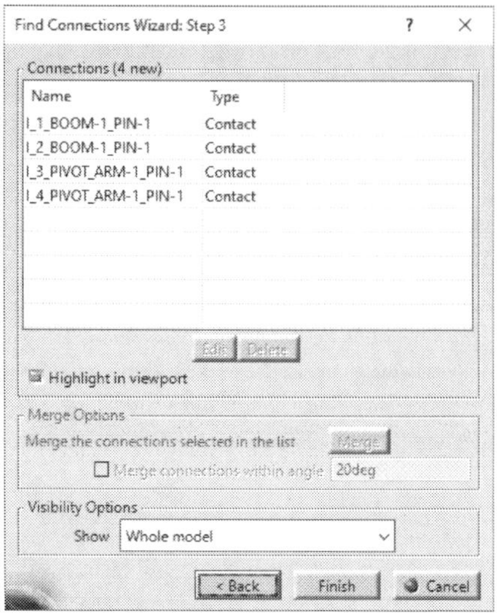

Figure 7–10

To visualize a connection, select it in the list, as shown in Figure 7–11. One surface will highlight in red, and the other in green.

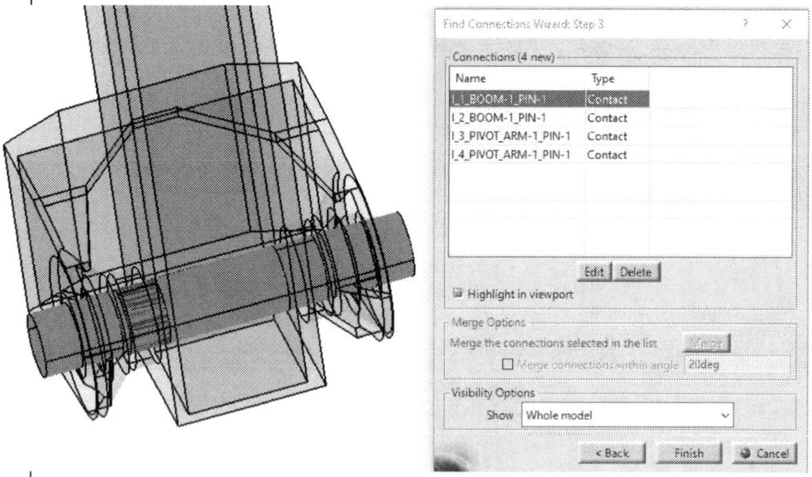

Figure 7–11

To change the connection type, click **Edit** and select the desired type in the Edit Connection dialog box that opens, as shown in Figure 7–12.

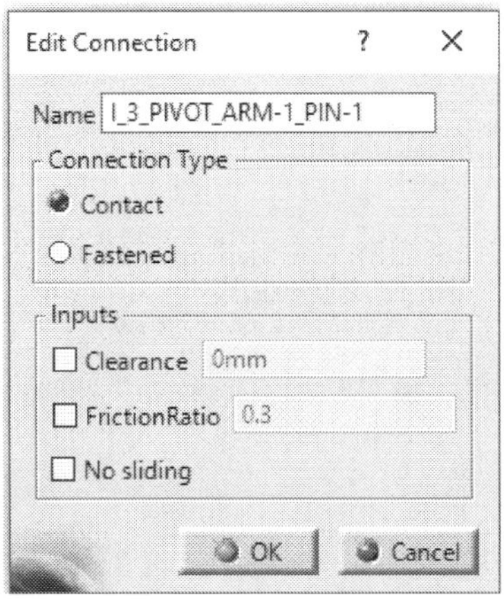

Figure 7–12

Once all the connections have been reviewed and edited as required, click **Finish**. The new connections are displayed in the tree, as shown in Figure 7–13.

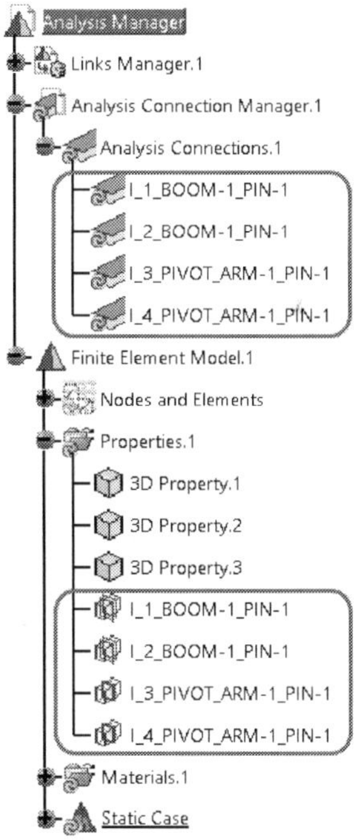

Figure 7–13

7.4 Mesh Refinement

The accuracy of the contact analysis is affected by the mesh density in the contact areas. The element size should be much smaller than the contact region.

Use the following guidelines to refine the mesh in contact areas.

- Separate areas of contact from the rest of the part surface by creating surface patches, as described in Chapter 3.
- Use the **Local size** mesh control to apply a smaller element size in the contact areas, as shown in Figure 7–14.

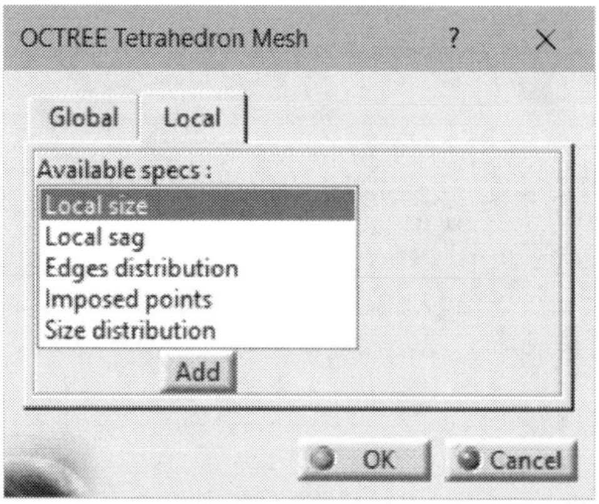

Figure 7–14

7.5 Contact Analysis Solution

Structural analysis with contact connections is a non-linear FEA analysis. A non-linear analysis is solved in small steps (controlled by the FEA solver), with the applied loads gradually incremented from no load to the full load, and with the equation system solved on every load increment.

A non-linear FEA takes much longer to solve than a comparable linear analysis. Therefore, use caution when setting up an analysis with many contact connections.

7.6 Contact Analysis Results

In addition to the usual result images, such as deformation, displacement, or Von Mises stress, you can also visualize contact pressures and contact clearances when you run analysis with contact connections.

Visualization of contact pressure and contact clearance requires the EST (Elfini) license.

To display the contact pressure image, right-click on **Static Case Solution.1** in the tree and select **Generate Image**, as shown in Figure 7–15.

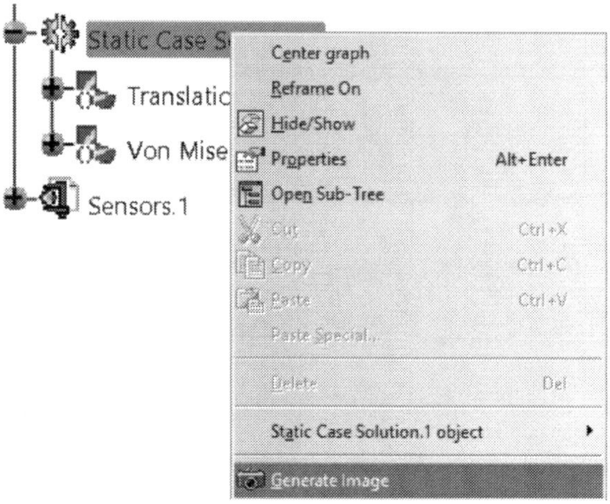

Figure 7–15

In the Image Generation dialog box, select **Pressure fringe** and click **OK**, as shown in Figure 7–16.

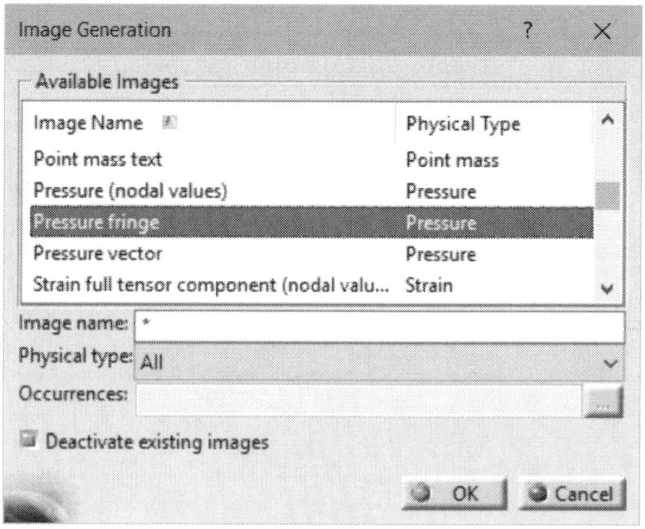

Figure 7–16

The contact pressure result plot displays as shown in Figure 7–17.

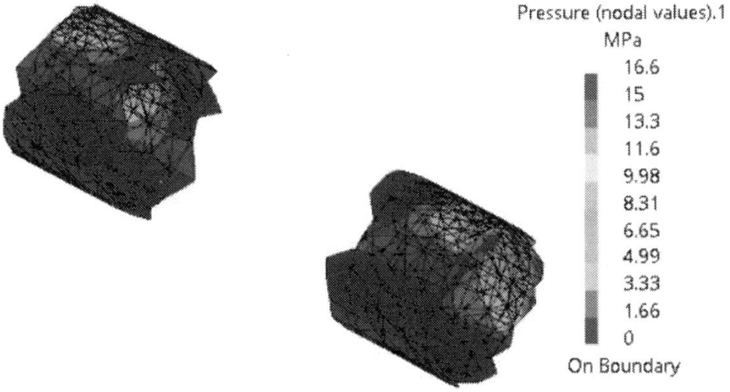

Figure 7–17

To visualize the contact clearance image, select the **Clearance iso** option in the Image Generation dialog box, as shown in Figure 7–18.

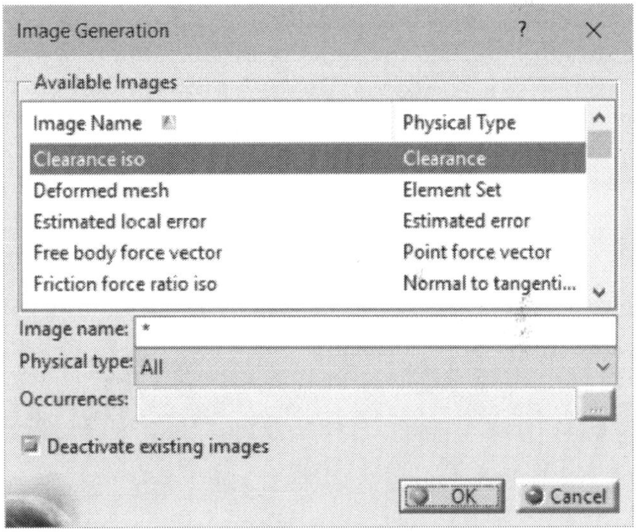

Figure 7–18

The contact clearance result plot displays as shown in Figure 7–19.

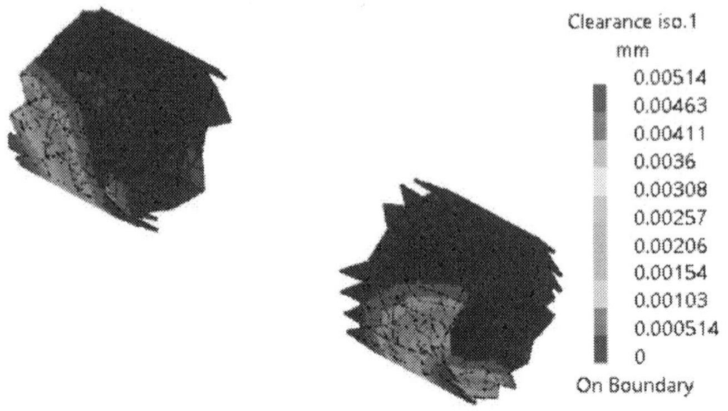

Figure 7–19

Practice 7a

Pin-Jointed Assembly

Practice Objectives

- Apply the materials and mesh the model.
- Create a fastened analysis connection.
- Create a contact analysis connection.
- Apply loads and restraints.
- Run the analysis with mesh adaptivity.
- Visualize the results.

In this practice, you will set up a contact analysis on a pin-jointed assembly model. The assembly that you will analyze consists of three parts; the exploded view is shown in Figure 7–20.

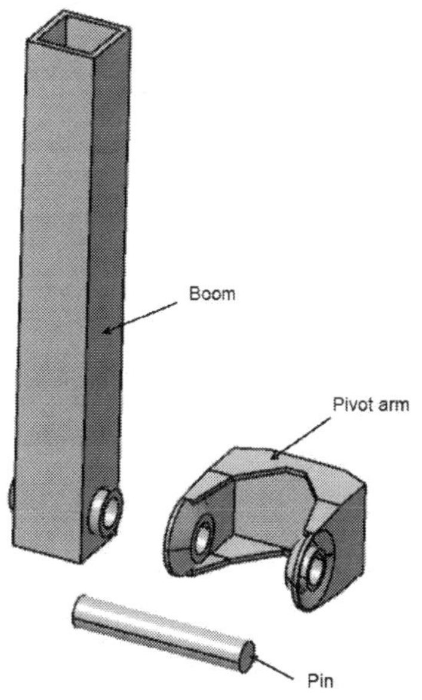

Figure 7–20

The pin is press-fit into the pivot arm holes. Therefore, the pin is fully fixed to the pivot arm. However, the boom is assembled on the pin with a small clearance to be able to rotate around the pin when the boom is moving.

Task 1 - Open the assembly in CATIA.

1. Open **PIN_JOINT_07.CATProduct** from the *CATIA Generative Structural Analysis Practice Files\Ch07* folder.

2. Set the model display as  (Shading with Edges). The assembly displays as shown in Figure 7–21.

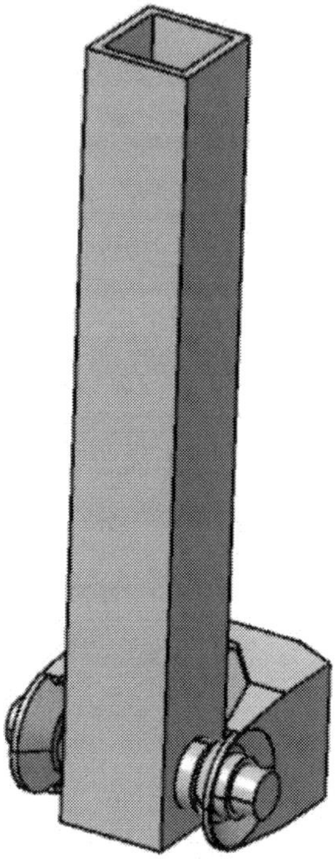

Figure 7–21

3. Select **Tools>Options>Parameters and Measures>Units** and set the units as follows:

   - Length: **Millimeter (mm)**
   - Force: **Newton (N)**
   - Moment: **Newton x Meter (Nxm)**
   - Pressure: **Megapascal (MPa)**

Task 2 - Switch the parts to Design Mode.

You only need to do this task if you opened the assembly in Visualization mode (the toggle **Tools>Options> Infrastructure>Product Structure>Work with the cache system** is on), because the parts must be in the Design mode for the analysis.

1. Right-click on the root assembly **PIN_JOINT_07** and select **Representations>Design Mode** in the contextual menu, as shown in Figure 7–22.

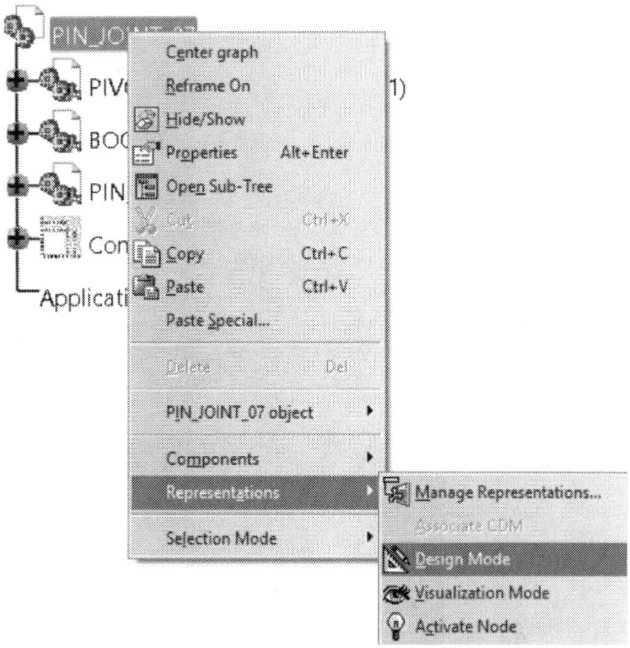

Figure 7–22

Task 3 - Apply the material.

1. Apply the **Steel** material to the entire assembly, as shown in Figure 7–23.

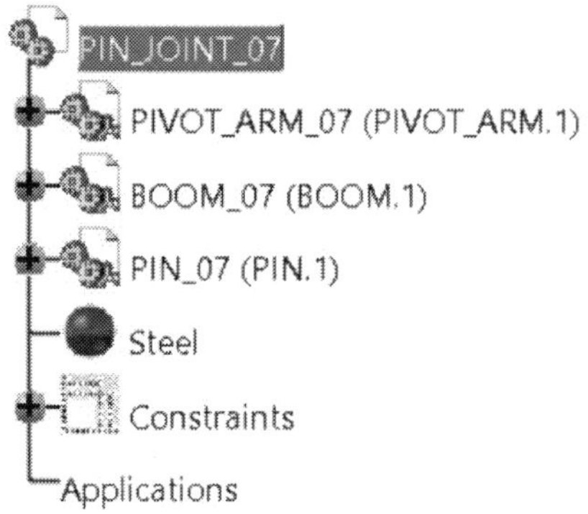

Figure 7–23

Task 4 - Start the GSA workbench.

1. Select **Start>Analysis & Simulation>Generative Structural Analysis**.
2. Select **Static Analysis** as the new analysis case.

Task 5 - Mesh the model.

For better stress accuracy in contact analysis, the mesh on the contact surfaces should be refined. This can be accomplished by using either local mesh refinement or the mesh adaptivity tool. You will use the mesh adaptivity tool later in this practice to ensure the accuracy of the analysis.

1. Set up the mesh specification for the parts in the assembly as follows:

- OCTREE Tetrahedron Mesh.1: PIVOT_ARM.1
  - Element type: **Parabolic**
  - Size: **20mm**
  - Absolute sag: **2mm**
- OCTREE Tetrahedron Mesh.1: BOOM.1
  - Element type: **Parabolic**
  - Size: **25mm**
  - Absolute sag: **2.5mm**

- OCTREE Tetrahedron Mesh.1: PIN.1
  - Element type: **Parabolic**
  - Size: **10mm**
  - Absolute sag: **1mm**

2. Right-click on **Nodes and Elements** in the tree and select **Mesh Visualization**. The mesh is displayed, as shown in Figure 7–24. Visually examine the mesh in various areas of the model.

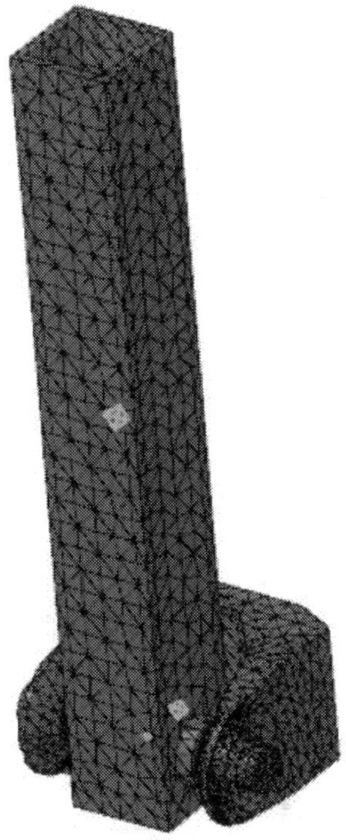

Figure 7–24

3. Right-click on **Mesh.1** in the tree and select **Delete** to delete the mesh visualization and return to the model view.

Task 6 - Create analysis connections.

The pin is press-fit into the pivot arm holes. Therefore, the pin is fully fixed to the pivot arm, which can be simulated by a fastened connection property between the pin and the pivot arm.

The boom is assembled on the pin in such a way that it can rotate around the pin when the boom is moving. At the same time, when a load is applied to the boom, the pin bends slightly and no longer contacts the holes in the boom over their entire surface areas. This behavior can be simulated by a contact connection property between the pin and the boom.

In this task, you will create both fastened and contact connection using the (Find interactions) tool.

1. In the Connection Properties toolbar, select (Find interactions). The Find Connections Wizard dialog box opens, as shown in Figure 7–25.

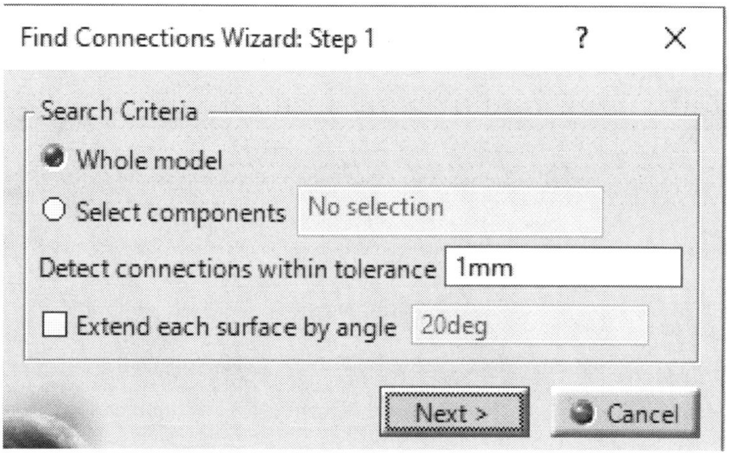

Figure 7–25

2. Click **Next**. The Find Connections Wizard dialog box displays, as shown in Figure 7–26.

Figure 7–26

3. The dialog box lets you select the default type of connection to create, which can be overridden later. Leave the default connection type as **Contact** and click **Run**. The Find Connections Wizard searches for contacting surfaces and displays the result, as shown in Figure 7–27.

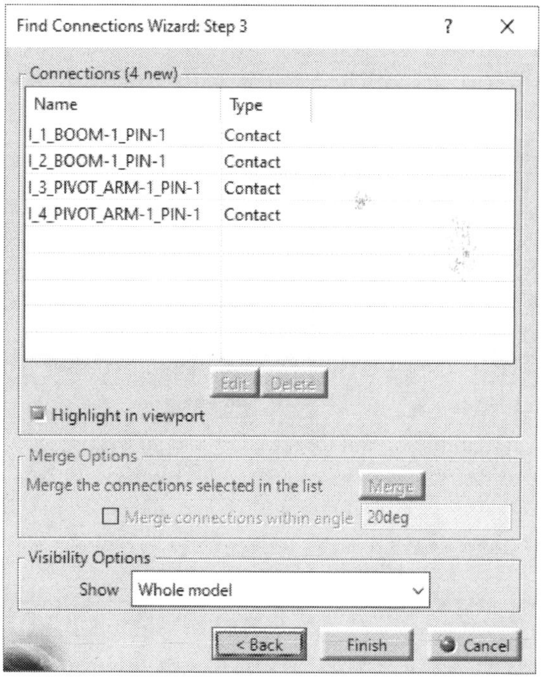

Figure 7–27

4. Select the first connection in the list. The surfaces of the pin and of one of the holes in the boom highlight, as shown in Figure 7–28. This connection should be of the contact type, so leave it as is.

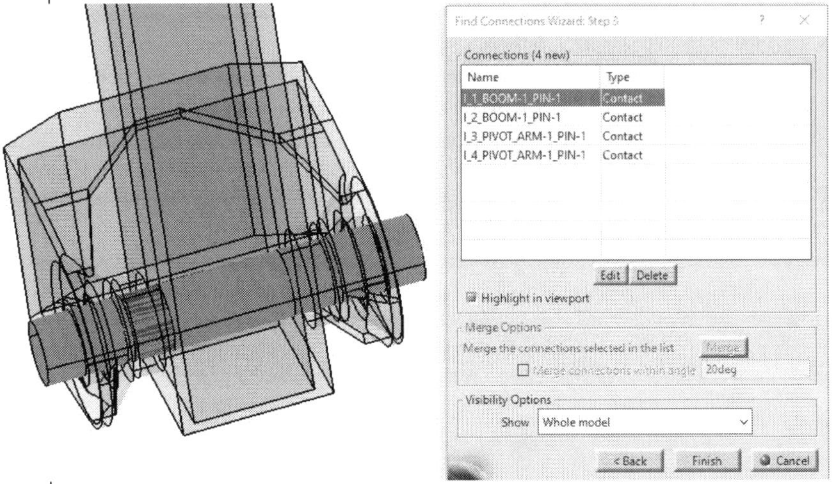

Figure 7–28

5. Select the second connection in the list. The surfaces of the pin and of the other hole in the boom highlight, as shown in Figure 7–29. This connection should also be of the contact type, so leave it as is.

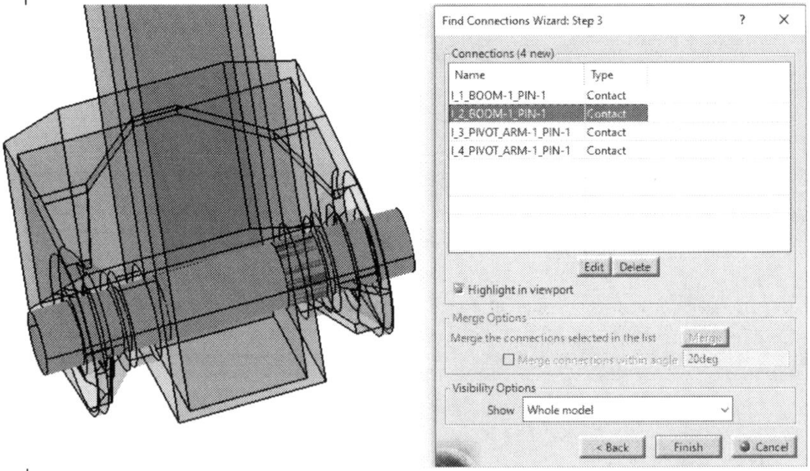

Figure 7–29

6. Select the third connection. The surfaces of the pin and of one of the holes in the pivot arm highlight, as shown in Figure 7–30.

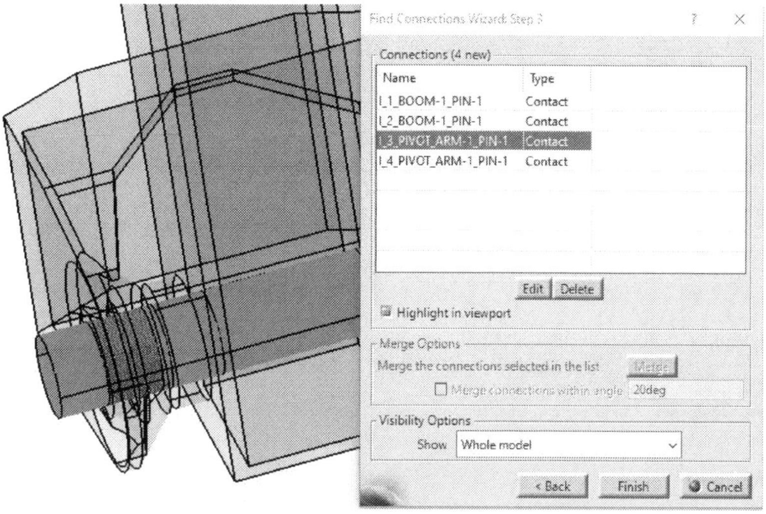

Figure 7–30

7. This should be a fastened connection. Click **Edit**. The Edit Connection dialog box opens, as shown in Figure 7–31.

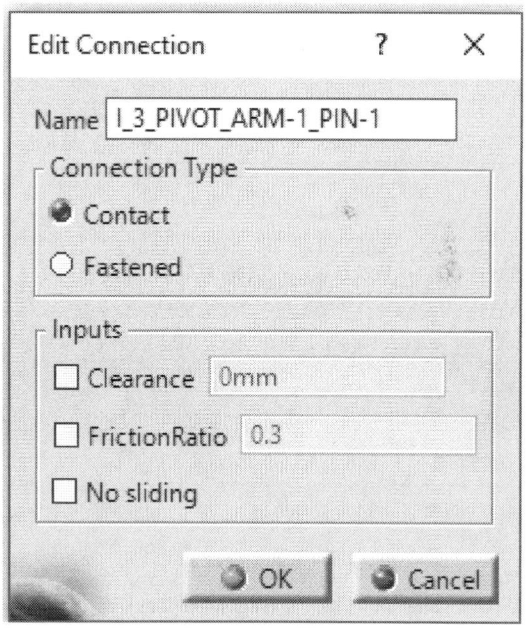

Figure 7–31

8. Activate **Fastened** and click **OK**, as shown in Figure 7–32.

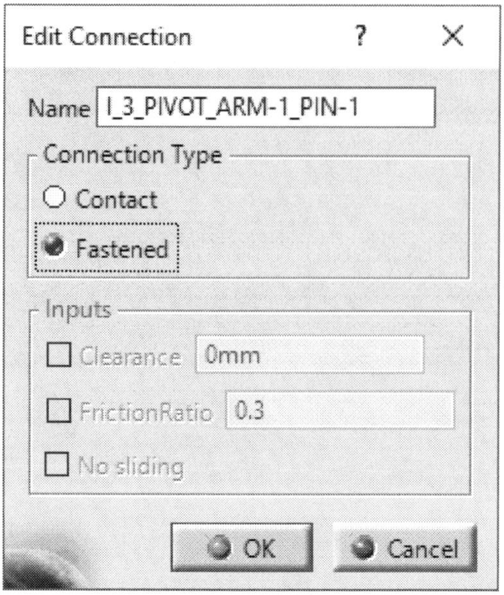

Figure 7–32

9. The fourth connection is between the pin and the other hole in the pivot arm. Change it to **Fastened** as well. The Find Connections Wizard dialog box displays, as shown in Figure 7–33.

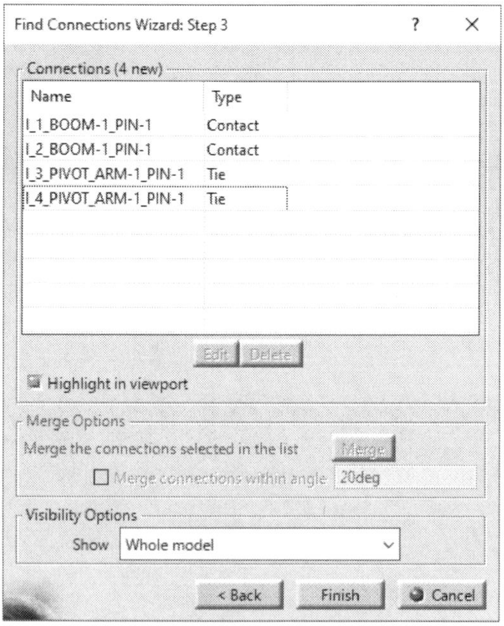

Figure 7–33

10. Click **Finish** to finalize the connections. The new connections are displayed in the tree, as shown in Figure 7–34.

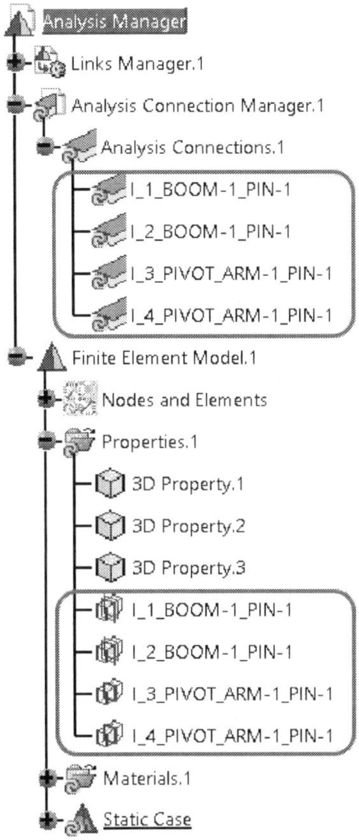

Figure 7–34

Task 7 - Apply the load.

1. Select 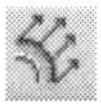 (Distributed Force) and apply **10000N** force in the **Y** direction to the top surface of the boom, as shown in Figure 7–35.

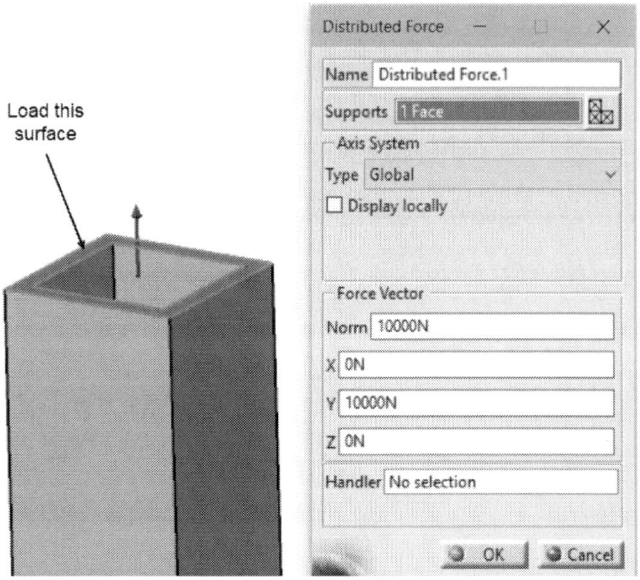

Figure 7–35

Task 8 - Apply the restraints.

This restraint is required to eliminate the rigid body rotation and sliding motions of the boom about the pin. The contact connection between the pin and the boom that you defined in Task 7 was frictionless.

1. Select  (User-defined Restraint) and restrain the **X**- and **Z**-directions on the end surface of the boom shown in Figure 7–36. Ensure that you leave the **Y**-direction free as this is the direction of the load.

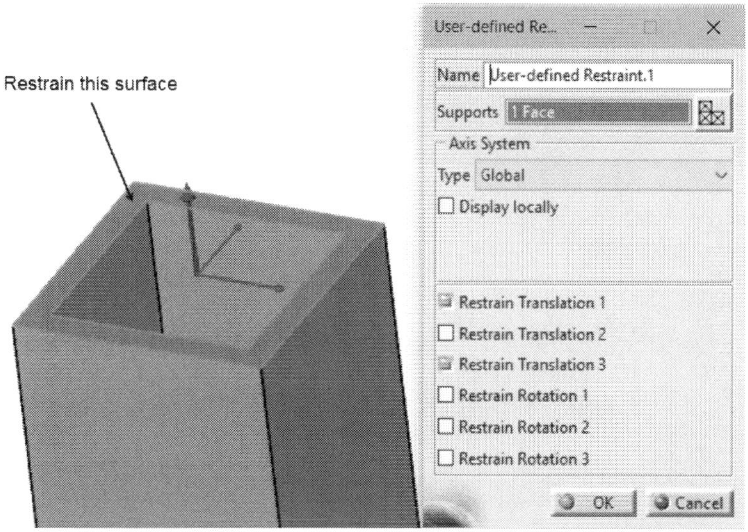

Figure 7–36

2. Apply the  (Clamp) restraint to the back surface of the pivot arm, as shown in Figure 7–37.

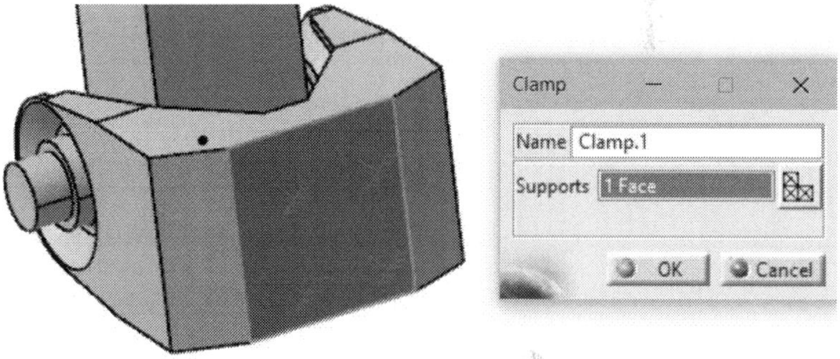

Figure 7–37

Task 9 - Run the analysis.

1. Select (Compute) and run the analysis, which should take under a minute.

2. Expand **Sensors.1** in the tree. Note that the value of the **Global Error Rate** sensor is about **14.4%**, as shown in Figure 7–38. In the following tasks, you will use the mesh adaptivity tool to improve the analysis accuracy to under 8% global error rate.

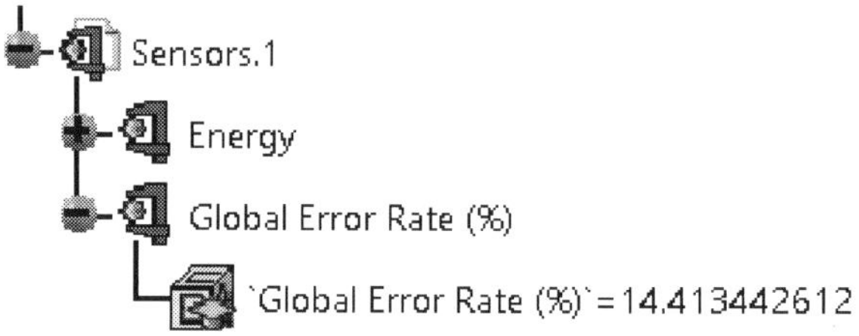

Figure 7–38

Task 10 - Set up Global Adaptivity.

1. Select (New Adaptivity Entity). In the Global Adaptivity dialog box that opens, select the **OCTREE Tetrahedron Mesh.1: PIVOT_ARM.1**, **OCTREE Tetrahedron Mesh.2: BOOM.1**, and **OCTREE Tetrahedron Mesh.3: PIN.1** meshes as the *Supports* and enter **8** in the *Objective Error* field, as shown in Figure 7–39. Click **OK** to finish.

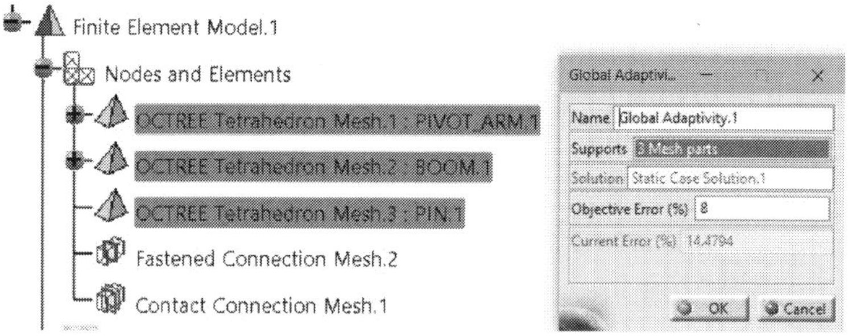

Figure 7–39

Task 11 - Run the analysis with adaptivity.

1. Select (Compute with Adaptivity). In the Adaptivity Process Parameters dialog box that opens, enter **3** in the *Iterations Number* field, activate the **Minimum Size** option and enter **4mm** as the minimum element size, as shown in Figure 7–40.

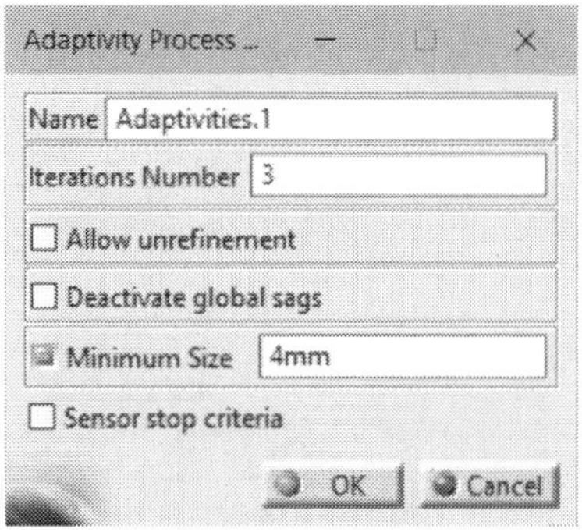

Figure 7–40

2. Click **OK** to start the computation. CATIA displays a series of messages informing you about the status of the computation process. Wait until computation completes, which may take a few minutes.

3. Once the computation is finished, CATIA may or may not automatically update the analysis sensors. To update all the sensors, right-click on **Sensors.1** in the tree and select **Update All Sensors**, as shown in Figure 7–41.

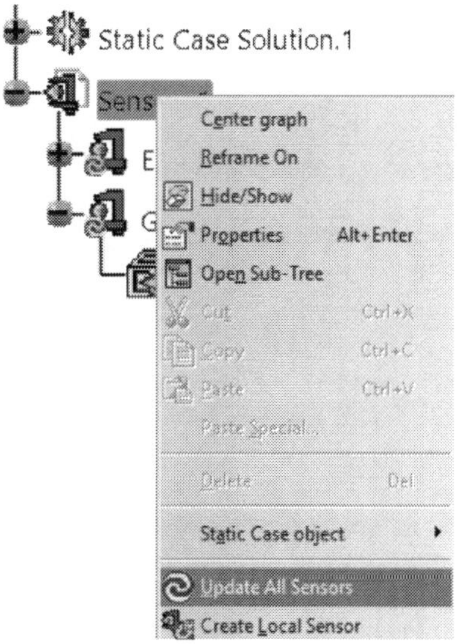

Figure 7–41

4. Expand **Sensors.1** in the tree and note that the value of the **Global Error Rate** sensor now reads **6.82%**, as shown in Figure 7–42. This is below the objective error in this analysis, which was 8%, so the mesh adaptivity process has succeeded.

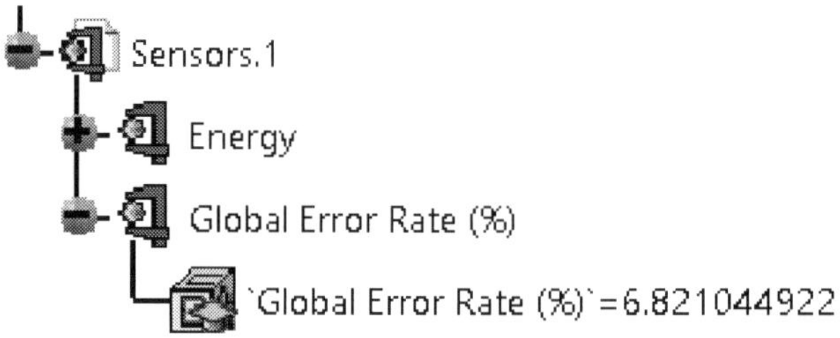

Figure 7–42

Task 12 - Display and animate the displacements.

1. Hide **Nodes and Elements**, **Properties.1**, **Restraints.1**, and **Loads.1**.

2. Select  (Customize View Parameters) and activate the options **Edges and points**, **Shading**, and **Material**.

3. Visualize the displacement vector () image, as shown in Figure 7–43.

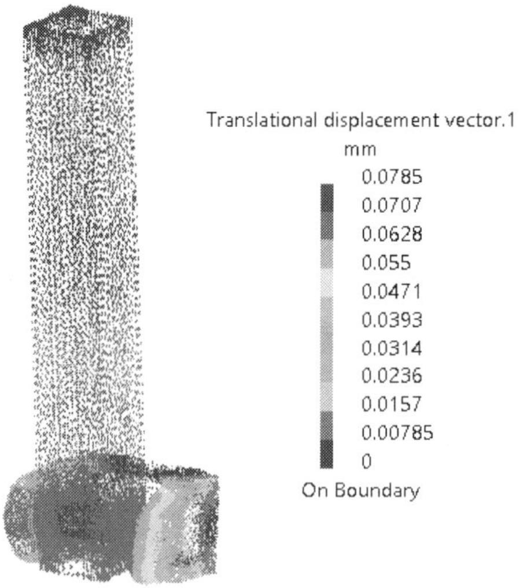

Figure 7–43

4. Double-click on **Translational displacement vector.1** in the tree and select **Average iso** in the *Types* list. The result displays as shown in Figure 7–44.

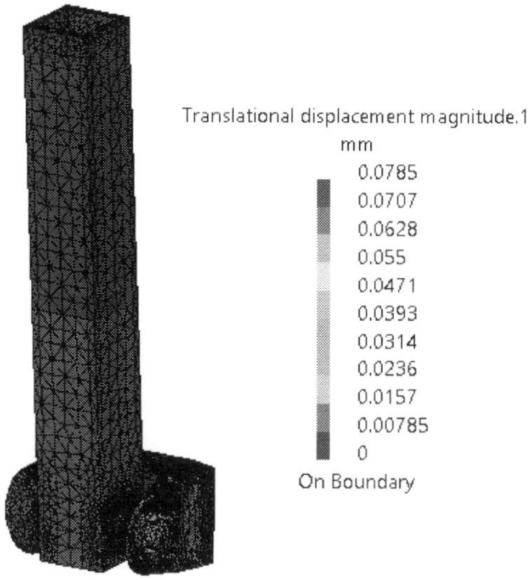

Figure 7–44

5. Animate the displacement result. Does the model deform according to the applied loads and restraints?

Task 13 - Display the Von Mises stress.

1. Select  (Von Mises Stress). The stress result displays as shown in Figure 7–45.

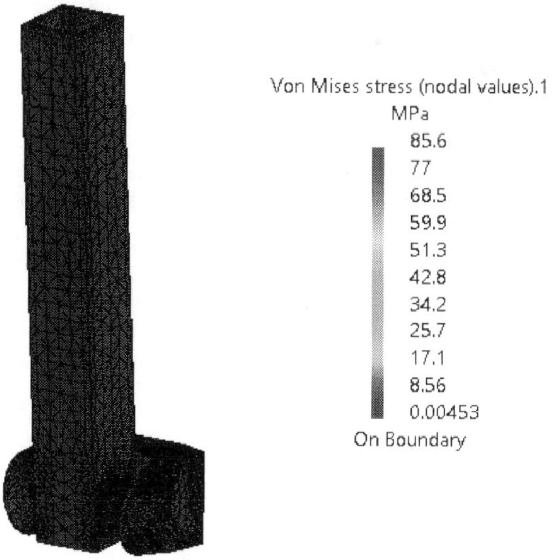

Figure 7–45

*The maximum stress in this model occurs in the pivot arm part near the clamp, while the stress level in the pin and the boom is much lower. Modifying the **Imposed max** value helps to reveal the stress image in the pin and boom parts.*

2. Double-click on the color map and set the **Imposed max** value to **30**, as shown in Figure 7–46.

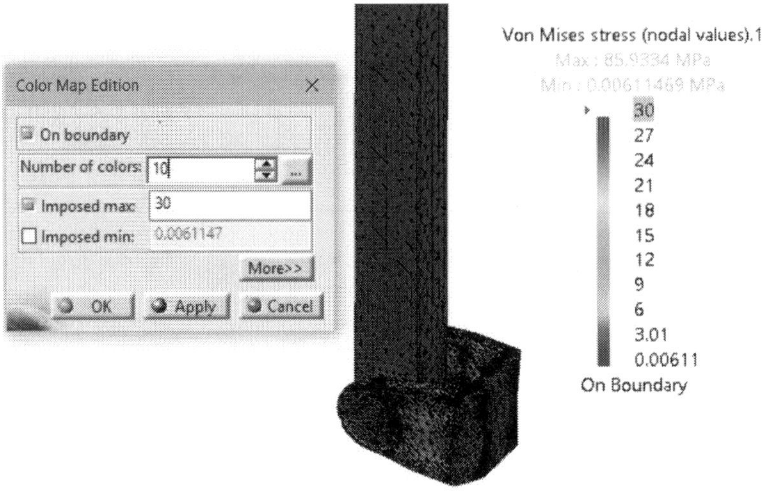

Figure 7–46

3. Select  (Back View). The result displays as shown in Figure 7–47.

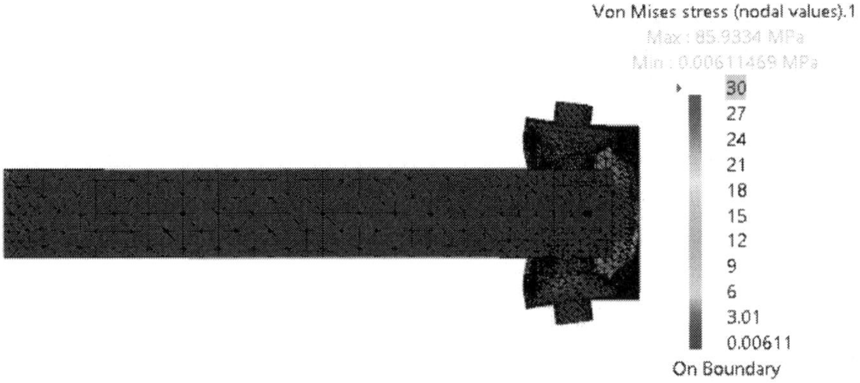

Figure 7–47

4. Select (Cut Plane Analysis). In the Cut Plane Analysis dialog box that opens, click **Init plane parameters**. The result displays as shown in Figure 7–48.

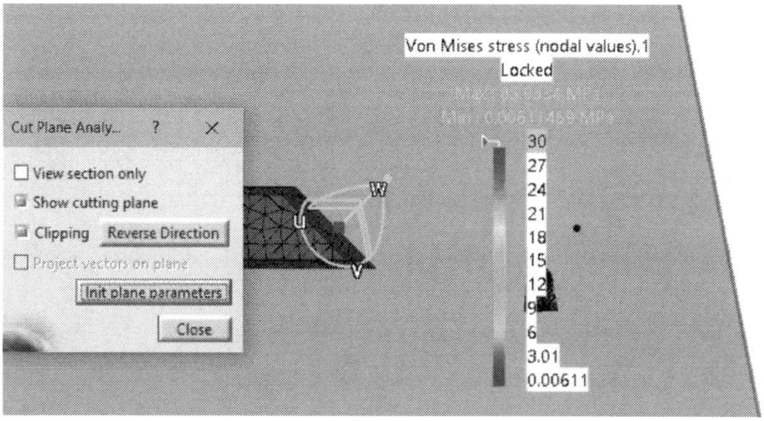

Figure 7–48

5. Right-click on the red square in the compass and select **Edit** in the contextual menu, as shown in Figure 7–49.

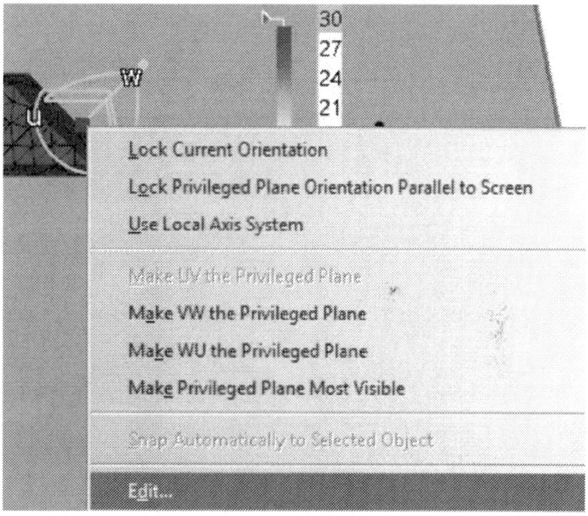

Figure 7–49

6. In the Parameters for Compass Manipulation dialog box that opens, enter the *Position* and *Angle* values as shown in Figure 7–50.

The specified position and angles make the cutting plane go through the axis of the pin.

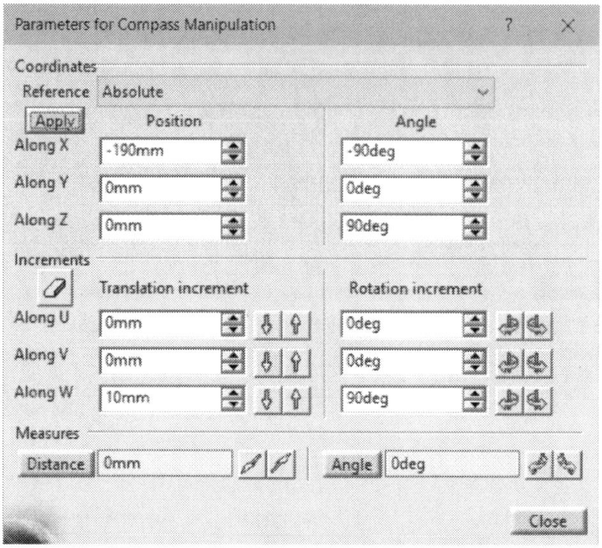

Figure 7–50

7. Click **Apply**, then click **Close**. The model displays as shown in Figure 7–51.

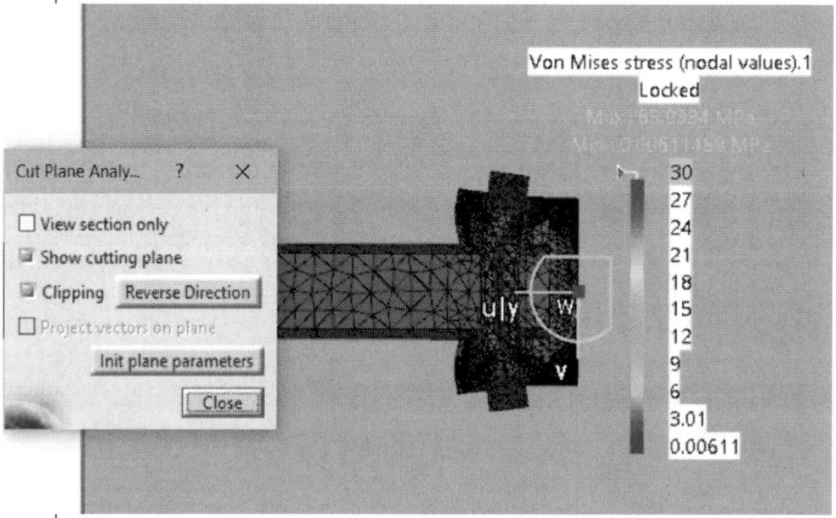

Figure 7–51

8. In the Cut Plane Analysis dialog box, deselect the **Show cutting plane** option. Using the **Reverse Direction** button, ensure that the front of the model is clipped out. The result plot displays as shown in Figure 7–52.

Figure 7–52

9. Zoom in on the area around the pin, as shown on Figure 7–53. Note the well-pronounced bending stress pattern in the pin.

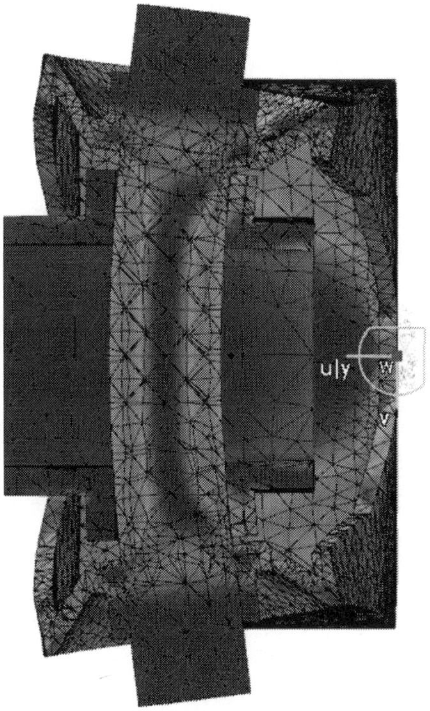

Figure 7–53

10. Close the Cut Plane Analysis dialog box. Right-click on **Von Mises stress (nodal values).1** in the tree and select **Activate/Deactivate** to delete the stress image from the screen and return to the model view.

Task 14 - Save and close the files.

1. Optionally, save the analysis document and the assembly for future reference.
2. Close both the analysis and the product documents.

Practice 7b Press-Fit Analysis

Practice Objectives

- Simplify the model.
- Apply the materials and create the mesh.
- Create a pressure fitting analysis connection.
- Apply loads and restraints.
- Run the analysis.
- Visualize the results.

In this practice, you will set up a press-fit contact analysis on a shaft and a ball bearing assembly model. The area of interest is the contact between the shaft and the inner ring of the bearing.

The exploded view of the assembly that you will analyze is shown in Figure 7–54.

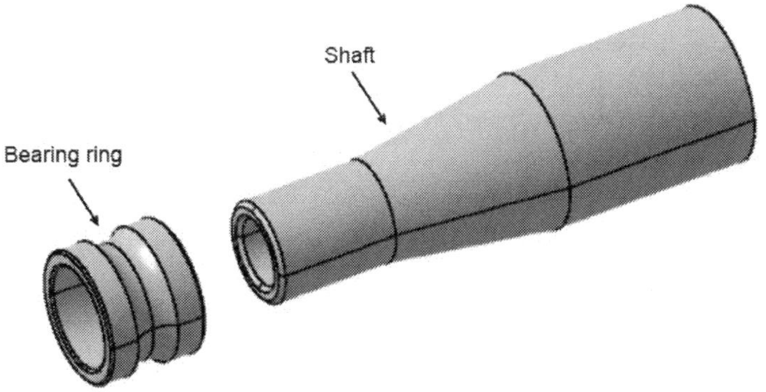

Figure 7–54

The bearing ring is press-fit onto the shaft. The outer diameter (OD) of the shaft is 20mm, and the inner diameter (ID) of the ring is 19.96mm. The objective is to determine deformation and stress in the parts due to the press-fit.

Task 1 - Open the assembly in CATIA.

1. Open **PRESS_FIT_07.CATProduct** from the *CATIA Generative Structural Analysis Practice Files\Ch07* folder.

2. Set the model display as  (Shading with Edges). The assembly displays as shown in Figure 7–55.

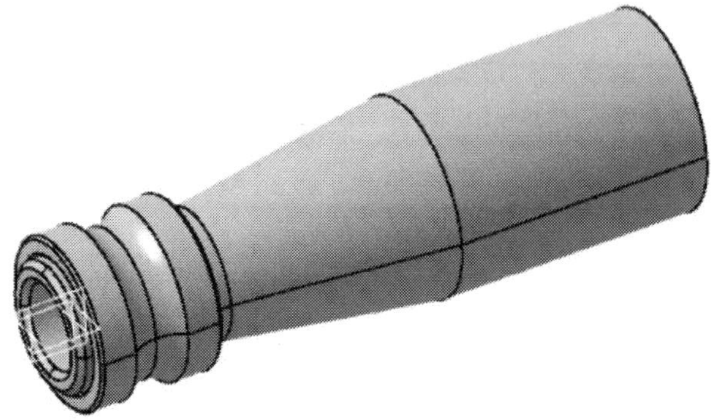

Figure 7–55

3. Select **Tools>Options>Parameters and Measures>Units** and set the units as follows:

   - Length: **Millimeter (mm)**
   - Force: **Newton (N)**
   - Moment: **Newton x Meter (Nxm)**
   - Pressure: **Megapascal (MPa)**

Task 2 - Switch the parts to Design Mode.

You only need to do this task if you opened the assembly in Visualization mode (the toggle **Tools>Options> Infrastructure>Product Structure>Work with the cache system** is on) because the parts must be in Design mode for the analysis.

1. Right-click on the root assembly **PRESS_FIT_07** and select **Representations>Design Mode** in the contextual menu, as shown in Figure 7–56.

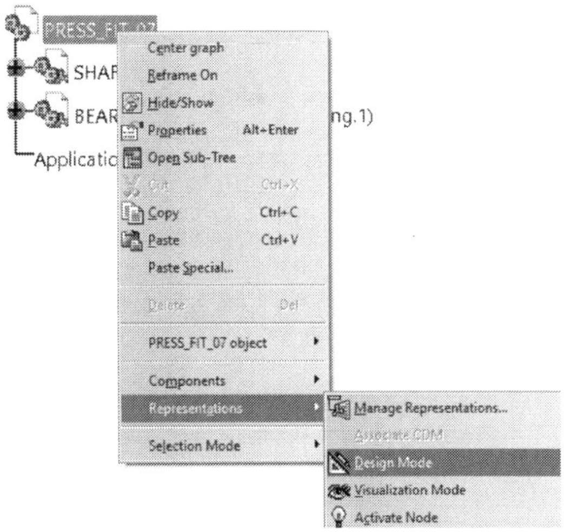

Figure 7–56

Task 3 - Apply the materials.

1. Apply the materials to the assembly parts, as shown in Figure 7–57:

   - SHAFT_07: **Aluminium**
   - BEARING_RING_07: **Steel**

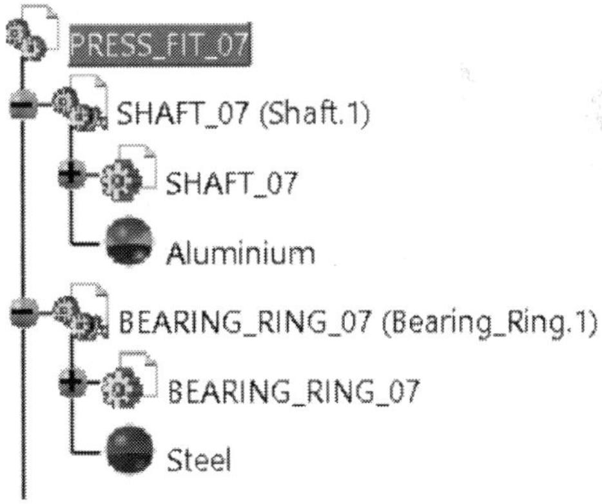

Figure 7–57

Task 4 - Simplify the model.

In this task, you will simplify the model in order to reduce the analysis runtime. Since the model is symmetric, you will analyze a quarter of the assembly.

1. Hide the **BEARING_RING_07** part.
2. Double-click on the **SHAFT_07** part to activate the **Part Design** workbench.
3. In the Surface-Based Features toolbar, select  (Split). The Split Definition dialog box opens, as shown in Figure 7–58.

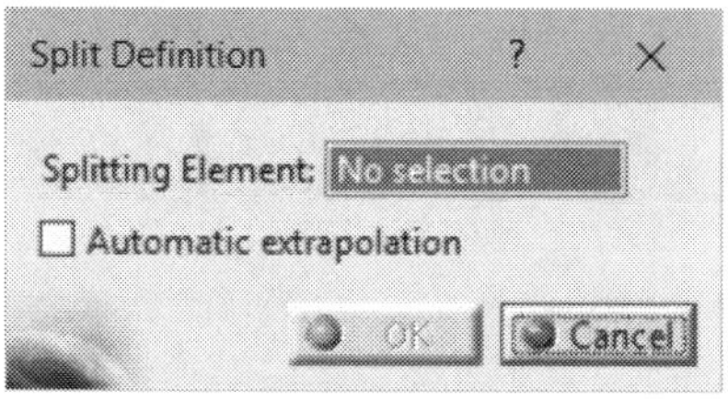

Figure 7–58

4. Select the **xy plane** as the *Splitting Element*. Make sure the orange arrow, which indicates the side to keep, points toward the +**Z** direction, as shown in Figure 7–59. If it does not, click on the orange arrow to flip the direction.

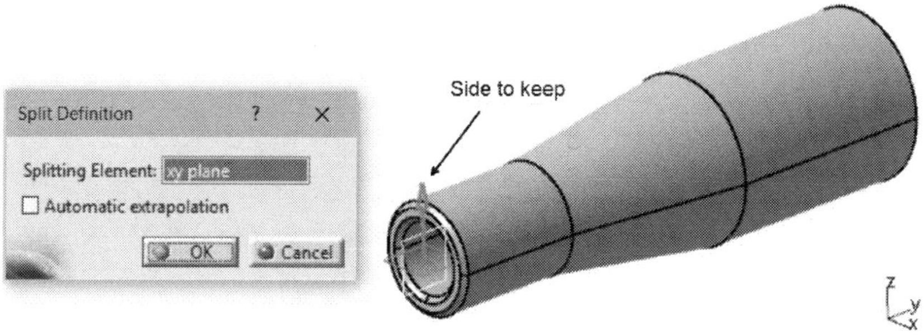

Figure 7–59

5. Click **OK**. The shaft part is cut in half, as shown in Figure 7–60.

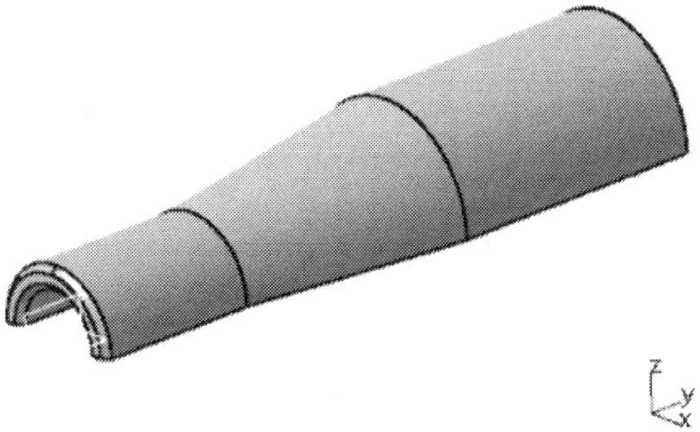

Figure 7–60

6. Select  (Split) and split the part again, now using the **yz plane** as the *Splitting Element*, keeping the side that is toward the -**X** direction, as shown in Figure 7–61.

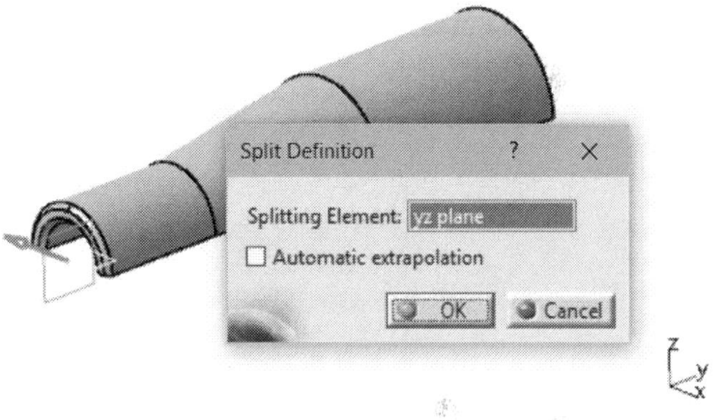

Figure 7–61

7. Click **OK**. The part displays as shown in Figure 7–62.

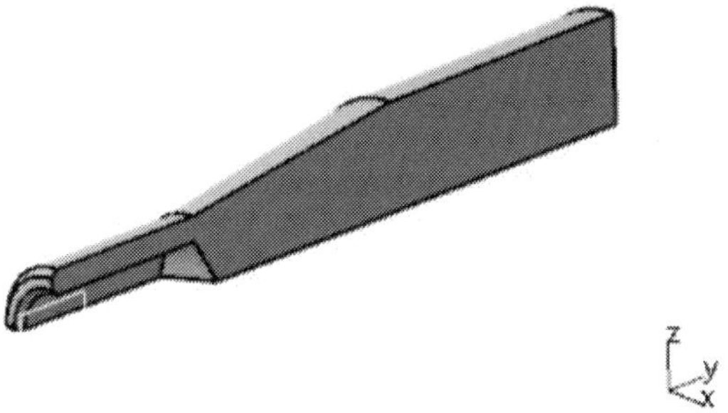

Figure 7–62

8. Double-click on the **PRESS_FIT_07** assembly in the tree to switch back to the **Assembly Design** workbench.

9. Using the previous steps as a guideline, split the bearing ring twice to obtain a quarter of the model. The quarter of the assembly should display as shown in Figure 7–63.

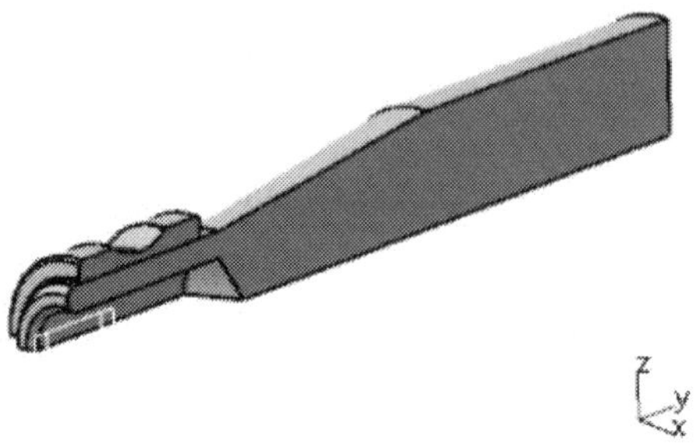

Figure 7–63

Task 5 - Start the GSA workbench.

1. Select **Start>Analysis & Simulation>Generative Structural Analysis**.

2. Select **Static Analysis** as the new analysis case.

Task 6 - Mesh the model.

For better stress accuracy in contact analysis, it is beneficial to use finer mesh on the contact surfaces. In this task, you will set up the global mesh parameters for the parts, as well as define a finer mesh specification on the contacting surfaces.

1. Double-click on **OCTREE Tetrahedron Mesh.1: Shaft.1** in the tree and in the *Global* tab, set up the global mesh parameters for the shaft part as shown in Figure 7–64:

    - Element type: **Parabolic**
    - Size: **2mm**
    - Absolute sag: **0.2mm**

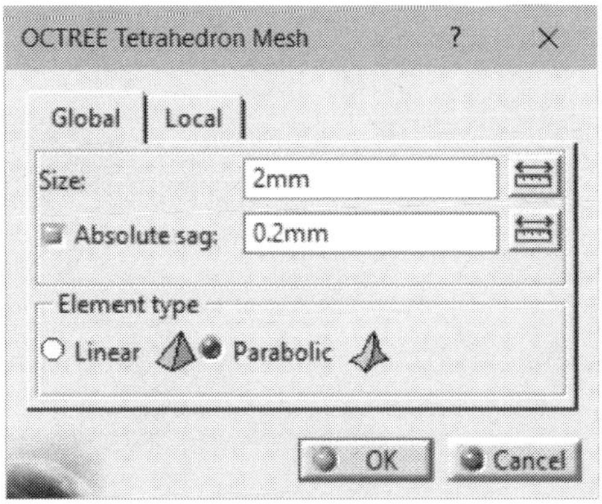

Figure 7–64

2. Select the *Local* tab and select the **Local size** option in the list, as shown in Figure 7–65.

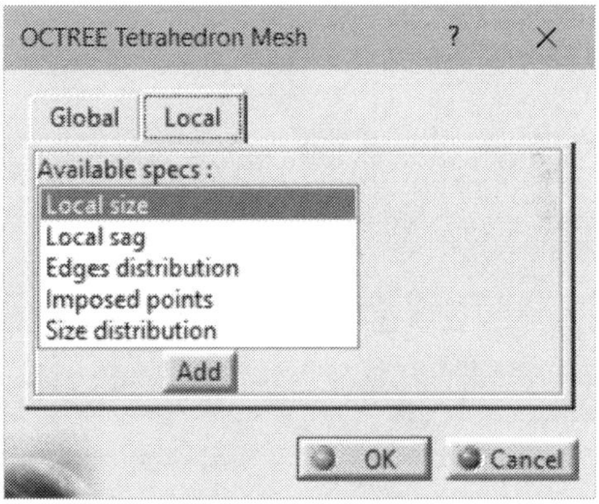

Figure 7–65

3. Click **Add**. The Local Mesh Size dialog box displays, as shown in Figure 7–66.

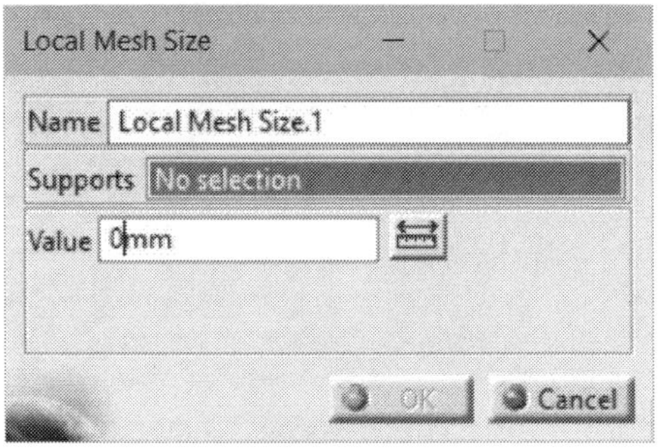

Figure 7–66

4. Hide the ring part and select the outer surface of the shaft under the bearing ring as the *Supports*. Enter **0.8mm** as the *Value*, as shown in Figure 7–67.

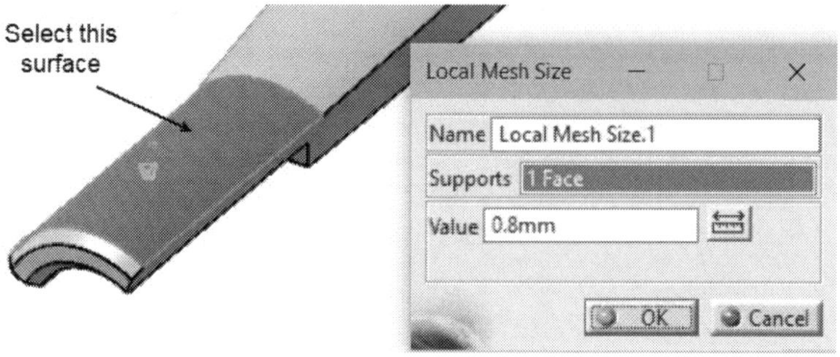

Figure 7–67

5. Click **OK** twice to close both the Local Mesh Size and the OCTREE Tetrahedron Mesh dialog boxes.
6. Unhide the ring part.
7. Double-click on **OCTREE Tetrahedron Mesh.1: Bearing_Ring.1** in the tree and in the *Global* tab, set up the global mesh parameters for the ring part as follows:
    - Element type: **Parabolic**
    - Size: **1.5mm**
    - Absolute sag: **0.1mm**
8. Using Steps 2 to 6 as a guideline, apply a **0.8mm** local mesh size specification to the inside surface of the bearing ring, as shown in Figure 7–68.

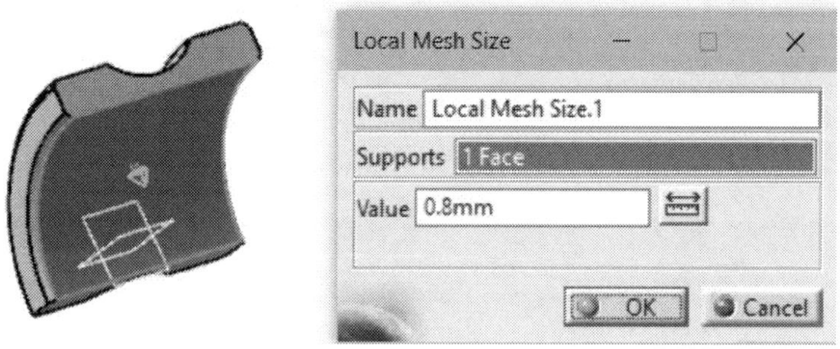

Figure 7–68

9. Right-click on **Nodes and Elements** in the tree and select **Mesh Visualization**. Zoom in on the mesh near the contacting surfaces and note the finer mesh in this area, as shown in Figure 7–69.

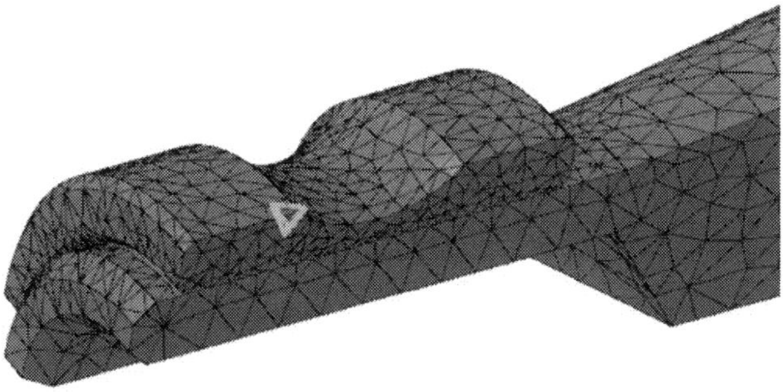

Figure 7–69

10. Right-click on **Mesh.1** in the tree and select **Delete** to delete the mesh visualization and return to the model view.

Task 7 - Create an analysis connection.

This assembly does not have any assembly constraints in the model. Therefore, in this task, you will create a general analysis connection as the support for the pressure fitting connection property.

Hide and unhide the parts as you go to facilitate the selections.

1. In the Analysis Supports toolbar, select  (General Analysis Connection). In the General Analysis Connection dialog box that opens, select the outside surface of the shaft as the *First component* and the inside surface of the ring as the *Second component*, as shown in Figure 7–70. Click **OK** when done.

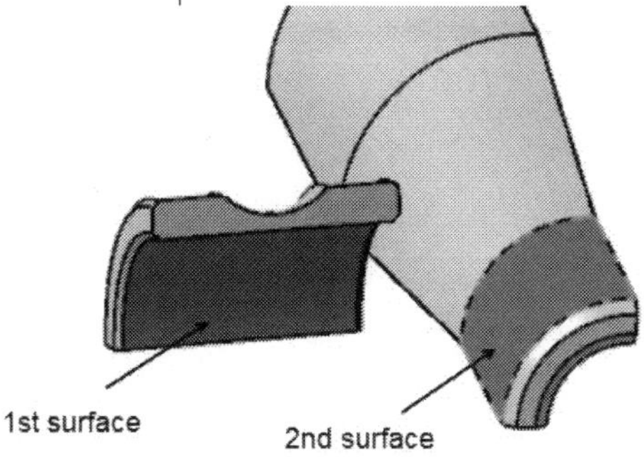

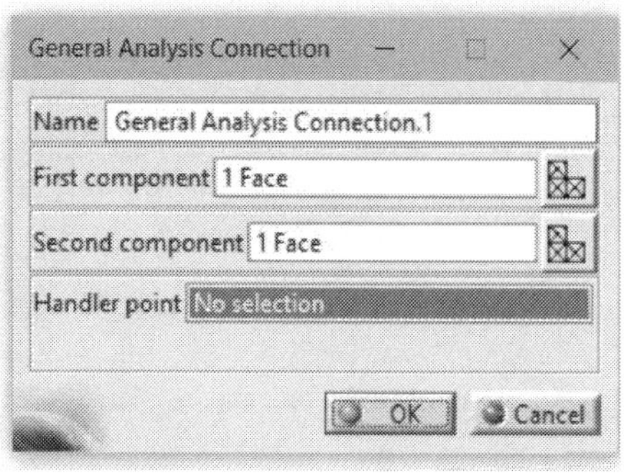

Figure 7–70

2. In the Connection Properties toolbar, select  (Pressure Fitting Connection Property). The Pressure Fitting Connection Property dialog box opens, as shown in Figure 7–71.

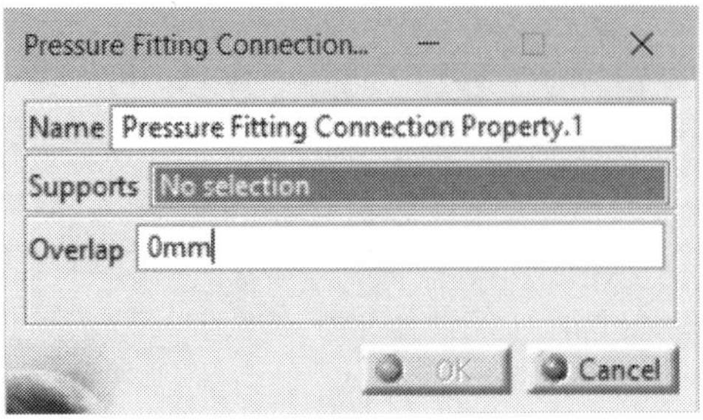

Figure 7–71

The shaft OD is 20mm while the ring ID is 19.96mm. Therefore, the amount of radial interference is (20mm – 19.96mm) / 2 = 0.02mm.

3. Select **General Analysis Connection.1** as the *Supports* and enter **0.02mm** as the *Overlap*, as shown in Figure 7–72. Click **OK** to finish.

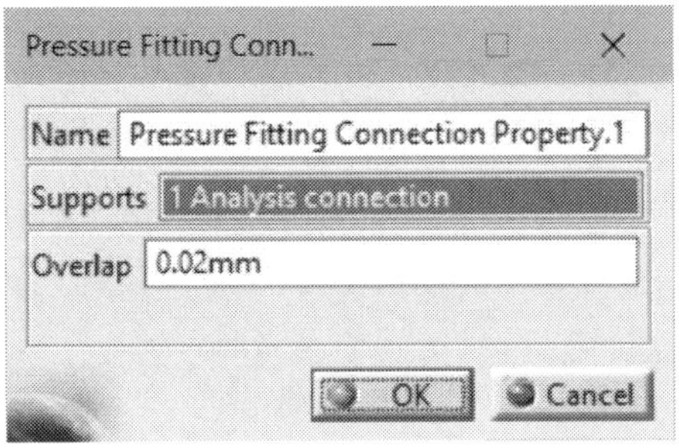

Figure 7–72

Task 8 - Apply the restraints.

1. Apply the  (Clamp) restraint to the back end of the shaft, as shown in Figure 7–73.

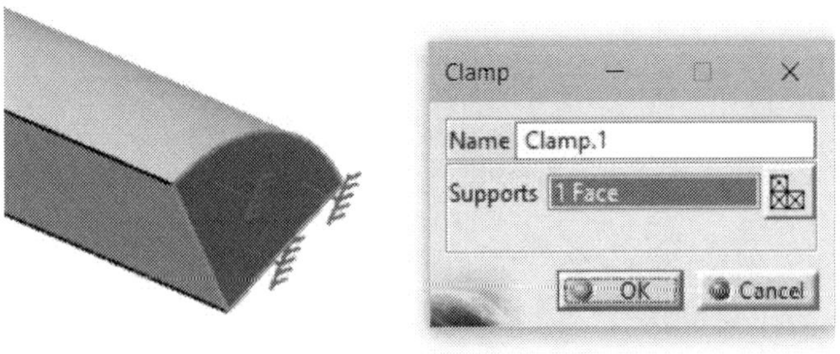

Figure 7–73

This restraint represents the mirror symmetry condition about the YZ plane.

2. Apply the (Surface Slider) restraint to the two cutout surfaces on the YZ plane, as shown in Figure 7–74.

Figure 7–74

This restraint represents the mirror symmetry condition about the XY plane.

3. Apply the (Surface Slider) restraint to the two cutout surfaces on the XY plane, as shown in Figure 7–75.

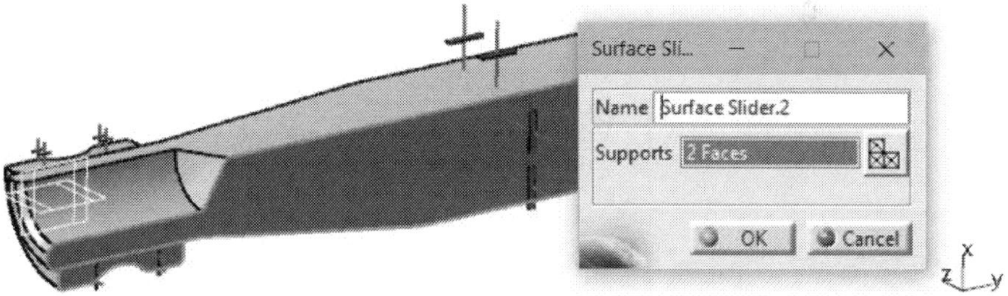

Figure 7–75

Task 9 - Run the analysis.

1. Select (Compute) and run the analysis, which should take a few minutes. Close the Warnings dialog box that appears in the process.

Task 10 - Display the deformation.

1. Hide the **Restraints**.
2. Visualize the deformation () image, as shown in Figure 7–76. Note that the deformed mesh image displays a substantial gap between the ring and the shaft (by default, CATIA scales up the displayed deformation).

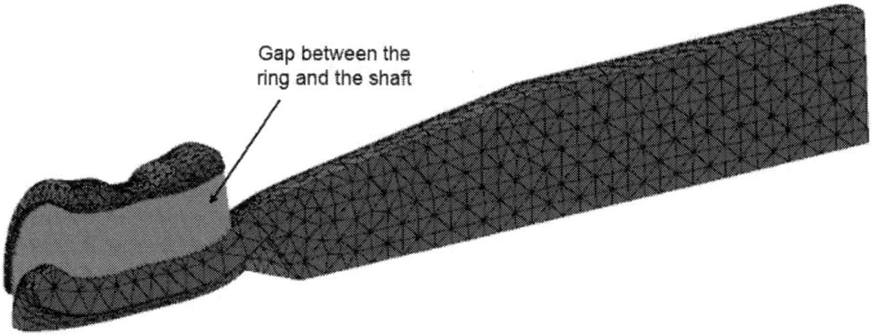

Figure 7–76

3. Select  (Amplification Magnitude), set the **Factor** value to **1**, and activate the **Set as default for future created images** option, as shown in Figure 7–77.

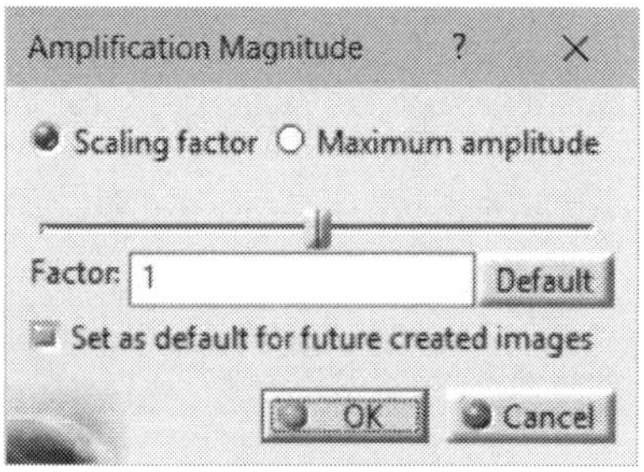

Figure 7–77

4. Click **OK**. The deformed mesh displays as shown in Figure 7–78. Note that now there is no gap between the ring and the shaft, as it should be.

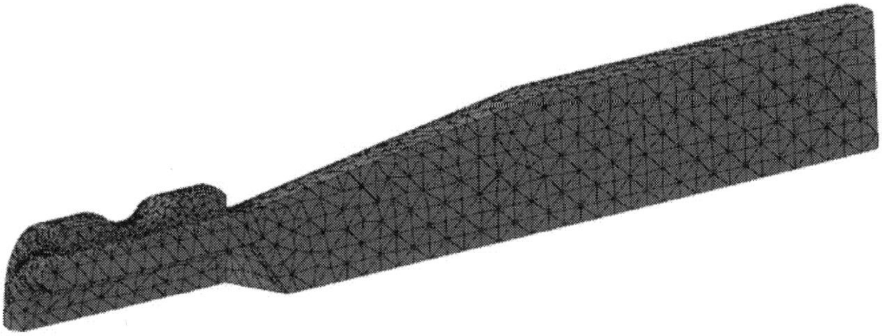

Figure 7–78

5. Zoom in on the contact area between the ring and the shaft, as shown in Figure 7–79. Note that the initial interference of 0.02mm between the ring and the shaft has been removed in the analysis.

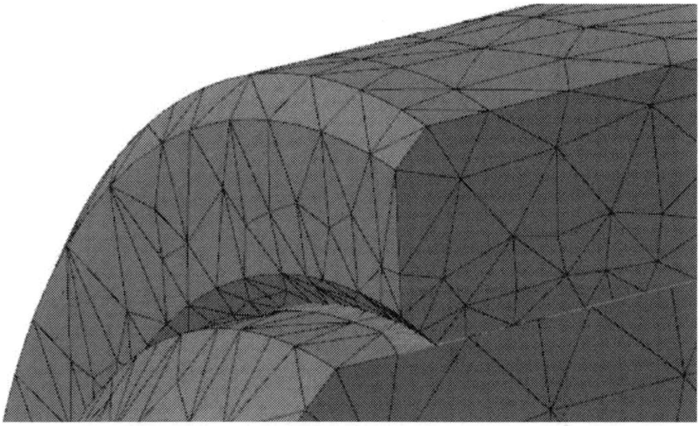

Figure 7–79

Task 11 - Determine the radial displacement.

1. Change the view mode to  (Shading with Material).

2. Visualize the displacement () image, as shown in Figure 7–80.

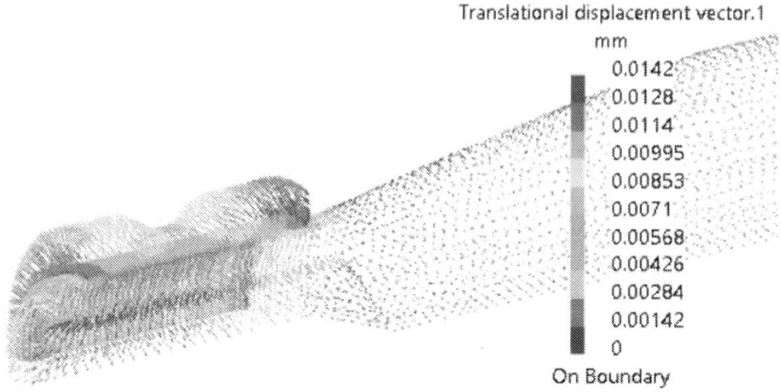

Figure 7–80

3. Double-click on the **Translational displacement vector.1** object in the tree. In the Image Edition dialog box that opens, select **Average iso** in the *Types* list, as shown in Figure 7–81. Do not close the Image Edition dialog box just yet.

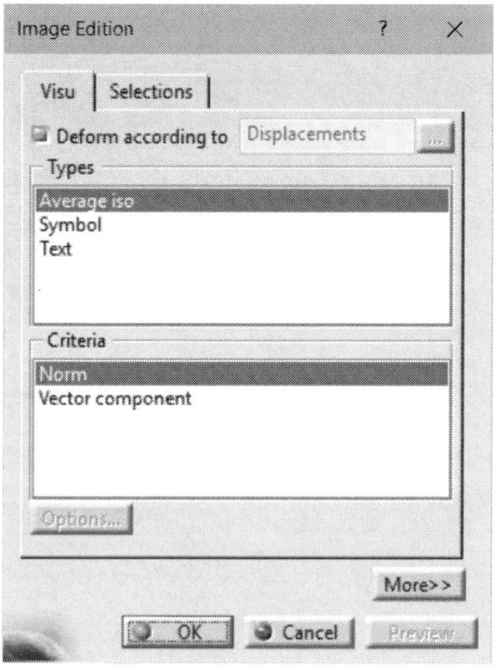

Figure 7–81

*The **C3** component in the Global Cartesian axis system is the **Z**-component.*

4. Click **More** to expand the dialog box. Select **Vector component** in the *Criteria* field and **C3** in the Component drop-down list, as shown in Figure 7–82.

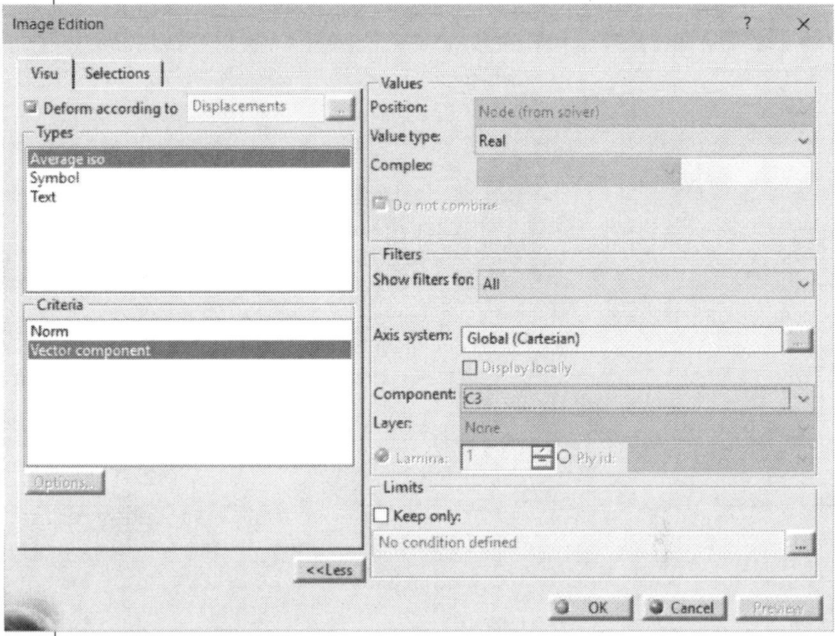

Figure 7–82

5. Click **OK** to close the Image Edition dialog box. The image is displayed as shown in Figure 7–83.

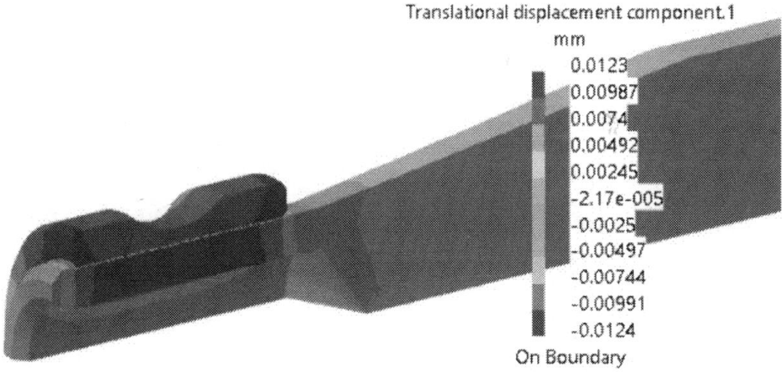

Figure 7–83

6. Select 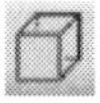 (Front View). Move the mouse pointer over the bottom of the ball race, as shown in Figure 7–84. Note that the **Z**-displacement at the bottom of the ball race is approximately 0.009mm.

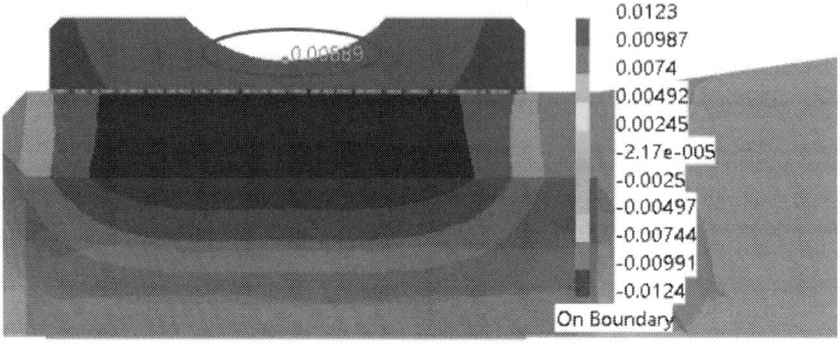

Figure 7–84

The **Z**-direction at this location corresponds to the radial direction on the shaft and the ring. Therefore, the increase in the OD of the ball race in the inner ring after assembling the bearing on the shaft is estimated to be 2x0.009 = 0.018mm, and the reduction of clearance between the inner and the outer rings of the bearing to be 0.009mm.

Task 12 - Display Von Mises stress in the bearing ring.

1. Select  (Von Mises Stress). The stress result for the assembly displays as shown in Figure 7–85.

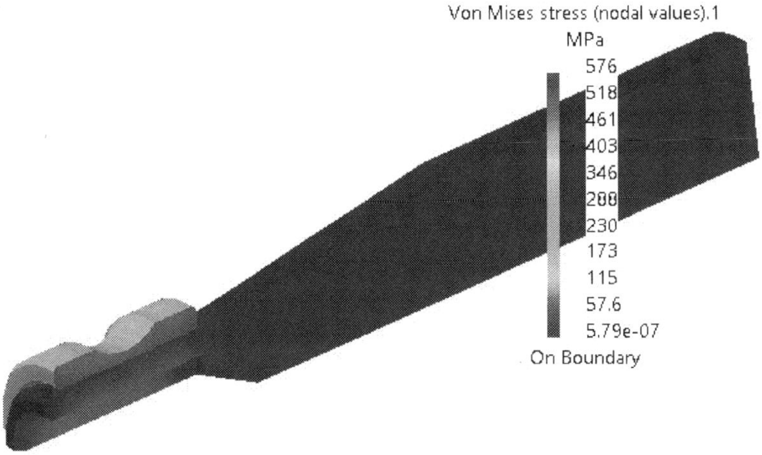

Figure 7–85

2. Double-click on **Von Mises stress (nodal values).1** in the tree. In the Image Edition dialog box that opens, activate the *Selections* tab. In the *Available Groups* section, select **OCTREE Tetrahedron Mesh.2: Bearing_Ring.1** and click the  button to move the part mesh into the *Activated Groups* section, as shown in Figure 7–86.

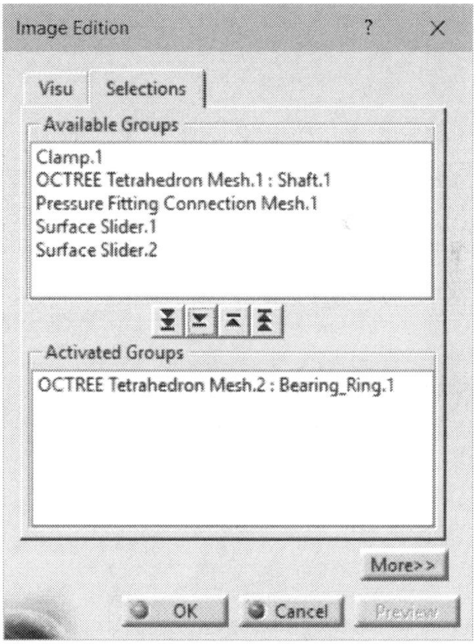

Figure 7–86

3. Click **OK** to close the Image Edition dialog box. Now the stress result is only displayed for the bearing ring, as shown in Figure 7–87.

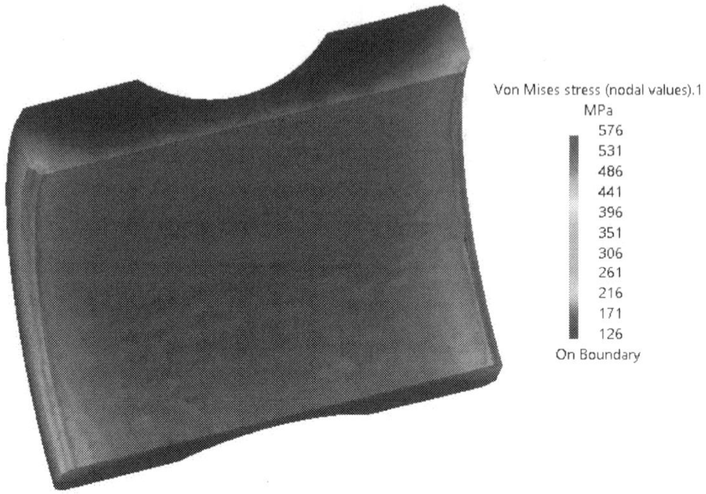

Figure 7–87

4. Rotate the model and examine the stress result. Note that the maximum stress occurs on the outer extremities of the ring.

Task 13 - Return to the model view.

1. Right-click on **Von Mises stress (nodal values).1** in the tree and select **Activate/Deactivate** to delete the stress image from the screen and return to the model view.

Task 14 - Save and close the files.

1. Optionally, save the analysis document and the assembly for future reference.
2. Close both the analysis and the product documents.

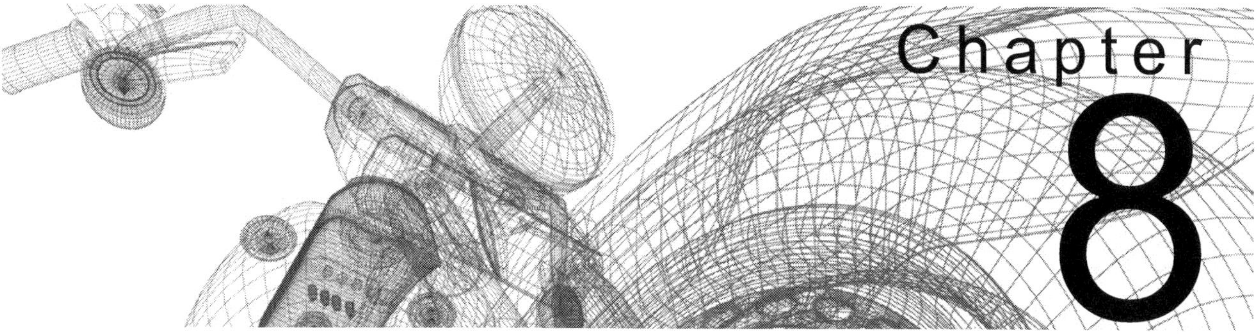

Fasteners

Many structural failures of mechanical assemblies and systems are found in joints rather than continuous material. Mechanical joints typically involve the use of bolts, screws, nuts, and other fasteners. Therefore, proper modeling of fasteners is important for accurate estimates of the strength of assembly joints.

In this chapter, you learn how to model fastened connections between assembly components.

Learning Objectives in This Chapter

- Understand the various fastener modeling methods.
- Use the rigid and smooth connection properties to simulate fasteners.
- Understand the virtual bolt tightening connection property.
- Understand the bolt tightening connection property.
- Obtain fastener loads from the analysis.

8.1 Fastener Modeling Methods in FEA

There is no singular commonly accepted method for fastener modeling in FEA. Instead, several techniques have been developed, based on the analysis accuracy and level of detail requirements.

The current commonly accepted fastener models in FEA fall into the following four categories, from the simplest to the most complex.

- Model Class 1:
  - The clamped parts are modeled as two separate bodies.
  - No bolt is in the model.
  - Bolt preload is ignored.
  - Bolt loads (tensile and shearing) are read out from the model.
  - With these bolt loads, the bolt is evaluated using hand calculations.
- Model Class 2:
  - The clamped parts are modeled as two contacting bodies.
  - The bolt is idealized using a beam or a spring element connected to the bolt head and nut contact areas.
  - Bolt preload is modeled with a pre-tension element.
  - Bolt loads (tensile and shearing) are read out from the model.
  - With these bolt loads, the bolt is evaluated using hand calculations.
- Model Class 3:
  - The clamped parts are modeled as two contacting bodies.
  - The bolt is modeled in a simplified way, as a prismatic body without thread.
  - Bolt preload is included.
  - Contact below the bolt head and the nut is modeled.
  - Nominal stresses in and around the bolt are obtained directly from the analysis.

- Model Class 4:
    - The bolt and nut geometry are modeled with thread and contacts on all contacting surfaces.
    - This model allows for a fully detailed view of what happens in the bolt and the connection.

CATIA enables implementation of these fastener modeling techniques with the following connection properties:

- Rigid connection property
- Smooth connection property
- Virtual bolt tightening connection property
- Virtual spring bolt tightening connection property
- Bolt tightening connection property

8.2 Rigid and Smooth Connection Properties

The use of either a rigid or a smooth connection property implements the Class 1 fastener model.

The schematic diagram of the connection is shown in Figure 8-1. The bolt geometry is not present in the model. Instead, the inside surfaces of the fastener holes are connected either with rigid or with smooth links, as shown in Figure 8–1. Optionally, you may use a contact connection to ensure there is no inter-penetration between the connected parts under the loading.

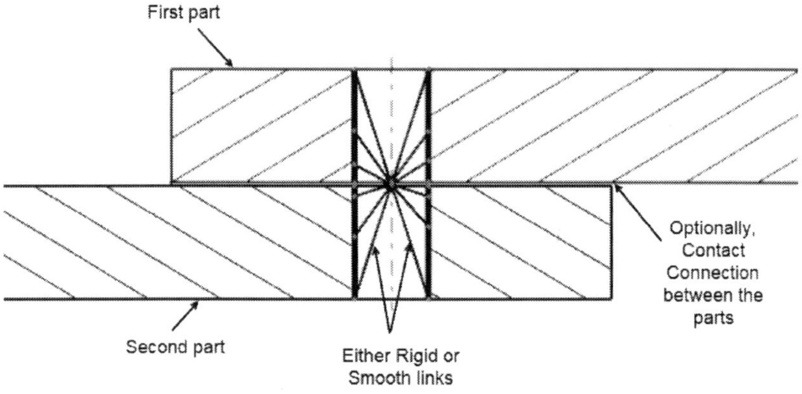

Figure 8–1

To create the connection support, select  (General Analysis Connection) and select the inside surfaces of the two holes, as shown in Figure 8–2.

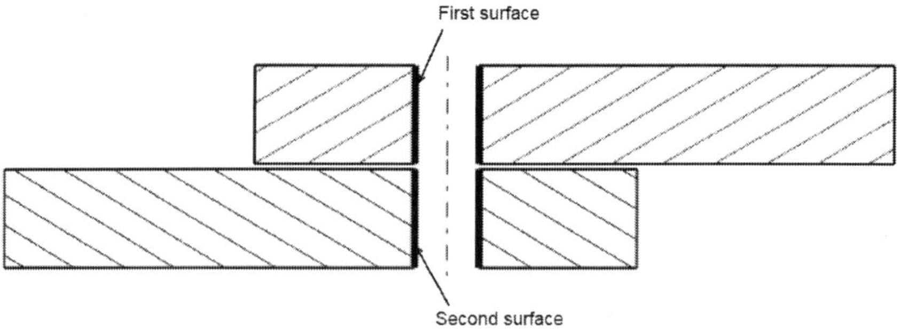

Figure 8–2

To create a rigid connection, select  (Rigid Connection Property) and select the *Supports*, as shown in Figure 8–3.

Figure 8–3

Optionally, select the **Transmitted Degrees of Freedom** checkbox and use the extended options to model fasteners other than bolts or screws. For example, the connection shown in Figure 8–4 models a dowel, since the degrees of freedom along the axis of the fastener are not transmitted.

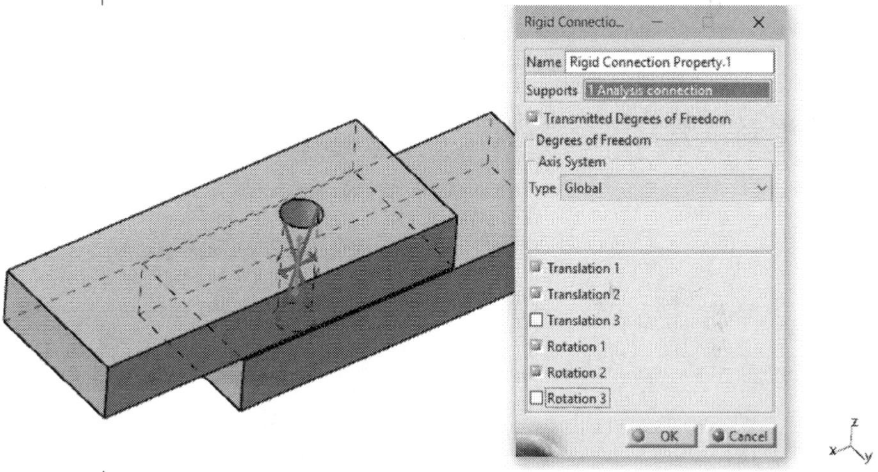

Figure 8–4

8.3 Virtual Bolt Tightening Connection Property

The virtual bolt tightening connection property implements the Class 2 fastener model.

The schematic diagram of the connection is shown in Figure 8–5. The bolt geometry is not present in the model. Behind the scenes, CATIA creates centroid points for the first and second holes. The centroid points are connected to the inside surfaces of the fastener holes with smooth links. The centroid points are connected to each other with a pre-tension element, which enables application of a bolt preload. Because of the bolt preload, a contact connection must be used to ensure there is no inter-penetration between the clamped parts under the loading, as shown in Figure 8–5.

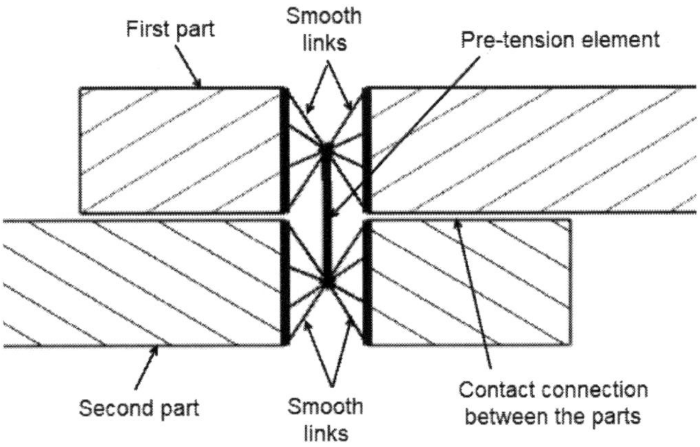

Figure 8–5

To create the connection support, select (General Analysis Connection) and select the inside surfaces of the two holes, as shown in Figure 8–6.

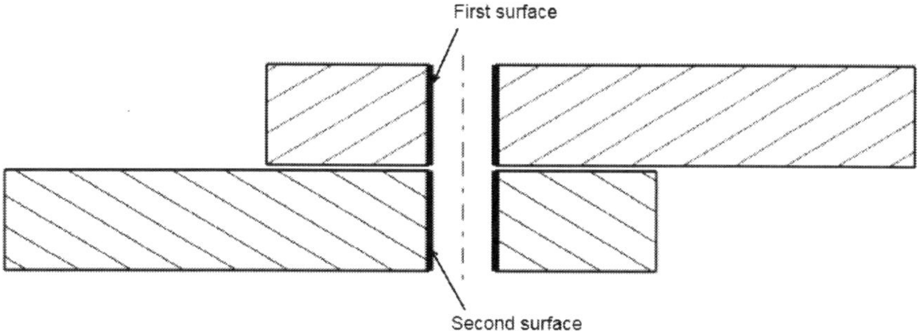

Figure 8–6

To create a virtual bolt tightening connection, select (Virtual Bolt Tightening Connection Property), select the *Supports*, and enter the *Tightening Force* value, as shown in Figure 8–7.

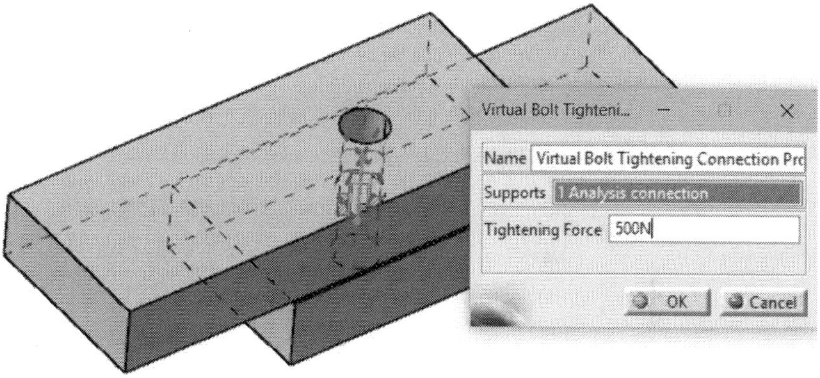

Figure 8–7

8.4 Virtual Spring Bolt Tightening Connection Property

The virtual spring bolt tightening connection property, similarly to the virtual bolt tightening connection property, implements the Class 2 fastener model. The difference is that the virtual spring bolt tightening connection property enables approximate modeling of the fastener's resilience using a spring element.

The schematic diagram of the connection is shown in Figure 8–8. The bolt geometry is not present in the model. Behind the scenes, CATIA creates centroid points for the first and second holes. The centroid points are connected to the inside surfaces of the fastener holes with smooth links. The centroid points are then connected to each other with a pre-tension element chained with a spring element. Because of the bolt preload, a contact connection must be used to ensure there is no inter-penetration between the clamped parts under the loading, as shown in Figure 8–8.

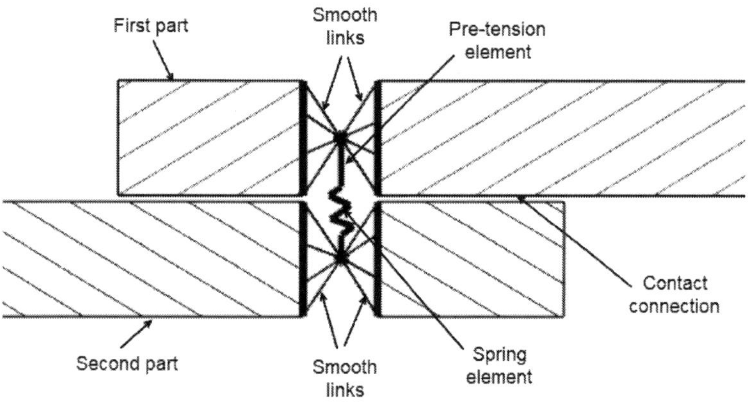

Figure 8–8

To create the connection support, select (General Analysis Connection) and select the inside surfaces of the two holes, as shown in Figure 8–9.

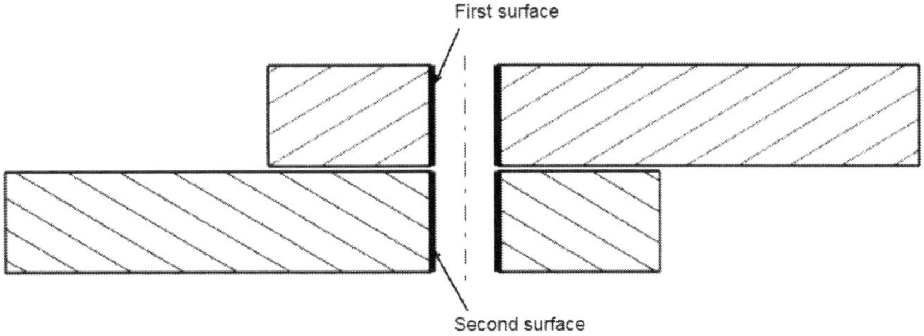

Figure 8–9

To create a virtual spring bolt tightening connection, select (Virtual Spring Bolt Tightening Connection Property), select the *Supports*, and enter the *Tightening force* and the spring stiffness values, as shown in Figure 8–10.

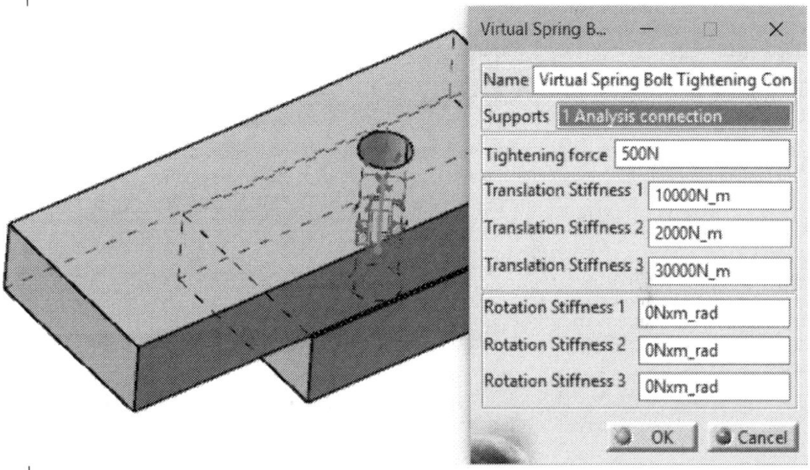

Figure 8–10

8.5 Bolt Tightening Connection Property

The bolt tightening connection property implements the Class 3 fastener model.

The schematic diagram of the connection is shown in Figure 8–11. The simplified (i.e., without thread) bolt geometry must be present in the model. The bolt tightening connection creates a preload force in the bolt axis direction and links the bolt shank and the tapped hole in the normal to the bolt axis direction. Because of the bolt preload, additional connections must be created in order to avoid inter-penetration of the parts, as shown in Figure 8–11:

- Either a contact connection with the **No sliding** option or a fastened connection under the bolt head (assuming the bolt is tightened well enough to eliminate surface sliding under the bolt head).
- A contact connection between the clamped parts.

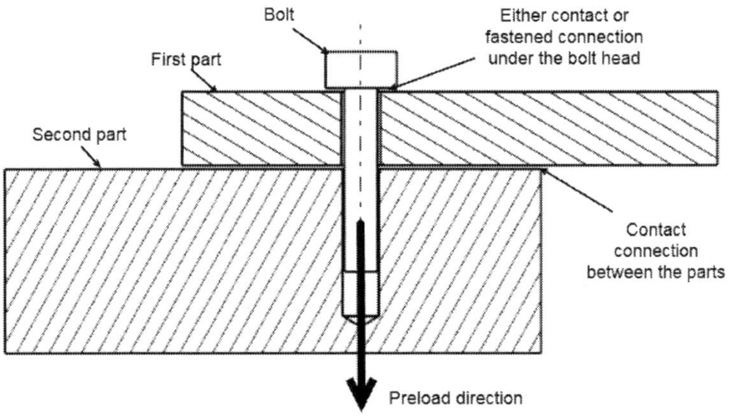

Figure 8–11

To create the connection support, select (General Analysis Connection) and select the outside surface of the bolt shank and the inside surface of the tapped hole, as shown in Figure 8–12.

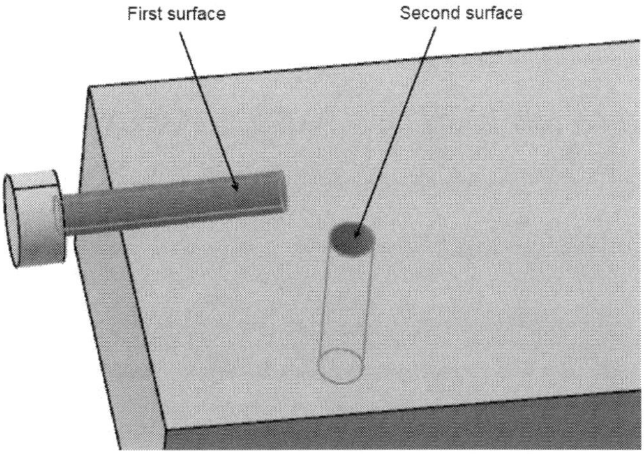

Figure 8–12

To create a bolt tightening connection, select (Bolt Tightening Connection Property), select the *Supports*, and enter the *Tightening force* value, as shown in Figure 8–13.

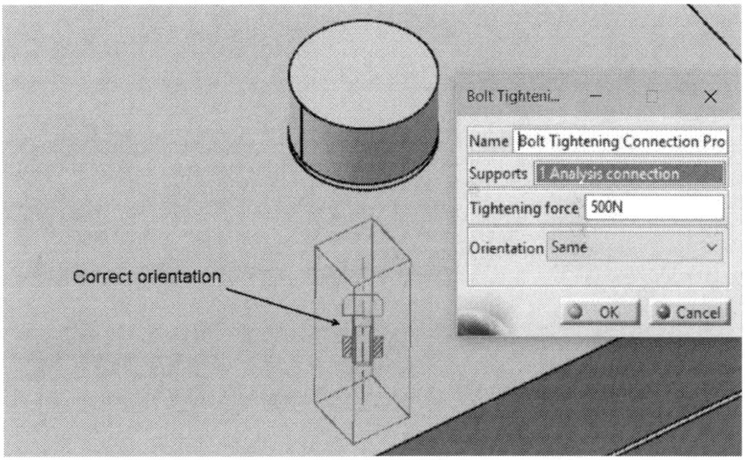

Figure 8–13

If the connection icon displays incorrect orientation (i.e., the icon is flipped compared to the actual bolt orientation in the model, as shown in Figure 8–14), use the Orientation drop-down list to ensure the correct orientation (as shown previously in Figure 8–13).

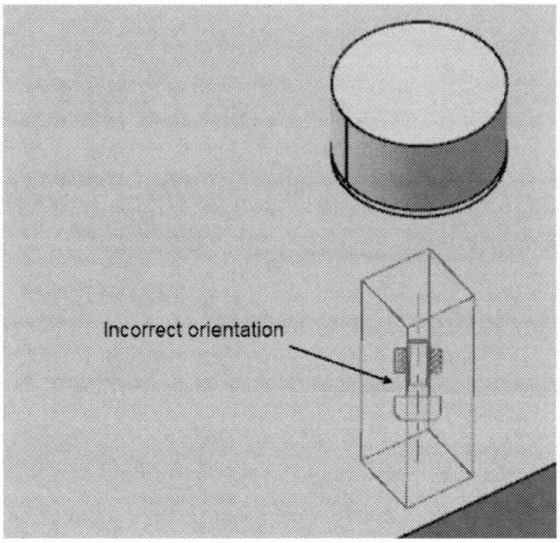

Figure 8–14

8.6 Obtaining Fastener Loads

Once the analysis is solved, you can extract the loads in the fasteners by creating reaction sensors.

To create a reaction sensor, right-click on **Sensors.1** in the tree and select **Create Resultant Sensor>Reaction Sensor**, as shown in Figure 8–15.

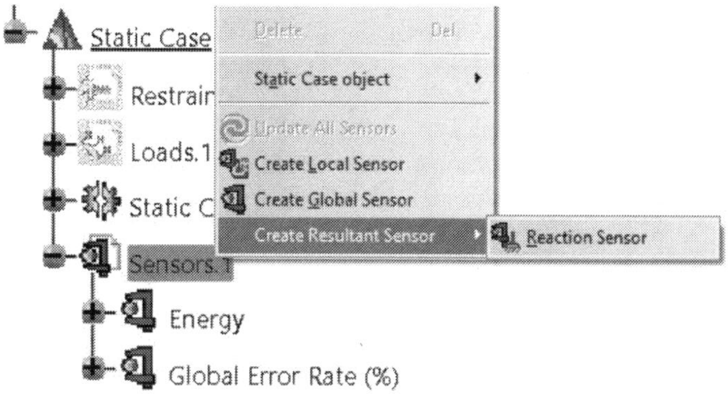

Figure 8–15

Once the Reaction Sensor dialog box opens, select the connection property for which you want to extract the loads, as shown in Figure 8–16.

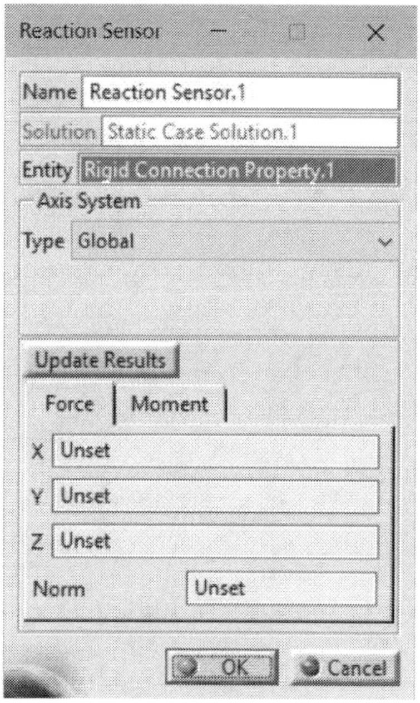

Figure 8–16

Click **Update Results**. The fastener loads are calculated and displayed, as shown in Figure 8–17.

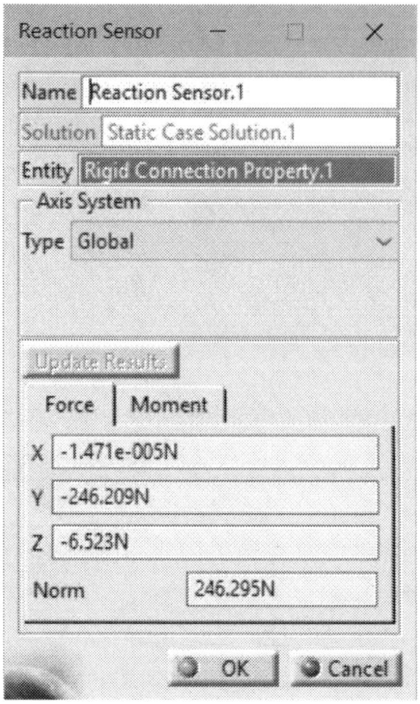

Figure 8–17

Practice 8a

Stress Analysis of a Fastened Assembly

Practice Objectives

- Mesh the model.
- Create contact connections.
- Create rigid connections.
- Create bolt tightening connections.
- Apply loads and restraints.
- Compute the analysis.
- Visualize the results.
- Extract fastener loads.

In this practice, you will set up and run a static stress analysis on the assembly shown in Figure 8–18.

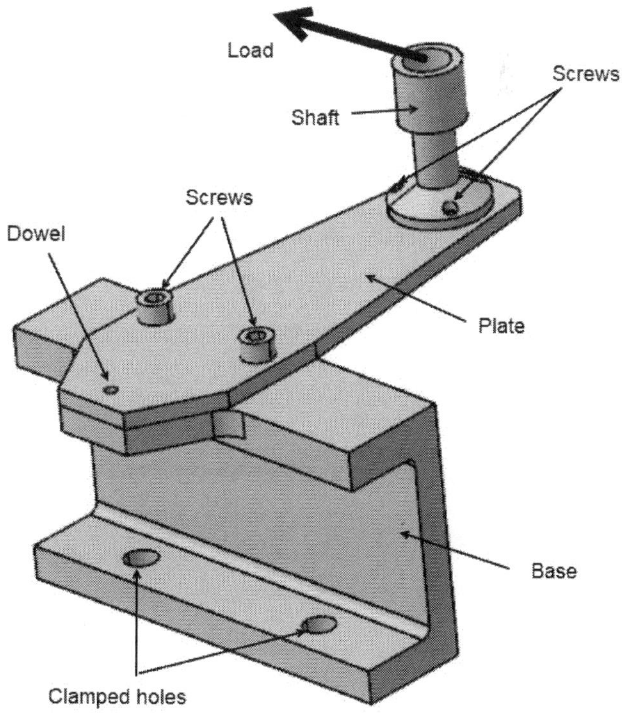

Figure 8–18

The assembly consists of three aluminum parts - the base, the plate, and the shaft. The assembly is clamped at the two bottom holes in the base part and is loaded by a horizontal force on the shaft, as shown previously in Figure 8–18. The plate is fastened to the base with two M6 screws. To alleviate shearing forces on the screws, a dowel is also used through the small hole at the end of the plate. The shaft part is fastened to the plate with three M2.5 screws.

Task 1 - Open the assembly in CATIA.

1. Open **Fasteners_08.CATProduct** from the *CATIA Generative Structural Analysis Practice Files\Ch08* folder.

2. Set the model display as  (Shading with Edges). The assembly displays as shown in Figure 8–19.

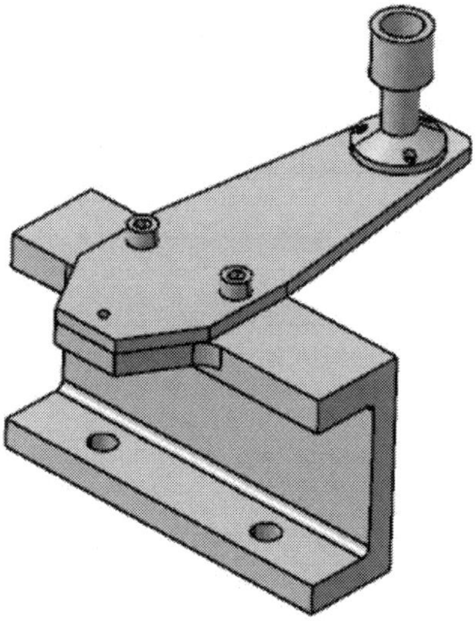

Figure 8–19

3. Select **Tools>Options>Parameters and Measures>Units** and set the units as follows:

   - Length: **Millimeter (mm)**
   - Force: **Newton (N)**
   - Moment: **Newton x Meter (Nxm)**
   - Pressure: **Megapascal (MPa)**

Task 2 - Switch the parts to Design Mode.

1. If you opened the assembly in Visualization mode, switch to Design mode by right-clicking on the root assembly **Fasteners_08** and selecting **Representations>Design Mode** in the contextual menu.

Task 3 - Examine the model.

1. Note that neither the M2.5 screws that attach the shaft to the plate nor the dowel are present in the assembly. You will use virtual bolt tightening connections to model those fasteners.
2. Expand the tree and note that all the parts have a material already applied.
3. Also note that the parts are assembled using parametric constraints. You will use these constraints as analysis connection supports.

Task 4 - Start the GSA workbench.

1. Select **Start>Analysis & Simulation>Generative Structural Analysis**.
2. Select **Static Analysis** as the new analysis case.

Task 5 - Mesh the model.

1. Set the mesh parameters for the assembly parts as follows:

- OCTREE Tetrahedron Mesh.1: Base_08.1
  - Element type: **Parabolic**
  - Size: **5mm**
  - Absolute sag: **1mm**
- OCTREE Tetrahedron Mesh.1: Plate_08.1
  - Element type: **Parabolic**
  - Size: **3mm**
  - Absolute sag: **0.5mm**
- OCTREE Tetrahedron Mesh.1: Shaft_08.1
  - Element type: **Parabolic**
  - Size: **2mm**
  - Absolute sag: **0.2mm**

- OCTREE Tetrahedron Mesh.1: Screw M6.1
  - Element type: **Parabolic**
  - Size: **2mm**
  - Absolute sag: **0.2mm**
- OCTREE Tetrahedron Mesh.1: Screw M6.2
  - Element type: **Parabolic**
  - Size: **2mm**
  - Absolute sag: **0.2mm**

2. Right-click on **Nodes and Elements** in the tree and select **Mesh Visualization**. The part mesh is displayed, as shown in Figure 8–20. Rotate the model and examine the mesh in various areas of the assembly.

Figure 8–20

3. Right-click on **Mesh.1** in the tree and select **Delete** to delete the mesh visualization and return to the model view.

Task 6 - Create contact analysis connections.

1. In the Connection Properties toolbar, select  (Contact Connection Property). Once the Contact Connection Property dialog box opens, expand the tree and select the **Surface contact.1** assembly constraint as the *Supports* and ensure that all other options in the dialog box are toggled off, as shown in Figure 8–21.

*The **Surface contact.1** constraint mates the top surface of the base part with the bottom surface of the plate.*

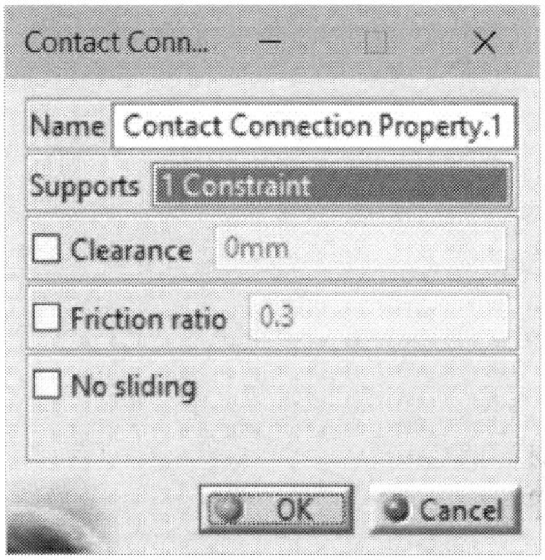

Figure 8–21

2. Click **OK** to finish.

3. Similarly, create another contact connection, now using the **Surface contact.2** constraint as the support.

*The **Surface contact.2** constraint mates the bottom surface of the shaft with the top surface of the plate.*

Task 7 - Create a rigid analysis connection.

In this task, you will model the dowel with a rigid analysis connection.

1. In the Connection Properties toolbar, select  (Rigid Connection Property). Once the Rigid Connection Property dialog box opens, select the **Coincidence.1** assembly constraint as the *Supports*, as shown in Figure 8–22.

*The **Coincidence.1** constraint aligns the axes of the holes in the plate and in the base part for the dowel.*

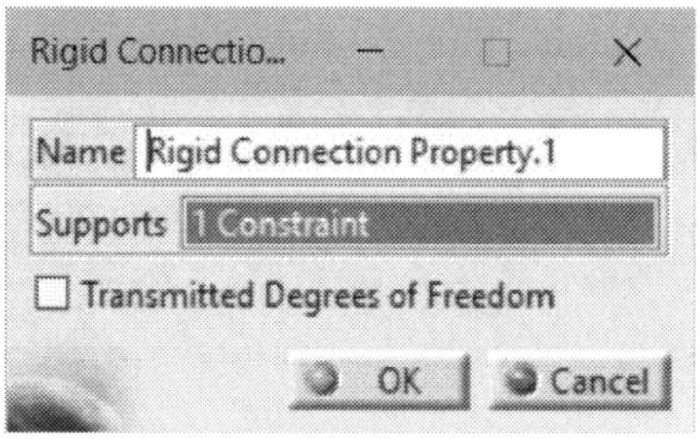

Figure 8–22

2. Activate the **Transmitted Degrees of Freedom** option. In the expanded Rigid Connection Property dialog box, deactivate the **Translation 1** and **Rotation 1** checkboxes, as shown in Figure 8–23.

*Dowel fasteners do not transfer forces along the axis of the dowel; therefore, the axial degrees of freedom in this connection should be deactivated. In this assembly, the axis of the dowel is aligned with the global **X**-direction, which corresponds to **Translation 1** and **Rotation 1** in the connection.*

Figure 8–23

3. Click **OK** to complete the connection.

Task 8 - Create analysis connections for the M6 screws.

The two M6 screws in this assembly are tightened to 500N preload, which you will model with a bolt tightening connection property. The preload ensures that there is sufficient friction between the screw head and the plate, so there is no relative sliding movement between the screw head and the plate. You will model this condition with a fastened connection property.

1. In the Connection Properties toolbar, select  (Bolt Tightening Connection Property). The Bolt Tightening Connection Property dialog box opens, as shown in Figure 8–24.

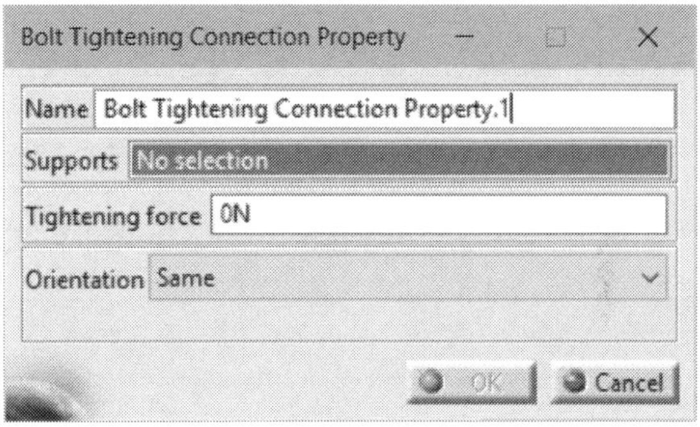

Figure 8–24

2. Select the **Coincidence.3** assembly constraint as the *Supports* and enter **500N** as the *Tightening force*, as shown in Figure 8–25. Leave the *Orientation* as **Same**.

*The **Coincidence.3** constraint aligns the axes of the tapped hole and in the shank of the first screw.*

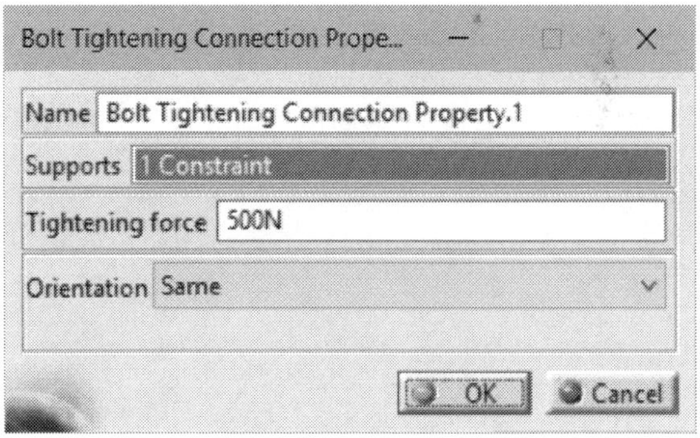

Figure 8–25

3. Click **OK** to finish.

4. In the Connection Properties toolbar, select (Fastened Connection Property). Once the Fastened Connection Property dialog box opens, select **Surface contact.3** assembly constraint as the *Supports*, as shown in Figure 8–26.

*The **Surface contact.3** constraint mates the bottom surface of the first screw head with the top surface of the plate.*

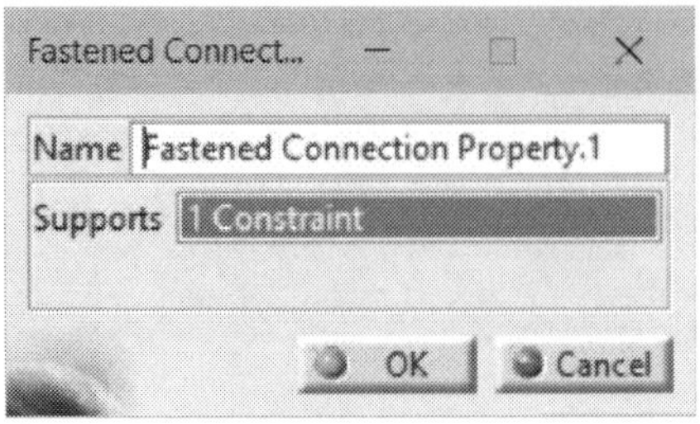

Figure 8–26

5. Click **OK** to finish.

6. Using Steps 1 to 5 as a guideline, create analysis connections for the second screw. Use the **Coincidence.4** constraint as the support for the bolt tightening connection property and **Surface contact.4** for the fastened connection property.

Task 9 - Create analysis connections for the M2.5 screws.

The three M2.5 screws that attach the shaft to the plate are tightened to 50N preload each. However, the screws themselves are not present in the assembly. Therefore, you will connect the shaft and the plate with a virtual bolt tightening connection property that does not require the fastener itself to be present in the model.

Also, there are no suitable assembly constraints in the model that could serve as supports for these connections. You will use a general analysis connection to create the supports.

Hide and unhide parts as you go to facilitate the selections.

1. In the Analysis Supports toolbar, select  (General Analysis Connection). In the General Analysis Connection dialog box, select the bottom surface of the counterbore in the shaft's hole as the *First component* and the inside surface of the hole in the plate as the *Second component*, as shown in Figure 8–27.

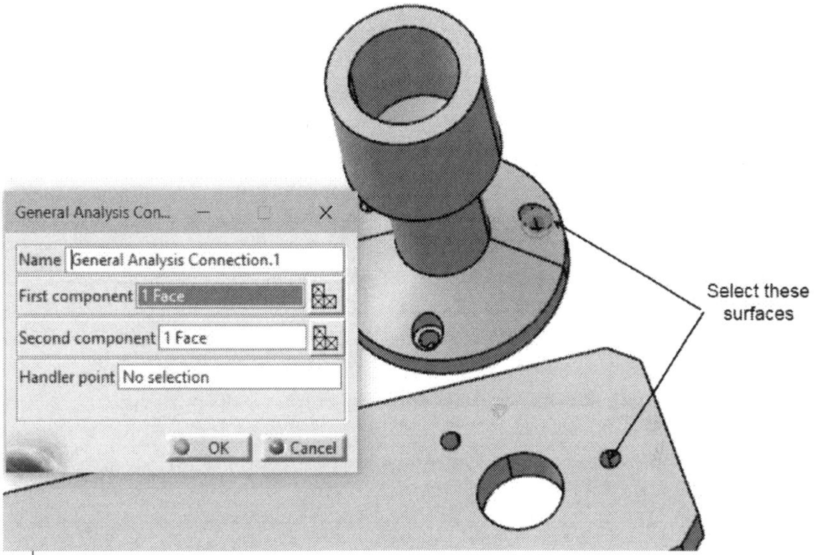

Figure 8–27

2. Click **OK** to finish.

3. In the Connection Properties toolbar, select  (Virtual Bolt Tightening Connection Property). The Virtual Bolt Tightening Connection Property dialog box opens, as shown in Figure 8–28.

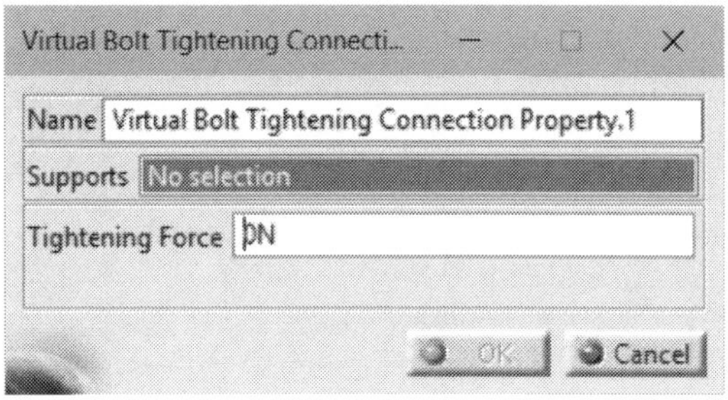

Figure 8–28

4. Select **General Analysis Connection.1** as the *Supports* and enter **50N** as the *Tightening force*, as shown in Figure 8–29.

Figure 8–29

5. Click **OK** to finish.

6. Using Steps 1 to 5 as a guideline, create virtual bolt tightening connections for the remaining two holes in the shaft.

7. The model with the connections displays as shown in Figure 8–30. Hide **Analysis Connection Manager.1** and **Properties.1** in the tree to de-clutter the view.

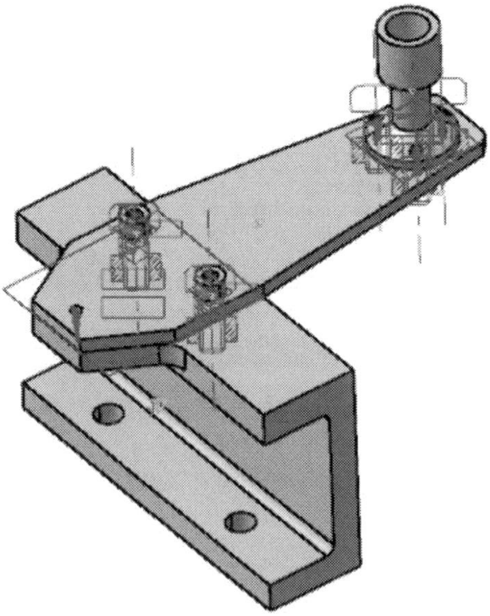

Figure 8–30

Task 10 - Apply the load.

1. Select  (Force Density) and apply **200N** force in the **Y** direction to the inside surface of the shaft, as shown in Figure 8–31.

Figure 8–31

Task 11 - Apply the restraints.

1. Apply the  (Clamp) restraint to the two large holes at the bottom of the base part, as shown in Figure 8–32.

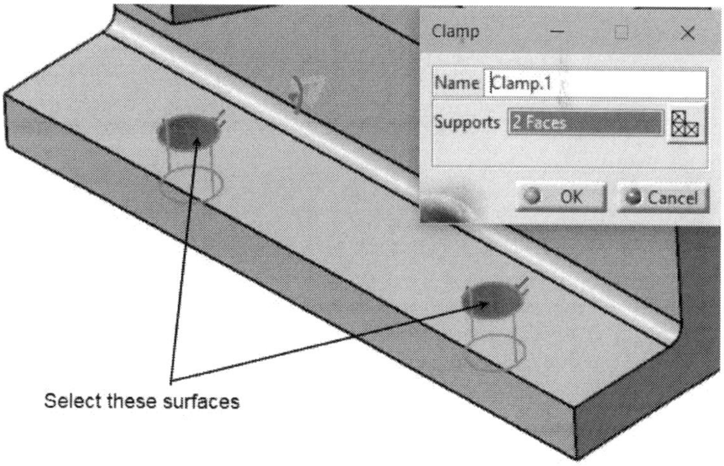

Figure 8–32

Task 12 - Run the analysis.

1. Select  (Compute) and run the analysis.
2. Once the computation completes, expand the tree and check the **Global Error Rate** sensor. For this analysis, the global error rate should be about **7.8%**, as shown in Figure 8–33.

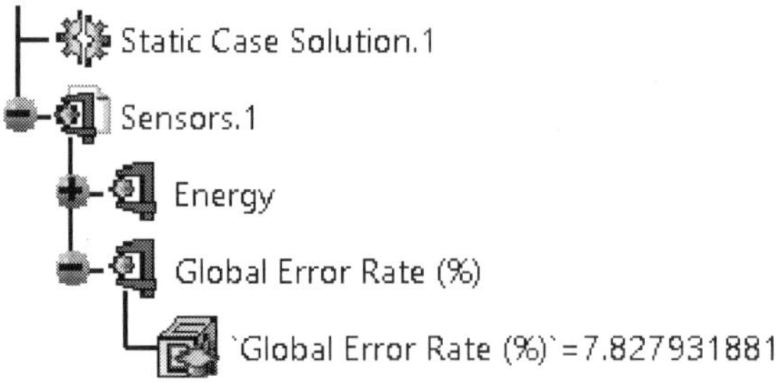

Figure 8–33

Task 13 - Display and animate the deformation.

1. Select  (Deformation) to display the deformed mesh image, as shown in Figure 8–34.

Figure 8–34

2. Animate the image and visually check whether the model deforms according to the applied loads and restraints.

Task 14 - Visualize the displacements.

1. Change the view mode to  (Shading with Material).

2. Select  (Displacement) to visualize the displacements, as shown in Figure 8–35. Note that the tip of the shaft deflects by about **0.683mm**.

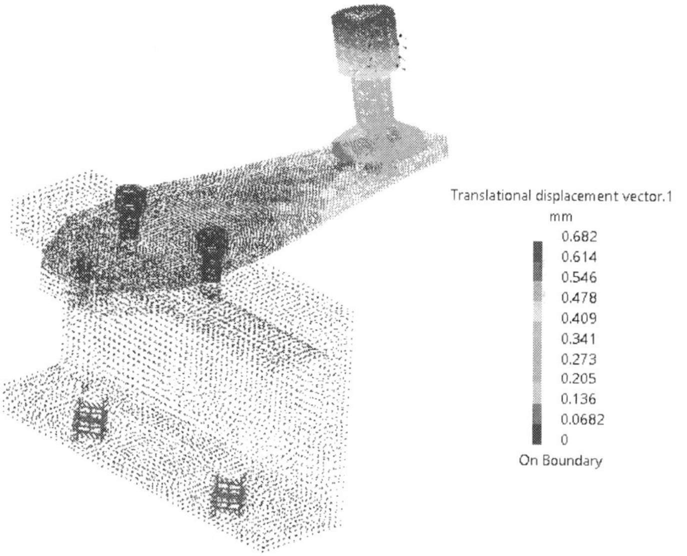

Figure 8–35

Task 15 - Display Von Mises stress.

1. Select (Von Mises Stress). The stress result for the entire assembly displays as shown in Figure 8–36.

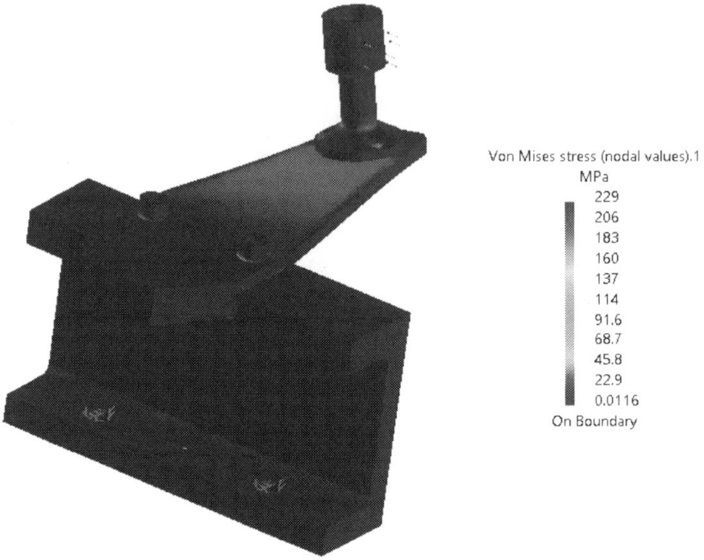

Figure 8–36

2. Double-click on **Von Mises stress (nodal values).1** in the tree. In the Image Edition dialog box that opens, activate the *Selections* tab. In the *Available Groups* section, select **OCTREE Tetrahedron Mesh.1: Base_08.1** and click the button to move the part mesh into the *Activated Groups* section, as shown in Figure 8–37.

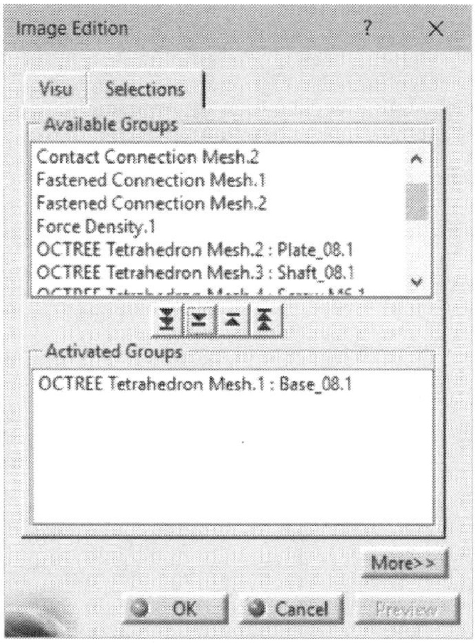

Figure 8–37

3. Click **OK** to close the Image Edition dialog box. Now the stress result is only displayed for the base part, as shown in Figure 8–38.

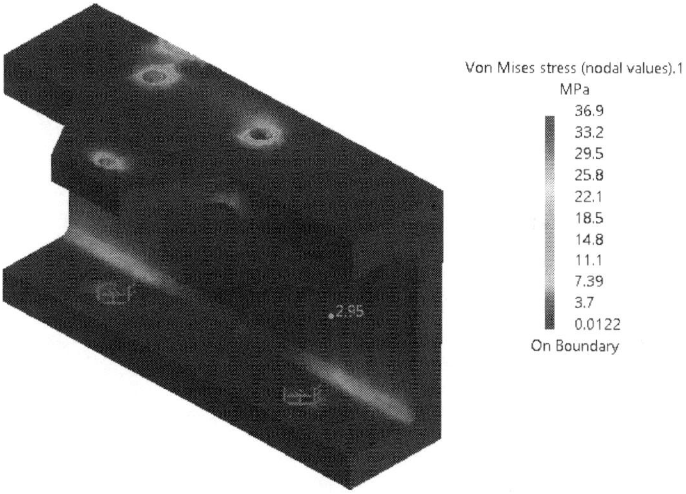

Figure 8–38

Note that the maximum stresses occur near the screw holes and the dowel hole.

4. Select  (Information) and click the **Von Mises stress (nodal values).1** object in the tree. The Information dialog box displays, as shown in Figure 8–39.

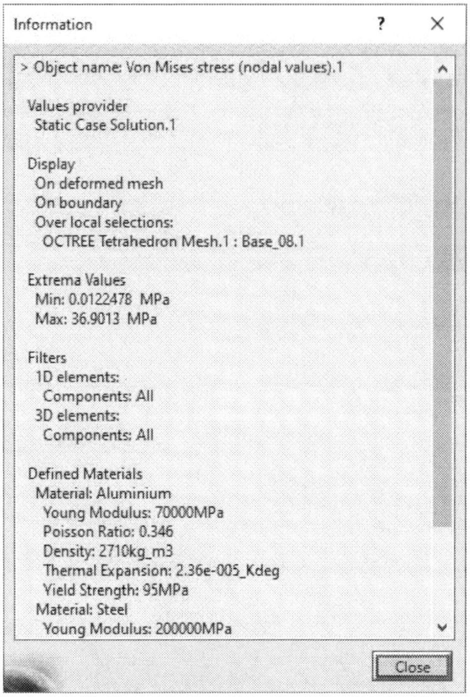

Figure 8–39

Note that the Aluminium material's **Yield Strength** is **95MPa.** The maximum Von Mises stress in the base part is approximately **36.9MPa**, which is well below 95MPa. Therefore, the base is predicted to withstand the load without failure.

5. Close the Information dialog box.

6. Using Steps 2 and 3 as a guideline, display Von Mises stress in the plate, as shown in Figure 8–40.

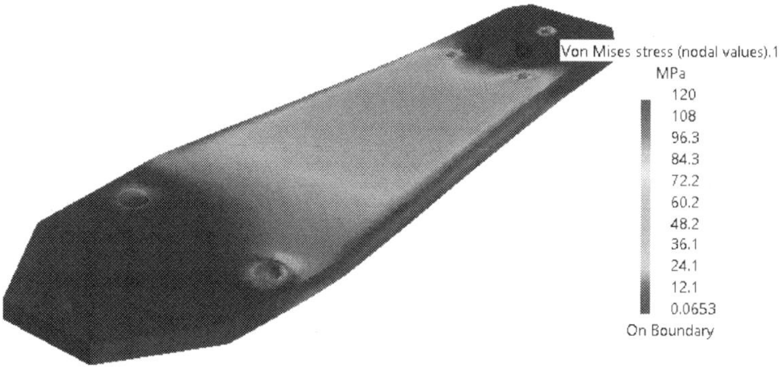

Figure 8–40

Note that the largest stresses in the plate occur near the M2.5 screw holes. Also, the maximum stress value **120MPa** exceeds the material's yield strength of **95MPa**.

7. Using Steps 2 and 3 as a guideline, display Von Mises stress in the shaft, as shown in Figure 8–41.

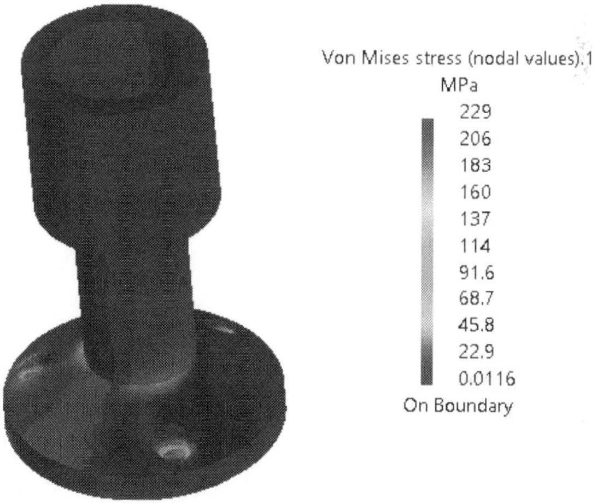

Figure 8–41

8. Using the  (Image Extrema) tool, locate the area of maximum stress in the shaft, as shown in Figure 8–42.

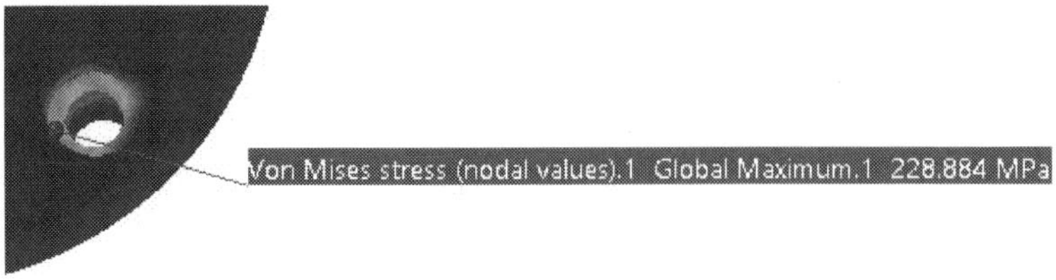

Figure 8–42

The maximum stress near one of the screws is approximately **229MPa**, which is twice as much as the material's yield strength of **95MPa**. Therefore, the shaft part is predicted to fail near the screw holes and the parts must be redesigned to reduce the stress to acceptable levels.

One of the possible design changes to alleviate high stresses in this area would be to increase the number of screws that attach the shaft to the plate.

Task 16 - Return to the model view.

1. Right-click on **Von Mises stress (nodal values).1** in the tree and select **Activate/Deactivate** to delete the stress image from the screen and return to the model view.

Task 17 - Obtain loads in the dowel.

In this task, you will extract the amount of load carried by the dowel fastener you created in Task 7.

1. Right-click on **Sensors.1** in the tree and select **Create Resultant Sensor>Reaction Sensor**, as shown in Figure 8–43.

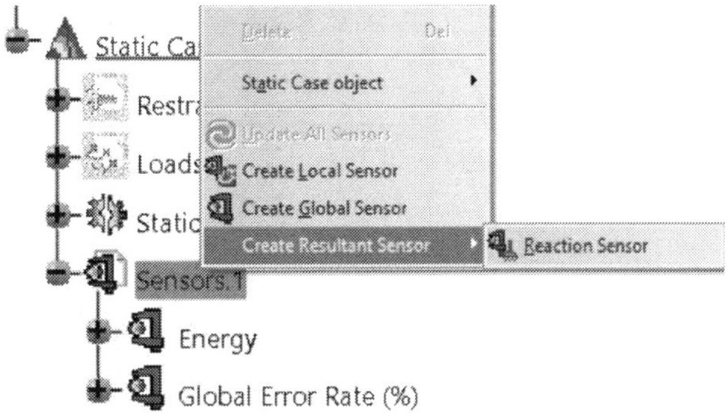

Figure 8–43

2. In the Reaction Sensor dialog box that opens, select the **Rigid Connection Prioperty.1** in the tree, as shown in Figure 8–44.

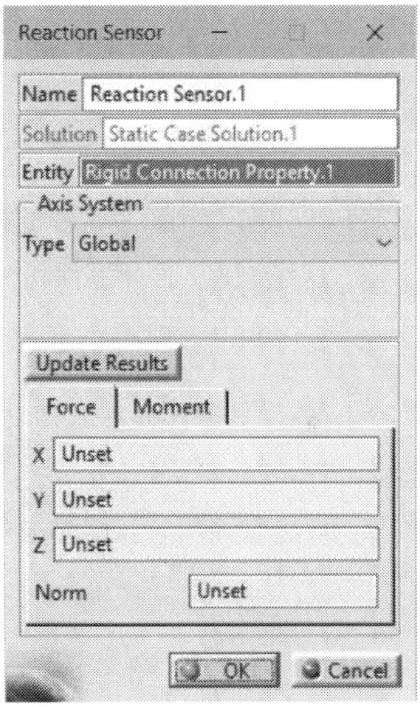

Figure 8–44

3. Click **Update Results**. The loads in the connection are calculated and displayed, as shown in Figure 8–45.

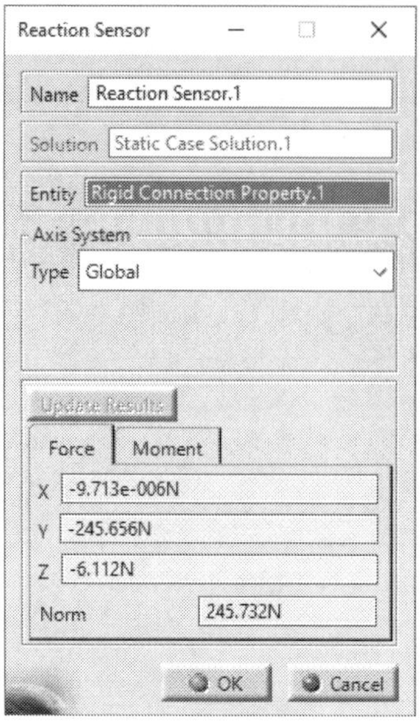

Figure 8–45

Note that the magnitude of the load carried by the dowel is approximately **246N**. Therefore, the dowel's diameter and material must be selected as to withstand this load without failure.

4. Click **OK**. The **Reaction Sensor.1** is saved in the tree, as shown in Figure 8–46.

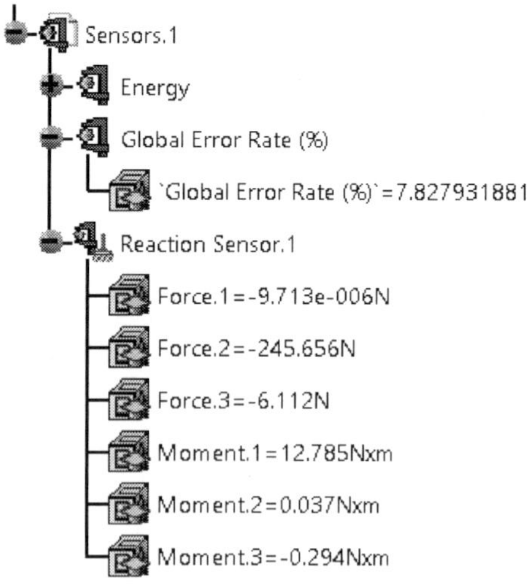

Figure 8–46

Task 18 - Save and close the files.

1. Optionally, save the analysis document and the assembly for future reference.
2. Close both the analysis and the product documents.

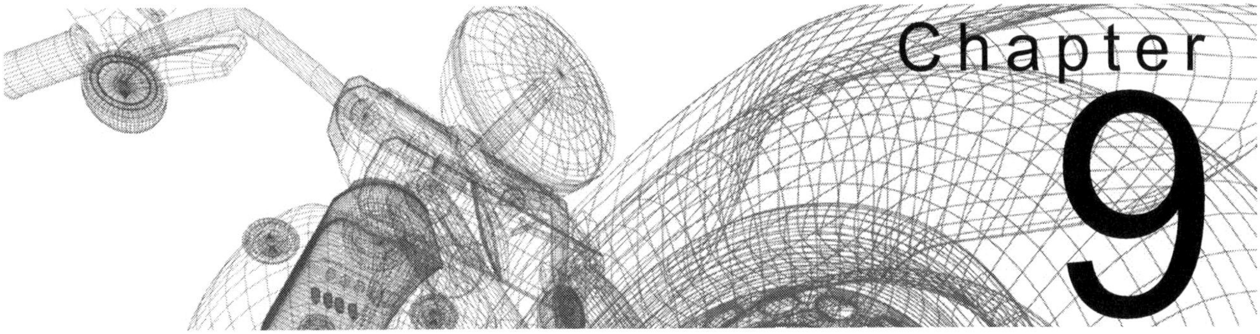

Shell Idealizations

Idealizations in FEA are the tools intended to simplify the general 3D solid analysis model, resulting in faster computation time. In this chapter, you learn how to use shell idealizations for thin-walled parts.

Learning Objectives in This Chapter

- Understand the shell idealization assumptions.
- Create mid-surface geometry.
- Create shell mesh and 2D Property.
- Apply loads and restraints.
- Visualize shell model results.
- Create welding connections.

9.1 Shell Idealization

The most common type of FEA idealization is shell idealization. Shell idealizations are used to simplify a thin-walled solid model. Shell models are less CPU-intensive and can be analyzed faster than solid models.

Shell elements are 3D, surface-like elements that are used to represent features that are thin in comparison to the length and width of the surface in your part. The rule of thumb is to use shell elements when the thickness dimension is less than 1/10 of the length and width of the feature. Shell elements must be placed on the mid-surface of the part, which is a surface that is equidistant from the side surfaces.

An example of a solid model that could be simplified using a shell idealization is shown in Figure 9–1. The part is a sheet-metal part 3mm thick, while the other dimensions in the part are over 100mm. The number of solid elements required to represent this part could be large. Therefore, the part model could be simplified for the analysis using the shell idealization.

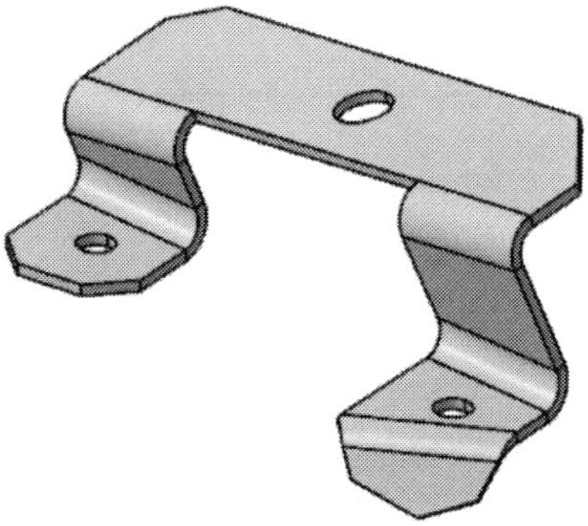

Figure 9–1

The shell idealization implemented in CATIA GSA is based on the Reissner-Mindlin plate theory, which is the extension of the Timoshenko beam theory onto thin plates and shells (i.e., it includes transversal shear effects). In terms of stresses, the Reissner-Mindlin plate theory assumes that normal stress in the out-of-plane direction (**Szz**) is nil, while normal stresses in the in-plane directions (**Sxx** and **Syy**) are varying linearly through the thickness, as shown in Figure 9–2.

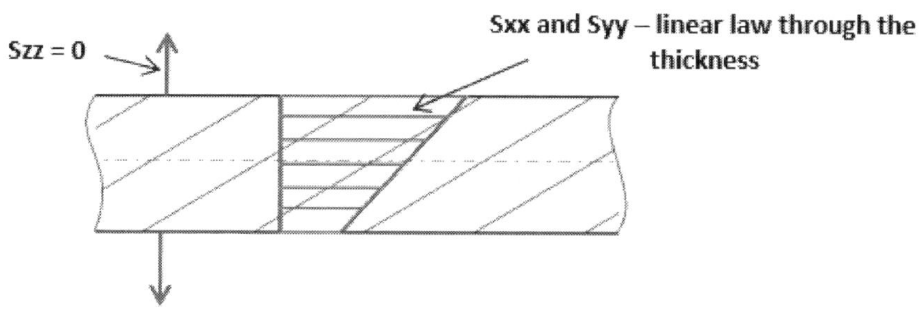

Figure 9–2

The in-plane stresses **Sxx** and **Syy** can be further broken down onto the sum of two components, as shown in Figure 9–3:

- Membrane stress, which is constant through the thickness and arises from loads acting in-plane.
- Bending stress, which is anti-symmetric through the thickness (i.e., changes from tension to compression) and arises from loads acting out-of-plane.

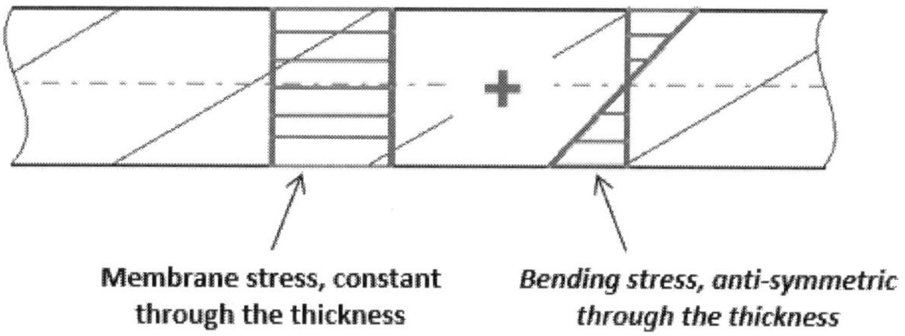

Figure 9–3

Once the shell idealization assumptions are applied, the result is that displacements, strains, and stresses at any point in the thin part can be described through the deformation of its mid-surface. Therefore:

- Only the mid-surface of the part must be meshed, onto 2D surface-like shell elements.
- The part's thickness and material are applied to this 2D mesh.
- All loads and restraints are applied to the mid-surface.
- Displacement results are calculated on the mid-surface.
- Stress results are calculated for the mid, top, and bottom surfaces of the part.

The workflow for working with shell idealizations in CATIA is shown in Figure 9–4. Note that the mid-surface geometry must be created in the Generative Shape Design (GSD) workbench rather than in the GSA workbench.

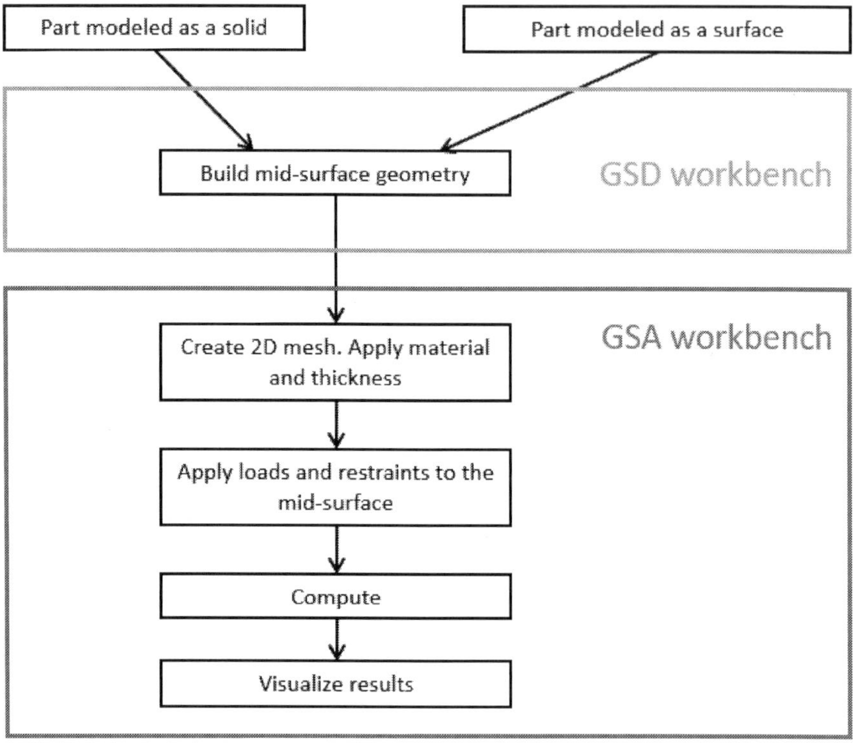

Figure 9–4

9.2 Mid-Surface Geometry

The mid-surface geometry must be created before entering the GSA workbench. This is typically done in the GSD workbench.

If your part is a solid, one of the suggested methods is as follows:

- Using the  (Extract) tool with **Tangent continuity**, extract one side of the part to a separate surface, as shown in Figure 9–5.

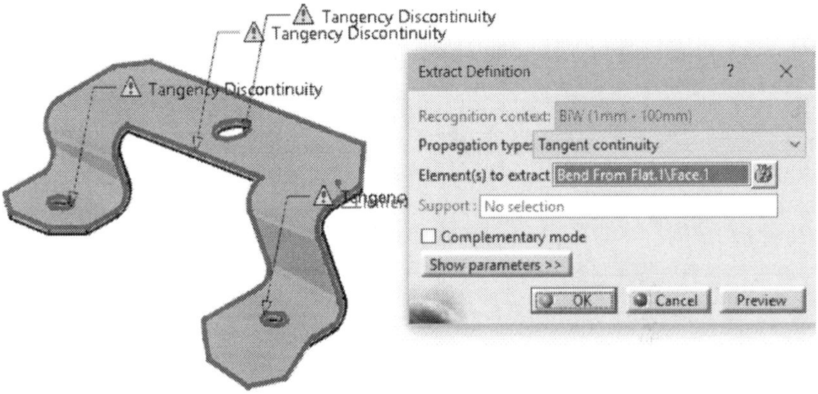

Figure 9–5

- Using the  (Offset) tool, offset the extracted side surface to the middle of the thickness of the part, as shown in Figure 9–6.

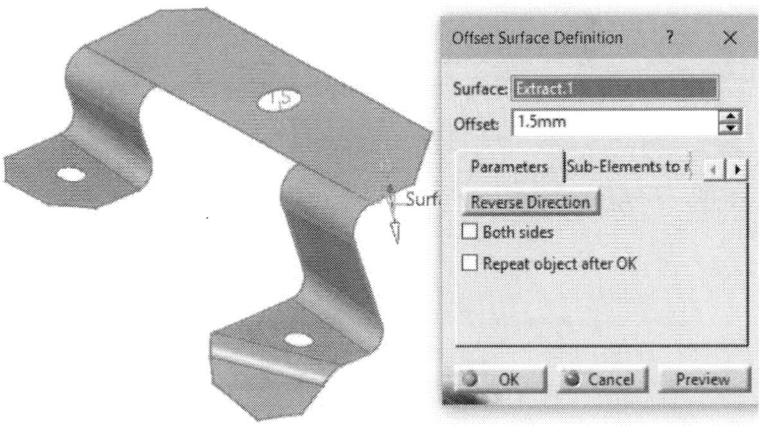

Figure 9–6

An alternative method would be to use the  (Mid Surface) tool, available with a full GSD license, as shown in Figure 9–7.

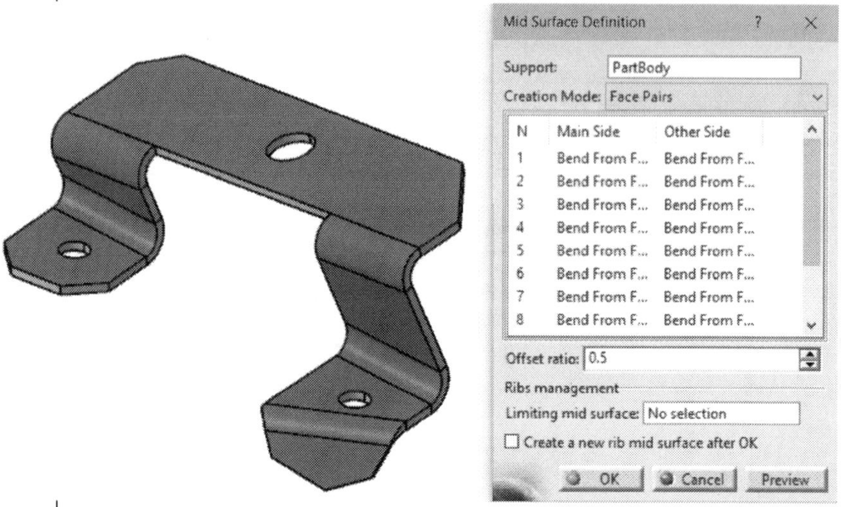

Figure 9–7

In general, you can use any suitable tool in the GSD workbench to create the mid-surface geometry. The goal is to create a surface that is equidistant from the inside and outside surfaces of the part. Note that the result must be joined into one quilt-like surface.

If your part is modeled as a surface rather than a solid, typically the surface represents one side of the part. In that case, the mid-surface model can be created by offsetting the side surface by half the thickness of the part.

However, if the part is very thin, such as a car body panel or an airplane skin, it is permissible to use a side surface for the analysis model instead of the mid-surface. The amount of introduced error would be negligible.

9.3 Shell Mesh and 2D Property

If your part is modeled as a solid (i.e., the PartBody is not empty), CATIA assumes that your intent is to use a solid 3D mesh for the analysis and automatically creates an **OCTREE Tetrahedron Mesh** and a **3D Property** for the part.

Use the following steps to use the shell idealization instead:

- Delete both the **OCTREE Tetrahedron Mesh** and **3D Property** for your part.
- In the Model Manager toolbar, select  (OCTREE Triangle Mesher) and create a 2D mesh for the mid-surface, as shown in Figure 9–8.

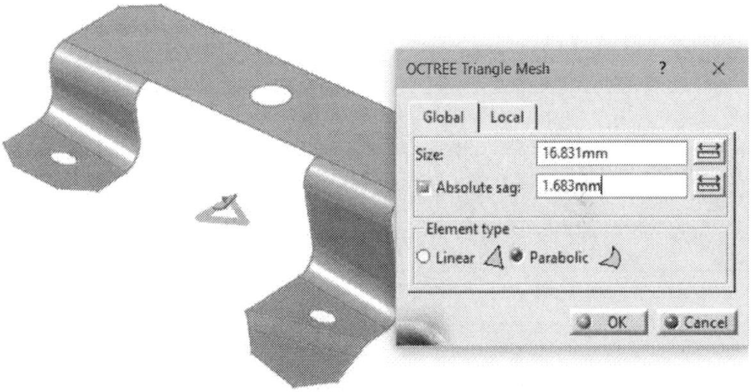

Figure 9–8

- Select  (2D Property) and apply thickness and material to the mid-surface, as shown in Figure 9–9.

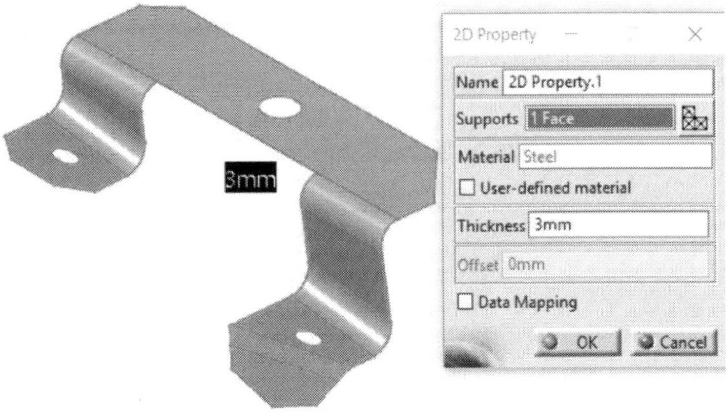

Figure 9–9

If your part is modeled as a surface rather than as a solid, upon entering the GSA workbench CATIA displays a warning message, as shown in Figure 9–10.

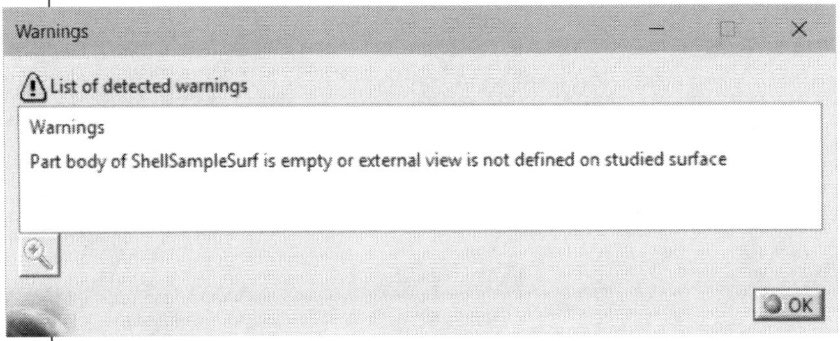

Figure 9–10

In that case, simply close the warning message box, then create the **OCTREE Triangle Mesh** () and **2D Property** () for the part, as described above.

9.4 Loads and Restraints

Loads and restraints in a shell model must be applied to the part's mid-surface elements, such as faces, edges, or vertices.

Note that shell mesh nodes, unlike solid mesh nodes, possess rotational degrees of freedom. Therefore, when applying a user-defined restraint, ensure that the selection of the rotational checkboxes models the desired boundary condition, as shown in Figure 9–11.

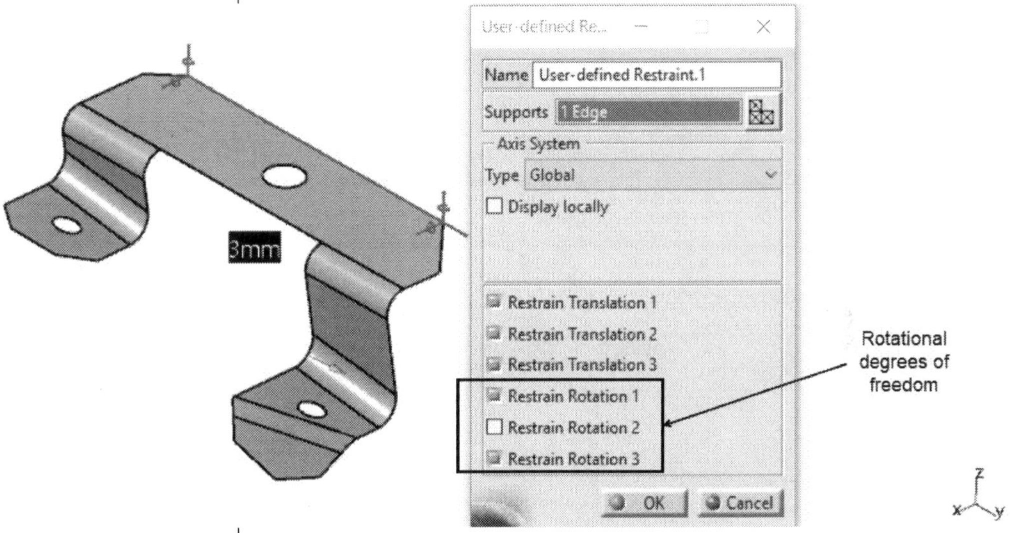

Figure 9–11

9.5 Result Visualization

Model deformations and displacements are displayed on the mid-surface only, as shown in Figure 9–12.

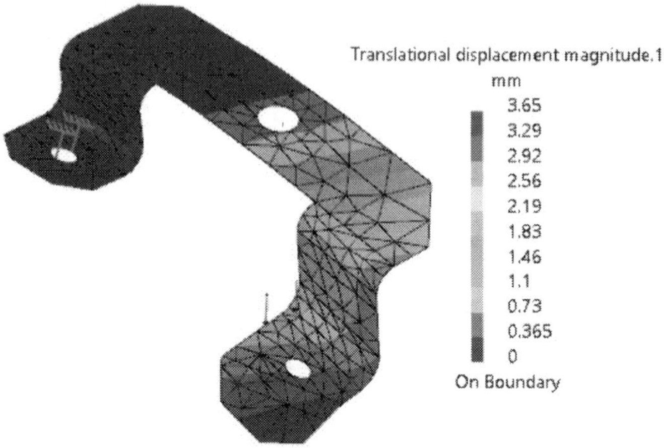

Figure 9–12

Stresses, however, can be displayed on the mid-surface, on either of the side surfaces, or on both of the side surfaces.

To select which surface to display the stress on, double-click on the stress image object in the tree. Click **More** to expand the Image Edition dialog box and select an appropriate option in the Layer drop-down list, as shown in Figure 9–13.

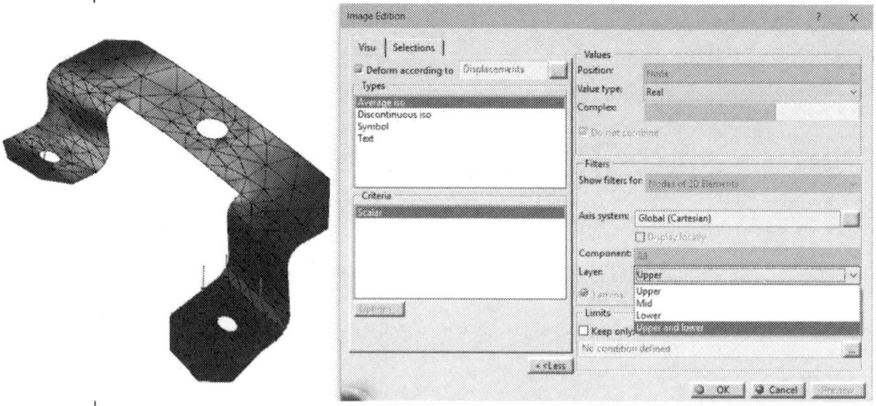

Figure 9–13

The recommended option is **Upper and lower**. This way, the stress image displays as a two-sided film, with appropriate values and colors shown on the upper and lower side of the mesh.

9.6 Welding Connections

Welding connections in GSA are intended for shell models and are designed to only approximately simulate the weld without detailed representation of the weld geometry.

The following connection types are available:

- Spot welding connection
- Seam welding connection
- Surface welding connection

Spot Welding Connection

A spot welding connection in GSA approximately models a spot weld without detailed representation of the weld diameter or area.

Each spot weld location must be specified by a 3D point placed on the mid-surface of one of the connected parts. If multiple spot welds need to be modeled, it is recommended that you place all the 3D points in a separate geometrical set.

Creating a spot welding connection is a three-step process:

- Create the connection support.
- Apply the connection property.
- Optionally, adjust the connection mesh parameters.

To create a spot welding connection support, select  (Point Analysis Connection). Once the Point Analysis Connection dialog box opens, select the mid-surface of the first part as the *First component* and the mid-surface of the second part as the *Second component*, then select the geometrical set that contains the spot weld location points, as shown in Figure 9–14.

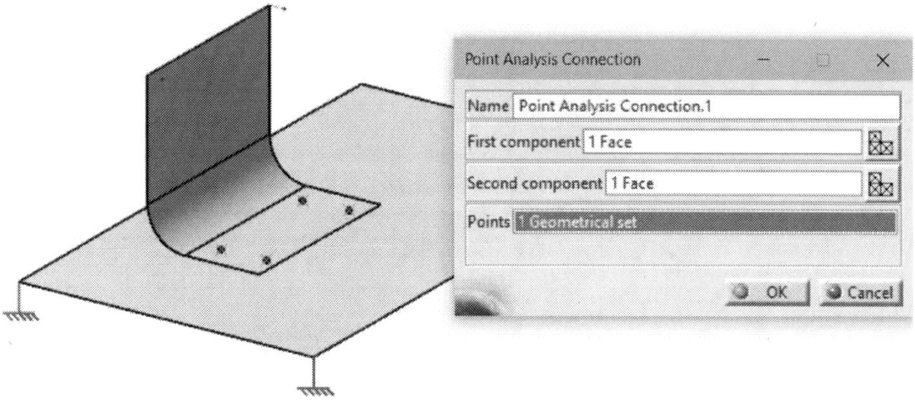

Figure 9–14

The created **Point Analysis Connection** displays in the tree, as shown in Figure 9–15.

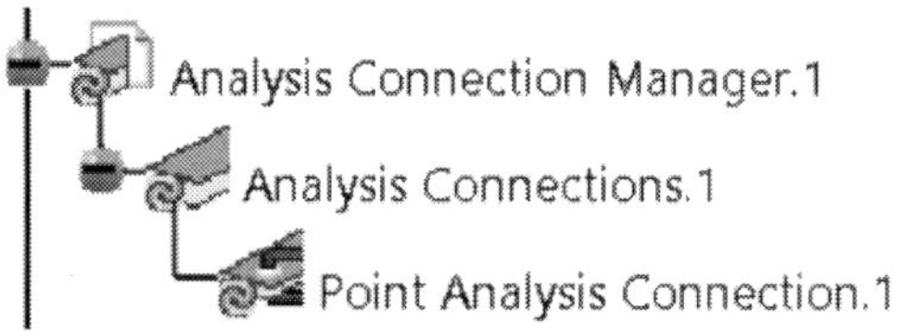

Figure 9–15

To apply the connection property, select  (Spot Welding Connection Property), select the connection support, and select the connection modeling method in the Type drop-down list, as shown in Figure 9–16. The connection modeling types are described in the following table.

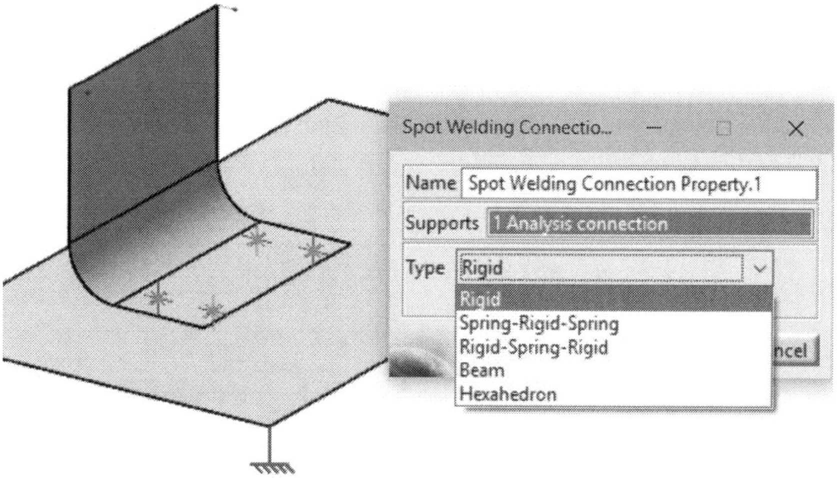

Figure 9–16

Connection Type		Description
	Rigid	Spot weld is modeled with a rigid bar.
	Spring-Rigid-Spring	Spot weld is modeled as a chain consisting of a spring element, a rigid bar, and another spring element.
	Rigid-Spring-Rigid	Spot weld is modeled as a chain consisting of a rigid bar, a spring element, and another rigid bar.
	Beam	Spot weld is modeled with a beam element.
	Hexahedron	Spot weld is modeled with a hexahedron element.

To edit the spot weld mesh parameters, double-click on **Spot Welding Connection Mesh.1** in the tree to open the Spot Welding Connection Mesh dialog box. For example, if **Hexahedron** was used as the connection modeling type, you could modify the diameter of the hexahedron element modeling the weld, as shown in Figure 9–17.

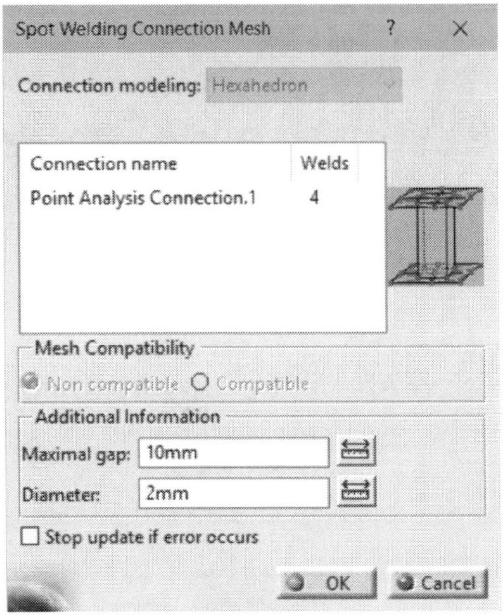

Figure 9–17

Seam Welding Connection

A seam welding connection in GSA approximately models a seam or a fillet weld without detailed representation of the weld shape and size.

The seam weld trajectory must be specified by a curve or an edge placed on the mid-surface of one of the connected parts.

Creating a seam welding connection is a three-step process:

- Create a connection support.
- Apply a connection property.
- Optionally, adjust the connection mesh parameters.

To create a seam welding connection support, select  (Line Analysis Connection). Once the Line Analysis Connection dialog box opens, select the mid-surface of the first part as the *First component* and the mid-surface of the second part as the *Second component*, then select the guide curve or edge that specifies the weld trajectory, as shown in Figure 9–18.

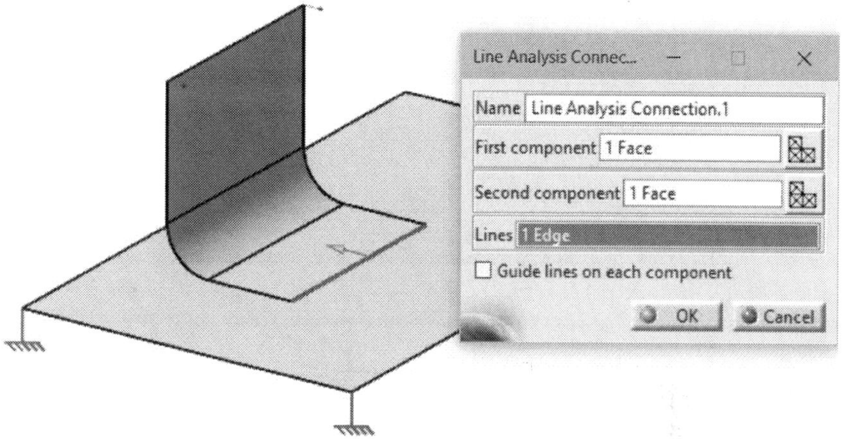

Figure 9–18

The created **Line Analysis Connection** displays in the tree, as shown in Figure 9–19.

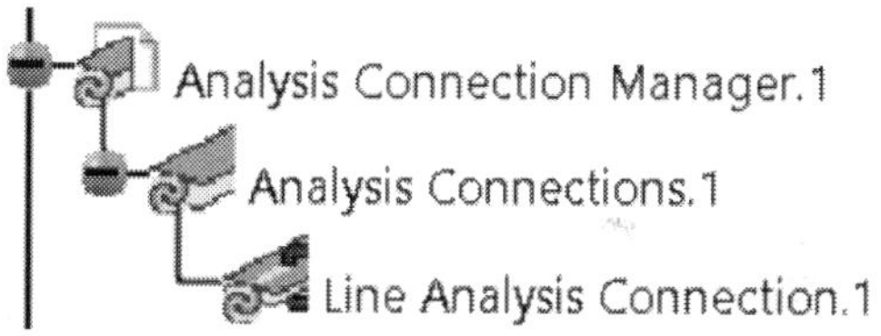

Figure 9–19

To apply the connection property, select  (Seam Welding Connection Property), select the connection support, and select the connection modeling method in the Type drop-down list, as shown in Figure 9–20. The connection modeling types are described in the following table.

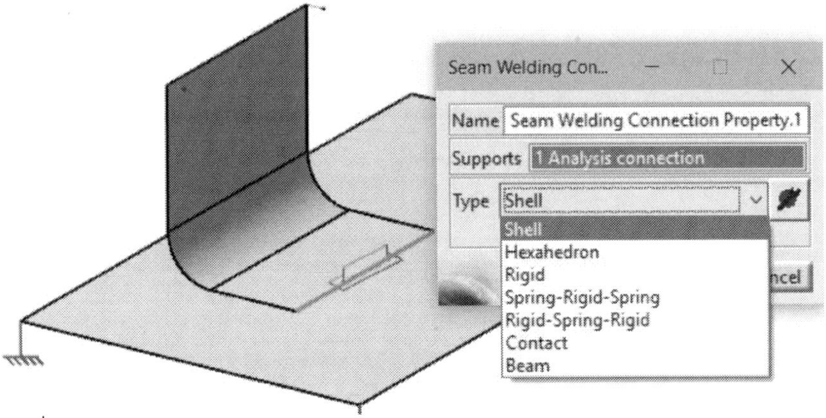

Figure 9–20

Connection Type		**Description**
	Shell	Seam weld is modeled with a continuous row of shell elements.
	Hexahedron	Seam weld is modeled with a continuous row of hexahedron elements.
	Rigid	Seam weld is modeled as a discrete row of rigid bars.
	Spring-Rigid-Spring	Seam weld is modeled as a row of discrete links, each link consisting of a spring element, a rigid bar, and another spring element.
	Rigid-Spring-Rigid	Seam weld is modeled as a row of discrete links, each link consisting of a rigid bar, a spring element, and another rigid bar.
	Contact	Seam weld is modeled as a discrete row of contact bars. Only applicable to connections between solid meshes.
	Beam	Spot weld is modeled as a discrete row of beams.

To edit the seam weld mesh parameters, double-click on **Seam Welding Connection Mesh.1** in the tree to open the Seam Welding Connection Mesh dialog box. For example, if **Hexahedron** was used as the connection modeling type, you could modify the mesh step and the width of the hexahedron elements modeling the weld material, as shown in Figure 9–21.

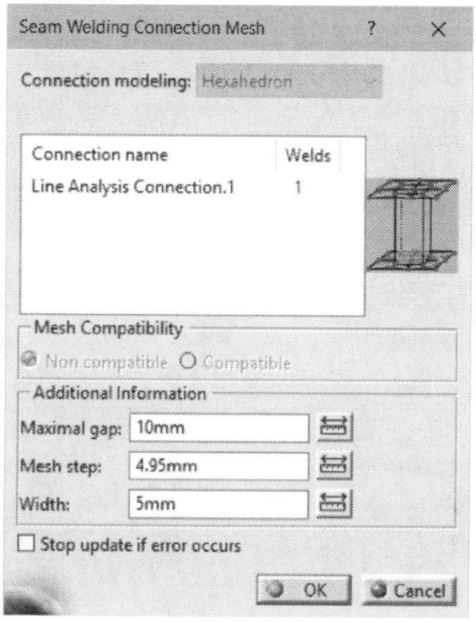

Figure 9–21

Surface Welding Connection

A surface welding connection in GSA approximately models a surface weld using a layer of hexahedron elements placed between the mid-surfaces of the connected parts.

The surface weld area must be specified by a surface placed on top of the mid-surface of one of the connected parts.

Creating a surface welding connection is a three-step process:

- Create a connection support.
- Apply a connection property.
- Optionally, adjust the connection mesh parameters.

To create a surface welding connection support, select  (Surface Analysis Connection). Once the Surface Analysis Connection dialog box opens, select the mid-surface of the first part as the *First component* and the mid-surface of the second part as the *Second component*, then select the surface that specifies the weld area, as shown in Figure 9–22.

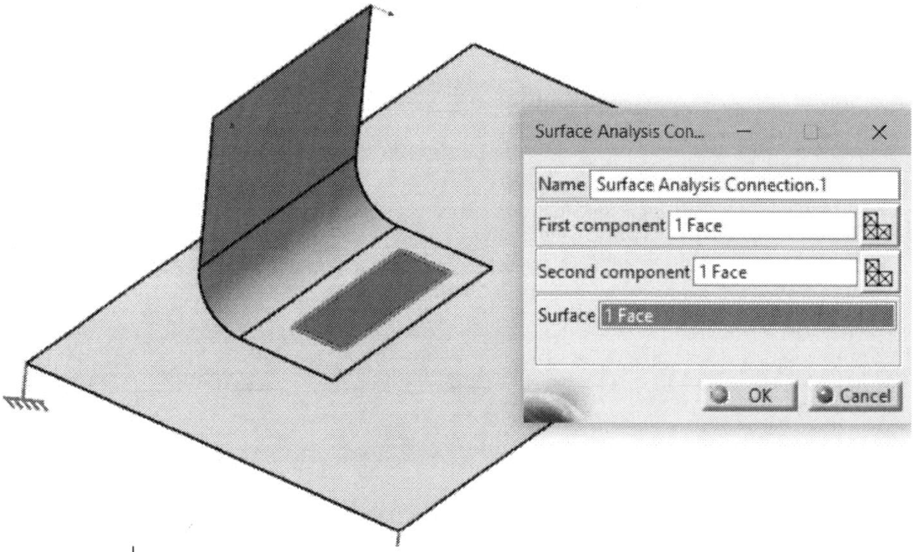

Figure 9–22

The created **Surface Analysis Connection** displays in the tree, as shown in Figure 9–23.

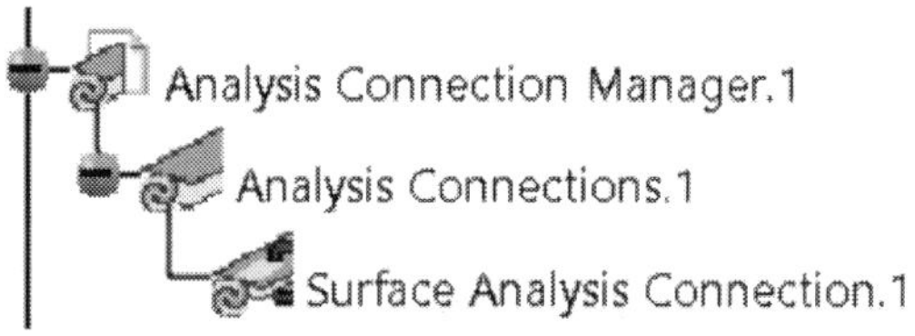

Figure 9–23

To apply the connection property, select  (Surface Welding Connection Property) and select the connection support, as shown in Figure 9–24.

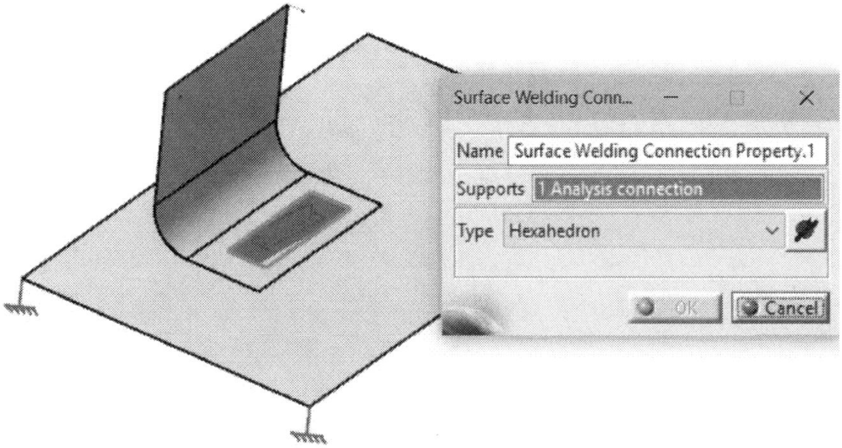

Figure 9–24

To edit the surface weld mesh parameters, double-click on **Surface Welding Connection Mesh.1** in the tree to open the Surface Welding Connection Mesh dialog box. You can modify the mesh step of the hexahedron elements modeling the weld, as shown in Figure 9–25.

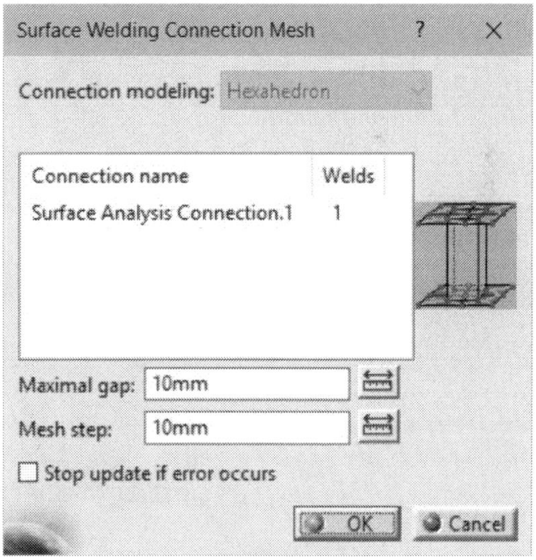

Figure 9–25

Practice 9a Sheet Metal Clip

Practice Objectives

- Create the mid-surface model.
- Create the shell mesh.
- Apply 2D Property.
- Set up loads and restraints.
- Run the analysis.
- Display the results.

In this practice, you will set up and run a static stress analysis on the small sheet metal clip shown in Figure 9–26. The clip has been designed in CATIA's Generative Sheetmetal Design workbench and is 0.12mm thick. You will use shell elements and shell mesh for the analysis instead of a solid mesh.

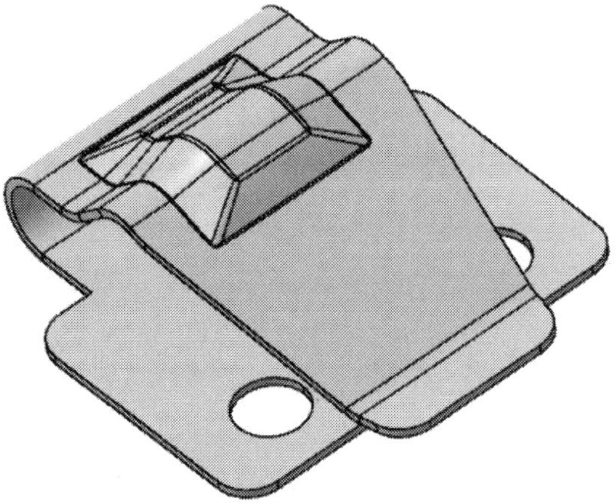

Figure 9–26

Task 1 - Open the part in CATIA.

1. Open **SheetMetal_09.CATPart** from the *CATIA Generative Structural Analysis Practice Files\Ch09* folder.

2. Set the model display as  (Shading with Edges). The part displays as shown in Figure 9–27.

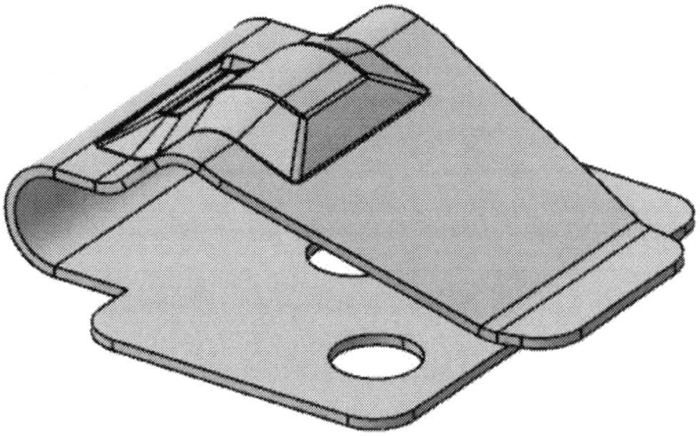

Figure 9–27

3. Select **Tools>Options>Parameters and Measures>Units** and set the units as follows:

   - Length: **Millimeter (mm)**
   - Force: **Newton (N)**
   - Moment: **Newton x Meter (Nxm)**
   - Pressure: **Megapascal (MPa)**

Task 2 - Create the mid-surface.

1. Activate the **Generative Shape Design**  workbench.
2. Create a new geometrical set named **MidSurf**.
3. Using the  (Extract) tool with **Tangent continuity**, extract the outside surface of the part, as shown in Figure 9–28.

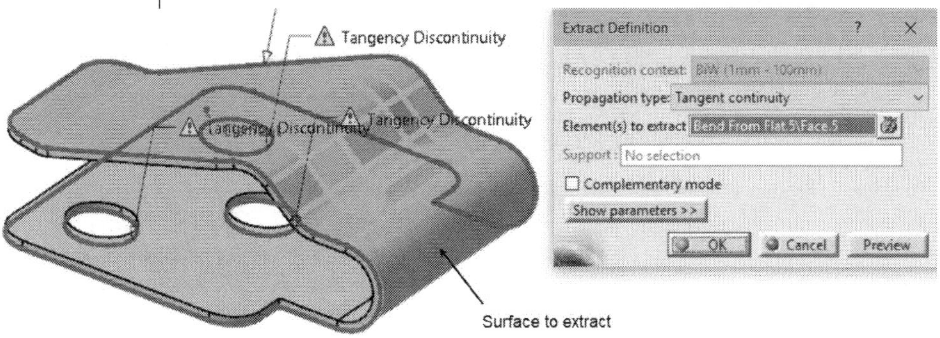

Figure 9–28

4. In the Surfaces toolbar, select  (Offset). In the Offset Surface Definition dialog box, select the extracted surface as the surface to offset, and, using the **Reverse Direction** button, ensure that the red arrow (which indicates the direction of the offset) points into the thickness of the part, as shown in Figure 9–29.

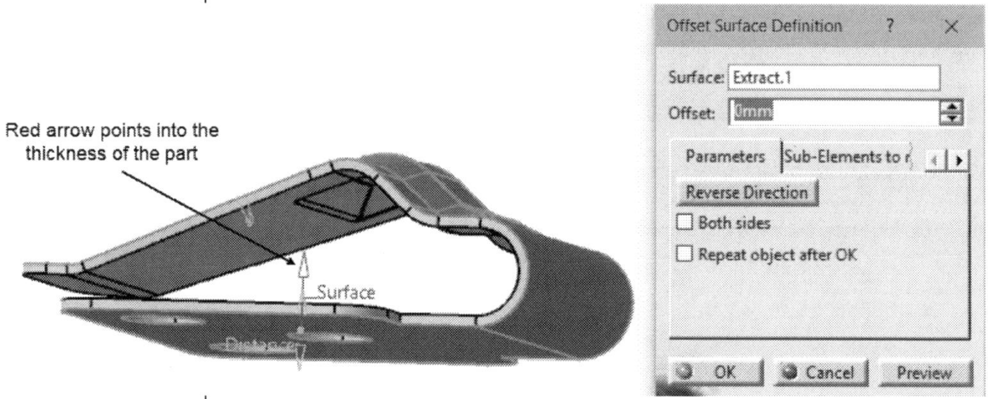

Figure 9–29

5. Right-click in the *Offset* field and select **Edit formula** in the contextual menu, as shown in Figure 9–30.

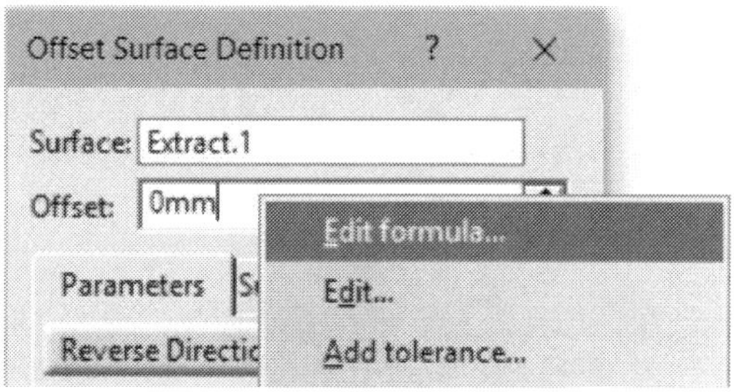

Figure 9–30

6. In the Formula Editor dialog box, create the formula shown in Figure 9–31. This ensures that the amount of the offset is exactly half of the thickness of the part.

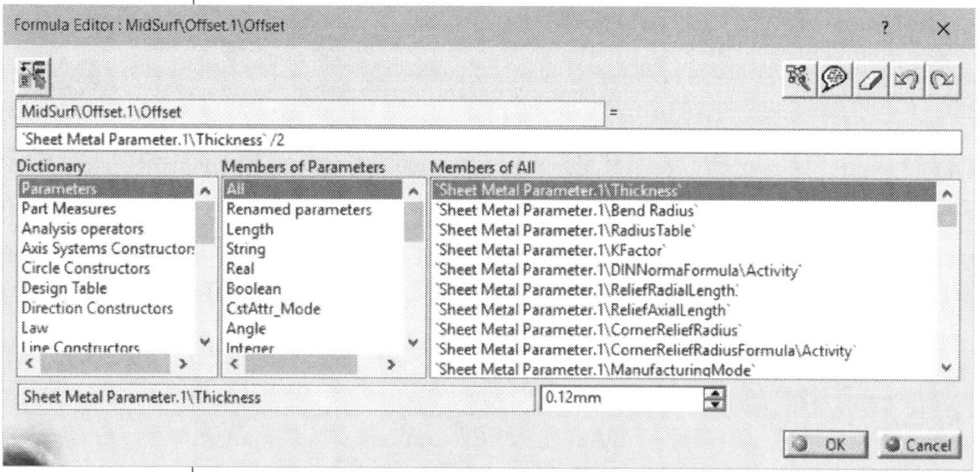

Figure 9–31

7. Click **OK** twice to close the Formula Editor and the Offset Surface Definition dialog boxes.

8. Hide **Extract.1**. Change the color for the **Offset.1** to **green** and set the transparency for the **PartBody** to **50%**. The model displays as shown in Figure 9–32. Note that the **Offset.1** surface goes exactly through the middle of the thickness of the part.

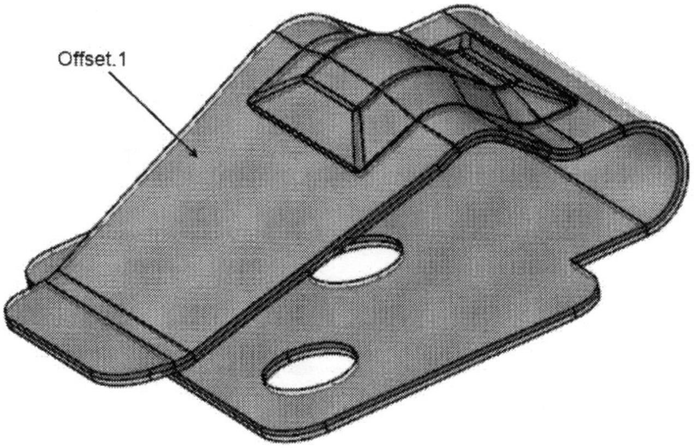

Figure 9–32

9. Hide the **PartBody**. The model displays as shown in Figure 9–33.

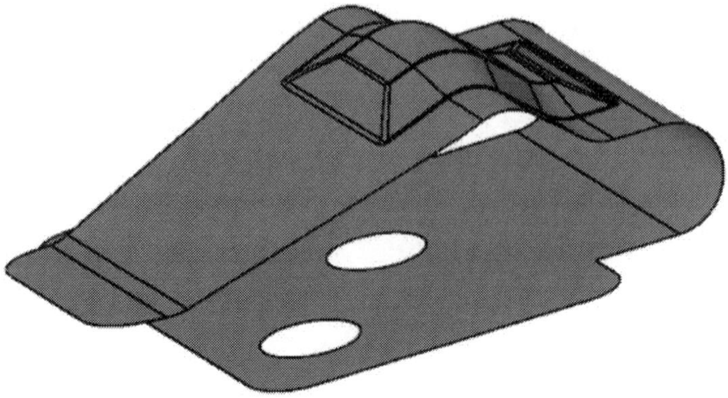

Figure 9–33

Task 3 - Create the axis system.

In this task, you will create an axis system that you will later use to specify the direction of the load.

1. Create an axis system in the middle of the edge of the flap, as shown in Figure 9–34. Ensure that the **Z**-axis points up and is normal to the flap's surface.

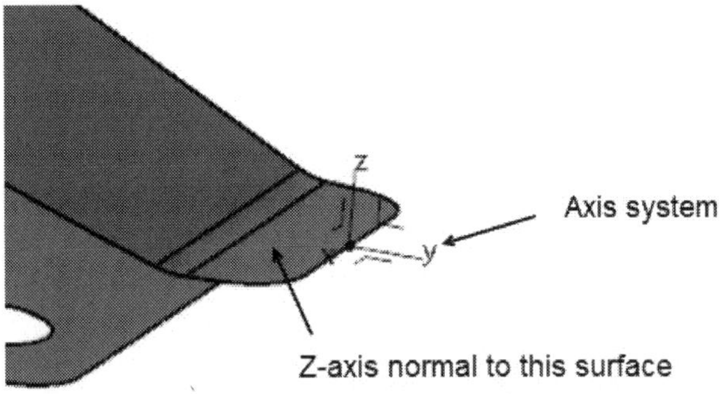

Figure 9–34

Task 4 - Apply the material.

1. Apply **Steel** to the entire part, as shown in Figure 9–35.

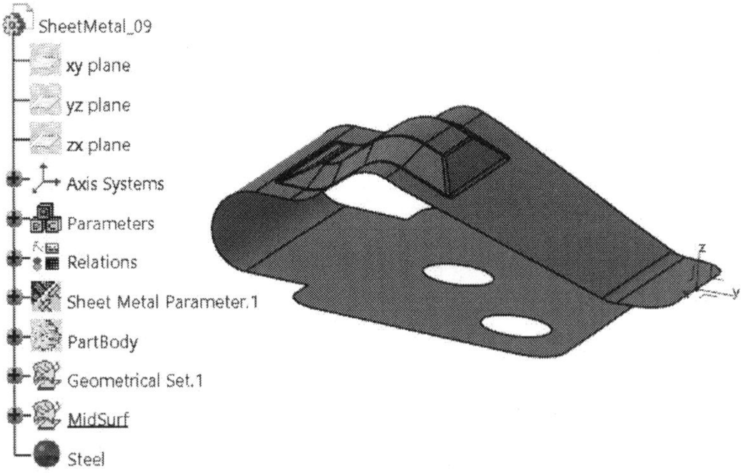

Figure 9–35

Task 5 - Launch the GSA workbench.

1. Select **Start>Analysis & Simulation>Generative Structural Analysis**.

2. Select **Static Analysis** as the new analysis case.

Task 6 - Mesh the part.

If the PartBody in the model is not empty, by default CATIA creates a solid mesh for the part. Since the intent is to use a shell mesh, in this task you will first delete the default solid mesh and its 3D Property, then create a shell mesh.

1. Right-click on **OCTREE Tetrahedron Mesh.1: SheetMetal_09** in the tree and select **Delete**, as shown in Figure 9–36.

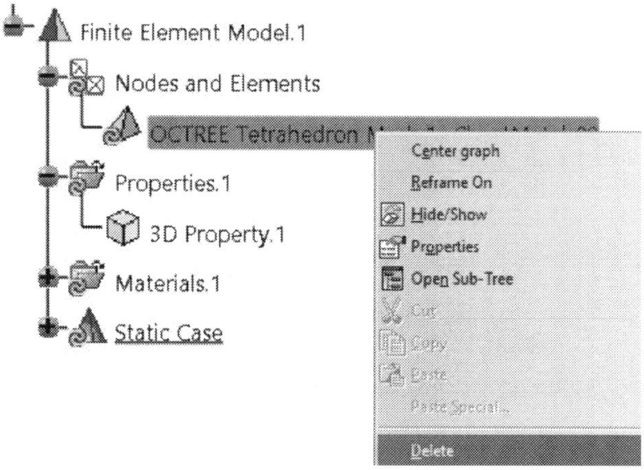

Figure 9–36

2. Right-click on **3D Property.1** in the tree and select **Delete**, as shown in Figure 9–37.

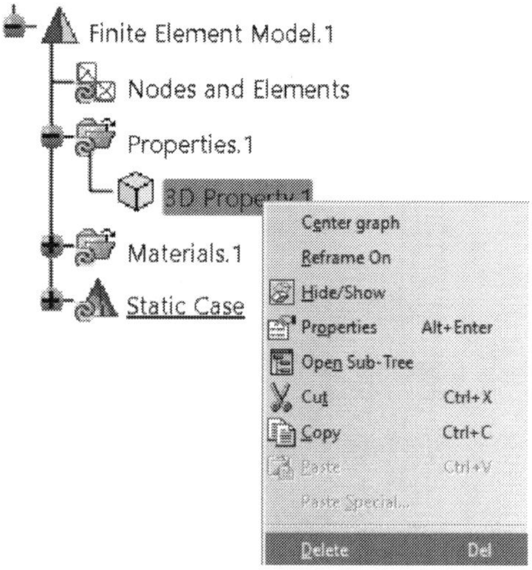

Figure 9–37

3. In the Model Manager toolbar, select  (OCTREE Triangle Mesher) and select the model. The OCTREE Triangle Mesh dialog box opens, as shown in Figure 9–38.

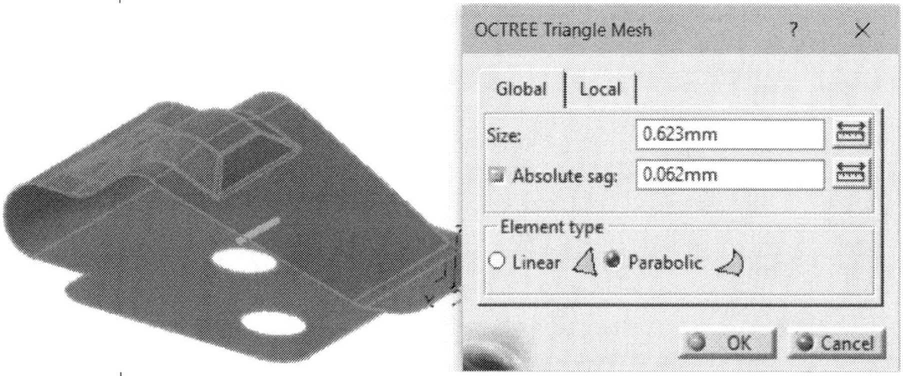

Figure 9–38

This model has some very small radii between the surfaces. Turning the sag control off helps to create a more regular mesh.

4. Ensure that the *Element type* is **Parabolic**. Enter **0.2mm** as the *Size* and toggle off the **Absolute sag** checkbox, as shown in Figure 9–39. Click **OK** to close the dialog box.

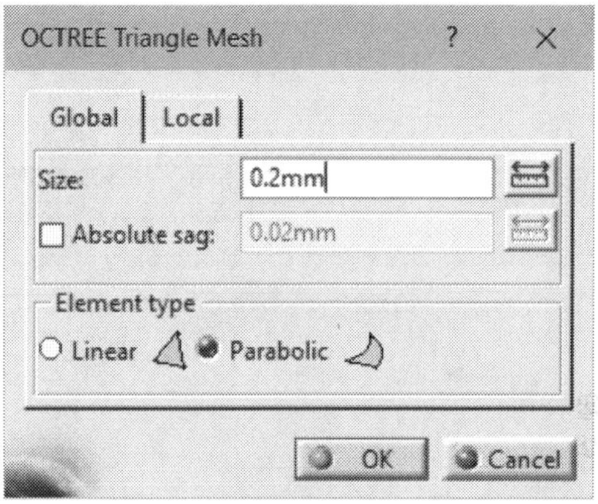

Figure 9–39

5. Right-click on **Nodes and Elements** in the tree and select **Mesh Visualization** to display the mesh, as shown in Figure 9–40. Rotate the model and examine the mesh in various areas of the part.

Figure 9–40

6. Right-click on **Mesh.1** in the tree and select **Delete** to delete the mesh image and return to the model view.

Task 7 - Apply 2D Property.

At this point in the process, neither material nor thickness are applied to the mesh. In this task, you will create a 2D Property, which assigns both material and thickness to the mesh.

1. Select  (2D Property) in the Model Manager toolbar. The 2D Property dialog box opens, as shown in Figure 9–41.

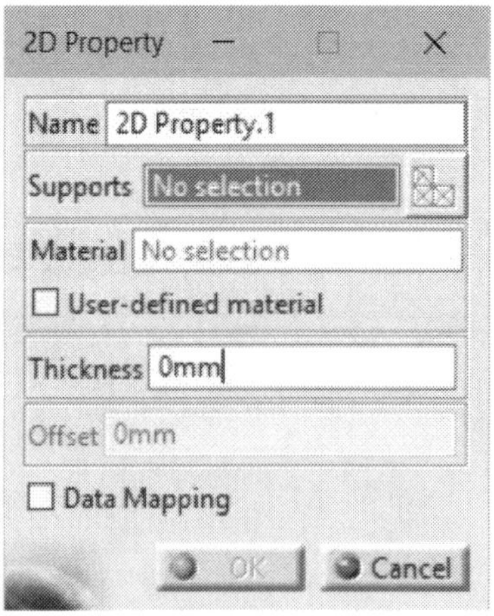

Figure 9–41

2. Select the model surface as the *Supports*. This automatically imports the material from the part and into the analysis, as shown in Figure 9–42.

Figure 9–42

3. Right-click in the *Thickness* field and select **Edit formula**, as shown in Figure 9–43.

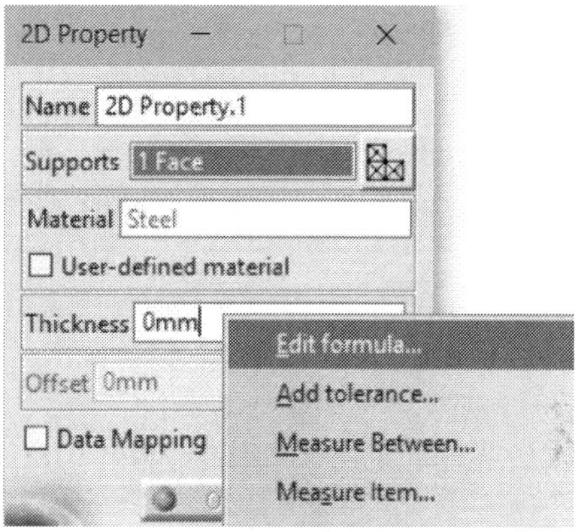

Figure 9–43

4. Using the Formula Editor dialog box, create a formula that links the mesh thickness with the part thickness, as shown in Figure 9–44.

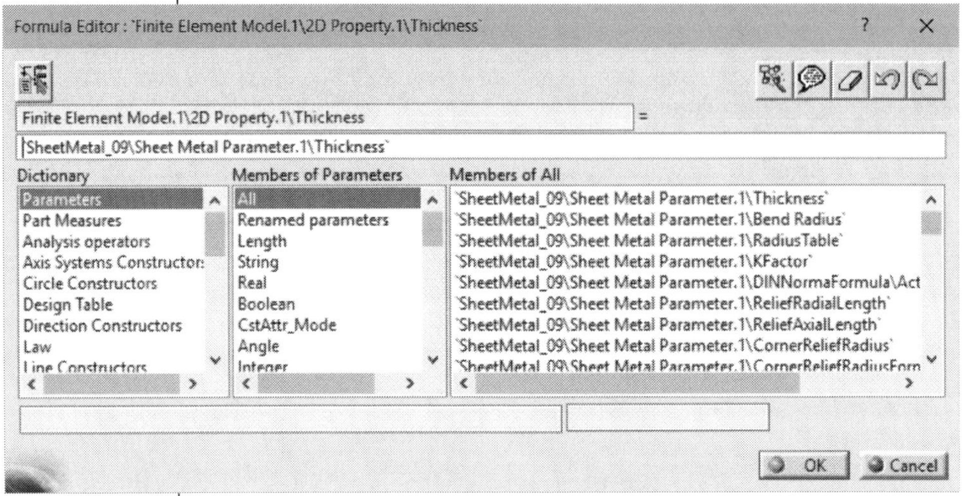

Figure 9–44

5. Click **OK** to close the Formula Editor. The 2D Property dialog box displays as shown in Figure 9–45.

Figure 9–45

6. Click **OK** to close the 2D Property dialog box.

Task 8 - Apply the restraints.

1. Apply the (Clamp) restraint to the edges of the three holes, as shown in Figure 9–46.

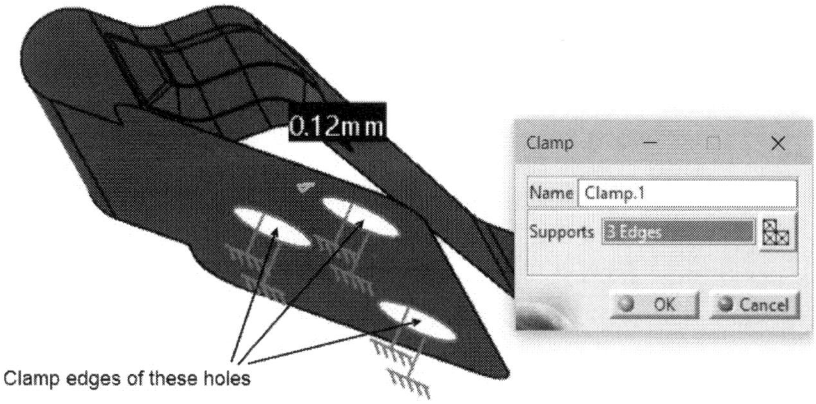

Figure 9–46

Task 9 - Apply the load.

You created Axis System.1 in Task 3.

1. Apply (Distributed Force) **0.2N** to the flap in the **Z**-direction of **Axis System.1**, as shown in Figure 9–47.

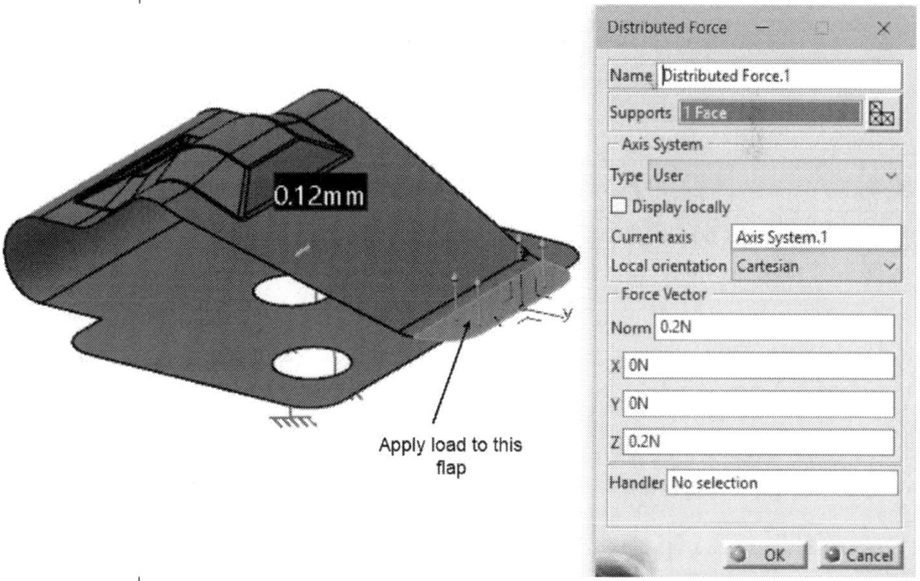

Figure 9–47

Task 10 - Run the analysis.

1. Run the analysis.

2. Expand **Sensors.1** in the tree. Note that the value of the **Global Error Rate** sensor is about **2.78%**, as shown in Figure 9–48. This indicates a good accuracy in the analysis.

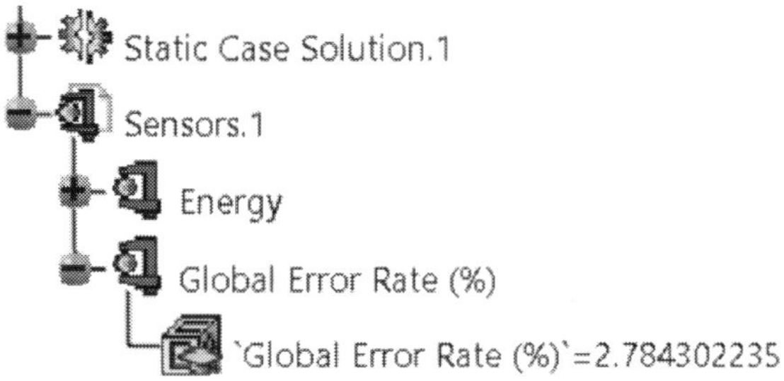

Figure 9–48

Task 11 - Display and animate the deformed mesh.

1. Hide **Nodes and Elements** and **Properties.1**.

2. Select  (Deformation) to visualize the deformed mesh image, as shown in Figure 9–49.

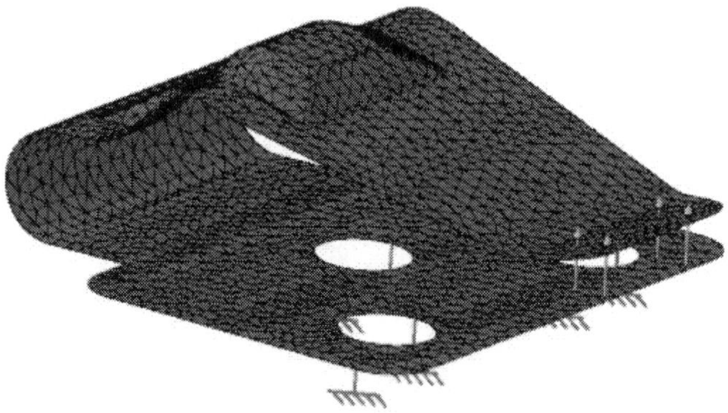

Figure 9–49

3. Animate the deformation. Does the model deform according to the applied loads and restraints?

Task 12 - Visualize the displacement magnitude.

1. Change the view mode to (Shading with Material).

2. Select (Displacement) to display the displacement vector image, as shown in Figure 9–50.

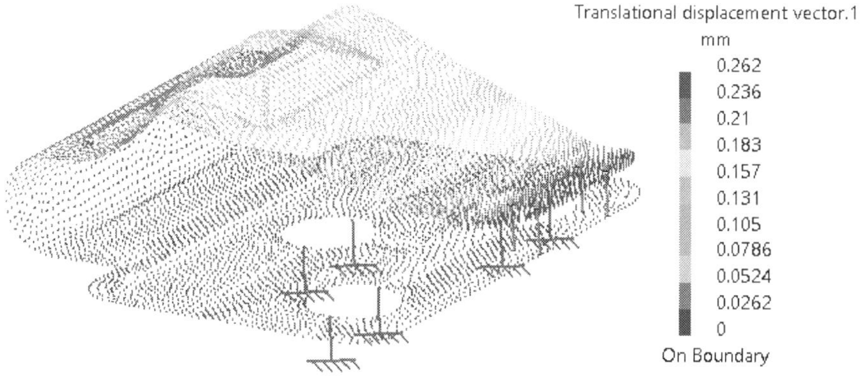

Figure 9–50

3. Double-click on the **Translational displacement vector.1** object in the tree. In the Image Edition dialog box that opens, select **Average iso** in the *Types* list and click **OK**. The displacement magnitude result is displayed, as shown in Figure 9–51. Note that the maximum displacement **0.262mm** occurs at the tip of the flap.

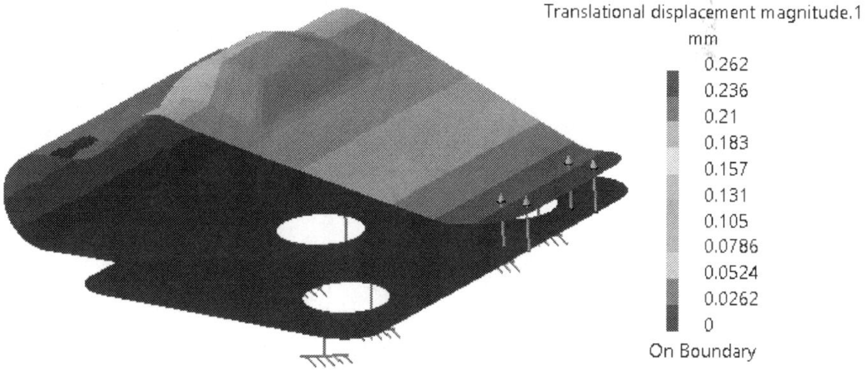

Figure 9–51

Task 13 - Display the stresses.

1. Select  (Von Mises Stress). The stress image displays, as shown in Figure 9–52.

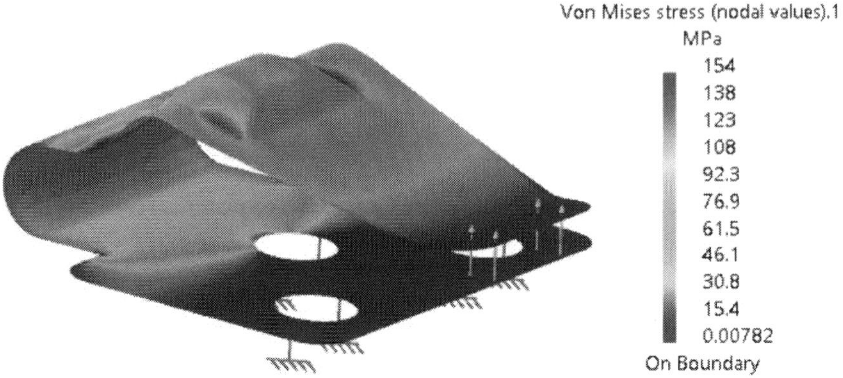

Figure 9–52

2. Double-click on **Von Mises stress (nodal values).1** in the tree and click **More** to expand the Image Edition dialog box, as shown in Figure 9–53.

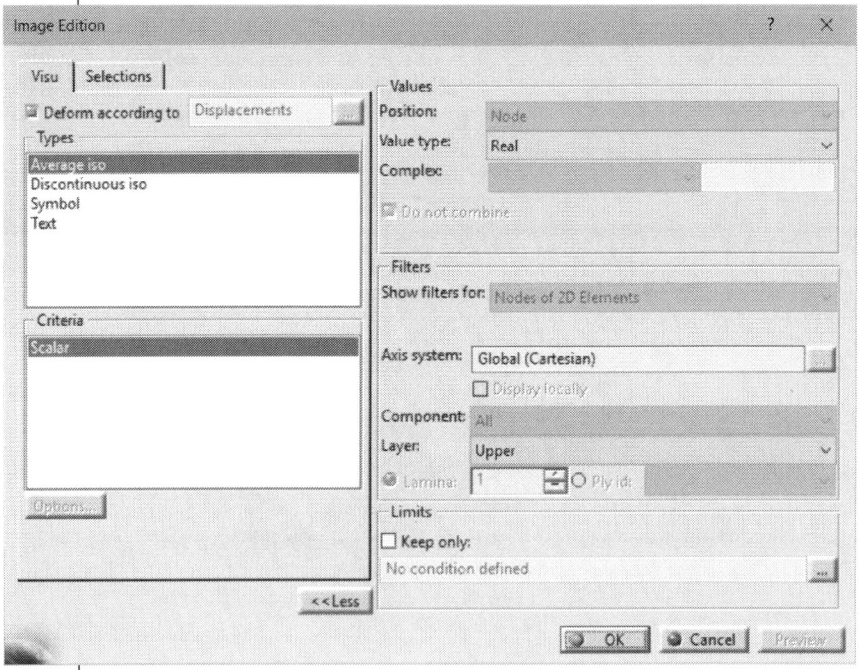

Figure 9–53

3. In the Layer drop-down list, select **Upper and lower**, as shown in Figure 9–54. This ensures that the computed stresses are shown on both sides of the part.

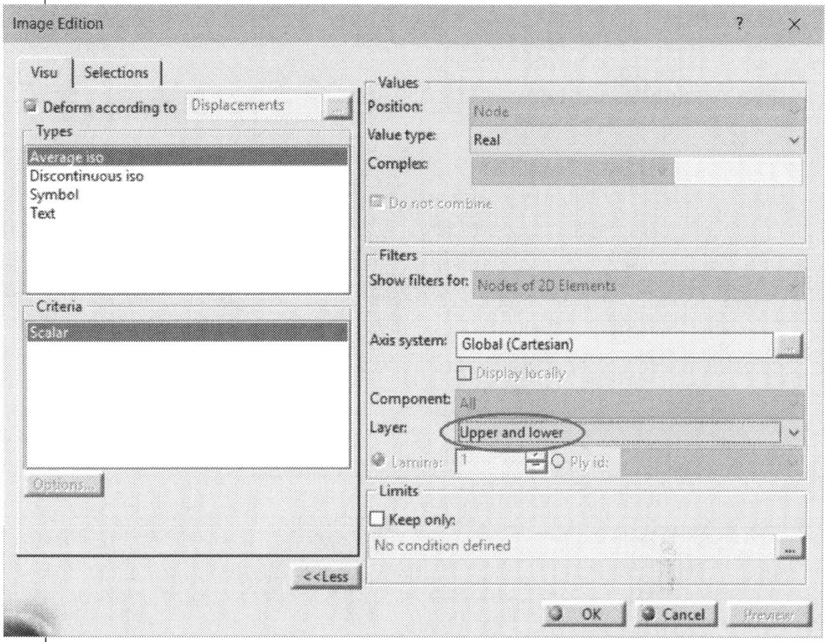

Figure 9–54

4. Click **OK** to close the Image Edition dialog box. The result displays as shown in Figure 9–55.

Figure 9–55

5. Using the  (Image Extrema) tool, locate the maximum stress in the model, as shown in Figure 9–56.

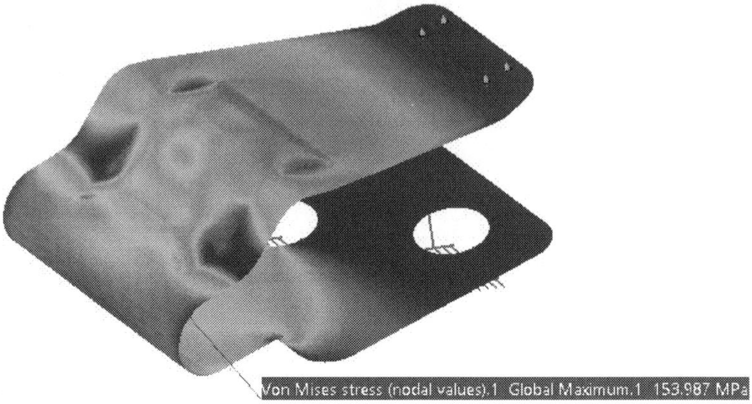

Figure 9–56

6. Right-click on **Von Mises stress (nodal values).1** and select **Activate/Deactivate** to deactivate the stress image and return to the model view.

Task 14 - Save and close the files.

1. Optionally, save the analysis document and the part for future reference.
2. Close both the analysis and the part documents.

Practice 9b Thin-Walled Bracket

Practice Objectives

- Create surface patches.
- Create shell mesh.
- Apply 2D Property.
- Apply loads and restraints.
- Compute the analysis with mesh adaptivity.
- Visualize the results.
- Obtain reaction forces in restraints.

In this practice, you will run a static stress analysis on the thin-walled bracket shown in Figure 9–57.

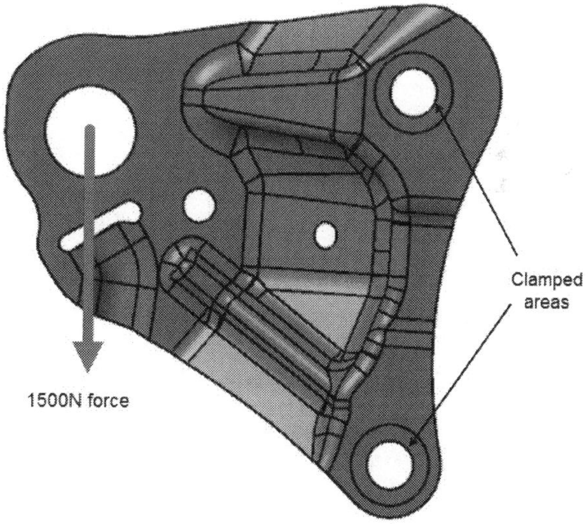

Figure 9–57

The bracket is loaded with 1500N vertical force and clamped by two bolts with washers over the two annular areas 15mm in diameter, as shown above in Figure 9–57. The part has been modeled as a surface rather than a solid; therefore, you will use shell elements and shell mesh for the analysis.

Task 1 - Open the part in CATIA.

1. Open **Bracket_09.CATPart** from the *CATIA Generative Structural Analysis Practice Files\Ch09* folder.

2. Set the model display as  (Shading with Edges). The part displays as shown in Figure 9–58.

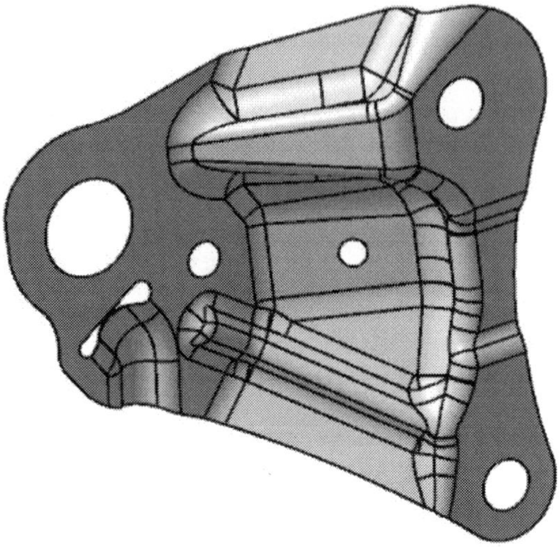

Figure 9–58

3. Examine the model. Note that the part is modeled as a surface (**Surface.1** in **Geometrical Set.1**) rather than a solid. There are no solid features in the **PartBody**.

4. Also note that the model has a parameter **Thickness** with the value **3mm**, which is the thickness of the part as manufactured.

5. Select **Tools>Options>Parameters and Measures>Units** and set the units as follows:

   - Length: **Millimeter (mm)**
   - Force: **Newton (N)**
   - Moment: **Newton x Meter (Nxm)**
   - Pressure: **Megapascal (MPa)**

Task 2 - Create surface patches for the bolts and washers.

1. Activate the **Generative Shape Design**  workbench.

2. Create a new geometrical set named **AnlsSurf**.

3. Create a circular sketch (**Sketch.1**), **15mm** in diameter and concentric with the hole, as shown in Figure 9–59.

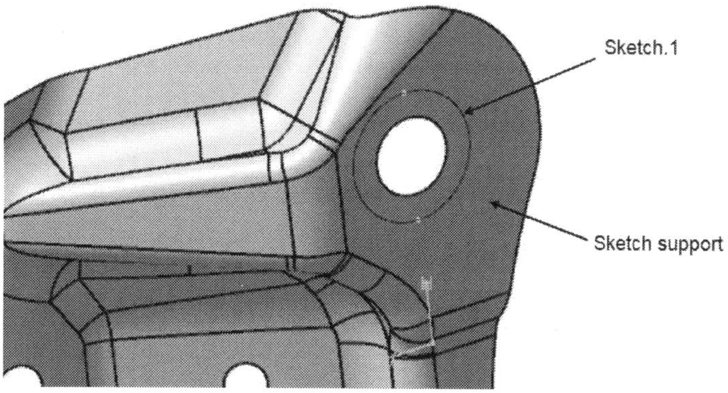

Figure 9–59

4. Select  (Extract) and extract the edge of the hole (**Extract.1**), as shown in Figure 9–60.

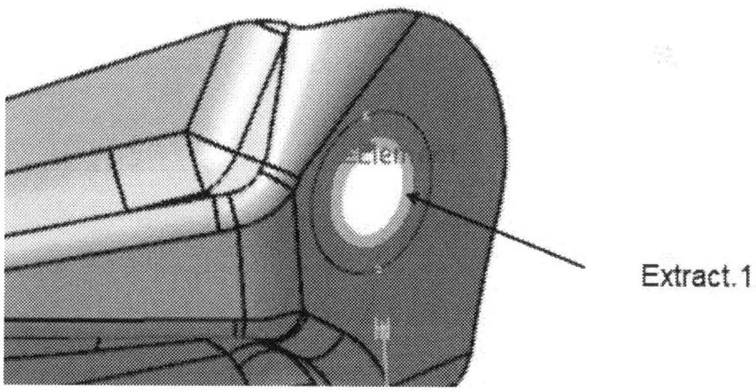

Figure 9–60

5. Select  (Split) and cut **Surface.1** with **Sketch.1**, keeping the side that is outside **Sketch.1**, as shown in Figure 9–61. The resulting surface should be named **Split.1**.

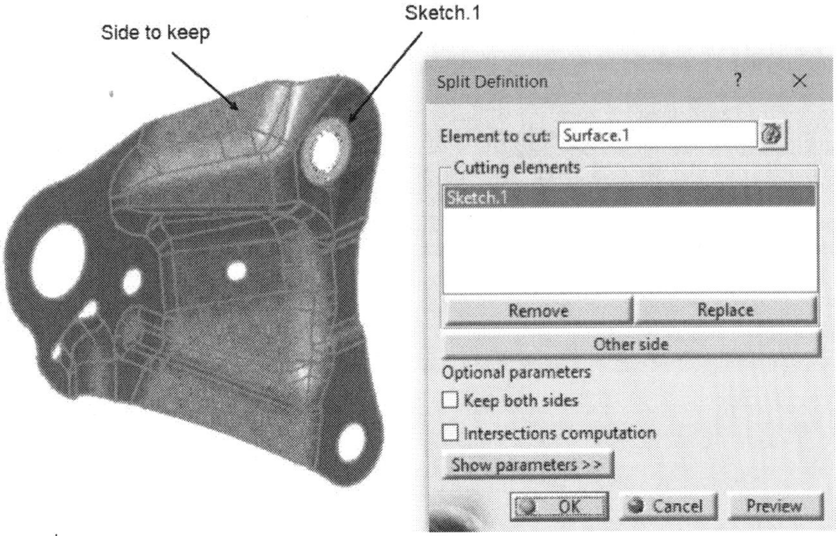

Figure 9–61

6. Select  (Fill) and fill the hole in the **Split.1** surface, as shown in Figure 9–62. The fill surface should be named **Fill.1**.

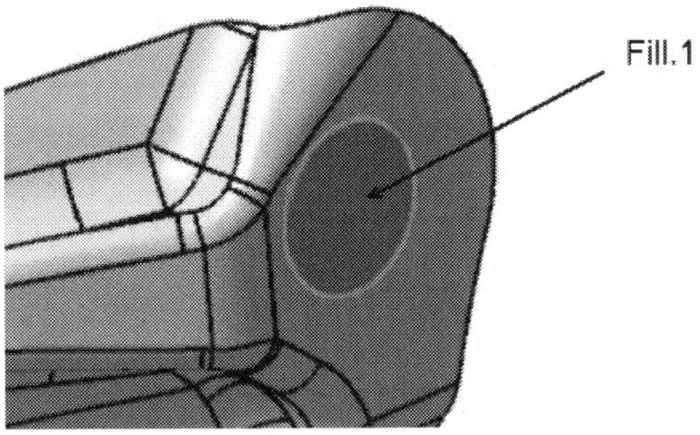

Figure 9–62

7. Split **Fill.1** with **Extract.1**, keeping the annular area as shown in Figure 9–63. The resulting surface should be named **Split.2**.

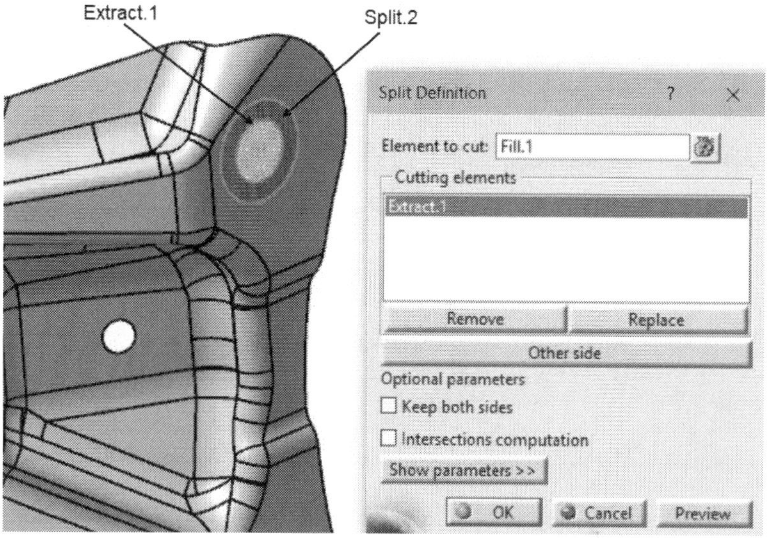

Figure 9–63

8. Hide **Sketch.1**, **Extract.1**, and **Fill.1**. The resulting model displays as shown in Figure 9–64.

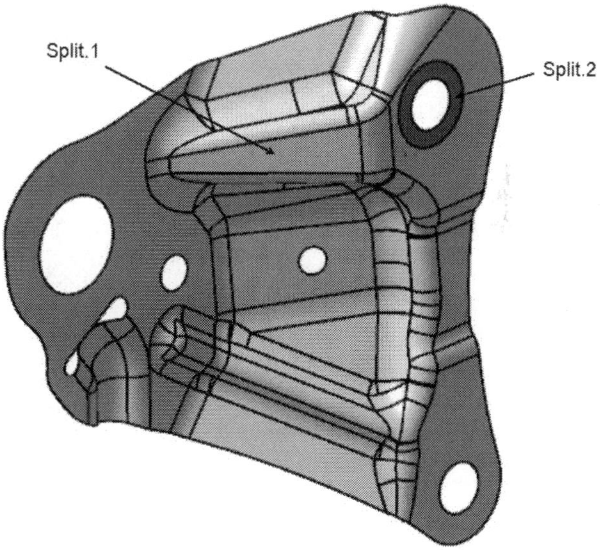

Figure 9–64

9. Using Steps 3 to 7 as a guideline, create another **15mm** annular area (**Split.4**) around the second hole, as shown in Figure 9–65. Note that the remainder of the bracket surface is automatically named Split.3

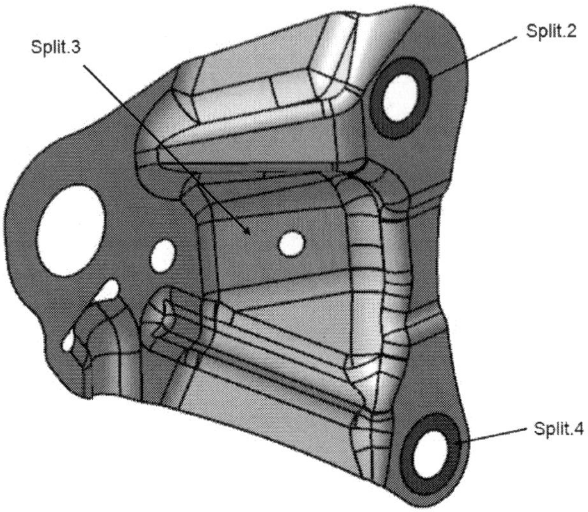

Figure 9–65

10. Select (Join) and join the **Split.2**, **Split.3**, and **Split.4** surfaces into one surface (**Join.1**), as shown in Figure 9–66.

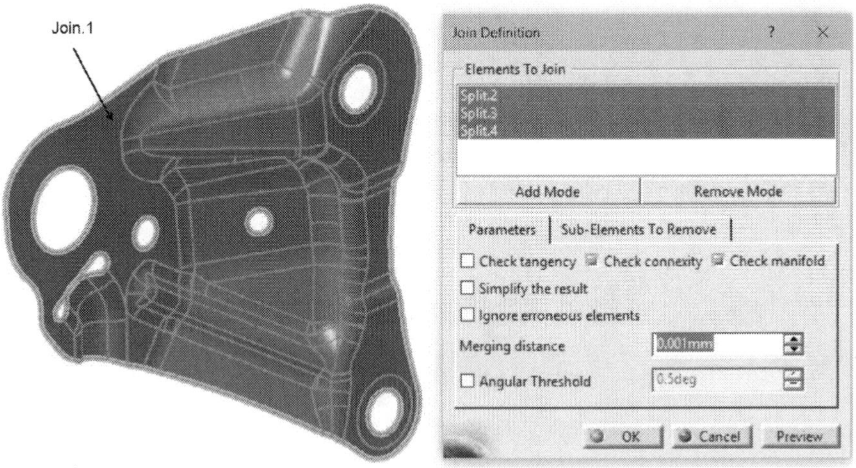

Figure 9–66

Task 3 - Apply the material.

1. Apply **Steel** to the entire part, as shown in Figure 9–67.

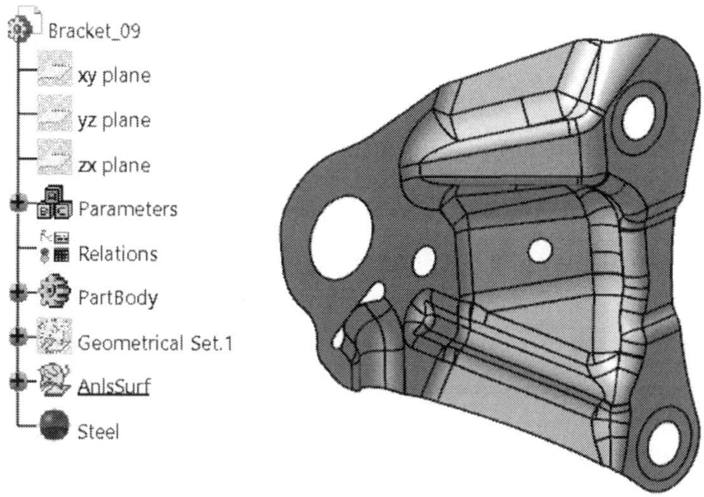

Figure 9–67

Task 4 - Launch the GSA workbench.

1. Select **Start>Analysis & Simulation>Generative Structural Analysis**.
2. CATIA displays the Warnings dialog box, saying that "PartBody of Bracket_09 is empty or external view is not defined on studied surface". This is because, by default, CATIA tries to create a solid mesh for the part, which in this case is not possible since the **PartBody** is indeed empty. Click **OK** to close the Warnings dialog box.
3. Select **Static Analysis** as the new analysis case and click **OK** to start the GSA workbench.

Task 5 - Mesh the part.

1. In the Model Manager toolbar, select  (OCTREE Triangle Mesher) and select the model. The OCTREE Triangle Mesh dialog box opens, as shown in Figure 9–68.

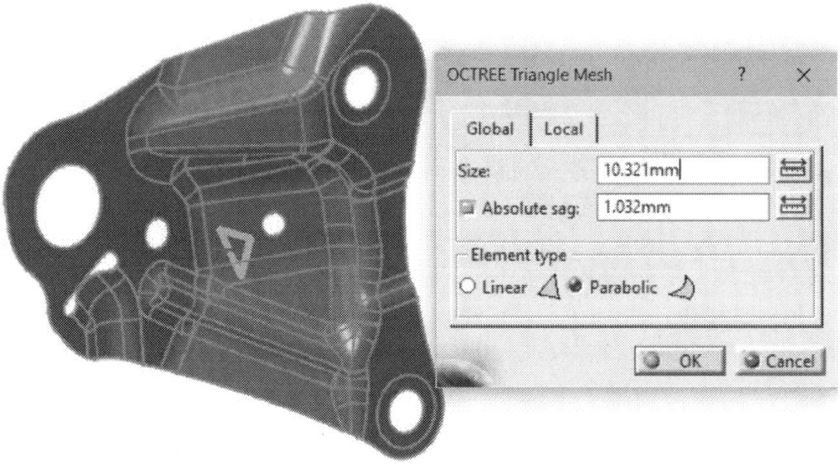

Figure 9–68

2. Ensure that the *Element type* is **Parabolic**. Enter **2mm** as the *Size* and **0.3mm** as the *Absolute sag*, as shown in Figure 9–69. Click **OK** to finish.

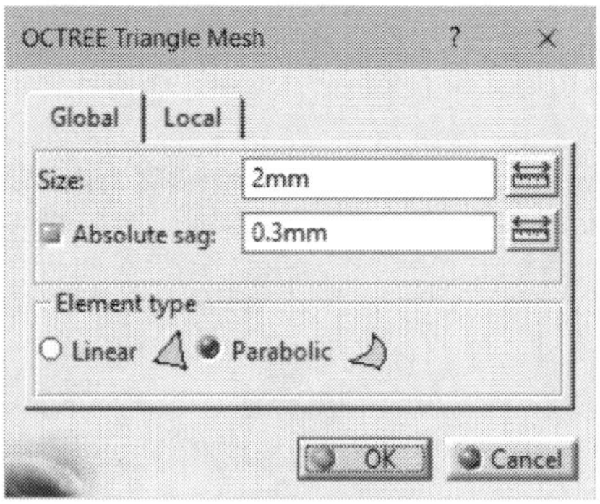

Figure 9–69

3. Right-click on **Nodes and Elements** in the tree and select **Mesh Visualization** to display the mesh, as shown in Figure 9–70. Rotate the model and examine the mesh in various areas of the part.

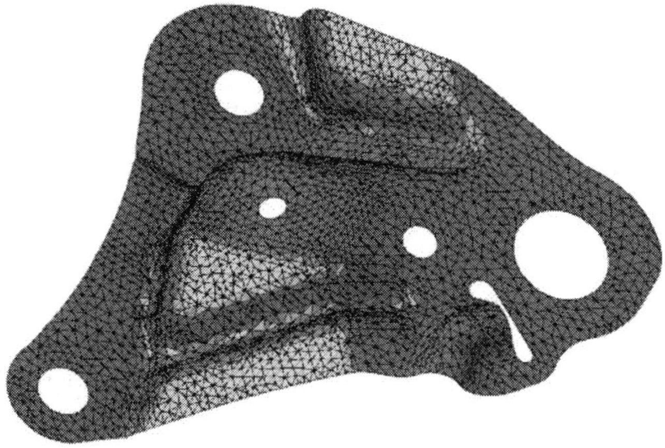

Figure 9–70

4. Right-click on **Mesh.1** in the tree and select **Delete** to delete the mesh image and return to the model view.

Task 6 - Apply 2D Property.

1. Select (2D Property) in the Model Manager toolbar. Once the 2D Property dialog box opens, select the model as the *Supports* and enter **3mm** as the *Thickness*, as shown in Figure 9–71.

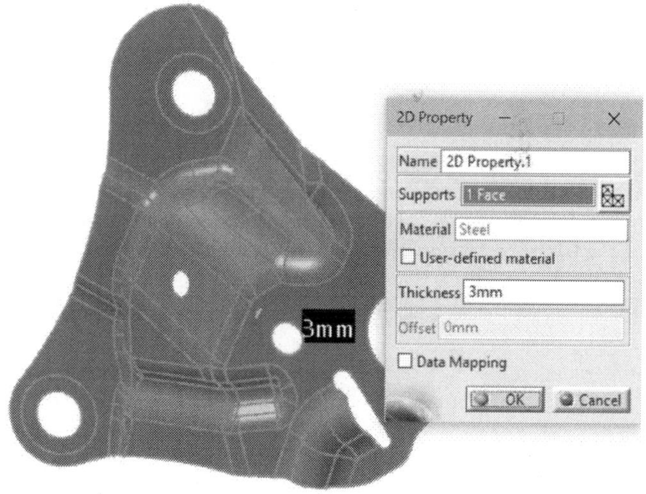

Figure 9–71

2. Click **OK** to close the 2D Property dialog box.

Task 7 - Apply the restraints.

In this task, you will apply clamp restraints to the two annular areas around the bolted holes. You will apply two separate restraints, which is necessary in order to be able to extract reaction forces in the holes after the analysis.

1. Apply the  (Clamp) restraint to the annular area around the upper hole, as shown in Figure 9–72.

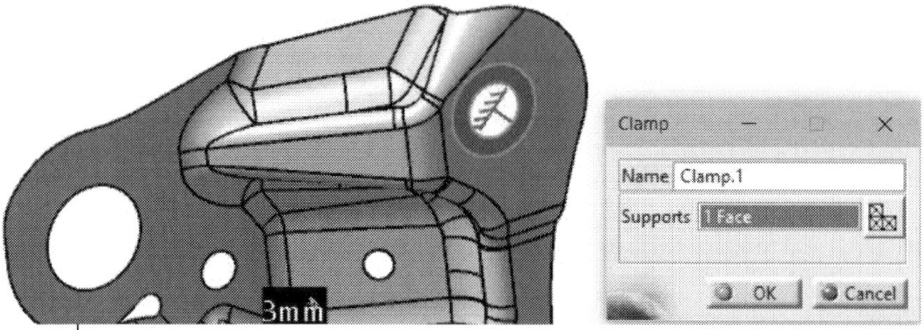

Figure 9–72

2. Apply the  (Clamp) restraint to the annular area around the lower hole, as shown in Figure 9–73.

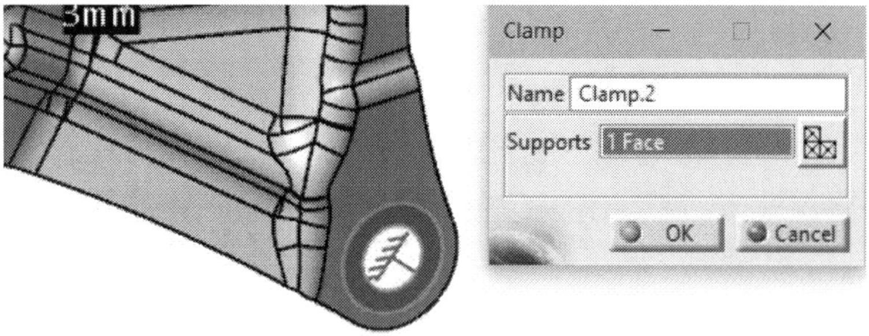

Figure 9–73

Task 8 - Apply the load.

1. Apply  (Distributed Force) **1500N** in the **Y**-direction to the edge of the larger hole, as shown in Figure 9–74.

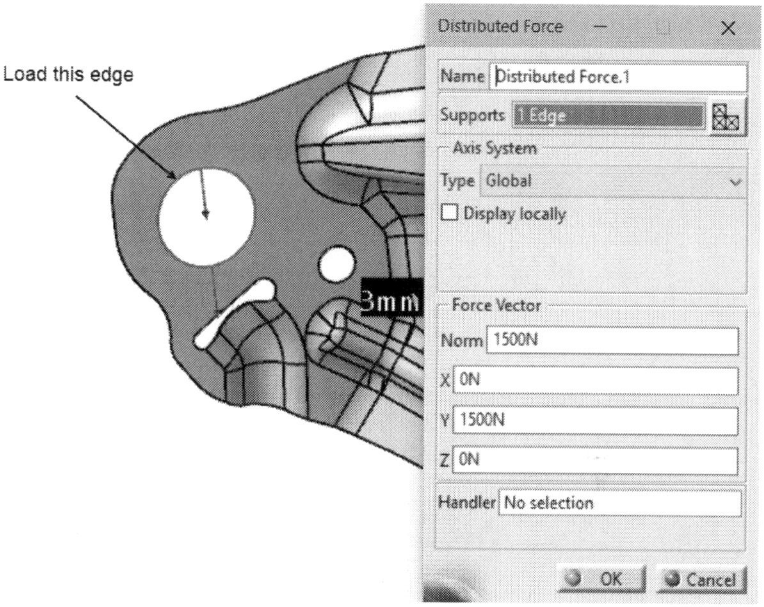

Figure 9–74

Task 9 - Run the analysis.

1. Run the analysis.

2. Expand **Sensors.1** in the tree. Note that the value of the **Global Error Rate** sensor is approximately **9.3%**, as shown in Figure 9–75.

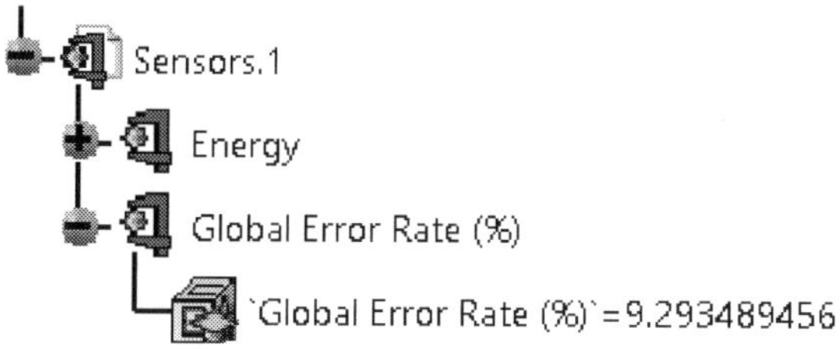

Figure 9–75

Task 10 - Set up Global Adaptivity.

The target error rate in this analysis is 5%. In this task, you will create a Global Adaptivity object and request the 5% error rate as the objective.

1. Select (New Adaptivity Entity). In the Global Adaptivity dialog box, select **OCTREE Triangle Mesh.1** as the *Supports* and enter **5** in the *Objective Error* field, as shown in Figure 9–76.

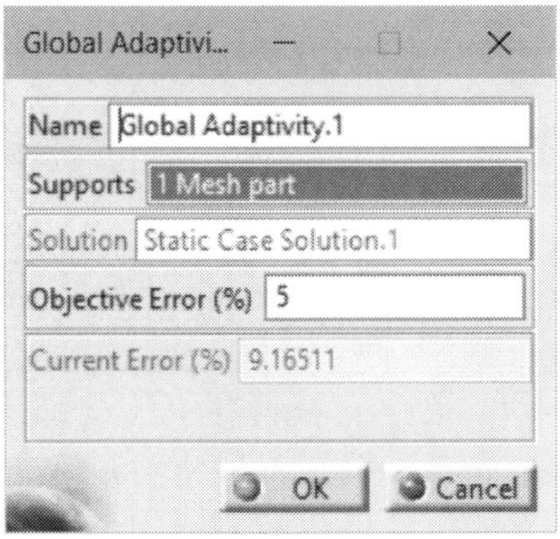

Figure 9–76

2. Click **OK** to close the Global Adaptivity dialog box.

Task 11 - Run the analysis with adaptivity.

1. Select (Compute with Adaptivity). In the Adaptivity Process Parameters dialog box that opens, enter **5** in the *Iterations Number* field, activate the **Minimum Size** option and enter **0.5mm** as the minimum element size, as shown in Figure 9–77.

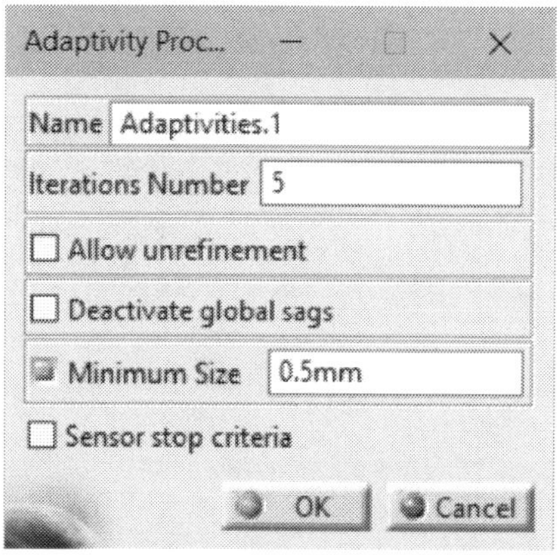

Figure 9–77

2. Click **OK** to start the computation. CATIA displays a series of messages informing you of the status of the computation process. Wait until computation completes.

3. CATIA may or may not automatically update the analysis sensors once the computation finishes. To update all the sensors, right-click on **Sensors.1** in the tree and select **Update All Sensors**.

4. Expand **Sensors.1** in the tree and note that the value of the **Global Error Rate** sensor now reads approximately **4.9%**, as shown in Figure 9–78. This is below the objective error in this analysis, which was 5%, so the adaptivity process has succeeded.

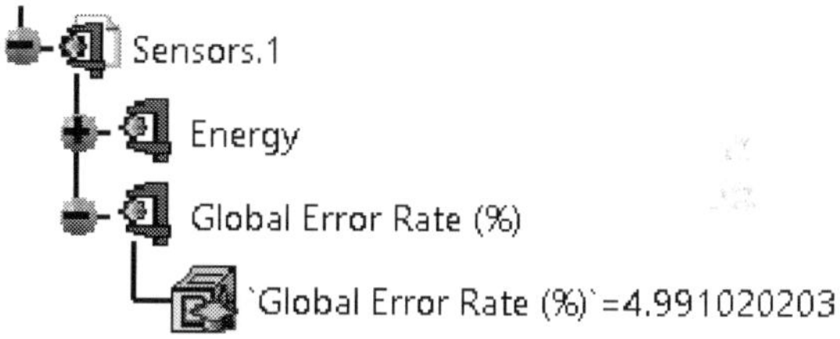

Figure 9–78

Task 12 - Display and animate the deformed mesh.

1. Hide **Nodes and Elements** and **Properties.1**.

2. Select (Deformation) to visualize the deformed mesh image, as shown in Figure 9–79.

Figure 9–79

3. Animate the deformation. Does the model deform according to the applied loads and restraints?

Task 13 - Display the stresses.

1. Change the view mode to (Shading with Material).

2. Select (Von Mises Stress). The stress image displays, as shown in Figure 9–80.

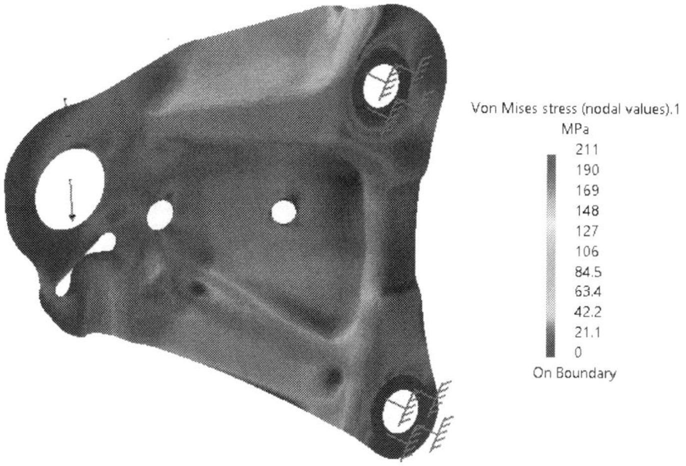

Figure 9–80

3. Double-click on **Von Mises stress (nodal values).1** in the tree and click **More** to expand the Image Edition dialog box. In the Layer drop-down list, select **Upper and lower**, as shown in Figure 9–81. This ensures that the computed stresses are shown on both sides of the part.

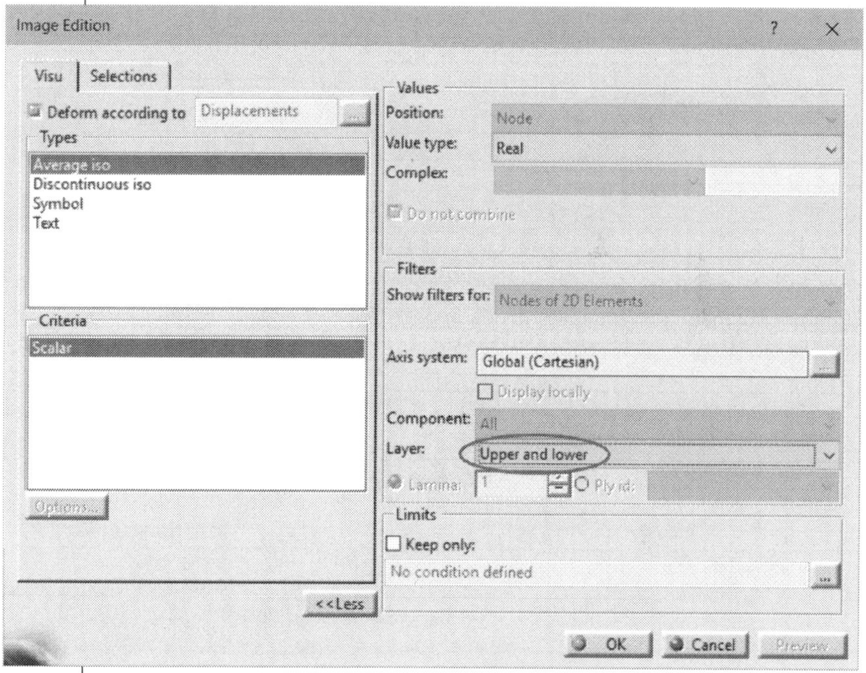

Figure 9–81

4. Click **OK** to close the Image Edition dialog box. The result displays as shown in Figure 9–82.

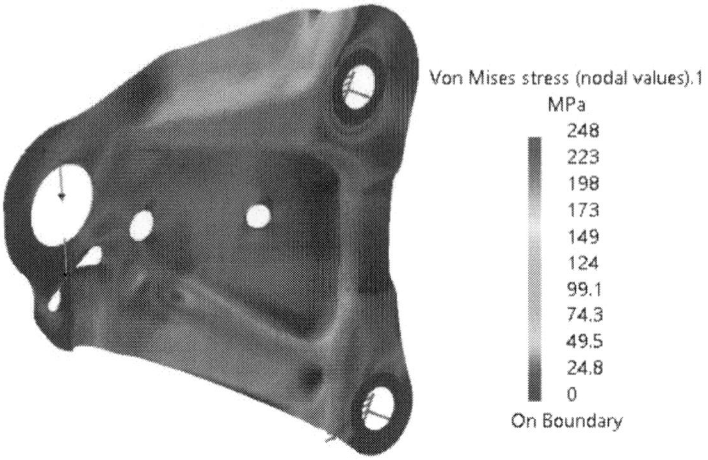

Figure 9–82

5. Using the (Image Extrema) tool, locate the maximum stress in the model, as shown in Figure 9–83. Does the maximum stress exceed the yield strength of the material?

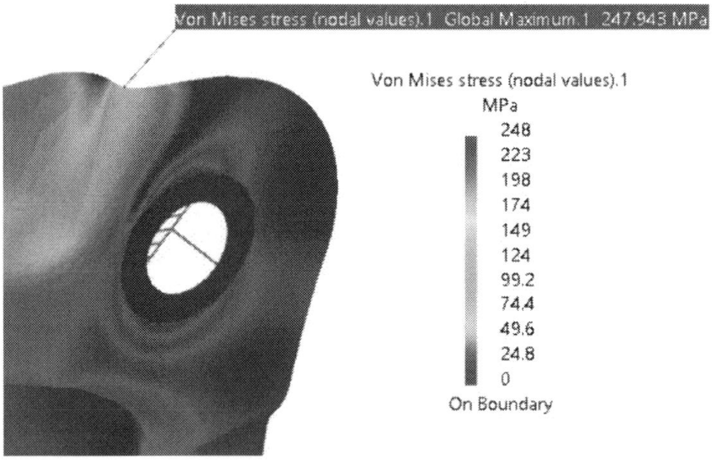

Figure 9–83

6. Right-click on **Von Mises stress (nodal values).1** and select **Activate/Deactivate** to deactivate the stress image and return to the model view.

Task 14 - Obtain reaction forces in the restraints.

In this task, you will create reaction sensors in order to obtain the amounts of force carried by each restraint under the given load on the bracket. This information would help you with proper sizing of the bolts used for mounting the bracket through the holes.

1. Right-click on **Sensors.1** in the tree and select **Create Resultant Sensor>Reaction Sensor** in the contextual menu, as shown in Figure 9–84.

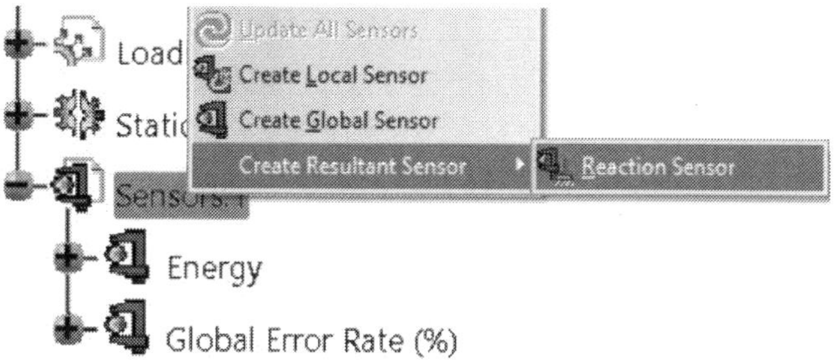

Figure 9–84

2. In the Reaction Sensor dialog box that opens, select **Clamp.1** in the tree and click **Update Results**. CATIA calculates the reaction forces and moments in the restraint at the upper hole and displays the results, as shown in Figure 9–85.

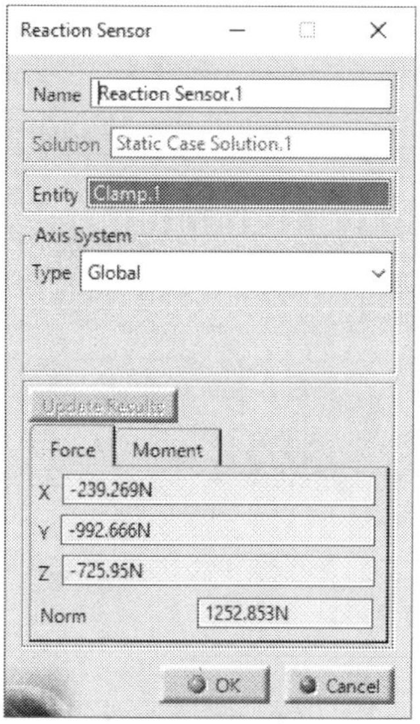

Figure 9–85

Note that the reaction force magnitude on the first clamped hole in the bracket is approximately **1253N**.

3. Click **OK** to close the Reaction Sensor dialog box.
4. Repeat Steps 1 to 3 to obtain the reaction force in the lower hole (**Clamp.2**), as shown in Figure 9–86.

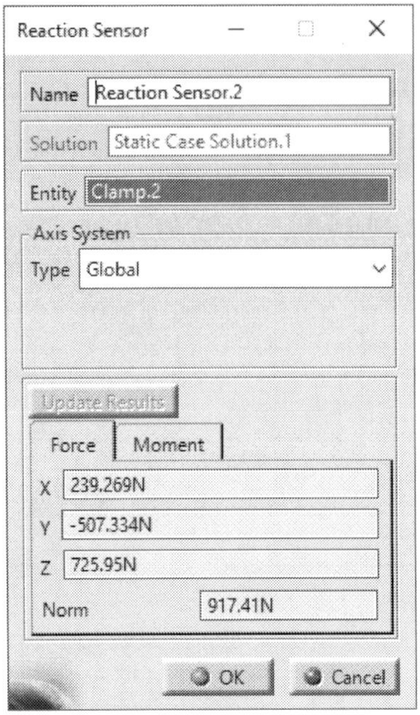

Figure 9–86

Task 15 - Save and close the files.

1. Optionally, save the analysis document and the part for future reference.
2. Close both the analysis and the part documents.

Practice 9c

Welding Connections

Practice Objectives

- Create shell mesh.
- Apply 2D Property.
- Create a seam welding analysis connection.
- Create a spot welding analysis connection.
- Apply loads and restraints.
- Compute the analysis.
- Visualize the results.

In this practice, you will run a static stress analysis on the sheet-metal assembly shown in Figure 9–87.

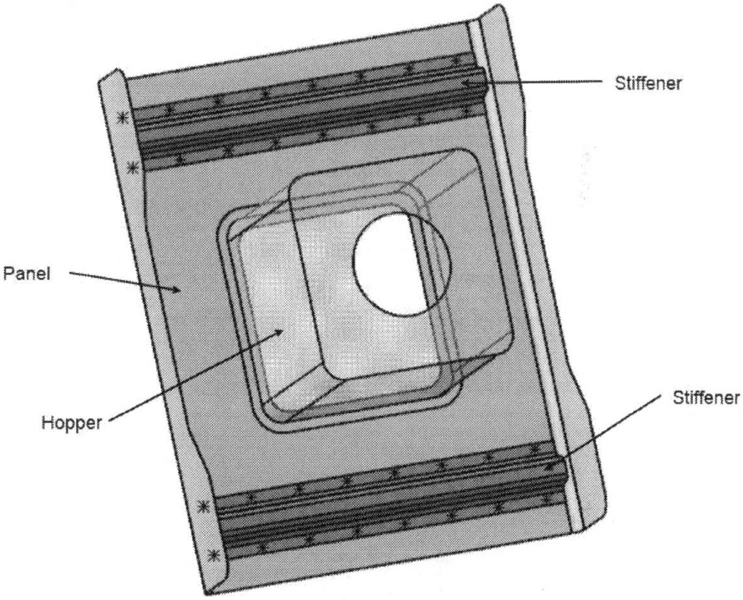

Figure 9–87

The assembly consists of four parts: the panel, the hopper, and two stiffeners. The hopper is welded to the panel by a continuous weld all around the bottom flange of the hopper, while the stiffeners are spot-welded to the panel.

Task 1 - Open the assembly in CATIA.

1. Open **Welds_09.CATProduct** from the *CATIA Generative Structural Analysis Practice Files\Ch09* folder.

2. Set the model display as  (Shading with Edges). The model displays as shown in Figure 9–88.

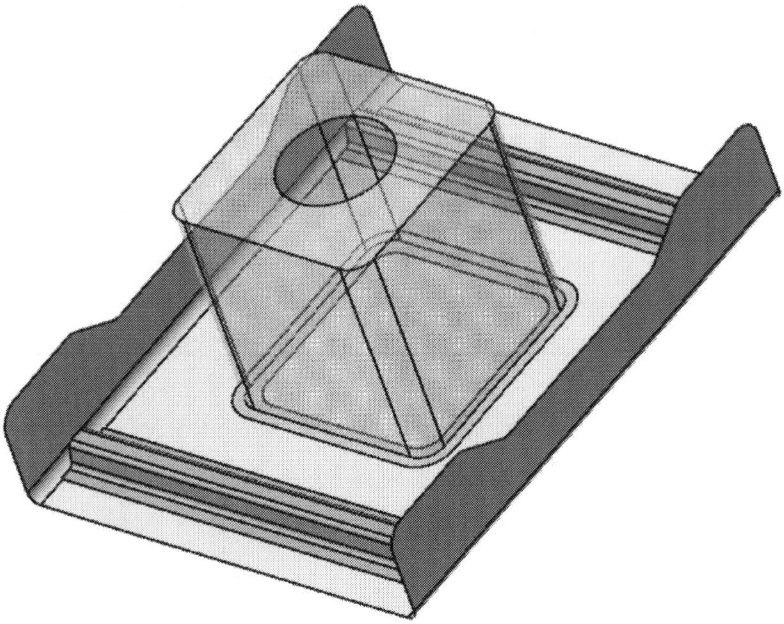

Figure 9–88

3. Select **Tools>Options>Parameters and Measures>Units** and set the units as follows:

   - Length: **Millimeter (mm)**
   - Force: **Newton (N)**
   - Moment: **Newton x Meter (Nxm)**
   - Pressure: **Megapascal (MPa)**

Task 2 - Switch the parts to Design Mode.

You only need to do this task if you opened the assembly in Visualization mode (the toggle **Tools>Options> Infrastructure>Product Structure>Work with the cache system** is on), because the parts must be in Design mode for the analysis.

1. Right-click on the root assembly **Welds_09** and select **Representations>Design Mode** in the contextual menu.

Task 3 - Examine the model.

1. Expand the tree and note that all the parts are modeled as surfaces rather than solids. The surfaces represent the mid-surfaces of the parts (i.e., through the middle of the thickness of each part).

2. Also note that each part has a parameter **Thickness**, which is the thickness of the part as manufactured, as shown in Figure 9–89.

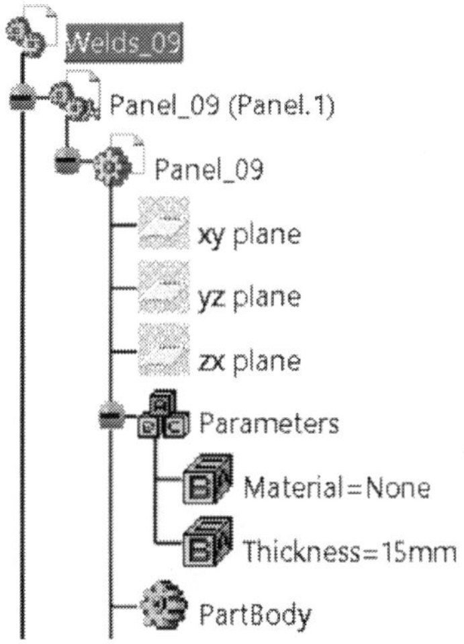

Figure 9–89

3. Expand the **Stiffener_09** part and note that it has a geometrical set named **WeldPnts**, which contains a set of points that indicate locations of the spot welds, as shown in Figure 9–90.

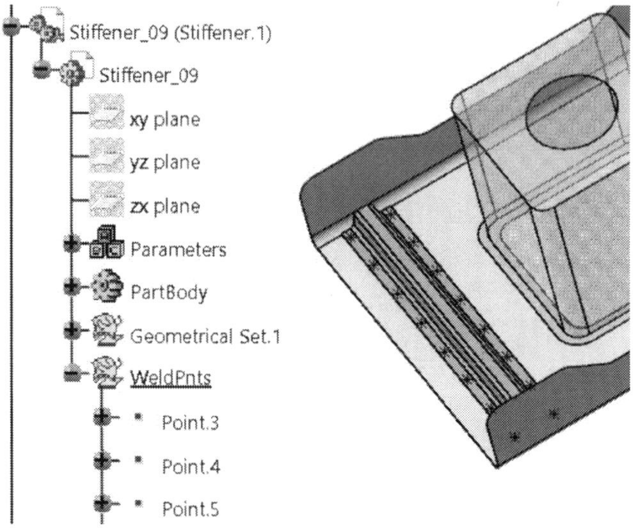

Figure 9–90

Task 4 - Create the weld path.

The hopper is welded to the panel by a continuous weld all around the bottom flange of the hopper. In this task, you will create a curve that represents the weld path.

1. Double-click on the **Hopper_09** part in the tree to switch to Part Design mode. Ensure that the **Generative Shape Design** workbench is activated.
2. Create a new geometrical set (**Geometrical Set.2**).
3. Select (Extract) and, using the **Tangent continuity** option, extract the entire all-around edge of the bottom flange of the hopper, as shown in Figure 9–91. Name the extracted curve as **WeldPath**.

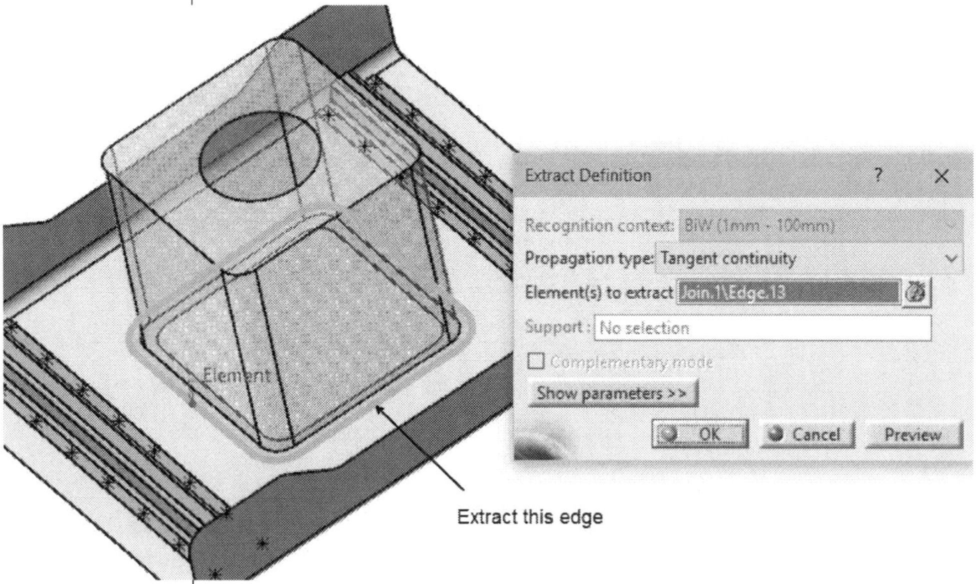

Figure 9–91

4. Double-click on the root assembly **Welds_09** in the tree to switch back to the Assembly Design mode.

Task 5 - Apply the material.

1. Apply **Steel** to the entire assembly, as shown in Figure 9–92.

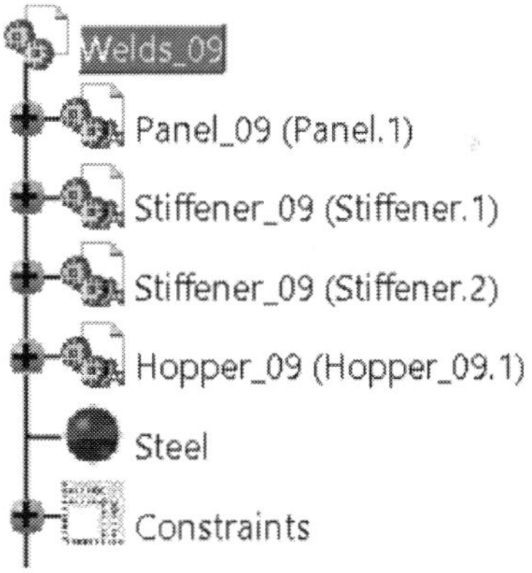

Figure 9–92

Task 6 - Launch the GSA workbench.

1. Select **Start>Analysis & Simulation>Generative Structural Analysis**.
2. CATIA displays the Warnings dialog box, saying that the part bodies of the parts in the assembly are empty. This is because the parts are modeled as surfaces rather than solids. Click **OK** to close the Warnings dialog box.
3. Select **Static Analysis** as the new analysis case and click **OK** to start the GSA workbench.

Task 7 - Mesh the parts.

1. Using the  (OCTREE Triangle Mesher) tool, create the shell meshes for the parts as follows:

- Panel_09 (Panel.1)
  - Element type: **Parabolic**
  - Size: **100mm**
  - Absolute sag: **20mm**
- Stiffener_09 (Stiffener.1)
  - Element type: **Parabolic**
  - Size: **100mm**
  - Absolute sag: **20mm**
- Stiffener_09 (Stiffener.2)
  - Element type: **Parabolic**
  - Size: **100mm**
  - Absolute sag: **20mm**
- Hopper_09 (Hopper_09.1)
  - Element type: **Parabolic**
  - Size: **100mm**
  - Absolute sag: **20mm**

2. Right-click on **Nodes and Elements** in the tree and select **Mesh Visualization** to display the mesh, as shown in Figure 9–93.

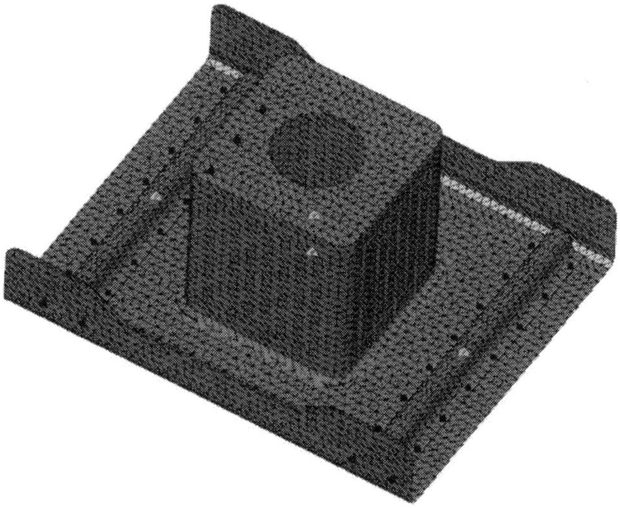

Figure 9–93

3. Right-click on **Mesh.1** in the tree and select **Delete** to delete the mesh image and return to the model view.

Task 8 - Apply 2D Property.

1. Select (2D Property). Once the 2D Property dialog box opens, select the surface of the **Panel_09** part as the *Supports* and enter **15mm** as the *Thickness*, as shown in Figure 9–94.

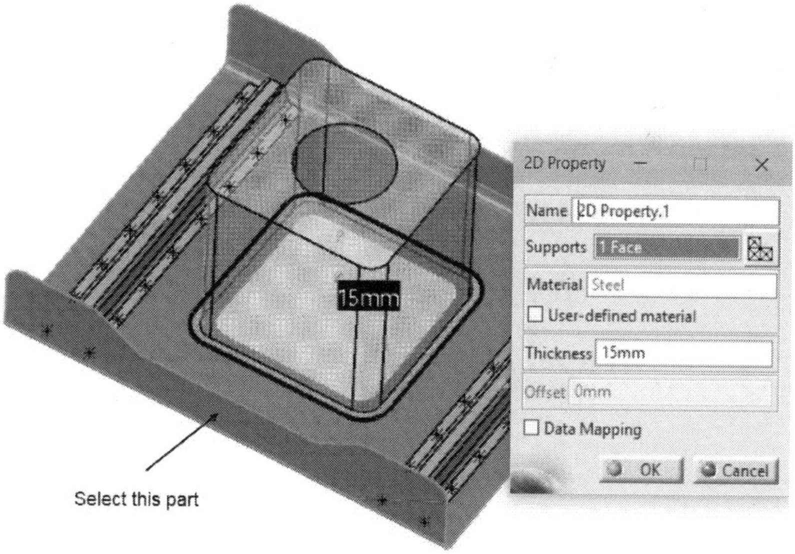

Figure 9–94

2. Click **OK** to close the 2D Property dialog box.
3. Using Steps 1 and 2 as a guideline, apply a **10mm** thickness to the hopper and to both stiffener parts.

Task 9 - Import weld material.

In this task, you will import into the analysis the material that you will later apply to the welding connections.

1. In the Model Manager toolbar, select  (User Material). The Library dialog box opens, as shown in Figure 9–95.

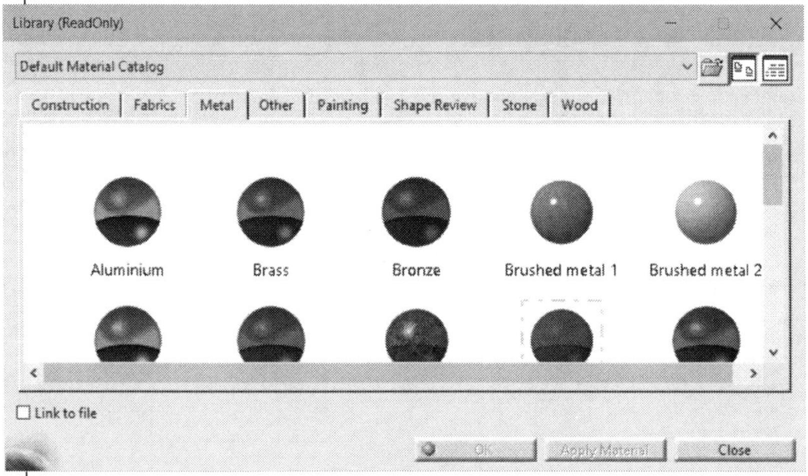

Figure 9–95

2. Select the *Metal* tab. In the list of materials, select **Steel** and click **OK** to import the material in the analysis model and close the material library, as shown in Figure 9–96.

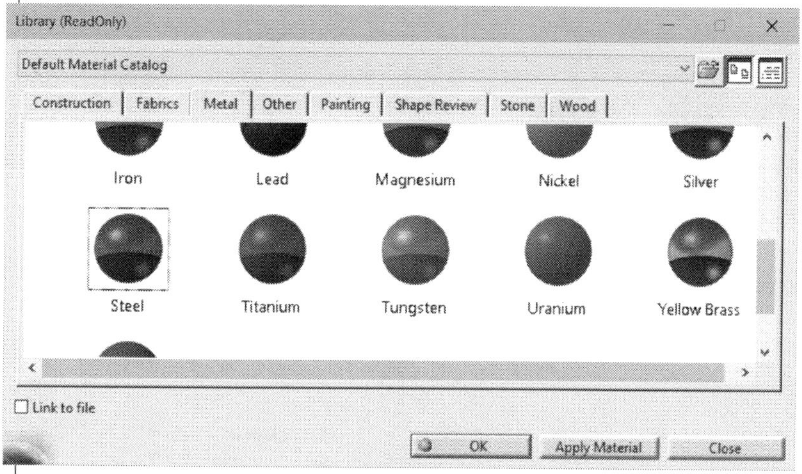

Figure 9–96

3. The imported material displays in the tree as **User Material.1**. Right-click on **User Material.1**, select **Properties**, and rename the material to **WeldMaterial**, as shown in Figure 9–97.

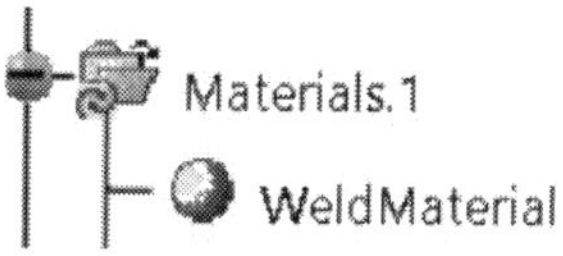

Figure 9–97

Task 10 - Create a seam welding analysis connection.

1. In the Analysis Supports toolbar, select  (Line Analysis Connection). The Line Analysis Connection dialog box opens, as shown in Figure 9–98.

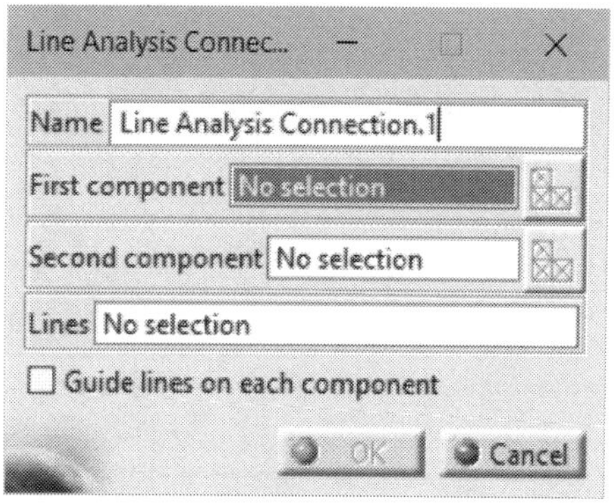

Figure 9–98

2. Select the hopper surface as the *First component*, the panel surface as the *Second component*, and the **WeldPath** curve as the *Lines*, as shown in Figure 9–99.

   Note: You created the **WeldPath** curve in Task 4. Make sure that you select the curve in the tree rather than in the graphics window.

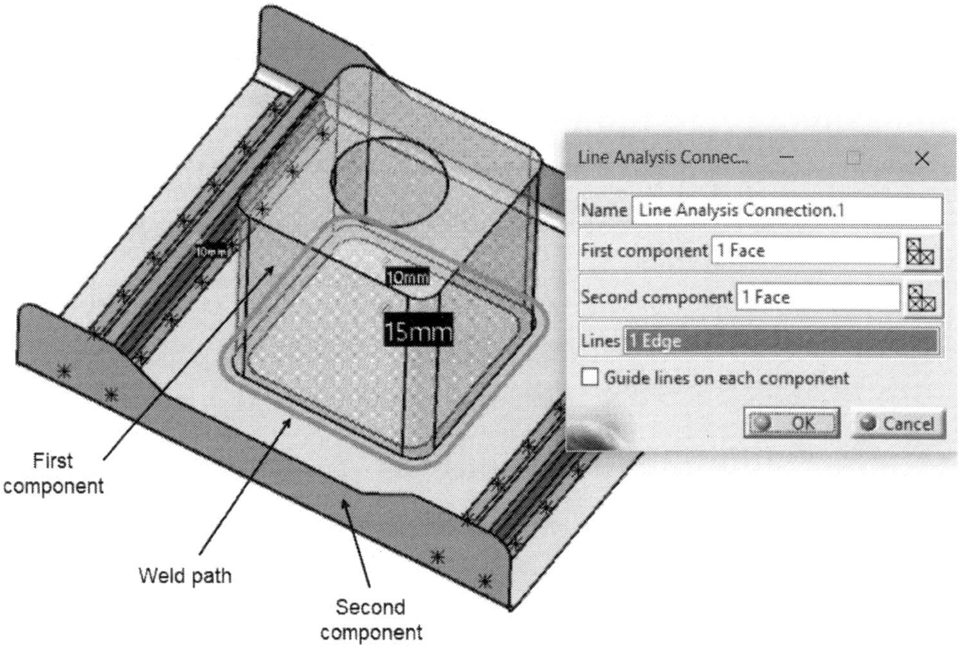

Figure 9–99

3. Click **OK** to finish. The new **Line Analysis Connection.1** is created and displayed in the tree in the **Analysis Connection Manager.1** section, as shown in Figure 9–100.

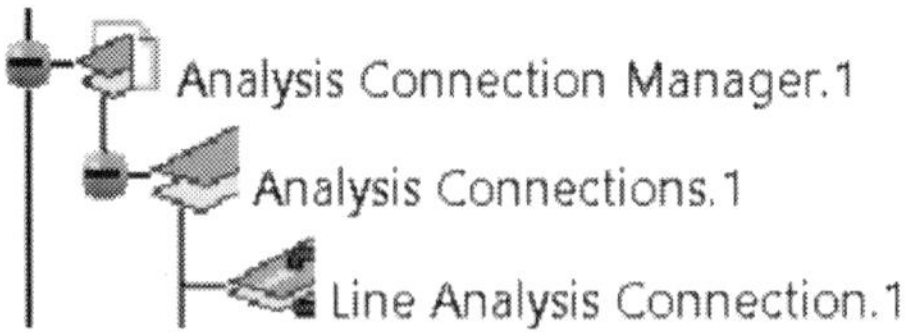

Figure 9–100

4. In the Connection Properties toolbar, select  (Seam Welding Connection Property). The Seam Welding Connection Property dialog box opens, as shown in Figure 9–101.

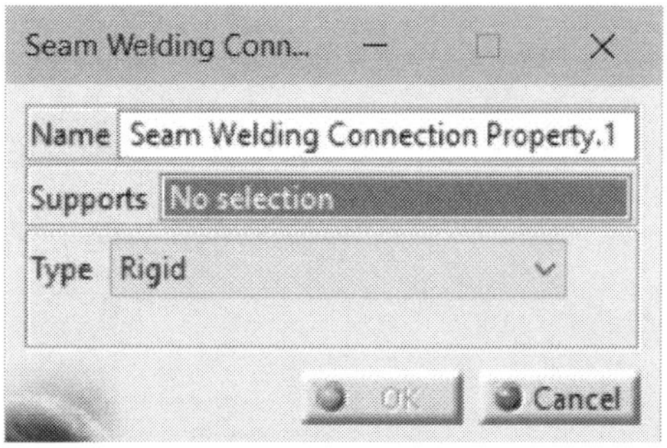

Figure 9–101

5. Select **Line Analysis Connection.1** as the *Supports* and select **Shell** in the Type drop-down list, as shown in Figure 9–102.

Figure 9–102

6. Click the  (Component edition) button. The Seam Welding Definition dialog box opens, as shown in Figure 9–103.

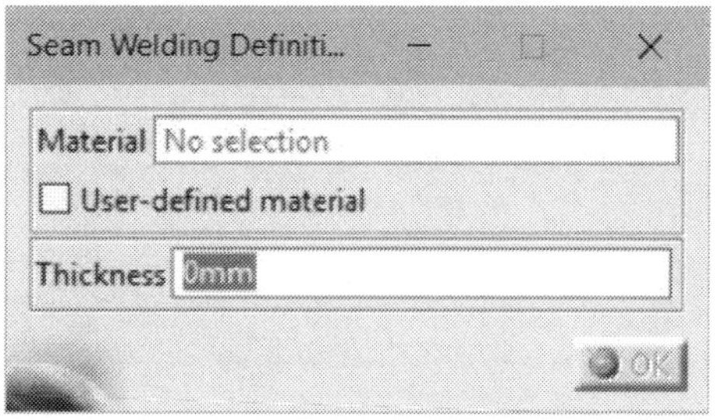

Figure 9–103

7. Toggle on the **User-defined material** checkbox and select the **WeldMaterial** in the tree. The Seam Welding Definition dialog box displays as shown in Figure 9–104.

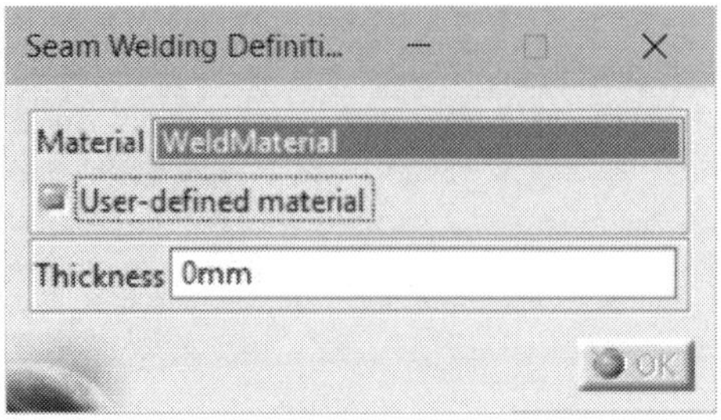

Figure 9–104

If shell elements are used to model a seam weld, the shell element thickness should be approximately equal to the average thickness of the connected parts. The hopper thickness is 10mm, while the panel thickness is 15mm. Therefore, the average thickness is 12.5mm.

8. Enter **12.5mm** as the *Thickness*, as shown in Figure 9–105.

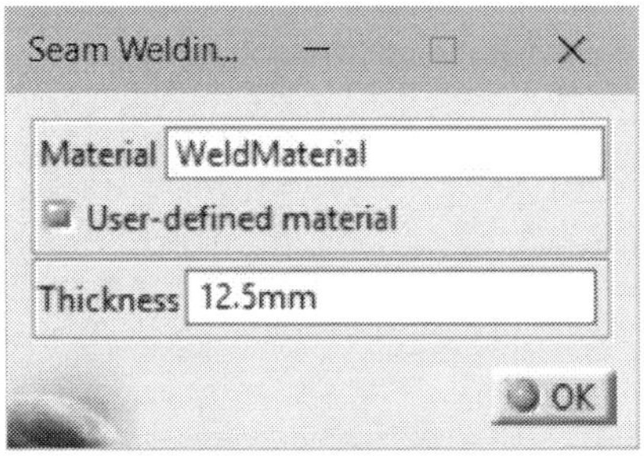

Figure 9–105

9. Click **OK** twice to close both the Seam Welding Definition and Seam Welding Connection Property dialog boxes. The new **Seam Welding Connection Property.1** and **Seam Welding Connection Mesh.1** display in the tree, as shown in Figure 9–106.

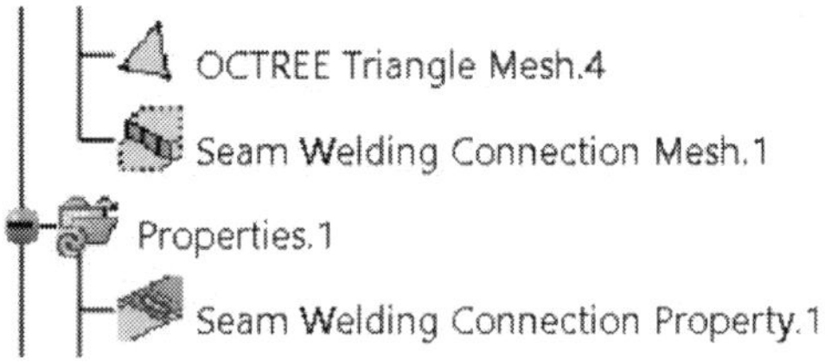

Figure 9–106

10. Double-click on **Seam Welding Connection Mesh.1** in the tree. In the Seam Welding Connection Mesh dialog box that opens, enter **20mm** as the *Maximal gap* and **100mm** as the *Mesh step*, as shown in Figure 9–107.

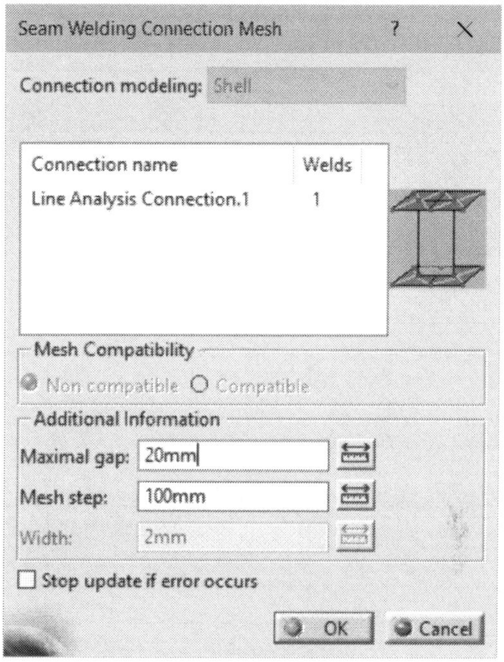

Figure 9–107

- The **Maximal gap** value should be equal or greater than the distance between the part surfaces connected with the seam weld.
- The **Mesh step** should be approximately the same as the mesh size for the connected parts.

11. Click **OK** to close the Seam Welding Connection Mesh dialog box.

Task 11 - Create spot welding analysis connections.

1. In the Analysis Supports toolbar, select  (Point Analysis Connection). The Point Analysis Connection dialog box opens, as shown in Figure 9–108.

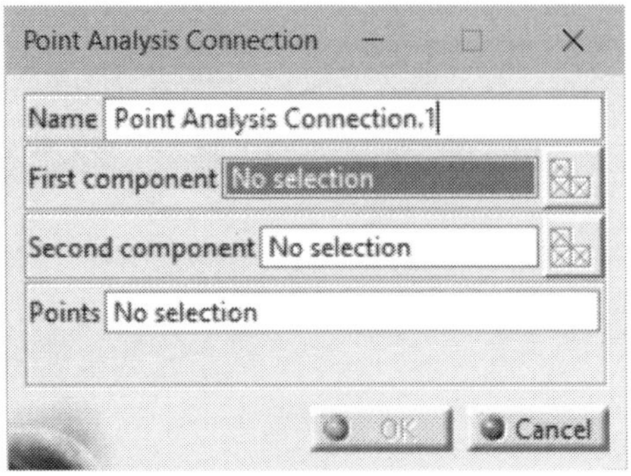

Figure 9–108

2. Select the stiffener surface as the *First component*, the panel surface as the *Second component*, and any one of the points on the stiffener as the *Points*, as shown in Figure 9–109.

   Note that selecting one point in fact selects all points in the geometrical set.

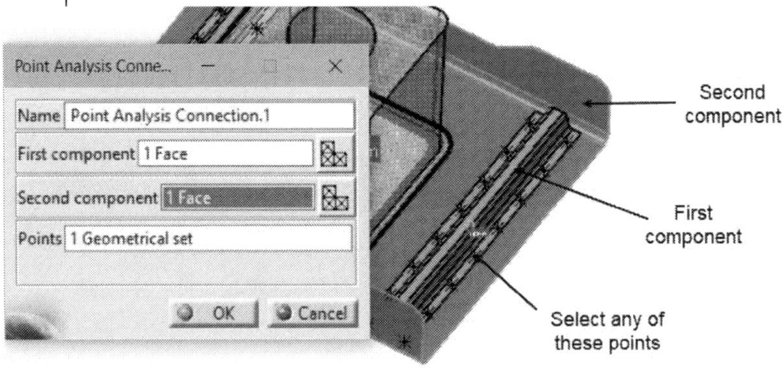

Figure 9–109

3. Click **OK** to finish. The new **Point Analysis Connection.1** is created and displayed in the tree, as shown in Figure 9–110.

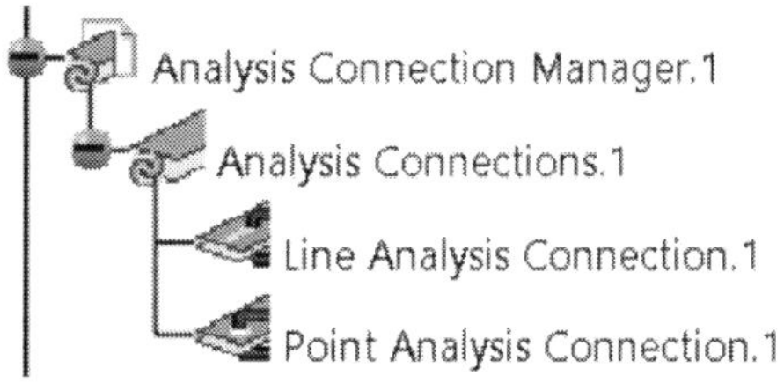

Figure 9–110

4. In the Connection Properties toolbar, select  (Spot Welding Connection Property). The Spot Welding Connection Property dialog box opens, as shown in Figure 9–111.

Figure 9–111

5. Select **Point Analysis Connection.1** as the *Supports* and select **Hexahedron** in the Type drop-down list, as shown in Figure 9–112.

Figure 9–112

6. Click the  (Component edition) button. The Spot Welding Definition dialog box opens, as shown in Figure 9–113.

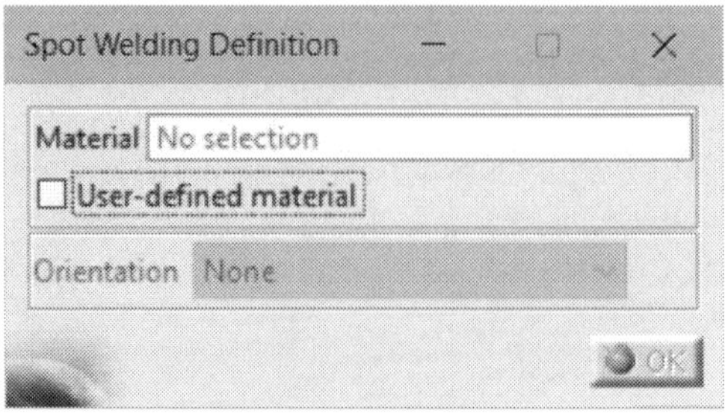

Figure 9–113

7. Toggle on the **User-defined material** checkbox and select the **WeldMaterial** in the tree. The Spot Welding Definition dialog box displays as shown in Figure 9–114.

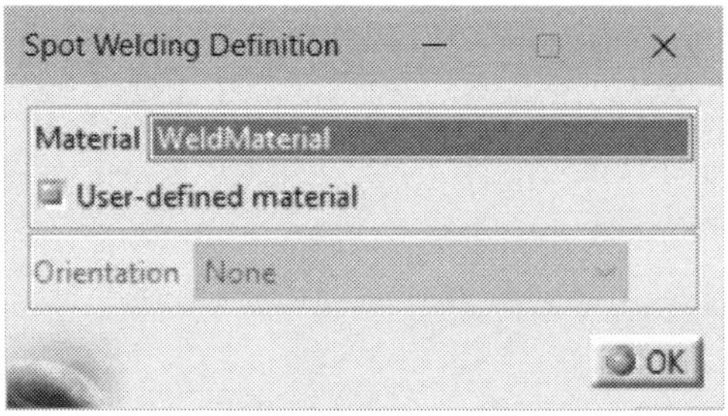

Figure 9–114

8. Click **OK** twice to close both the Spot Welding Definition and Spot Welding Connection Property dialog boxes. The new **Spot Welding Connection Property.1** and **Spot Welding Connection Mesh.1** display in the tree, as shown in Figure 9–115.

Figure 9–115

*The **Maximal gap** value should be equal or greater than the distance between the part surfaces connected with the spot weld.*

9. Double-click on **Spot Welding Connection Mesh.1** in the tree. In the Spot Welding Connection Mesh dialog box that opens, enter **20mm** as the *Maximal gap* and **40mm** as the *Diameter*, as shown in Figure 9–116.

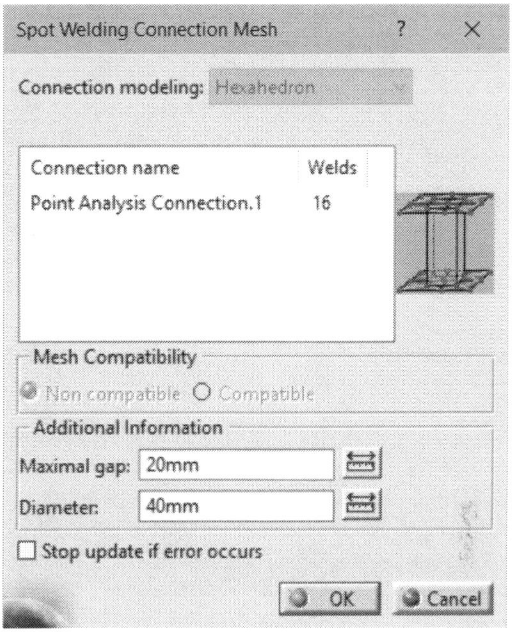

Figure 9–116

10. Click **OK** to close the Spot Welding Connection Mesh dialog box.

11. Using Steps 1 to 10 as a guideline, create a spot welding connection for the second stiffener.

Task 12 - Visualize welding connection meshes.

1. Hide both the **Analysis Connection Manager.1** and **Properties.1** objects in the tree to de-clutter the model view.

2. Select **Seam Welding Connection Mesh.1** in the tree. Right-click, select **Properties**, and change the fill color to **bright green**.

3. Select both **Spot Welding Connection Mesh.1** and **Spot Welding Connection Mesh.2** in the tree. Right-click, select **Properties**, and change the fill color to **pink**.

4. Right-click on **Nodes and Elements** in the tree and select **Mesh Visualization** to display the mesh, as shown in Figure 9–117.

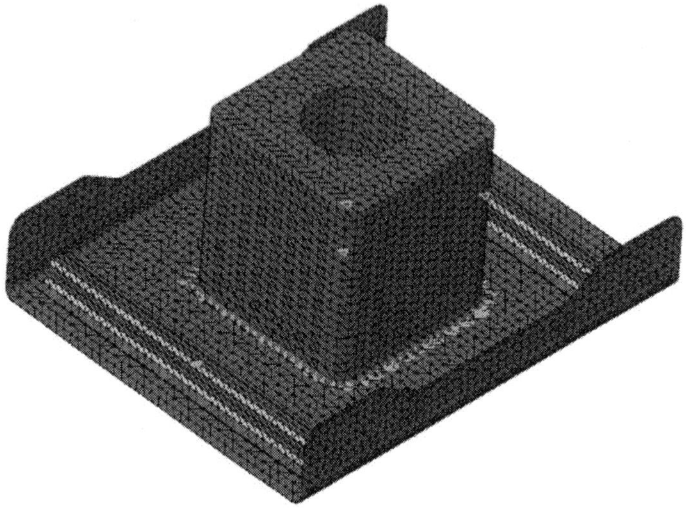

Figure 9–117

5. Double-click on **Mesh.1** in the tree. In the Image Edition dialog box that opens, activate the *Selections* tab and move **OCTREE Triangle Mesh.1**, **Seam Welding Connection Mesh.1**, **Spot Welding Connection Mesh.1**, and **Spot Welding Connection Mesh.2** into the *Activated Groups* section, as shown in Figure 9–118.

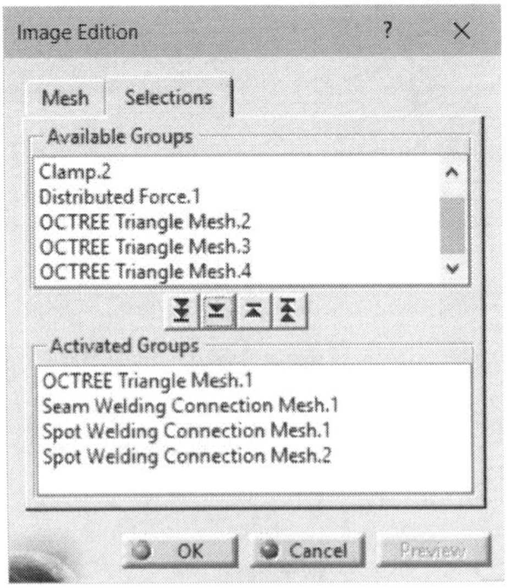

Figure 9–118

6. Click **OK**. Now the mesh is only displayed for the panel part and for the welding connections, as shown in Figure 9–119. Zoom in on the connections meshes and note that the seam weld is modeled with shell elements (colored in bright green) while the spot welds are modeled with hexahedron elements (colored in pink).

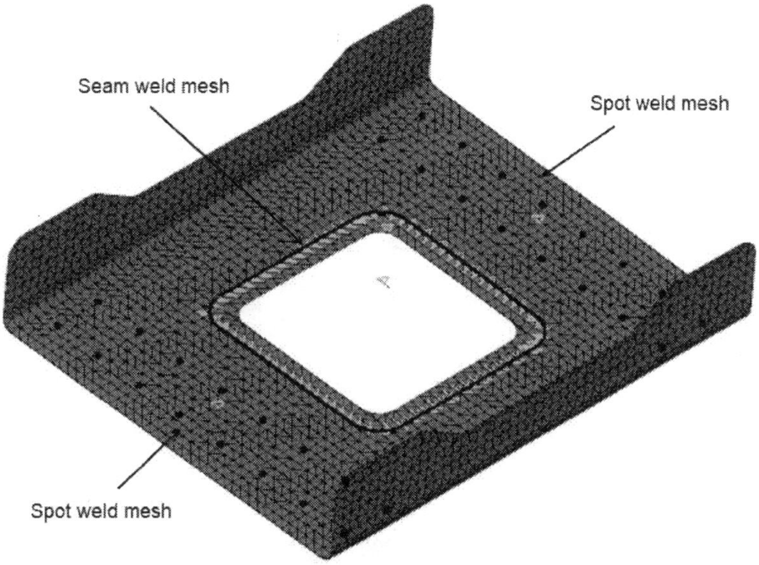

Figure 9–119

7. Right-click on **Mesh.1** in the tree and select **Delete** to delete the mesh image and return to the model view.

Task 13 - Apply the restraints.

1. Apply the (Clamp) restraint to the two flange surfaces on the panel part, as shown in Figure 9–120.

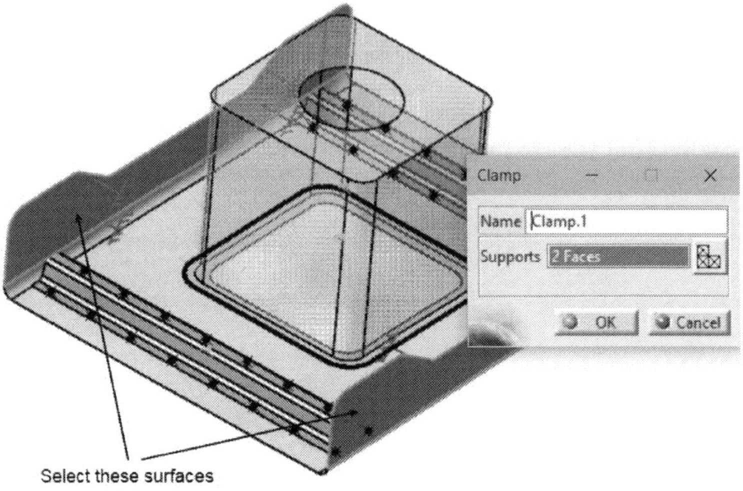

Figure 9–120

Task 14 - Apply the load.

1. Apply (Distributed Force) **10000N** in the **Z**-direction to the top surface of the hopper, as shown in Figure 9–121.

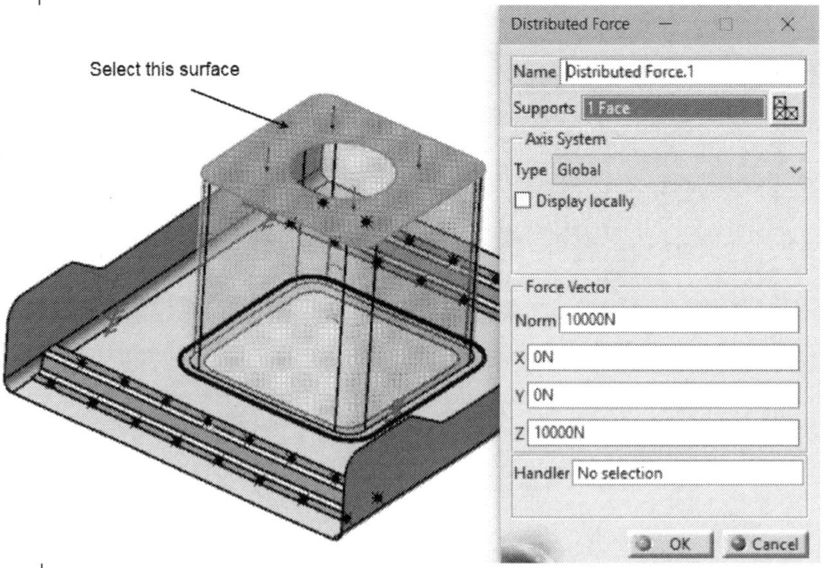

Figure 9–121

Task 15 - Run the analysis.

1. Select (Compute) and run the computation.

Task 16 - Visualize the displacement magnitude.

1. Change the view mode to (Shading with Material).

2. Select (Displacement) to display the displacement vector image, as shown in Figure 9–122.

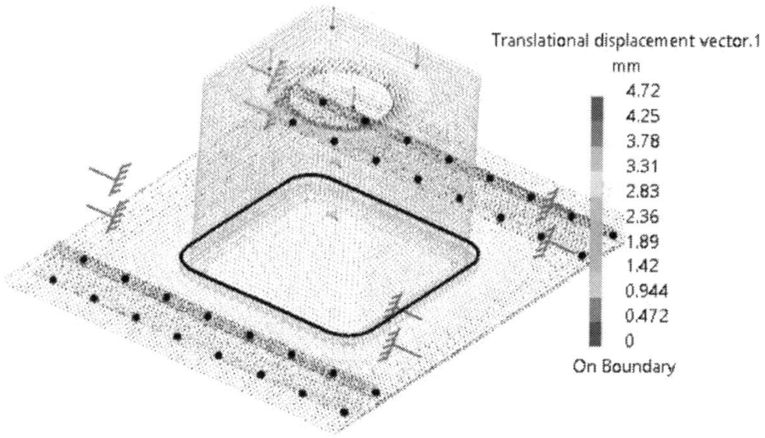

Figure 9–122

3. Double-click on the **Translational displacement vector.1** object in the tree. In the Image Edition dialog box that opens, select **Average iso** in the *Types* list and click **OK**. The displacement magnitude result is displayed, as shown in Figure 9–123. Note that the maximum displacement **4.72mm** occurs at the top of the hopper.

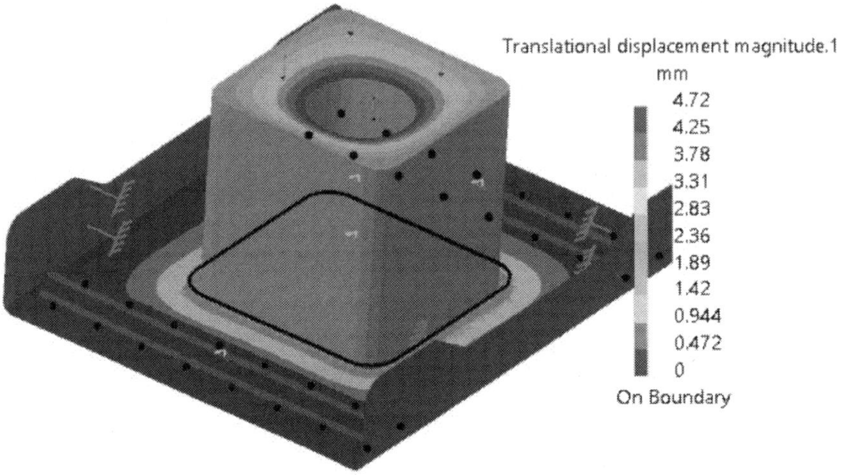

Figure 9–123

4. Animate the displacements. Does the model deform according to the applied loads and restraints?

Task 17 - Display the stresses.

1. Select (Von Mises Stress). The stress image displays, as shown in Figure 9–124.

Figure 9–124

2. Using the  (Image Extrema) tool, locate the maximum stress in the model, as shown in Figure 9–125. Note that the maximum stress occurs at one of the spot welds at the end of the stiffener part.

Figure 9–125

3. Right-click on **Von Mises stress (nodal values).1** and select **Activate/Deactivate** to deactivate the stress image and return to the model view.

Task 18 - Save and close the files.

1. Optionally, save the analysis document and the assembly for future reference.

2. Close both the analysis and the product documents.

Chapter 10

Frequency Analysis

A frequency analysis helps you to determine the natural frequencies and natural modes of vibration for a model. These factors are important for models that are subjected to cyclic or vibration loads, because resonance occurs at vibrational loads that are at or close to the natural frequencies for the model.

Learning Objectives in This Chapter

- Understand the natural frequency and natural mode of vibration.
- Review the frequency analysis equation.
- Set up a frequency analysis.
- Create non-structural masses.
- Display the frequency analysis results.

10.1 Natural Frequency

All objects vibrate when hit, struck, plucked, or otherwise disturbed. When an object vibrates, it tends to do so at a specific frequency or set of frequencies. For example, it could be a guitar string or a tuning fork.

The frequency (or frequencies) at which an object tends to vibrate when disturbed is called the *characteristic* or *natural frequency* of the object.

Natural frequencies are numbered (1st, 2nd, 3rd, etc.), with the 1st natural frequency being the lowest. The 1st natural frequency is sometimes called the *fundamental frequency* of an object.

If a dynamic load is applied to a model close to its natural frequency, the model exhibits a larger than normal oscillation. This phenomenon is called *resonance*. Without correct damping, the resonance can become uncontrollable and cause the model to collapse.

Frequency analysis predicts the natural frequencies of your model so that you can determine whether the applied dynamic loads might cause resonance. The results of a modal analysis also help to determine whether a model requires redesign, such as more or less damping to prevent failure.

10.2 Frequency Analysis Equation

The equation solved in a frequency analysis is the equation of dynamic equilibrium (i.e., Newton's equation) with neither damping nor external loads included. In matrix notation, the equation is written as follows:

$$[M] \cdot \ddot{u} + [K] \cdot u = 0 \qquad (10.1)$$

The first member in the equation represents the inertia force (i.e., mass times acceleration), while the second member represents the resistance force (i.e., stiffness times displacement).

Note that no external loads are included in the equation. Indeed, the magnitude of the external force that causes the vibration does not affect the vibration frequency. Consider the example of a tuning fork. Whether barely hit or hit hard, the tuning fork emits the same sound tone (i.e., the same frequency).

If equation (10.1) is solved for one mass, one degree of freedom system shown in Figure 10–1, the solution produces the well-known equation for the natural frequency ω:

$$\omega = \sqrt{K/_{M}} \qquad (10.2)$$

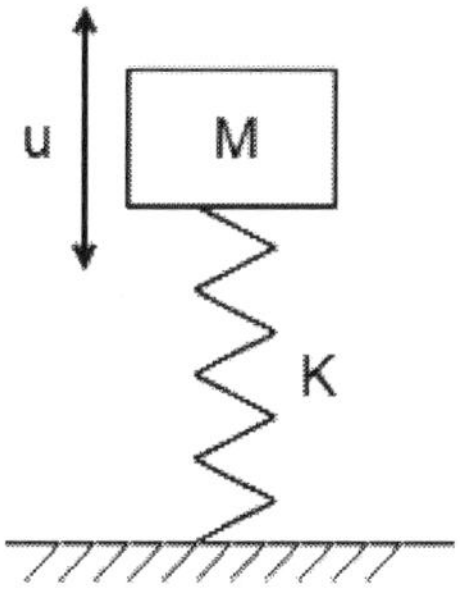

Figure 10–1

It follows from equation (10.2) that when dealing with unwanted resonance, you have two major variables at your disposal – stiffness and mass. To raise the natural frequency, the system should be designed stiffer and lighter. Alternatively, to lower the natural frequency, the system should be designed more flexible and heavier.

10.3 Natural Modes

An object vibrating at a natural frequency creates a physical deformation, or shape, of the object. This shape is called the *natural mode* of vibration.

Using frequency analysis, you can visualize these shapes and the frequency that is associated with them. Two mode shapes are shown in Figure 10–2. By viewing mode shapes, you can determine how a part reacts to different frequencies of vibration.

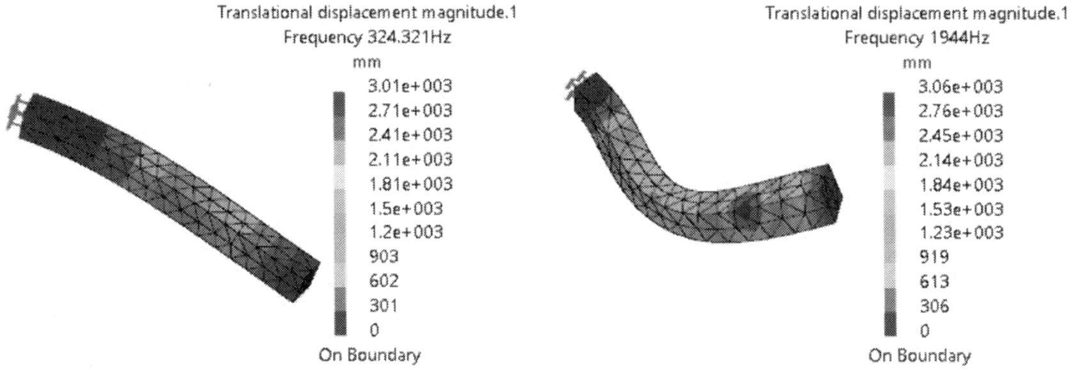

Figure 10–2

Since no external loads are included in the analysis, the displayed natural modes are essentially dimensionless. When mode shapes display in GSA, only some imaginary magnitudes display, scaled to an arbitrary value.

10.4 Creating a Frequency Analysis Case

A frequency analysis is the type of analysis that allows solving models without restraints. This is called free frequency analysis in GSA.

To create either a frequency analysis or a free frequency analysis, select the appropriate option in the New Analysis Case dialog box upon starting the GSA workbench, as shown in Figure 10–3.

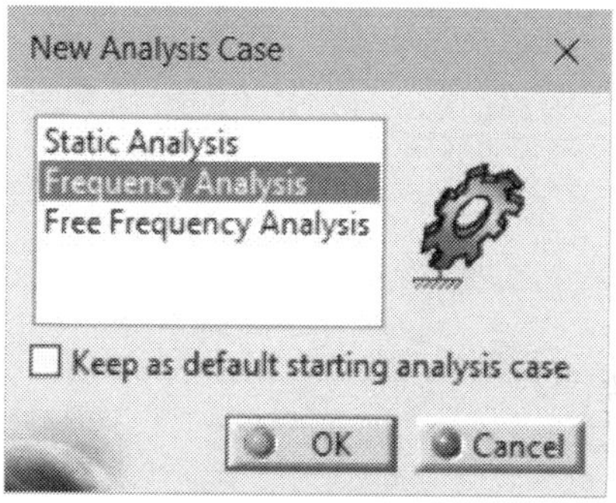

Figure 10–3

Alternatively, you can create a new frequency case from within the GSA workbench by selecting **Insert>Frequency Case**, as shown in Figure 10–4.

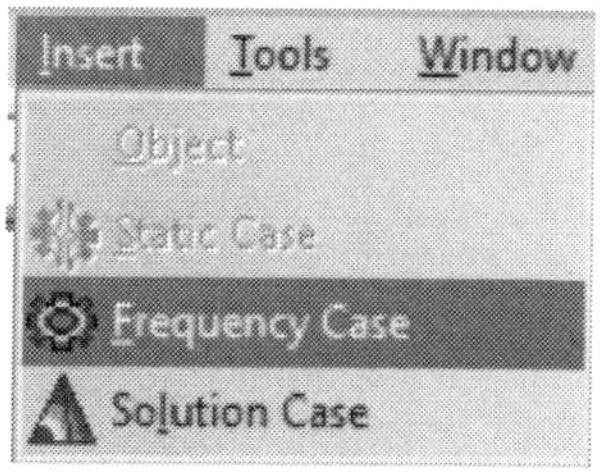

Figure 10–4

The default number of frequencies and modes that CATIA computes for a frequency analysis is **10**. To request a different number of frequencies and modes, double-click on **Frequency Case Solution.1** in the tree to open the Frequency Solution Parameters dialog box, as shown in Figure 10–5.

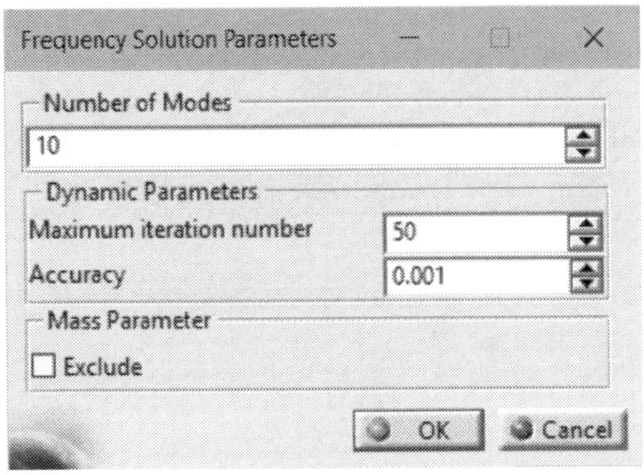

Figure 10–5

10.5 Non-Structural Masses

It follows from equation (10.2) that non-structural masses (i.e., those that do not affect the stiffness of the product) must also be included in the model for an accurate frequency analysis.

Consider the example of simulating the dynamic behavior of a pickup truck. The frame of the truck is the main structural element that ensures necessary stiffness and structural integrity of the vehicle. As such, the frame should be accurately modeled with a detailed finite element mesh.

At the same time, there are also many non-structural parts mounted on the frame, such as the engine, gas tank, etc. The non-structural parts could be modeled in the analysis as lumped masses placed at their center of gravity and attached to the frame with, for example, virtual parts.

The GSA workbench offers the following options for modeling of non-structural masses: distributed mass, line mass density, and surface mass density.

Distributed Mass

A distributed mass applies a lumped mass to a geometrical entity or to a virtual part.

To create a distributed mass, select  (Distributed Mass) in the Masses toolbar. In the Distributed Mass dialog box that opens, select the *Supports* and enter the *Mass* value, as shown in Figure 10–6.

Figure 10–6

Line Mass Density

A line mass density applies a linear mass intensity, as mass per unit length, to an edge of a curve. For example, a line mass density could be used to account for the mass of the insulation when analyzing cable structures.

To create a line mass density, select  (Line Mass Density) in the Masses toolbar. In the Line Mass Density dialog box that opens, select the *Supports* and enter the *Line Mass Density* value, as shown in Figure 10–7.

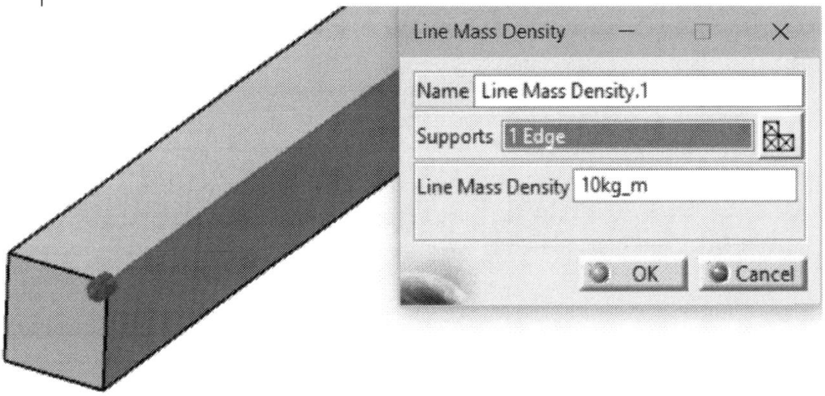

Figure 10–7

Surface Mass Density

A surface mass density applies a mass intensity, as mass per unit area, to a surface. For example, a surface mass density could be used to account for the mass of the copper conductor in the vibration analysis of printed circuit boards.

To create a surface mass density, select (Surface Mass Density) in the Masses toolbar. In the Surface Mass Density dialog box that opens, select the *Supports* and enter the *Surface Mass density* value, as shown in Figure 10–8.

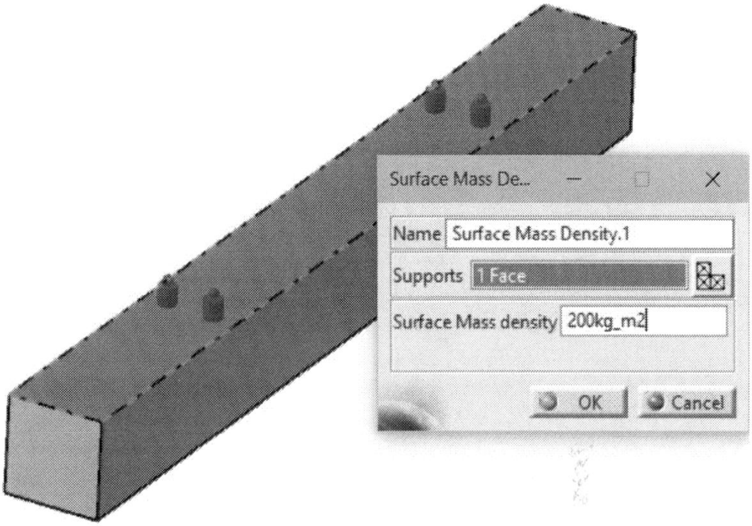

Figure 10–8

10.6 Result Visualization

Once the frequency analysis is completed, CATIA creates a list of computed frequencies in the **Sensors.1** section in the tree, as shown in Figure 10–9.

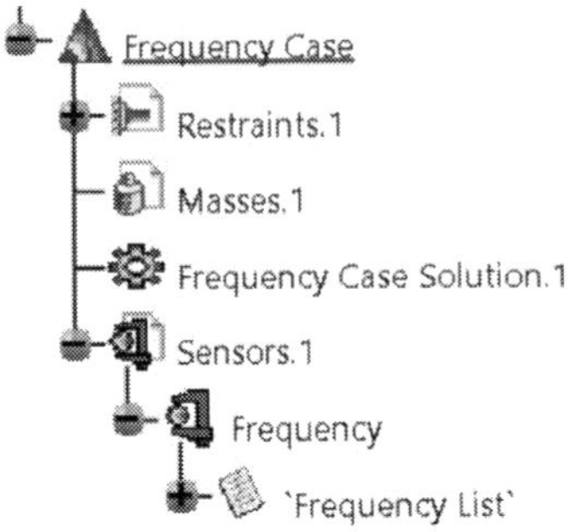

Figure 10–9

Double-click on **Frequency List** in the tree to display the values of the frequencies, as shown in Figure 10–10.

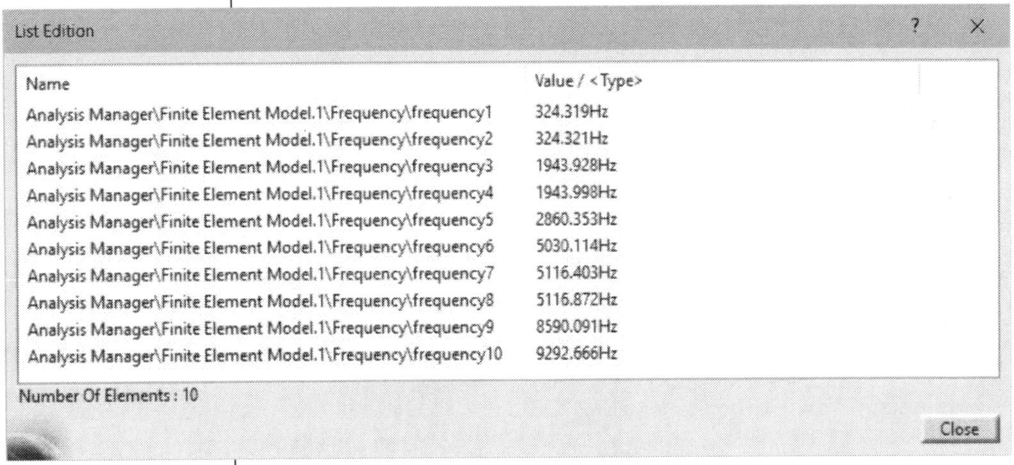

Figure 10–10

To display the natural modes, create any result image (such as deformation, displacement, or Von Mises stress). Double-click on the image object in the tree to open the Image Edition dialog box and switch to the *Occurrences* tab to display the list of modes and frequencies, as shown in Figure 10–11.

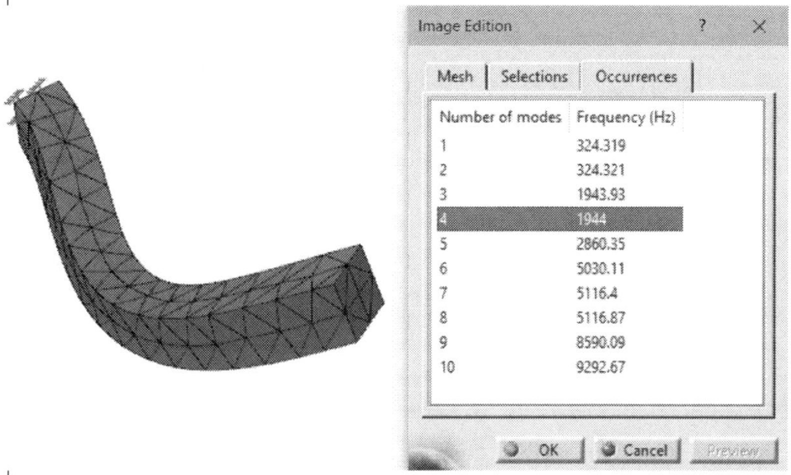

Figure 10–11

Selecting a mode in the list will display the result image for that mode.

Practice 10a Frequency Analysis of a Bracket

Practice Objectives

- Set up and run a frequency analysis.
- Display the results.

In this practice, you will set up and run a frequency analysis on the bracket model shown in Figure 10–12.

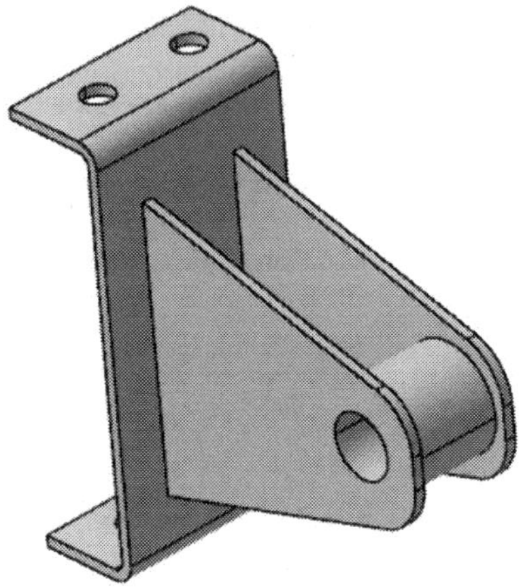

Figure 10–12

Task 1 - Open the part in CATIA.

1. Open **Bracket_10.CATPart** from the *CATIA Generative Structural Analysis Practice Files\Ch10* folder.

2. Set the model display as  (Shading with Edges). The part displays as shown in Figure 10–13.

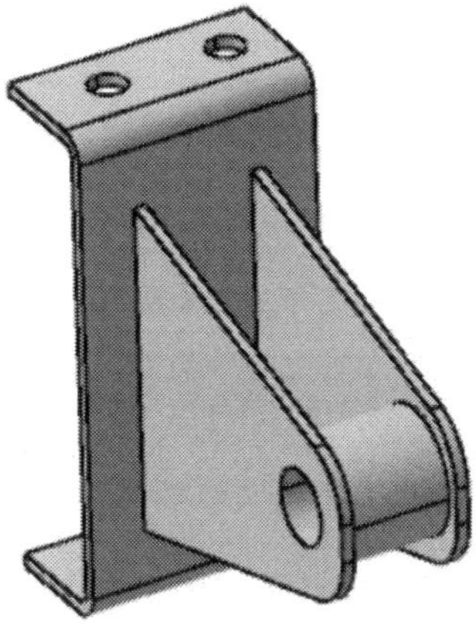

Figure 10–13

3. Select **Tools>Options>Parameters and Measures>Units** and set the units as follows:

   - Length: **Millimeter (mm)**
   - Force: **Newton (N)**
   - Moment: **Newton x Meter (Nxm)**
   - Pressure: **Megapascal (MPa)**

Task 2 - Apply the material.

1. Apply **Steel** to the part.

Task 3 - Launch the GSA workbench.

1. Select **Start>Analysis & Simulation>Generative Structural Analysis**

2. In the New Analysis Case dialog box, select **Frequency Analysis** and click **OK**, as shown in Figure 10–14.

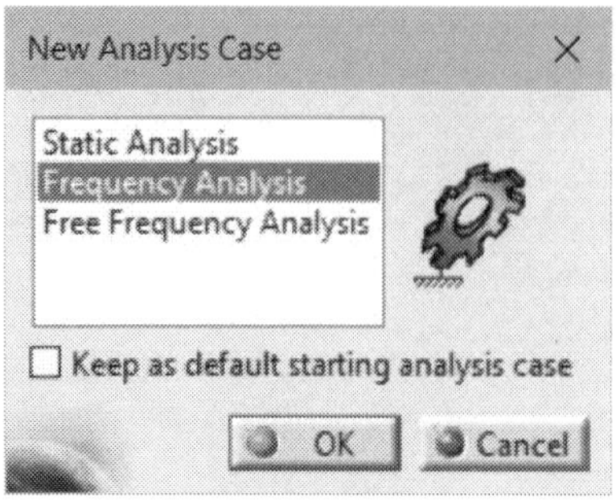

Figure 10–14

Task 4 - Mesh the part.

1. Measure the thickness of the part, as shown in Figure 10–15.

Figure 10–15

A size of 9mm is 1.8 times the thickness of the part, which is the recommended ratio for thin-walled parts. A sag of 1.8mm is 20% of the size, which is the rule of thumb for most of the parts.

2. Double-click on **OCTREE Tetrahedron Mesh.1: Bracket_10** in the tree. In the OCTREE Tetrahedron Mesh dialog box, select **Parabolic** as the *Element type*, enter the *Size* as **9mm** and the *Absolute sag* as **1.8mm**, as shown in Figure 10–16.

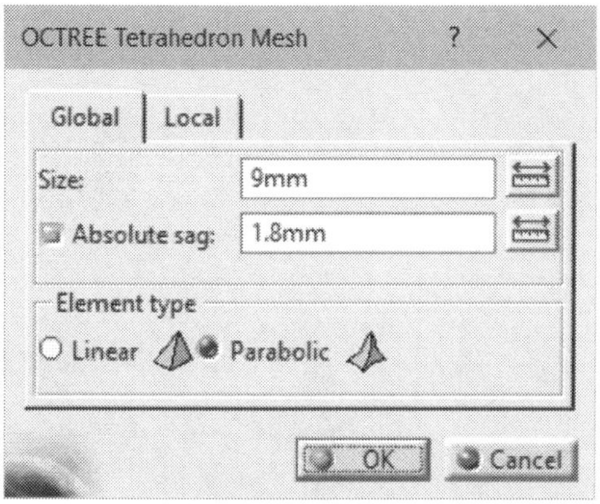

Figure 10–16

3. Click **OK** to close the OCTREE Tetrahedron Mesh dialog box.

4. Right-click on **Nodes and Elements** in the tree and select **Mesh Visualization**. The part mesh is displayed, as shown in Figure 10–17.

Figure 10–17

5. Right-click on **Mesh.1** in the tree and select **Delete** to delete the mesh visualization and return to the model view.

Task 5 - Apply the restraints.

1. Select  (Clamp) and clamp the inside surfaces of the four holes, as shown in Figure 10–18.

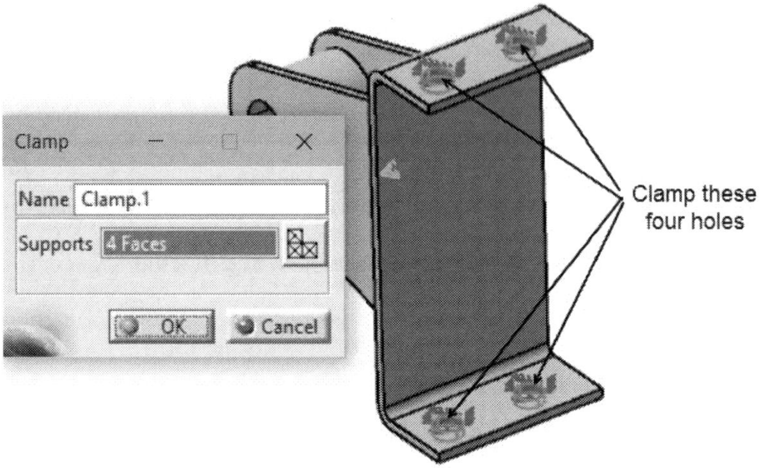

Figure 10–18

Task 6 - Request the number of modes.

1. Double-click on **Frequency Case Solution.1** in the tree. The Frequency Solution Parameters dialog box opens, as shown in Figure 10–19.

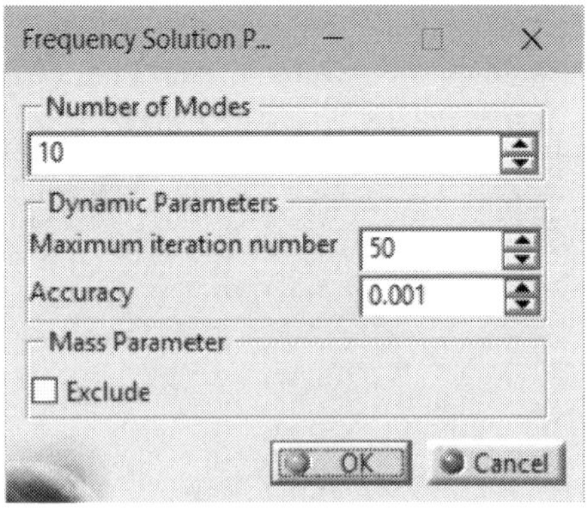

Figure 10–19

2. Enter **6** as the *Number of Modes* and leave all other solution parameters at their default values, as shown in Figure 10–20.

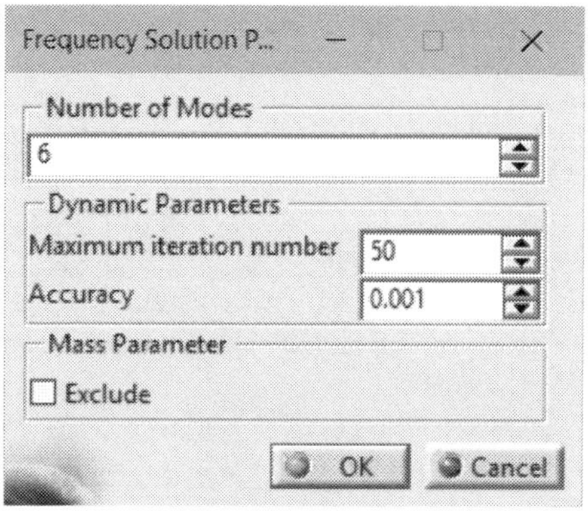

Figure 10–20

3. Click **OK** to close the Frequency Solution Parameters dialog box.

Task 7 - Run the analysis.

1. Select (Compute) and run the analysis. Wait until the computation completes, which should take a few seconds.

Task 8 - Display the natural frequencies.

1. Expand the **Sensors.1** object in the tree. Note that there is the **Frequency List** object, as shown in Figure 10–21.

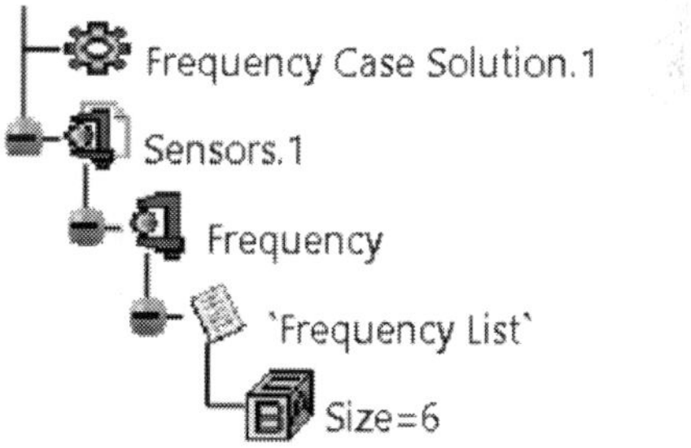

Figure 10–21

2. Double-click on **Frequency List** in the tree. The List Edition dialog box displays, listing all the computed natural frequencies, as shown in Figure 10–22.

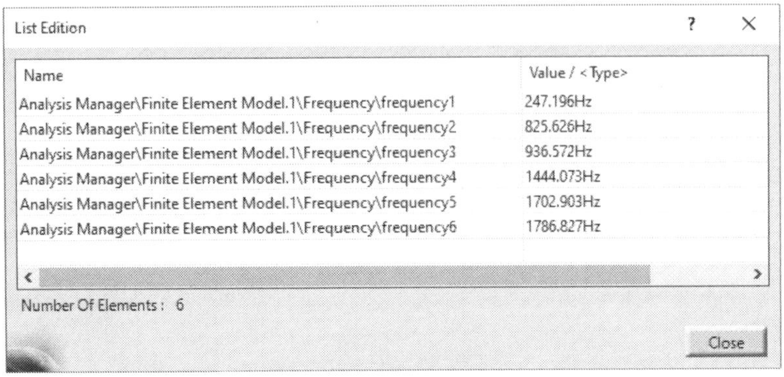

Figure 10–22

3. Click **Close** to close the List Edition dialog box.

Task 9 - Display and animate the natural modes.

1. Select  (Deformation). The deformation image for the first natural mode displays, as shown in Figure 10–23.

Figure 10–23

2. Animate the deformation. Note that the first natural mode of vibration causes bending of the bracket in the horizontal direction.

3. Double-click on **Deformed mesh.1** in the tree. In the Image Edition dialog box, activate the *Occurrences* tab and select the second mode in the list, as shown in Figure 10–24.

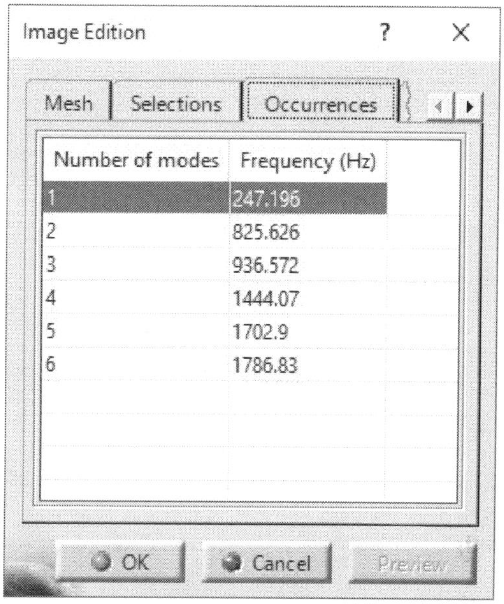

Figure 10–24

4. Click **OK**. The deformation image for the second natural mode displays, as shown in Figure 10–25.

Figure 10–25

5. Animate the deformation. Note that the second natural mode of vibration causes bending of the bracket in the vertical direction.

6. Display and animate the remaining modes of vibration. Which mode of vibration causes the twisting deformation of the bracket?

Task 10 - Save and close the files.

1. Optionally, save the analysis document and the part for future reference.

2. Close both the analysis and the part documents.

Practice 10b Frequency Analysis of a PCB Assembly

Practice Objectives

- Create the mid-surface and the shell mesh.
- Create a rigid virtual part and distributed mass.
- Set up and run a frequency analysis.
- Display the results.

In this practice, you will set up and run a frequency analysis on the assembly shown in Figure 10–26.

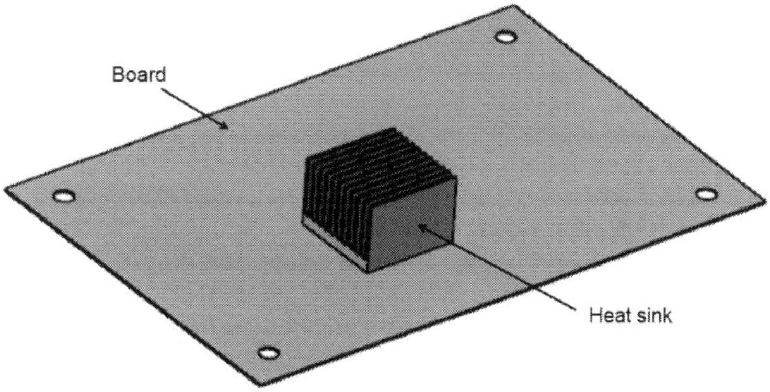

Figure 10–26

The assembly consists of two parts – a printed circuit board (PCB) made of plastic and a heat sink made of aluminum. The electronics chip between the heat sink and the board has negligible mass and is omitted in the analysis; therefore, the heat sink is assumed to be bonded to the PCB over their contacting area.

During the vibration, the thin PCB is expected to significantly flex, while the heat sink would be acting as a rigid body moving along with the flexing of the PCB. Given these considerations, the most efficient way to set up the analysis is to model the heat sink with a rigid virtual part with a lumped mass placed at its center of gravity (CoG), while modeling the PCB using a shell idealization.

Task 1 - Open the assembly in CATIA.

1. Open **Pcb_asm_10.CATProduct** from the *CATIA Generative Structural Analysis Practice Files\Ch10* folder.

2. Set the model display as  (Shading with Edges). The assembly displays as shown in Figure 10–27.

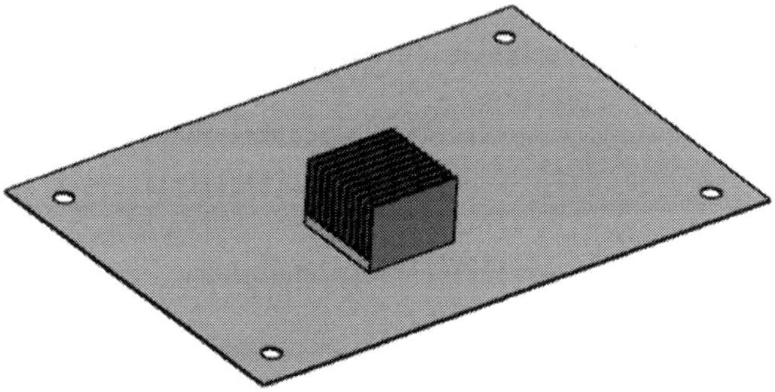

Figure 10–27

3. If you opened the assembly in Visualization mode (the toggle **Tools>Options>Infrastructure>Product Structure>Work with the cache system** is on), switch it to Design mode by right-clicking on the root assembly **PCB_ASM_10** and selecting **Representations>Design Mode** in the contextual menu.

4. Expand the model tree and note that the parts already have materials applied:

   - PCB_10: **Plastic**
   - HS_10: **Aluminium**

5. Select **Tools>Options>Parameters and Measures>Units** and set the units as follows:

   - Length: **Millimeter (mm)**
   - Force: **Newton (N)**
   - Moment: **Newton x Meter (Nxm)**
   - Pressure: **Megapascal (MPa)**

Task 2 - Create the contact patch.

In this task, you will create a surface patch for the contact area between the heat sink and the PCB. This contact patch will be used later as a support for the rigid virtual part.

1. Double-click on the **PCB_10** part in the tree to activate it and to switch to Part Design mode.
2. Make sure the **Generative Shape Design** 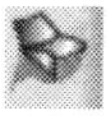 workbench is active. Otherwise, activate the workbench.
3. Create a new geometrical set (**Geometrical Set.1**).
4. In the Wireframe toolbar, select  (Projection). Project one of the four bottom edges of the heat sink onto the top surface of the PCB, as shown in Figure 10–28.

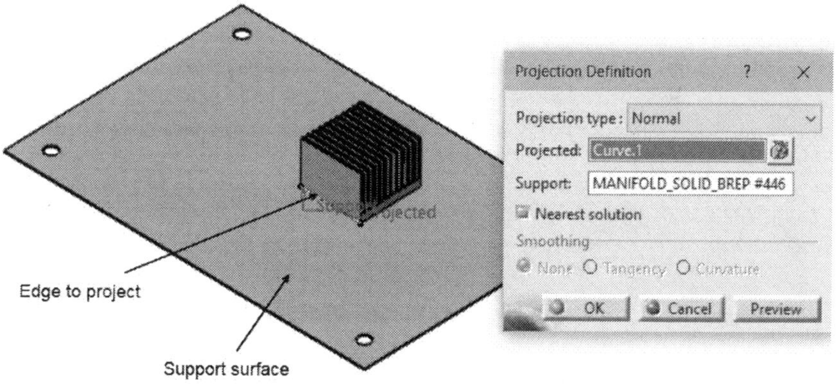

Figure 10–28

5. Project the remaining three bottom edges of the heat sink onto the PCB. Hide the heat sink part. The model displays as shown in Figure 10–29.

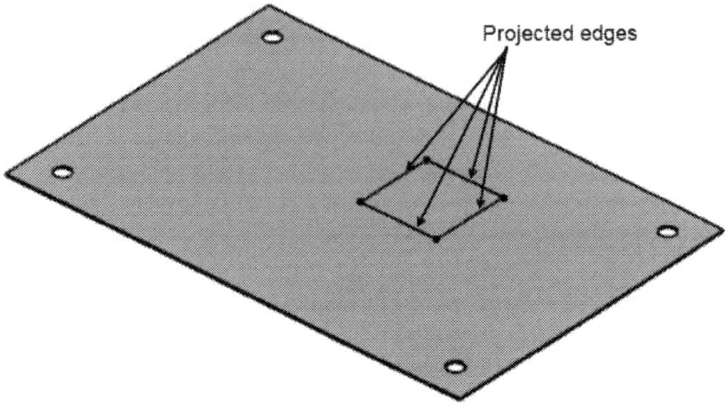

Figure 10–29

6. In the Surfaces toolbar, select (Fill). Using the four projection curves created in Steps 4 and 5, create a fill surface, as shown in Figure 10–30.

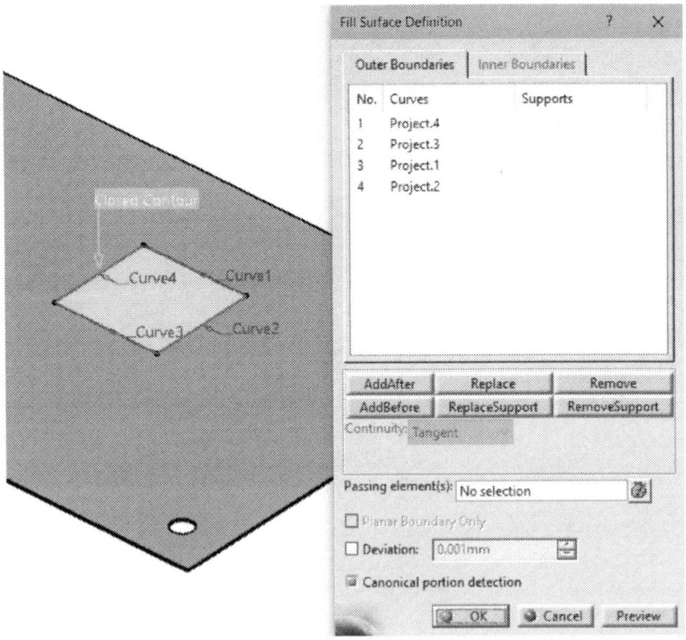

Figure 10–30

7. Switch to the **Part Design** workbench.

8. Right-click on the **PartBody** and select **Define In Work Object** in the contextual menu.

9. In the Surface-Based Features toolbar, select  (Sew Surface). In the Sew Surface Definition dialog box that opens, select **Fill.1** as the *Object to sew*, deselect the **Simplify geometry** option, and ensure that the orange arrow points toward the PCB body, as shown in Figure 10–31.

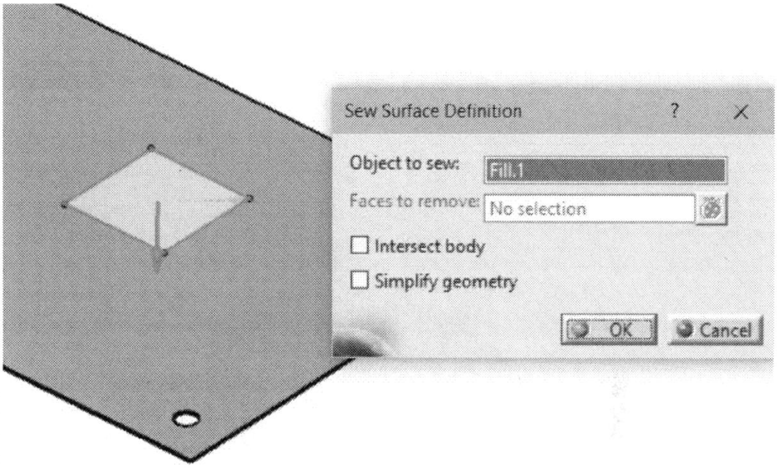

Figure 10–31

10. Click **OK** to complete the Sew Surface operation. Hide **Geometrical Set.1**. The PCB part with the contact patch displays as shown in Figure 10–32.

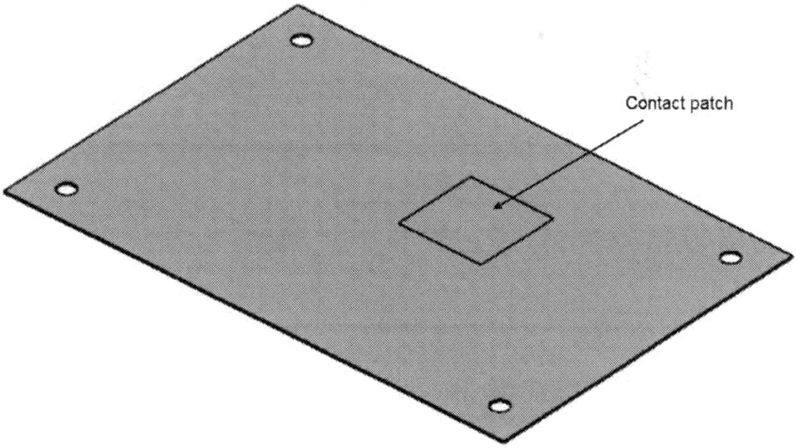

Figure 10–32

Task 3 - Create the mid-surface.

You will use the shell mesh to model the PCB. In this task, you will create the mid-surface for the PCB.

1. At this point, the **PCB-10** part must still be active and in Part Design mode. Activate the **Generative Shape Design** workbench.
2. Create a new geometrical set (**Geometrical Set.2**).
3. Using the (Extract) tool with **Tangent continuity**, extract the top surface of the PCB part, as shown in Figure 10–33.

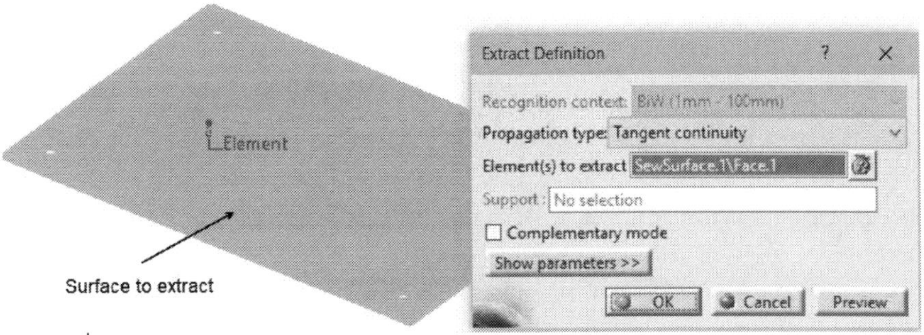

Figure 10–33

The thickness of the PCB is 1mm.

4. Using the (Offset) tool, offset the extracted surface toward the middle of the thickness of the part by **0.5mm**, as shown in Figure 10–34.

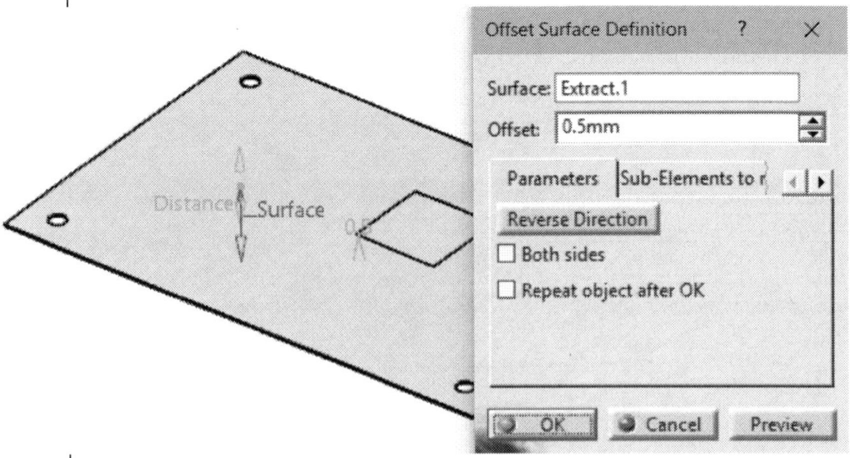

Figure 10–34

5. Hide **Extract.1** and **PartBody**. The model displays as shown in Figure 10–35.

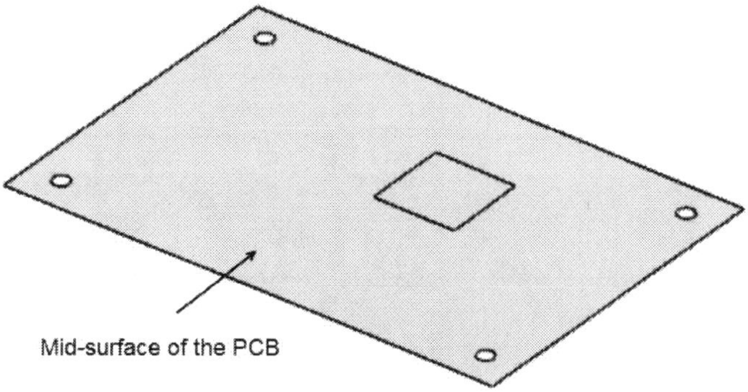

Figure 10–35

Task 4 - Obtain the mass analysis information for the heat sink.

In this task, you will measure the mass and create the CoG point for the heat sink part.

1. Unhide the **HS_10** part and hide the **PCB_10** part.
2. Double-click on the **HS_10** part in the tree to activate it and to switch to Part Design mode.
3. In the Measure toolbar, select  (Measure Inertia). The Measure Inertia dialog box opens, as shown in Figure 10–36.

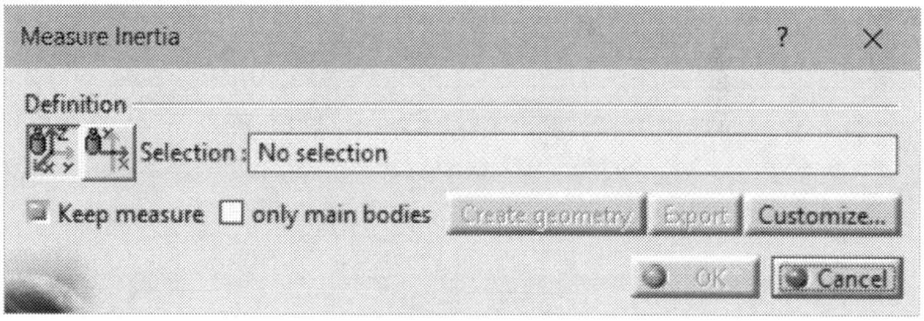

Figure 10–36

4. Click **Customize**. In the Measure Inertia Customization dialog box, select the options shown in Figure 10–37.

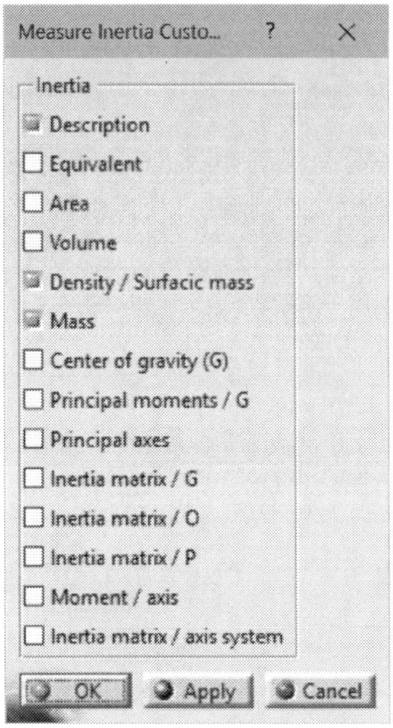

Figure 10–37

5. Click **OK** to close the Measure Inertia Customization dialog box.

6. Select the heat sink's **PartBody** in the tree and activate the **Keep measure** option. The Measure Inertia dialog box displays, as shown in Figure 10–38.

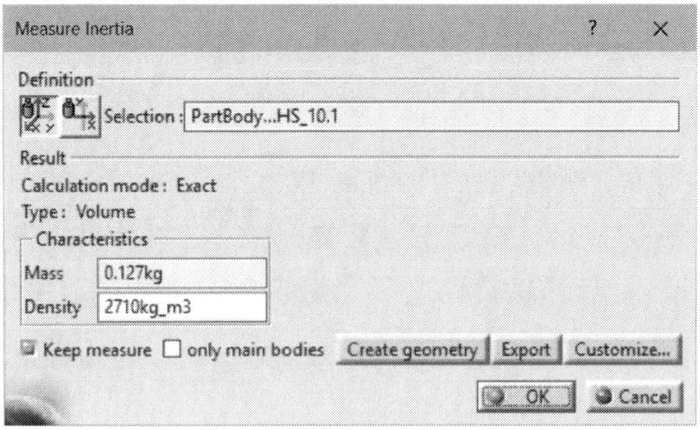

Figure 10–38

7. Click **Create geometry**. In the Creation of Geometry dialog box that opens, click **Center of gravity** and select **OK**, as shown in Figure 10–39.

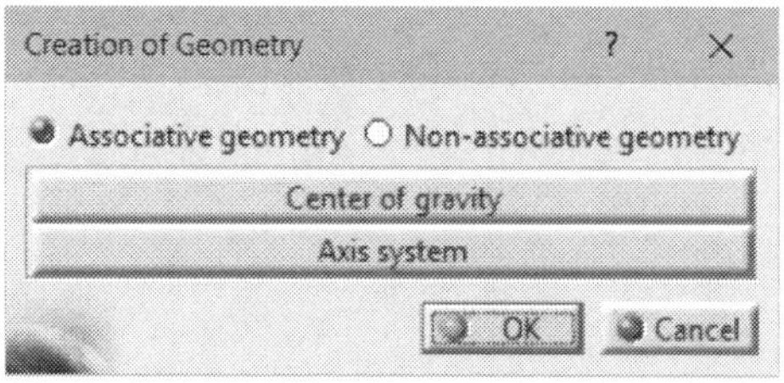

Figure 10–39

8. Click **OK** to close the Measure Inertia dialog box. CATIA creates the **Inertia Volume.1** measurement in the tree, as well as the CoG point (as shown in Figure 10–40).

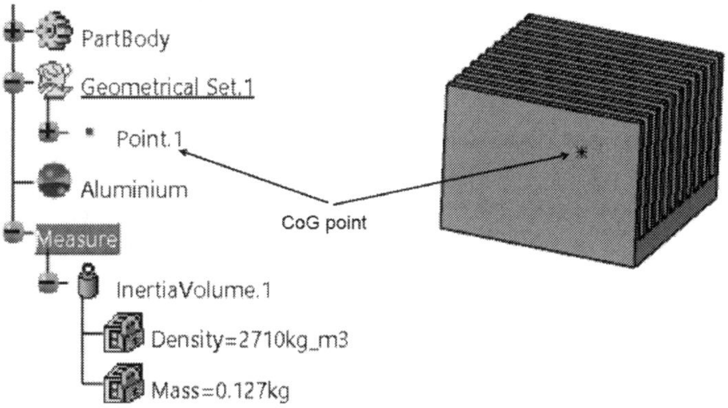

Figure 10–40

9. Hide the heat sink's **PartBody** and unhide the **PCB_10** part. Double-click on the root product **PCB_ASM_10** in the tree to activate and return to the Assembly Design mode. The model displays as shown in Figure 10–41.

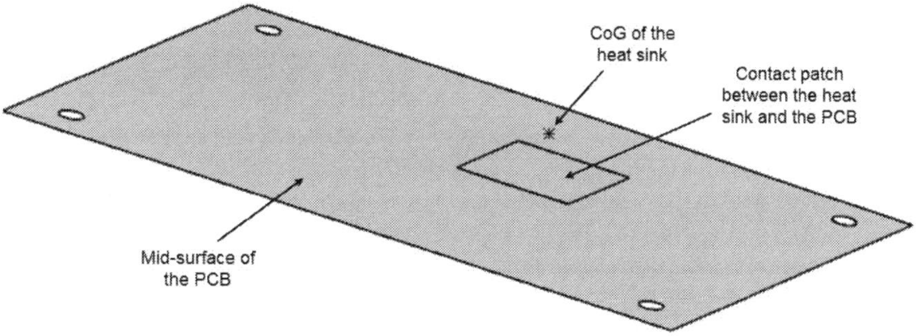

Figure 10–41

Task 5 - Launch the GSA workbench.

1. Select **Start>Analysis & Simulation>Generative Structural Analysis.**
2. In the New Analysis Case dialog box, select **Frequency Analysis** and click **OK**, as shown in Figure 10–42.

Figure 10–42

Task 6 - Create the mesh and the 2D Property.

By default, CATIA assumes that the analysis intent is to use a solid 3D mesh for the parts and automatically creates an **OCTREE Tetrahedron Mesh** and a **3D Property** for every part in the assembly. Since the heat sink part in this analysis will be simulated with a virtual part and a shell idealization will be used for the PCB part, those default meshes and 3D properties must be deleted.

1. Expand the tree and delete the following entities:
   - **OCTREE Tetrahedron Mesh.1: PCB_10.1**
   - **OCTREE Tetrahedron Mesh.2: HS_10.1**
   - **3D Property.1**
   - **3D Property.2**
2. In the Model Manager toolbar, select  (OCTREE Triangle Mesher) and select the mid-surface of the PCB part. The OCTREE Triangle Mesh dialog box opens, as shown in Figure 10–43.

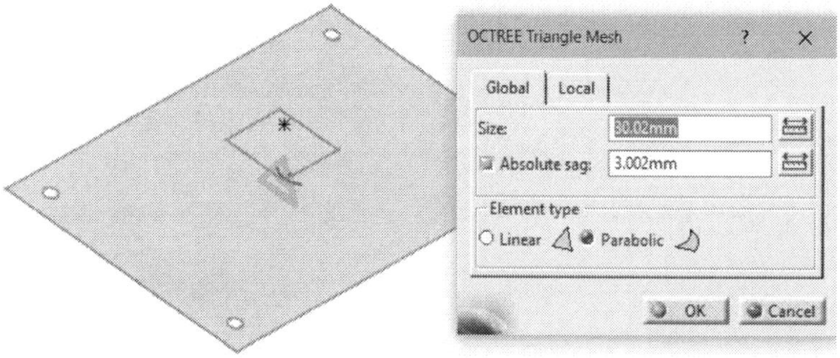

Figure 10–43

3. Ensure that the *Element type* is **Parabolic**. Enter **10mm** as the *Size* and **1mm** as the *Absolute sag*, as shown in Figure 10–44. Click **OK** to close the dialog box.

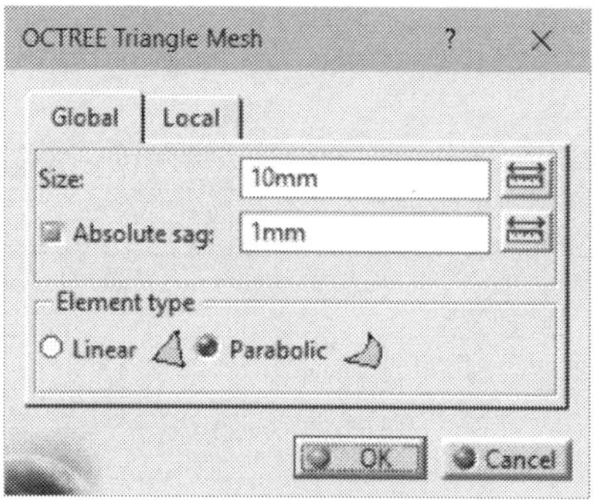

Figure 10–44

4. Right-click on **Nodes and Elements** in the tree and select **Mesh Visualization** to display the mesh, as shown in Figure 10–45.

Figure 10–45

5. Right-click on **Mesh.1** in the tree and select **Delete** to delete the mesh image and return to the model view.

6. Select  (2D Property) in the Model Manager toolbar. Once the 2D Property dialog box opens, select the mid-surface of the PCB as the *Supports* and enter **1mm** as the *Thickness*, as shown in Figure 10–46.

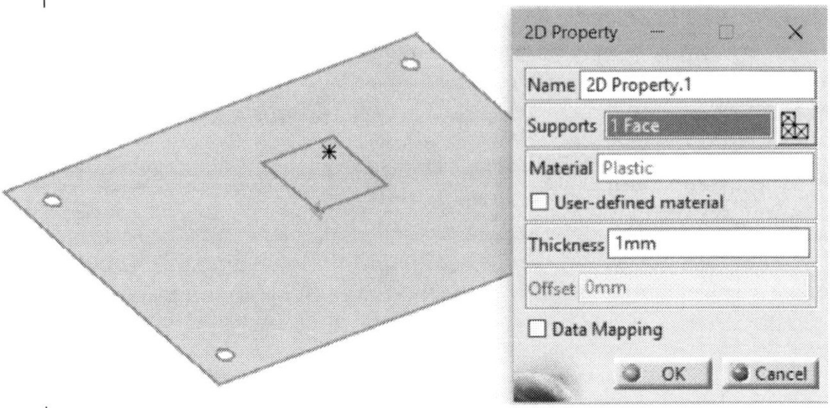

Figure 10–46

7. Click **OK** to finish.

Task 7 - Apply the restraints.

1. Select  (Clamp) and clamp the edges of the four holes in the PCB, as shown in Figure 10–47.

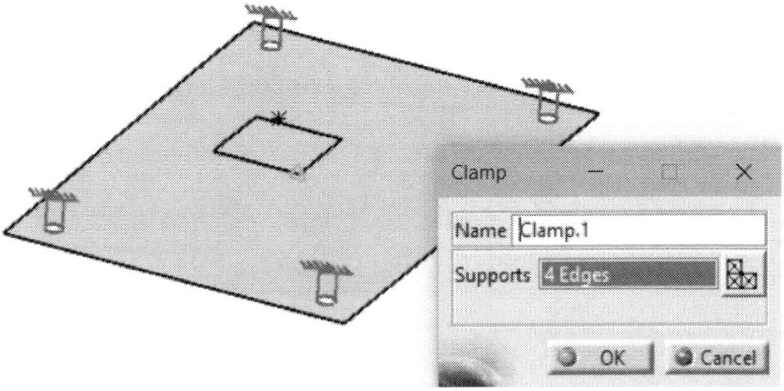

Figure 10–47

Task 8 - Create the virtual part.

In this task, you will create a rigid virtual part that simulates the heat sink in the analysis.

1. Select (Rigid Virtual Part). Once the Rigid Virtual Part dialog box opens, select the contact patch on the PCB surface as the *Supports* and the CoG point of the heat sink as the *Handler*, as shown in Figure 10–48.

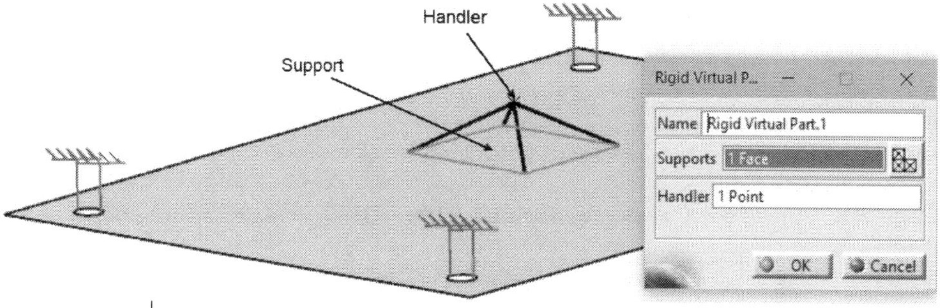

Figure 10–48

2. Click **OK** to close the Rigid Virtual Part dialog box.

Task 9 - Create the distributed mass.

The mass of the heat sink in the analysis is simulated as a lumped mass placed at the CoG of the heat sink. In this task, you will apply a distributed mass to the handler of the virtual part that models the heat sink.

1. In the Masses toolbar, select (Distributed Mass). The Distributed Mass dialog box opens, as shown in Figure 10–49.

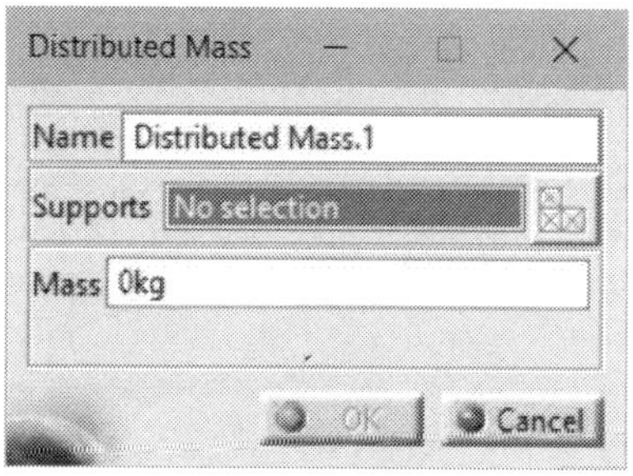

Figure 10–49

Applying a mass to a virtual part effectively applies the mass to the virtual part's handler point.

2. Select the virtual part as the *Supports*, as shown in Figure 10–50.

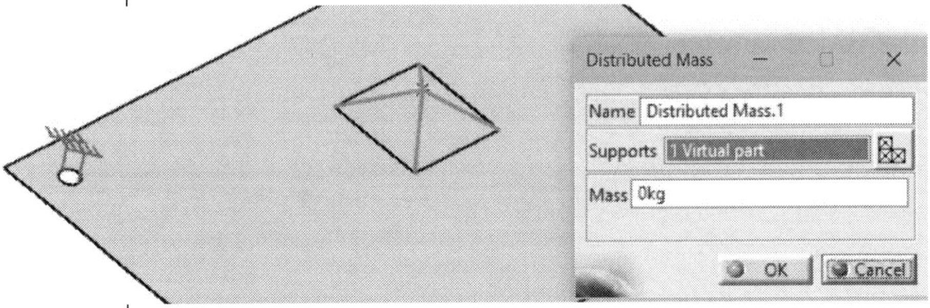

Figure 10–50

3. Right-click in the *Mass* field and select **Edit formula**, as shown in Figure 10–51.

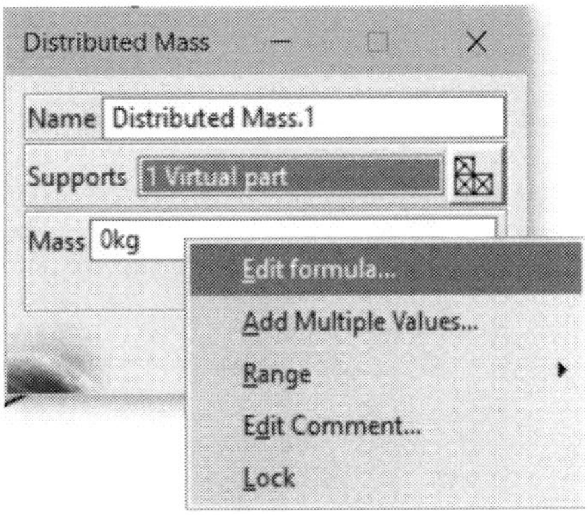

Figure 10–51

4. The Formula Editor dialog box opens, as shown in Figure 10–52.

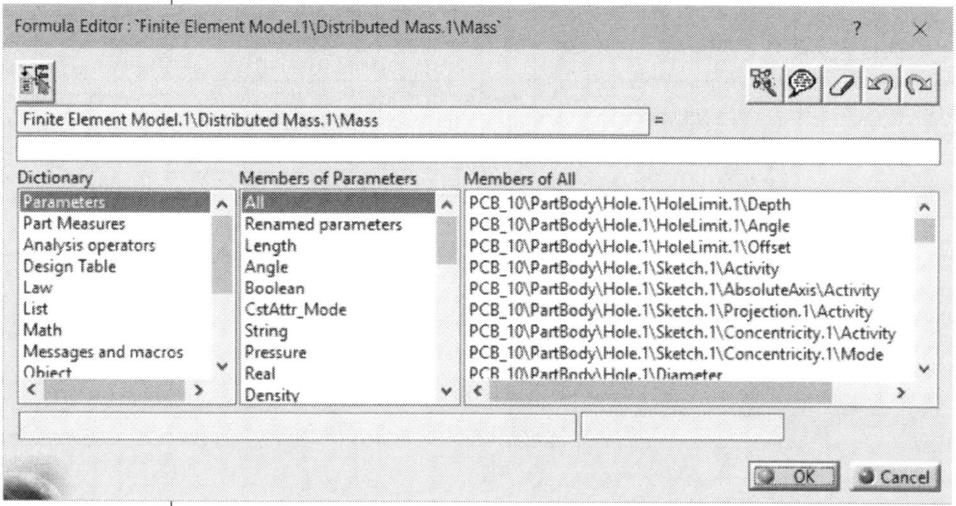

Figure 10–52

5. Expand the tree and select the **Mass** parameter in the **Inertia Volume.1** measurement in the **HS_10** part. The heat sink mass gets automatically entered into the formula, as shown in Figure 10–53.

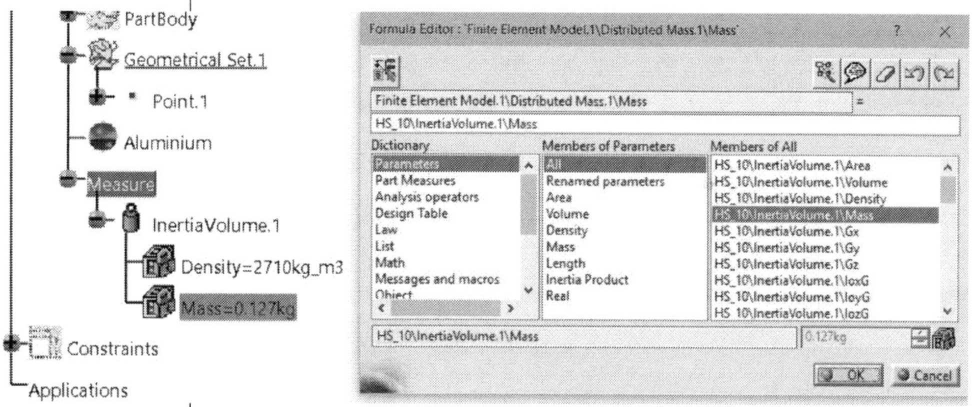

Figure 10–53

Now the distributed mass value is linked to the actual mass of the heat sink. If the heat sink design or dimensions change, the distributed mass value will update accordingly.

6. Click **OK** to close the Formula Editor dialog box. The Distributed Mass dialog box displays, as shown in Figure 10–54.

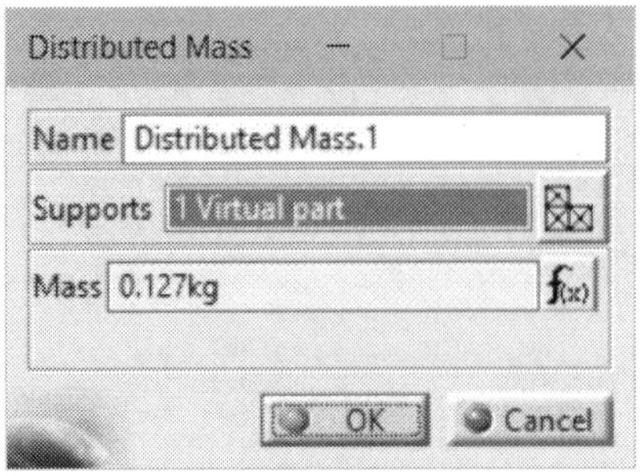

Figure 10–54

7. Click **OK** to close the Distributed Mass dialog box. The model displays as shown in Figure 10–55.

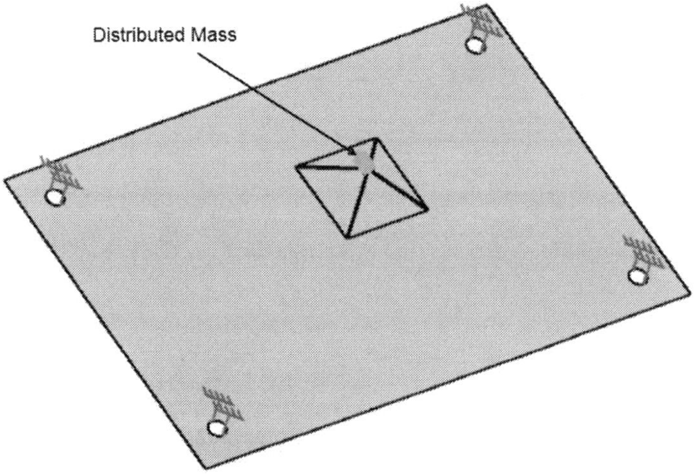

Figure 10–55

Task 10 - Specify the number of modes.

1. Double-click on **Frequency Case Solution.1** in the tree. Once the Frequency Solution Parameters dialog box opens, enter **4** as the *Number of Modes* and leave all other solution parameters at their default values, as shown in Figure 10–56.

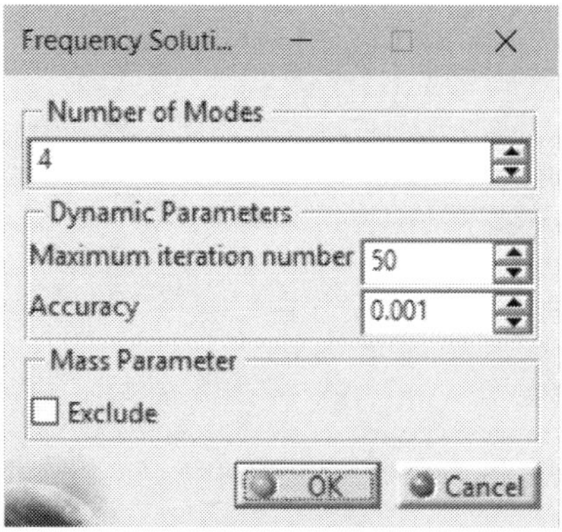

Figure 10–56

2. Click **OK** to close the Frequency Solution Parameters dialog box.

Task 11 - Run the analysis.

1. Select  (Compute) and run the analysis. Wait until the computation completes, which should take a few seconds.

Task 12 - Display the natural frequencies.

1. Expand the **Sensors.1** heading in the tree and double-click on the **Frequency List** object. The List Edition dialog box displays, listing all the computed natural frequencies, as shown in Figure 10–57.

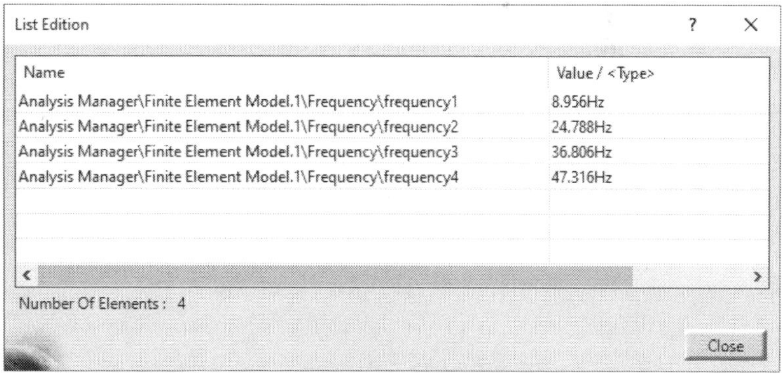

Figure 10–57

2. Click **Close** to close the List Edition dialog box.

Task 13 - Display and animate the natural modes.

1. Hide **Nodes and Elements**, **Properties.1**, and **Distributed Mass.1**.

2. Select  (Deformation). The deformation image for the first natural mode displays, as shown in Figure 10–58.

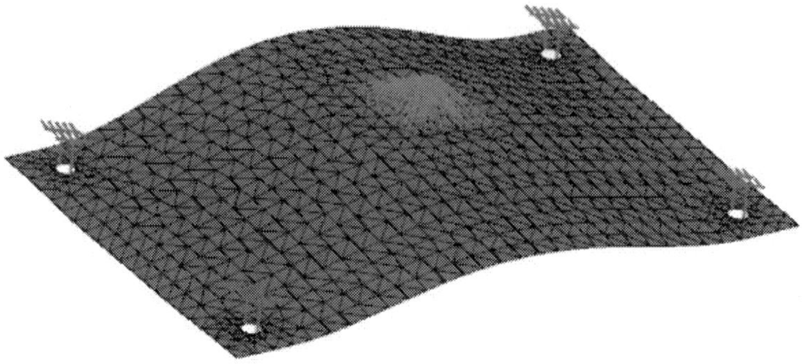

Figure 10–58

3. Animate the deformation. Note that the first natural mode of vibration causes flexing of the PCB in the up and down direction.

4. Double-click on **Deformed mesh.1** in the tree. In the Image Edition dialog box, activate the *Occurrences* tab and select the second mode in the list, as shown in Figure 10–59.

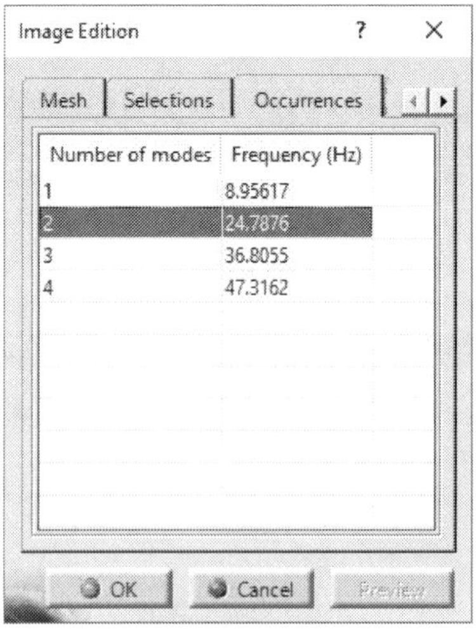

Figure 10–59

5. Click **OK**. The deformation image for the second natural mode displays, as shown in Figure 10–60.

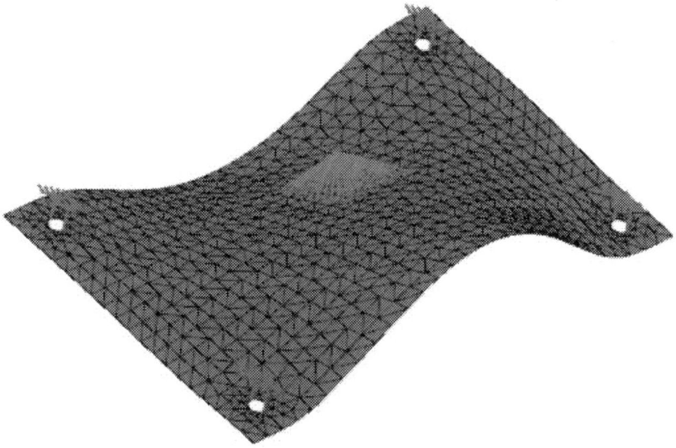

Figure 10–60

6. Animate the deformation. Note that the second natural mode of vibration causes twisting deformation of the PCB.
7. Display and animate the remaining two modes of vibration.

Task 14 - Save and close the files.

1. Optionally, save the analysis document and the part for future reference.
2. Close both the analysis and the part documents.

Made in United States
Orlando, FL
05 November 2026

90230606R00321